Syrian Chemical Weapons and International Law

Tatsuya Abe

Syrian Chemical Weapons and International Law

Springer

Tatsuya Abe
School of International Politics, Economics
and Communication
Aoyama Gakuin University
Tokyo, Japan

ISBN 978-981-99-3699-1 ISBN 978-981-99-3700-4 (eBook)
https://doi.org/10.1007/978-981-99-3700-4

This Springer imprint is published by the registered company Springer Nature Singapore Pte Ltd.
The registered company address is: 152 Beach Road, #21-01/04 Gateway East, Singapore 189721, Singapore

Acknowledgments

This monograph is an expansion of ideas originally outlined in "Syrian Chemical Weapons Issues" in *Dimensions of Disarmament and Non-Proliferation* (Shinzansha, 2019) (in Japanese). It also includes revised elements from the following: "Syria: The Chemical Weapons Question and Autonomous Sanctions," in Masahiko Asada (ed.), *Economic Sanctions in International Law and Practice* (Routledge, 2020); "Challenge inspections under the Chemical Weapons Convention: between ideal and reality," *The Nonproliferation Review*, Vol. 24, Nos. 1–2 (2017); and "Effectiveness of the Institutional Approach to an Alleged Violation of International Law: The Case of Syrian Chemical Weapons," *Japanese Yearbook of International Law*, Vol. 57 (2014).

I thank the School of International Politics, Economics and Communication, at Aoyama Gakuin University, for giving me the opportunity to concentrate on researching this monograph in my capacity as Professor of International Law on the school's faculty.

I also thank my colleagues for much useful feedback over the years. And I am particularly beholden to Prof. Masahiko Asada of Doshisha University for the invaluable advice.

This work was made possible by grants from the Japan Society for the Promotion of Science (JSPS) KAKENHI, Nos. 19K01317 and 21H04384.

Tatsuya Abe

Contents

About the Author

Tatsuya Abe is Professor of International Law at the School of International Politics, Economics and Communication, Aoyama Gakuin University, Japan. Having received his Doctor of Laws degree from Kyoto University, Prof. Abe specializes in disarmament and arms control law, having been involved for over 20 years with the Nobel Peace Prize-winning Organisation for the Prohibition of Chemical Weapons (OPCW). Recent publications include *Weapons of Mass Destruction and International Law* (2011) (in Japanese), as well as articles in *The Nonproliferation Review* and *Japanese Yearbook of International Law*.

Chapter 1
Introduction

Abstract The purpose of this monograph is to discuss the issue of Syrian chemical weapons from an international law perspective. Its particular focus is on Syria's compliance and non-compliance with relevant obligations under international humanitarian and disarmament law. Taking this as the analytical framework, the author proposes to address the following questions: how the international community ensures Syria's compliance with the obligation to eliminate its chemical weapons stockpiles; how the international community has dealt with potential and actual non-compliance of Syria with this obligation; how the international community has addressed allegations of use of chemical weapons by the Assad regime; and how the international community has responded to Syria's non-compliance with the obligation not to use chemical weapons.

1.1 Context

In 2013, the international community suddenly confronted the Syrian chemical weapons problem. Admittedly, it had been alleged prior to that time that Syria was developing and maintaining a chemical weapons arsenal.[1] Given Syria's involvement alongside other Middle East Arab States in armed conflict with Israel, and that Syria

[1] Testimony of William H. Webster, Director, Central Intelligence Agency, Washington, DC, Global Spread of Chemical and Biological Weapons, Hearing Before the Committee on Governmental Affairs and Its Permanent Subcommittee on Investigations, United States Senate, one hundred first Congress, first session, 9 February 1989, p. 12. See also Julian Perry Robinson, "Chemical-Weapons Proliferation in the Middle East," in Efraim Karsh, Martin S. Navias and Philip Sabin (eds.), *Non-Conventional-Weapons Proliferation in the Middle East: Tackling the Spread of Nuclear, Chemical, and Biological Capabilities* (Clarendon Press, 1993), p. 69, p. 96; Philipp C. Bleek and Nicholas J. Kramer, "Eliminating Syria's chemical weapons: implications for addressing nuclear, biological and chemical threats," *The Nonproliferation Review*, Vol. 23, Nos. 1–2 (2016), p. 197, pp. 198–201.

T. Abe, *Syrian Chemical Weapons and International Law*,
https://doi.org/10.1007/978-981-99-3700-4_1

had not signed the Chemical Weapons Convention (CWC) since it was open for signature in January 1993,[2] it came as little surprise that Syria was stockpiling chemical weapons for security reasons. The Assad regime first officially acknowledged doing so, however, at a news conference on 24 July 2012, when Jihad Makdissi, a Syrian Foreign Ministry spokesman, stressed that "[a]ny stock of W.M.D. or unconventional weapons that the Syrian Army possesses will never, never be used against the Syrian people or civilians during this crisis, under any circumstances" and that "[t]hese weapons are made to be used strictly and only in the event of external aggression against the Syrian Arab Republic."[3] Syria has reiterated the same position on other occasions.[4] United States (US) President Barack Obama responded with his declaration of 20 August 2012, in which he referred to "a red line" and warned of "enormous consequences" should the Assad regime use or even move chemical weapons in the ongoing armed conflict in Syria.[5] This statement was widely recognized as signifying the possible US military actions against Syria.

Such concerns become more tangible in December 2012, when the press reported that "Syrian opposition groups have accused the regime of using chemical weapons against rebels in Homs, while the regime said rebel fighters used poison gas against the army in Damascus."[6] Another allegation was reported in March 2013: "Syria's government accused rebels of firing a chemical weapon Tuesday…Rebels and their international backers denied the allegations and said they don't have access to

---

[2] Syria thus has no legal obligation to eliminate its chemical weapons program, which some commentators misunderstand. See Patrick Butchard and Christian Henderson, "A Functional Typology of Commissions of Inquiry," in Christian Henderson (ed.), *Commissions of Inquiry: Problems and Prospects* (Hart Publishing, 2017), p. 11, p. 24.

[3] New York Times, Syria Threatens Chemical Attack on Foreign Force, By Neil MacFarquhar and Eric Schmitt, 23 July 2012, https://www.nytimes.com/2012/07/24/world/middleeast/chemical-weapons-wont-be-used-in-rebellion-syria-says.html, accessed 6 September 2020. See also https://www.youtube.com/watch?v=r0sI3Y_OlDA, accessed 22 April 2023.

[4] UN Doc. A/67/628–S/2012/917, 10 December 2012, p. 2; UN Doc. S/2013/171, 19 March 2013, p. 2.

[5] The White House, Office of the Press Secretary, Remarks by the President to the White House Press Corps, 20 August 2012, https://obamawhitehouse.archives.gov/the-press-office/2012/08/20/remarks-president-white-house-press-corps, accessed 22 April 2023. ("We have been very clear to the Assad regime, but also to other players on the ground, that a red line for us is we start seeing a whole bunch of chemical weapons moving around or being utilized. That would change my calculus. That would change my equation… We have communicated in no uncertain terms with every player in the region that that's a red line for us and that there would be enormous consequences if we start seeing movement on the chemical weapons front or the use of chemical weapons. That would change my calculations significantly.").

[6] Al Bawaba, Syria regime and rebels both claim use of chemical weapons, 24 December 2012, https://www.albawaba.com/amp/news/syria-chemical-weapons-458972, accessed 22 April 2023. See also AlArabiya News, Syrian regime used gas on opposition fighters: activists, 25 December 2012, https://english.alarabiya.net/News/2012/12/25/Syrian-regime-used-gas-on-opposition-fighters-activists, accessed 22 April 2023.

chemical weapons."[7] Syria requested that the UN Secretary-General investigate in accordance with UN General Assembly Resolution 42/37C.[8] The United Kingdom (UK) and France almost immediately responded to this action by requesting that the Secretary-General investigate other allegations under the same procedures.[9] Syrian chemical weapons became the international community's agenda.

One issue the international community has addressed was to eliminate Syrian chemical weapons program in response to the use of said weapons in East Ghouta on 21 August 2013. This attack had raised the possibility of serious dispute between the US, the UK, and France, which were exploring military options, and Russia and Syria, which strongly opposed same. However, the US and Russia found a diplomatic solution, agreeing to a joint proposal to eliminate the Syrian chemical weapons program "in the soonest and safest manner."[10] For its part, Syria accepted the proposal, opting also to accede to the CWC. The Organization for the Prohibition of Chemical Weapons (OPCW) Executive Council and the UN Security Council established the "Resolution 2118 Regime"[11] in effectuation thereof, showing the united resolve of the international community in achieving the ultimate goal of the elimination of the Syrian chemical weapons program. While relevant tasks, including removal and destruction of declared chemical weapons and destruction of declared chemical weapons production facilities, were completed through systematic compliance control under the Resolution 2118 Regime, the completeness of Syria's declaration has not yet been verified. Outstanding issues remain to be resolved.

In tandem with these efforts, the international community has encountered another chemical weapons issue. There have been many allegations of chemical weapons use in Syria which began in April 2014. If true, they constitute clear non-compliance with the obligations under the CWC and UN Security Council Resolution 2118. The chemical first allegedly used was chlorine, which was not declared as a weapon by Syria, and thus not subject to the elimination obligation under the Resolution 2118 Regime. Thus, the further use of chemical weapons was regarded as distinct from the elimination of declared Syrian chemical weapons. These issues subsequently became intertwined, however, when it was confirmed that the Assad regime was using sarin—whose precursors were supposed to be removed from Syria under the Resolution 2118 Regime, showing that Syria was not complying with its obligations not to use chemical weapons and to submit full and complete declarations. A permanent Member veto prevented the UN Security Council from acting however, leaving the OPCW policy-making organs to respond instead with sanctions against Syria. There is no prospect of the situation improving.

---

[7] Wall Street Journal, Syria Alleges Rebels Launched Chemical Attack, 19 March 2013, https://www.wsj.com/articles/SB10001424127887323415304578370314003599212, accessed 22 April 2023.

[8] UN Doc. S/2013/184, 25 March 2013.

[9] *Ibid.*

[10] OPCW Doc. EC-M-33/NAT.1, 17 September 2013, Annex, p. 2.

[11] UN Doc. S/RES/2118 (2013), 27 September 2013; OPCW Doc. EC-M-33/DEC.1, 27 September 2013.

1.2 Review of the Literature

Syrian chemical weapons concerns have drawn some attention in academia, with virtually all of the literature taking a thematic approach to the topic. Michelle Bentley published *Syria and the Chemical Weapons Taboo* (Manchester University Press, 2016), one of the few research monographs on the subject, in which she analyzes the role of Syrian chemical weapons in relation to US foreign policy from an international relations perspective. Another relevant monograph is *The Syrian Conflict's Impact on International Law* (Cambridge University Press, 2020), by Michael P. Scharf, Milena Sterio, and Paul R. Williams, although it discusses chemical weapons only slightly.

Conversely, many international law scholars have demonstrated an interest in the issue of the use of chemical weapons. The most popular such topic is the legality of unilateral military action in response to the alleged use of same. The attempt to use force by the US, the UK, and France against Syria in 2013 became an important subject of publications[12] and also ignited some online debate.[13] The same is true of

[12] Andrew M. Bell, "Using Force against the Weapons of the Weak: Examining a Chemical-Biological Weapons Usage Criterion for Unilateral Humanitarian Intervention under the Responsibility to Protect," *Cardozo Journal of International and Comparative Law*, Vol. 22, Issue 2 (2014), p. 261, pp. 261–320; John R. Crook, "United States Threatens Military Strikes Against Syria, Then Joins in Diplomatic Efforts to Control Syrian Chemical Weapon," *American Journal of International Law*, Vol. 107, No. 4 (2013), p. 900, pp. 900–907; Michael N. Schmitt, "The Syrian Intervention: Assessing the Possible International Law Justifications," *International Law Studies Series*, US Naval War College, Vol. 89 (2013), p. 744, pp. 744–756; Manisuli Ssenyonjo, "Unilateral Military Action in the Syrian Arab Republic: A Right to Humanitarian Intervention or a Crime of Aggression," *International Human Rights Law Review*, Vol. 2, Issue 2 (2013), p. 323, pp. 323–343; Carsten Stahn, "Syria and the Semantics of Intervention, Aggression and Punishment; On Red Lines and Blurred Lines," *Journal of International Criminal Justice*, Vol. 11, Issue 5 (December 2013), p. 955, pp. 955–977; Carsten Stahn, "Between Law-Breaking and Law-Making: Syria, Humanitarian Intervention and What the Law Ought to Be," *Journal of Conflict and Security Law*, Vol. 19, Issue 1 (2014), p. 25, pp. 25–48; Kenneth R. Mayer, "Executive Power in the Obama Administration and the Decision to Seek Congressional Authorization for a Military Attack against Syria: Implications for Theories of Unilateral Action," *Utah Law Review*, Vol. 2014, Issue 4 (2014), p. 821, pp. 821–842; Chelsea O'Donnell, "The Development of the Responsibility to Protect: An Examination of the Debate over the Legality of Humanitarian Intervention," *Duke Journal of Comparative and International Law*, Vol. 24, Issue 3 (Spring 2014), p. 557, pp. 557–588; Christian Henderson, "The UK Government's Legal Opinion on Forcible measures in Response to the Use of Chemical Weapons by the Syrian Government," *International and Comparative Law Quarterly*, Vol. 64, No. 1 (2015), p. 179, pp. 179–196; Anne Lagerwall, "Threats of and Actual Military Strikes Against Syria—2013 and 2017," in Tom Ruys and Olivier Corten (eds.), *The Use of Force in International Law: A Case-based Approach* (Cambridge University Press, 2018), p. 828, pp. 828–847; Yasmine Nahlawi, *The Responsibility to Protect in Libya and Syria: Mass Atrocities, Human Protection, and International Law* (Routledge 2020), pp. 133–139.

[13] Dapo Akande, "The Legality of Military Action in Syria: Humanitarian Intervention and Responsibility to Protect," *EJIL Talk!*, 28 August 2013, https://www.ejiltalk.org/humanitarian-intervention-responsibility-to-protect-and-the-legality-of-military-action-in-syria/, accessed 22 April 2023; Daniel Bethlehem, "Stepping Back a Moment-The Legal Basis in Favour of a Principle of Humanitarian Intervention," *EJIL: Talk!*, 12 September 2013, https://www.ejiltalk.org/stepping-back-a-moment-the-legal-basis-in-favour-of-a-principle-of-humanitarian-intervention/, accessed 22 April

the 2017 and 2018 airstrikes against Syria.[14] Another related topic to draw comments is accountability for perpetrators, with some articles addressing attribution mechanisms, i.e., means for identifying parties who use chemical weapons,[15] while others go further into questions raised vis-à-vis international criminal law.[16] A few writers

---

2023; Harold Hongju Koh, "Syria and the Law of Humanitarian Intervention (Part II: International Law and the Way Forward)," *EJIL: Talk!*, 4 October 2013, https://www.ejiltalk.org/syria-and-the-law-of-humanitarian-intervention-part-ii-international-law-and-the-way-forward/, accessed 22 April 2023.

[14] Marko Milanovic, "The Clearly Illegal US Missile Strike in Syria," *EJIL:Talk!*, 7 April 2017, https://www.ejiltalk.org/the-clearly-illegal-us-missile-strike-in-syria/, accessed 22 April 2023; Daniela Abratt, "U.S. Intervention in Syria: A Legal Responsibility to Protect," *Denver Law Review*, Vol. 95, Issue 1 (2017), p. 21, pp. 21–72; Mika Hayashi, "The U.S. Airstrike After the Use of Chemical Weapons in Syria: National Interest, Humanitarian Intervention, or Enforcement Against War Crimes?," *ASIL Insights*, Vol. 21, Issue 8, 13 July 2017, https://www.asil.org/insights/volume/21/issue/8/us-airstrike-after-use-chemical-weapons-syria-national-interest, accessed 22 April 2023; Lagerwall, *supra* note 12, pp. 848–854; Anders Henriksen, "Trump's Missile Strike on Syria and the Legality of Using Force to Deter Chemical Warfare," *Journal of Conflict and Security Law*, Vol. 23, Issue 1 (2018), p. 33, pp. 33–48; Marko Milanovic, "The Syria Strikes: Still Clearly Illegal," *EJIL:Talk!*, 15 April 2018, https://www.ejiltalk.org/the-syria-strikes-still-clearly-illegal/, accessed 22 April 2023; Monica Hakimi, "The Attack on Syria and the Contemporary Jus ad Bellum," *EJIL Talk!*, 15 April 2018, https://www.ejiltalk.org/the-attack-on-syria-and-the-contemporary-jus-ad-bellum/, accessed 22 April 2023; Jacob Behmer, "The Legality of President Trump's Missile Strike on Al-Shayrat Air Force Base in Syria," *University of St. Thomas Journal of Law and Public Policy (Minnesota)*, Vol. 13, Issue 2 (2019), p. 83, pp. 83–102; Aniel Caro de Beer and Dire Tladi, "The Use of Force against Syria in Response to Alleged Use of Chemical Weapons by Syria: A Return to Humanitarian Intervention?" *Zeitschrift Für Ausländisches öffentliches Recht Und Vökerrecht*, Vol. 79 (2019), p. 205, pp. 205–239; Agata Kleczkowska, "The Illegality of Humanitarian Intervention: The Case of the UK's Legal Position concerning the 2018 Strikes in Syria," *Utrecht Journal of International and European Law*, Vol. 35, Issue 1 (2020), p. 35, pp. 35–49; Kenneth Watkin, "Humanitarian Intervention and the Responsibility to Protect: Where It Stands in 2020: Fighting in the Law's Gaps," *Southwestern Journal of International Law*, Vol. 26, Issue 2 (2020), p. 213, pp. 213–240; Simon Chesterman, "Responsibility to Protect and Humanitarian Intervention From Apology to Utopia and Back Again", in Robin Geiß and Nils Melzer (eds.), *The Oxford Handbook of the International Law of Global Security* (Oxford University Press, 2021), p. 808, pp. 808–820; Vincent Nordin, "A Humanitarian Exception: The International Legal Justification for U.S. Military Action Against the Syrian Regime," *Santa Clara Law Review*, Vol. 61, Issue 3 (2021), p. 811, pp. 811–838; Nadia Ahmad, "Legalizing Humanitarian Intervention in Response to Chemical Weapon Usage: Syrian Conflict's Impact on International Law," *Willamette Journal of International Law and Dispute Resolution*, Vol. 29, Issue 2 (2022), p. 155, pp. 155–186.

[15] Alexander Orakhelashvili, "The Attribution Decision Adopted by the OPCW's Conference of States Parties and Its Legality," *International Organizations Law Review*, Vol. 17, Issue 3 (2020), p. 664, pp. 664–681; Mirko Sossai, "Identifying the Perpetrators of Chemical Attacks in Syria: The Organisation for the Prohibition of Chemical Weapons as Part of the Fight against Impunity," *Journal of International Criminal Justice*, Vol. 17, Issue 2 (May 2019), p. 211, pp. 211–227.

[16] Yasmine Nahlawi, "The Responsibility to Protect and Obama's Red Line on Syria," *Global Responsibility to Protect*, Vol. 8, Issue 1 (2016), p. 76, pp. 76–101; Yasmin Naqvi, "Crossing the red line: The use of chemical weapons in Syria and what should happen now," *International Review of the Red Cross*, Vol. 99, No. 3 (2017), p. 959, pp. 959–993; Michelle Almary, "The Necessity for a Permanent Disincentive: Examining the Use of Chemical Weapons with a Focus on Syria's Civil War," *Southwestern Journal of International Law*, Vol. 24, Issue 2 (2018), p. 301, pp. 301–336; Yasmin Naqvi and Olfemi Elias, "Chemical Weapons and Non-State Actors," in Ezequiel

discuss the development of international law.[17] Relatively few authors have examined Syrian chemical weapons disarmament,[18] however, and even most that do have dealt with specific topics regarding the elimination of such or work relating thereto. As of this writing, no publication has treated both the issues of humanitarian law and disarmament law from an international law perspective.

1.3 Compliance/Non-compliance Control as Analytical Framework

In order to discuss both issues of humanitarian law and disarmament law in terms of Syrian chemical weapons, this paper introduces "compliance/non-compliance control" as an analytical framework. In academia, the concept of "international control (contrôl international)"[19] or "international supervision"[20] has been used to explain the practice of "a new system of inducing compliance with international rules."[21] Beginning after the First World War, and with renewed impetus after the Second World War, States have resorted to treaties to regulate matters which used to

Heffes, Marcos D. Kotlik and Manuel J. Ventura (eds.), *International Humanitarian Law and Non-State Actors* (Springer, 2020), p. 115, pp. 115–148.

[17] Masahiko Asada, "A Path to a Comprehensive Prohibition of the Use of Chemical Weapons under International Law: From the Hague to Damascus," *Journal of Conflict and Security Law*, Vol. 21, No. 2 (2016), p. 153, pp. 153–208; Michael P. Scharf, "Striking a Grotian Movement: How the Syrian Airstrikes Changed International Law Relating to Humanitarian Intervention," *Chicago Journal of International Law*, Vol. 19, Issue 2 (2019), p. 586, pp. 586–614.

[18] Ralf Trapp, "Elimination of the Chemical Weapons Stockpile of Syria," *Journal of Conflict and Security Law*, Vol. 19, Issue 1 (2014), p. 7, pp. 7–24; Paul Walker, "Syrian Chemical Weapons Destruction: Taking Stocks and Looking Ahead," *Arms Control Today* (December 2014), https://www.armscontrol.org/act/2014-12/features/syrian-chemical-weapons-destruction-taking-stock-looking-ahead, accessed 22 April 2023; Marie Jacobsson, "Syria and the Issue of Chemical Weapons: A Snapshot of a Legal Time-frame: the United Nations Security Council Resolution 2118 (2013) and the OPCW Executive Council Decision," in Jonas Ebbesson et al. (eds.), *International Law and Changing Perceptions of Security: liber amicorum Said Mahmoudi* (Brill Nijhoff, 2014), p. 134, pp. 134–151; Bleek and Kramer, *supra* note 1, pp. 197–230; Karim Makdisi and Coralie Pison Hindawi, "The Syrian Chemical Weapons Disarmament Process in Context: Narratives of Coercion, Consent, and Everything in Between," *Third World Quarterly*, Vol. 38, Issue 8 (2017), p. 1691, pp. 1691–1709; Mika Hayashi, "Benefits of a Legally Non-Binding Agreement: The Case of the 2013 US-Russian Agreement on the Elimination of Syrian Chemical Weapons," *International Community Law Review*, Vol. 20, Issue 2 (2018), p. 252, pp. 252–277; Karim Makdisi and Coralie Pison Hindawi, "Exploring the UN and OPCW Partnership in Syrian Chemical Weapons Disarmament: Interorganizational Cooperation and Autonomy," *Global Governance*, Vol. 25, Issue 4 (2019), p. 535, pp. 535–562; Dominique Anelli, "Old Chemical Weapons: Moving the OPCW to an Active Role," *Arms Control Today*, June 2020, https://www.armscontrol.org/act/2020-06/features/old-chemical-weapons-moving-opcw-active-role, accessed 22 April 2023.

[19] Pierre-Marie Dupuy and Yann Kerbrat, *Droit international public, 16e édition* (Dalloz, 2022), pp. 606–607.

[20] Antonio Cassese, *International Law,* second edition (Oxford University Press, 2005), p. 291.

[21] *Ibid.*, p. 291.

be within their domestic jurisdictions. At heart, these treaties impose non-reciprocal obligations[22] on States Parties within their respective territories. The problem is that a State Party's compliance and non-compliance with such obligations may go unnoticed by other States Parties. It is therefore necessary for third parties, typically international monitoring organs, to observe treaty implementation—i.e., whether obligations are being complied with.[23]

It has been indicated that international control is equipped with mechanisms for establishing compliance and redressing non-compliance. According to a commentator, the aim of international supervision is "to make a contribution to the realization of the objectives of the system within which supervision is exercised" and this contribution is made by "(1) reviewing the behaviour of those forming part of the system for its conformity with norms which have been created within the system for the realization of its objectives, and (2), in case of apparent lack of conformity between behaviour and norms, the promotion and, where necessary and possible, enforcement of measures for restoring the conformity."[24] To begin with, it is critical to ascertain State behavior.[25] To this end, international monitoring organs consider the implementation of respective norms based on reports by Member States, as well as the information collected by personnel tasked with verifying effectuation of norms on-site.[26] When the facts show that State behavior conforms to obligations, the State concerned is in compliance, and no action is to be taken. Full compliance is not always easy, however; non-compliance may happen for a variety of reasons. Once non-compliance is established, the next step is redress, and international monitoring organs tend to take non-punitive measures. They explore means and methods and make recommendations to assist the concerned State in restoring compliance as well as preventing like failures in future.[27] Experience indicates that providing technical and financial assistance to build capacity can substantially improve performance.[28]

---

[22] *Ibid.*, p. 293. See also Antonio Cassese, "Fostering Increased Conformity with International Standards: Monitoring and Institutional Fact-finding," in Antonio Cassese (ed.), *Realizing Utopia: The Future of International Law* (Oxford University Press, 2012), p. 295, pp. 298–299.

[23] Cassese, *supra* note 20, p. 293. See also Cassese, *supra* note 22, pp. 298–299. See also I. I. Lukashuk, "Control in Contemporary International Law," in W. E. Butler (ed.), *Control over Compliance with International Law* (Martinus Nijhoff Publishers, 1991), p. 5, pp. 5–7.

[24] Pieter van Dijk, "Normative Force and Effectiveness of International Norms," *Germany Yearbook of International Law*, Vol. XXX (1987), p. 9, p. 26.

[25] W. E. Butler, "Ensuring Compliance with Arms Control Agreements: Legal Responses," in W. E. Butler (ed.), *Control over Compliance with International Law* (Martinus Nijhoff Publishers, 1991), p. 31, p. 34.

[26] Lukashuk, *supra* note 23, p. 7; Butler, *supra* note 25, p. 32. See also Abram Chayes and Antonia Handler Chayes, *The New Sovereignty: Compliance with International Regulatory Agreements* (Harvard University Press, 1995), p. 23.

[27] M. I. Lazarev, "On a Theoretical Concept of Control over the Fulfilment of International Obligations of State," in W. E. Butler (ed.), *Control over Compliance with International Law* (Martinus Nijhoff Publishers, 1991), p. 17, p. 19; van Dijk, *supra* note 24, pp. 26–27. See also Lukashuk, *supra* note 23, p. 5.

[28] Chayes and Chayes, *supra* note 26, p. 23.

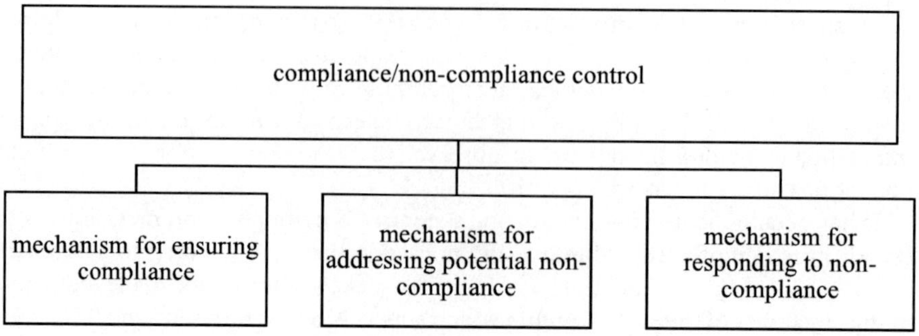

Fig. 1.1 Compliance/non-compliance control framework

This author concurs in principle with the two-step mechanism of international control, as they offer useful tools for practical analysis, but with the caveat that they do not seem to reflect the full range of international control. First, a mechanism for ensuring compliance is a very important component of international control, especially in the field of disarmament. States Parties to disarmament treaties are mutually obliged to destroy weapons specified therein that they may possess. As non-compliance by one State Party will become a threat to other States Parties, such treaties include intrusive routine verification systems, which aim to ensure compliance with relevant obligations rather than investigating such compliance. Second, practice suggests that intermediate space exists between the mechanism for ensuring compliance and that for responding to non-compliance. There is a case where the status of compliance of the State concerned is unclear. International monitoring organs thus conduct clarifications of ambiguities based on the facts.[29] If the fact is in conformity with the obligation, it means compliance. If not, it does non-compliance. Cassese seems to recognize this intermediate space, as he acknowledges that "supervisory bodies do not put States in the dock, but tend to persuade them, *even before any possible breach occurs*, by dint of cautious diplomatic and moral pressure, to abide by those rules which they may be inclined to disregard" (emphasis added).[30] He also points out the "unique form of 'preventive' supervision" of "[a]daption of measures designed to *forestall the possible commission of international delinquency* by State" (emphasis added).[31] In order to reflect the aforementioned practice, this monograph describes mechanisms of international control, which will be referred to hereinafter as compliance/non-compliance control. The mechanisms in question are intended to ensure compliance, address potential non-compliance, and respond to non-compliance (Fig. 1.1).

[29] See Butler, *supra* note 25, p. 34.

[30] Cassese, *supra* note 20, p. 294.

[31] *Ibid.*, p. 294.

1.4 Format of this Monograph

The format of this monograph is as follows. Chapter 2 outlines international law relevant to Syrian chemical weapons and lays the foundation for the core discussion thereof in Chapters. 3 and 4. It covers the 1925 Geneva Protocol, which prohibits the use of chemical weapons in war, the 1993 Chemical Weapons Convention (CWC), which bans chemical weapons comprehensively, the 1998 Rome Statute of the International Criminal Court (ICC), which identifies the use of chemical weapons as a war crime in both international and non-international armed conflict, customary international law on non-use of chemical weapons, and UN Security Council Resolution 1540, which explores non-proliferation to non-State actors of weapons of mass destruction, including chemical weapons. The details of each of these instruments are addressed therein, including history, development, and how they pertain to Syria.

Chapters 3 and 4 make separate intensive discussions of compliance/non-compliance control, predicated on an assumption that compliance/non-compliance controls may vary depending on aspects of substantive obligations: act or omission. As the literature has thus far paid little attention to this difference, this monograph accordingly offers a new perspective on compliance/non-compliance control analysis. Chapter 3 examines international humanitarian law, i.e., non-use of chemical weapons. While the use of chemical weapons is prohibited under international law as recited above, the ongoing Syrian non-international armed conflict has nonetheless experienced numerous chemical attacks. This chapter offers in-depth inquiries into questions raised by this situation about how the international community responds, in particular, how that community characterizes institutional compliance/non-compliance control mechanisms in this instance, *ex post* measures against potential or real non-compliance and their effectiveness, and alternatives in the event that such institutional mechanisms fail. Chapter 4 examines international disarmament law. The Resolution 2118 Regime introduced a systematic and continuous compliance/non-compliance control based on both *ex ante* and *ex post* measures. In order to achieve the stated goal of the elimination of Syria's chemical weapons program, the Resolution 2118 Regime obliged Syria to submit declarations, dispose of their chemical weapons, and destroy their chemical weapons production facilities. Specific questions that this chapter addresses in this regard include how the Resolution 2118 Regime verifies performance and responds to missed deadlines and incomplete declarations.

Chapter 5, the conclusion, summarizes the foregoing by highlighting characteristics of compliance/non-compliance control in the context of Syrian chemical weapons, as well as implications for the CWC and beyond.

Chapter 2
International Law Pertaining to Syrian Chemical Weapons

Abstract This chapter outlines sources of international law on chemical weapons and their relevance to the Syrian situation. In the contemporary context, the following treaties cover chemical weapons issues. First is the 1925 Geneva Protocol, which prohibits the use of chemical and biological weapons in war, and which Syria signed on 17 December 1968. Second is the 1993 Chemical Weapons Convention (CWC), which envisions a comprehensive ban on chemical weapons, subject to international verification. Use of sarin in Ghouta in August 2013 caused Syria to accede to the CWC on 14 September 2013. And third is the 1998 Rome Statute of the International Criminal Court (ICC), which enumerates employment of chemical weapons among war crimes in international armed conflict which individuals may be charged with, and which was amended in 2010 to expand the scope of this crime to encompass non-international armed conflict as well. Given that Syria remains a non-State Party to the Rome Statute, UN Security Council resolutions would be required to refer the situation in Syria to the ICC. It is also widely held that there exists customary international law prohibiting use of chemical weapons in international armed conflict, and that such prohibition extends likewise to non-international armed conflict.

2.1 Introduction

Article 38, para. 1 of the Statute of the International Court of Justice (ICJ Statute) lists sources of international law.[1] International treaties (Article 38, para. 1a), represent one of the two prime such cited sources. Vienna Convention on the Law of Treaties (VCLT) defines a treaty as "an international agreement concluded between States in written form and governed by international law, whether embodied in a single instrument or in two or more related instruments and whatever its particular designation" (Article 2, para. 1(a)). A treaty binds only on those States that consent to be bound by it. In the context of Syrian chemical weapons, it is important to specify when treaties

[1] Vaughan Lowe, *International Law* (Oxford University Press, 2007), p. 35; Andrew Clapham, *Brierly's Law of Nations*, seventh edition (Oxford University Press, 2012), p. 54; Malcolm N. Shaw, *International Law,* ninth edition (Cambridge University Press, 2021), p. 59; Hugh Thirlway, *The Sources of International Law,* second edition (Oxford University Press, 2019), p. 8.

T. Abe, *Syrian Chemical Weapons and International Law*,
https://doi.org/10.1007/978-981-99-3700-4_2

on chemical weapons become binding on Syria and to clarify their applicability due to reservations on Syria's part.

International custom (Article 38, para. 1b) is the other cited prime source. In its *North Sea Continental Shelf* cases, the ICJ established the so-called two-element theory, under which the existence of customary international law is affirmed if there exist both general practice and *opinio juris*, or objective and subjective elements of customary international law.[2] By definition, customary international law binds on all States.[3] In the context of Syrian chemical weapons, it is essential to identify the substance of such customary international law that applies to Syria and the situation in Syria when events of interest occur. UN Security Council resolutions under Chapter VII of the Charter of the United Nations (UN Charter) may also bind on UN Member States in accordance with Article 25 of same.

2.2 International Treaties on Chemical Weapons

In the contemporary context, the following treaties are relevant to chemical weapons in general: the 1925 Protocol for the Prohibition of the Use in War of Asphyxiating, Poisonous or Other Gases, and of Bacteriological Methods of Warfare (Geneva Protocol),[4] the 1993 Convention on the Prohibition of the Development, Production, Stockpiling and Use of Chemical Weapons and on their Destruction (Chemical Weapons Convention: CWC),[5] and the 1998 Rome Statute of the International Criminal Court (Rome Statute/ICC Statute).[6]

(1) International Treaty in General

Article 2, para. 1(a) of the VCLT defines a treaty as "an international agreement concluded between States in written form and governed by international law, whether embodied in a single instrument or in two or more related instruments and whatever its particular designation." Treaties are only binding on the parties to a given treaty, i.e., States which consent to be bound by said treaty and for which the treaty is in force (VCLT, Article 2, para. 1(g)). States Parties are allowed to make reservations to multilateral treaties in order to modify particular provisions unless prohibited by a given treaty and so long as such reservations are compatible with the object and purpose of the treaty (VCLT, Articles 19–21). In an exceptional case, Treaties may

---

[2] *North Sea Continental Shelf, Judgment, I.C.J. Reports 1969*, p. 3, p. 44, para. 77. See also Conclusion 2, Conclusions on the Identification of Customary International Law (*Yearbook of the International Law Commission 2018*, Vol. II, Part Two, p. 90).

[3] Thirlway, *supra* note 1, p. 63. The International Law Commission (ILC) includes "a persistent objector theory" concept in its Conclusion 15 of the Conclusions on the Identification of Customary International Law (*Yearbook of the International Law Commission 2018*, Vol. II, Part Two, p. 91).

[4] *League of Nations Treaty Series*, Vol. XCIV, pp. 66–74 (No. 2138).

[5] *United Nations Treaty Series*, Vol. 1974, p. 45 (No. 33757).

[6] *United Nations Treaty Series*, Vol. 2187, p. 3 (No. 38544).

also be binding on non-State Parties through applicable procedures (VCLT, Article 25).

(2) 1925 Geneva Protocol

(a) Adoption

The Geneva Protocol was adopted at the Geneva Conference for the Supervision of the International Trade in Arms and Ammunition on 17 June 1925. As its official title indicates, it prohibits the use in war of "asphyxiating, poisonous or other gases, and of all analogous liquids, materials or devices"—a classical formulation of contemporary chemical weapons.

During the First World War, a variety of chemical weapons were used by both Germany and the Allies chiefly in the European theater, resulting in more than ten thousand deaths and one million injuries. At that time, chemical weapons were literally the most powerful "weapons of mass destruction." The international community thus sought to ban the use of these heinous weapons in war.

This was not the first international treaty to address chemical weapons, as the Geneva Protocol itself acknowledged: "the prohibition of such use has been declared in Treaties to which the majority of Powers of the world are Parties." Such prior treaties include the Declaration concerning Asphyxiating Gases (Hague Declaration IV, 2), adopted at the First Peace Conference at the Hague in 1899, which prohibited "the use of projectiles the sole object of which is the diffusion of asphyxiating or deleterious gases." The peace treaties of 1919 also included obligations regarding chemical weapons. Article 171 of the Treaty of Versailles provides: "The use of asphyxiating, poisonous or other gases and all analogous liquids, materials or devices being prohibited, their manufacture and importation are strictly forbidden in Germany." However, the Hague Declaration IV, 2 would not apply to a war between parties to the declaration should one of the belligerents be joined by a non-party thereto (*clausula si omnes*), while obligations of the aforementioned peace treaties applied only to the States Parties specified therein. It thus became necessary to adopt an international treaty that would ban the use of chemical weapons in war universally and unconditionally.

(b) After the Entry into Force

The Geneva Protocol entered into force on 8 February 1928, with many States participating, including great powers other than the US and Japan, though it was by no means perfect. One problem was that it only prohibited using chemical weapons; development, manufacture, and possession of same were outside its scope, and States Parties to the Protocol, including France, Germany, Italy, the USSR, and the UK, had developed and stockpiled chemical weapons in large quantities by the end of the Second World War. Another problem was that many States Parties made reservations on ratification or accession by which they would not be bound by their obligations under the Protocol if an enemy State or any of its allies "fails to respect the prohibitions laid down in the Protocol."[7] In effect, the Geneva Protocol would only prohibit chemical (or biological) first strikes.

Irrespective of these deficiencies, the Geneva Protocol has generally functioned as intended since the Second World War. The number of States Parties stood at 146 as of 31 December 2022[8] and more than half of all reservations have been withdrawn.[9] This does not mean, however, that the Geneva Protocol has been fully observed by States Parties, as allegations of violations have been submitted to the UN against Portugal,[10] the USSR,[11] Viet Nam[12] and Iraq.[13]

Portugal faced allegations of use of chemical substances in territories under its administration in early 1970s. In 1970 and 1971, the UN General Assembly adopted Resolutions 2707 (XXV) and 2795 (XXVI), which condemned Portugal for "the use of chemical and bacteriological methods of warfare against the peoples of Angola, Mozambique and Guinea (Bissau)", and explicitly indicated that such use

---

[7] Algeria (8 January 1992), Angola (2 March 1990), Australia (24 May 1930), Bahrain (20 October 1988), Bangladesh (6 January 1989), Belgium (4 December 1928), Bulgaria (7 March 1934), Cambodia (15 March 1983), Canada (6 May 1930), Chile (2 July 1935), People's Republic of China (13 July 1952), Czechoslovakia (16 August 1938), Democratic Peoples' Republic of Korea (8 December 1988), Estonia (28 August 1931), Fiji (26 January 1973), France (10 May 1926), India (13 June 1929), Iraq (7 April 1931), Ireland (18 August 1930), Israel (22 January 1969), Jordan (10 October 1976), Kuwait (3 January 1971), Libya (17 October 1971), Mongolia (18 November 1968), Netherlands (31 October 1930), New Zealand (22 January 1930), Nigeria (23 September 1968), Pakistan (13 April 1960), Papua New Guinea (2 September 1980), Portugal (30 May 1930), Republic of Korea (26 December 1988), Romania (23 August 1929), Solomon Islands (1 June 1981), South Africa (24 May 1930), Spain (22 August 1929), USSR (5 April 1928), UK, (9 April 1930), US (22 January 1975), Viet Nam (23 September 1980), and Yugoslavia (12 April 1929) (United Nations, Office for Disarmament Affairs, Protocol for the Prohibition of the Use in War of Asphyxiating, Poisonous or Other Gases, and of Bacteriological Methods of Warfare, https://treaties.unoda.org/t/1925, accessed 22 April 2023); cf. Dietrich Schindler and Jiří Toman, *The Laws of Armed Conflicts: A Collection of Conventions, Resolutions, and Other Documents*, third revised and completed edition (Kluwer Academic Publishers, 1988), pp. 117–121.

[8] United Nations, Office for Disarmament Affairs, Protocol for the Prohibition of the Use in War of Asphyxiating, Poisonous or Other Gases, and of Bacteriological Methods of Warfare, https://treaties.unoda.org/t/1925, accessed 22 April 2023.

[9] States that have withdrawn their reservations include: Australia (25 November 1986), Belgium (17 February 1997), Bulgaria (2 October 1991), Canada (20 August 1991 and 28 October 1999), Chile (11 September 1991), Czech and Slovak Federal Republic (25 September 1990), Estonia (28 May 1999), France (25 November 1996), Ireland (10 February 1972), Mongolia (15 May 1990), Netherlands (17 July 1995), New Zealand, (6 January 1989) Portugal (23 December 2002 and 21 March 2014), Romania (16 July 1991), Russia (18 January 2001), South Africa (12 July 1996), Spain (27 November 1992), and UK (8 November 1991 and 20 December 2002) (United Nations, Office of the Disarmament Affairs, Protocol for the Prohibition of the Use in War of Asphyxiating, Poisonous or Other Gases, and of Bacteriological Methods of Warfare, https://treaties.unoda.org/t/1925, accessed 22 April 2023).

[10] Ratification on 1 July 1930 with reservation.

[11] Ratification on 5 April 1928 with reservation.

[12] Accession on 15 December 1980 with reservation.

[13] Accession on 18 August 1931 with reservation.

is "contrary to the generally recognized rules of international law embodied in the [Geneva] Protocol."[14] While these resolutions were adopted overwhelmingly, they also received a few votes against.[15] Since no international body investigated these allegations, the question was left unanswered.

The USSR and Viet Nam were accused of using chemical and toxin weapons in Afghanistan and against Cambodia[16] in the late 1970s and early 1980s. In its note verbale dated 21 February 1984, the US explicitly mentioned that the use of chemical and toxin weapons in Afghanistan and southeast Asia was "in violation of the Geneva Protocol of 1925."[17] Cambodia also condemned Viet Nam for using chemical weapons "in flagrant violation of the 17 June 1925 Geneva Protocol"[18] and "in violation of the Geneva Convention of 17 June 1925."[19] The UN General Assembly introduced two ad hoc investigation procedures for the alleged use of chemical weapons,[20] the second of which requested "the Secretary-General to investigate...information that may be brought to his attention by any Member State concerning activities that may constitute a violation of the [Geneva] Protocol...in order to ascertain thereby the facts of the matter..." (Resolution 37/98D).[21] However, lack of cooperation on the part of both the USSR and Viet Nam obstructed efforts to use these procedures to verify the allegations in question.

Unlike these ambiguous cases, Iraq frequently used chemical weapons against Iran[22] during their war in the 1980s. Beginning in 1983, Iran submitted numerous letters to the UN Secretary-General alleging Iraqi chemical weapons attacks[23] in

---

[14] UN Doc. A/RES/2707(XXV), 14 December 1970, para. 9; UN Doc. A/RES/2795(XXVI), 10 December 1971, para. 6.

[15] Resolution 2707 (XXV) was adopted by a vote 94 in favor to six (Brazil, Portugal, South Africa, Spain, UK, and US) against, with 16 abstentions (UN Doc. A/PV.1928, 14 December 1970, p. 8, para. 56; Resolution 2795 (XXVI) was adopted by a vote of 105 in favor to eight (Brazil, Costa Rica, France, Portugal, South Africa, Spain, UK, and US) against, with five abstentions (UN Doc. A/PV.2012, 10 December 1971, p. 4, para. 29).

[16] Accession on 15 March 1983 with reservation.

[17] UN Doc. A/39/113, 22 February 1984, p. 2.

[18] UN Doc. A/39/92 S/16383, 30 January 1984, p. 3.

[19] UN Doc. A/39/121, 5 March 1984, p. 3.

[20] UN Doc. A/RES/35/144C, 12 December 1980; UN Doc. A/RES/37/98D, 13 December 1982.

[21] UN Doc. A/RES/37/98D, 13 December 1982, operative para. 4.

[22] Accession on 3 August 1929 without reservation.

[23] UN Doc. S/15934, 18 August 1983; UN Doc. S/16139, 10 November 1983; UN Doc. S/16140, 10 November 1983; UN Doc. S/16154, 16 November 1983; UN Doc. S/16235, 28 December 1983; UN Doc. S/16378, 1 March 1984; UN Doc. S/16380, 1 March 1984; UN Doc. S/16408, 12 March 1984; UN Doc. A/40/176 S/17028, 14 March 1985; UN Doc. S/17031, 14 March 1985; UN Doc. S/17039, 18 March 1985; UN Doc. A/40/189 S/17046, 21 March 1985; UN Doc. S/17059, 26 March 1985; UN Doc. S/17088, 9 April 1985; UN Doc. S/17089, 9 April 1985; UN Doc. S/17095, 11 April 1985; UN Doc. S/17096, 11 April 1985; UN Doc. S/17129, 25 April 1985; UN Doc. S/17143, 2 May 1985; UN Doc. S/17181, 13 May 1985; UN Doc. S/17217, 24 May 1985; UN Doc. A/40/487 S/17342, 16 July 1985; UN Doc. A/40/849 S/17606, 4 November 1985; UN Doc. S/17782, 31 January 1986; UN Doc. S/17790, 4 February 1986; UN Doc. S/17822, 12 February 1986; UN Doc. S/17829, 14 February 1986; UN Doc. S/17833, 14 February 1986; UN Doc. S/17887, 3 March

violation of Geneva Protocol of 1925,[24] and requesting investigations of same.[25]

1986; UN Doc. S/17888, 3 March 1986; UN Doc. S/17944, 26 March 1986; UN Doc. S/18028, 22 April 1986; UN Doc. S/18036, 24 April 1986; UN Doc. S/18104, 27 May 1986; UN Doc. S/18322, 5 September 1986; UN Doc. S/18324, 10 September 1986; UN Doc. S/18549, 29 December 1986; UN Doc. S/18553, 2 January 1987; UN Doc. S/18555, 5 January 1987; UN Doc. S/18556, 5 January 1987; UN Doc. S/18574, 9 January 1987; UN Doc. S/18600, 14 January 1987; UN Doc. S/18605, 15 January 1987; UN Doc. S/18614, 19 January 1987; UN Doc. S/18635, 27 January 1987; UN Doc. S/18675, 6 February 1987; UN Doc. S/18679, 9 February 1987; UN Doc. S/18723, 25 February 1987; UN Doc. S/18788, 8 April 1987; UN Doc. S/18796, 10 April 1987; UN Doc. A/42/219 S/18799, 13 April 1987; UN Doc. A/42/220 S/18800, 13 April 1987; UN Doc. S/18809, 16 April 1987; UN Doc. S/18810, 16 April 1987; UN Doc. A/42/238 S/18820, 21 April 1987; UN Doc. A/42/253 S/18825, 27 April 1987; UN Doc. A/42/255 S/18828, 28 April 1987; UN Doc. A/42/257 S/18829, 28 April 1987; UN Doc. A/42/263 S/18837, 30 April 1987; UN Doc. A/42/269 S/18844, 4 May 1987; UN Doc. A/42/279 S/18851, 7 May 1987; UN Doc. A/42/282 S/18855, 8 May 1987; UN Doc. A/42/286 S/18859, 11 May 1987; UN Doc. A/42/294 S/18866, 15 May 1987; UN Doc. A/42/315 S/18890, 2 June 1987; UN Doc. A/42/334 S/18910, 10 June 1987; UN Doc. A/42/350 S/18928, 17 June 1987; UN Doc. A/42/360 S/18941, 23 June 1987; UN Doc. A/42/366 S/18947, 25 June 1987; UN Doc. A/42/370 S/18952, 29 June 1987; UN Doc. A/42/371 S/18953, 29 June 1987; UN Doc. A/42/373 S/18955, 30 June 1987; UN Doc. A/42/375 S/18956, 30 June 1987; UN Doc. S/18962, 2 July 1987; UN Doc. A/42/382 S/18966, 6 July 1987; UN Doc. A/42/384 S/18967, 7 July 1987; UN Doc. A/42/397 S/18973, 13 July 1987; UN Doc. A/42/426 S/19006, 30 July 1987; UN Doc. S/19191, 9 October 1987; UN Doc. S/19193, 9 October 1987; UN Doc. S/19619, 15 March 1988; UN Doc. S/19665, 21 March 1988; UN Doc. A/43/239 S/19682, 25 March 1988; UN Doc. S/19816, 21 April 1988; UN Doc. S/19822, 22 April 1988; UN Doc. S/19892, 19 May 1988; UN Doc. S/19902, 25 May 1988; UN Doc. S/20049, 22 July 1988; UN Doc. S/20051, 22 July 1988; UN Doc. S/20058, 25 July 1988; UN Doc. S/20084, 3 August 1988; UN Doc. S/20085, 3 August 1988. In response, Iraq categorically rejected several Iranian allegations (UN Doc. A/38/650 S/16193, 30 November 1983; UN Doc. S/17611, 6 November 1985; UN Doc. S/19948, 20 June 1988).

[24] UN Doc. A/40/118 S/16941, 5 February 1985, p. 3; UN Doc. A/40/176 S/17028, 14 March 1985, p. 2; UN Doc. A/40/189 S/17046, 21 March 1985, p. 1; UN Doc. S/17096, 11 April 1985, p. 1; UN Doc. S/17129, 25 April 1985, p. 1; UN Doc. S/17217, 24 May 1985, p. 2; UN Doc. A/40/487 S/17342, 16 July 1985, p. 1; UN Doc. A/40/849 S/17606, 4 November 1985, p. 1; UN Doc. S/17782, 31 January 1986, p. 1; UN Doc. S/17843, 18 February 1986, p. 1; UN Doc. S/17888, 3 March 1986, p. 1; UN Doc. S/17925, 18 March 1986, p. 1; UN Doc. S/18028, 22 April 1986, p. 1; UN Doc. S/18104, 27 May 1986, p. 1; UN Doc. S/18553, 2 January 1987, p. 1; UN Doc. S/18555, 5 January 1987, p. 1; UN Doc. S/18574, 9 January 1987, p. 1; UN Doc. S/18600, 14 January 1987, p. 1; UN Doc. S/18605, 15 January 1987, p. 1; UN Doc. S/18614, 19 January 1987, p. 1; UN Doc. S/18635, 27 January 1987, p. 1; UN Doc. S/18675, 3 February 1987, p. 1; UN Doc. S/18675, 6 February 1987, p. 1; UN Doc. S/18679, 9 February 1987, p. 1; UN Doc. S/18723, 25 February 1987, p. 1; UN Doc. A/42/220 S/18800, 13 April 1987, p. 2; UN Doc. A/42/238 S/18820, 21 April 1987, p. 2; UN Doc. A/42/257 S/18829, 28 April 1987, p. 1; UN Doc. A/42/269 S/18844, 4 May 1987, p. 1; UN Doc. A/42/282 S/18855, 8 May 1987, p. 1; UN Doc. A/42/306 S/18878, 26 May 1987, p. 2; UN Doc. S/19193, 9 October 1987, p. 2; UN Doc. S/19664, 21 March 1988, p. 2; UN Doc. S/20074, 29 July 1988, p. 1.

[25] UN Doc. S/16128, 7 November 1983; UN Doc. S/16154, 16 November 1983; UN Doc. S/16397, 8 March 1984; UN Doc. S/16446, 28 March 1984; UN Doc. A/39/182 S/16481, 13 April 1984; UN Doc. S/16498, 19 April 1984; UN Doc. A/39/333 S/16652, 29 June 1984; UN Doc. A/40/176 S/17028, 14 March 1985; UN Doc. S/17039, 18 March 1985; UN Doc. S/17089, 9 April 1985; UN

In response, the UN Secretary-General dispatched fact-finding missions,[26] which concluded that chemical weapons were used[27] and that Iraqi armed forces were responsible.[28] In his report to the Security Council, the Secretary-General described the use of chemical weapons in the armed conflict between Iran and Iraq as acts "in contravention of the Geneva Protocol of 1925"[29] and constituting the "violation of the Geneva Protocol".[30] Pursuant to this report, the Security Council adopted four presidential statements and three resolutions. The first two presidential statements only stressed the necessity for strict compliance with the Geneva Protocol,[31] while the third and fourth presidential statements and all three resolutions either deplored or strongly condemned the use of chemical weapons "contrary to obligations under the 1925 Geneva Protocol"[32] or "in violation of Geneva Protocol."[33]

Doc. S/17181, 13 May 1985; UN Doc. S/17822, 12 February 1986; UN Doc. S/17833, 14 February 1986; UN Doc. S/17835, 17 February 1986; UN Doc. S/17836, 17 February 1986; UN Doc. S/ 17843, 18 February 1986; UN Doc. S/17888, 3 March 1986; UN Doc. S/17944, 26 March 1986; UN Doc. S/18036, 24 April 1986; UN Doc. S/18104, 27 May 1986; UN Doc. S/18553, 2 January 1987; UN Doc. S/18555, 5 January 1987; UN Doc. S/18635, 27 January 1987; UN Doc. S/18675, 6 February 1987; UN Doc. S/18723, 25 February 1987; UN Doc. A/42/237 S/18819, 21 April 1987; UN Doc. A/42/371 S/18953, 29 June 1987; UN Doc. S/19665, 21 March 1988; UN Doc. A/43/ 233 S/19669, 22 March 1988; UN Doc. A/43/239 S/19682, 25 March 1988; UN Doc. S/20084, 3 August 1988; UN Doc. S/20085, 3 August 1988.

[26] Rather than act under General Assembly Resolution 37/98D, the UN Secretary-General instead carried out the investigation on his own authority to establish fact-finding missions (Howard Mann, "Arms Control Verification and the United Nations: The Chemical Weapons Experience of the 1980s," *Canadian Yearbook of International Law*, Vol. 26 (1988), p. 185, p. 200). This was because the Security Council was deadlocked over the Iran-Iraq issue and the Eastern bloc States were reluctant to accept the investigation mechanism under the aforementioned Resolution 37/98D (*ibid.*).

[27] UN Doc. S/16433, 26 March 1984, pp. 11–12, para. 35; UN Doc. S/17127, 24 April 1985, p. 4, paras. 1–4; UN Doc. S/17911, 12 March 1986, p. 18, para. 57; UN Doc. S/18852, 8 May 1987, p. 18, para. 65; UN Doc. S/19823, 25 April 1988, pp. 17–18, para. 54; UN Doc. S/20060, 20 July 1988, pp. 15–16, para. 46; UN Doc. S/20063, 25 July 1988, pp. 11–12, para. 32; UN Doc. S/20134, 19 August 1988, p. 11, para. 23.

[28] UN Doc. S/17911, 12 March 1986, p. 18, para. 58; UN Doc. S/18852, 8 May 1987, pp. 18–19, para. 66; UN Doc. S/20060, 20 July 1988, p. 15, para. 46(d); UN Doc. S/20134, 19 August 1988, p. 11, para. 23(c). Iraq insisted that it "has not used" chemical weapons (UN Doc. S/16438, 27 March 1984).

[29] UN Doc. S/16663, 12 March 1986, p. 1.

[30] UN Doc. S/17911, 12 March 1986, p. 4, para. 14; UN Doc. S/18852, 8 May 1987, pp. 1 and 2, paras. 1 and 6; UN Doc. S/19823, 25 April 1988, p. 1, para. 1; UN Doc. S/20063, 25 July 1988, p. 2, para. 4; UN Doc. S/20134, 19 August 1988, p. 3, para. 9.

[31] UN Doc. S/16454, 30 March 1984, p. 1; UN Doc. S/17130, 25 April 1985, p. 1.

[32] UN Doc. S/RES/598 (1987), 20 July 1987, preamble para. 4. Italy argued that "[t]he conflict between Iran and Iraq is the cause of repeated and serious violations of the fundamental principles of international law, including … the Geneva Protocol of 1925" (UN Doc. S/PV.2750, 20 July 1987, p. 33 (Italy)). Venezuela pointed out that "such practices violate the provisions of the 1925 Geneva Protocol" (*ibid.*, p. 56 (Venezuela)). UN Doc. S/RES/612 (1988), 9 May 1988, operative para. 2.

[33] UN Doc. S/17932, 21 March 1986, p. 1; UN Doc. S/18863, 14 May 1987, p. 1; UN Doc. S/RES/ 620 (1998), 26 August 1988, operative para. 1. Several States also condemned Iraq for violating the Geneva Protocol. For example, Israel argued that "[t]hese acts [of the use of chemical weapons] constitute a violation of the 1925 Geneva Protocol" (UN Doc. A/43/262 S/19699, 28 March 1988).

In addition, Iraq used chemical weapons against Kurds within its territory in March 1988, in an incident known as the Halabja massacre. Several States explicitly referred to the Geneva Protocol and condemned Iraq's violation thereof. Iran stated that the attack was carried out "in flagrant violation of the 1925 Geneva Protocol."[34] US State Department spokesman Charles E. Redman said that the reported gas attack by Iraq against its Iranian-occupied city of Halabja "appears to be a particularly grave violation of the 1925 Geneva Protocol Against Chemical Warfare."[35] Sweden stressed that "[t]he large-scale use of chemical weapons against the city of Halabja was a flagrant violation of the 1925 Geneva Protocol."[36] These views were based on the premise that the Geneva Protocol applies to use of chemical weapons in non-international armed conflicts, though the use of the term "war" indicates that the Geneva Protocol does not apply to civil wars or to domestic disturbances.[37] The abovementioned allegations against Portugal and the USSR could also be understood as possible cases of the use of chemical weapons in non-international armed conflicts. While one might argue that the Protocol's scope extends to non-international armed conflict through subsequent practice in accordance with the rule codified in Article 31, para. 3(b) of the VCLT,[38] a majority of States have instead rooted such discussion in the context of customary international law,[39] that is, the emergence of newly established customary international law or the expanded scope of existing customary international law, which, in the view of some States, is reflected in the Geneva Protocol, as will be discussed hereinafter.

In 1987 the UN General Assembly adopted a resolution establishing a standing mechanism under the authority of the Secretary-General to investigate "the possible use of chemical and bacteriological (biological) or toxin weapons that may constitute a violation of the 1925 Geneva Protocol or other relevant rules of customary

---

Japan held that "such use of chemical weapons is in violation of the Geneva Protocol of 1925" (UN Doc. A/43/268 S/19715, 31 March 1988). Argentina asserted that "[t]he use of chemical weapons and asphyxiating, toxic and similar gases in the war between two countries [Iran and Iraq] constitutes a serious violation of the 1925 Geneva Protocol and of customary international law" (UN Doc. A/43/303 S/19774, 14 April 1988).

[34] UN Doc. S/19639, 17 March 1988; UN Doc. S/19647, 18 March 1988.

[35] Washington Post, 23 March 1988, p. a37.

[36] UN Doc. A/S-15/PV.2, 1 June 1988, p. 23, para. 89.

[37] R.R. Baxter and Thomas Buergenthal, "Legal Aspects of the Geneva Protocol of 1925," *American Journal of International Law*, Vol. 64, No. 5 (1970), p. 853, p. 869.

[38] The general rule is recognized as customary by the ICJ (See *Territorial Dispute (Libyan Arab Jamahiriya/Chad), Judgment, I.C.J. Reports 1994*, p. 6, pp. 34–37, paras. 66–71; *Legality of the Use by a State of Nuclear Weapons in Armed Conflict, Advisory Opinion, I.C.J. Reports 1996(I)*, p. 66, p. 75, para. 19; *Kasikili/Sedudu Island (Botswana/Namibia), Judgment, I.C.J. Reports 1999(II)*, p. 1045, p. 1075, para. 48; *Sovereignty over Pulau Ligitan and Pulau Sipadan (Indonesia/Malaysia), Judgment, I.C.J. Reports 2002*, p. 625, p. 645, para. 37). The ILC's conclusions on subsequent agreements and subsequent practice in relation to the interpretation of treaties acknowledges in its Conclusion 7 the possibility that such may result in "widening" the range of possible interpretation (*Yearbook of the International Law Commission 2018*, Vol. II, Part Two, pp. 24–25).

[39] Sandesh Sivakumaran, *The Law of Non-International Armed Conflict* (Oxford University Press, 2012), p. 394.

international law in order to ascertain the facts of the matter..."[40] In 1989, the States participating in the Conference of States Parties to the 1925 Geneva Protocol and other interested States on the prohibition of chemical weapons reaffirmed "their full support for the [UN] Secretary-General in carrying out his responsibilities for investigations in the event of alleged violations of the Geneva Protocol."[41]

(c) **Syria**

Syria signed the Geneva Protocol on 17 December 1968,[42] albeit with the reservation that such accession did not imply its recognition of Israel,[43] which does not affect the scope of *ratione materiae*. Since its accession, Syria has explicitly and implicitly reiterated its commitment to the Protocol. In December 1969, it voted for UN General Assembly Resolution 2603A (XXIV),[44] which declared the use in international armed conflict of any chemical agents as contrary to the generally recognized rules of international law, as embodied in the Geneva Protocol.[45] In January 1989, it participated in the Conference of States Parties to the 1925 Geneva Protocol and other Interested States on the Prohibition of Chemical Weapons held in Paris, and adhered to the final declaration condemning chemical weapons use.[46] In November 2005, Syria identified the Geneva Protocol as one of the international treaties relevant to UN Security Council Resolution 1540 in its report submitted to the Security Council, albeit under the heading of biological materials.[47] In December 2012, even

[40] UN Doc. A/RES/42/37C, 30 November 1987. See also UN Doc. S/RES/620 (1988), 26 August 1988, para. 2. Upon UN General Assembly request (UN Doc. A/RES/42/37C, 30 November 1987, operative para. 5; UN Doc. A/RES/43/74A, 7 December 1988, operative para. 6), the Secretary-General developed the Guidelines and Procedures for the Timely and Efficient Investigation of Reports of the Possible Use of Chemical and Bacteriological (Biological) or Toxin Weapons (Guidelines and Procedures) (UN Doc. A/44/561, 4 October 1989, Annex, paras. 90 and 102). The UN General Assembly endorsed the Guidelines and Procedures by welcoming the proposals of the group of qualified experts (UN Doc. A/RES/44/115B, 15 December 1989, operative para. 5).

[41] UN Doc. A/44/88, 20 January 1989, p. 3.

[42] United Nations, Office for Disarmament Affairs, Syrian Arab Republic: Accession to 1925 Geneva Protocol, https://treaties.unoda.org/a/1925/syrianarabrepublic/ACC/paris, accessed 22 April 2023; UN. Doc. S/AC.44/2004/(02)/70/Add.3, 7 November 2005, Annex, pp. 7 and 11.

[43] United Nations, Office for Disarmament Affairs, Syrian Arab Republic: Accession to 1925 Geneva Protocol, https://treaties.unoda.org/a/1925/syrianarabrepublic/ACC/paris, accessed 22 April 2023 ("l'adhésion de la République Arabe Syrienne à ce protocole et sa ratification par son gouvernement ne signifient en aucun cas la reconnaissance d'Israël et ne sauraient conduire à établir des rapports avec ce dernier au sujet des dispositions prévues par ce protocole."); Schindler and Toman, *supra* note 7, p. 126 ("The accession by the Syrian Arab Republic to this Protocol and the ratification of the Protocol by its Government does not in any case imply the recognition of Israel or lead to the establishment of relations with the latter concerning the provisions laid down in the Protocol").

[44] UN Doc. A/RES/2603A (XXIV), 16 December 1969.

[45] UN Doc. A/PV.1836, 16 December 1969, p. 4. See also UN Doc. A/7890, 13 December 1969, p. 9, para. 19.

[46] UN Doc. A/44/88, 20 January 1989. *International Legal Materials,* Vol. 28, No. 4 (July 1989), p. 1020.

[47] UN. Doc. S/AC.44/2004/(02)/70/Add.3, 7 November 2005, p. 7, para. 33.

after the breakout of domestic conflict, Syria stressed that "[i]t has also emphasized its adherence to its legal obligations under the conventions and protocols that it has ratified."[48]

If a State is a party to the Geneva Protocol without second strike reservation, it may logically have no incentive to possess chemical weapons, and thus face no obstacle to joining a treaty banning same. In this context, Syria clearly stated in its national report to the 1540 Committee that it "does not possess any chemical weapons, their means of delivery, or any related materials," while at the same time acknowledging the possession of "chemical materials which are all used for peaceful industrial or agricultural purposes."[49] Despite this, Syria did not accede to the CWC until September 2013, and it had long been suspected that Syria might be developing and stockpiling chemical weapons. For instance, at a session in the Committee on Governmental Affairs and Its Permanent Subcommittee on Investigations, United States Senate, the Director of the Central Intelligence Agency (CIA) testified that "Syria began producing chemical warfare agents and munitions in the mid-1980's, and currently has a chemical warfare production facility."[50]

(2) **1993 Chemical Weapons Convention**

(a) **Adoption**

The Chemical Weapons Convention (CWC) was adopted at the UN General Assembly on 30 November 1992[51] and opened for signature on 13 January 1993. It was the first multilateral disarmament treaty to purpose a comprehensive ban on one category of weapon under international verification. Negotiations lasted nearly twenty years prior to that time, owing to the Cold War and the arrangements required for the verification regime. Regarding the former, while the US and the USSR agreed to biological weapons disarmament in 1972, they both maintained chemical weapons as a military option, with the US insisted on a right to maintain minimum stockpiles up to the end of the negotiations on the convention. It was thus necessary for the Cold War to end before a non-discriminatory treaty comprehensively banning chemical weapons could be adopted. As to the latter, the CWC introduced a stringent verification regime, carried out by the Organization for the Prohibition of Chemical Weapons (OPCW), the Convention's implementing body, to ensure States Parties' compliance with their obligations under the CWC and to address their non-compliance. It primarily targets military sites such as storage and destruction facilities, though it also extends to commercial facilities. The scope of access for verification purposes

---

[48] UN Doc. A/67/628–S/2012/917, 10 December 2012, p. 2.

[49] UN. Doc. S/AC.44/2004/(02)/70/Add.3, 7 November 2005, p. 6, paras. 24 and 26.

[50] Testimony of William H. Webster, Director, Central Intelligence Agency, Washington, DC, Global Spread of Chemical and Biological Weapons, Hearing Before the Committee on Governmental Affairs and Its Permanent Subcommittee on Investigations, United States Senate, one hundred first Congress, first session, 9 February 1989, p. 12. See also Philipp C. Bleek and Nicholas J. Kramer, "Eliminating Syria's chemical weapons: implications for addressing nuclear, biological and chemical threats," *The Nonproliferation Review*, Vol. 23, Nos. 1-2 (2016), p. 197, pp. 198–201.

[51] UN Doc. A/RES/47/39, 30 November 1992.

was one of the most sensitive issues to be resolved in the negotiations, as the dual-use nature of toxic chemicals and their precursors necessitated verifying non-diversion of such substances from legitimate peaceful purposes.

(b) After the Entry into Force

The CWC entered into force on 29 April 1997. As of August 2013, the number of States Parties stands at 189, and 76.07% of declared category 1 chemical weapons have been destroyed.[52]

(c) Syria

At first, Syria neither signed nor acceded to the CWC. As mentioned, its inaction in this regard raised suspicions that it might have a chemical weapons arsenal. The international community eventually discovered that it was right to be concerned on this point.

Finally, on 14 September 2013, twenty-four days after the alleged use of sarin in East Ghouta, Syria submitted its instrument of CWC accession to the UN Secretary-General.[53] As a consequence, the Convention would enter into force for Syria thirty days later, on 14 October 2013, in accordance with Article XXI, para. 2 thereof. In the meantime, Syria expressed its intent about the provisional application of the CWC as follows: "[Syria]…shall comply with the stipulations contained [in the Chemical Weapons Convention] and observe them faithfully and sincerely, applying the [Chemical Weapons] Convention provisionally pending its entry into force for the Syrian Arab Republic."[54] The reason for such a provisional application was that the political situation at the time did not allow Syria to follow the formal timeline of accession to the Convention, despite the relatively short period of time involved.[55] The provisional application was thus meant to fill a status gap between the date Syria submitted the instrument of accession and that of entry into force, to address ambiguous relations between Syria and the OPCW, and to meet expectations to speed up the CWC's implementation on Syria's part. Syria also needed technical assistance from the OPCW.[56]

Article 25 of the VCLT, on provisional application of treaties, envisages cases wherein (a) the treaty itself so provides and (b) the negotiating States have so agreed in some other manner. The CWC, however, contains no such provision, and the

---

[52] OPCW Doc. EC-74/DG.20, 8 October 2013, para. 20.

[53] UN. Doc. C.N.592.2013.TREATIES-XXVI.3 (Depositary Notification), 14 September 2013.

[54] *Ibid.* See also UN Treaty Collection, https://treaties.un.org/Pages/ViewDetails.aspx?src=TREATY&mtdsg_no=XXVI-3&chapter=26&clang=_en#EndDec, accessed 22 April 2023.

[55] Juan Manuel Gómez-Robledo, "The Provisional Application of Treaties," *University of Vienna Law Review*, Vol. 2:2 (2018), p. 182, p. 189.

[56] Marie Jacobsson, "Syria and the Issue of Chemical Weapons: A Snapshot of a Legal Time-frame: the United Nations Security Council Resolution 2118 (2013) and the OPCW Executive Council Decision," in Jonas Ebbesson et al (eds.), *International Law and Changing Perceptions of Security: liber amicorum Said Mahmoudi* (Brill Nijhoff, 2014), p. 134, p. 138.

negotiating States had no such agreement.[57] Therefore, these rules are neither relevant nor applicable in this instance. The relevant OPCW Executive Council decision indicates that the question of provisional application was accordingly addressed based on the ad hoc consent, or, more precisely, lack of objection, of the States Parties.[58]

At all events, on 12 September 2013, Syria notified the UN Secretary-General, depositary of the CWC, of its intent to apply the Convention provisionally,[59] and formally registered the abovementioned declaration two days later.[60] The Secretary-General circulated it to all States Parties to the CWC and "received no communications to the contrary from the States Parties with regard to this declaration."[61] The OPCW Executive Council referred to the necessity of an immediate start to the destruction of the Syrian chemical weapons program pending the formal entry into force of the CWC,[62] emphasizing that "the provisional application of the Convention gives immediate effect to its provisions with respect to the Syrian Arab Republic."[63] It also noted Syria's actions in accordance with the provisional application, such as its offer to cooperate with the OPCW and the designation of its National Authority.[64] This suggests that the OPCW Executive Council was not in a position to approve or endorse the provisional application, but merely acknowledge the context and subsequent developments.[65] While Russia and the US took into account "the commitment

---

[57] Lisa Tabassi and Olufemi Elias, "18—Disarmament," in Michael J. Bowman (ed.), *Conceptual and Contextual Perspectives on the Modern Law of Treaties* (Cambridge University Press, 2018), p. 578, p. 594; Gómez-Robledo, *supra* note 55, p. 189.

[58] OPCW Doc. EC-M-33/DEC.1, 27 September 2013.

[59] *Ibid.*, preamble para. 6.

The OPCW Director-General received a letter from the Syrian Foreign Minister informing him of the decision to join the CWC that same day, and a request from the Syrian Deputy Minister for OPCW technical assistance the following day (OPCW News, OPCW to Review Request from Syria, 13 September 2013, https://www.opcw.org/media-centre/news/2013/09/opcw-review-request-syria, accessed 22 April 2023).

[60] UN Doc. C.N.592.2013.TREATIES-XXVI.3 (Depositary Notification), 14 September 2013. See also https://treaties.un.org/Pages/ViewDetails.aspx?src=TREATY&mtdsg_no=XXVI-3&chapter=26&clang=_en#EndDec, accessed 22 April 2023.

[61] OPCW Doc. EC-M-33/DEC.1, 27 September 2013, preamble para. 7. The OPCW Director-General also forwarded the Syrian request for provisional application to States Parties "for consideration" (OPCW News, OPCW to Review Request from Syria, 13 September 2013, https://www.opcw.org/media-centre/news/2013/09/opcw-review-request-syria, accessed 22 April 2023).

[62] *Ibid.*, preamble para. 9.

[63] *Ibid.*, preamble para. 11.

[64] *Ibid.*, preamble para. 10.

[65] In this regard, the Second ILC Report seems to misinterpret the text of the OPCW Executive Council decision. According to the report, the OPCW Executive Council "affirmed that 'the provisional application of the Convention gives immediate effect to its provisions with respect to the Syrian Arab Republic'" and it was the OPCW Executive Council decision "recognizing the legal effects of provisional application that made it possible to implement the treaty immediately…" (ILC Second report on the provisional application of treaties By Juan Manuel Gómez-Robledo, Special Rapporteur, UN Doc. A/CN.4/675, 9 June 2014, p. 13, paras. 67–68). As seen above, however, the OPCW Executive Council decision made no mention of "affirm" or "recognize."

of the Syrian authorities to provisionally apply the Chemical Weapons Convention prior to its entry into force" in their joint national paper (about which see Chapter. 3),[66] it was still possible for one or more States Parties to object to Syria's declaration.[67] No such objection was raised,[68] however, illustrating that a unilateral declaration can give rise to provisional application if a pressing need exists and all States Parties consent.[69] If so, this case might theoretically be understood as the unilateral declaration of Syria accepting all obligations under the CWC, rather than the agreement between Syria and all States Parties on provisional application.[70] For its part, the International Law Commission (ILC) was neutral in this regard. While including in its commentary the text that "a declaration by a State or an international organization that is accepted by the other States or international organizations concerned" as a form of agreement "in cases where the treaty remains silent or when it is not otherwise agreed," the ILC simply indicated that the declaration of Syria is "an example" of a State making a unilateral declaration about provisional application,[71] without clarifying whether doing so fell within the legal regime of provisional application or that of unilateral declarations of States giving rise to legal obligations.[72] In any event, as described above, the CWC formally entered into force for Syria on 14 October 2013, making it the Convention's 190th State Party.[73]

(3) **1998 ICC Rome Statute**

(a) **Adoption**

The ICC Rome Statute was adopted at a diplomatic conference on 17 July 1998. Its purpose is "to establish a permanent institution which has the power to exercise the jurisdiction over persons for the most serious crimes of concern" to the international community as a whole (Article 1). It identifies "war crimes" as one of four categories of crimes within its jurisdiction (Article 5, para. 1(c)) and lists such war crimes which individuals may be charged with (Article 8).

International law has been traditionally concerned with State responsibility for violations of international humanitarian law. The idea of international criminal tribunals dates back to the early twentieth century. Article 227 of the Versailles Treaty requested that the Netherlands surrender Kaiser Wilhelm II to the Allied Powers for trial following the First World War, a provision that the Netherlands rejected. At the end of the Second World War, however, the international community witnessed the

---

[66] OPCW Doc. EC-M-33/NAT.1, 17 September 2013, p. 2.

[67] Tabassi and Elias, *supra* note 57, p. 594.

[68] It is stressed that "[t]he principle of duty to cooperate prevailed" (Jacobsson, *supra* note 56, p. 151).

[69] Gómez-Robledo, *supra* note 55, p. 189.

[70] Jacobsson, *supra* note 56, p. 140; Sean D. Murphy, "Current Developments," *American Journal of International Law*, Vol. 115, Issue 4 (2021), p. 671, p. 673.

[71] Report of the International Law Commission on the Work of Its Seventy-Second Session, UN GAOR, 76th session, Supp. No. 10, UN Doc. A/76/10, 10 September 2021, pp. 76–77.

[72] Murphy, *supra* note 70, p. 673.

[73] OPCW Doc. EC-M-33/DEC.1, 27 September 2013, preamble para. 8.

Nurnberg and Tokyo Military Tribunals, which at last ushered in the era of criminal trials at the international level.

In December 1948, in conjunction with the adoption of the Convention on the Prevention and Punishment of the Crime of Genocide (Genocide Convention), which envisaged an international trial system, the UN General Assembly invited the ILC "to study the desirability and possibility of establishing an international judicial organ for the trial of persons charged with genocide or other crimes over which jurisdiction will be conferred upon that organ by international conventions."[74] In response, the ILC submitted positive views on the establishment of an international tribunal, based on which the General Assembly embarked on preparations. A newly created committee presented a draft statute in 1951 and a revised one in 1953. However, the General Assembly postponed the initiative under the circumstance of the Cold War.

The end of the Cold War provided an opportunity to revive the idea of international criminal tribunal. In December 1989, the General Assembly asked the ILC to resume its work. In 1993, the UN Security Council established ad hoc international criminal tribunals for the former Yugoslavia and Rwanda. This development spurred the ILC to submit a final draft statute to the General Assembly in 1994.[75] Following Ad Hoc Committee meetings in 1995 and six Preparatory Committee sessions between 1996 and 1998, the aforementioned diplomatic conference took place, at which the ICC Rome Statute was adopted, making it possible to hold individuals accountable for serious breaches or violations of relevant rules. In other words, international law was ultimately equipped with a two-pronged approach to addressing violations of international humanitarian law, on the State and individual levels.

(b) **Chemical Weapons Provisions**

Regarding war crimes involving chemical weapons, the Rome Statute specifies "[e]mploying asphyxiating, poisonous or other gases, and all analogous liquids, materials or devices" among "serious violations of the laws and customs applicable in international armed conflict" (Article 8, para. 2(b)(xviii)). This language, almost identical to that of the Geneva Protocol, follows the classical formulation of chemical weapons. In 2010, the Review Conference of the Rome Statute successfully added such crimes to "serious violations of the laws and customs applicable in armed conflicts not of an international character" by amendment (Article 8, para. 2(e)(xiv)).[76] Moreover, the indiscriminate nature thereof means that use of chemical weapons against civilians may fall under other crimes against humanity or war

[74] UN Doc. A/RES/260B (III), 9 December 1948.

[75] *Yearbook of the International Law Commission 1994*, Vol. II, Part Two, p. 26, para. 91.

[76] ICC Doc. RC/Res.5, 10 June 2010 (ICC Doc. RC/11, pp. 13–16). This amendment "shall enter into force for those States Parties which have accepted the amendment one year after the deposit of their instruments of ratification or acceptance" (Article 121, para. 5). As of 20 January 2023, it was ratified or accepted by 45 States Parties (UN Treaty Collection, https://treaties.un.org/Pages/ViewDetails.aspx?src=TREATY&mtdsg_no=XVIII-10-a&chapter=18&clang=_en, accessed 22 April 2023).

crimes under Article 7, para. 1(a), Article 8, para. 2(c)(i), and Article 8, para. 2(e)(i) of the Statute.

(c) **Syria**

To date, Syria remains a non-State Party to the Rome Statute since the latter's entry into force on 1 July 2002. Thus, the ICC is unable to exercise jurisdiction over situations in Syria in accordance with Article 13, para. (a) or (c), as these provisions are predicated on crimes committed by a national of a State Party, in the territory of a State Party, or on board a vessel or aircraft registered by a State Party (Article 12, para. 2). Nor has it consented as a non-State Party to the exercise of ICC jurisdiction in accordance with Article 12, para. 3. The only remaining option for bringing parties responsible for using chemical weapons in Syria to international justice is the referral of the UN Security Council, acting under Chapter VII of the UN Charter, to the ICC Office of the Prosecutor (OTP) in accordance with Article 13, para. (b).

2.3 Customary International Law on Chemical Weapons

Chemical weapons have also been addressed by customary international law, though the scope thereof is limited to the use of same. As discussed hereinafter, however, the scope of non-use of chemical weapons has been expanded to include international as well as non-international armed conflicts.

(1) **Customary International Law in General**

Customary international law, an unwritten source of international law, is binding on all States by definition.[77] The existence of customary international law is determined on the basis of the aforementioned two-element theory,[78] which the ILC has elaborated as follows:

- To determine the existence and content of a rule of customary international law, it is necessary to ascertain whether there is a general practice that is accepted as law (*opinio juris*).[79]

[77] Thirlway, *supra* note 1, p. 63. The International Law Commission (ILC) included "a persistent objector theory" concept in its Conclusion 15 of the Conclusions on the Identification of Customary International Law (*Yearbook of the International Law Commission 2018*, Vol. II, Part Two, p. 91).

[78] *North Sea Continental Shelf, Judgment, I.C.J. Reports 1969*, p. 3, p. 44, para. 77; *Continental Shelf (Libyan Arab Jamahiriya/Malta), Judgment, I.C.J. Reports 1985*, p. 13, pp. 29–30, para. 27; *Military and Paramilitary Activities in and against Nicaragua (Nicaragua v. United States of America), Merits, Judgment, I.C.J. Reports 1986*, p. 14, p. 97, para. 183; *Legality of the Threat or Use of Nuclear Weapons, Advisory Opinion, I.C.J. Reports 1996*, p. 226, p. 253, para. 64; *Jurisdictional Immunities of the State (Germany v. Italy: Greece intervening), Judgment, I.C.J. Reports 2012*, p. 99, pp. 122–123, para. 55; *Legal Consequences of the Separation of the Chagos Archipelago from Mauritius in 1965, Advisory Opinion, I.C.J. Reports 2019*, p. 95, pp. 131–132, para. 149.

[79] Conclusion 2, Conclusions on the Identification of Customary International Law (*Yearbook of the International Law Commission 2018*, Vol. II, Part Two, p. 90).

- The relevant practice must be general, meaning that it must be sufficiently widespread and representative, as well as consistent.[80]
- The requirement, as a constituent element of customary international law, that the general practice be accepted as law (*opinio juris*) means that the practice in question must be undertaken with a sense of legal right or obligation.[81]

Despite wide acceptance of this formulation, however, the two-element theory does not necessarily apply to obligations of omission. In normal circumstances, States refrain from taking action. One could argue that there is general practice because State practice of inaction is fully general and consistent. If this argument is acceptable, then the next question is whether *opinio juris* exists. However, this is a very difficult question to answer. Inaction as such does not offer an indication as to whether States refrain from doing something in the belief that they feel obliged to do so. The existence of *opinio juris* will thus be evaluated abstractly. Given non-recourse to nuclear weapons over the past fifty years, the ICJ issued a denial in its *Nuclear Weapons* advisory opinion of the existence of a customary obligation not to use nuclear weapons because of "substantial negative votes and abstentions" to relevant UN General Assembly resolutions, which "still fall short of establishing the existence of an *opinio juris* on the illegality of the use of such weapons."[82]

Due to the nature of obligation of omission as indicated herein, a paradox arises: an inconsistent practice will offer a good opportunity to analyze whether customary obligation of omission exists, a position of the ICJ in the *Nicaragua* case, pointing out that "instances of State conduct inconsistent with a given rule should generally have been treated as breaches of that rule, not as indications of the recognition of a new rule."[83] In other words, the existence of *opinio juris* in an actual case supersedes and even cures lack of consistency in State practice. In this regard, the attitude of the State concerned is of importance. As the ICJ elaborated in the aforementioned case, "[i]f a State acts in a way prima facie incompatible with a recognized rule, but defends its conduct by appealing to exceptions or justifications contained within the rule itself, then whether or not the State's conduct is in fact justifiable on that basis, the significance of that attitude is to confirm rather than to weaken the rule."[84] If the State concerned categorically denies the fact without mentioning a "rule," the attitude thus expressed suggests that said State does not deny said "rule" per se. The reaction of other States is also valuable. If overwhelming majority of other States, in some cases through resolutions of regional or international organizations, condemn the act inconsistent with the "rule," this should be regarded as collective *opinio juris*.

---

[80] Conclusion 8, Conclusions on the Identification of Customary International Law (*ibid.*, p. 91).

[81] Conclusion 9, para. 1, Conclusions on the Identification of Customary International Law (*ibid.*, p. 91).

[82] *Legality of the Threat or Use of Nuclear Weapons, Advisory Opinion, I.C.J. Reports 1996*, p. 226, p. 255, para. 71.

[83] *Military and Paramilitary Activities in and against Nicaragua (Nicaragua v. United States of America), Merits, Judgment, I.C.J. Reports 1986*, p. 14, p. 98, para. 186.

[84] *Ibid.*, p. 98, para. 186.

Having discussed the approach to the identification of customary obligation of omission in general, we turn to the specific instance of non-use of chemical weapons under customary international law.

(2) Non-use of Chemical Weapons in International Armed Conflicts

Following the Second World War, the international community did not witness the use of chemical weapons in international armed conflict until the Iran-Iraq War of the 1980s. An important development during this period was the adoption of UN General Assembly Resolution 2603A (XXIV) in December 1969.[85] The relevant portion of same for present purposes is as follows:

> *Declares* as contrary to the generally recognized rules of international law, as embodied in the Protocol for the Prohibition of the Use in War of Asphyxiating, Poisonous or Other Gases, and of Bacteriological Methods of Warfare, signed at Geneva on 17 June 1925, in international armed conflicts of:
>
> (a) Any chemical agents of warfare—chemical substances, whether gaseous, liquid or solid—which might be employed because of their direct toxic effects on man, animals or plants;
>
> (b) Any biological agents of warfare—living organisms, whatever their nature, or infective material derived from them—which are intended to cause disease or death in man, animals or plants, and which depend for their effects on their ability to multiply in the person, animal or plant attacked.

Whether this resolution can be evidence of customary international law needs to be examined in light of the formulation that was established by the ICJ in the *Nuclear Weapons* advisory opinion and reaffirmed in the *Chagos* case. In sum, the Court held that while UN General Assembly resolutions themselves are not legally binding, they "may sometimes have normative value" and "can, in certain circumstances, provide evidence important for establishing the existence of a rule or the emergence of an *opinio juris*."[86] Factors for consideration of such resolutions are "its content," "the conditions of its adoption," "whether an *opinio juris* exists as to its normative character," and "a series of resolutions."[87]

The UN General Assembly took the position that the Geneva Protocol embodies "the generally recognized rules of international law,"[88] i.e., existing customary international law. As implied in Article 38 of the VCLT, a treaty rule binds on States not

[85] UN Doc. A/RES/2603A(XXIV), 16 December 1969. A draft resolution was submitted by Argentina, Brazil, Burma, Ethiopia, India, Mexico, Morocco, Nigeria, Pakistan, Sweden, United Arab Republic, and Yugoslavia (UN Doc. ENDC/265, 26 August 1969). Algeria, Ceylon, Cyprus, Ghana, Ireland, Jamaica, Kenya, and Nepal joined the co-sponsoring States (UN Doc. A/7890, 13 December 1969, pp. 5–6).

[86] *Legality of the Threat or Use of Nuclear Weapons, Advisory Opinion, I.C.J. Reports 1996*, p. 226, pp. 254–255, para. 70; *Legal Consequences of the Separation of the Chagos Archipelago from Mauritius in 1965, Advisory Opinion, I.C.J. Reports 2019*, p. 95, p. 132, para. 151.

[87] *Legality of the Threat or Use of Nuclear Weapons, Advisory Opinion, I.C.J. Reports 1996*, p. 226, p. 255, para. 70. See also *Legal Consequences of the Separation of the Chagos Archipelago from Mauritius in 1965, Advisory Opinion, I.C.J. Reports 2019*, p. 95, p. 132, para. 151.

[88] UN Doc. A/RES/2603A(XXIV), 16 December 1969, preamble para. 5.

party to said treaty if it becomes a customary rule, and by the 1950s, the assertion was being made that the Geneva Protocol had become just such customary international law.[89] This position itself thus demonstrates the substance of customary rule and the existence of *opinio juris* as to its normative character.

Nor did the conditions of its adoption interfere with this conclusion. While the resolution was adopted by a vote of 80 in favor to three against, with 36 abstentions,[90] the States that did not vote in favor objected only against inclusion of "plants" among prohibited targets of chemical warfare agents, as well as to procedural aspects of reliance on a General Assembly resolution.[91] No State denied the existence of "generally recognized rules of international law" on the prohibition of the use of chemical weapons. The conditions of the adoption, thus, did not affect the evidential value of this resolution to the existence of customary international law.[92]

Subsequent resolutions also implicitly and explicitly reflect the general acceptance of the existence of customary international law. As seen above, the UN General Assembly adopted two resolutions in the specific context of "the use of chemical and bacteriological methods of warfare" in territories under Portuguese administration. Resolutions 2707 (XXV) and 2795 (XXVI) explicitly mentioned that such use is "contrary to the generally recognized rules of international law embodied in the [Geneva] Protocol… and to General Assembly resolution 2603 (XXIV)."[93] While some States did not vote in favor,[94] once again, there was no dispute over the existence of "generally recognized rules of international law."

The UN General Assembly also adopted three resolutions which introduced procedures for investigating allegations of use of chemical weapons. The first of these is Resolution 35/144C,[95] which contains this text in its fourth preamble paragraph:

> *Believing* that the continued authority of the [Geneva] Protocol and relevant rules of customary international law require that full and proper attention be given to all report

---

[89] Hersch Lauterpacht (ed.), *Oppenheim's International Law: a treatise*, seventh edition (Longmans, Green and Co., 1955), p. 344; Robert W. Tucker, *The Law of War and Neutrality at Sea* (United States Government Printing Office, 1957), p. 52; Morris Greenspan, *The Modern Law of Land Warfare* (University of California Press, 1959), p. 354. See also Myres S. McDougal and Florentino P. Feliciano, *Law and Minimum World Public Order* (Yale University Press, 1961), p. 634; George Bunn, "Banning Poison Gas and Germ Warfare: Should the United States Agree?," *Wisconsin Law Review*, Vol. 1969, No. 2 (1969), p. 375, pp. 381–389.

[90] UN Doc. A/PV.1836, 16 December 1969, p. 4.

[91] UN Doc. A/7890, 13 December 1969, p.10. UN Doc. A/C.1/PV.1716, 9 December 1969, pp. 13–14, paras. 145–146(Canada), p.18, para. 202 (France); UN Doc. A/C.1/PV.1717, 10 December 1969, p. 2, paras. 12–13 (Netherlands), p. 5, para. 56 (Japan), p. 6, para. 60 (Belgium), p. 6, paras. 63–64 (El Salvador), p. 7, para. 81 (China), p. 10, para. 120 (Australia); Masahiko Asada, "A Path to a Comprehensive Prohibition of the Use of Chemical Weapons under International Law: From the Hague to Damascus," *Journal of Conflict and Security Law*, Vol. 21, No. 2 (2016), p. 153, p. 160.

[92] Wil D. Verwey, *Riot Control Agents and Herbicides in War: Their humanitarian, toxicological, ecological, military, polemological, and legal aspects* (A. W. Sijthoff, 1977), pp. 283–284.

[93] UN Doc. A/RES/2707 (XXV), 14 December 1970, para. 9; UN Doc. A/RES/2795 (XXVI), 10 December 1971, para. 6.

[94] See footnote 15.

[95] UN Doc. A/RES/35/144C, 12 December 1980.

regarding the alleged use of chemical weapons and to their harmful effects, both immediate and long-term, to humans and to the environment of the victim countries.

The General Assembly adopted the resolution on 12 December 1980, by a vote of 78 in favor to 17 against, with 36 abstentions.[96] During the negotiation, there were no objections to the language "the continued authority of the [Geneva] Protocol and relevant rules of customary international law," suggesting that there was thus a general consensus among States on the existence of customary international law on non-use of chemical weapons despite the vote tallies.

Second came Resolution 37/98D, titled "Provisional procedures to uphold the authority of the 1925 Geneva protocol."[97] Its fourth operative paragraph requests "the Secretary-General to investigate…information that may be brought to his attention by any Member State concerning activities that may constitute a violation of the Protocol or of the relevant rules of customary international law in order to ascertain thereby the facts of the matter…"[98] The General Assembly adopted the resolution on 13 December 1982 by a vote of 86 in favor to 19 against, with 33 abstentions.[99] Again, the existence of "the relevant rules of customary international law" was not questioned, the conditions of the resolution's adoption notwithstanding. Those States that did not support the resolution argued that it indirectly amended the Geneva Protocol to establish a right of States not Parties to same to pass judgment on the conduct of States

---

[96] UN Doc. A/35/PV.94, 12 December 1980, para. 58. The original text of this passage in the draft resolution, sponsored by Canada, France, Federal Republic of Germany, Netherlands, New Zealand, Norway, Spain, and Turkey (UN Doc. A/C.1/35/L.43, 18 November 1980, preamble para. 4 and UN Doc. A/C.1/35/L.43/Rev.1, 20 November 1980, preamble para. 4 ("*Believing* that the continued authority of the [Geneva] Protocol and relevant rules of customary international law require that full and proper attention be given to all report regarding the alleged use of chemical weapons.")) was followed by an amendment proposed by Afghanistan, Bulgaria, Czechoslovakia, Laos, Mongolia, Poland, and Viet Nam (UN Doc. A/C.1/35/L.57, 25 November 1980, preamble para. 4 ("*Believing* that the continued authority of the [Geneva] Protocol and relevant rules of customary international law require that full and proper attention be given to all report regarding the alleged use of chemical weapons and to their harmful effects, both immediate and long-term, to humans and to the environment of the victim countries and to the military personnel of the belligerent parties.")), a revised draft that incorporated a partial amendment offered by New Zealand on behalf of the sponsors of the original draft (UN Doc. A/C.1/35/L.43/Rev.2, 26 November 1980, preamble para. 4 ("*Believing* that the continued authority of the [Geneva] Protocol and relevant rules of customary international law require that full and proper attention be given to all report regarding the alleged use of chemical weapons and to their harmful effects")), and an amendment to the revised draft proposed by Viet Nam on behalf of the sponsors of the initial amendment (UN Doc. A/C.1/35/L.61, 28 November 1980, preamble para. 4 ("*Believing* that the continued authority of the [Geneva] Protocol and relevant rules of customary international law require that full and proper attention be given to all report regarding the alleged use of chemical weapons and to their harmful effects both immediate and long-term, to humans and to the environment of the victim countries.")).

[97] UN Doc. A/RES/37/98D, 13 December 1982.

[98] *Ibid.*, operative para. 4.

[99] UN Doc. A/37/PV.101, 13 December 1982, para. 46.

Parties.[100] No State denied the existence of customary international law on non-use of chemical weapons, however.[101] In fact, several States explicitly endorsed this position. For instance, France, a sponsor, stated that "according to the most widely expressed opinion, its provisions are part of customary international law."[102] For their part, India and Canada explicitly referred to Resolution 2603A (XXIV),[103] while the US took the position that "[t]he prohibition contained in the 1925 Geneva Protocol has become part of customary international law and is thus binding on all states,"[104] that "[t]he use of these [chemical and toxin] weapons is a flagrant contravention of two major international agreements and customary international law,"[105] and that "[s]uch use of chemical weapons would constitute yet another serious breach of the Protocol, and related rules of customary international law…"[106] And the Federal Republic of Germany expressed the view that "the objective of resolution 37/98D is simply to ensure compliance with the actual obligations deriving from the Protocol and from international customary law."[107]

Third and most important of these is Resolution 42/37C, titled "Measures to uphold the authority of the 1925 Geneva Protocol and to support the conclusion of a chemical weapons convention."[108] Its first preamble paragraph recalled "the provisions of the [Geneva] Protocol…, and other relevant rules of customary international law,"[109] while its fourth operative paragraph requests "the Secretary-General to carry out investigation in response to reports that may be brought to his attention by any Member State concerning the possible use of chemical and bacteriological (biological) or toxin weapons that may constitute a violation of the 1925 Geneva Protocol or other relevant rules of customary international law in order to ascertain the facts of the matter…"[110] The General Assembly adopted this resolution without a vote on 30

[100] UN Doc. A/C.1/37/PV.47, 29 November 1982, pp. 21 (Hungary), 27 (India), 32 (Bulgaria), 36 (Argentine), 41 (Czechoslovakia), 43–45 (Algeria), 46–47 (USSR), 61 (Ukrainian SSR), 66 (Mexico), 67–70 (Viet Nam), and 72 (Byelorussian SSR).

[101] While the German Democratic Republic indicated that "it is not clear what is mean by so-called relevant rules of customary international law" (UN Doc. A/C.1/37/PV.47, 29 November 1982, p. 28 (German Democratic Republic)) and Argentina pointed out that the concept of "the relevant rules of customary international law" is "too vague to be included in a verification system" (*ibid.*, p. 37 (Argentina)), they did not question the existence of these rules per se under customary international law.

[102] UN Doc. A/C.1/37/PV.38, 19 November 1982, pp. 89–90 (France).

[103] UN Doc. A/C.1/37/PV.47, 29 November 1982, pp. 27 (India), and 56 (Canada).

[104] UN Doc. A/38/184, 9 May 1983, p. 3.

[105] UN Doc. A/38/326, 5 August 1983, p. 2.

[106] UN Doc. A/39/113, 22 February 1984, p. 3.

[107] UN Doc. A/38/281, 22 June 1983, p. 2.

[108] UN Doc. A/RES/42/37C, 30 November 1987.

[109] *Ibid.*, preamble para. 1.

[110] *Ibid.*, operative para. 4.

November 1987.[111] In 1992, this mechanism was implemented to investigate alleged use of chemical weapons during international armed conflict between Azerbaijan and Armenia.[112] The fact that both were non-State Parties to the Geneva Protocol at that time indicates that they agreed about the aforementioned existence of customary international law in this regard.

The same belief is also widely held in academia. For example, Baxter and Buergenthal reached the conclusion that "[t]he weight of opinion appears today to favor the view that customary international law proscribes the use in war of lethal chemical and biological weapons."[113] Goldblat pointed out that "[a]ccording to a widely shared opinion, the [Geneva] Protocol is part of customary international law, to be complied with by parties and non-parties alike."[114] Boothby was of the view that "[t]his norm is started to apply in both international and non-international armed conflicts."[115] Dinstein indicated that "even prior to the American ratification, the prevailing view was that the Protocol had come to reflect customary international law."[116] And Fleck argued that "[t]he general prohibition against the use of poisonous gases…now constitutes a rule of customary law."[117] Despite this uncontroversial and unanimous consensus on the existence of customary international law, however, it remains unclear whether the use of chemical weapons is prohibited without exception thereunder.[118] By the 1970s, Thomas and Thomas were of the view that "the existence of a binding customary norm prohibiting at least the first use of the lethal or severely injurious types of chemical agents."[119] Moore argued that "the weight of opinion seems to support the view that customary international law prohibits at

---

[111] UN Doc. A/42/PV.84, 30 November 1987, p. 36. In 1988, the General Assembly also adopted Resolution 43/74A, containing nearly identical elements to Resolution 42/37C, without a vote (UN Doc. A/43/PV.73, 7 December 1988, p. 38).

[112] UN Doc. S/24344, 24 July 1992.

[113] Baxter and Buergenthal, *supra* note 37, p. 853.

[114] Jozef Goldblat, *Arms Control: The New Guide to Negotiations and Agreements*, second edition (SAGE Publications, 2002), p. 137.

[115] William H. Boothby, *Weapons and the Law of Armed Conflict* (Oxford University Press, 2009), p. 137.

[116] Yoram Dinstein, *The Conduct of Hostilities under the Law of International Armed Conflict*, third edition (Cambridge University Press, 2016), p. 92.

[117] Dieter Fleck, "6. Means of Combat, III. Weapons of Mass Destruction," in Dieter Fleck (ed.), *The Handbook of International Humanitarian Law*, fourth edition (Oxford University Press, 2021), p. 156, p. 165. This text remains the same since the first edition (Stefan Oeter, "Methods and Means of Combat," in Dieter Fleck (ed.), *The Handbook of International Humanitarian Law* (Oxford University Press, 1999), p. 105, p. 148; Stefan Oeter, "Methods and Means of Combat," in Dieter Fleck (ed.), *The Handbook of International Humanitarian Law*, second edition (Oxford University Press, 2008), p. 119, p. 171; Stefan Oeter, "Methods and Means of Combat," in Dieter Fleck (ed.), *The Handbook of International Humanitarian Law*, third edition (Oxford University Press, 2013), p. 115, p. 162).

[118] Mika Hayashi, "Reacting to the Use of Chemical Weapons: Options for Third States," *Journal on Use of Force and International Law*, Vol. 1, No.1 (2014), p. 80, pp. 83–84.

[119] Ann Van Wynen Thomas and Aaron Joshua Thomas, *Legal Limits on the Use of Chemical and Biological Weapons* (Southern Methodist University Press, 1970), p. 185.

least the first use of lethal chemical agents in war."[120] These ideas arose the practice of reservations to the Geneva Protocol regarding right of reprisal, which "cannot effectively be invoked" by States Parties to the CWC following the latter's entry into force.[121] This understanding does not apply to Israel or the Democratic People's Republic of Korea, however, as they are States Parties to the Geneva Protocol with reservation, but non-State Parties to the CWC. It would thus be safer to conclude that customary international law obliges all States not to carry out at least the first use of chemical weapons instead.

(3) Non-use of Chemical Weapons in Non-international Armed Conflicts

While Resolution 2603A (XXIV) limited the scope of customary international law to international armed conflicts, subsequent developments suggested that customary international law extends the prohibition of the use of chemical weapons to non-international armed conflicts as well. The aforementioned Halabja incident offers a more useful reference.[122]

As described, in March 1988 Iraq made a large chemical attack against the Kurdish population within its territory in. In 1995, the International Criminal Tribunal for the former Yugoslavia (ICTY) in its *Tadić* case referred to various statements, declarations, and attitudes of states in response to the incident, including the declaration of the twelve Member States of the European Community,[123] the position of the British authorities,[124] the statement by the German authorities,[125] the view of the US,[126] the attitude of Iraq,[127] and the response of Middle Eastern States to US accusations,[128] concluding that "there undisputedly emerged a general consensus in the international community on the principle that the use of those weapons is also prohibited in

---

[120] John Norton Moore, "Ratification of the Geneva Protocol on Gas and Bacteriological Warfare: A Legal and Political Analysis," *Virginia Law Review*, Vol. 58, No. 3 (1972), p. 419, p. 449.

[121] Asada, *supra* note 91, p. 183.

[122] Sivakumaran, *supra* note 39, p. 394.

[123] Prosecutor v. Dusko Tadić a/k/a "Dule", Decision on the Defence Motion for Interlocutory Appeal on Jurisdiction, IT-94–01, 2 October 1995, para. 120 (*European Political Cooperation Documentation Bulletin*, Vol. 4, No. 2 (European University Institute, 1988), p. 92; UN Doc. A/C.1/43/PV.4, 18 October 1988, p. 47; UN Doc. A/C.1/43/PV.31, 9 November 1988, p. 23; UN Doc. A/C.3/43/SR.49, 22 November 1988, p. 16; Report on European Union [EPC Aspects], *European Political Cooperation Documentation Bulletin*, Vol. 4, No. 2 (European University Institute, 1988), p. 330; Question No 362/88 by Mr. Arbeloa Muru (S-E) Concerning the Poisoning of Opposition Members in Iraq, *European Political Cooperation Documentation Bulletin*, Vol. 4, No. 2 (European University Institute, 1988), p. 187.

[124] Prosecutor v. Dusko Tadić a/k/a "Dule", Decision on the Defence Motion for Interlocutory Appeal on Jurisdiction, IT-94–01, 2 October 1995, para. 121.

[125] *Ibid.*, para. 121.

[126] *Ibid.*, para. 122.

[127] *Ibid.*, para. 123 (*New York Times*, Iraq's Right to Chemical Arms Upheld by Official, 16 September 1988, p. A11).

[128] *Ibid.*, para. 123 (*New York Times*, Turkey Opposes an Inquiry into Poison Gas Issue, 15 September 1988, p. A13; *Washington Post*, Yelling "Palestine," 20 September 1988, p. A 21).

internal armed conflicts."[129] Commentators regard this judicial view as a key instance of international practice demonstrating the existence of customary international law in this regard.[130]

Dutch courts as well as the European Court of Human Rights (ECHR) had also taken up the matter. In its 2009 judgment in the *van Anraat* case, the Supreme Court of the Netherlands endorsed the decision of the Court of Appeal, which was premised on the very existence of a customary international rule prohibiting the use of chemical weapons in non-international armed conflict when the incident occurred.[131] The ECHR also referred to the decision by the ICTY *Tadić* case which noted "the existence, at the relevant time, of a rule of customary international law prohibiting the use of chemical weapons by States against civilian populations within their own territory."[132]

There have been other allegations of the use of chemical weapons in non-international armed conflicts following the Halabja incident. In 1992, Mozambique requested that the UN Secretary-General investigate a case in which anti-government forces allegedly attacked government troops with chemical weapons.[133] In 2007, it was reported that an Iraqi opposition group used chlorine gas in that country's non-international armed conflict, an act that the UN Security Council and the OPCW condemned in strong terms.[134] Furthermore, as indicated above, the ICC Rome Statute was amended in 2010 to add use of chemical weapons to a list of war crimes in non-international armed conflict, albeit by only the 84 States Parties to the Statute,

129 Prosecutor v. Dusko Tadić a/k/a "Dule", Decision on the Defence Motion for Interlocutory Appeal on Jurisdiction, IT-94–01, 2 October 1995, para. 124.

130 Kenneth Watkin, "Chemical Agents and Expanding Bullets: Limited Law Enforcement Exceptions or Unwarranted Handcuffs," *Israel Yearbook on Human Rights*, Vol. 36 (2006), p. 43, p. 47; Sivakumaran, *supra* note 39, pp. 394–395.

131 Judgment LJN: BG4822, Hoge Raad der Nederlanden (Supreme Court of the Netherlands), 07/10742, 30 June 2009. See also Judgment LJN: AX6406, Rechtbank 's-Gravenhage (Regional Court of The Hague), 09/751003–04, 23 December 2005; Judgment LJN: BA6734, Gerechtshof' 's-Gravenhage (Court of Appeal of The Hague), 2,200,050,906–2, 9 May 2007.

132 Third Section Decision as to the Admissibility of Application No. 65389/09, by Frans Cornelis Adrianus van Anraat against the Netherlands, 6 July 2010, para. 94.

133 UN Doc. S/24065, 12 June 1992, p. 1, para. 1. This document does not refer to the UN Secretary-General's investigation mechanism created by UN General Assembly Resolution 42/37C. The UN publication indicates, however, that the investigation was carried out pursuant to this mechanism (*United Nations Disarmament Yearbook, Vol. 38 (Part II): 2013* (United Nations Publication, 2014), p. 66, footnote 3). Customary international law was considered applicable, given that Mozambique remains a non-State Party to the Geneva Protocol as of this writing.

134 Security Council Press Statement on Iraq, UN Doc. SC/8963, 22 February 2007 ("The members of the Security Council are following with concern the situation in Iraq, and condemn all terrorist attacks, including the recent chlorine gas…"); UN Doc. S/PV.5635, 23 February 2007, p. 4 (OPCW Director-General); OPCW News, OPCW Director-General Condemns Renewed Chemical Attacks in Iraq, 19 March 2007, https://www.opcw.org/media-centre/news/2007/03/opcw-director-general-condemns-renewed-chemical-attacks-iraq, accessed 22 April 2023; *Chemical Disarmament*, Vol. 5, No. 2 (2007), p. 5.

representing less than half the number of States in the international community and excluding major powers such as the US, Russia, China, India, and Pakistan.[135]

International law scholars have confronted this issue as well. Some have previously raised doubts about the existence of positive law at the time of the Halabja incident. For Zwanenburg and den Dekker, "it is difficult to determine if this rule of international law was already established back in the 1980s." They further point out that "[a]part from (consistent) normative reactions of states to instances of such use, proof can only be derived from the absence of contrary practice based on a sense of legal…obligation" and that "[s]trong proof…seems to be lacking."[136] Asada conducted a detailed critical analysis on relevant State practice cited by the ICTY in the Tadić case, concluding that "our examination could not lead to the same conclusion as the ICTY's."[137]

These days, however, there is consensus in academia that customary international law prohibits use of chemical weapons in non-international armed conflicts. Sivakumaran holds that "at least since 1988, if not earlier, the prohibition on the use of asphyxiating, poisonous, and other gases, and chemical weapons in non-international armed conflict has been recognized as a norm of customary international law."[138] Dinstein regarded the abovementioned amendment to the ICC Rome Statute as reflecting customary international law on the prohibition of use of chemical weapons in non-international armed conflicts.[139] Fleck states that "the prohibition on the use of chemical weapons is applicable irrespective of whether the conflict is international or non-international."[140] Solis seems to combine the two approaches when he argues that "[t]oday, there are 145 States Parties, and the Protocol's prohibitions are customary law with regard to both international armed conflicts (IACs) and non-international armed conflicts (NIACs)."[141] The International Committee of the Red Cross (ICRC) also takes the same approach.[142]

---

[135] Asada, *supra* note 91, p. 198.

[136] Marten Zwanenburg and Guido den Dekker, "Prosecutor v. Frans van Anraat—Case No. 07/10742.2009 Nederlandse Jurisprudentie 481," *American Journal of International Law*, Vol. 104, No. 1 (2010), p. 86, p. 91.

[137] Asada, *supra* note 91, p. 192.

[138] Sivakumaran, *supra* note 39, p. 394.

[139] Yoram Dinstein, *Non-International Armed Conflicts in International Law* (Cambridge University Press, 2014), p. 12.

[140] Fleck, *supra* note 117, p. 166. The cited text remains unchanged from the first three editions (Oeter, "Methods and Means of Combat," in Dieter Fleck (ed.), *The Handbook of International Humanitarian Law* (Oxford University Press, 1999), p. 105, p. 148; Oeter, "Methods and Means of Combat," in Dieter Fleck (ed.), *The Handbook of International Humanitarian Law*, second edition (Oxford University Press, 2008), p. 119, p. 171; Oeter, "Methods and Means of Combat," in Dieter Fleck (ed.), *The Handbook of International Humanitarian Law*, third edition (Oxford University Press, 2013), p. 115, p. 162).

[141] Gary D. Solis, *The Law of Armed Conflict: International Humanitarian law in War*, third edition (Cambridge University Press, 2022), p. 613.

[142] Jean-Marie Henckaerts and Louise Doswald-Beck, *Customary International Humanitarian Law*, Volume I Rules (Cambridge University Press, 2005), pp. 261–263.

It follows that today customary international law encompasses the prohibition of use of chemical weapons in non-international armed conflict, by States and non-State actors alike, through the emergence of a new customary rule or an expansion of the scope of existing such law, which, in views of some States, is included in the Geneva Protocol. State practice in the early stages of the Syrian chemical weapons question will prove this conclusion, as will be discussed hereinafter.

As customary international law is binding on all States, it follows that same is also binding on Syria. The "persistent objector theory,"[143] even if stipulated, is not relevant in this instance, as Syria has never asserted any persistent objection to the emergence of customary rules governing prohibitions on use of chemical weapons.

2.4 UN Security Council Resolution

(1) "Law-Making" Resolutions

A "law-making" UN Security Council resolution may be binding on States, based on the aforementioned Article 25 of the UN Charter, which stipulates that "[t]he Members of the United Nations agree to accept and carry out the decisions of the Security Council in accordance with the present Charter." Thus, a paragraph using the term "decides" in a resolution adopted under Chapter VII would create a legally binding obligation. While each such instrument typically addresses a single specific issue, it is theoretically possible to include general obligations that would apply to all States.

(2) Resolution 1540

(a) Adoption

In a rare example of a law-making resolution, UN Security Council Resolution 1540, on non-proliferation of weapons of mass destruction to non-State actors, was adopted unanimously on 28 April 2004.[144] During open debate, many States mentioned the legally binding status of draft resolutions.[145] The Syrian Representative also made general comments on the elimination of weapons of mass destruction (WMD), grave

143 Conclusion 15, Conclusions on the Identification of Customary International Law (*Yearbook of the International Law Commission 2018*, Vol. II, Part Two, p. 91).

144 UN Doc. S/RES/1540 (2004), 28 April 2004.

145 UN Doc. S/PV. 4950, 22 April 2004, pp. 4 (Brazil), 5 (Algeria), 7 (Spain), 10 (Chile), 11 (UK), 16 (Russia), 17 (US), 18 (Germany), 27 (Ireland), 28 (Japan); UN Doc. S/PV. 4950 (Resumption), 22 April 2004, pp. 6 (Norway), 11 (Jordan), 17 (Kuwait); UN Doc. S/PV. 4956, 28 April 2004, pp. 3 (Pakistan), 7 (UK), 8 (Spain). A few States expressed concern about the legislative function of the Security Council (UN Doc. S/PV. 4950, 22 April 2004, pp. 23 (India), 32 (Iran)).

concerns about the possibility of WMD falling into the hands of terrorists, and the importance of coordinated international cooperation in stemming the threat.[146]

(b) **Substance**

It is widely understood that Resolution 1540 establishes binding obligations, calling on all States to "refrain from providing any form of support to non-State actors that attempt to develop, acquire, manufacture, possess, transport, transfer or use…chemical…weapons and their means of delivery" (operative para. 1); to adopt and enforce appropriate effective laws (operative para. 2); and to take and enforce effective measures to establish domestic controls (operative para. 3).

(c) **Syria**

All States are required to submit reports to the 1540 Committee, a subsidiary organ of the Security Council established in operative para. 4 of the Resolution 1540, whose mandate is to monitor implementation.[147] Syria has submitted five such national reports.[148] In its initial reports of 2004 and 2005, Syria made it clear that it does not possess weapons of mass destruction including chemical weapons,[149] though it acknowledged the possession of "chemical materials which are all used for peaceful industrial or agricultural purposes" and added that it had introduced a series of measures to regulate the handling of chemical materials employed in various applications with a view to preventing such substances from falling into the hands of non-State actors.[150] In its 2013 report, Syria mentioned media coverage regarding the possible production of chemical weapons by Al-Qaida members who were threating to use them against Syrian civilians.[151] As of this writing, Syria has submitted no further reports.

---

[146] UN Doc. S/PV. 4950, 22 April 2004, p. 33 (Syria).

[147] Subsequent resolutions extended the 1540 Committee mandate six times. The current mandate will expire by the end of November 2032 (UN Doc. S/RES/1673 (2006), 27 April 2006; UN Doc. S/RES/1810 (2008), 25 April 2008; UN Doc. S/RES/1977 (2011), 20 April 2011; UN Doc. S/RES/2572 (2021), 22 April 2021; UN Doc. S/2622 (2022), 25 February 2022; UN Doc. S/2663 (2022), 30 November 2022).

[148] UN. Doc. S/AC.44/2004/(02)/70, 14 October 2004; UN. Doc. S/AC.44/2004/(02)/70/Add.1, 26 August 2005; UN. Doc. S/AC.44/2004/(02)/70/Add.2, 29 September 2005; UN. Doc. S/AC.44/2004/(02)/70/Add.3, 7 November 2005; UN. Doc. S/AC.44/2013/21, 29 May 2013.

[149] UN. Doc. S/AC.44/2004/(02)/70, 14 October 2004, p. 2; UN. Doc. S/AC.44/2004/(02)/70/Add.3, 7 November 2005, p. 6, para. 24.

[150] UN. Doc. S/AC.44/2004/(02)/70/Add.3, 7 November 2005, p. 6, para. 26.

[151] UN. Doc. S/AC.44/2013/21, 29 May 2013, pp. 2–3.

2.5 Conclusion

A historical analysis indicates that the international community takes an incremental approach to the regulation and prohibition of chemical weapons, beginning with their use. Having witnessed the loss and damage caused by chemical attacks in the First World War, the international community adopted the Geneva Protocol in 1925, prohibiting use of chemical weapons in wartime. During the Cold War, a consensus emerged on customary international law prohibiting use of chemical weapons in international armed conflict, with the scope of customary international law further expanded to cover non-international armed conflict at a later stage. The CWC strengthened the prohibition of use to cover "any circumstances," while also prohibiting the development, production, stockpiling, and transfer of chemical weapons and imposing the obligation to destruct them.

Other institutions cover the acts of non-State actors. In the context of punishing individuals involved in chemical weapons use, the ICC Rome Statute included the use of chemical weapons in the list of war crimes in international armed conflict in the original text of 1998 and added the same act in the list of war crimes under non-international armed conflict in the 2010 amendment. UN Security Council Resolution 1540 likewise addresses non-proliferation to non-State actors of weapons of mass destruction, including chemical weapons.

As mentioned above, the CWC is the most important such instrument, for its comprehensive scope and stringent verification regime for ensuring compliance. In this regard, Syria's unexpected accession was significant, even if avoiding military action by the US, the UK, and France was its primary motivation. At the same time, the Convention is not perfect. It is not binding on non-State Parties. It cannot enforce sanctions. It lacks a mechanism to identify the perpetrators. It does not have criminal procedures. The Syrian chemical weapons issues have revealed these deficiencies and the necessity for coordination in relevant legal and institutional frameworks, as discussed hereinafter.

Chapter 3
International Humanitarian Law: *Ad Hoc* Compliance/Non-compliance Control Through *Ex Post* Measures

Abstract International law prohibits the use of chemical weapons. The compliance/non-compliance control is focused on how to deal with potential and actual non-compliance with this obligation on an *ad hoc* base through *ex post* measures. In the case of alleged use of chemical weapons, the fact-finding organs investigate allegations in order to determine whether chemical weapons were used and to identify the perpetrators. When use of chemical weapons has been ascertained, non-compliance needs to be addressed. The UN Security Council and the OPCW Executive Council took such measures in response to the chemical weapons attacks on 21 August 2013 as imposing a comprehensive ban of chemical weapons on Syria and tightening the non-proliferation regime. The Security Council's failure to adopt legally binding sanctions against further use of chemical weapons led the OPCW policy-making organs to suspend Syrian rights and privileges. In the meantime, like-minded States took unilateral action against Syria, while raising questions about the legality of use of force.

3.1 Introduction

There have been multiple allegations of chemical substances being used as weapons in the non-international armed conflict in Syria since December 2012. On 23 December 2012, Syrian rebels claimed that the government killed rebel fighters in a gas attack on Homs.[1] On 19 March 2013, the government and the opposition criticized each other for reportedly killing 25 people in Aleppo with chemical weapons.[2] In response, both Syria and the UK and France requested that the UN Secretary-General investigate this allegation on 20 and 21 March respectively. The UK and France also asked the Secretary-General to investigate other allegations, claiming that the Syrian

[1] The Times, Syrian rebels in Homs claim gas attack by government, 25 December 2012, https://www.thetimes.co.uk/article/syrian-rebels-in-homs-claim-gas-attack-by-government-g2bjcxxmmv8, accessed 22 April 2023.

[2] Reuters, Alleged chemical attack kills 25 in northern Syria, 19 March 2013, https://www.reuters.com/article/us-syria-crisis-chemical-idUSBRE92I0A220130319, accessed 22 April 2023.

T. Abe, *Syrian Chemical Weapons and International Law*,
https://doi.org/10.1007/978-981-99-3700-4_3

government used chemical weapons against anti-government forces. The Secretary-General established a UN Mission to investigate, in conjunction with the OPCW and the World Health Organization (WHO).[3] Then another alleged use of chemical weapons, this time in East Ghouta, was reported on 21 August 2013 while the UN Mission was deployed in Syria. It shifted the investigation to this allegation, concluding that "chemical weapons have been used in the ongoing conflict between the parties in the Syrian Arab Republic, also against civilians, including children, on a relatively large scale."[4] Unprecedented measures were instituted in response, which would have forestalled similar incidents if fully implemented.

In April 2014, both parties to the non-international armed conflict in Syria further alleged chemical attacks by the other. The Syrian government insisted that five States and terrorist organizations were "fully responsible for the crimes that were committed in Syria with chemical weapons, including the recent attack in Kafr Zayta."[5] For its part, the Special Representative of [the] Syrian Coalition to the United Nations claimed that Syrian regime air assets "bombarded the opposition-held town of Kafr Zita with explosive barrels loaded with chemical and toxic gases."[6] While investigation of the allegations was called for, it was unclear why either party to non-international armed conflict in Syria would be able to use weapons that were supposedly being disposed of under international control. If the government's account was true, Syria had failed to prevent proliferation of chemical weapons to non-State actors within its territory. If, on the other hand, the Syrian Coalition was right, then the government was using chemical agents as weapons which were undeclared. The international community's response to further use of chemical weapons in Syria runs the gamut from creating fact-finding missions and attribution mechanisms to ascertain their use and identify both the Syrian government and ISIL as responsible parties to making efforts to take sanctions against Syrian non-compliance. The situation became more complicated due to a number of allegations on the ground, and an ongoing political confrontation between the US and its European allies on the one hand and Russia, Syria, and Iran on the other.

This chapter clarifies the relevant substantive obligation, then discusses how the international community has dealt with the issue of the use of chemical weapons in Syria through compliance/non-compliance control. It consists of brief comments on ensuring compliance, intensive discussion on addressing potential non-compliance, and a relatively comprehensive analysis of institutional and unilateral responses to non-compliance, followed by a conclusion.

---

[3] UN Doc. S/2013/184, 25 March 2013, p. 1. This marked the first time since 1992 that the UN had implemented the mechanism. It was also the OPCW's first experience of making its personnel available to a UN investigation mission in accordance with relevant CWC provisions. In the meantime, the Independent International Commission of Inquiry (COI) on the Syrian Arab Republic, which the United Nations Human Rights Council (UNHRC) had established in 2011, initiated its own investigation pursuant to its own mandate.

[4] UN Doc. A/67/997–S/2013/553, 16 September 2013, p. 8, para. 27.

[5] UN Doc. S/2014/271, 16 April 2014, p. 2.

[6] UN Doc. S/2014/285, 17 April 2014, p. 2. See also UN Doc. S/2014/274, 11 April 2014.

3.2 Substantive Obligation: Obligation of Omission

(1) Context

International law establishes a prohibition against use of chemical weapons, which is typical of the obligation of omission. As discussed above, relevant sources in this regard are the Geneva Protocol, the CWC, and customary international law. Which of these sources applies depends on when a given incident occurred.

(2) Applicable Law

(a) Prior to September 2013

Prior to September 2013, the CWC did not apply to alleged use of chemical weapons in the non-international armed conflict in Syria because Syria remained a non-State Party to the Convention, as previously described. Applicable law was thus confined to customary international law and the Geneva Protocol. As early as in September 2012, the illegality of the use of chemical weapons was already mentioned. Cyprus stated on behalf of the EU that "use of chemical weapons is prohibited by general international law and by conventions including the 1925 Geneva Protocol, and [we] stress that the use of chemical weapons by Syria would be unlawful."[7] For its part, Norway indicated that "[i]nternational law, binding also for Syria, strictly prohibits the use of chemical weapons."[8]

After Syria, the UK, and France requested that the UN Secretary-General activate his investigation mechanism, the opinions of the States Parties to the CWC on this matter became clearer. The third Review Conference in April 2013 offered States Parties with timely opportunities to express their views in this regard. Some States Parties explicitly referred to the relevant sources. Luxembourg argued that "[i]f the use of chemical weapons were confirmed, that would represent a clear violation of the 1925 Geneva Protocol or other applicable regulations under traditional international law."[9] Romania mentioned that "[i]f the allegations are confirmed it would most probably constitute a violation of the 1925 Geneva Protocol…"[10] Mongolia reminded Syria of "the prohibition of the use of chemical weapons by international customary law and by the 1925 Geneva Protocol."[11] France stressed that "[c]eci constituerait une violation grave du Protocole de Genève de 1925 et d'autres règles pertinentes du droit international coutumier."[12] And Germany claimed that the use of

---

[7] OPCW Doc. EC-70/NAT.14 (Cyprus on behalf of the EU), 25 September 2012, p. 2.

[8] OPCW Doc. EC-70/NAT.12 (Norway), 25 September 2012, p. 1.

[9] OPCW Doc. RC-3/NAT.36 (Luxembourg), 8 April 2013.

[10] OPCW Doc. RC-3/NAT.37 (Romania), 9 April 2013.

[11] OPCW Doc. RC-3/NAT.31 (Mongolia), 10 April 2013.

[12] France, https://www.opcw.org/sites/default/files/documents/CSP/RC-3/national-statements/France_rc3.pdf, accessed 22 April 2023. In response to the chemical attack of 21 August 2013, France argued that "the [Assad] regime has violated the commitments under the Geneva Protocol of 1925, which it has signed in 1968, concerning the prohibition of use at war of suffocating gas, toxic or similar weapons as well as biological weapons" (Syria/Syrian chemical programme—National

chemical weapons "would be a grave violation of the 1925 Geneva Protocol and other rules of customary international law."[13] Curiously, all of these States Parties cited both the Geneva Protocol and customary international law.[14] Other States Parties indirectly endorsed the applicability of the Geneva Protocol and/or customary international law through their support of the UN investigation mission initiated by the UN Secretary-General pursuant to General Assembly Resolution 42/37C.[15] At the Third

---

executive summary of declassified intelligence, https://www.diplomatie.gouv.fr/IMG/pdf/Syrian_Chemical_Programme.pdf, accessed 22 April 2023).

[13] OPCW Doc. RC-3/NAT.28 (Germany), 9 April 2013.

[14] The UN Secretary-General also referred to the Geneva Protocol and customary international law when he condemned the use of chemical weapons in Ghouta on 21 August 2013 in his report (UN Doc. A/67/997–S/2013/553, 16 September 2013, p. 1, para. 1). The COI indicated that "[t]he use of chemical weapons is prohibited in all circumstances under customary international humanitarian law, and is a war crime under the Rome Statute" (UN Doc. A/HRC/23/58, 18 July 2013, para. 136).

[15] Argentina, http://www.opcw.org/index.php?eID=dam_frontend_push&docID=16290, accessed 22 April 2023; OPCW Doc. RC-3/NAT.62 (Australia), 9 April 2013, p. 1; OPCW Doc. RC-3/NAT23 (Belgium), 9 April 2013, pp. 2–3; OPCW Doc. RC-3/NAT.68 (Bolivia), 9 April 2013, p. 2; OPCW Doc. RC-3/NAT.32 (Croatia), 9 April 2013, p. 1; France, http://www.opcw.org/index.php?eID=dam_frontend_push&docID=16319, accessed 22 April 2023; OPCW Doc. RC-3/NAT.28 (Germany), 9 April 2013, p. 2; OPCW Doc. RC-3/NAT.38 (Hungary), 9 April 2013, p. 1; OPCW Doc. RC-3/NAT.29 (India), 8 April 2013, p. 2; Indonesia, http://www.opcw.org/index.php?eID=dam_frontend_push&docID=16333, accessed 22 April 2023; OPCW Doc. RC-3/NAT.74 (Iraq), 8 April 2013, p. 3; OPCW Doc. RC-3/NAT.51 (Ireland), 9 April 2013, p. 1; OPCW Doc. RC-3/NAT.43 (Japan), 9 April 2013, p. 2; Kazakhstan, http://www.opcw.org/index.php?eID=dam_frontend_push&docID=16357, accessed 22 April 2023; OPCW Doc. RC-3/NAT.36 (Luxembourg), 8 April 2013, p. 2; Malaysia, http://www.opcw.org/index.php?eID=dam_frontend_push&docID=16299 accessed 22 April 2023; OPCW Doc. RC-3/NAT.31 (Mongolia), 10 April 2013, p. 2; OPCW Doc. RC-3/NAT.35 (New Zealand), 9 April 2013, p. 1; OPCW Doc. RC-3/NAT.25 (Norway), 8 April 2013, p. 1; OPCW Doc. RC-3/NAT.34 (Pakistan), 8 April 2013, p. 1; Paraguay, http://www.opcw.org/index.php?eID=dam_frontend_push&docID=16360, accessed 22 April 2023; OPCW Doc. RC-3/NAT.18 (Peru), 8 April 2013, p. 2; OPCW Doc. RC-3/NAT.66 (Qatar), 8 April 2013, p. 2; OPCW Doc. RC-3/NAT.52 (Republic of Korea), 9 April 2013, p. 2; OPCW Doc. RC-3/NAT.37 (Romania), 9 April 2013, p. 3; OPCW Doc. RC-3/NAT.21 (Russia), 9 April 2013, p. 3; Saudi Arabia, http://www.opcw.org/index.php?eID=dam_frontend_push&docID=16305, accessed 22 April 2023; OPCW Doc. RC-3/NAT.27 (Slovakia), 9 April 2013, p. 2; OPCW Doc. EC-M-32/NAT.3 (South Africa), 27 March 2013, p. 2; Sweden, http://www.opcw.org/index.php?eID=dam_frontend_push&docID=16308, accessed 22 April 2023; Switzerland, http://www.opcw.org/index.php?eID=dam_frontend_push&docID=16325, accessed 7 January 2023; Thailand, http://www.opcw.org/index.php?eID=dam_frontend_push&docID=16289, accessed 22 April 2023; OPCW Doc. RC-3/NAT.69 (United Arab Emirates), 8 April 2013, p. 2; UK, http://www.opcw.org/index.php?eID=dam_frontend_push&docID=16326, accessed 22 April 2023; OPCW Doc. EC-M-32/NAT.1 (US), 27 March 2013, p. 1; OPCW Doc. RC-3/NAT.45 (US), 9 April 2013, p. 4; OPCW Doc. RC-3/NAT.50 (Ireland on behalf of the EU), 8 April 2013, p. 2; NAM CWC States Parties and China, http://www.opcw.org/index.php?eID=dam_frontend_push&docID=16296, accessed 22 April 2023. The UN Secretary-General explicitly cited UN General Assembly Resolution 42/37C (Off-the-Cuff, Secretary-General's Press Encounter on Syrian Government Request, New York, 21 March 2013, http://www.un.org/sg/offthecuff/index.asp?nid=2745, accessed 22 April 2023; UN Doc. A/67/997–S/2013/553, 16 September 2013, p. 4, para. 1; UN Doc. A/68/663-S/2013/735, 13 December 2013, p. 5, para. 1). The OPCW Director-General also referred to the UN Secretary-General's "mandate pursuant to UN General Assembly resolution 42/37C of 1987" (OPCW Doc. EC-M-32/DG.1, 27 March 2013, p. 1, para. 3).

Review Conference, States Parties expressed their collective support for the close cooperation between the OPCW Director-General and the UN Secretary-General in the investigation,[16] a sign of the understanding among States Parties that the UN Secretary-General's investigation mechanism applies to alleged use of chemical weapons in Syria. This implies that they shared the view that such use "may constitute a violation of the 1925 Geneva Protocol or other relevant rules of customary international law."[17] Furthermore, other States Parties used the expression "the use of chemical weapons by anyone under any circumstances would be reprehensible and [is] completely contrary to the legal norms and standards of the international community" in their statements,[18] language which rapidly attracted broad support. As a result, the Third Review Conference succeeded in including it in its political declaration on possible use of chemical weapons in Syria, as follows:

> Recalling the Thirty-Second Meeting of the Executive Council...underlined that the use of chemical weapons by anyone under any circumstances would be reprehensible and completely contrary to the legal norms and standards of the international community.[19]

The language has become boilerplate in subsequent collective decisions.[20] From a normative perspective, this expression implies the existence of "legal norms" on prohibitions of use of force beyond the CWC's scope. While the term is so ambiguous that it may not be decisive, in the author's view, it could be understood as an indication

16 OPCW Doc. RC-3/3*, 19 April 2013, para. 9.19.

17 UN Doc. A/RES/42/37C, 30 November 1987, operative para. 4.

18 Argentina, https://www.opcw.org/sites/default/files/documents/CSP/RC-3/national-statements/Argentina_rc3.pdf, accessed 22 April 2023; OPCW Doc. RC-3/NAT.25 (Norway), 8 April 2013, p. 2; OPCW Doc. RC-3/NAT.34 (Pakistan), 8 April 2013, p. 1; RC-3/NAT.78 (Indonesia), 9 April 2013, p. 2; Thailand, https://www.opcw.org/sites/default/files/documents/CSP/RC-3/national-statements/Thailand_rc3.pdf, accessed 22 April 2023; NAM CWC States Parties and China, https://www.opcw.org/sites/default/files/documents/CSP/RC-3/national-statements/Iran_NAM_rc3.pdf, accessed 22 April 2023.

19 OPCW Doc. RC-3/3*, 19 April 2013, para. 9.18. This language appeared in the Executive Council Chairperson's read-out statement at the thirty-second meeting of the Executive Council held on 27 March 2013 (OPCW Doc. EC-M-32/2/Rev.1, 27 March 2013, p. 2). It seems that she reflected the discussion at the meeting and gave due regard to the statement of South Africa, which proposed to include almost exactly same language as in the Chairperson's statement (OPCW Doc. EC-M-32/NAT.3, 27 March 2013, p. 1). South Africa appears to have "borrowed" the language from the statement of the OPCW Director-General, who used this expression as early as 19 March 2013 when he delivered his statement on the alleged use of chemical weapons in Khan-Al Assal (OPCW News, Statement by the OPCW Director-General on Allegations of Chemical Weapons Use in Syria, https://www.opcw.org/media-centre/news/2013/03/statement-opcw-director-general-allegations-chemical-weapons-use-syria, accessed 22 April 2023). He used it again in his statement to the thirty-second meeting of the Executive Council (OPCW Doc. EC-M-32/DG.1, 27 March 2013, p. 2, para. 11). The US also included a version of the language in its own statement at the thirty-second meeting of the Executive Council (OPCW Doc. EC-M-32/NAT.1, 27 March 2013, p. 1).

20 OPCW Doc. EC-M-33/DEC.1, 27 September 2013, preamble paras. 1 and 2; OPCW Doc. EC-M-48/DEC.1, 4 February 2015, preamble para. 1; OPCW Doc. EC-84/DEC.8, 9 March 2017, preamble para. 1.

of *opinion juris* among States Parties in terms of state of (customary) international law.[21]

It follows that there was a consensus among States on the existence of "international law" prohibiting use of chemical weapons in non-international armed conflicts. While there may be some statements that suggest the scope of the Geneva Protocol extending this far, it would be safer to argue that there at least exists relevant customary international law which is implicitly endorsed and logically confirmed by State practice.

(b) **After 27 September 2013**

Syria's accession to the CWC and the adoption of the Resolution 2118 added two more sources to its obligations. First, Syria is obliged not to use chemical weapons in accordance with Article I, para. 1(b) of the CWC. On 14 September 2013, Syria declared provisional application of the CWC,[22] becoming a State Party to the CWC on 14 October 2013.[23] Second, Syria is also obliged not to use chemical weapons under Resolution 2118. In the operative para. 4, the UN Security Council "[d]ecide[d] that the Syrian Arab Republic shall not use, develop, produce, otherwise acquire, stockpile or retain chemical weapons, or transfer, directly or indirectly, chemical weapons to other States or non-State actors."[24] Explicit reference to Article 25 of the UN Charter in the fourteenth preamble paragraph makes the decision binding on Syria.[25]

While the Geneva Protocol and customary international law remain applicable to Syria, the issue of further use of chemical weapons has almost always been discussed per the Resolution 2118 Regime, as it includes relevant compliance/non-compliance control procedures. The UN Security Council frequently recalled the formulation of operative para. 4 of Resolution 2118 in the subsequent resolutions.[26] The same language was also used in three different draft resolutions in response to the alleged use of chemical weapons in Douma in April 2018.[27]

---

[21] For a different view, see Masahiko Asada, "A Path to a Comprehensive Prohibition of the Use of Chemical Weapons under International Law: From the Hague to Damascus," *Journal of Conflict and Security Law*, Vol. 21, No. 2 (2016), p. 153, p. 199.

[22] OPCW Doc. EC-M-33/DEC.1, 27 September 2013, preamble para. 7.

[23] UN Doc. C.N.592.2013.TREATIES-XXVI.3.

[24] UN Doc. S/RES/2118 (2013), 27 September 2013, para. 4.

[25] Asada, *supra* note 21, p. 203.

[26] UN Doc. S/RES/2209 (2015), 6 March 2015, preamble para. 2 and operative para. 3; UN Doc. S/RES/2235 (2015), 7 August 2015, para. 2; UN Doc. S/RES/2319 (2016), 17 November 2016, para. 2.

[27] UN Doc. S/2018/175 (Russia), 10 April 2018, operative para. 2; UN Doc. S/2018/321 (Albania, Australia, Bulgaria, Canada, Denmark, Estonia, Finland, France, Germany, Italy, Latvia, Lithuania, Montenegro, Netherlands, Norway, Peru, Poland, Qatar, Republic of Moldova, Slovenia, Sweden, The former Yugoslav Republic of Macedonia, Turkey, Ukraine, UK and US), 10 April 2018, operative para. 3; UN Doc. S/2018/322 (Russia), 10 April 2018, preamble para. 4. See also UN Doc. A/RES/71/203, 19 December 2016, operative para. 5; UN Doc. A/RES/72/191, 19 December 2017, operative para. 6; UN Doc. A/RES/73/182, 17 December 2018, operative para. 5; UN Doc. A/RES/

Furthermore, the Resolution 2118 included language related to non-use of chemical weapons by non-State actors in Syria. Operative para. 5 targeted "party in Syria" and "[u]nderscore[d] that no party in Syria should use, develop, produce, acquire, stockpile, retain, or transfer chemical weapons,"[28] while operative para. 19 covered "non-State actors" in general and "[d]emand[ed] that non-State actors not develop, acquire, manufacture, possess, transport, transfer, or use nuclear, chemical or biological weapons and their means of delivery."[29] As was the case with non-use of chemical weapons by Syria, the UN Security Council frequently referred to the formulation of these paragraphs as well.[30] Two draft resolutions on renewing the mandate of the OPCW-UN Joint Investigative Mechanism (JIM) in November 2017 alluded to same,[31] as did three different draft resolutions addressing alleged use of chemical weapons in Douma in April 2018.[32] Unlike the aforementioned operative para. 4 of Resolution 2118, these passages did not include the term "decide,"though this does not necessarily mean that use of chemical weapons by non-state actors is not prohibited under international law. Instead, given that customary international law prohibits use of chemical weapons in non-international armed conflict, this provision applies to rebels and insurgents, as well as to a State or its government, as suggested in Resolution 2118, preamble para. 8, "affirming that the use of chemical weapons constitutes a serious violation of international law," and operative para. 2, "condemn[ing] in the strongest terms any use of chemical weapons in the Syrian Arab Republic, in particular the attack on 21 August 2013, in violation of international law."[33]

74/169, 18 December 2019, operative para. 5; UN Doc. A/RES/75/193, 16 December 2020, operative para. 5. UN Doc. A/HRC/RES/30/10, 1 October 2015, operative para. 9; UN Doc. A/HRC/RES/31/17, 23 March 2016, operative para. 14; UN Doc. A/HRC/RES/32/25, 1 July 2016, operative para. 18; UN Doc. A/HRC/RES/33/23, 30 September 2016, operative para. 19; UN Doc. A/HRC/RES/34/26, 24 March 2017, operative para. 24; UN Doc. A/HRC/RES/35/26, 23 June 2017, operative para. 21; UN Doc. A/HRC/RES/36/20, 29 September 2017, operative para. 21; UN Doc. A/HRC/RES/37/29, 23 March 2018, operative para. 23.

[28] UN Doc. S/RES/2118 (2013), 27 September 2013, operative para. 5.

[29] *Ibid.*, operative para. 19.

[30] UN Doc. S/RES/2209 (2015), 6 March 2015, preamble para. 2 and operative para. 4; UN Doc. S/RES/2235 (2015), 7 August 2015, operative para. 3; UN Doc. S/RES/2319 (2016), 17 November 2016, preamble para. 7.

[31] UN Doc. S/2017/962 (France, Italy, Japan, Sweden, Ukraine, UK, and US), 17 November 2017, operative para. 3; UN Doc. S/2017/968 (Bolivia), 17 November 2017, preamble para. 5.

[32] UN Doc. S/2018/175 (Russia), 10 April 2018, operative para. 3; UN Doc. S/2018/321 (Albania, Australia, Bulgaria, Canada, Denmark, Estonia, Finland, France, Germany, Italy, Latvia, Lithuania, Montenegro, Netherlands, Norway, Peru, Poland, Qatar, Republic of Moldova, Slovenia, Sweden, The former Yugoslav Republic of Macedonia, Turkey, Ukraine, UK, and US), 10 April 2018, operative para. 2; UN Doc. S/2018/322 (Russia), 10 April 2018, preamble para. 4.

[33] Asada, *supra* note 21, p. 204.

3.3 Compliance/Non-compliance Control

Regarding the obligation not to use chemical weapons, a typical obligation of omission, no mechanism is required to ensure compliance with it, because in ordinary circumstances, compliance with this type of obligation is always ensured without action being taken. Potential or real non-compliance always happens *ad hoc*, and *ad hoc* compliance/non-compliance control accordingly responds *ex post*. The relevant procedures vary depending on when chemical attacks occur, which directly concerns applicable law.

For use of chemical weapons prior to and on 21 August 2013, again, the only applicable obligation is that of customary international law. The international community has had to address non-compliance, potential or real, with this obligation by relying on existing procedures per UN General Assembly Resolution and the UN Security Council's primary responsibility for maintaining international peace and security. The provisional application of the CWC to Syria made it possible for the OPCW to be involved in the international efforts to eliminate Syrian chemical weapons.

For use of chemical weapons since September 2013, the relevant obligations come under the CWC and UN Security Council Resolution 2118. The OPCW policy-making organs and the Security Council have considered the issue of further use of chemical weapons and taken measures in accordance with the relevant provisions. The UN General Assembly, including the United Nations Human Rights Council (UNHRC), has also expressed views based on the above-mentioned information. In addition, several States have taken unilateral measures as well, in tandem with the aforementioned activities of the relevant organizations.

3.3.1 Ensuring Compliance

As mentioned above, it is infeasible to introduce procedures for ensuring compliance with the obligation of omission. Any type of obligation of omission will be fully observed in ordinary circumstances where a State does not carry out an act incompatible with this obligation. It means that in ordinary circumstances the compliance with the obligation of omission is *always* ensured without taking actions. Only when non-compliance is alleged does obligation of omission draw States' attention. Again, no mechanism is required to ensure compliance with the obligation against use of chemical weapons.

3.3.2 *Addressing Potential Non-compliance*

(1) **Background**

Allegations of chemical weapons use in Syria have come to the attention of the international community since December 2012. As mentioned above, in many cases, the Syrian government and opposition groups alike have criticized each other for using chemical weapons while categorically denying their own use of same. Allegations do not mean a violation of international law. At this juncture, the situation is still in the potential non-compliance stage, raising the question of how the international community should address the allegations.

As a first step, a fact-finding organ should be established. As the name indicates, their primary task is to establish facts. While policy-making organs of international organizations can take actions including sanctions against users of chemical weapons, it is premature to do so where allegations remain unconfirmed. For the alleged use of chemical weapons in Syria, five fact-finding organs have thus far been tasked to investigate these allegations: the United Nations Mission to Investigate Allegations of the Use of Chemical Weapons in the Syrian Arab Republic (UN Mission), the OPCW Fact-Finding Mission (FFM), the OPCW-UN Joint Investigative Mechanism (JIM), the OPCW Investigation and Identification Team (IIT), and the Independent International Commission of Inquiry on the Syrian Arab Republic (COI). These organs report to such concerned policy-making organs as the UN Security Council, the OPCW Executive Council, and the UNHRC.[34] As of this writing, in multiple instances, these organs have ascertained chemical weapons use and identified the responsible parties. Their findings and conclusions provide a basis for the aforementioned policy-making organs to act.

This section discusses fact-finding as a means to address potential non-compliance with obligations under international law. It begins with an overview of fact-finding, follows with a comprehensive analysis of the abovementioned fact-finding organs regarding use of chemical weapons in Syria, addressing their legal basis, mandates, Syrian obligations, and implementation, before concluding with an evaluation.

(2) **Overview**

(a) **Definition**

Fact-finding is defined as "a recognized from of international dispute settlement through the process of elucidating facts."[35] Its primary purpose is to clarify facts in a dispute through impartial investigation, thereby facilitating the process of identifying

---

[34] Michael Bothe, "Fact-finding as a means of ensuring respect for international humanitarian law," in W Heintschel von Heinegg and V Epping (eds), *International Humanitarian Law Facing New Challenges* (Springer, 2007), p. 249, p. 258. See also Antonio Cassese, "Fostering Increased Conformity with International Standards: Monitoring and Institutional Fact-finding," in Antonio Cassese (ed.), *Realizing Utopia: The Future of International Law* (Oxford University Press, 2012), p. 295, pp. 302–303.

[35] Agnieszka Jachec Neale, "Human Rights Fact-Finding into Armed Conflict and Breaches of the Laws of War," *American Society of International Law Proceedings*, Vol. 105 (2011), p. 85, p. 85; Agnieszka Jachec-Neale, "Fact-Finding," in Rüdiger Wolfrum (ed.), *The Max Planck Encyclopedia of Public International Law*, Vol. 4 (Oxford University Press, 2012), p. 1077, p. 1077. See also Théo

the final solutions.[36] It is to be carried out by "an impartial and neutral body carrying out the inquiry ... or a joint body consisting of the representatives of the disputing parties."[37]

(b) **Significance**

It has been pointed out that fact-finding is of significance in both deterrence and dispute resolution.[38] First, clarifying facts is an indispensable component of the dispute resolution process.[39] In summary, a legal dispute comprises issues of fact and law, which are resolved through application of law to fact. If parties to a legal conflict disagree on the facts, facts must be established before law can be applied to them. In this regard, fact-finding organs play the same function as judicial organs, though they differ from each other in substance. The former have a limited mandate to clarify facts in non-binding reports,[40] while the latter settle dispute both through finding facts and applying law to same in binding decisions.

Second, fact-finding per se has a deterrent effect; it prevents future violations and promotes compliance with international law.[41] This matters because unlike domestic societies, the international community does not accommodate procedural enforcement mechanisms by default. Even if procedures exist, they usually require aforementioned consent of States concerned in accordance with relevant treaty provisions. Be that as it may, the existence of procedures itself is of significance. Without it, States

---

Boutruche, "Credible Fact-Finding and Allegations of International Humanitarian Law Violations: Challenges in Theory and Practice," *Journal of Conflict and Security Law*, Vol. 16, No. 1 (2011), p. 105, p. 106.

[36] Jachec Neale, "Human Rights Fact-Finding into Armed Conflict and Breaches of the Laws of War," *supra* note 35, p. 85; Jachec-Neale, "Fact-Finding," *supra* note 35, p. 1078.

[37] Jachec-Neale, "Fact-Finding," *supra* note 35, p. 1078.

[38] Jachec Neale, "Human Rights Fact-Finding into Armed Conflict and Breaches of the Laws of War," *supra* note 35, p. 85; Thilo Marauhn, "Sailing Close to the Wind: Human Rights Council Fact-Finding in Situations of Armed Conflict—The Case of Syria," *California Western International Law Journal*, Vol. 43, No. 2 (2013), p. 401, p. 448; Théo Boutruche, "Credible Fact-Finding and Allegations of International Humanitarian Law Violations: Challenges in Theory and Practice," *Journal of Conflict and Security Law*, Vol. 16, No. 1 (2011), p. 105, p. 109.

[39] Article 15, para. 3 of the Covenant of the League of Nations refers to "facts" of disputes as one of three elements of the "statement" made public by the Council for a settlement of the dispute.

[40] Despite this limited function, facts, once established, can have an impact on dispute settlement, especially findings of violations of international law, as suggested by Article 36, para. 2c of the ICJ Statue. Moreover, it may not matter much that reports by fact-finding organs are non-binding, because once reported, such facts cannot be retracted (Alexander Orakhelashvili, "Commissions of Inquiry and Traditional Mechanisms of Dispute Settlement," in Christian Henderson (ed.), *Commissions of Inquiry: Problems and Prospects* (Hart Publishing, 2017), p. 119, pp. 123 and 142). It has also been argued that in practice it is not easy to draw a clear distinction between the factual and legal dimensions of a given conflict (Larissa J. Van Den Herik, "An Inquiry into the Role of Commissions of Inquiry in International Law: Navigating the Tensions between Fact-Finding and Application of International Law," *Chinese Journal of International Law*, Vol. 13, No. 3 (2014), p. 507, pp. 512 and 536; See also Boutruche, *supra* note 38, p. 108).

[41] Rob Grace, "From Design to Implementation: The Interpretation of Fact-Finding Mandates," *Journal of Conflict and Security Law*, Vol. 20, No. 1 (2015), p. 27, pp. 27–28.

have almost no incentive to comply with international law. And while fact-finding may not be the most powerful such procedure, because it is not involved with findings of law or other binding rulings, facts established by such organs which are inconsistent with obligations under international law are themselves tantamount to violations of international law,[42] which is the situation that States most wish to avoid, thus explaining the deterrent effect of fact-finding.

(c) Types of Fact-Finding Operations

Fact-finding can generally be categorized into traditional dispute resolution means based on consent of parties to a dispute, and contemporary dispute settlement mechanisms within the broader institutional framework of international organizations.

The first traditional type of fact-finding, or "international commissions for inquiry" procedures, was introduced in the 1899 Convention for the Pacific Settlement of International Disputes.[43] The relevant provisions of this Convention have been implemented in five instances: the 1905 Dogger Bank case involving the UK and Russia, the 1912 Tavignano case involving France and Italy, the 1918 Tiger case involving Germany and Spain, the 1922 Tubantia case involving Germany and the Netherlands, and the 1962 Red Crusader Incident involving the UK and Denmark. This type of fact-finding procedure requires agreement between the parties to the dispute,[44] which has its pros and cons. On the one hand, fact-finding activities, including on-site investigations, are carried out in a cooperative and smooth manner, and the findings and conclusions will be accepted by the parties. On the other hand, reaching agreement on establishing fact-finding organs is not easy, and fact-finding per se does not include dispute resolution in its mandate. Article 90 of the 1977 First Protocol to the Geneva Conventions also established another traditional type of fact-finding, the International Humanitarian Fact-Finding Commission (IHFFC), which will investigate situations of armed conflict on condition that all Parties involved have equally recognized the competence thereof. This Commission, however, has only participated in a single case to-date, where the Organization for Security and Co-operation in Europe (OSCE) requested that the Commission lead an independent forensic investigation in relation to an accident during the activities of its Special Monitoring Mission to Ukraine (SMM) in 2017.[45]

---

[42] Orakhelashvili, *supra* note 40, p. 132.

[43] Articles 9–14, 1899 Convention for the Pacific Settlement of International Disputes; Articles 9–36, 1907 Convention for the Pacific Settlement of International Disputes.

[44] Article 10, 1899 Convention for the Pacific Settlement of International Disputes; Article 10, 1907 Convention for the Pacific Settlement of International Disputes. It has been pointed out that "this mechanism was still based on respect for sovereignty and the notion of reciprocity" (Cassese, *supra* note 34, p. 296).

[45] International Humanitarian Fact-Finding Commission, OSCE Special Monitoring Mission was not targeted, concludes Independent Forensic Investigation into tragic incident of 23 April 2017, https://www.ihffc.org/index.asp?mode=shownews&ID=831, accessed 22 April 2023. It has been pointed out that the consent requirement discourages States from using the IHFFC (H. E. Nicolas Lang, "The Path to Better Compliance with International Humanitarian Law," *Military Law and Law of War Review*, Vol. 52, No. 1 (2013), p. 131, p. 134).

The reality is that traditional fact-finding, based on consent of the parties, is becoming less attractive. Two other approaches are emerging in its place. First, the recent proliferation of international courts and tribunals has coincided with the relative decline in relevance of the aforementioned traditional type.[46] States seem to find advantage in binding decisions of judicial settlement rather than non-binding finding of facts. Second, also as described above, the contemporary type of fact-finding has developed within a broader institutional framework of international organizations.[47] While this type of fact-finding may not explicitly be referred to in relevant treaties, practice indicates that it has frequently been used on an *ad hoc* basis in the dynamic process of settling disputes.[48]

This second, contemporary, type of fact-finding is established by international organizations, without requiring consent of States concerned in principle.[49] Lack of consent in this regard does not matter because the fact-finding organs exercise their competence as elements of principal and subsidiary organs of international organizations.[50] This type of fact-finding has sometimes been tasked not only with "pure" fact-finding, but also determining whether violations of international law have taken place, monitoring compliance with the obligations under international treaties, and making recommendations.[51] Their reports may serve as important inputs for policy-making organs to act on, and thus play a primary role in contributing to dispute settlement.[52] UN organs have accumulated experiences in this regard. The UN Security Council established the first such fact-finding organ in 1979, in the Middle Eastern context,[53] thereafter dispatching fact-finding missions to such locales as Seychelles, Rwanda, Burundi, the Middle East, Darfur, and the Central African Republic.[54] The UN General Assembly established a fact-finding mechanism under

---

46 Orakhelashvili, *supra* note 40, p. 120.

47 Van Den Herik, *supra* note 40, p. 520.

48 *Ibid.*, p. 523. In this regard, the legal basis should lie in "implied powers" (*ibid.*, p. 527).

49 Orakhelashvili, *supra* note 40, p. 121. See also Cassese, *supra* note 34, p. 302.

50 Orakhelashvili, *supra* note 40, p. 130. It has also been pointed out that "unlike the inspection missions which require the territorial state's consent to entry into and operate in their territory, commissions of inquiry do not seem to require such consent for merely pronouncing on the relevant state's conduct" (*ibid.*, p. 131). This argument holds only so long as fact-finding organs can find facts without on-site visits.

51 Patrick Butchard and Christian Henderson, "A Functional Typology of Commissions of Inquiry," in Christian Henderson (ed.), *Commissions of Inquiry: Problems and Prospects* (Hart Publishing, 2017), p. 11, pp. 13–33; Orakhelashvili, *supra* note 40, p. 133; Triestino Mariniello, "The Impact of International Commissions of Inquiry on the Proceedings before the International Criminal Court," in Christian Henderson (ed.), *Commissions of Inquiry: Problems and Prospects* (Hart Publishing, 2017), p. 171, p. 175.

52 Bothe, *supra* note 34, p. 258.

53 Jachec-Neale, "Fact-Finding," *supra* note 35, p. 1080. UN Doc. S/RES/446 (1979), 22 March 1979, para. 4.

54 UN Doc. S/RES/496 (1981), 15 December 1981, para. 2; UN Doc. S/RES/935 (1994), 1 July 1994, para. 1; UN Doc. S/RES/1012 (1995), 28 August 1995, para. 1; UN Doc. S/RES/1013 (1995), 7 September 1995, para. 1; UN Doc. S/RES/1405 (2002), 19 April 2002, para. 2; S/RES/1564 (2004), 18 September 2004, para. 12; UN Doc. S/RES/2127 (2013), 5 December 2013, para. 24.

the authority of the UN Secretary-General to investigate allegations of chemical weapons use, which was implemented in Afghanistan and Southeast Asia in the 1980s, as described hereinafter. The Secretary-General has also taken the initiative in investigating situations in Georgia, Burundi, Iraq, and Djibouti, in addition to the abovementioned chemical weapons allegation in the Iran-Iraq War, as seen below, upon request.[55] The UNOHCHR and UNHRC have also conducted many fact-finding missions of their own.[56] In 1991, the UN General Assembly adopted a resolution on Declaration on Fact-Finding by the United Nations in the Field of the Maintenance of International Peace and Security, which identified generic elements of fact-finding activities under UN auspices.[57]

Contrary to the high reliance on such fact-finding on the part of UN agencies, current practice receives "the overall generally negative assessment."[58] The primary reason lies in the fact that international organizations establish fact-finding organs without consent of States subject to investigation. Such fact-finding might thus be confrontational and risks non-cooperation on the part of investigated States. Their reports may also be criticized in terms of quality and their impact on the decision-making processes of policy-making organs diminished.[59] It remains to be seen whether this holds for fact-finding organs in the context of Syrian chemical weapons use.

(d) **Practice in the chemical weapons usage context**

As mentioned, the UN took two approaches in investigating chemical weapons allegations in the 1980s and early 1990s. One approach is the UN General Assembly resolutions requesting that the UN Secretary-General investigate relevant information provided by States.[60] The 1980 and 1982 resolutions introduced *ad hoc* and provisional procedures. A group of experts investigated chemical weapons allegations in Southeast Asia and Afghanistan, but was unable to reach a definitive conclusion.[61] The 1987 resolution established the aforementioned standing UN Secretary-General Investigation Mechanism.[62] In 1989, the States participating in the Conference of

---

[55] UN Doc. S/26795, 17 November 1993; UN Doc. S/1994/1152, 11 October 1994; UN Doc. S/2004/140, 23 February 2004; UN Doc. S/2008/602, 12 September 2008.

[56] See John P. Pace, *The United Nations Commission on Human Rights: "A Very Great Enterprise"* (Oxford University Press, 2020). The UNHRC has established more than thirty fact-finding bodies since its inauguration (OHCHR, List of HRC-mandated Commissions of Inquiries / Fact-Finding Missions & Other Bodies (as of March 2022), https://www.ohchr.org/EN/HRBodies/HRC/Pages/ListHRCMandat.aspx, accessed 22 April 2023).

[57] UN Doc. A/RES/46/59, 9 December 1991, Annex.

[58] Jachec-Neale, "Fact-Finding," *supra* note 35, p. 1081.

[59] *Ibid.*, p. 1081; Orakhelashvili, *supra* note 40, p. 128.

[60] UN Doc. A/RES/35/144C, 12 December 1980, operative paras. 4–6; UN Doc. A/RES/37/98D, 13 December 1982, operative para. 4; UN Doc. A/RES/42/37C, 30 November 1987, operative para. 4.

[61] UN Doc. A/37/259, 1 December 1982, pp. 48–50. Provisional procedures have not been subsequently invoked.

[62] Upon request of the General Assembly (UN Doc. A/RES/42/37C, 30 November 1987, operative para. 5; UN Doc. A/RES/43/74A, 7 December 1988, operative para. 6), the Secretary-General

States Parties to the 1925 Geneva Protocol and other interested States on the prohibition of chemical weapons reaffirmed "their full support for the Secretary-General in carrying out his responsibilities for investigations."[63] In 1992, Mozambique and Armenia requested that the UN Secretary-General investigate chemical weapons allegations.[64] In the first instance, the mission "cannot conclude that a chemical warfare agent was used in the attack."[65] In the second instance, the mission was of the view that "no evidence of use of chemical weapons was presented to the team."[66]

The other approach is the good-office function of the UN Secretary-General. During the Iran–Iraq war, the UN Secretary-General relied on this function in dispatching fact-finding missions upon request of Iran. The reports confirmed the use of chemical weapons[67] and identified Iraqi forces as perpetrators.[68]

Separately, the CWC was adopted in September 1992, following twenty years of negotiations. As expected in 1987 UN General Assembly resolution, it included "investigation of alleged use of chemical weapons" in its Verification Annex Part XI. Such investigation may be carried out either upon request of any State Party, in other words, without the consent of the investigated State Party in accordance with Article IX or upon request of the State Party to be investigated in accordance with Article

developed the Guidelines and Procedures for the Timely and Efficient Investigation of Reports of the Possible Use of Chemical and Bacteriological (Biological) or Toxin Weapons ("Guidelines and Procedures") (UN Doc. A/44/561, 4 October 1989, Annex I, pp. 11–47). The UN General Assembly endorsed the Guidelines and Procedures by welcoming the proposals of the group of qualified experts (UN Doc. A/RES/44/115B, 15 December 1989, operative para. 5).

63 UN Doc. A/44/88, 20 January 1989, p. 3.

64 UN Doc. S/24065, 12 June 1992, p. 1, para. 1; UN Doc. S/24344, 24 July 1992, p. 1, para. 3.

65 *Ibid.*, p. 11, para. 36.

66 UN Doc. S/24344, 24 July 1992, p. 8, para. 24.

67 UN Doc. S/16433, 26 March 1984, pp. 11–12, para. 35; UN Doc. S/17127, 24 April 1985, p. 4, paras. 1–4; UN Doc. S/17911, 12 March 1986, p. 18, para. 57; UN Doc. S/18852, 8 May 1987, p. 18, para. 65; UN Doc. S/19823, 25 April 1988, pp. 17–18, para. 54; UN Doc. S/20060, 20 July 1988, pp. 15–16, para. 46; UN Doc. S/20063, 25 July 1988, pp. 11–12, para. 32; UN Doc. S/20134, 19 August 1988, p. 11, para. 23.

68 UN Doc. S/17911, 12 March 1986, p. 18, para. 58; UN Doc. S/18852, 8 May 1987, pp. 18–19, para. 66; UN Doc. S/20060, 20 July 1988, p. 15, para. 46(d); UN Doc. S/20134, 19 August 1988, p. 11, para. 23(c). Iraq insisted that it "has not used" chemical weapons (UN Doc. S/16438, 27 March 1984).

X.[69] The CWC also envisages the OPCW as cooperating with the UN Secretary-General upon request in cases of alleged use of chemical weapons in relation to non-State Parties.[70]

(3) **Addressing Potential Non-compliance: Fact-Finding organs**

(a) **Legal Basis**

All fact-finding organs concerned with use of chemical weapons in Syria have legal bases for their establishment. Four of these rely on resolutions or decisions by relevant policy-making organs, while the OPCW FFM is based on the "general authority" of the OPCW Director-General.[71]

The legal bases for the UN Mission and the OPCW-UN JIM have not been disputed. The UN Secretary-General created the former by activating the existing UN Secretary-General Investigation Mechanism under the UN General Assembly Resolution 42/37C, and the UN Security Council unanimously adopted the resolution establishing the latter.[72] By contrast, the legal basis for the COI, the OPCW FFM, and the OPCW IIT, was questioned by some States, despite all but the OPCW FFM having been established based on the aforementioned resolution or decision of the relevant policy-making organs.

The COI was established by the UNHRC.[73] At the meeting when the resolution was adopted, Russia pointed out one-sided and politicized elements in it. China stressed the resolution of crisis through the promotion of dialogue and cooperation and the restoration of social stability rather than accusations. Syria criticized the State co-sponsors for their determination to politically condemn Syria and to pass

---

[69] At the ninety-ninth session of the OPCW Executive Council in March 2022, Ukraine explicitly referred to Article X of the CWC ("My country reserves the right to request assistance and protection, as provided for in Article X of the Convention, should we be threatened with chemical weapons use. My country is in grave peril, under constant attack by Russia and with many civilian casualties. Should chemical weapons be used, we will ask for help with establishing the facts on the territory of Ukraine. Russia must be held to account.") (OPCW Doc. EC-99/NAT.7 (Ukraine), 8 March 2022, p. 2).

[70] Verification Annex Part XI, para. 27. As discussed below, this provision was invoked when Syria, the UK, and France requested that the UN Secretary-General investigate chemical weapons allegations in March 2012. At the eighty-fourth session of the OPCW Executive Council, Sweden indicated that "Malaysia may have the option to consider requesting an investigation pursuant to the United Nations Secretary-General's mechanism" depending on the results of its investigation into the alleged assassination of Kim Jong-nam with VX at Kuala Lumpur International Airport (OPCW Doc. EC-84/NAT.14 (Sweden), 7 March 2017, p. 2).

[71] OPCW Doc. S/1191/2014, 16 June 2014, p. 3.

[72] UN Doc. S/PV.7501, 7 August 2015, p. 2.

[73] The resolution was adopted by a vote of 33 in favor (Austria, Belgium, Benin, Botswana, Burkina Faso, Chile, Congo, Costa Rica, Czech Republic, Guatemala, Hungary, Indonesia, Italy, Jordan, Kuwait, Kyrgyzstan, Maldives, Mauritius, Mexico, Nigeria, Norway, Peru, Poland, Qatar, Republic of Moldova, Romania, Saudi Arabia, Senegal, Spain, Switzerland, Thailand, US, and Uruguay) to four against (China, Cuba, Ecuador, and Russia) with nine abstentions (Angola, Bangladesh, Cameroon, Djibouti, India, Malaysia, Mauritania, Philippines, Uganda). The report of the COI included the terms of reference (UN Doc. A/HRC/S-17/2/Add.1, 23 November 2011, p. 4).

over any proposals for reform.[74] After 2017, Syria also argued that the COI was overstepping its mandate and encroaching on the activities of the OPCW FFM and the OPCW-UN JIM.[75] These assertions received little support, however.

As described above, the OPCW FFM has a different legal basis from that of the other organs: "the general authority of the OPCW Director-General." It is necessary to assess how to understand this basis from a legal standpoint. Further use of chemical weapons in Syria was reported in the media on 11 April 2014,[76] followed by expressions of concern on the part of the US and UK at a meeting of the OPCW Executive Council.[77] Despite the relevant provision on the investigation of alleged use of chemical weapons in Verification Annex Part XI being theoretically available, however, no action was taken by any State Party. And while the Syrian opposition drew the attention of the UN Security Council president to the incident in Kafr Zita and "the urgent need for an immediate investigation" in a letter submitted through the United Arab Emirates,[78] no action was taken here either. The situation became more complicated as it was further reported that "[b]oth sides said chlorine gas had been used."[79] Against this backdrop, the OPCW Director-General announced the creation of "an OPCW mission to establish facts surrounding allegations of use of chlorine in Syria" on 29 April 2014.[80] States Parties expressed their support for this initiative,[81] and Syria agreed to accept the mission on its territory.[82]

According to the OPCW Technical Secretariat, the basis for the establishment of the OPCW FFM lies in "the general authority of the OPCW Director-General to

[74] Human Rights Council, Press Release, Human Rights Council decides to dispatch a commission of inquiry to investigate human rights violations in the Syrian Arab Republic, 23 August 2011, https://www.ohchr.org/en/press-releases/2011/08/human-rights-council-decides-dispatch-commission-inquiry-investigate-human?LangID=E&NewsID=11326, accessed 22 April 2023.

[75] UN Doc. A/HRC/36/G/10 (Syria), 12 September 2017 p. 2; UN Doc. A/HRC/38/G/7 (Syria), 15 August 2018, p. 2; UN Doc. A/HRC/39/G/7 (Syria), 16 November 2018, p. 3.

[76] The Times, Assad "spreading terror with new chemical attacks," 11 April 2014, p. 36.

[77] OPCW Doc. EC-M-40/NAT.4 (US), 11 April 2014, p. 2; OPCW Doc. EC-M-40/NAT.7 (UK), 11 April 2014, p. 2.

[78] UN Doc. S/2014/285, 17 April 2014.

[79] Reuter, Syria opposition claims has evidence of chlorine gas attack, 14 April 2014, https://www.reuters.com/article/us-syria-crisis-chemicals-idUSBREA3D0GM20140414, accessed 22 April 2023.

[80] OPCW News, OPCW to Undertake Fact-Finding Mission in Syria on Alleged Chlorine Gas Attacks, 29 April 2014, https://www.opcw.org/media-centre/news/2014/04/opcw-undertake-fact-finding-mission-syria-alleged-chlorine-gas-attacks, accessed 22 April 2023.

[81] OPCW Doc. EC-M-40/NAT.13 (UK), 29 April 2014, p. 2; OPCW Doc. EC-M-40/NAT.15 (Turkey), 29 April 2014; OPCW Doc. EC-M-40/NAT.24 (Mexico), 29 April 2014; Remarks, Robert P. Mikulak, U.S. Permanent Representative to the Organization for the Prohibition of Chemical Weapons, United States Delegation to the Executive Council, The Hague, Netherlands, 29 April 2014, https://2009-2017.state.gov/t/avc/rls/2014/225340.htm, accessed 22 April 2023; OPCW Doc. EC-M-40/NAT.20 (UK), 8 May 2014, p. 2; OPCW Doc. EC-M-40/NAT.21 (Greece on behalf of the EU), 8 May 2014, p. 2; OPCW Doc. EC-M-40/NAT.23 (US), 8 May 2014, pp. 1–2.

[82] OPCW Doc. EC-M-42/DG.1, 23 May 2014, para. 15.

seek to uphold at all times the object and purpose of the Chemical Weapons Convention,"[83] rather than the investigation procedures on alleged use in accordance with Articles IX and X of the Convention.[84] The OPCW Technical Secretariat further indicated that this authority is reinforced by relevant decisions of the OPCW Executive Council and UN Security Council Resolution 2118, OPCW Executive Council general endorsement, and Syria's acceptance through exchange of letters.[85]

Perhaps the starting point should be the concept of "implied powers." It is widely accepted in theory and practice that international organizations have and can exercise "implied powers" which are not explicitly provided for in their founding instruments to achieve their objectives.[86] If the term of "general authority" is used as a variation of "implied powers," there may be no serious problem from a conceptual point of view. The question that follows, of whether this general authority covers the establishment of fact-finding missions, bears close examination.

The use of chemical weapons is a core issue confronting the OPCW, and the aforementioned CWC Verification Annex Part XI provides detailed procedures for investigating alleged use of chemical weapons, to be carried out by the OPCW Technical Secretariat. Establishing fact-finding missions to investigate allegations is thus fully consistent with the objective of the CWC and necessary for the OPCW to function. This raises the question of which internal organ should retain and exercise "general authority" or "implied powers" to establish fact-finding organs.

International organizations such as the OPCW typically comprise policy-making organs and a secretariat. The former make decisions and supervise the latter, which carries out its tasks under the guidance of the former, in accordance with the organization's constituent documents. When it comes to investigating alleged use of chemical weapons, the CWC does not provide the OPCW Director-General with explicit authority to initiate such investigations. Instead, it only requires a State Party to make a motion.[87] Upon such request, the OPCW Director-General implements relevant provisions, by design. It has also been argued that implied powers may not change the distribution of functions within an organization.[88] The general

[83] OPCW Doc. S/1191/2014, 16 June 2014, p. 3.

[84] Mirko Sossai, "Identifying the Perpetrators of Chemical Attacks in Syria: The Organisation for the Prohibition of Chemical Weapons as Part of the Fight against Impunity," *Journal of International Criminal Justice*, Vol. 17, Issue 2 (May 2019), p. 211, p. 213.

[85] OPCW Doc. S/1191/2014, 16 June 2014, p. 3. The characterization of "the acceptance by Syria" as one of the elements reinforcing the "general authority" suggests that the OPCW Technical Secretariat did not regard "the acceptance by Syria" as a sufficient basis for the establishment of the OPCW FFM. It has also been pointed out that said establishment of the OPCW FFM reflects "the combination of consent and coercion" (Sossai, *supra* note 84, p. 214).

[86] *Reparation for injuries suffered in the service of the United Nations, Advisory Opinion: I.C.J. Reports 1949*, p. 174, p. 182; *Legality of the Use by a State of Nuclear Weapons in Armed Conflict, Advisory Opinion, I.C.J. Reports 1996*, p. 66, p. 79, para. 25; Henry G. Schermers and Niels M. Blokker, *International Institutional Law: Unity within Diversity*, fifth revised edition (Martinus Nijhoff Publishers, 2011), pp. 180–189.

[87] Verification Annex Part XI, para. 1. The UK pointed out that "the Director-General has the requisite mandate to make such an undertaking" (OPCW Doc. EC-M-40/NAT.13 (UK), 29 April 2014, p. 2); albeit without elaboration.

[88] Schermers and Blokker, *supra* note 86, p. 185.

authority of the OPCW Director-General per se may not be sufficient for establishing fact-finding missions, raising the question of what happens should the policy-making organs reject the OPCW Director-General's decision.

One way to address such ambiguities in legal basis, perhaps the only way, is by the endorsement of said policy-making organs,[89] and in fact, the OPCW Executive Council has repeatedly endorsed the OPCW FFM. For instance, at the forty-second meeting on 17 June 2014, having received positive statements from States Parties,[90] it "emphasised its unequivocal support for the Director-General's decision to continue the Mission;"[91] at the seventy-sixth session in the following month, it "reaffirmed the broad support for the Director-General's decision to send a mission" and "re-emphasised its unequivocal support for the Director-General's decision to continue the Mission;"[92] at the forty-eighth and fiftieth meetings in February and November 2015, it adopted decisions which included the language "[e]xpressing support for the continuation of the work of the Fact-Finding Mission."[93] The UN Security Council subscribed to these endorsements of the OPCW Executive Council and "[e]xpresses support for the OPCW Executive Council decision of 4 February 2015 to continue the work of the OPCW Fact-Finding Mission" in its resolution of March 2015.[94] Furthermore, the OPCW Technical Secretariat explicitly referred to these developments under the headings of "introduction," "executive summary," and "legal framework" in the OPCW FFM's reports.[95] Nor is Syrian cooperation at issue, because

[89] Article VIII, para. 37 stipulates that "[t]he Technical Secretariat … shall carry out the other functions entrusted to it under this Convention as well as those functions delegated to it by the Conference and the Executive Council.".

[90] OPCW Doc. EC-M-41/NAT.1 (Turkey), 22 May 2014; OPCW Doc. EC-M-41/NAT.2 (Iran), 22 May 2014, p. 1; OPCW Doc. EC-M-41/NAT.3 (UK), 22 May 2014, p. 2; OPCW Doc. EC-M-41/NAT.4 (Netherlands), 22 May 2014, p. 2; OPCW Doc. EC-M-41/NAT.5 (Germany), 22 May 2014, p. 2; OPCW Doc. EC-M-41/NAT.6 (Denmark and Norway), 22 May 2014, pp. 1–2; OPCW Doc. EC-M-41/NAT.7 (Greece on behalf of the EU), 22 May 2014, p. 2; OPCW Doc. EC-M-41/NAT.8 (US), 22 May 2014, p. 3; OPCW Doc. EC-M-42/NAT.1 (Greece on behalf of the EU), 17 June 2014, p. 2; OPCW Doc. EC-M-42/NAT.2 (Turkey), 17 June 2014, p. 1; OPCW Doc. EC-M-42/NAT.3 (New Zealand), 17 June 2014, pp. 1–2; OPCW Doc. EC-M-42/NAT.4 (UK), 17 June 2014, p. 2; OPCW Doc. EC-M-42/NAT.12 (US), 17 June 2014, pp. 2–3.

[91] OPCW Doc. EC-M-42/3, 30 June 2014, para. 7.4.

[92] OPCW Doc. EC-76/6, 11 July 2014, paras. 6.42 and 6.45.

[93] OPCW Doc. EC-M-48/DEC.1, 4 February 2015, preamble para. 8 (adopted by vote of 41 in favor to one against (OPCW Doc. EC-M-48/3, 4 February 2015, para. 3.4)); OPCW Doc. EC-M-50/DEC.1, 23 November 2015, preamble para. 10 (adopted without vote (OPCW Doc. EC-M-50/2, 23 November 2015, para. 3.4)).

[94] UN Doc. S/RES/2209 (2015), 6 March 2015, operative para. 5 (adopted by vote of 14 in favor with one abstention (UN Doc. S.PV.7401, 6 March 2015, p. 2)).

[95] OPCW Doc. S/1318/2015, 29 October 2015, p. 4, para. 1.1; OPCW Doc. S/1444/2016, 21 December 2016, p. 3, para. 1.1; OPCW Doc. S/1445/2016, 27 December 2016, p. 1, para. 1; OPCW Doc. S/1491/2717, 1 May 2016, p. 3, para. 1.1; OPCW Doc. S/1510/2017, 29 June 2017, p. 4, para. 2.3; OPCW Doc. S/1548/2017, 2 November 2017, p. 2, para. 2.3; OPCW Doc. S/1626/2018, 15 May 2018, p. 2, para. 2.3; OPCW Doc. S/1636/2018*, 13 June 2018, p. 2, para. 2.3; OPCW Doc. S/1642/2018, 15 May 2018, p. 3, para. 1.1; OPCW Doc. S/1645/2018, 6 July 2018, p. 1, para. 1; OPCW Doc. S/1731/2019, 15 May 2019, p. 2, para. 1; OPCW Doc. S/1901/2019, 1 October 2019,

as mentioned above, Syria has allowed the OPCW FFM to conduct investigations within its borders.

The OPCW IIT was established in accordance with the decision of the OPCW Conference of the States Parties at its fourth special session,[96] which tasked the OPCW Technical Secretariat with operating a mechanism to identify those who used chemical weapons in Syria. This session was a stormy one. During preparations, on the OPCW Executive Council, where the provisional agenda of the special session of the Conference of the States Parties was drafted,[97] China, Iran, Russia, Syria, and Venezuela jointly expressed dissatisfaction with the request for special session by Australia, Bulgaria, Canada, France, Germany, Japan, New Zealand, Poland, Romania, the UK, and the US.[98] The special session itself required votes seven times, once to adopt the agenda,[99] five to reject as many proposals to amend the UK draft decision,[100] and once to adopt said draft decision,[101] in order to conclude

---

p. 1, para. 1; OPCW Doc. S/1902/2019, 1 October 2019, p. 1, para. 1; OPCW Doc. S/2017/2022*, 24 January 2022, p. 3, para. 2.1; OPCW Doc. S/2020/2022, 31 January 2022, p. 3, para. 2.1.

[96] OPCW Doc. C-SS-4/DEC.3, 27 June 2018.

[97] Article VIII, para. 12 of the CWC stipulates that a special session of the Conference of the States Parties, not a review Conference but the regular Conference, shall be convened (a) when decided by the Conference; (b) when requested by the Executive Council; or (c) when requested by any member and supported by one third of the members. The first special session was requested by the US in accordance with subparagraph (c) (OPCW Doc. C-SS-1/1, 3 April 2002, para. 1), while the second and third special sessions were requested by the Executive Council in accordance with subparagraph (b) (OPCW Doc. C-SS-2/3, 30 April 2003, para. 1.2; OPCW Doc. C-SS-3/3, 7 April 2008, para. 1.2).

Rule 6 of the Rules of Procedures of the Conference of the States Parties (OPCW Doc. C-I/3/Rev.2, 8 April 2013) elaborates on the relevant process as follows:

- [a]ny Member of the Organisation may request the Director-General to convene a special session of the Conference;
- [t]he Director-General shall immediately inform the other Members of the Organisation of the request and inquire whether they concur with it; and
- [i]f one third of the Members concur with the request, a special session of the Conference shall be convened by the Director-General not later than 30 days after the receipt by him or her of such request.

[98] They argued that the "concern" of eleven States Parties over the continuing use of chemical weapons cannot be regarded as sufficient reason for convening a special session of the Conference of the States Parties because the same issue should be discussed either during a regular session or at a review Conference scheduled for late 2018 (OPCW Doc. EC-M-60/NAT.1, 4 June 2018, p. 1).

[99] OPCW Doc. C-SS-4/3, 27 June 2018, para. 2. The vote was 98 in favor to nine against.

[100] *Ibid.*, paras. 3.6–3.10. The votes were 22 in favor to 76 against the amendment proposed by Kazakhstan, 23 in favor to 78 against the amendment proposed by Belarus, 21 in favor to 78 against the amendment proposed by Bolivia 19 in favor to 79 against the amendment proposed by Iran, and 23 in favor to 78 against the amendment proposed by Burundi.

[101] OPCW Doc. C-SS-4/3, 27 June 2018, para. 3.17. The draft decision was adopted by a vote of 82 in favor to 24 against.

its business.[102] During the session, it became clear that many States Parties had a common belief in the necessity of attribution mechanisms concerning chemical weapons use in Syria.[103] There were, however, significant differences of opinion on whether adopting such attribution mechanisms was allowed under the CWC, and whether such attribution mechanisms on the part of the OPCW encroached on the functions of the UN, especially the Security Council.

Regarding the compatibility with the CWC, those States Parties who supported the UK draft decision affirmed that it was compatible with the CWC, without offering detailed legal opinions or interpretations,[104] while those who rejected the UK draft decision seemed to rely on a strict interpretation of the Convention,

---

[102] There were 152 States Parties in attendance, meaning that approximately 50 States Parties did not participate in each vote, while China, Iran, Myanmar, Nicaragua, Russia, Syria, and Venezuela took the same positions on all of the votes.

[103] OPCW Doc. C-SS-4/NAT.1 (Poland), 26 June 2018, p. 2; OPCW Doc. C-SS-4/NAT.3 (Albania), 27 June 2018, p. 2; OPCW Doc. C-SS-4/NAT.4 (New Zealand), 26 June 2018, p. 2; OPCW Doc. C-SS-4/NAT.5 (Bulgaria on behalf of the EU), 26 June 2018, p. 3; OPCW Doc. C-SS-4/NAT.6 (US), 26 June 2018, p. 2; OPCW Doc. C-SS-4/NAT.7 (Ireland), 27 June 2018, p. 2; OPCW Doc. C-SS-4/NAT.8 (Iceland), 27 June 2018, p. 2; OPCW Doc. C-SS-4/NAT.9 (Germany), 26 June 2018, p. 3; OPCW Doc. C-SS-4/NAT.13 (Lithuania), 27 June 2018, p. 2; OPCW Doc. C-SS-4/NAT.14 (Republic of Korea), 27 June 2018, p. 2; OPCW Doc. C-SS-4/NAT.15 (Austria), 27 June 2018, p. 1; OPCW Doc. C-SS-4/NAT.22 (Estonia), 26 June 2018, p. 2; OPCW Doc. C-SS-4/NAT.23 (Sweden), 27 June 2018, p. 2; OPCW Doc. C-SS-4/NAT.24 (Portugal), 26 June 2018, p. 2; OPCW Doc. C-SS-4/NAT.27 (Ukraine), 26 June 2018, p. 2; OPCW Doc. C-SS-4/NAT.29 (Australia), 26 June 2018, p. 2; OPCW Doc. C-SS-4/NAT.31 (Canada), 26 June 2018, p. 1; OPCW Doc. C-SS-4/NAT.36 (Morocco), 27 June 2018, p. 1; OPCW Doc. C-SS-4/NAT.38 (Uruguay), 27 June 2018, p. 1 (Uruguay did not participate in the voting on the UK draft decision); OPCW Doc. C-SS-4/NAT.39 (Mexico), 26 June 2018, p. 3; OPCW Doc. C-SS-4/NAT.40 (Russia), 26 June 2018, p. 1; OPCW Doc. C-SS-4/NAT.44 (India), 26 June 2018, p. 1; OPCW Doc. C-SS-4/NAT.45 (India), 26 June 2018, p. 1; OPCW Doc. C-SS-4/NAT.50 (Peru), 27 June 2018, p. 2; OPCW Doc. C-SS-4/NAT.52 (Ecuador), 27 June 2018, p. 2 (Ecuador did not participate in the vote on the UK draft decision); Tanzania on behalf of the African group, https://www.opcw.org/sites/default/files/documents/CSP/C-SS-4/en/CSPSS4-_AFRICAN_GROUP_STATEMENT_-_26-06-2018__2_.pdf, accessed 22 April 2023; Indonesia, https://www.opcw.org/sites/default/files/documents/CSP/C-SS-4/en/Indonesia_National_Statement.pdf, accessed 22 April 2023 (Indonesia did not participate in the vote on the UK draft decision); Latvia, https://www.opcw.org/sites/default/files/documents/CSP/C-SS-4/en/Latvia_-_National_Statement.pdf, accessed 22 April 2023; Finland, https://www.opcw.org/sites/default/files/documents/CSP/C-SS-4/en/Finland_-_National_Statement.pdf, accessed 22 April 2023; Netherlands, https://www.opcw.org/sites/default/files/documents/CSP/C-SS-4/en/Iran_-_National_Statement.pdf, accessed 22 April 2023.

[104] OPCW Doc. C-SS-4/NAT.3 (Albania), 27 June 2018, p. 2; OPCW Doc. C-SS-4/NAT.5 (Bulgaria on behalf of the EU), 26 June 2018, p. 3; OPCW Doc. C-SS-4/NAT.9 (Germany), 26 June 2018, p. 3; OPCW Doc. C-SS-4/NAT.13 (Lithuania), 27 June 2018, p. 2; OPCW Doc. C-SS-4/NAT.22 (Estonia), 26 June 2018, p. 1; OPCW Doc. C-SS-4/NAT.23 (Sweden), 27 June 2018, p. 2; OPCW Doc. C-SS-4/NAT.24 (Portugal), 26 June 2018, p. 2; OPCW Doc. C-SS-4/NAT.29 (Australia), 26 June 2018, p. 2; OPCW Doc. C-SS-4/NAT.31 (Canada), 26 June 2018, p. 1. OPCW Doc. C-SS-4/NAT.50 (Peru), 27 June 2018, p. 2; OPCW Doc. C-SS-4/NAT.51 (Denmark), 27 June 2018, p. 2; France, https://www.opcw.org/sites/default/files/documents/CSP/C-SS-4/en/France_National_Statement.pdf, accessed 22 April 2023; Finland, https://www.opcw.org/sites/default/files/documents/CSP/C-SS-4/en/Finland_-_National_Statement.pdf, accessed 22 April 2023. The Decision recalled Verification Annex Part XI, para. 26 (OPCW Doc. C-SS-4/DEC.3, 27 June 2018,

arguing that adopting attribution mechanisms by the OPCW exceeds the scope of the CWC,[105] necessitating amendment thereof.[106] It was also pointed out that "granting the Director-General 'unprecedented and unchecked powers'...would open itself to partisan use of the institution of the Director-General"[107] and that "attribution...entails a serious risk for the staff of the Secretariat as a technical body."[108]

In his critical analysis of the attribution mechanism question, Orakhelashvili divided it into the overall powers of the OPCW and the delegation of powers from the Conference of the States Parties to the Technical Secretariat. Regarding the former, while he noted the broadly formulated provision of Article VIII, para. 1 of the CWC, which does not inherently exclude "dealing with attribution issues" from the OPCW's competence, he also indicated that a more crucial issue is whether attribution matters fall within the generic competence of its internal organs, because an international organization is the sum thereof.[109] He concluded, however, that the CWC did not confer any power on the OPCW to generically subsume the establishment of attribution mechanisms for the following reasons. First, the attribution task is about "the conduct of the state in a particular conflict situation," and is thus qualitatively different from the verification task the CWC assigns to the OPCW, which is about the correctness of declarations of possession of chemical weapons. Second, approaching such verification activities in the least intrusive manner possible under Article VIII, para. 5 of the CWC does not offer room for attribution mechanisms. And third, the OPCW itself has not considered the establishment of attribution mechanisms.[110]

preamble para. 8), which includes "to identify the origin of any chemical weapons used" in the mandate of the teams that investigate alleged use in accordance with the CWC.

[105] OPCW Doc. C-SS-4/NAT.19 (Syria), 27 June 2018, p. 1; Iran, https://www.opcw.org/sites/default/files/documents/CSP/C-SS-4/en/Iran_-_National_Statement.pdf, accessed 22 April 2023 ("The Convention has not given the right or obligation of attributing the responsibility of the use of chemical weapons to the Director-General or Technical Secretariat"). This position was shared by Cuba (OPCW Doc. C-SS-4/NAT.32, 27 June 2018, p. 1) and Pakistan (https://www.opcw.org/sites/default/files/documents/CSP/C-SS-4/en/Pakistan_-_National_Statement.pdf, accessed 22 April 2023) who did not participate in the vote on the UK draft decision.

[106] OPCW Doc. C-SS-4/NAT.40 (Russia), 26 June 2018, p. 3; OPCW Doc. C-SS-4/NAT.42 (Russia), 27 June 2018, p. 1; OPCW Doc. C-SS-4/NAT.45 (India), 26 June 2018, p. 2; Iran, https://www.opcw.org/sites/default/files/documents/CSP/C-SS-4/en/Iran_-_National_Statement.pdf, accessed 22 April 2023; Burundi, https://www.opcw.org/sites/default/files/documents/CSP/C-SS-4/en/Burundi_National_Statement_English.pdf, accessed 22 April 2023.

[107] OPCW Doc. C-SS-4/NAT.45 (India), 26 June 2018, p. 2. See also Beth Van Schaack, *Imagining Justice for Syria: Water Always Finds its Way* (Oxford University Press, 2020), p. 365.

[108] Iran, https://www.opcw.org/sites/default/files/documents/CSP/C-SS-4/en/Iran_-_National_Statement.pdf, accessed 22 April 2023. Pakistan, which, as mentioned above, did not participate in the UK draft decision vote, also pointed out a lack of measures to prevent misuse of the mechanism for political purposes by powerful states (https://www.opcw.org/sites/default/files/documents/CSP/C-SS-4/en/Pakistan_-_National_Statement.pdf, accessed 22 April 2023).

[109] Orakhelashvili, *supra* note 40, pp. 670–671 ("an organ of an international organization can adopt a decision on matters not expressly mentioned in its constituent instrument, as long as those matters generically belong to the kind of activities to which the organ in question is expressly authorized.").

[110] *Ibid.*, p. 671.

With respect to the latter, Orakhelashvili pointed out "a certain degree of hierarchy" among the Conference of the States Parties as the OPCW's most pre-eminent organ and other internal organs, and wondered why the Conference of the States Parties was able to expand the statutory competence of the Technical Secretariat, whose function was rather modest, being limited to preparatory, assisting, and advisory activities under the CWC. While the relevant provisions of the Convention assigned the role in considering matters of compliance, including attribution, to the Executive Council and the Conference of the States Parties, the decision of the OPCW Conference of the States Parties refers these matters back to the Technical Secretariat.[111] He also raised doubts about the operational aspects of the decision of the OPCW Conference of the States Parties, because it gave the Technical Secretariat almost a blank check without reference to safeguards or controls by the Conference of the States Parties.[112] He thus concluded in this instance that "the Decision…has exceeded the authority of the Conference [of the States Parties] on the ground of distorting the intra-institutional balance under the Chemical Weapons Convention."[113]

These arguments do not seem persuasive. The CWC accommodates not only routine verification aimed at ensuring compliance but also a challenge inspection and an investigation of alleged use of chemical weapons, thereby addressing doubts about non-compliance. The fact that the OPCW itself has not considered the establishment of attribution mechanisms in the past cannot deny the OPCW overall power to introduce such mechanisms. Such prior lack of consideration was due mainly to the fact that there have been no major issues of chemical weapons use since the OPCW's inauguration.[114] Rather, the Verification Annex Part XI, para. 26 tasks inspection teams to collect information "that serve to identify the origin of any chemical weapons used" during investigations of alleged use, suggesting that the function of attributing responsibility is "inherent" in the powers of the OPCW.[115] Moreover, given the hierarchy among internal organs of the OPCW, Article VIII, para. 37 of the CWC explicitly envisages the possibility that the Technical Secretariat shall carry out functions "delegated" by the Conference of the States Parties. Finally, the purpose

---

[111] *Ibid.*, pp. 673–674.

[112] *Ibid.*, p. 679.

[113] *Ibid.*, p. 680. As a consequence, "[t]he Technical Secretariat's activities conducted on the basis of the Decision would similarly be ultra vires and not opposable to member states" (*ibid.*) and "… member states are not under any obligation to cooperate with IIT or accept their findings as authoritative" (*ibid.*, p. 681).

[114] There were two issues related to the use of chemical weapons prior to 2013. One was the allegations of such usage in Darfur, Sudan in 2004 (OPCW News, Sudan's Official Position Regarding Allegations of Use of Chemical Weapons in the Darfur Region, 8 October 2004, https://www.opcw.org/media-centre/news/2004/10/sudans-official-position-regarding-allegations-use-chemical-weapons, accessed 22 April 2023); the other was multiple chlorine gas attacks by groups in Iraq in 2007 (OPCW News, OPCW Director-General Condemns the Chlorine Attacks in Iraq, 23 February 2007, https://www.opcw.org/media-centre/news/2007/02/opcw-director-general-condemns-chlorine-attacks-iraq, accessed 22 April 2023). However, these issues were treated either as allegations without sufficient evidence or as incidents involving a non-State Party.

[115] Sossai, *supra* note 84, p. 221.

of attribution mechanisms is not to determine violations but to clarify facts about perpetrators.

That said, perhaps one cannot but find the legal basis for attribution mechanisms in the aforementioned so-called implied power theory. As indicated, it is generally accepted in theory and practice alike that international organizations have implied powers which are not explicitly mentioned in their institutive instruments.[116] The problem here is that unlike the OPCW FFM, this newly introduced attribution mechanism did not receive overall endorsement by the OPCW but faced objections from twenty-four States Parties and silence from more than eighty others. Under the current situation, the issue of the compatibility with the CWC has not definitively been resolved. The most effective remedy would be a ruling by a competent judicial organ.[117]

Regarding the "transfer" of mandate from the UN Security Council to the OPCW, those States Parties who favored the UK draft decision regretted the non-renewal of the attribution mechanism at the UN Security Council, indicating or implying their preference for a Security Council resolution, but endorsed the adoption of the same mechanism within the OPCW in light of the political stalemate at the Security Council,[118] while those opposing the UK draft decision insisted on the Security Council's exclusive role in this regard and paid less attention to its being deadlocked.[119]

Orakhelashvili indicated that this was "an attempt to transfer the authority from the UN to the OPCW and consequently to evade the unanimity of permanent members

[116] *Reparation for injuries suffered in the service of the United Nations, Advisory Opinion: I.C.J. Reports 1949*, p. 174, p. 182; *Legality of the Use by a State of Nuclear Weapons in Armed Conflict, Advisory Opinion, I.C.J. Reports 1996,* p. 66, p. 79, para. 25; Schermers and Blokker, *supra* note 86, pp. 180–189.

[117] Schermers and Blokker, *supra* note 86, p. 182.

[118] OPCW Doc. C-SS-4/NAT.1 (Poland), 26 June 2018, p. 2; OPCW Doc. C-SS-4/NAT.5 (Bulgaria on behalf of the EU), 26 June 2018, p. 3; OPCW Doc. C-SS-4/NAT.12 (Bulgaria on behalf of the EU), 27 June 2018, p. 1; OPCW Doc. C-SS-4/NAT.6 (US),, 26 June 2018 p. 2; OPCW Doc. C-SS-4/NAT.7 (Ireland), 27 June 2018, p. 2; OPCW Doc. C-SS-4/NAT.8 (Iceland), 27 June 2018, p. 1; OPCW Doc. C-SS-4/NAT.9 (Germany), 26 June 2018, pp. 2–3; OPCW Doc. C-SS-4/NAT.13 (Lithuania), 27 June 2018, pp. 1–2; OPCW Doc. C-SS-4/NAT.14 (Republic of Korea), 27 June 2018, pp. 1–2; OPCW Doc. C-SS-4/NAT.15 (Austria), 27 June 2018, p. 1; OPCW Doc. C-SS-4/NAT.23 (Sweden), 27 June 2018, p. 2; OPCW Doc. C-SS-4/NAT.24 (Portugal), 26 June 2018, p. 2; OPCW Doc. C-SS-4/NAT.26 (Czech Republic), 26 June 2018, pp. 1–2; OPCW Doc. C-SS-4/NAT.27 (Ukraine), 26 June 2018, p. 2; OPCW Doc. C-SS-4/NAT.29 (Australia), 26 June 2018, p. 2; OPCW Doc. C-SS-4/NAT.31 (Canada), 26 June 2018, p. 1; OPCW Doc. C-SS-4/NAT.39 (Mexico), 26 June 2018, p. 1; OPCW Doc. C-SS-4/NAT.51 (Denmark), 27 June 2018, p. 1; France, https://www.opcw.org/sites/default/files/documents/CSP/C-SS-4/en/France_National_Statement.pdf, accessed 22 April 2023; Latvia, https://www.opcw.org/sites/default/files/documents/CSP/C-SS-4/en/Latvia_-_National_Statement.pdf, accessed 22 April 2023; Slovenia, https://www.opcw.org/sites/default/files/documents/CSP/C-SS-4/en/Slovenia.pdf, accessed 7 January 2023.

[119] OPCW Doc. C-SS-4/NAT.17 (Syria), 26 June 2018, p. 2; OPCW Doc. C-SS-4/NAT.40 (Russia), 26 June 2018 p. 3; OPCW Doc. C-SS-4/NAT.42 (Russia), 27 June 2018, pp. 1–2; Iran, https://www.opcw.org/sites/default/files/documents/CSP/C-SS-4/en/Iran_-_National_Statement.pdf, accessed 22 April 2023.

of the Security Council."[120] His concerns lie in the feasibility of the decision of the OPCW Conference of the States Parties. Having noted a lack of binding powers on the part of the OPCW, particularly the Technical Secretariat, he wondered "how the OPCW Secretariat can examine potential violations of the Chemical Weapons Convention if it cannot enter the territory of the relevant state," and estimated that "[t]his may actually be the reason why the Convention's authors did not include the accountability and attribution task in its text, as being generically outside the OPCW organ's expressly defined tasks."[121]

Notwithstanding, a theoretical possibility of the transfer of authority from the UN Security Council to the OPCW Conference of the States Parties is one thing; the feasibility of attribution mechanisms within the OPCW is another. There may be ways to address the obvious lack of binding force of the OPCW IIT. In this regard, the Technical Secretariat refers to Article VII, para. 7 under which a State Party is obliged "to cooperate with the Organization in the exercise of all its functions" in its reports.[122] While this may be a self-evident obligation of States Parties in relation to the OPCW, it is legally binding. If a State Party fails to fulfil this obligation, it will face consequences in the form of measures taken by the policy-making organs to redress the situation. The OPCW Technical Secretariat further mentioned operative para. 7 of the UN Security Council Resolution 2118 which decided that Syria shall "cooperate fully with the OPCW and the United Nations."[123] On their part, the Executive Council and the Conference of the States Parties also cited Article VII, para. 7 of the CWC,[124] and referred to operative para. 7 of UN Security Council Resolution 2118 in the context of the cooperation with and the provision of access to the OPCW IIT in demanding Syria's full cooperation with the Technical Secretariat.[125] Whether operative para. 7 of the UN Security Council Resolution 2118 obliges Syria

[120] Orakhelashvili, *supra* note 40, p. 677.

[121] *Ibid.*, p. 678.

[122] OPCW Doc. S/1867/2020, 8 April 2020, p. 3, para. 7, pp. 19–20, para. 4.3; OPCW Doc. S/1943/2021, 12 April 2021, pp. 2–3, para. 6, p. 53, para. 3.

[123] OPCW Doc. EC-91/S/3, 28 June 2019, p. 3, para. 10; OPCW Doc. S/1867/2020, 8 April 2020, p. 3, para. 7, p. 19, para. 4.3; OPCW Doc. S/1943/2021, 12 April 2021, p. 2, para. 6, p. 53, para. 3.

[124] OPCW Doc. EC-94/DEC.2. 9 July 2020, preamble para. 11; OPCW Doc. C-25/DEC.9, 21 April 2021, preamble para. 5. See also OPCW Doc. EC-94/NAT.4 (Germany), 15 April 2020, pp. 1–2; OPCW Doc. EC-94/NAT.6 (UK), 14 April 2020, p. 2; OPCW Doc. EC-94/NAT.16 (Mexico), 19 June 2020, p. 2; OPCW Doc. EC-94/NAT.60 (Peru), 7 July 2020, p. 2; France, https://www.opcw.org/sites/default/files/documents/2020/07/France%20EC-94%20National%20Statement%20%28French%29.pdf, accessed 22 April 2023; OPCW Doc. C-25/NAT.119 (France), 20 April 2021, p. 2; OPCW Doc. C-25/NAT.121 (Mexico), 21 April 2021, p. 1.

[125] OPCW Doc. EC-94/DEC/2. 9 July 2020, operative para. 3; OPCW Doc. C-25/DEC.9, 21 April 2021, operative para. 6.

to cooperate with fact-finding organs regarding the alleged use of chemical weapons will be discussed hereinafter.

(b) **Modalities**

(i) **Mandates**

The fact-finding organs have mandates of varying scope. The UN Mission and the OPCW FFM are tasked with determining whether chemical weapons were used in Syria,[126] while the OPCW-UN JIM and the OPCW IIT are mandated to identify responsible parties.[127] The COI, an international human rights-related organ, has both aspects in its mandate, which further extends to "the investigation of violation of international law."[128] Even if the fact-finding organs are not tasked with the investigation of violation of international law, their findings of fact as such have implications.[129] There is a consensus in the international community that use of chemical weapons is prohibited under international law. Thus, the confirmation of the use of chemical weapons means that there was a violation of international law and the identification of perpetrators does that they violated international law.

Practice suggests that fact-finding mandates should include identifying users of chemical weapons, in addition to determining whether chemical weapons were used.[130] It is anticipated that attribution mechanisms will contribute as follows.[131] One is dispute settlement. Establishing use of chemical weapons itself is not sufficient to settle disputes, particularly when all parties to a given dispute criticize one other such use. It is thus necessary to identify violators of such international law with a view to settling the dispute by holding those who used chemical weapons accountable. Another potential contribution is deterrence. The international community has witnessed the continued use of chemical weapons, despite affirmative conclusions in several reports by fact-finding organs. When all parties to armed conflict claim use of chemical weapons by another, it is only natural that the fact-finding organs drew affirmative conclusions. Hence, determining whether chemical weapons were used did not have a deterrent effect per se, necessitating additional measures. The data

[126] For the UN Mission, UN Doc. A67/997–S/2013/553, 16 September 2013, p. 4; UN Doc. A68/663 –S/2013/735, 13 December 2013, p. 5. For the OPCW FFM, OPCW Doc. S/1255/2015*, 10 March 2015, Annex, p. 3, para. 3; OPCW Doc. EC-M-48/DEC.1, 4 February 2015, preamble para. 5; UN Doc. S/RES/2235 (2015), 7 August 2015, preamble para. 9; OPCW Doc. EC-M-50/DEC.1, 23 November 2015, preamble para. 6.

[127] For the OPCW-UN JIM, UN Doc. S/RES/2235 (2015), 7 August 2015, operative para. 5. For the OPCW IIT, OPCW Doc. C-SS-4/DEC.3, 27 June 2018, operative para. 10.

[128] UN Doc. A/HRC/RES/S-17/1, 22 August 2011, operative para. 13.

[129] It has been pointed out that the mandates of commissions of inquiry established by the UNHRC are "inherently contradictory" because they apparently predetermine that violations have been committed, while at the same time ask the commissions to "establish facts" and that "[f]actual findings may … have as many or even more legal implications as legal characterizations" (Van Den Herik, *supra* note 40, pp. 509, 536).

[130] In general, commissions of inquiry in the field of international human rights have an explicit mandate to identify those responsible (*ibid.*, p. 537).

[131] UN Doc. S/PV.7798, 31 October 2016, p. 4 (UK).

indicated a significant decrease in the number of allegations since the OPCW-UN JIM's establishment.[132]

Regarding the COI mandate, two questions can be raised: whether it might extend to use of chemical weapons, and whether it should investigate in parallel with the OPCW-related fact-finding organs. The first question should be generalized to whether the mandates of fact-finding organs that specify only human rights also encompass international humanitarian law, a subject that is attracting considerable attention.[133] While its mandate was originally limited to alleged violations of international human rights law, following its August 2012 report its scope expanded to alleged violations of international humanitarian law as well.[134] The reason was clear: the COI "determined that the intensity and duration of the conflict, combined with the increased organizational capabilities of anti-Government armed groups, had met the legal threshold for a non-international armed conflict."[135] UNHRC Resolution 21/26 of October 2012 stressed the need "to conduct an international, transparent, independent and prompt investigation into abuses and violations of international law, with a view to hold to account those responsible for violations and abuses, including those that may amount to crimes against humanity and war crimes,"[136] thereby adding "war crimes" to the mandates of the COI.

This is not an isolated practice but a general tendency. The UNHRC has established many other fact-finding organs which are involved in investigating violations of international humanitarian law.[137] The practice of the commissions of inquiry has been understood as follows: international human rights law and international humanitarian law are closely related with each other and cannot be completely separable;[138] the interface between these branches of international law is a growing

---

[132] UN Doc. S/PV.7798, 31 October 2016, p. 3 (US); UN Doc. S/PV.7815, 17 November 2016, p. 3 (US).

[133] Bothe, *supra* note 34, p. 261.

[134] UN Doc. A/HRC/21/50, 16 August 2012, p. 6, operative para. 12.

[135] *Ibid.*, p. 6, operative para. 12.

[136] UN Doc. A/HRC/RES/21/26, 17 October 2012, operative para. 10.

[137] Marco Odello, "The Interplay between International Human Rights Law and International Humanitarian Law in the Practice of Commissions of Inquiry," in Christian Henderson (ed.), *Commissions of Inquiry: Problems and Prospects* (Hart Publishing, 2017), p. 199, p. 204. For example, the Fact-Finding Mission to investigate violations of international law, including international humanitarian and human rights law, resulting from Israeli attacks on a flotilla carrying humanitarian aid (UN Doc. A/HRC/RES/14/1, 2 June 2014, operative para. 8); the UN Independent International Commission of Inquiry on the 2014 Gaza Conflict (UN Doc. A/HRC/RES/S-21/1, 23 July 2014, operative para. 13); the Commission of Inquiry on the 2018 protests in the Occupied Palestinian Territory (UN Doc. A/HRC/RES/S-28/1, 18 May 2018, operative para. 5); the UN Independent International Commission of Inquiry on the Occupied Palestinian Territory and Israel (UN Doc. A/HRC/RES/S-30/1, 28 May 2021, operative para. 1); the Independent International Commission of Inquiry on Ukraine (UN Doc. A/HRC/RES/49/1, 7 March 2022, operative para. 11(a) and (d)).

[138] See Grace, *supra* note 41, pp. 40–41; Boutruche, *supra* note 38, p. 123.

phenomenon,[139] in its Nuclear Weapons and Wall in Palestine advisory opinions, the ICJ acknowledged the possibility that some rights may be matters of both international human rights law and international humanitarian law in a situation of armed conflict,[140] there were no objections at the UNHRC to incorporating international humanitarian law in mandates of commissions of inquiry.[141] There has been criticism, however. A commentator indicated that the determination of the "legal lenses" that commissions of inquiry choose is often controversial because "a wide range of factors…influence perceptions about the appropriate 'legal lenses.'"[142] Another law scholar complained that commissions of inquiry blur the lines between international human rights law and international humanitarian law and insisted that these bodies of law should be "more clearly separated from each other—not just in theory, but in practice."[143] Another writer also stressed the differences between the parameters to evaluate violations of international human rights law and those to assess violations of international humanitarian law: international human rights law fact-finding mainly concerns ascertaining State responsibility, and placing pressure on States to end violations; while international humanitarian law fact-finding may focus more directly on the further prosecution of war crimes and other serious crimes.[144]

Even if the COI is allowed to investigate alleged violations of international humanitarian law in practice, whether it should investigate in tandem with other fact-finding organs is another question. On 16 September 2013, the Chairperson of the COI expressed the intent to conduct investigations in tandem with the activities of the UN Mission under the UN Secretary-General Investigation Mechanism.[145] While violations of non-use of weapons, including chemical weapons, are easier to investigate than violations of prohibitions on methods of combat because the former does not require assessment of proportionality, as far as the question of whether chemical weapons were used is concerned, the UN Mission plays a more technically professional investigative role than the COI. The former is equipped with expertise through OPCW personnel and technical and scientific resources, including analysis of samples at designated laboratories. There is no doubt that the OPCW-related fact-finding organs have used these resources more smoothly than the UN Mission. The fact that the COI was not even allowed to enter Syria should also be taken into

[139] See Micaela Frulli, "Fact-Finding or Paving the Road to Criminal Justice: Some Reflections on United Nations Commissions of Inquiry," *Journal of International Criminal Justice*, Vol. 10, No. 5 (December 2012), p. 1323, p. 1333; Marauhn, *supra* note 38, p. 439.

[140] *Legality of the Threat or Use of Nuclear Weapons, Advisory Opinion, I.C.J. Reports 1996*, p. 226, p. 240, para. 25; *Legal Consequences of the Construction of a Wall in the Occupied Palestinian Territory, Advisory Opinion, I.C.J. Reports 2004*, p. 136, p. 178, para. 106.

[141] Grace, *supra* note 41, pp. 40–41.

[142] *Ibid.*, p. 42.

[143] Marauhn, *supra* note 38, p. 460.

[144] Frulli, *supra* note 139, pp. 1334 and 1337–1338.

[145] Statement by Paulo Sérgio Pinheiro, Chair of the Independent International Commission of Inquiry on the Syrian Arab Republic, at the HRC twenty-fourth regular session, Geneva, 16 September 2013, https://newsarchive.ohchr.org/EN/NewsEvents/Pages/DisplayNews.aspx?NewsID=13733&LangID=E, accessed 22 April 2023.

account. For these reasons, it is doubtful whether the COI can conduct meaningful fact-finding activities in terms of allegations of use of chemical weapons, and should be involved in investigation in parallel with the OPCW-related fact-finding organs.

(ii) **Establishment**

The OPCW-UN JIM, the OPCW IIT, and the COI are contemporary fact-finding organs, in the sense that international organizations initiated their establishment unilaterally, without consent of State concerned.[146] By contrast, the UN Mission and OPCW FFM were established with the involvement of Syria. Whether this development can be understood as consent of the State concerned, an important aspect of traditional fact-finding procedures, demands careful consideration.

As mentioned previously, the OPCW Technical Secretariat found the basis for establishing the OPCW FFM in the "general authority" of the Director-General, referring to Syrian "acceptance" among other reinforcing elements. The distinction between the "general authority" and the reinforcing elements thereof suggests that the OPCW Technical Secretariat may not regard Syrian "acceptance" an indispensable condition for the establishment of the OPCW FFM. According to the OPCW Technical Secretariat, Syria expressed its "acceptance" through the aforementioned exchange of letters on the subject between the Director-General and the Syrian government.[147] Subsequent official OPCW documents reveal that "an exchange of letters" addressed the terms of reference of the OPCW FFM.[148] Thus, what Syria accepted was the terms of reference, which elaborates on modalities of OPCW FFM activities in the territory of Syria. The Director-General could not have created the OPCW FFM without the "acceptance" of Syria in advance. The OPCW FFM, thus, should be understood as a traditional fact-finding procedure in the sense that it required the consent of the State concerned. Later on, Syria requested that the OPCW Technical Secretariat start "in-depth and comprehensive discussions on the terms of reference of the FFM to fill the existing loopholes and make its working methods transparent and fully consistent with the standards and provisions stipulated

[146] In accordance with operative para. 5 of the UN Security Council Resolution 2235 (2015), the UN Secretary-General elaborated on the terms of reference of the OPCW-UN JIM (UN Doc. S/2015/669, 27 August 2015), which were authorized by the Security Council (UN Doc. S/2015/697, 10 September 2015). In this regard, the UN and Syria concluded an agreement on the status of the OPCW-UN JIM, the sole fact-finding organ among three whose entry was accepted by Syria, to ensure a timely, safe, and secure fact-finding mandate (UN Doc. S/2016/142, 12 February 2016, p. 8, para. 33). The COI adopted its terms of reference (UN Doc. A/HRC/S-17/2/Add.1, 23 November 2011, p. 4 and Annex I).

[147] OPCW Doc. S/1191/2014, 16 June 2014, p. 3, para. 4.

[148] OPCW Doc. S/1255/2015*, 10 March 2015, Annex; OPCW Doc. S/1255/2015*/Add.1, 13 March 2015. See also OPCW Doc. S/1510/2017, 29 June 2017, p. 4, para. 2.2; OPCW Doc. S/1548/2017, 2 November 2017, p. 2, para. 2.2; OPCW Doc. S/1628/2018, 15 May 2018, p. 2, para. 2.2; OPCW Doc. S/1636/2018*, 13 June 2018, p. 2, para. 2.2; OPCW Doc. S/1901/2020, 1 October 2020, p. 1, para. 1.2; OPCW Doc. S/1902/2020, 1 October 2020, p. 2, para. 1.2; OPCW Doc. S/2017/2022*, 24 January 2022, p. 3, para. 2.2; OPCW Doc. S/2020/2022, 31 January 2022, p. 3, para. 2.2.

in the Convention and its Verification Annex,"[149] indicating that Syria considers the terms of reference binding.

Syria triggered the UN Mission investigation with its own request, as previously described. The UN Secretary-General created the UN Mission, however. The requests from Syria on 20 March 2013[150] and from the UK and France on the next day 21 March 2013[151] showcase the UN Mission's dual aspects. Syria's request was decisive in establishing the UN Mission. Syria was willing to accept an on-site visit investigation in Khan al-Asal, enabling the UN Mission to conduct a traditional cooperative fact-finding investigation with the consent of the concerned State. Syria was, however, unable to prevent the UK and France's own request, despite its possible reluctancy to receive an investigation into the chemical incidents that they alleged. The UN Mission would thus become a contemporary confrontational fact-finding organ without consent of the concerned State. Despite the UN Mission's latter aspect, Syria retained some control over the team's investigations. Even after a UN Mission is established, the UN and the investigated State must agree on investigation modalities before the UN Mission enters the territory of the State to be investigated, including locations to be visited. The UN Secretary-General was thus in a difficult position. At the outset, he expressed the intent to respond to Syria's request as a matter of priority.[152] Rather than citing specific incidents, however, he instead took the principled position that all serious claims should be investigated.[153] It took nearly four months for the UN and Syria to reach an agreement. The issue of which locations the UN Mission would visit seemed to be resolved in an ambiguous and compromised way, as indicated by the statement that "the Mission will travel to Syria as soon as

---

149 OPCW Doc. EC-91/NAT.41 (Syria), 10 July 2019, p. 2; OPCW Doc. EC-91/NAT.43 (Syria), 11 July 2019, p. 3. See also OPCW Doc. EC-M-56/NAT.7 (Russia), 9 November 2017, p. 3; OPCW Doc. EC-92/NAT.44 (Russia), 9 July 2019, p. 3; OPCW Doc. EC-92/NAT.30 (Russia), 10 October 2019, p. 1.

150 UN Doc. S/2013/184, 25 March 2013, p. 1. It is noteworthy that Syria "officially requested that the investigation should determine who it was that used chemical weapons in Khan Asal" in its letter to the UN Secretary-General (UN Doc. S/2013/520, 3 September 2013, p. 3).

151 UN Doc. S/2013/184, 25 March 2013, p. 1. In light of Bothe's argument that "States have been extremely reluctant to lodge complaints as a kind of *actio popularis* in the 'public,' in the common interest," (Bothe, *supra* note 40, p. 262) the UK and France took exceptional action in this instance.

152 United Nations, Note to Correspondents on Syria, New York, 23 March 2013, https://www.un.org/sg/en/content/sg/note-correspondents/2013-03-23/note-correspondents-syria, accessed 22 April 2023.

153 Secretary-General's remarks to the Third Review Conference of the States Parties to the Chemical Weapons Convention, The Hague (Netherlands), 8 April 2013, https://www.un.org/sg/en/content/sg/speeches/2013-04-08/remarks-third-review-conference-states-parties-chemical-weapons, accessed 22 April 2023.

possible to contemporaneously investigate three of the reported incidents, including Khan al-Asal."[154]

(iii) Organizational Status and the Relationship with Other Organs

Each fact-finding organ has its own organizational and institutional status, while some make cooperative and complimentary relations with each other with a view to exploring ways to facilitate the efficiency of their work.

UN Mission

The UN Mission, an *ad hoc* independent UN fact-finding organ, benefits from OPCW support.[155] UN General Assembly Resolution 42/37C, which, as previously mentioned, forms the UN Mission's basis, anticipated such external support because of a lack of expertise on the part of the UN. Accordingly, it requested, on the one hand, "the [UN] Secretary-General to [s]eek…assistance as appropriate from Member States and the relevant international organizations" (operative para. 7), and on the other hand, "Member States and the relevant international organizations to co-operate fully with the Secretary-General" (operative para. 8). In this regard, the CWC includes a legal basis for the OPCW to cooperate with the UN Secretary-General in Verification Annex Part XI, para. 27, which stipulates that "[i]n the case of alleged use of chemical weapons involving a State not Party to this Convention or in territory not controlled by a State Party, the Organization shall closely cooperate with the Secretary-General of the United Nations. If so requested, the Organization shall put its resources at the disposal of the Secretary-General of the United Nations."

There are practical and legal problems alike with this provision. The first issue was a lack of modalities for implementation. In this regard, the Supplementary Arrangement concerning the Implementation of Article II (2) of the Relationship Agreement between the United Nations and the Organisation for the Prohibition of Chemical Weapons (Supplementary Arrangement)[156] was concluded on 14 September 2012 to establish a framework of cooperation between the organizations in cases of alleged use of chemical weapons in relation to non-State Parties to the CWC (Article I, para. 1). It incorporates detailed provisions about a wide range of practical and operational aspects including resources to be provided by the OPCW to the UN Secretary-General (Article I, para. 2(a)–(d)), the status of OPCW personnel and equipment (Article I, para. 3), fact-finding scope and working procedures (Article I, para. 5(b)–(c)), coordination of necessary arrangements by the UN Secretary-General (Article I, para. 6),

[154] United Nations, Note to Correspondents on Syria, New York, 31 July 2013, https://www.un.org/sg/en/content/sg/note-correspondents/2013-07-31/note-correspondents-syria, accessed 22 April 2023.

[155] Fourteen OPCW staff members joined the UN Mission (UN Doc. A/68/663–S/2013/735, 13 December 2013, Appendix 11, p. 85).

[156] *United Nations Treaty Series*, Vol. 2160, II-1240, pp. 207–221. Article XIV of the UN-OPCW Relationship Agreements stipulates the powers of the UN Secretary-General and the OPCW Director-General to "enter into such supplementary arrangements and develop such practical measures for the implementation of this Agreement as may be found desirable".

submission of the final report from the OPCW Director-General to the UN Secretary-General (Article I, para. 7),[157] and reimbursement of the costs of the OPCW by the UN (Article III, para. 1).[158]

Second was the ambiguity in the term "the Organization" in Verification Annex Part XI, para. 27, which became apparent when the OPCW Director-General informed the Executive Council at its seventieth session about the Supplementary Arrangement being concluded.[159] It raised the question of who is empowered to put the resources of the OPCW at the disposal of the UN Secretary-General on behalf of the OPCW. Does the OPCW Director-General act on their own initiative? Or is a decision by a competent policy-making organ required? During the debate, Russia insisted on the full control of the Executive Council over actions to be taken by the Director-General in response to request by the UN Secretary-General by pointing out that the issue related to "the functions of the Executive Council, including on supervising the activities of the Technical Secretariat."[160] For its part, the US rejected Russia's argument, emphasizing the mandatory nature of OPCW cooperation and the importance of a rapid response in the cases of suspected chemical weapons use.[161] The Executive Council addressed their difference of opinion by requesting that the Director-General "promptly inform the [Executive] Council and all States Parties of the request [by the UN Secretary-General] and of the actions that the Technical Secretariat is undertaking to respond to the request."[162] This measure made it clear that the Director-General can take actions in response to the request without any Executive Council involvement, while the Executive Council monitors activities to be carried out by the Technical Secretariat and subsequent developments pursuant to its functions under Article VIII. In response to a request from the UN Secretary-General on 23 March 2013, the OPCW Director-General immediately sent a copy of the UN Secretary-General's letter to States Parties, and informed the Executive

[157] Types of arrangements and contents of the report are almost identical to those identified in the Guidelines and Procedures (UN Doc. A/44/561, 4 October 1989, Annex, paras. 90 and 102). The final report shall include information on the composition of the fact-finding mission, all relevant data gathered during the mission including reports on the analysis of samples, a description of the fact-finding process, and the factual finding of the investigation.

[158] A similar arrangement was concluded between the WHO and the UN in January 2011, when the WHO and the UN Office for Disarmament Affairs (UNODA) agreed on the Memorandum of Understanding between the World Health Organization and the United Nations Concerning WHO's Support to the Secretary-General's Mechanism for Investigation of the Alleged Use of Chemical, Biological or Toxin Weapons, https://unoda-web.s3-accelerate.amazonaws.com/wp-content/uploads/assets/WMD/Secretary-General_Mechanism/UN_WHO_MOU_2011.pdf, accessed 22 April 2023. Article I, para 1.1 provides an indicative list of activities that the WHO takes in case of alleged chemical weapons use that are brought to the attention of the UN Secretary-General, including but not necessarily limited to seconding WHO personnel to UNODA, providing health information, sharing disease outbreak control methodologies, and contributing harmonizing outbreak response procedures and field operations.

[159] OPCW Doc. EC-70/5, 28 September 2012, para. 3.2.

[160] OPCW Doc. EC-70/NAT.7 (Russia), 27 September 2012.

[161] OPCW Doc. EC-70/NAT.16 (US), 25 September 2012, p. 1.

[162] OPCW Doc. EC-70/5, 28 September 2012, para 3.3.

Council of further developments at its twenty-second meeting on 27 March 2013.[163] The Third Review Conference of April 2013 included the following language in its political declaration: "[r]ecalling the expertise in the OPCW for the investigation of alleged use of chemical weapons, the States Parties expressed their support for the close cooperation, in accordance with paragraph 27 of Part XI of the Verification Annex of the Convention, between the Director-General of the OPCW and the Secretary-General of the United Nations in this regard."[164]

OPCW FFM, OPCW-UN JIM, and OPCW IIT

The OPCW-related organs, the OPCW FFM, the OPCW-UN JIM, and the OPCW IIT, differ from one another organizationally. The OPCW FFM is an *ad hoc* mission of the OPCW Technical Secretariat, the OPCW-UN JIM is an *ad hoc* independent OPCW-UN joint organ,[165] and the OPCW IIT is an *ad hoc* unit of the OPCW Technical Secretariat. They are, however, linked with one other both directly and indirectly. The relevant UN Security Council resolution and OPCW Conference of the States Parties decision established institutional connections between the activities of the OPCW FFM with the mandates of the other organs, in that both the OPCW-UN JIM and the OPCW IIT are tasked with investigating incidents where the OPCW FFM ascertains the probable or actual use of chemical weapons, in order to fulfill their respective mandates to identify perpetrators.[166] The OPCW Conference of the States Parties decision clarified the division of roles between these attribution mechanisms by excluding "cases for which the OPCW-UN JIM has not issued a report" from the OPCW IIT's investigative scope.[167] The relevant UN Security Council resolution addressed issues of exchange and retention of information between the OPCW FFM

---

[163] OPCW Doc. EC-M-32/DG.1, 27 March 2013, para 5.

[164] OPCW Doc. RC-3/3*, 19 April 2013, para 9.19. Several delegations expressed their disappointment with the lack of explicit reference to the ongoing investigation under the UN Mission (OPCW Doc. RC-3/NAT.55 (Ireland), 19 April 2013, p. 1; OPCW Doc. RC-3/NAT.56 (US), 19 April 2013, p. 1; OPCW Doc. RC-3/NAT.57 (Switzerland), 19 April 2013, p. 1; OPCW Doc. RC-3/NAT.60 (Netherlands), 19 April 2013, p. 1).

[165] In November 2015, the OPCW and the UN concluded the Supplementary Arrangement Concerning the Implementation of the United Nations Security Council Resolution 2235 (2015) between the United Nations and the Organisation for the Prohibition of Chemical Weapons (B-1240), "intended to establish the framework" for coordination between two international organizations (Article I, para. 1).

[166] UN Doc. S/RES/2235 (2015), 7 August 2015, operative para. 5; OPCW Doc. C-SS-4/DEC.3, 27 June 2018, operative para. 10. The OPCW Conference of the States Parties regretted that the OPCW-UN JIM mandate was not renewed (*ibid.*, preamble para. 4).

[167] OPCW Doc. C-SS-4/DEC.3, 27 June 2018, operative para. 10.

and the OPCW-UN JIM,[168] whereon the OPCW and the OPCW-UN JIM concluded a memorandum of understanding.[169]

COI

The COI has the status of subsidiary body of the UNHRC, with no formal relations with the other OPCW fact-finding organs.

(iv) **Guiding Principles**

The Declaration on Fact-Finding by the United Nations indicates that "[f]act-finding should be comprehensive, objective, impartial and timely."[170] A commentator also points out that a fact-finding organ should ensure that they establish facts "in a transparent, independent, objective, and impartial manner."[171] In this regard, the United Nations Office of the High Commissioner for Human Rights (UNOHCHR) identifies eleven elements as principles of human rights and international humanitarian law fact-finding and investigations: do no harm, independence, impartiality, transparency, objectivity, confidentiality, credibility, visibility, integrity, professionalism, and consistency.[172] Five fact-finding organs have acted essentially in line with these elements, whether explicitly or implicitly, except for timeliness, which, even as an aspect of professionalism, may not always be taken into account.[173]

When the UN Secretary-General announced his decision to establish the UN Mission, he referred to Syria's request for "a specialized, impartial and independent mission."[174] The terms of reference of the OPCW FFM mentioned "the impartial

---

[168] UN Doc. S/RES/2235 (2015), 7 August 2015, operative paras. 9 and 12. The UN Security Council envisaged the possibility that the OPCW-UN JIM might obtain evidence related to possible uses of chemical weapons in cases in which the OPCW FFM was not involved. Should that happen, the OPCW-UN JIM is requested to transmit that evidence to the OPCW FFM via the OPCW Director-General.

[169] UN Doc. S/2016/142, 12 February 2016, p. 8, para. 28.

[170] The Declaration on Fact-Finding by the United Nations in the Field of the Maintenance of International Peace and Security (UN Doc. A/RES/46/59, 9 December 1991, Annex), operative para. 3.

[171] Théo Boutruche, "Selectivity and Choices in Human Rights Fact-finding: Reconciling Subjectivity with Objectivity?" in Christian Henderson (ed.), *Commissions of Inquiry: Problems and Prospects* (Hart Publishing, 2017), p. 287, p. 290.

[172] United Nations Office of the High Commissioner for Human Rights, *Commissions of Inquiry and Fact-Finding Missions on International Human Rights and Humanitarian Law, Guidance and Practice* (2015), pp. 33–35.

[173] The OPCW-UN JIM and the OPCW IIT commence investigating only after the OPCW FFM confirmed chemical weapons use.

[174] United Nations, Secretary-General's Press Encounter on Syrian Government Request, 21 March 2013, https://www.un.org/sg/en/content/sg/press-encounter/2013-03-21/secretary-generals-press-encounter-syrian-government-request, accessed 22 April 2023; UN Doc. A/68/663–S/2013/735, 13 December 2013, p. 6, para. 6. See also UN Doc. S/2013/187 (Iran), 25 March 2013, p. 2 ("such an investigation will be done in full impartiality, objectivity and seriousness.").

The UN Secretary-General also expressed his intent to conduct a thorough, impartial, and prompt investigation at a closed-door session of the UN Security Council on 21 August 2013, in response to allegations of chemical weapons attacks in Ghouta (United Nations, and international nature of their duties,"[175] characterizing privileges and immunities of its personnel as "necessary to ensure the independent exercise of the Mission's activities."[176] The UN Secretary-General also made it clear that the OPCW-UN JIM shall demonstrate "objectivity," and conduct its work in an "independent and impartial manner," and that its composition shall reflect "comprehensive, professional and multidisciplinary expertise" to meet the mandate of the resolution.[177] The OPCW Technical Secretariat stressed that the OPCW IIT will carry out its operations in an "independent, impartial, and objective manner."[178] The UNHRC urgently dispatched an "independent international" commission of inquiry (COI) in response.[179]

States have also shared and stressed elements that fact-finding organs should respect, especially the OPCW FFM, the OPCW-UN JIM, and the OPCW IIT, as illustrated by their statements at OPCW and UN meetings. These include the aforementioned independence, objectivity, impartiality and professionalism, although different States have assigned them different priorities. When the OPCW-related fact-finding organs published their reports, a majority of States commended them for conducting investigation activities in line with these elements,[180] while a minority

Syria: Ban sending official request to allow UN probe of alleged chemical weapons use, 22 August 2013, https://news.un.org/en/story/2013/08/447282-syria-ban-sending-official-request-allow-un-probe-alleged-chemical-weapons-use, accessed 22 April 2023; UN Doc. A/68/663–S/2013/735, 13 December 2013, p. 10, para. 35).

[175] OPCW Doc. S/1255/2015*, 10 March 2015, Annex, p. 3, para. 6.

[176] *Ibid.*, p. 4, para. 7.

[177] UN Doc. S/2015/669, 27 August 2015, pp. 2–3.

[178] OPCW Doc. EC-91/S/3, 28 June 2019, p. 2, para. 6; OPCW Doc. EC-92/S/8, 3 October 2019, p. 2, para. 8.

[179] UN Doc. A/HRC/RES/S-17/1, 22 August 2011, operative para. 13.

[180] OPCW FFM: OPCW Doc. EC-M-49/NAT.5 (Chile), 7 May 2015, p. 1; OPCW Doc. EC-79/NAT.6 (Luxembourg on behalf of the EU), 7 July 2015, p. 2; OPCW Doc. EC-79/NAT.24 (Chile), 7 July 2015, pp. 2–3; OPCW Doc. EC-83/NAT.9 (Slovakia on behalf of the EU), 11 October 2016, p. 2; OPCW Doc. EC-M-54/NAT.2 (Norway), 13 April 2017, p. 1; OPCW Doc. EC-M-54/NAT.8 (Australia), 13 April 2017, p. 2; OPCW Doc. EC-M-54/NAT.18 (UK), 13 April 2017, p. 2; OPCW Doc. EC-M-54/NAT.7 (Japan), 19 April 2017, p. 1; OPCW Doc. EC-M-54/NAT.5 (Germany), 20 April 2017, p. 1; OPCW Doc. EC-M-55/NAT.3 (Turkey), 5 July 2017, p. 1; OPCW Doc. EC-M-55/NAT.4 (UK), 5 July 2017, p. 2; OPCW Doc. EC-M-55/NAT.6 (Slovakia), 5 July 2017, p. 1; OPCW Doc. EC-M-55/NAT.11 (Belgium), 5 July 2017, p. 1; OPCW Doc. EC-86/NAT.5 (Estonia on behalf of the EU), 10 October 2017, p. 2; OPCW Doc. EC-90/NAT.32 (Switzerland), 13 March 2019, p. 1; OPCW Doc. EC-90/NAT.44 (Mexico), 12 March 2019, pp. 1–2; OPCW Doc. EC-91/NAT.9 (Finland), 9 July 2019, p. 2; OPCW Doc. EC-91/NAT.13 (Germany), 9 July 2019, p. 1; OPCW Doc. EC-91/NAT.38 (Peru), 9 July 2019, p. 2; OPCW Doc. EC-92/NAT.11 (Republic of Korea), 8 October 2019, pp. 1–2; OPCW Doc. EC-92/NAT.12 (Switzerland), 8 October 2019, p. 2; OPCW Doc. EC-93/NAT.23 (Finland), 10 March 2020, p. 1; OPCW Doc. EC-93/NAT.15 (Croatia on behalf of the EU), 10 March 2020, p. 1; OPCW Doc. EC-95/NAT.24 (Germany), 6 October 2020, p. 1; OPCW Doc. EC-95/NAT.36 (France), 6 October 2020, p. 1; OPCW Doc. EC-96/NAT.16 (Republic of Korea), 9 March 2021, p. 2; OPCW Doc. EC-96/NAT.18 (Italy), 9 March 2021, p. 1. OPCW-UN JIM: UN Doc. S/PV.7815, 17 November 2016, p. 6 (Ukraine); UN Doc. S/PV. 7893, 28 February 2017, pp. 8 (Japan), 10 (Italy); OPCW Doc. EC-M-55/NAT.3 (Turkey), 5 July 2017, p. 1; OPCW Doc. EC-M-55/NAT.11 (Belgium), 5 July 2017, p. 1; UN Doc. S/PV.8090, 7 November 2017, pp. 8 (Ukraine), 9 (France), 12 (Japan), 14 (Uruguay), 22 (Sweden), 23 (Italy); OPCW Doc. EC-M-56/

demanded respect for them,[181] with the rest merely mentioning their importance.[182] In response to the media reports on serious allegations, States have often stressed the timely deployment of fact-finding teams to locations concerned.[183] When an attribution mechanism's extension or re-establishment was on the agenda, many

NAT.1 (Joint statement of UK, France, Germany and US), 9 November 2017, p. 1; OPCW Doc. EC-M-56/NAT.4 (Germany), 9 November 2017, p. 1; OPCW Doc. EC-90/NAT.32 (Switzerland), 13 March 2019, p. 1. OPCW IIT: OPCW Doc. EC-93/NAT.23 (Finland), 10 March 2020, p. 1; OPCW Doc. EC-94/NAT.1 (US), 14 April 2020, p. 2; OPCW Doc. EC-94/NAT.7 (France), 9 April 2020, p. 1; OPCW Doc. EC-94/NAT.4 (Germany), 15 April 2020, p. 1; OPCW Doc. EC-94/NAT.10 (Czech Republic), 16 April 2020, p. 1; OPCW Doc. EC-94/NAT.8 (New Zealand), 21 April 2020, p. 2; OPCW Doc. EC-94/NAT.9 (Slovenia), 25 May 2020, p. 1; OPCW Doc. EC-94/NAT.14 (Costa Rica), 15 June 2020, p. 1; OPCW Doc. EC-94/NAT.15 (Italy), 18 June 2020, p. 1; OPCW Doc. EC-94/NAT.16 (Mexico), 19 June 2020, p. 2; OPCW Doc. EC-94/NAT.21 (Austria), 7 July 2020, p. 1; OPCW Doc. EC-94/NAT.24 (Republic of Korea), 7 July 2020, p. 2; OPCW Doc. EC-94/NAT.33 (Lithuania), 7 July 2020, p. 1; OPCW Doc. EC-94/NAT.34 (Finland), 7 July 2020, p. 1; OPCW Doc. EC-94/NAT.35 (Germany on behalf of the EU), 7 July 2020, p. 2; OPCW Doc. EC-94/NAT.37 (US), 7 July 2020, p. 2; OPCW Doc. EC-94/NAT.45 (Germany), 7 July 2020, p. 2; OPCW Doc. EC-94/NAT.46 (Denmark), 7 July 2020, p. 1; OPCW Doc. EC-94/NAT.60 (Peru), 7 July 2020, p. 2; OPCW Doc. EC-95/NAT.8 (Slovenia), 6 October 2020, p. 1; OPCW Doc. EC-95/NAT.9 (Estonia), 6 October 2020, p. 1; OPCW Doc. EC-95/NAT.25 (Germany on behalf of the EU), 6 October 2020, p. 1; OPCW Doc. EC-95/NAT.44 (Lithuania), 6 October 2020, p. 1; OPCW Doc. EC-95/NAT.52 (Canada), 6 October 2020, p. 1; OPCW Doc. EC-95/NAT.57 (Republic of Korea), 6 October 2020, p. 2; OPCW Doc. EC-96/NAT.18 (Italy), 9 March 2021, p. 1.

181 OPCW FFM: OPCW Doc. EC-80/NAT.10 (Russia), 7 October 2015, p. 2; OPCW Doc. EC-81/NAT.29 (Cuba), 15 March 2016, p. 2; OPCW Doc. EC-M-56/NAT.15 (Iran), 9 November 2017, p. 1; OPCW Doc. EC-90/NAT.23 (Iran), 13 March 2019, p. 2; OPCW Doc. EC-91/NAT.27 (Iran), 10 July 2019, p. 3; OPCW Doc. EC-92/NAT.9 (Iran), 9 October 2019 p. 2; OPCW Doc. EC-94/NAT.29 (Iran), 7 July 2020, p. 2; OPCW Doc. EC-96/NAT.51 (Iran), 9 March 2021, p. 3. OPCW-UN JIM: UN Doc. S/PV.7915, 5 April 2017, pp. 6 (Bolivia), 17 (Russia); UN Doc. A/72/526–S/2017/848 (Russia), 10 October 2017; UN Doc. S/PV.8073, 24 October 2017, pp. 4–5 (Russia); UN Doc. S/PV.8090, 7 November 2017, pp. 23 (Senegal), 20 (Bolivia); OPCW Doc. EC-M-56/NAT.2 (Russia), 9 November 2017, p. 1. For more general context: UN Doc. S/PV.7922, 12 April 2017, pp. 6 (Russia), 9 (Bolivia); OPCW Doc. EC-M-54/NAT.9 (Iran), 13 April 2017, p. 2; OPCW Doc. EC-M-54/DEC/CPR.1/Rev.1 (The Islamic Republic of Iran and the Russian Federation: Draft Decision), 19 April 2017, preamble para. 4, https://london.mid.ru/en/press-centre/gb_en_fnapr_6064/, accessed 22 April 2023; OPCW Doc. EC-86/NAT.24 (Russia), 10 October 2017, p. 2; OPCW Doc. C-25/NAT.95 (Brazil), 20 April 2021, p. 2; OPCW Doc. C-25/NAT.113 (India), 21 April 2021, p. 3; OPCW Doc. C-25/NAT.115 (Cuba), 21 April 2021, p. 2. OPCW IIT: OPCW Doc. EC-94/NAT.5 (Syria), 16 April 2020, p. 1,

182 OPCW FFM: OPCW Doc. EC-78/NAT.32 (China), 17 March 2015, p. 1; OPCW Doc. EC-79/NAT.13 (China), 7 July 2015, p. 2; OPCW Doc. EC-81/NAT.27 (China), 15 March 2016, p. 2; OPCW Doc. EC-94/NAT.41 (China), 7 July 2020, p. 2. OPCW-UN JIM: UN Doc. S/PV.7815, 17 November 2016, p. 5 (China); UN Doc. S/PV.7915, 5 April 2017, p. 7 (China); UN Doc. S/PV.7922, 12 April 2017, pp. 6 (China), 9–10 (Kazakhstan); OPCW Doc. EC-M-56/NAT.14 (Brazil), 9 November 2017, p. 1; OPCW Doc. EC-96/NAT.37 (China), 9 March 2021, p. 2. OPCW IIT: OPCW Doc. EC-94/NAT.39 (India), 7 July 2020, p. 2, OPCW Doc. EC-94/NAT.59 (India), 9 July 2020, p. 1.

183 Incident in Khan Shaykhun: UN Doc. S/PV.7915, 5 April 2017, pp. 10 (Uruguay), 10 (Kazakhstan), 13 (Ethiopia), 14 (Senegal); UN Doc. S/PV.7919, 7 April 2017, p. 10 (Japan); UN Doc. S/PV.7922, 12 April 2017, pp. 3 (UK), 7–8 (Russia), 9 (Sweden); OPCW Doc. EC-M-54/DEC/CRP.1/Rev.1 (The Islamic Republic of Iran and the Russian Federation: Draft Decision), 19 April 2017, preamble para. 4, https://london.mid.ru/en/press-centre/gb_en_fnapr_6064/, accessed

States again attached importance to the independence, objectivity, impartiality, and professionalism thereof.[184]

(c) Syrian Obligations

The cooperation of States concerned, especially that of the State in which fact-finding organs are deployed to investigate, is essential if such organs are to collect information sufficient to base findings of fact on.

Syria is not obliged to cooperate with fact-finding organs established by the UN General Assembly, including the UNHRC, as resolutions by either organ are not binding on it. Regarding the UN Mission, the UN General Assembly simply "[r]equests Member States…to co-operate fully with the Secretary-General in the…-work."[185] With respect to the COI, the UNHRC also "[c]alls upon the Syrian authorities to cooperate fully with the commission of inquiry."[186]

On the contrary, it is crystal-clear that Syria is obligated to cooperate with the OPCW-UN JIM, as the UN Security Council established it in accordance with its Resolution 2235, in which it recalled Syria's obligation to cooperate with the OPCW and the UN under operative para. 7 of Resolution 2118[187] and "stress[ed] that this [obligation] includes an obligation to cooperate with the OPCW Director-General

---

22 April 2023. Incident in Douma: UN Doc. S/PV.8225, 9 April 2018, pp. 10 (Netherlands), 15 (Sweden), 19 (Kazakhstan) 20 (Kazakhstan), 22 (Peru), 25–26 (Syria) ("as soon as possible to investigate and verify these allegations").

[184] UN Doc. S/PV.8105, 16 November 2017, pp. 8 (Bolivia), 10 (China), 12 (Egypt), 16 (Russia); UN Doc. S/PV.8107, 17 November 2017, pp. 3 (US), 6 (Bolivia); UN Doc. S/PV.8225, 9 April 2018, pp. 9 (Netherlands), 14 (UK), 14 (China), 16 (Sweden), 18 (Equatorial Guinea), 20 (Kuwait), 21 (Bolivia); UN Doc. S/PV.8228, 10 April 2018, pp. 3 (US), 6 (China), 7 (Bolivia) OPCW Doc. C-SS-4/NAT.23 (Sweden), 27 June 2018, p. 2; OPCW Doc. C-SS-4/NAT.6 (US), 26 June 2018, p. 2; OPCW Doc. C-SS-4/NAT.9 (Germany), 26 June 2018, p. 3; OPCW Doc. C-SS-4/NAT.15 (Austria), 27 June 2018, p. 1; OPCW Doc. C-SS-4/NAT.27 (Ukraine), 26 June 2018, p. 2; OPCW Doc. C-SS-4/NAT.29 (Australia), 26 June 2018, p. 2; OPCW Doc. C-SS-4/NAT.36 (Morocco), 27 June 2018, p. 1; OPCW Doc. RC-4/NAT.19* (Austria, Australia, Belgium, Bulgaria, Canada, Côte d'Ivoire, Czech Republic, Denmark, Estonia, Finland, France, Germany, Ghana, Ireland, Italy, Japan, Kuwait, Latvia, Lithuania, Luxembourg, Montenegro, Morocco, Netherlands, New Zealand, Norway, Peru, Poland, Republic of Korea, Senegal, Slovenia, Spain, Sweden, Switzerland, Tunisia, Turkey, UK, US, and Ukraine: Joint Paper Shared Views of the Participating States of the International Partnership against Impunity for the Use of Chemical Weapons Implementation of Decision C-SS-4/DEC.3, dated 27 June 2018), 29 November 2018, p. 1. See also UN Doc. S/2017/962, 16 November 2017 (draft resolution of France, Italy, Japan, Sweden, Ukraine, UK, and US), preamble para. 9; UN Doc. S/2017/968, 16 November 2017 (draft resolution of Bolivia), preamble para. 9; UN Doc. S/ 2018/175, 10 April 2018 (draft resolution of Russia), preamble para. 11; UN Doc. S/2018/321, 10 April 2018 (draft resolution of Albania, Australia, Bulgaria, Canada, Denmark, Estonia, Finland, France, Germany, Italy, Latvia, Lithuania, Montenegro, Netherlands, Norway, Peru, Poland, Qatar, Moldova, Slovenia, Sweden, The former Yugoslav Republic of Macedonia, Turkey, Ukraine, UK, and US), preamble para. 8.

[185] UN Doc. A/RES/42/37C, 30 November 1987, operative para. 8.

[186] UN Doc. A/HRC/RES/S–17/1, 22 August 2011, operative para. 16.

[187] UN Doc. S/RES/2235 (2015), 7 August 2015, preamble para. 10 and operative para. 7.

and…the United Nations Secretary-General and the Joint Investigative Mechanism."[188] The OPCW FFM is a different story. When the OPCW Director-General announced its establishment, he did not refer to Syria's obligation to cooperate. Nor did the terms of reference agreed to through the exchange of letters between the OPCW Technical Secretariat and Syria allude to such obligation. In August 2015, its status was clarified when the Security Council Resolution 2335 encompassed Syria's obligation to cooperate with the OPCW FFM within the scope of its abovementioned obligation to cooperate with the OPCW under Resolution 2118.[189] Operative para. 7 of Resolution 2118 apparently focused on Syrian cooperation with OPCW and UN personnel in the context of eliminating chemical weapons. One item in a list of modalities for cooperation is almost identical with language that appears in OPCW Executive Council decision on the elimination of Syrian chemical weapons.[190] This list may not be comprehensive, but rather, indicative, as suggested by the term "including" after the phrase "the Syrian Arab Republic shall cooperate fully with the OPCW and the United Nations." Thus, it can be said that this obligation encompasses the obligation to cooperate with the OPCW FFM. As mentioned, the UN Security Council clarified the point in its subsequent resolutions.

The OPCW IIT is still another matter. Despite no indication in the relevant OPCW Conference of the States Parties decision of Syrian obligation to cooperate with an organ to be established,[191] the OPCW Technical Secretariat referred to the obligation of State Party under Article VII, para. 7 to cooperate with the OPCW beginning in preparatory stages.[192] While this may suffice in legal terms, the OPCW IIT added operative para. 7 of UN Security Council Resolution 2118 in its reports in response to the refusal of Syria to issue visas and its argument that the relevant OPCW Conference of the States Parties decision was inconsistent with the CWC.[193] Both the OPCW Executive Council and the Conference of the States Parties "[e]xpresse[d] deep concern that the Syrian Arab Republic did not cooperate with, and provide

[188] *Ibid.*, operative para. 7. The UN Security Council identified "full access to all locations, individuals, and materials in Syria" as part of said cooperation (*ibid.*). The UN Security Council reaffirmed this language in November 2016 (UN Doc. S/RES/2319 (2016), 17 November 2016, operative para. 7).

[189] UN Doc. S/RES/2235 (2015), 7 August 2015, operative para. 7. See also UN Doc. S/RES/2319 (2016), 17 November 2016, operative para. 7.

[190] UN Doc. S/RES/2235 (2015), 7 August 2015, operative para. 7; OPCW Doc. EC-M-33/DEC.1, 27 September 2013, operative para. 1(e).

[191] The OPCW Conference of the States Parties decision tasked the OPCW Technical Secretariat to submit regular reports on the investigation to the UN Secretary-General for consideration (OPCW Doc. C-SS-4/DEC.3, 27 June 2018, operative para. 10).

[192] OPCW Doc. EC-91/S/3, 28 June 2019, p. 3, para. 10; OPCW Doc. EC-92/S/8, 3 October 2019, p. 4, para. 16.

[193] OPCW Doc. S/1867/2020, 8 April 2020, p. 11, para. 2.7; pp. 19–20, para. 4.3; OPCW Doc. S/1943/2021, 12 April 2021, p. 3, para. 6; Annex 3, p. 53, para. 3.

access to, the IIT as required by United Nations Security Council resolution 2118 (2013)."[194]

(d) Implementation

(i) Conduct and Results

As described above, five fact-finding organs have been involved in the investigation of chemical incidents since the international community received the first allegations of chemical weapons use in Syria. The conduct and results of investigation are as follows. Additional information is included in Appendix B and C.

First, the UN Secretary-General Investigation Mechanism was activated for the first time in twenty years, establishing the UN Mission in March 2013[195] upon request of Syria on the one hand[196] and the UK and France on the other.[197] By the end of August 2013, UN Member States requested the UN Mission investigate a total of sixteen allegations, of which it took on seven,[198] concluding that chemical weapons were used in Ghouta on 21 August 2013,[199] and completing its investigations by December 2013.

Second, the OPCW Director-General launched the OPCW FFM in April 2014.[200] In more than twenty reports, it ascertained the following chemical attacks: Kafr-Zita between 10 April and 30 August 2014, Al-Tamanah on 12, 18 and 30 April 2014 and 22 and 25 May 2014, and Talmenes on 21 and 24 April 2014;[201] Idlib Governorate

---

[194] OPCW Doc. EC-94/DEC.2, 9 July 2020, operative para. 3; OPCW Doc. C-25/DEC.9, 21 April 2021, operative para. 6. See also OPCW Doc. EC-94/NAT.6 (UK), 14 April 2020, p. 2; OPCW Doc. EC-94/NAT.16 (Mexico), 19 June 2020, p. 2; OPCW Doc. EC-94/NAT.65 (Guatemala), 7 July 2020, p. 2; OPCW Doc. EC-94/NAT.37 (US), 7 July 2020; UN Doc. S/2020/1202, 16 December 2020, pp. 29–30 (UK); OPCW Doc. C-25/NAT.111 (UK), 20 April 2021, p. 1; OPCW Doc. C-25/NAT.121 (Mexico), 21 April 2021; UN Doc. S/PV.8982, 28 February 2022, p. 15 (Turkey).

[195] UN News, UN chief announces independent probe into allegations of chemical attack in Syria, 21 March 2013, https://news.un.org/en/story/2013/03/435082-un-chief-announces-independent-probe-allegations-chemical-attack-syria, accessed 22 April 2023. The UN Secretary-General implemented General Assembly resolution 42/37C, which was reaffirmed by Security Council resolution 620. While the UN Mission reports included the terms of reference (UN Doc. A/67/997–S/2013/553, 16 September 2013, p. 4; UN Doc. A/68/663–S/2013/735, 13 December 2013, p. 5), they merely recited the Mission's purpose and made reference to its Guidelines, without citing detailed modalities or procedures.

[196] UN Doc. S/2013/184, 25 March 2013, p. 1. Syria warned that "the terrorist groups could use those weapons against the Syrian people" (UN Doc. A/67/628–S/2012/917, 10 December 2012, p. 2).

[197] UN Doc. S/2013/184, 25 March 2013, p. 1.

[198] UN Doc. A/68/663–S/2013/735, 13 December 2013, para. 45.

[199] UN Doc. A/67/997–S/2013/553, 16 September 2013, p. 8, paras. 27–29; UN Doc. A/68/663–S/2013/735, 13 December 2013, p. 21, paras. 108–110.

[200] OPCW News, OPCW to Undertake Fact-Finding Mission in Syria on Alleged Chlorine Gas Attacks, 29 April 2014, https://www.opcw.org/media-centre/news/2014/04/opcw-undertake-fact-finding-mission-syria-alleged-chlorine-gas-attacks, accessed 22 April 2023. The OPCW published the terms of reference in its official documents (OPCW Doc. S/1255/2015*, 10 March 2015, Annex; OPCW Doc. S/1255/2015*/Add.1, 13 March 2015).

[201] OPCW Doc. S/1212/2014, 10 September 2014; OPCW Doc. S/1230/2014, 18 December 2014.

(Qmenas, Sarmin, Binnish, Idlib City, Al-Nerab, and Saraqib) between 16 March and 20 May 2015;[202] Marea on 21 August 2015;[203] Marea on 1 and 3 September 2015;[204] Um-Housh on 15 and 16 September 2016;[205] Kafr Zeita on 1 October 2016;[206] Ltamenah on 24 and 25 March 2017;[207] Ltamenah on 30 March 2017;[208] Khan Shaykhun on 4 April 2017;[209] Saraqib 4 February 2018;[210] and Douma on 7 April 2018.[211] At the same time, it was unable to definitively ascertain chemical weapons use in the following instances: Jober on 29 August 2014, Al-Maliha on 16 April 2014, Al-Maliha on 11 July 2014, Al Kabbas on 10 September 2014, Nubel and Al-Zahraa on 8 January 2015, Darrayya on 15 February 2015;[212] Aleppo on 2 August 2016;[213] Al-Hamadaniyah on 30 October 2016, Karm Al-Tarrab on 13 November 2016;[214] Saraqib on 1 August 2016;[215] and Aleppo on 24 November 2018.[216] It continues to operate as of this writing.

Third, the UN Security Council created the OPCW-UN JIM in August 2015, tasking it with identifying those responsible for chemical attacks.[217] In its third, fourth, and seventh reports, it identified the Syrian government as having perpetrated the attacks in Talmenes on 21 April 2014, Qmenas on 16 March 2015, Sarmin on 16 March 2015, and Khan Shaykhun on 4 April 2017,[218] and ISIL the attacks in Marea on 21 August 2015, and Um-Housh on 15 and 16 September 2016, respectively.[219] The mission's mandate was extended temporarily in October 2016[220] and for an additional year in November 2016,[221] only to be terminated in November 2017 owing to failure of renewal on part of the Security Council.[222] In April 2018, the Security Council

[202] OPCW Doc. S/1319/2015, 29 October 2015.

[203] OPCW Doc. S/1320/2015, 29 October 2015.

[204] OPCW Doc. S/2017/2022*, 24 January 2022.

[205] OPCW Doc. S/1491/2017, 12 May 2017.

[206] OPCW Doc. S/2020/2022, 31 January 2022.

[207] OPCW Doc. S/1636/2018*, 13 June 2018.

[208] OPCW Doc. S/1548/2017, 2 November 2017.

[209] OPCW Doc. S/1497/2017, 12 May 2017; OPCW Doc. S/1510/2017, 29 June 2017.

[210] OPCW Doc. S/1626/2018, 15 May 2018.

[211] OPCW Doc. S/1645/2018, 6 July 2018; OPCW Doc. S/1731/2019, 1 March 2019.

[212] OPCW Doc. S/1318/2015/Rev.1, 17 December 2015.

[213] OPCW Doc. S/1444/2016, 27 December 2016.

[214] OPCW Doc. S/1642/2018, 2 July 2018.

[215] OPCW Doc. S/1901/2020, 1 October 2020.

[216] OPCW Doc. S/1902/2020, 1 October 2020.

[217] UN Doc. S/RES/2335 (2015), 7 August 2015. This resolution was adopted unanimously (UN Doc. S/PV. 7501, 7 August 2015, p. 2).

[218] UN Doc. S/2016/738/Rev.1, 24 August 2016; UN Doc. S/2016/888, 21 October 2016.

[219] UN Doc. S/2017/904, 26 October 2017.

[220] UN Doc. S/RES/2314 (2016), 31 October 2016.

[221] UN Doc. S/RES/2319 (2016), 16 November 2016.

[222] Russia vetoed a draft resolution sponsored by 41 States (UN Doc. S/2017/884, 24 October 2017) (UN Doc. S/PV.8073, p. 5, 11 in favor (Egypt, Ethiopia, France, Italy, Japan, Senegal, Sweden,

deliberated on proposals to re-establish this attribution mechanism, which came to naught.[223]

Fourth, the OPCW Conference of the States Parties adopted an attribution mechanism by vote at its fourth special session in June 2018,[224] which was embodied as the OPCW IIT. This unit, established within the OPCW Technical Secretariat, has concluded that the Syrian government used chemical weapons in Ltamenah on 24, 25 and 30 March 2017,[225] Saraqib on 4 February 2018,[226] and Douma on 7 April 2018.[227] Its investigations are ongoing as of this writing.

Fifth, the UNHRC established the COI by vote in August 2011.[228] It has established 38 instances of chemical weapons use, 32 of which met its standard of proof for attribution to Syrian government forces, and one of which was similarly attributed to ISIL. These include Kafr Zeita on 11, 12, 16, and 18 April 2014, Al-Tamana'a on 12, 18, and 29 April 2014, Tal Minnis on 21 April 2014;[229] al-Sukkari on 6 September 2016, Eastern Aleppo on 1 October 2016, and al-Kalasa on 8 December 2016;[230] Al-Latamneh on 30 March 2017, Khan Shaykhun on 4 April 2017, Ayn Tarma on 1 July 2017, Zamalka on 2 July 2017, and Jowbar on 6 July 2017;[231] Saraqueb on 4

Ukraine, UK, US, and Uruguay) to two against (Bolivia and Russia), with two abstentions (China and Kazakhstan)), another sponsored by seven States (UN Doc. S/2017/962, 16 November 2017) (UN Doc. S/PV.8105, p. 3, 11 in favor (Ethiopia, France, Italy, Japan, Kazakhstan, Senegal, Sweden, Ukraine, UK, US, and Uruguay) to two against (Bolivia and Russia), with two abstentions (China and Egypt)), and a Japanese-sponsored draft resolution (UN Doc. S/2017/970, 17 November 2017) (UN Doc. S/PV.8107, p. 2, 12 in favor (Egypt, Ethiopia, France, Italy, Japan, Kazakhstan, Senegal, Sweden, Ukraine, UK, US, and Uruguay) to two against (Bolivia and Russia), with one abstention (China)). A Russian draft resolution failed to obtain the required number of votes (UN Doc. S/PV.8105, p. 19, four in favor (Bolivia, China, Kazakhstan and Russia) to seven against (France, Italy, Sweden, Ukraine, UK, US, and Uruguay), with four abstentions (Egypt, Ethiopia, Japan and Senegal)).

[223] A draft resolution sponsored by Albania, Australia, Bulgaria, Canada, Denmark, Estonia, Finland, France, Germany, Italy, Latvia, Lithuania, Montenegro, Netherlands, Norway, Peru, Poland, Qatar, Moldova, Slovenia, Sweden, The former Yugoslav Republic of Macedonia, Turkey, Ukraine, UK, and US (UN Doc. S/2018/321, 10 April 2018) was defeated by Russian veto (UN Doc. S/PV.8228, 10 April 2018, p. 5). A Russian draft resolution (UN Doc. S/2018/175, 10 April 2018) did not receive sufficient supports (UN Doc. S/PV.8228, 10 April 2018, p. 9, six in favor (Bolivia, China, Equatorial Guinea, Ethiopia, Kazakhstan, and Russia) to seven against (France, Netherlands, Peru, Poland, Sweden, UK, and US), with two abstentions (Côte d'Ivoire and Kuwait)).

[224] OPCW Doc. C-SS-4/DEC.3, 27 June 2018. The decision was adopted by a vote of 82 in favor to 24 against (OPCW Doc. C-SS-4/3, 27 June 2018, para. 3.17), indicating that 46 States Parties were absent from the voting and that 41 States Parties did not participate in the special session.

[225] OPCW Doc. S/1867/2020, 8 April 2020.

[226] OPCW Doc. S/1943/2021, 12 April 2021.

[227] OPCW Doc. S/2125/2023, 27 January 2023.

[228] UN Doc. A/HRC/RES/S-17/1, 22 August 2011. The resolution was adopted by a vote of 33 in favor to four against, with nine abstentions.

[229] UN Doc. A/HRC/27/60, 13 August 2014.

[230] UN Doc. A/HRC/34/64, 2 February 2017.

[231] UN Doc. A/HRC/36/55, 8 August 2017.

February 2018.[232] In the other five instances, including Khan Al-Assal on 19 March 2013, Saraqib on 29 April 2013 and Al-Ghouta on 21 August 2013,[233] the COI was unable to make such attribution of responsibility.[234] The UNHRC has repeatedly extended the COI's pursuant to relevant resolutions.[235]

(ii) **Value**

The most valuable work of the fact-finding organs is their reports, especially their affirmative conclusions. Findings of chemical weapons use means violations of international law. Identifying perpetrators means their violations of international law. The reports of fact-finding organs have thus served as an objective basis for relevant policy-making organs to take necessary measures as will be discussed hereinafter, which should put an end to arguments by interested States based on their subjective assessments.[236] The following sections examine several aspects of the fact-finding organs and their reports, mostly procedural.[237]

(iii) **Independence**

The principle of independence requires that members of fact-finding organs not seek or accept instructions from, or be influenced by, anyone in carrying out their mandates.[238] All fact-finding organs have maintained their independence, given that relevant "mandating authorities"[239] make appointments to such organs without State involvement. For the UN Mission, the UN Secretary-General directly appoints

---

[232] UN Doc. A/HRC/39/65, 9 August 2018.

[233] UN Doc. A/HRC/25/65, 12 February 2014.

[234] UN Doc. A/HRC/46/54, 21 January 2020, p. 8, para. 32.

[235] UN Doc. A/HRC/RES/19/22 (41 in favor to 3 against, with 2 abstentions), 10 April 2012, operative para. 14; UN Doc. A/HRC/RES/21/26, 17 October 2012 (41–3–3), operative para. 17; UN Doc. A/HRC/RES/22/24, 12 April 2013 (41–1–5), operative para. 28; UN Doc. A/HRC/RES/25/23, 28 March 2014 (32–4–11), operative para. 2; UN Doc. A/HRC/RES/28/20, 27 March 2015 (29–6–12), operative para. 3; UN Doc. A/HRC/RES/31/17, 23 March 2016 (27–6–14), operative para. 4; UN Doc. A/HRC/RES/34/26, 24 March 2017 (27–7–13), operative para. 3; UN Doc. A/HRC/RES/37/29, 23 March 2018 (27–4–16), operative para. 45; UN Doc. A/HRC/RES/40/17 (28–5–14), 22 March 2019, operative para. 55; UN Doc. A/HRC/RES/43/28, 22 June 2020 (42–2–18), operative para. 67; UN Doc. A/HRC/RES/46/22, 24 March 2021 (27–6–14), operative para. 38.

[236] Grace, *supra* note 41, p. 29; Michael A. Becker and Sarah M.H. Nouwen, "International Commissions of Inquiry: What Difference Do They Make? Taking an Empirical Approach," *The European Journal of International Law*, Vol. 30, No. 3 (2019), p. 819, pp. 833–834.

[237] It has been pointed out that procedures are key to channeling matters under consideration to their proper conclusions (Alison Bisset, "Community of Inquiry and Procedural Fairness," in Christian Henderson (ed.), *Commissions of Inquiry: Problems and Prospects* (Hart Publishing, 2017), p. 309, p. 311).

[238] United Nations Office of the High Commissioner for Human Rights, *Commissions of Inquiry and Fact-Finding Missions on International Human Rights and Humanitarian Law, Guidance and Practice* (2015), p. 33; Boutruche, *supra* note 171, p. 291.

[239] United Nations Office of the High Commissioner for Human Rights, *Commissions of Inquiry and Fact-Finding Missions on International Human Rights and Humanitarian Law, Guidance and Practice* (2015), p. 18.

qualified experts for participation in an investigation,[240] while the OPCW Director-General assembles a suitably sized team with requisite qualifications and capabilities to conduct fact-finding missions and makes same available to the UN Secretary-General.[241] The OPCW Director-General selects members from OPCW Technical Secretariat officials and a list of qualified experts for the OPCW FFM,[242] and is asked to ensure a balanced composition, per the foregoing.[243] The UN Secretary-General is similarly requested to recruit for the OPCW-UN JIM, with due regard for drawing from as wide a geographical basis as is practicable.[244] The OPCW Technical Secretariat recruits for the OPCW IIT, again, with due regard for geographical basis and gender balance.[245]The UNHRC president makes appointments to the COI.[246]

While no State raised the question of independence of these fact-finding organs in the early periods of their missions, since early 2017, or more specifically, after the OPCW-UN JIM confirmed that the Syrian government was responsible for the use of chemical weapons in some incidents, Russia expressed concern about a composition of the OPCW fact-finding organs including its geographical balance,[247] and made several proposals in this regard at the OPCW Executive Council and the UN Security Council.

First, in April 2017, in response to alleged use of chemical weapons in Khan Shaykoun and airstrikes by the US against Syria, Russia and Iran submitted a joint draft decision to the OPCW Executive Council that originally included the idea of establishing "an impartial and professional international team of experts"[248] that could bring OPCW FFM personnel together with "national experts from a number of countries" selected on the basis of balanced geographical representation,[249] the

---

[240] UN Doc. A/44/561, 4 October 1989, para. 92(b).

[241] Supplementary Arrangement Concerning the Implementation of Article II (2)(c) of the Relationship between the United Nations and the Organisation for the Prohibition of Chemical Weapons, 14 and 20 September 2012, Article I, para. 2(a).

[242] OPCW Doc. S/1255/2015*, 10 March 2015, Annex (Terms of Reference of the OPCW Fact-Finding Mission in Syria, agreed through Exchange of Letters with the Syrian Arab Republic), p. 4, para. 8.

[243] *Ibid.*

[244] UN Doc. S/RES/2235 (2015), 7 August 2015, operative para. 6.

[245] OPCW Doc. EC-91/S/3, 28 June 2019, Annex 1, p. 4.

[246] UN Doc. A/HRC/S-17/2/Add.1, 23 November 2011, Annex I, para. 6.

[247] UN Doc. S/PV. 7893, 28 February 2017, p. 7 (Russia); UN Doc. S/PV. 7915, 5 April 2017, p. 17 (Russia); OPCW Doc. EC-M-54/NAT.13 (Russia), 19 April 2017, p. 3; Russia, https://www.mid.ru/en/web/guest/general_assembly/-/asset_publisher/lrzZMhfoyRUj/content/id/2904623, accessed 22 April 2023; UN Doc. S/2017/897–A/72/579 (Russia), 25 October 2017, p. 4; UN Doc. S/PV.8090, 7 November 2017, p. 15 (Russia); OPCW Doc. EC-M-56/NAT.7 (Russia), 9 November 2017, p. 2. In its rebuttal, the US pointed out that OPCW FFM personnel fulfil the prerequisite of broad geographical distribution, and the OPCW-UN JIM comprises experts from geographically diverse backgrounds (UN Doc. S/2018/35, 16 January 2018 (US), p. 3).

[248] OPCW Doc. EC-M-54/NAT.9 (Iran), 13 April 2017, p. 2.

[249] OPCW Doc. EC-M-54/NAT.15 (Russia), 13 April 2017, p. 5. In this regard, Russia also submitted a draft resolution to the UN Security Council, stating that, "[t]he operative part should be limited to

composition or technical operations whereof subject to Security Council approval.[250] This was controversial because it allowed the UN Security Council, especially permanent members, to be involved in determining the composition of fact-finding teams, undermining their independence. Several States Parties objected,[251] showing confidence in the OPCW FFM's impartiality, independence, and professionalism.[252] Russia and Iran revised their draft, replacing the abovementioned new mechanism[253] with "the possible participation in the investigation [of the OPCW Fact-Finding Mission (FFM)] by representatives of the OPCW-UN Joint Investigative Mechanism (JIM)…as well as national experts of interested States Parties,"[254] again apparently to undermine OPCW FFM independence. The revised draft decision was rejected.[255]

Second, when the UN Security Council debated renewing the OPCW-UN JIM in November 2017, Russia referred to "wide geographical basis" for the OPCW-UN JIM and "balanced composition" of the OPCW FFM in its draft resolution.[256] In response, a draft resolution sponsored by France, Italy, Japan, Sweden, Ukraine, the UK, and the US recalled the relevant language of UN Security Council Resolution

one paragraph indicating that the OPCW Fact-finding Mission should conduct a thorough investigation of the reports on the ground, but with one important condition—the staff of the investigative Mission should be introduced to the Council and should reflect a geographical balance" (UN Doc. S/PV.7915, 5 April 2017, p. 16 (Russia); see also UN Doc. S/PV. 7919, 7 April 2017, pp. 11–12 (Russia)). It appears that Russia made this proposal informally, as no official record of it exists.

250 See Sweden, https://www.opcw.org/sites/default/files/documents/EC/M-54/en/Sweden_ECM-54.pdf, accessed 22 April 2023.

251 OPCW Doc. EC-M-54/NAT.8 (Australia), 13 April 2017, p. 2; OPCW Doc. EC-M-54/NAT.11 (France), 13 April 2017, p. 1; OPCW Doc. EC-M-54/NAT.18 (UK), 13 April 2017, p. 2; Canada, https://www.opcw.org/sites/default/files/documents/EC/M-54/en/Canada_ECM-54.pdf, accessed 22 April 2023; Sweden, https://www.opcw.org/sites/default/files/documents/EC/M-54/en/Sweden_ECM-54.pdf, accessed 22 April 2023.

252 OPCW Doc. EC-M-54/NAT.2 (Norway), 13 April 2017, p. 1; OPCW Doc. EC-M-54/NAT.11 (France), 13 April 2017, p. 1; OPCW Doc. EC-M-54/NAT.18 (UK), 13 April 2017, p. 2; Sweden, https://www.opcw.org/sites/default/files/documents/EC/M-54/en/Sweden_ECM-54.pdf, accessed 22 April 2023.

253 See OPCW Doc. EC-M-54/NAT.10 (Guatemala), 20 April 2017, p. 1.

254 OPCW Doc. EC-M-54/DEC/CRP.1/Rev.1 (The Islamic Republic of Iran and the Russian Federation: Draft Decision), 19 April 2017, operative para. 3, https://www.rusemb.org.uk/fnapr/6064, accessed 22 April 2023.

255 OPCW Doc. EC-M-54/2, 20 April 2017, para. 3.9. The vote was six in favor (Algeria, China, the Islamic Republic of Iran, Russia, South Africa, and the Sudan) to 21 against (Australia, Belgium, Chile, France, Germany, Guatemala, Italy, Japan, Latvia, Mexico, Panama, Peru, Poland, Republic of Korea, Saudi Arabia, Slovakia, Spain, Sweden, Switzerland, UK, and US), with 13 abstentions (Argentina, Armenia, Bangladesh, Brazil, Cameroon, Ghana, India, Iraq, Kenya, Morocco, Pakistan, Senegal, and Viet Nam). See OPCW Doc. EC-M-54/NAT.7 (Japan), 19 April 2017, p. 1; OPCW Doc. EC-M-54/NAT.5 (Germany), 20 April 2017, p. 1.

256 UN Doc. S/2017/968, 16 November 2017 (Bolivia draft resolution), preamble para. 10 and operative para. 10. Bolivia re-submitted a withdrawn Russian draft resolution (UN Doc. S/2017/933) as its own (UN Doc. S/PV. 8105, 16 November 2017, pp. 13, 17 (Russia)).

2235 without mentioning geographical balance.[257] The former received only four votes in favor, while Russia vetoed the latter.[258]

Third, when the media reported the allegation of use of chemical weapons in Douma in April 2018 and the US, the UK, and France took military action against Syria in response, Russia submitted a draft resolution to the UN Security Council to establish a new attribution mechanism, including language that "due regard should be paid to the importance of recruiting the staff on as wide of a geographical basis as is practicable," requiring personnel be subject to Security Council approval,[259] and tasked the Security Council with thorough assessments of conclusions reached by said organ.[260] Several States objected,[261] leading to its rejection.[262] Russia also offered to facilitate OPCW FFM domestic travel arrangements.[263] While the UK expressed interest in this offer, it also made sure to stress the importance of complete freedom of action and access.[264] While Russia and Syria continue to emphasize the importance of geographical basis in the OPCW FFM,[265] a majority of States seem satisfied with the status quo.

When it comes to the OPCW IIT, the Technical Secretariat disclosed that it comprises personnel from all five of its regional groups: Africa (Kenya and South Africa), Asia (Republic of Korea), Eastern Europe (Romania and Serbia), Latin America and the Caribbean (Brazil and Mexico), and Western Europe and Other States (Belgium, Canada, Ireland, Italy, Netherlands, and Portugal).[266] While Russia

---

[257] UN Doc. S/2017/962, 16 November 2017 (France, Italy, Japan, Sweden, Ukraine, UK and US: draft resolution), preamble para. 10.

[258] UN Doc. S/PV. 8105, 16 November 2017, pp. 3, 19. The vote was four in favor (Bolivia, China, Kazakhstan, and Russia) to seven against (France, Italy, Sweden, Ukraine, UK, US, and Uruguay), with four abstentions (Egypt, Ethiopia, Japan, and Senegal).

[259] UN Doc. S/2018/175, 10 April 2018 (Russia draft resolution), operative para. 7.

[260] *Ibid.*, operative para. 5.

[261] UN Doc. S/PV.8228, 10 April 2018, pp. 8 (Netherlands), 9 (UK), 10 (US), 11 (Kuwait). See also UN Doc. S/PV.8174, 5 February 2018, p. 5 (UK).

[262] UN Doc. S/PV.8225, 9 April 2018, p. 9. The vote was six in favor Bolivia, China, Equatorial Guinea, Ethiopia, Kazakhstan, and Russia) to seven against (France, Netherlands, Peru, Poland, Sweden, UK, and US), with two abstentions (Côte d'Ivoire and Kuwait). A draft resolution on the same matter sponsored by Albania, Australia, Bulgaria, Canada, Denmark, Estonia, Finland, France, Germany, Italy, Latvia, Lithuania, Montenegro, Netherlands, Norway, Peru, Poland, Qatar, Moldova, Slovenia, Sweden, The former Yugoslav Republic of Macedonia, Turkey, Ukraine, the UK, and the US (UN Doc. S/2018/321, 10 April 2018) was vetoed by Russia (UN Doc. S/PV.8228, 10 April 2018, p. 5).

[263] UN Doc. S/PV.8225, 9 April 2018, p. 7 (Russia).

[264] *Ibid.*, p. 14 (UK).

[265] OPCW Doc. C-SS-4/NAT.40 (Russia), 26 June 2018, p. 4; Press Release of the Permanent Representative of the Russian Federation to the OPCW, 15 October 2018, https://www.mid.ru/en/web/guest/foreign_policy/international_safety/conflicts/-/asset_publisher/xIEMTQ3OvzcA/content/id/3373474, accessed 22 April 2023; Russia, https://www.opcw.org/sites/default/files/documents/2019/02/Russian%20Statement_0.pdf, accessed 22 April 2023; UN Doc. S/PV.8390, 5 November 2018, p. 16 (Syria); UN Doc. S/2019/221 (Syria), 15 March 2019, p. 5.

[266] OPCW Doc. EC-91/S/3, 28 June 2019, Annex 1, p. 4.

and China complain about the team having a geographically unbalanced composition, arguing that most of its personnel were recruited from the West,[267] this remains a minority opinion.

(iv) **Objectivity**

Fact-finding organs collect information pertaining to allegations and base their conclusions on such information.[268] Samples constitute valuable evidence, as facts can be derived from scientific analysis thereof. Important examples are direct samples including neat agents, munitions (intact and used), remnants of components, environmental samples including air, soil, vegetation, water, and snow, and biomedical samples including hair, urine, tissues, and blood.[269] Testimonials also contribute,[270] with first-hand testimony gathered interviews considered primary evidence,[271] especially when on-site visits are not possible.[272] Fact-finding organs are called on to interview representatives of parties to dispute who may be involved in any way in alleged use of chemical weapons.[273] Survivors and casualties alike can also provide important information, through medical records, witnesses, first responders, and medical personnel.[274]

267 OPCW Doc. EC-91/NAT.44 (Russia), 9 July 2019, p. 2; UN Doc. A/74/825–S/2020/311 (Russia), 28 April 2020, p. 2; OPCW Doc. EC-94/NAT.41 (China), 7 July 2020, p. 1; UN Doc. S/2020/1197 (Russia), 11 December 2020, pp.2–3; OPCW Doc. C-25/NAT.124 (Russia on behalf of the Collective Security Treaty Organization), 20 April 2021, p. 1; OPCW Doc. EC-98/NAT.32 (China), 5 October 2021, p. 2.

268 United Nations Office of the High Commissioner for Human Rights, *Commissions of Inquiry and Fact-Finding Missions on International Human Rights and Humanitarian Law, Guidance and Practice* (2015), p. 34; Boutruche, *supra* note 171, p. 291.

269 UN Doc. A/44/561, 4 October 1989, p. 27, para. 97(b)(ii); UN Doc. A/67/997–S/2013/553, 16 September 2013, p. 4, para. 6; UN Doc. A/68/663–S/2013/735, 13 December 2013, p. 12, para. 41; OPCW Doc. S/1255/2015*, 10 March 2015, Annex, p. 5, para. 14.

270 UN Doc. A/68/663–S/2013/735, 13 December 2013, p. 12, para. 41; OPCW Doc. S/1510/2017, 29 June 2017, p. 6, para. 3.8; UN Doc. S/2016/738/Rev.1, 24 August 2016, p. 7, para. 21; UN Doc. S/PV.8090, 7 November 2017, p. 4 (Mulet, OPCW-UN JIM); OPCW Doc. EC-92/S/8, 3 October 2019, p. 2.

271 OPCW Doc. S/1319/2015, 29 October 2015, Annex 2, p. 8, para. 2.7; OPCW Doc. S/1510/2017, 29 June 2017, p. 49, para. 5.113.

272 OPCW Doc. S/1230/2014, 18 December 2014, p. 6, para. 2.6; OPCW Doc. S/1319/2015, 29 October 2015, Annex 2, p. 14, para. 2.42; OPCW Doc. S/1548/2017, 2 November 2017, p. 4, para. 4.6; OPCW Doc. S/1626/2018, 15 May 2018, p. 3, para. 4.4; OPCW Doc. S/1636/2018*, 13 June 2018, p. 4, para. 4.6; OPCW Doc. S/1901/2020, 1 October 2020, p. 2, para. 2.4.

273 UN Doc. A/44/561, 4 October 1989, p. 29, para. 100.

274 UN Doc. A/44/561, 4 October 1989, pp. 28–29, para. 98; UN Doc. A/67/997–S/2013/553, 16 September 2013, p. 4, para. 6; UN Doc. A/68/663–S/2013/735, 13 December 2013, p. 12, para. 41; OPCW Doc. S/1255/2015*, 10 March 2015, Annex, p. 5, paras. 15–16.

On-site visits

On-site visits provide golden opportunities to collect as much credible information as possible.[275] Samples that fact-finding organs find directly on-site and maintain complete custody constitute the best evidence.[276] In the context of the alleged use of chemical weapons in Syria, the fact-finding organs carried out only three on-site visits: the UN Mission visits to Ghouta[277] and Jobar[278] and the OPCW FFM to Douma.[279]

It has been pointed out that conducting fact-finding activities outside of the State being investigated would be more difficult if alleged violations of international humanitarian law were to be investigated,[280] and that the evidentiary value of information gathered outside of the State being investigated, including interviews, is relatively limited.[281] Syria barred the COI and the OPCW IIT, thus preventing any on-site visits by these teams.[282] The relevant policy-making organs have condemned or expressed concern about Syrian action in this regard.[283] The UN Mission, the OPCW FFM, and the OPCW-UN JIM were allowed to deploy into Syria, but unable

---

[275] UN Doc. A/44/561, 4 October 1989, p. 26, para. 94. See also OPCW Doc. S/1319/2015, 29 October 2015, Annex 2, p. 8, para. 2.10; OPCW Doc. S/1320/2015, 29 October 2015, Annex, p. 4, para. 2.6; OPCW Doc. S/1510/2017, 29 June 2017, p. 6, para. 3.11; OPCW Doc. S/1548/2017, 2 November 2017, p. 4, para. 4.5; OPCW Doc. S/1626/2018, 15 May 2018, p. 3, para. 4.3; OPCW Doc. S/1636/2018*, 13 June 2018, p. 3, para. 4.5; UN Doc. S/2016/738/Rev.1, 24 August 2016, Annex I, p. 24, para. 26.

[276] UN Doc. A/44/561, 4 October 1989, p. 27, para. 97(b)(i).

[277] UN Doc. A/67/997–S/2013/553, 16 September 2013, p. 6, para. 18. The UN Mission stayed in Moadamiyah, West Ghouta, for two hours on 26 August 2013, and Zamalka and Ein Tarma, East Ghouta, for a total of five and a half hours on 28–29 August 2013, collecting environmental, chemical, and medical samples (*ibid*., pp. 7–8, paras. 23, 24, 26, 28).

[278] UN Doc. A/68/663–S/2013/735, 13 December 2013, p. 19, paras. 90, 92. While the UN Mission investigated allegations of chemical attacks in Khan-Al Asal on 19 March 2013, Saraqueb on 29 April 2013, Sheik Maqsood on 13 April 2013, Jobar on 24 August 2013, Bahhariyeh on 22 August 2013, and Ashrafiah Sahnaya on 25 August 2013, it was unable to conduct on-site visits in any of these instances (UN Doc. A/68/663–S/2013/735, 13 December 2013, pp. 13, 16, 17–18, 20, paras. 28, 68–69, 81–82, 102–103).

[279] OPCW Doc. S/1645/2018, 6 July 2018, pp. 6–7, paras. 6.7–6.9; OPCW Doc. S/1731/2019, 1 March 2019, p. 8, paras. 6.7–6.9. The OPCW FFM took environmental samples, ensuring the full chain of custody throughout the operation (OPCW Doc. S/1645/2018, 6 July 2018, p. 7, para. 7.2; OPCW Doc. S/1731/2019, 1 March 2019, p. 7, para. 7.2.).

[280] Frulli, *supra* note 139, p. 1337.

[281] Marauhn, *supra* note 40, p. 447.

[282] UN Doc. A/HRC/27/60, 13 August 2014, p. 3, para. 2; UN Doc. A/HRC/30/48, 13 August 2015, p. 3, para. 2; UN Doc. A/HRC/31/68, 11 February 2016, p. 3, para. 2; UN Doc. A/HRC/33/55, 11 August 2016, p. 3, para. 2; UN Doc. A/HRC/36/55, 8 August 2017, p. 3, para. 6; UN Doc. A/HRC/38/CRP.3, 20 June 2018, p. 4, para. 4; UN Doc. A/HRC/39/65, 9 August 2018, p. 3, para. 3; UN Doc. A/HRC/40/70, 31 January 2019, p. 3, para. 3.

OPCW Doc. S/1867/2020, 8 April 2020, p. 3, para. 7; OPCW Doc. S/1943/2021, 12 April 2021, p. 2, para. 6.

[283] UN Doc. A/HRC/RES/24/22, 27 September 2013, preamble para. 5; UN Doc. A/HRC/RES/25/23, 28 March 2014, preamble para. 5; UN Doc. A/HRC/RES/26/23, 27 June 2014, preamble para. 6; UN Doc. A/HRC/RES/27/16, 25 September 2014, preamble para. 10; UN Doc. A/HRC/RES/28/

to make on-site visits except for the incidents indicated above, primarily for security reasons,[284] another being the elapsed time between the incidents and the investigations.[285] Russia and Syria have repeatedly accused both organs for not visiting the sites of the allegations,[286] raising particular doubts about the OPCW-UN JIM

20, 27 March 2015, preamble para. 8; UN Doc. A/HRC/RES/29/16, 2 July 2015, preamble para. 7; UN Doc. A/HRC/RES/30/10, 1 October 2015, preamble para. 8; UN Doc. A/HRC/RES/31/17, 23 March 2016, preamble para. 12; UN Doc. A/HRC/RES/32/25, 1 July 2016, preamble para. 10; UN Doc. A/HRC/RES/33/23, 30 September 2016, preamble para. 19; UN Doc. A/HRC/RES/34/26, 24 March 2017, preamble para. 13; UN Doc. A/HRC/RES/35/26, 23 June 2017, preamble para. 13; UN Doc. A/HRC/RES/36/20, 29 September 2017, preamble para. 18; UN Doc. A/HRC/RES/37/29, 23 March 2018, preamble para. 17; UN Doc. A/HRC/RES/38/16, 6 July 2018, preamble para. 15; UN Doc. A/HRC/RES/39/15, 28 September 2018, preamble para. 15; UN Doc. A/HRC/RES/40/17, 22 March 2019, preamble para. 17; UN Doc. A/HRC/RES/41/23, 12 July 2019, preamble para. 18; UN Doc. A/HRC/RES/42/27, 27 September 2019, preamble para. 18; UN Doc. A/HRC/RES/43/28, 22 June 2020, preamble para. 18; UN Doc. A/HRC/RES/45/21, 6 October 2020, preamble para. 6; UN Doc. A/HRC/RES/46/22, 24 March 2021, preamble para. 8; UN Doc. A/HRC/RES/47/18, 13 July 2021, preamble para. 9; UN Doc. A/HRC/RES/48/15, 8 October 2021, preamble para. 11.

OPCW Doc. EC-94/DEC.2, 9 July 2020, operative para. 3; UN Doc. A/HRC/RES/46/22, 24 March 2021, operative para. 33; OPCW Doc. C-25/DEC.9, 21 April 2021, operative para. 6.

[284] Both the UN Mission and the OPCW FFM identified "the risk assessment of conducting such visits in the midst of the ongoing armed conflict in Syria" as a key factor in deciding to conduct on-site visits (UN Doc. A/68/663–S/2013/735, 13 December 2013, p. 12, para. 44; OPCW Doc. S/1319/2015, 29 October 2015, Annex 2, pp. 8–9, para. 2.10; OPCW Doc. S/1320/2015, 29 October 2015, Annex, pp. 4–5, para. 2.6).

UN Doc. A/68/663–S/2013/735, 13 December 2013, p. 14, paras. 56, 57 ("Due to the deteriorating security situation, the United Nations Mission was not able to conduct an on-site visit to Khan Al Asal").

OPCW Doc. S/1319/2015, 29 October 2015, Annex 2, p. 9, para. 2.12; OPCW Doc. S/1320/2015, 29 October 2015, Annex, p. 5, para. 2.8; OPCW Doc. S/1491/2017, 1 May 2017, p. 4, para. 1.7; OPCW Doc. S/1510/2017, 29 June 2017, p. 6, para. 3.13; OPCW Doc. S/1548/2017, 2 November 2017, p. 4, para. 4.5; OPCW Doc. S/1626/2018, 15 May 2018, p. 3, para. 4.3; OPCW Doc. S/1636/2018*, 13 June 2018, p. 3, para. 4.5; OPCW Doc. S/1901/2020, 1 October 2020, p. 4, para. 5.2; OPCW Doc. S/1902/2020, 1 October 2020, p. 7, para. 5.1; OPCW Doc. S/2017/2022*, 24 January 2022, p. 9, para. 6.4; OPCW Doc. S/2020/2022, 31 January 2022, p. 14, para. 6.6.

UN Doc. S/2016/738/Rev.1, 24 August 2016, Annex I, p. 24, para. 26; UN Doc. S/2016/888, 21 October 2016, p. 5, para. 13; UN Doc. S/2017/904, 26 October 2017, p. 5, para. 14; UN Doc. S/2017/904, 26 October 2017, p. 5, para. 15; UN Doc. S/2017/904, 26 October 2017, p. 5, para. 17.

[285] UN Doc. S/2016/888, 21 October 2016, p. 5, para. 13; UN Doc. S/2017/904, 26 October 2017, p. 5, para. 14; UN Doc. UN Doc. S/2017/904, 26 October 2017, p. 5, para. 16.

[286] OPCW Doc. EC-M-50/NAT.3 (Russia), 23 November 2015, p. 2; UN Doc. S/2016/844 (Syria), 20 October 2016, p. 8; OPCW Doc. EC-M-54/NAT.13 (Russia), 19 April 2017, pp. 3–4; OPCW Doc. EC-M-55/NAT.9* (Russia), 5 July 2017, pp. 1, 4; UN Doc. S/2017/576 (Russia), 14 July 2017, pp. 2, 5; UN Doc. A/72/526–S/2017/848 (Russia), 10 October 2017, p. 1; UN Doc. S/PV.8090, 7 November 2017, p. 25 (Syria); UN Doc. S/2017/935* (Syria), 14 November 2017, p. 2; UN Doc. S/2017/991 (Syria), 5 December 2017, p. 1; UN Doc. S/PV.8221, 4 April 2018, p. 15 (Russia); UN Doc. S/PV.8221, 4 April 2018, p. 18 (Syria); UN Doc. A/72/848–S/2018/397 (Russia), 4 May 2018, p. 4; OPCW Doc. C-SS-4/NAT.40 (Russia), 26 June 2018, p. 4; OPCW Doc. EC-92/NAT.28 (Syria), 9 October 2019, pp. 1–2; UN Doc. A/C.1/74/PV.23, 4 November 2019, p. 10 (Syria); OPCW Doc. EC-93/NAT.31 (Russia), 11 March 2020, p. 1; OPCW Doc. EC-94/NAT.17 (Russia), 19 June 2020, pp. 2–4; UN Doc. S/2021/22, 7 January 2021, Annex XVI (Syria), p. 31; UN Doc. S/2021/226, 9

not making on-site visits to Khan Shaykhun despite there being an agreement with the groups controlling the area on the experts' visit,[287] and insisting that such on-site visits be made.[288] In this regard, in April 2017, Russia and Iran tabled a joint draft decision to the OPCW Executive Council, requesting that the OPCW Director-General dispatch the OPCW FFM to undertake a full-scale and thorough investigation in the Khan Shaykhun area and the Shayrat airbase,[289] which was rejected.[290] Russia also circulated two draft UN Security Council resolutions in November 2017 and April 2018. In the first draft, Russia sought to extend the OPCW-UN JIM mandate, so that it might dispatch on-site investigation teams to Khan Shaykhun and the Shayrat airbase,[291] while the second one was to re-establish an attribution mechanism which Russia would urge to investigate on the basis of evidence collected "in the course of on-site visits."[292] Both drafts included language stressing the imperative for the OPCW FFM not to act remotely,[293] endorsing the request of the relevant organs for the OPCW's assistance to "conduct timely on-site visits,"[294] and calling upon the OPCW Director-General to notify the UN Security Council of any difficulties in organizing on-site visits.[295] In response, the UK drew attention to CWC provisions

March 2021, Annex XV (Syria), p. 22; OPCW Doc. C-25/NAT.124 (Russia), 20 April 2021, p. 1; UN Doc. S/2021/446, 10 May 2021, Annex XI (Russia), p. 17; UN Doc. S/PV.8785, 3 June 2021, p. 8 (Russia). See also OPCW Doc. EC-M-56/NAT.12 (Cuba), 9 November 2017, pp. 1–2.

[287] UN Doc. S/2017/968, 16 November 2017, preamble para. 16; UN Doc. S/PV.8090, 7 November 2017, p. 14 (Russia).

[288] UN Doc. S/PV.7915, 5 April 2017, p. 17 (Russia); UN Doc. S/PV.7922, 12 April 2017, p. 8 (Russia); OPCW Doc. EC-85/NAT.1 (Russia), 30 May 2017, p. 2; UN Doc. S/2017/455 (Russia), 1 June 2017, p. 2; UN Doc. A/72/578–S/2017/901 (Russia), 1 November 2017, p. 1; UN Doc. S/PV.8090, 7 November 2017, p. 14 (Russia); OPCW Doc. EC-M-56/NAT.7 (Russia), 9 November 2017, p. 1; OPCW Doc. EC-88/NAT.24 (Russia), 12 July 2018, pp. 1–2; OPCW Doc. EC-92/NAT.28 (Syria), 9 October 2019, pp. 1–2; UN Doc. S/2021/446, Annex XVIII (Syria), 10 May 2021, p. 29. See also OPCW Doc. EC-M-54/NAT.9 (Iran), 13 April 2017, p. 2; OPCW Doc. EC-M-56/NAT.14 (Brazil), 9 November 2017, p. 1; OPCW Doc. EC-M-56/NAT.15 (Iran), 9 November 2017, p. 2; OPCW Doc. EC-M-58/NAT.16 (Iran), 16 April 2018, p. 2.

[289] OPCW Doc. EC-M-54/DEC/CRP.1/Rev.1 (The Islamic Republic of Iran and the Russian Federation: Draft Decision), 19 April 2017, operative para. 1, https://london.mid.ru/en/press-centre/gb_en_fnapr_6064/, accessed 22 April 2023.

[290] OPCW Doc. EC-M-54/2, 20 April 2017, para. 3.9. The voting was as follows: six in favor (Algeria, China, Iran, Russia, South Africa, and Sudan) to 21 against (Australia, Belgium, Chile, France, Germany, Guatemala, Italy, Japan, Latvia, Mexico, Panama, Peru, Poland, Republic of Korea, Saudi Arabia, Slovakia, Spain, Sweden, Switzerland, UK, and US), with 13 abstentions (Argentina, Armenia, Bangladesh, Brazil, Cameroon, Ghana, India, Iraq, Kenya, Morocco, Pakistan, Senegal, and Viet Nam) (EC-M-54/2. 20 April 2017, para. 3.9).

[291] UN Doc. S/2017/968, 16 November 2017, operative paras. 1, 11, 13.

[292] UN Doc. S/2018/175, 10 April 2018, operative para. 5.

[293] UN Doc. S/2017/968, 16 November 2017, preamble para. 6; UN Doc. S/2018/175, 10 April 2018, preamble para. 6.

[294] UN Doc. S/2017/968, 16 November 2017, operative para. 5; UN Doc. S/2018/175, 10 April 2018, operative para. 16.

[295] UN Doc. S/2017/968, 16 November 2017, operative para. 7; UN Doc. S/2018/175, 10 April 2018, operative para. 18.

that envisaged other ways to gather relevant evidence in cases where safe and timely visits would be difficult,[296] and the Netherlands argued that the "[t]he necessity of on-site investigations is up to the team to decide."[297] These Russian drafts were also rejected.[298] As counter-proposals, the US, the UK, France, and other States submitted two draft resolutions to the UN Security Council in November 2017 and April 2018, including language of "safe travel to the sites" relevant to fact-finding investigations and where the investigators determine "there are reasonable grounds to believe access is justified based on their assessment of the facts and circumstances known to them at the time."[299] Russia vetoed both drafts.[300]

Chain of custody

Even if fact-finding organs are unable to visit the location in question, they can rely on information provided by others.[301] As mentioned above, samples can be valuable in this regard. Handling them to ensure credibility is key. When they are collected by other actors, maintaining chain of custody is essential.[302] Fact-finding organs must establish that samples were retrieved from sites of alleged chemical attacks, and that the security, integrity, and preservation of said samples have been ensured prior to their being received by said organs.

The UN Mission seems to have strictly verified its chain of custody, relying neither on environmental samples collected by Russia which found traces of sarin, nor on a report presented by France containing results of environmental samples that tested

[296] UN Doc. S/PV.8174, 5 February 2018, p. 5 (UK).

[297] UN Doc. S/PV.8228, 10 April 2018, p. 18 (Netherlands).

[298] UN Doc. S/PV.8105, 16 November 2017, p. 19 (four in favor (Bolivia, China, Kazakhstan and Russia) to seven against (France, Italy, Sweden, Ukraine, UK, US and Uruguay), with four abstentions (Egypt, Ethiopia, Japan and Senegal)); UN Doc. S/PV.8228, 10 April 2018, p. 9 (six in favor (Bolivia, China, Equatorial Guinea, Ethiopia, Kazakhstan and Russia) to seven against (France, Netherlands, Peru, Poland, Sweden, UK and US), with two abstentions (Côte d'Ivoire and Kuwait)).

[299] UN Doc. S/2017/962, 16 November 2017, operative para. 6; UN Doc. S/2018/321, 10 April 2018, preamble para. 8.

[300] UN Doc. S/PV.8105, 16 November 2017, p. 3 (eleven in favor (Ethiopia, France, Italy, Japan, Kazakhstan, Senegal Sweden, Ukraine, UK, US and Uruguay) to two against (Bolivia and Russia), with two abstentions (China and Egypt)); UN Doc. S/PV.8228, 10 April 2018, p. 5 (twelve in favor (Côte d'Ivoire, Equatorial Guinea, Ethiopia, Kazakhstan, Kuwait, France, Netherlands, Peru, Poland, Sweden, UK, and US) to two against (Bolivia and Russia), with one abstention (China)).

[301] The OPCW FFM clarified principal methods for collecting and evaluating credibility of information in situations where on-site visits are not possible (OPCW Doc. S/1548/2017, 2 November 2017, p. 4, para. 4.6; OPCW Doc. S/1626/2018, 15 May 2018, p. 3, para. 4.4; OPCW Doc. S/1636/2018*, 13 June 2018, p. 4, para. 4.6).

[302] The UN Mission, the OPCW FFM, the OPCW-UN JIM, and the OPCW IIT explicitly mention chain of custody in their reports (UN Doc. A/68/663–S/2013/735, 13 December 2013, p. 12, para. 42; OPCW Doc. S/1319/2015, 29 October 2015, Annex 2, p. 7, para. 2.1; OPCW Doc. S/1320/2015, 29 October 2015, Annex, p. 4, para. 2.1; OPCW Doc. S/1510/2017, 29 June 2017, p. 5, para. 3.1; UN Doc. S/2016/888, 21 October 2016, p. 13, para. 5; OPCW Doc. S/1867/2020, 8 April 2020, p. 20, para. 4.8). By contrast, the COI does not address the subject.

positive for sarin, nor on soil samples provided by Syria that tested positive for sarin.[303]

The OPCW FFM has confronted the chain of custody issue throughout practically its entire mandate. Its approach to this issue seems to vary over time. Before May 2017, it strictly verified chain of custody, explicitly admitting that the chain of custody was not verified for samples provided either by interviewees,[304] or NGOs,[305] or by the Syrian government,[306] instead finding evidentiary value only in biomedical samples, collection of which was witnessed by the team and collected from casualties the team encountered.[307] After June 2017, however, the OPCW FFM apparently relaxed its chain of custody requirements. Having acknowledged in its June 2017 report that "the evidentiary value of samples taken close to the time of the allegation, supported by photographic and video evidence and in association with witness testimony, needs to be balanced against the evidentiary value of the FFM visiting the site at a later date to collect its own samples,"[308] it combined biomedical specimens for which it had full chain of custody[309] with samples lacking full chain of custody,[310] categorizing the former as "primary" evidence and the latter as "secondary" or "tertiary" evidence.[311] Furthermore, having explained that "interviews, review of video evidence supplied at interview, the documentation, digital photo/video files provided, subsequently assessed through metadata and geolocation, still and video photography, and the metadata of the media files enabled it to determine the relevant samples were retrieved from or located at the sites of the respective allegations,"[312] the OPCW FFM has relied solely on samples obtained from others, in particular an NGO, to verify the use of chemical weapons since November 2017.[313] At the same time, it did not find any evidential value in samples provided by the Syrian government, either because

[303] UN Doc. A/68/663–S/2013/735, 13 December 2013, pp. 14, 16, 19, 21, 22, paras. 58, 70, 93, 111, 113, 115. See also *ibid.*, p. 23, para. 117.

[304] OPCW Doc. S/1230/2014, 18 December 2014, pp. 6, 21, paras. 2.6, 5.53.

[305] OPCW Doc. S/1319/2015, 29 October 2015, Annex 2, pp. 16, 17, paras. 2.50, 2.52.

[306] OPCW Doc. S/1318/2015/Rev.1, 17 December 2015, pp. 47–48, para. 3.92; OPCW Doc. S/1444/2016, 27 December 2016, p. 5, para. 3.2 and Annex 8, p. 29, para. 11.

[307] OPCW Doc. S/1320/2015, 29 October 2015, Annex, p. 19, para. 3.27; OPCW Doc. S/1491/2017, 12 May 2017, pp. 7, 20, paras. 5.7, 5.46.

[308] OPCW Doc. S/1510/2017, 29 June 2017, p. 7, para. 3.14; OPCW Doc. S/1548/2017, 2 November 2017, p. 3, para. 3.3; OPCW Doc. S/1548/2017, 2 November 2017, pp. 4–5, para. 4.8; OPCW Doc. S/1626/2018, 15 May 2018, p. 2, para. 3.3; OPCW Doc. S/1636/2018*, 13 June 2018, p. 3, para. 3.3.

[309] OPCW Doc. S/1510/2017, 29 June 2017, p. 11, para. 3.52.

[310] *Ibid.*, pp. 11, 14, paras. 3.46, 3.66.

[311] *Ibid.*, p. 49, paras. 5.113–5.115.

[312] OPCW Doc. S/1548/2017, 2 November 2017, p. 25, para. 6.5; OPCW Doc. S/1626/2018, 15 May 2018, p. 26, para. 7.3; OPCW Doc. S/1636/2018*, 13 June 2018, p. 29, para. 6.2; OPCW Doc. S/2017/2022*, 24 January 2022, p. 16, para. 7.39.

[313] OPCW Doc. S/1548/2017, 2 November 2017, pp. 5, 25, paras. 4.10–4.11, 6.1; OPCW Doc. S/1626/2018, 15 May 2018, pp. 4, 26, paras. 4.9, 7.1; OPCW Doc. S/1636/2018*, 13 June 2018, pp. 4, 12, 22, 29, paras. 4.11, 4.12, 5.33, 5.61, 6.1; OPCW Doc. S/2017/2022*, 24 January 2022, p. 9, para. 5.5; OPCW Doc. S/2020/2022, 31 January 2022, p. 37, para. 8.4.

analyses of same did not find any scheduled chemicals[314] or supporting information was lacking.[315]

In July 2017, Russia raised doubts whether the chain of custody had been observed during the OPCW FFM investigation of the incident in Khan Shaykhun on 4 April 2017,[316] and has continued to criticize the OPCW FFM for not maintaining chain of custody, with Syria, Cuba, and Iran following suit.[317] Russia further tabled draft UN Security Council resolutions in which the Security Council would express regret that the samples the OPCW FFM relied on in the course of its investigation lacked full chains of custody[318] and stress the importance of respecting chain of custody to preserve the integrity of material evidence.[319] While the US and other States did not address this point in their counter draft resolutions, they did not necessarily ignore the importance of chain of custody either. Rather, their consistent support for the OPCW FFM implies their satisfaction with its approach to the requirement of chain of custody. In the author's opinion, whether the chain of custody is respected depends on the quality and quantity of supportive evidence the OPCW FFM can offer.

The OPCW-UN JIM and the OPCW IIT encountered the same issue. For some samples, they confirmed that the chain of custody was established,[320] while they acknowledged a lack thereof for others.[321] In this regard, Syria, Russia, and Iran have complained about the chain of custody practices of these attribution mechanisms,[322]

314 OPCW Doc. S/1642/2018, 2 July 2018, p. 37, paras. 9.9–9.10.

315 OPCW Doc. S/1902/2020, 1 October 2020, p. 40, para. 8.4.

316 OPCW Doc. EC-M-55/NAT.9* (Russia), 5 July 2017, pp. 2–3; UN Doc. S/2017/576(Russia), 14 July 2017, pp. 3–4.

317 UN Doc. A/72/526–S/2017/848 (Russia), 10 October 2017, p. 1; UN Doc. A/72/579–S/2017/897 (Russia), 25 October 2017, p. 2; UN Doc. S/PV.8090, 7 November 2017, p. 14 (Russia); OPCW Doc. EC-M-56/NAT.12 (Cuba), 9 November 2017, pp. 1–2; OPCW Doc. EC-M-56/NAT.15 (Iran), 9 November 2017, p. 1; UN Doc. S/2017/935* (Syria), 14 November 2017, p. 2; OPCW Doc. EC-M-58/NAT.16 (Iran), 16 April 2018, p. 2; OPCW Doc. C-SS-4/NAT.40 (Russia),, 26 June 2018 pp. 3–4; OPCW Doc. EC-88/NAT.23 (Russia), 10 July 2018, p. 3; UN Doc. S/PV.8390, 5 November 2018, p. 16 (Syria); OPCW Doc. EC-90/NAT.41 (Russia), 26 April 2019, Annex, p. 4; OPCW Doc. EC-92/NAT.28 (Syria), 9 October 2019, p. 2; UN Doc. A/C.1/74/PV.23, 4 November 2019, p. 20 (Syria); OPCW Doc. EC-93/NAT.31 (Russia), 11 March 2020, p. 1; UN Doc. S/2021/226, 9 March 2021, Annex XV (Syria), p. 23; UN Doc. S/2021/446, 10 May 2021, Annex XVIII (Syria), p. 29; UN Doc. S/PV.8785, 3 June 2021, p. 7 (Russia); UN Doc. S/PV.8849, 2 September 2021, p. 16 (Syria); UN Doc. S/PV.8872, 4 October 2021, p. 15 (Syria); UN Doc. S/PV.8982, 28 February 2022, p. 14 (Syria).

318 UN Doc. S/2017/968, 16 November 2017, preamble para. 17.

319 UN Doc. S/2017/968, 16 November 2017, preamble para. 7; UN Doc. S/2018/175, 10 April 2018, preamble para. 7.

320 UN Doc. S/2016/738/Rev.1, 24 August 2016, p. 17, para. 70; UN Doc. S/2016/738/Rev.1, 24 August 2016, Annex IX, p. 91, para. 48; OPCW Doc. S/1867/2020, 8 April 2020, p. 37, para. 7.26; OPCW Doc. S/1867/2020, 8 April 2020, p. 38, para. 7.31.

321 UN Doc. S/2016/738/Rev.1, 24 August 2016, Annex IV, p. 47, para. 30; UN Doc. S/2016/738/Rev.1, 24 August 2016, Annex VIII, p. 79, para. 35; UN Doc. S/2017/904, 26 October 2017, Annex II, pp. 28, 31, paras. 58, 78; OPCW Doc. S/1867/2020, 8 April 2020, p. 37, para. 7.26.

322 UN Doc. S/2016/844 (Syria), 20 October 2016, p. 5; UN Doc. S/PV.8090, 7 November 2017, p. 25 (Syria); UN Doc. S/2017/935* (Syria), 14 November 2017, p. 3; UN Doc. S/2017/991 (Syria),

with Russia in particular asserting that the chain of custody requires the relevant evidence to be collected by the investigation team itself.[323] This position seems too strict for chain of custody maintenance, however, making it difficult for fact-finding organs to reach conclusions without on-site visits. In practice, the OPCW-UN JIM relied on records, documents, and laboratory analysis,[324] while the OPCW IIT made use of contemporaneous video recordings, OPCW documentation, and interviewing witnesses about the videos themselves, as well as the actual collection and the procedures undertaken between such collection and the transfer to the OPCW FFM.[325] The COI has faced like complaints from Syria, about non-observation of credible norms on handling of samples and lack of reliability or neutrality of parties who transport said samples.[326] As with the OPCW FFM, these attribution mechanisms are required to provide supportive evidence both in quality and quantity to demonstrate chain of custody.

Open-source materials

Another controversy is whether fact-finding organs can also rely on open-source materials for evidence, because the credibility of open-source information is not necessarily guaranteed. All fact-finding organs but the UN Mission do refer to open-source information and acknowledge its collection and usefulness. For instance, the COI notes that open sources "are invaluable for gathering background information" and that open-source material "could also be mined for information…which will assist in identifying key incidents, help to define the priorities for investigations, provide leads for investigations and identify sources."[327] For the OPCW-UN JIM, "[e]xtensive material is available on open sources and social media relating to the cases under investigation" and "[m]aterial deemed central to the investigation was subjected to forensic analysis."[328] The OPCW IIT also confirms that its

5 December 2017, p. 6; UN Doc. S/PV.8221, 4 April 2018, p. 15 (Russia); OPCW Doc. EC-94/NAT.17 (Russia), 19 June 2020, p. 3; UN Doc. S/2021/337, 9 April 2021, Annex XI (Russia), p. 14; UN Doc. S/2021/446, 10 May 2021, Annex XI (Russia), p. 17; UN Doc. S/2021/446, 10 May 2021, Annex XVII (Iran), p. 27; UN Doc. S/PV.8785, 3 June 2021, p. 8 (Russia); UN Doc. S/PV.8830, 4 August 2021, p. 5 (Russia); UN Doc. S/PV.8849, 2 September 2021, p. 5 (Russia); UN Doc. S/PV.8921, 8 December 2021, p. 5 (Russia); UN Doc. S/PV.8982, 28 February 2022, p. 12 (Russia).

323 UN Doc. A/74/825–S/2020/311 (Russia), 28 April 2020, p. 2; UN Doc. S/2020/902, 15 September 2020, Annex III (Russia), p. 13; OPCW Doc. EC-97/NAT.50 (Russia), 6 July 2021, p. 1.

324 UN Doc. S/2016/738/Rev.1, 24 August 2016, p. 17, para. 70; UN Doc. S/2016/738/Rev.1, 24 August 2016, Annex IX, p. 91, para. 48.

325 OPCW Doc. S/1867/2020, 8 April 2020, p. 37, para. 7.26; OPCW Doc. S/1867/2020, 8 April 2020, p. 38, para. 7.31.

326 UN Doc. A/HRC/36/G/10 (Syria), 12 September 2017, p. 2.

327 United Nations Human Rights Office of the High Commissioner, *Commissions of Inquiry and Fact-Finding Missions on International Human Rights and Humanitarian Law* (2015), p. 37.

328 OPCW-UN JIM: UN Doc. S/2016/738/Rev.1, 24 August 2016, p. 22, para. 14. It should be noted that the original version included "open source and social media" before "material deemed central to the investigation." (UN Doc. S/2016/738, 24 August 2016, p. 22, para. 14). The deletion suggests an intent not to focus on open-source information.

"activities…include interviews with victims and other witnesses of the incidents, with experts in the various subjects relevant to the investigation, and evaluation of open-source material."[329] The OPCW FFM seemed to change its approach to open-source information. Prior to June 2017, the OPCW FFM characterized open-source materials as "tertiary evidence" and/or "supporting information,"[330] especially when on-site visits are not possible. However, in its July 2018 report, the OPCW FFM slightly downgraded the status of open-source materials, limiting the purpose of their use to planning and comparison with material the FFM team collected during its investigations. In subsequent reports, it further clarified that open-source information was used for comparison purposes with material "directly" collected by the FFM during investigation,[331] and that the mission's conclusions do not rely on such open-source information.[332]

Complaints about use of open-source information began in March 2017, when the Non-Aligned Movement (NAM) CWC States Parties and China expressed concern about "the attempt to accuse States Parties of using chemical weapons on the basis of unsubstantiated allegations made by media reports or other open source" in their collective statement at the OPCW Executive Council.[333] In November, Iran argued that "[t]he report of the Joint Investigative Mechanism…is the result of interviews and information received from open sources and terrorist groups,"[334] and Syria subsequently pointed out that "[t]he Mechanism…was satisfied with photographs,

[329] OPCW Doc. EC-92/S/8, 3 October 2019, p. 2.

[330] OPCW Doc. S/1319/2015, 29 October 2015, Annex 2, p. 8, para. 2.7; OPCW Doc. S/1319/2015, 29 October 2015, Annex 2, pp. 14, 93, paras. 2.42, 5.1, 5.3; OPCW Doc. S/1510/2017, 29 June 2017, p. 48, para. 5.108; OPCW Doc. S/1510/2017, 29 June 2017, p. 49, para. 5.115.

[331] OPCW Doc. S/1645/2018, 6 July 2018, p. 7, para. 7.5; OPCW Doc. S/1731/2019, 1 March 2019, p. 9, para. 7.5; OPCW Doc. S/1901/2020, 1 October 2020, p. 4, para. 5.5; OPCW Doc. S/1902/2020, 1 October 2020, p. 12, para. 6.31; OPCW Doc. S/2017/2022*, 24 January 2022, p. 9, para. 5.4; OPCW Doc. S/2020/2022, 31 January 2022, p. 11, para. 5.4.

[332] OPCW Doc. S/1731/2019, 1 March 2019, p. 9, para. 7.5; OPCW Doc. S/2020/2022, 31 January 2022, p. 11, para. 5.4.

[333] OPCW Doc. EC-84/NAT.18 (Venezuela on behalf of the NAM CWC States Parties and China), 7 March 2017, pp. 2–3. See also OPCW Doc. EC-85/NAT.33 (Venezuela on behalf of the NAM CWC States Parties and China), 11 July 2017, p. 3; OPCW Doc. EC-86/NAT.32 (Venezuela on behalf of the NAM CWC States Parties and China), 10 October 2017, p. 2; OPCW Doc. EC-87/NAT.33 (Venezuela on behalf of the NAM CWC States Parties and China), 13 March 2018, p. 2; OPCW Doc. EC-89/NAT.16 (Venezuela on behalf of the NAM CWC States Parties and China), 9 October 2018, p. 2; OPCW Doc. EC-91/NAT.46 (Venezuela on behalf of the NAM CWC States Parties and China), 9 July 2019, p. 2; OPCW Doc. EC-92/NAT.22 (Bolivia on behalf of the NAM CWC States Parties and China), 8 October 2019, p. 2; OPCW Doc. EC-93/NAT.11 (Azerbaijan on behalf of the NAM CWC States Parties and China), 10 March 2020, p. 2; OPCW Doc. EC-94/NAT.70 (Azerbaijan on behalf of the NAM CWC States Parties and China), 7 July 2020, p. 2; OPCW Doc. EC-95/NAT.10 (Azerbaijan on behalf of the NAM CWC States Parties and China), 6 October 2020, p. 2; OPCW Doc. EC-96/NAT.12 (Azerbaijan on behalf of the NAM CWC States Parties and China), 9 March 2021, p. 2.

[334] UN Doc. A/C.1/72/PV.28, 2 November 2017, p. 9 (Iran). See also UN Doc. A/C.1/73/PV.28, 5 November 2018, p. 10 (Iran).

video recordings and other material obtained from open sources that lack any credibility."[335] They criticized the OPCW FFM and the OPCW IIT for relying on open-source information,[336] with Cuba, Russia, and Venezuela following suit.[337] While these States explicitly or implicitly oppose use of open-source information, their objection seems inconsistent. They had many opportunities to raise questions prior to 2017, but they did not seize them. On the contrary, Syria itself relied on open-source information to justify its position during the OPCW FFM's first investigation in 2014,[338] and complained that the COI ignored information available through open sources that Syria itself referred to,[339] indicating that those who claimed open-source information supported their position endorsed its use, while those who found it unfavorable to their position rejected it. Perhaps the point is not whether open-source information should be used, but how.

Standards of proof

Fact-finding must be credible. A key aspect of such credibility is a sound and elaborated methodology.[340] As a matter of practice, fact-finding organs establish standards of proof and examine whether evidence collected satisfies same, putting

[335] UN Doc. S/2017/935* (Syria), 14 November 2017, p. 2. See also UN Doc. S/PV.8105, 16 November 2017, p. 15 (Syria); UN Doc. S/2017/991, 5 December 2017 (Syria), p. 1; UN Doc. S/PV.8221, 4 April 2018, p. 18 (Syria); UN Doc. S/PV.8228, 10 April 2018, p. 20 (Syria); UN Doc. A/C.1/73/PV.28, 5 November 2018, p. 5 (Syria). See also UN Doc. A/HRC/36/G/10 (Syria), 12 September 2017, pp. 2–3.

[336] UN Doc. A/73/PV.63, 20 December 2018, p. 9 (Syria); OPCW Doc. EC-90/NAT.23 (Iran), 13 March 2019, p. 2; OPCW Doc. EC-92/NAT.22 (Syria), 9 October 2019, pp. 1–2; UN Doc. A/C.1/74/PV.23, 4 November 2019, p. 20 (Syria); UN Doc. A/C.1/74/PV.23, 4 November 2019, p. 21 (Iran); OPCW Doc. EC-94/NAT.3 (Iran), 15 April 2020, pp. 1–2; OPCW Doc. EC-94/NAT.29 (Iran), 7 July 2020, p. 1; OPCW Doc. EC-95/NAT.18 (Iran), 6 October 2020, p. 2; OPCW Doc. EC-95/NAT.58 (Syria), 6 October 2020, p. 2; UN Doc. S/2021/22, 7 January2021, Annex XVI (Syria), p. 31; UN Doc. S/2021/226, 8 March 2021, Annex XV (Syria), p. 23; OPCW Doc. EC-96/NAT.51 (Iran), 9 March 2021, p. 2; OPCW Doc. C-25/NAT.108 (Iran), 21 April 2021, pp. 1–2; UN Doc. S/2021/446, 10 May 2021, Annex XVII (Iran), p. 27; UN Doc. S/2021/446, 10 May 2021, Annex XVIII (Syria), p. 29; UN Doc. S/2021/446, 10 May 2021, Annex XVIII (Syria), p. 30; UN Doc. S/PV.8785, 3 June 2021, p. 28 (Syria); OPCW Doc. EC-97/NAT.46 (Syria), 6 July 2021, p. 3; OPCW Doc. EC-97/NAT.2 (Iran),1, 6 July 2021 p. 2; UN Doc. S/PV.8849, 2 September 2021, p. 16 (Syria); UN Doc. S/PV.8872, 4 October 2021, p. 15 (Syria); UN Doc. S/PV.8982, 28 February 2022, p. 14 (Syria); UN Doc. S/PV.8990, 10 March 2022, p. 13 (Syria).

[337] OPCW Doc. EC-90/NAT.34 (Cuba), 12 March 2019, p. 2; OPCW Doc. EC-95/NAT.29 (Cuba), 6 October 2020, p. 3; UN Doc. S/2020/1202, 16 December 2020, Annex XI (Russia), p. 23; UN Doc. S/2021/109, 5 February 2021, Annex XI (Russia), p. 15; OPCW Doc. EC-96/NAT.45 (Venezuela), 9 March 2021, p. 3; OPCW Doc. EC-97/NAT.8 (Russia), 5 July 2021, p. 2. Syria also complained about use of open-source information by the COI regarding the Khan Shaykhun incident. (UN Doc. A/HRC/36/G/10 (Syria), 12 September 2017, p. 2).

[338] OPCW Doc. S/1191/2014, 16 June 2014, Annex 2, p. 7 ("In addition, several videos from social media websites and other open source information was provided to the FFM in support of the position of the Syrian Government, together with other documents, such as reports about intercepted communications.").

[339] UN Doc. A/HRC/36/G/10 (Syria), 12 September 2017, p. 2.

[340] Boutruche, *supra* note 38, pp. 106–107.

such standards of proof at the heart of the objective nature of findings,[341] directly concerning degrees of certainty regarding facts and potentially characterizing fact-finding organs' activities. There are five standards of proof for fact-finding, as follows:[342]

- Reasonable suspicion: Grounds for suspicion that the incident in question occurred, but other conclusions are possible.
- Balance of probabilities (Sufficient evidence): More evidence supports the finding than contradicts it.
- Clear and convincing evidence: Very solid support for the finding; significantly more evidence supports the finding and limited information suggests the contrary.
- Overwhelming evidence: Conclusive or highly convincing evidence supports the finding.
- Beyond reasonable doubt: Specific term applied for criminal conviction in many legal systems.

Different fact-finding organs use different standards of proof. It would be useful to examine this issue in light of the aforementioned mandates. First, the UN Mission and the OPCW FFM are tasked with determining whether chemical weapons were used or not. UN Mission reports give almost no indication about standards of proof. While it confirmed the collection of "clear and convincing evidence" with regard to the chemical attacks in Ghouta on 21 August 2013,[343] it might be reaching to say that "clear and convincing evidence" meant standards of proof were satisfied. As for the OPCW FFM, only three of its reports explicitly referred to "reasonable grounds" as the apparent standard of proof that it relied on.[344] Despite lack of reference in its other reports, the OPCW FFM has also implicitly relied on the same standard of proof, stressing that it "adhered to the most stringent protocols available"[345] or

[341] Boutruche, *supra* note 171, p. 303.

[342] Stephen Wilkinson, "Finding the Facts' Standards of Proof and Information Handling in Monitoring, Reporting and Fact-Finding Missions," Working Paper, Monitoring, Reporting, and Fact-Finding (MRP) project, Program on Humanitarian Policy and Conflict Research (HPCR) at Harvard University (2014), p. 8, https://ssrn.com/abstract=2400927, accessed 22 April 2023; See also Stephen Wilkinson, "Standards of Proof in International Humanitarian and Human Rights Fact-Finding and Inquiry Missions," Geneva academy of international humanitarian law and human rights (2012), p. 49, https://www.geneva-academy.ch/joomlatools-files/docman-files/Standards%20of%20Proof%20in%20Fact-Finding.pdf, accessed 22 April 2023.

[343] UN Doc. A/67/997–S/2013/553, 16 September 2013, p. 8, para. 28; UN Doc. A/68/663–S/2013/735, 13 December 2013, p. 21, para. 109.

[344] OPCW Doc. S/1731/2019, 1 March 2019, para. 7.1, footnote 9; OPCW Doc. S/1901/2020, 1 October 2020, para. 5.6; OPCW Doc. S/1902/2020, 1 October 2020, para. 3.9.

[345] OPCW Doc. S/1319/2015, 29 October 2015, p. 7, para. 2.3; OPCW Doc. S/1320/2015, 29 October 2015, p. 4, para. 2.3; OPCW Doc. S/1510/2017, 29 June 2017, p. 5, para. 3.6; OPCW Doc. S/1645/2018, 6 July 2018, p. 7, para. 7.1; OPCW Doc. S/1731/2019, 1 March 2019, para. 7.1; OPCW Doc. S/1901/2020, 1 October 2020, para. 5.6; OPCW Doc. S/1902/2020, 1 October 2020, para. 3.9; OPCW Doc. S/2017/2022*, 24 January 2022, p. 8, para. 5.1; OPCW Doc. S/2020/2022, 31 January 2022, p. 11, para. 5.1.

"followed the same methodology,"[346] which should perhaps be inferred as subsuming said standards of proof.

Second, the COI's mandate encompasses both establishing facts and identifying perpetrators. Regarding the former, the COI explicitly referred to "reasonable suspicion"—a variation of "reasonable grounds" as indicated hereinafter, and "a lower standard of proof than that applied in a criminal proceeding"—which would be met when it "obtained a reliable body of evidence, consistent with other information, indicating the occurrence of a particular incident or event."[347] In fact, commissions/missions have most commonly adopted "reasonable suspicion" or "reasonable grounds to believe," and less frequently "balance of probabilities," as the standard for making findings of fact.[348] The COI thus simply followed common practice.[349] Moreover, specific paragraphs regarding chemical weapons use make clear that "reasonable grounds" relate to both fact-finding and attribution.[350]

Third, the OPCW-UN JIM and the OPCW IIT are attribution-specific organs who identify users of chemical weapons. The standards of proof of the former seem to be higher than that of the latter. The OPCW-UN JIM described three standards: "overwhelming evidence (highly convincing evidence to support a finding)," "substantial evidence (very solid evidence to support a finding)," and "sufficient evidence (there is evidence of a credible and reliable nature for the Mechanism to make a finding that a party was involved in the use of chemicals as weapons)," and decided that the third standard at least was required.[351] The OPCW-UN JIM stressed in its third report of

[346] OPCW Doc. S/1548/2017, 2 November 2017, p. 3, para. 3.1; OPCW Doc. S/1626/2018, 15 May 2018, p. 2, para. 3.1; OPCW Doc. S/1636/2018*, 13 June 2018, p. 2, para. 3.1; OPCW Doc. S/1645/2018, 6 July 2018, p. 7, para. 7.1; OPCW Doc. S/1731/2019, 1 March 2019, para. 7.1; OPCW Doc. S/1901/2020, 1 October 2020, para. 5.6; OPCW Doc. S/1902/2020, 1 October 2020, para. 3.9; OPCW Doc. S/2017/2022*, 24 January 2022, p. 8, para. 5.1; OPCW Doc. S/2020/2022, 31 January 2022, p. 11, para. 5.1.

[347] UN Doc. A/HRC/S-17/2/Add.1, 23 November 2011, p. 4, para. 5.

[348] United Nations Office of the High Commissioner for Human Rights, *Commissions of Inquiry and Fact-Finding Missions on International Human Rights and Humanitarian Law, Guidance and Practice* (2015), p. 62. This means that "commissions/missions are not required to establish guilt in the way courts do and as such they do not apply a criminal law standard of proof of 'beyond reasonable doubt'" (*ibid.*).

[349] See also UN Doc. A/HRC/21/50, 16 August 2012, p. 6, para. 10; UN Doc. A/HRC/22/59, 5 February 2013, p. 6, para. 10; UN Doc. A/HRC/23/58, 18 July 2013, p. 4, para. 9; UN Doc. A/HRC/24/46, 16 August 2013, p. 4, para. 10; UN Doc. A/HRC/25/65, 12 February 2014, p. 4, para. 6; UN Doc. A/HRC/27/60, 13 August 2014, p. 4, para. 6; UN Doc. A/HRC/28/69, 5 February 2015, p. 4, para. 5; UN Doc. A/HRC/30/48, 13 August 2015, p. 3, para. 6; UN Doc. A/HRC/31/68, 11 February 2016, p. 3, para. 6; UN Doc. A/HRC/33/55, 11 August 2016, p. 3, para. 6.

[350] UN Doc. A/HRC/27/60, 13 August 2014, p. 19, para. 118; UN Doc. A/HRC/36/55, 8 August 2017, p. 15, para. 70; UN Doc. A/HRC/36/55, 8 August 2017, p. 16, para. 77; UN Doc. A/HRC/36/55, 8 August 2017, Annex II, p. 29, para. 35. cf. UN Doc. A/HRC/46/54, 21 January 2021, p. 8, para. 32; UN Doc. A/HRC/RES/46/22, 24 March 2021, operative para. 32.

[351] UN Doc. S/2016/142, 12 February 2016, p. 4, para. 20; UN Doc. S/2016/738/Rev.1, 24 August 2016, p. 8, para. 24 and Annex I, p. 23, para. 23; UN Doc. S/2016/888, 21 October 2016, p. 4, para. 7; UN Doc. S/2017/904, 26 October 2017, p. 7, para. 25.

October 2016 that it is not "a judicial or quasi-judicial body" with "authority or jurisdiction…to make a formal or binding judicial determination of criminal liability," but "a non-judicial investigative body within its mandate identifying 'to the greatest extent feasible' individuals and other actors involved in the use of chemicals as weapons and the roles that they played."[352]

Be that as it may, the OPCW-UN JIM clearly applied a higher threshold than the COI. While they identified the same perpetrators in the incidents in Talmenes on 21 April 2014,[353] Um-Housh on 16 September 2016,[354] and Khan Shaykoun on 4 April 2017,[355] they differed over allegations of chemical attacks in Kafr Zita on 11 and 18 April 2014 and Al-Tamanah on 29 April 2014. The COI concluded that Syrian government helicopters dropped barrel bombs containing chemical agents,[356] while the OPCW-UN JIM reported that it was unable to confirm the use of chemical weapons because "the remnants of the device allegedly used had been removed from the site"[357] and "there was insufficient information."[358]

In April 2018, the UN Security Council had an opportunity to discuss the possible reinstatement of attribution mechanism. Russia proposed "beyond reasonable doubt" as the standard of proof to be used by this mechanism in a new guise.[359] The UK objected, pointing out that this standard had not been used in any other comparable past or current UN investigation but only in relation to criminal prosecutions in courts of law, which have significantly greater investigative powers and independence than investigations based on UN Security Council resolutions.[360] In the event, this proposal was voted down.[361]

Unlike the OPCW-UN JIM, the OPCW IIT adopted "reasonable grounds,"[362] the same standard of proof as that which the COI employed. According to its first report, the OPCW IIT followed "standard practice of international fact-finding bodies

352 UN Doc. S/2016/888, 21 October 2016, p. 4, para. 6.

353 OPCW Doc. S/2016/738/Rev.1, 24 August 2016, Annex IV, p. 50, para. 56; UN Doc. A/HRC/27/60, 13 August 2014, p. 19, para. 118.

354 OPCW Doc. S/2017/904, 26 October 2017, p. 9, para. 36; UN Independent International Commission of Inquiry on the Syrian Arab Republic, Chemical Weapons Attacks as of 18 February 2021.

355 OPCW Doc. S/2017/904, 26 October 2017, p. 10, para. 46; UN Doc. A/HRC/36/55, 8 August 2017, p. 16, para. 77 and Annex II, p. 29, para. 35.

356 UN Doc. A/HRC/27/60, 13 August 2014, p. 19, para. 118.

357 OPCW Doc. S/2016/738/Rev.1, 24 August 2016, Annex II, p. 34, para. 75; OPCW Doc. S/2016/738/Rev.1, 24 August 2016, Annex III, p. 42, para. 51.

358 OPCW Doc. S/2016/738/Rev.1, 24 August 2016, Annex V, p. 58, para. 52.

359 UN Doc. S/2018/175 (Russian draft resolution), 10 April 2018, operative para. 6.

360 UN Doc. S/PV.8174, 5 February 2018, p. 5 (UK); UN Doc. S/PV.8228, 10 April 2018, p. 9 (UK).

361 UN Doc. S/PV.8228, 10 April 2018, p. 9. The vote was six in favor (Bolivia, China, Equatorial Guinea, Ethiopia, Kazakhstan, and Russia) to seven against (France, Netherlands, Peru, Poland, Sweden, UK, and US), with two abstentions (Côte d'Ivoire and Kuwait).

362 OPCW Doc. S/1867/2020, 8 April 2020, pp. 14–15, paras. 2.18; OPCW Doc. S/1943/2021, 12 April 2021, p. 7, para. 1.4.

and commissions of inquiry,"[363] and would reach its conclusions on identification of perpetrators based on "a sufficient and reliable body of information which, consistent with other information, would allow an ordinarily prudent person to reasonably believe that an individual or entity was involved in the use of chemical weapons (i.e., 'reasonable grounds')."[364] Both the OPCW IIT and COI reached the same conclusions on the chemical attacks in Ltamenah on 30 March 2017[365] and Saraqib on 4 February 2018.[366]

(v) **Impartiality**

The principle of impartiality requires that fact-finding organs investigate all parties to allegations with equal thoroughness, avoiding any perception of favoritism.[367]

One challenge lies with the selection of witnesses for interview.[368] According to the OPCW FFM, "[i]n the best case during an investigation, potential interviewees would be identified by one of two means: (1) through the investigation team canvassing the area of the alleged incident to identify witnesses; and (2) through the identification of potential interviewees as possible leads by another source deemed reliable by virtue of proximity or involvement."[369]

Circumstances may vary depending on the possibility of on-site visits. If the fact-finding body is able to visit the alleged location, it should be relatively easy to identify witnesses. The UN Mission interviewed survivors, health care workers, patients, doctors, and nurses,[370] with no complaint from the parties to the armed conflict. The OPCW FFM also held interviews with 39 witnesses during its on-site investigation of the chemical incidents in Douma.[371] If the fact-finding body cannot make on-site visits, it must find witnesses with the assistance of the parties to the armed conflict themselves and/or third parties. The reports indicate that the OPCW FFM made arrangements with both parties in some instances,[372] and with one or

---

363 The relevant footnote includes a reference to the COI (OPCW Doc. S/1867/2020, 8 April 2020, p. 15, footnote 31).

364 OPCW Doc. S/1867/2020, 8 April 2020, pp. 14–15, paras. 2.18.

365 OPCW Doc. S/1867/2020, 8 April 2020, p. 58, para. 14; UN Doc. A/HRC/36/55, 8 August 2017, p. 15, para. 70.

366 OPCW Doc. S/1943/2021, 12 April 2021, p. 45, para. 10.1; UN Doc. A/HRC/39/65, 9 August 2018, p. 11, para. 55.

367 United Nations Office of the High Commissioner for Human Rights, *Commissions of Inquiry and Fact-Finding Missions on International Human Rights and Humanitarian Law, Guidance and Practice* (2015), p. 33; Boutruche, *supra* note 171, p. 291.

368 Boutruche, *supra* note 171 , p. 301.

369 OPCW Doc. S/1319/2015, 29 October 2015, Annex 2, p. 9, para. 2.11; OPCW Doc. S/1320/2015, 29 October 2015, Annex, p. 5, para. 2.7; OPCW Doc. S/1510/2017, 29 June 2017, p. 6, para. 3.12.

370 UN Doc. A/67/997 S/2013/552, 16 September 2013, p. 8, para. 20; UN Doc. A/68/663–S/2013/735, 13 December 2013, p. 11, para. 39.

371 OPCW Doc. S/1731/2019, 1 March 2019, p. 21, paras. 8.41. While Russia and Syria commented about these interviews (UN Doc. S/2019/211, 15 March 2019, p. 4; UN Doc. A/73/883 S/2019/415, 23 May 2019, Annex I, p. 3), they did not appear to have complaint about their impartiality.

372 OPCW Doc. S/1510/2017, 29 June 2017, p. 7, paras. 3.17–3.20.

another of the parties in other instances.[373] During the investigation of chemical attack in Khan Shaykhun, it interviewed witnesses identified through "liaison with the representatives of several NGOs" and "two people…presented as interviewees by the Government of the Syrian Arab Republic."[374] While Russia criticized the OPCW FFM for emphasizing the divergence between their statements,[375] it is clear that the OPCW FFM conducted interviews with representatives of both parties, ensuring the impartiality of its investigation.

Russia, Syria, and Iran have stressed that the conclusions of the OPCW FFM and the OPCW-UN JIM lacked credibility because they were based on the testimony of "terrorists."[376] However, interviewing "terrorists" per se does not impugn impartiality. Even if the Syrian government labels the opposition groups as "terrorists," they are still parties to the armed conflict. It is also curious that they began this argument only in October 2016, after the OPCW-UN JIM identified the Syrian government as the perpetrator.

Russia and Syria have also complained about lack of clarity in interviewee selection,[377] arguing that reports by fact-finding organs have often omitted descriptions of their selection procedures, especially factors for selection, instead inclining toward

[373] Arrangements with the Syrian government: OPCW Doc. S/1318/2015/Rev.1, 17 December 2015, pp. 10–11 and 21, paras. 3.22, 3.23 and 3.47; OPCW Doc. S/1444/2016, 21 December 2016, pp. 5–6, para. 4.3; OPCW Doc. S/1902/2020, 1 October 2020, p. 10, para. 6.17; OPCW Doc. S/2020/2022, 31 January 2021, p. 13, para. 5.17. Arrangements with opposition groups: OPCW Doc. S/1319/2015, 29 October 2015, Annex 2, pp. 9–10 and 14, paras. 2.15, 2.16 and 2.42; OPCW Doc. S/1320/2015, 29 October 2015, Annex, p. 5, para. 2.9; OPCW Doc. S/1548/2017, 2 November 2017, p. 4, para. 4.7; OPCW Doc. S/1626/2018, 15 May 2018, p. 3, paras. 4.5 and 4.6; OPCW Doc. S/1636/2018*, 13 June 2018, p. 4, paras. 4.7 and 4.8.

[374] OPCW Doc. S/1510/2017, 29 June 2017, p. 7, paras. 3.17 and 3.20.

[375] OPCW Doc. EC-M-55/NAT.9* (Russia), 5 July 2017, p. 3; UN Doc. S/2017/576 (Russia), 14 July 2017, p. 4.

[376] UN Doc. S/2016/844 (Syria), 20 October 2016, pp. 8 and 11; UN Doc. S/2016/903 (Syria), 2 November 2016, p. 3; OPCW Doc. EC-85/NAT.1 (Russia), 30 May 2017, p. 3; UN Doc. A/C.1/72/PV.28, 2 November 2017, p. 9 (Iran); UN Doc. S/PV.8105, 16 November 2017, pp. 16–17 (Russia); UN Doc. S/2017/991 (Syria), 5 December 2017, p. 1; UN Doc. S/PV.8105, 16 November 2017, p. 15 (Syria); UN Doc. S/PV.8221, 4 April 2018, p. 18 (Syria); UN Doc. S/PV.8228, 10 April 2018, p. 20 (Syria); OPCW Doc. C-SS-4/NAT.40 (Russia), 26 June 2018, p. 4; UN Doc. A/C.1/73/PV.28, 2 November 2018, p. 20 (Iran); UN Doc. S/2019/221 (Syria), 15 March 2019, p. 4; UN Doc. A/73/833–S/2019/415 (Russia), 23 May 2019, p. 3; OPCW Doc. EC/92/NAT.28 (Syria), 9 October 2019, p. 2; UN Doc. A/C.1/74/PV.23, 4 November 2019, p. 21 (Iran); OPCW Doc. EC-94/NAT.5 (Syria), 16 April 2020, p. 2; OPCW Doc. EC-94/NAT.40 (Syria), 7 July 2020, p. 2; UN Doc. S/2021/22, 7 January 2021, Annex XVI (Syria), p. 31; UN Doc. S/2021/109, 5 February 2021, Annex XI (Russia), p. 15; UN Doc. S/2021/226, 8 March 2021, Annex XV (Syria), p. 23; UN Doc. S/2021/446, 10 May 2021, Annex XI (Russia), p. 17; UN Doc. S/PV.8785, 3 June 2021, p. 8 (Russia); UN Doc. S/PV.8785, 3 June 2021, p. 29 (Syria); OPCW Doc. EC-97/NAT.46 (Syria), 6 July 2021, p. 3. Iran raised concerns about "terrorists" as early as January 2015 (Iran, https://www.opcw.org/sites/default/files/documents/EC/M-48/Iran.pdf, accessed 22 April 2023). See also UN Doc. A/HRC/36/G/10 (Syria), 12 September 2017, p. 2.

[377] OPCW Doc. EC-M-48/NAT.1 (Russia), 21 January 2015, p. 3; UN Doc. S/PV.7401, 6 March 2015, p. 6 (Russia); OPCW Doc. EC-M-50/NAT.3 (Russia), 23 November 2015, p. 2; UN Doc. S/2016/903 (Syria), 2 November 2016, p. 3; OPCW Doc. EC-91/NAT.43 (Syria), 11 July 2019, p. 2;

concentrating on factual information about the conduct of the interviews themselves. This does not mean, however, that the fact-finding organs made these selections arbitrarily. As mentioned above, Syria and Russia did not raise this point when the Syrian government requested investigations,[378] but expressed concerns when the fact-finding organs reached conclusions unacceptable to them.

(vi) **Professionalism**

Sampling and Analysis

As mentioned, samples may constitute valuable evidence, and their scientific analysis demonstrates objective fact. In this regard, both the UN Mission and the OPCW FFM have relied extensively on the OPCW-designated laboratory network.

Since its inauguration, the OPCW has established and enhanced the technical capabilities needed to carry out sampling and analysis in accordance with relevant CWC provisions. One of the main aspects of this effort is a global network of designated laboratories which are qualified to conduct off-site sampling and analysis. This network enables the OPCW not only to fulfill the requirements under Verification Annex Part II, para. 57 that samples be analyzed in at least two designated laboratories but also to contribute to the implementation of Verification Annex Part XI, para. 27, envisaging the OPCW role in cooperating with the UN Secretary-General upon activation of the latter's investigation mechanism.[379] For an institution to maintain the status of "designated" laboratory, it must pass proficiency testing under relevant guidelines.[380] As of the UN Mission deployment to Syria, 21 laboratories from 17 States Parties were so designated.[381] The OPCW-designated laboratories network system proved its scientific and technical professionalism when, for the first time, these laboratories took part in off-site sampling and analysis during the UN Mission investigation.[382] The results were as follows:

- The UN mission was able to collect environmental and biomedical samples relating to the alleged chemical attack in Ghouta of 21 August 2013.[383] Several

UN Doc. A/74/825–S/2020/311 (Russia), 28 April 2020, p. 2; OPCW Doc. EC-97/NAT.46 (Syria), 6 July 2021, p. 3.

378 OPCW Doc. EC-M-50/NAT.3 (Russia), 23 November 2015, p. 2.

379 The Supplementary Arrangement also stipulates that the fact-finding mission would carry out its sampling and analysis in accordance with OPCW procedures (*United Nations Treaty Series*, Vol. 2160, II-1240, paras. 5(a), 6(b), 6(d), 7(b), and 7(c)).

380 OPCW Doc. C-I/DEC.61, 22 May 1997; OPCW Doc. C-I/DEC.62, 22 May 1997; OPCW Doc. C-I/DEC.65, 22 May 1997; OPCW Doc. EC-XX/DEC.3, 19 May 2000. See also OPCW Doc. C-20/DEC.4, 2 December 2015.

381 OPCW Doc. S/1123/2013, 12 August 2013.

382 The UN Secretary-General implicitly indicated that five OPCW designated laboratories in Finland, Germany, Sweden, Switzerland and the Netherlands were involved in the off-site sampling and analysis (UN Doc. A/68/663-S/2013/735, 13 December 2013, p. 2; See also UN Doc. A/C.1/68/PV.17, p. 7 (Finland).

383 UN Doc. A/67/997-S/2013/553, 16 September 2013, pp. 6–8, paras. 18, 23, 24, 26.

samples tested positive. Results were consistent between the two designated laboratories concerned.[384]

- The UN mission relied only on biomedical samples relating to the alleged chemical attack in Jobar of 24 August 2013. Several samples tested positive. Results were identical between the two designated laboratories concerned.[385]
- The UN mission collected biomedical samples relating to the alleged chemical attacks in Saraqueb of 29 April 2013 and Ashrafiah Sahnaya of 25 August 2013 which tested positive at two designated laboratories.[386]
- The UN mission analyzed blood samples and corresponding DNA samples of two civilians who were allegedly exposed to secondary contamination relating to the alleged chemical attack in Khan Al Asal of 19 March 2013. The samples tested negative.[387]
- The UN mission received blood samples relating to the alleged chemical attack in Bahhariyeh of 22 August 2013 which tested negative.[388]

It follows that the validity and reliability of the OPCW designated laboratories network system were fully demonstrated, which does not necessarily mean that there were no problems with the investigation. The OPCW faced an obstacle when the UN Secretary-General requested its assistance. While the CWC envisaged that relevant off-site sampling and analysis procedures would be considered and approved by the first Conference of the States Parties (Verification Annex Part II, para. 56), there was no consensus among the States Parties, a situation that persists as of this writing. The 2013 OPCW annual report indicated that the Technical Secretariat addressed the matter with an alternative bilateral approach. Between March and July 2013, the Technical Secretariat concluded a "technical arrangement" with seven designated laboratories.[389] The question thus arises of whether relevant CWC provisions are

[384] *Ibid.*, Appendix 4 and 6; UN Doc. A/68/663-S/2013/735, 13 December 2013, Appendix 5.

[385] UN Doc. A/68/663-S/2013/735, 13 December 2013, Appendix 7.

[386] *Ibid.*, Appendix 4 and 8.

[387] *Ibid.*, Appendix 3.

[388] *Ibid.*, Appendix 6.

[389] IAR 302 Exchange of letters between the OPCW Technical Secretariat and the Swedish Defence Research Agency (FOI): Technical arrangement on the off-site analysis of samples taken in a fact-finding mission as part of an investigation of alleged use of chemical weapons (signed 5 and 9 April 2013; entered into force 12 April 2013), IAR 303 Exchange of letters between the OPCW Technical Secretariat and the Netherlands Organisation for Applied Scientific Research (TNO): Technical Arrangement on the off-site analysis of samples taken in a fact-finding mission as part of an investigation of alleged use of chemical weapons (signed 15 and 26 April 2013; entered into force 2 May 2013), IAR 304 Exchange of letters between the OPCW Technical Secretariat and the Finnish Institute for Verification of the Chemical Weapons Convention (VERIFIN): Technical arrangement regarding the off-site analysis of samples (signed 4 April and 18 March 2013; entered into force 4 April 2013), IAR 305 Technical Arrangement regarding the off-site analysis of samples between the OPCW Technical Secretariat and the Chemical Analysis and Testing Laboratory (Romania) (signed 4 April and 12 March 2013; entered into force 4 April 2013), IAR 306 Technical Arrangement regarding the off-site analysis of samples between the OPCW Technical Secretariat and the Spiez Laboratory, Switzerland (signed 4 April and 22 March 2013; entered into force 4 April 2013),

bypassed, as well as whether the Technical Secretariat is competent to conclude such instruments.

The CWC tasks the Technical Secretariat only with negotiating "agreements or arrangements relating to the implementation of verification activities with States Parties, subject to approval by the Executive Council" (Article VIII, para. 39(a)). It could be argued that this provision does not require Executive Council approval of agreements or arrangements by the Technical Secretariat or with entities that are not States or international organizations. In practice, the Technical Secretariat has been a party to several such international agreements or instruments with counterparts who are neither States nor international organizations, as indicated in the lists of "International Agreements and Instruments registered by the Technical Secretariat" in the OPCW annual reports.[390] Apparently, the OPCW Conference of the States Parties has implicitly endorsed this practice by acknowledging these same reports, and the Technical Secretariat has accordingly continued to explore this approach subsequently.[391]

The OPCW FFM has taken much more advantage of the OPCW-designated laboratory network than the UN Mission. The results of off-site sampling and analysis in the former's investigations are as follows:

- Chlorine and chlorine-related chemicals were detected from samples relating to the alleged chemical attacks in Idlib between 16 March and 20 May 2015,[392] although none of the samples were collected by the OPCW FFM.[393]

IAR 309 Technical arrangement regarding off-site analysis of samples between the OPCW Technical Secretariat and the ECBC Forensic Analytical Center, Edgewood Arsenal, Aberdeen Proving Ground, Maryland, the United States of America (signed 7 June and 11 June 2013; entered into force 7 June 2013), and IAR 312 Cooperation arrangement (off-site analysis of samples taken in a fact-finding mission as part of an investigation of alleged use of chemical weapons) between the OPCW Technical Secretariat and the Bundeswehr Joint Medical Service Headquarter on behalf of the Laboratory of the Bundeswehr Institute of Pharmacology and Toxicology for Med C-Agent Special Diagnostics, Verification and Analytics, Germany (signed 23 and 8 July 2013; entered into force 23 July 2013) (OPCW Doc. C-19/4, 3 December 2014, Annex 11).

[390] IAR 229 Letter of Agreement Between the Technical Secretariat and the Preparatory Commission for the Comprehensive Nuclear Test-Ban Treaty Organization (CTBTO) on the Provision of Personnel for the OPCW Challenge-Inspection Exercise, IAR 230 Letter of Agreement Between the Technical Secretariat and the Spiez Laboratory on the Provision of Personnel for the OPCW Challenge-Inspection Exercise (OPCW Doc. C-17/4, 6 November 2007, Annex 13). See also bilateral instruments regarding sample preparation or evaluation of results for official OPCW Proficiency Test between OPCW and designated laboratories (IAR 244, IAR 245, IAR 246, IAR 247 (OPCW Doc. C-17/4, 6 November 2007, Annex 13)).

[391] The Technical Secretariat concluded additional technical arrangements with designated laboratories or their supervising authorities: five in 2015 (OPCW Doc. C-21/4, 30 November 2016, Annex 11), one in 2016 (OPCW Doc. C-22/4, 29 November 2017, Annex 8), two in 2017 (OPCW Doc. C-23/4, 19 November 2018, Annex 8), three in 2018 (OPCW Doc. C-24/4, 28 November 2019, Annex 8), and two in 2019 (OPCW Doc. C-25/4, 20 April 2021, Annex 8).

[392] OPCW Doc. S/1319/2015, 29 October 2015, Annex 2, pp. 79–80, paras. 3.162, 3.163, 3.167, 3.168, 3.171.

[393] OPCW Doc. S/1319/2015, 29 October 2015, Annex 2, p. 75, para. 3.153.

- Blood sample analysis indicated sarin exposure relating to the alleged chemical attack in Darayya on 15 February 2015,[394] although the OPCW FFM was unable to link these results to the alleged incident,[395] as these samples were provided by Syrian authorities and the chain of custody was not verified.[396]
- Methyl diethanolamine, a precursor for nitrogen mustard, was identified in a textile sample relating to the alleged chemical attack in Aleppo on 2 August 2016,[397] although this result does not confirm the use of chemical weapons, because methyl diethanolamine can be found in commercial detergents, and no signs of nitrogen mustard exposure were found among the casualties.[398]
- Sulfur mustard was found in biomedical and neat agent samples relating to the alleged chemical attack in Um-Housh on 15–16 September 2016.[399] The former were collected by the medical staff of Hospital 601, witnessed by two FFM team members,[400] while the latter were handed over by Syrian authorities.[401]
- Biomedical specimens and environmental and other samples tested positive for sarin or sarin-like substances relating to the alleged chemical attack in Khan Shaykhun on 4 April 2017.[402] Some samples were collected in the presence of the FFM team,[403] while others were taken in its absence.[404]
- Sarin and related chemicals were detected relating to the alleged chemical attack in Ltamenah on 30 March 2017,[405] although all samples were collected by an NGO.[406]
- Analysis of samples relating to the alleged chemical attack in Saraqib on 4 February 2018 revealed the presence of chlorine,[407] albeit collected by an NGO.[408]
- Sarin, chlorine, and related chemicals were identified relating to the alleged chemical attack in in Ltamenah on 24–25 March 2017,[409] albeit collected by an NGO.[410]
- The OPCW FFM collected environmental samples, including from two cylinders, relating to the alleged chemical attack in Douma on 7 April 2018, which were

[394] OPCW Doc. S/1318/2015/Rev.1, 17 December 2015, p. 48, para. 3.93 and Annex 8.
[395] *Ibid.*, p. 48, para. 3.93.
[396] *Ibid.*, pp. 48–49, para. 3.92(e) and (h).
[397] OPCW Doc. S/1444/2016, 27 December 2016, Annex 8, p. 29, para. 14.
[398] *Ibid.*, Annex 8, p. 30, para. 18.
[399] OPCW Doc. S/1491/2017, 12 May 2017, pp. 19, 20, paras. 5.44, 5.49, Annexes 10 and 11.
[400] *Ibid.*, p. 20, para. 5.46.
[401] *Ibid.*, p. 19, paras. 5.38–5.40.
[402] OPCW Doc. S/1510/2017, 29 June 2017, pp. 36–48, paras. 5.81–5.107.
[403] *Ibid.*, p. 38, para. 5.83.
[404] *Ibid.*, pp. 39, 45, 47, paras. 5.87, 5.99, 5.100, 5.103.
[405] OPCW Doc. S/1548/2017, 2 November 2017, pp. 15–23.
[406] *Ibid.*, p. 13, para. 5.30.
[407] OPCW Doc. S/1626/2018, 15 May 2018, pp. 4, 15–24, paras. 4.10, 5.53–5.60.
[408] *Ibid.*, p. 4, paras. 4.9–4.10.
[409] OPCW Doc. S/1636/2018*, 13 June 2018, pp. 12–16, 22–28, paras. 5.36, 5.37, 5.63.
[410] *Ibid.*, pp. 12, 22, paras. 5.33, 5.35, 5.61, 5.62.

analyzed at the OPCW-designated laboratories.[411] Various chlorinated organic chemicals were detected.[412]

- While samples relating to the alleged chemical attack in Aleppo on 24 November 2018 were analyzed by the OPCW-designated laboratories,[413] no chemical substance was detected.[414]
- Thiodiglycol, a precursor of sulfur mustard and itself a scheduled chemical, and thiodiglycol sulfoxide, which is an oxidation product of thiodiglycol, were detected in samples relating to the alleged chemical attack in Marea on 1 and 3 September 2015,[415] albeit collected by an NGO.[416]

No State has disputed the analyses conducted by the OPCW-designated laboratories per se. While Russia raised questions about sampling and analysis in the case of alleged use in Douma in April 2018, it did not dispute the results directly, but instead alluded to selection of the designated laboratories, the limited number of identical results at said laboratories, and the assessments of the results.[417] By contrast, Russia used its own OPCW-designated laboratory to demonstrate chemical weapons use in Khan al-Asal in March 2013,[418] indicating its endorsement of the system.

It should be noted that the COI does not possess relevant expertise or technical capabilities,[419] and thus relies on other evidence, including interviews, medical records, and open-source information. The COI explicitly referred to the findings of the OPCW FFM relating to the alleged chemical attack in Khan Shaykhun on

---

[411] OPCW Doc. S/1731/2019, 1 March 2019, pp. 8–9, 12–13 and 14, paras. 7.2, 8.5 and 8.18. While Syrian authorities initially did not accept the sealing of the cylinders, the OPCW Technical Secretariat did ultimately tag and seal them (*ibid*, pp. 40–41). On 9 July 2021, Syria informed the Technical Secretariat of an attack on 8 June 2021 against the declared former chemical weapons production facility, which resulted the destruction of two chlorine cylinders related to the chemical weapons incident in Douma on 7 April 2018 (OPCW Doc. EC-98/NAT.1 (Syria), 9 July 2021, p. 1).

[412] OPCW Doc. S/1731/2019, 1 March 2019, p. 13, para. 8.6 and Annex 5.

[413] OPCW Doc. S/1902/2020, 1 October 2020, pp. 9, 14, 37, 38, paras. 6.5, 6.50, 7.47, 7.51, 7.55 and Annex 9.

[414] *Ibid.*, p. 38, para. 7.53.

[415] OPCW Doc. S/2017/2022*, 24 January 2022, p. 18, paras. 7.43–7.44.

[416] *Ibid.*, p. 16, para. 7.39.

[417] UN Doc. A/73/883–S/2019/415 (Russia), 23 May 2019, Annex I, pp. 3–4.

[418] Press statement by H.E. Ambassador Vitaly Churkin, Permanent Representative of the Russian Federation to the United Nations, on the use of chemical weapons in Syria, 9 July 2013, https://russiaun.ru/en/news/sc_press_statement_syria, accessed 22 April 2023; Comment by the Information and Press Department of the Russian Ministry of Foreign Affairs regarding the investigations into the use of chemical weapons in Syria, 4 September 2013, https://www.mid.ru/en/web/guest/foreign_policy/international_safety/conflicts/-/asset_publisher/xIEMTQ3OvzcA/content/id/97974, accessed 22 April 2023.

[419] Van Schaack, *supra* note 107, p. 101.

4 April 2017, especially regarding sampling and analysis, to reinforce its conclusion.[420] While this approach may be indispensable, it would also tend to reduce the independence of COI investigations.

(vii) **Syrian Cooperation**

There is a stark contrast in the degree of Syrian cooperation with the various fact-finding organs. Syria has cooperated more or less with the UN Mission, the OPCW FFM, and the OPCW-UN JIM, allowing them into its territory. Policy-making organs have called upon all parties in Syria to extend their full cooperation,[421] as have many States.[422] On the other hand, Syria has refused to cooperate with the COI and the OPCW IIT. While Syria is not obliged to cooperate with the former, the UNHRC has repeatedly condemned or deplored Syria's lack of cooperation with the COI and demanded its full cooperation therewith, including by granting the COI immediate, full and unfettered access.[423] By contrast, Syria is clearly obligated to cooperate with

[420] UN Doc. A/HRC/36/55, 8 August 2017, pp. 26–28, 29, paras. 21–27, 34.

[421] OPCW Doc. EC-M-48/DEC.1, 4 February 2015, operative para. 6; UN Doc. S/RES/2209 (2015), 6 March 2015, operative para. 6; OPCW Doc. EC-M-50/DEC.1, 23 November 2015, operative para. 7.

[422] OPCW Doc. EC-M-48/NAT.7 (Peru), 21 January 2015, p. 1; OPCW Doc. EC-79/NAT.6 (Luxembourg on behalf of the EU), 7 July 2015, p. 2; OPCW Doc. EC-79/NAT.23 (Switzerland), 7 July 2015, p. 1; OPCW Doc. EC-79/NAT.24 (Chile), 7 July 2015, p. 2; OPCW Doc. EC-80/NAT.28 (Luxembourg on behalf of the EU), 6 October 2015, p. 2; OPCW Doc. EC-80/NAT.14 (Malaysia), 6 October 2015, p. 2; OPCW Doc. EC-M-50/NAT.16 (Luxembourg on behalf of the EU), 23 November 2015, p. 2; OPCW Doc. EC-M-50/NAT.6 (Japan), 23 November 2015, p. 1; OPCW Doc. EC-81/NAT.13 (Japan), 16 March 2016, p. 2; OPCW Doc. EC-82/NAT.22 (Slovakia on behalf of the EU), 12 July 2016, p. 2; OPCW Doc. EC-82/NAT.17 (Japan), 12 July 2016, p. 1; OPCW Doc. EC-83/NAT.9 (Slovakia on behalf of the EU), 11 October 2016, p. 2; OPCW Doc. EC-84/NAT.10 (Malta on behalf of the EU), 7 March 2017, p. 1; OPCW Doc. EC-84/NAT.14 (Sweden), 7 March 2017, p. 1; OPCW Doc. EC-M-54/NAT.1 (Brazil), 13 April 2017, p. 1; OPCW Doc. EC-M-55/NAT.5 (Japan), 5 July 2017, p. 2; OPCW Doc. EC-85/NAT.7 (Estonia on behalf of the EU), 11 July 2017, p. 2; OPCW Doc. EC-86/NAT.5 (Estonia on behalf of the EU), 10 October 2017, p. 2; OPCW Doc. EC-86/NAT.21 (Chile), 10 October 2017, p. 2; OPCW Doc. EC-87/NAT.20* (Bulgaria on behalf of the EU), 13 March 2018, p. 2; OPCW Doc. EC-87/NAT.35 (Italy), 13 March 2018, p. 2; OPCW Doc. EC-89/NAT.33 (Italy), 9 October 2018, p. 1; OPCW Doc. EC-90/NAT.22 (Italy), 13 March 2019, p. 2; OPCW Doc. EC-92/NAT.7 (Finland on behalf of the EU), 8 October 2019, p. 3; OPCW Doc. EC-95/NAT.68 (Nigeria), 6 October 2020, p. 2; OPCW Doc. EC-96/NAT.25 (Nigeria), 9 March 2021, p. 1.

[423] UN Doc. A/HRC/RES/24/22, 27 September 2013, preamble para. 5 and operative para. 2; UN Doc. A/HRC/RES/25/23, 28 March 2014, preamble para. 5 and operative para. 3; UN Doc. A/HRC/RES/26/23, 27 June 2014, preamble para. 6 and operative para. 2; UN Doc. A/HRC/RES/27/16, 25 September 2014, preamble para. 10 and operative para. 2; UN Doc. A/HRC/RES/28/20, 27 March 2015, preamble para. 8 and operative para. 2; UN Doc. A/HRC/RES/29/16, 2 July 2015, preamble para. 7 and operative para. 2; UN Doc. A/HRC/RES/30/10, 1 October 2015, preamble para. 8 and operative para. 2; UN Doc. A/HRC/RES/31/17, 23 March 2016, preamble para. 12 and operative para. 3; UN Doc. A/HRC/RES/32/25, 1 July 2016, preamble para. 10 and operative para. 4; UN Doc. A/HRC/RES/33/23, 30 September 2016, preamble para. 9 and operative para. 6; UN Doc. A/HRC/RES/34/26, 24 March 2017, preamble para. 13 and operative para. 5; UN Doc. A/HRC/RES/35/26, 23 June 2017, preamble para. 13 and operative para. 3; UN Doc. A/HRC/RES/36/20, 29 September 2017, preamble para. 18 and operative para. 3; UN Doc. A/HRC/RES/37/29, 23 March

the latter, and States Parties initially urged Syria to fulfill this obligation.[424] Lack of cooperation on Syria's part eventually became inescapable, however, which many States Parties criticized.[425] The OPCW Executive Council and the Conference of the States Parties likewise "[e]xpresse[d] deep concern that the Syrian Arab Republic

2018, preamble para. 17 and operative para. 5; UN Doc. A/HRC/RES/38/16, 6 July 2018, preamble para. 15 and operative para. 4; UN Doc. A/HRC/RES/39/15, 28 September 2018, preamble para. 15 and operative para. 4; UN Doc. A/HRC/RES/40/17, 22 March 2019, preamble para. 17 and operative para. 4; UN Doc. A/HRC/RES/41/23, 12 July 2019, preamble para. 18 and operative para. 4; UN Doc. A/HRC/RES/42/27, 27 September 2019, preamble para. 18 and operative para. 4; UN Doc. A/HRC/RES/43/28, 22 June 2020, preamble para. 18 and operative para. 4; UN Doc. A/HRC/RES/46/22, 24 March 2021, preamble para. 8 and operative para. 6; UN Doc. A/HRC/RES/47/18, 13 July 2021, preamble para. 9 and operative para. 4; UN Doc. A/HRC/RES/48/15, 8 October 2021, preamble para. 11 and operative para. 4.

424 OPCW Doc. EC-90/NAT.30 (Peru), 12 March 2019, p. 1; OPCW Doc. EC-91/NAT.20 (Czech Republic), 10 July 2019, p. 1; OPCW Doc. EC-91/NAT.29 (Netherlands), 9 July 2019, p. 2; OPCW Doc. EC-91/NAT.38 (Peru), 9 July 2019, p. 1; OPCW Doc. EC-91/NAT.45 (Guatemala), 10 July 2019, p. 1; OPCW Doc. EC-92/NAT.7 (Finland on behalf of the EU), 8 October 2019, p. 3; OPCW Doc. EC-92/NAT.10 (Germany), 8 October 2019, p. 1. See also OPCW Doc. EC-94/NAT.8 (New Zealand), 21 April 2020, p. 1; OPCW Doc. EC-94/NAT.16 (Mexico), 19 June 2020, p. 2; OPCW Doc. EC-94/NAT.31 (Nigeria), 7 July 2020, pp. 1–2; OPCW Doc. EC-95/NAT.40 (Ireland), 6 October 2020, p. 2; OPCW Doc. EC-95/NAT.53 (Saudi Arabia), 6 October 2020, p. 2; OPCW Doc. EC-95/NAT.68 (Nigeria), 6 October 2020, p. 2; OPCW Doc. EC-96/NAT.25 (Nigeria), 9 March 2021, p. 1; OPCW Doc. EC-96/NAT.44 (Saudi Arabia), 9 March 2021, p. 2; OPCW Doc. EC-97/NAT.20 (Slovakia), 6 July 2021, p. 2; OPCW Doc. EC-97/NAT.31 (UK), 6 July 2021, pp. 1–2; OPCW Doc. EC-97/NAT.54 (Switzerland), 6 July 2021, p. 1; OPCW Doc. EC-97/NAT.58 (Saudi Arabia), 6 July 2021, p. 2; OPCW Doc. EC-99/NAT.45 (Switzerland), 8 March 2022, p. 1; OPCW Doc. EC-99/NAT.55 (Mexico), 8 March 2022, p. 2; OPCW Doc. EC-100/NAT.11 (Switzerland), 5 July 2022, p. 1; OPCW Doc. EC-100/NAT.36 (Australia), 5 July 2022, p. 1; OPCW Doc. EC-100/NAT.43 (Peru), 5 July 2022, p. 1.

425 OPCW Doc. EC-92/NAT.18 (UK), 8 October 2019, p. 2; OPCW Doc. EC-94/NAT.4 (Germany), 15 April 2020, p. 2; OPCW Doc. EC-94/NAT.6 (UK), 14 April 2020, p. 2; OPCW Doc. EC-94/NAT.25 (Ireland), 7 July 2020, p. 2; OPCW Doc. EC-94/NAT.34 (Finland), 7 July 2020, p. 1; OPCW Doc. EC-94/NAT.60 (Peru), 7 July 2020, p. 2; OPCW Doc. EC-94/NAT.65 (Guatemala), 7 July 2020, p. 2; OPCW Doc. EC-94/NAT.37 (US), 7 July 2020; OPCW Doc. EC-95/NAT.51 (Peru), 6 October 2020, p. 2; UN Doc. S/2020/1202, 16 December 2020, pp. 29–30 (UK); OPCW Doc. EC-96/NAT.15 (Peru), 9 March 2021, pp. 1–2; OPCW Doc. C-25/NAT.111 (UK), 20 April 2021, p. 1; OPCW Doc. C-25/NAT.121 (Mexico), 21 April 2021; UN Doc. S/2021/446, 10 May 2021, Annex XIX (Turkey), p. 31; UN Doc. S/PV.8982, 28 February 2022, p. 15 (Turkey); OPCW Doc. EC-99/NAT.13 (Germany), 8 March 2022, p. 2. See also OPCW Doc. EC-94/NAT.4 (Germany), 15 April 2020, p. 2; UN Doc. S/2020/1088, 9 November 2020, Annex II (Belgium), p. 4; UN Doc. S/2020/1088, 9 November 2020, Annex V (Estonia), p. 10; UN Doc. S/2020/1088, 9 November 2020, Annex VI (France), p. 11; UN Doc. S/2020/1202, 16 December 2020, Annex VI (Estonia), p. 15; UN Doc. S/2021/226, 8 March 2021, Annex III (Estonia), p. 5; UN Doc. S/2021/446, 10 May 2021, Annex XIX (Turkey), p. 31; OPCW Doc. EC-96/NAT.42 (France), 9 March 2021, p. 2; OPCW Doc. C-25/NAT.103 (France), 20 April 2021, p. 2; OPCW Doc. C-25/NAT.123 (Estonia), 20 April 2021, p. 1; OPCW Doc. EC-97/NAT.34 (Czech Republic), 6 July 2021, p. 1; OPCW Doc. EC-97/NAT.55 (Spain), 6 July 2021, p. 2; UN Doc. S/PV.8872, 4 October 2021 (UK), p. 13; OPCW Doc. EC-98/NAT.14 (Austria), 5 October 2021, p. 1; OPCW Doc. EC-98/NAT.16 (Lithuania), 5 October 2021, p. 2; UN Doc. S/PV.8921, 8 December 2021, pp. 6 (US), 8 (Norway), 9 (Estonia); UN Doc. S/PV.8982, 28 February 2022, p. 9 (Albania); OPCW Doc. EC-99/NAT.13 (Germany), 8 March 2022, p. 2; OPCW Doc. EC-99/NAT.18 (Sweden), 8 March 2022, p. 1; OPCW Doc. EC-99/NAT.26 (Czech), 8 March 2022, p. 2; UN Doc. S/PV.8990, 10 March 2022, p. 7 (Albania); OPCW

did not cooperate with, and provide access to, the OPCW IIT as required by United Nations Security Council resolution 2118 (2013)."[426]

(4) **Evaluation**

(a) **Potential References**

Fortunately, the international community never heard of investigations of alleged use of chemical weapons by a State between the OPCW's inauguration in 1997 and March 2013, because there were no such allegations in that period. One should thus go back to the investigations between the late 1970s and the early 1990s for potential references:

- In the early 1980s, the USSR and Viet Nam were criticized for using toxic chemicals in Afghanistan and against Cambodia in the late 1970s and early 1980s, respectively.[427] In response, the UN General Assembly introduced *ad hoc* investigation procedures for alleged use of chemical weapons, based on which the group of experts investigated these allegations, albeit without reaching definitive conclusions due to lack of cooperation by the concerned States.[428]
- During the Iran-Iraq war of the 1980s, Iraq used chemical weapons against Iran. Despite the former's categorical denial of same, investigation missions dispatched by the UN Secretary-General in exercise of his good-office function upon the latter's request confirmed the use of chemical weapons[429] and identified Iraqi forces as perpetrators.[430] The Security Council deliberated on these findings and took action in response.[431]
- In 1992, Mozambique and Armenia requested that the UN Secretary-General investigate alleged use of chemical weapons in accordance with UN General

Doc. EC-100/NAT.17 (Norway), 5 July 2022, p. 2; OPCW Doc. EC-100/NAT.24 (Germany), 5 July 2022, p. 2; UN Doc. S/PV.9141, 29 September 2022, p. 6 (Albania); UN Doc. S/PV.9164, 25 October 2022, p. 7 (Albania).

426 OPCW Doc. EC-94/DEC.2, 9 July 2020, operative para. 3; OPCW Doc. C-25/DEC.9, 21 April 2021, operative para. 6.

427 UN Doc. A/39/113, 22 February 1984, p. 2.

428 UN Doc. A/37/259, 1 December 1982, pp. 48–50.

429 UN Doc. S/16433, 26 March 1984, pp. 11–12, para. 35; UN Doc. S/17127, 24 April 1985, p. 4, paras. 1–4; UN Doc. S/17911, 12 March 1986, p. 18, para. 57; UN Doc. S/18852, 8 May 1987, p. 18, para. 65; UN Doc. S/19823, 25 April 1988, pp. 17–18, para. 54; UN Doc. S/20060, 20 July 1988, pp. 15–16, para. 46; UN Doc. S/20063, 25 July 1988, pp. 11–12, para. 32; UN Doc. S/20134, 19 August 1988, p. 11, para. 23.

430 UN Doc. S/17911, 12 March 1986, p. 18, para. 58; UN Doc. S/18852, 8 May 1987, pp. 18–19, para. 66; UN Doc. S/20060, 20 July 1988, p. 15, para. 46(d); UN Doc. S/20134, 19 August 1988, p. 11, para. 23(c). Iraq insisted that it "has not used" chemical weapons (UN Doc. S/16438, 27 March 1984).

431 UN Doc. S/16454, 30 March 1984, pp. 1–2; UN Doc. S/17130, 25 April 1985, pp. 1–2; UN Doc. S/17932, 21 March 1986, pp. 1–2; UN Doc. S/18863, 14 May 1987, pp. 1–2; UN Doc. S/RES/598 (1987), 20 July 1987; UN Doc. S/RES/612 (1988), 9 May 1988; UN Doc. S/RES/620 (1998), 26 August 1988.

Assembly Resolution 42/37C.[432] While the missions were dispatched, they were unable to reach definitive conclusions in either case.[433]

These cases suggest that affirmative conclusions of fact-finding organs provide the UN Security Council with bases on which to act.

(b) **Effectiveness**

The most significant achievement of the relevant fact-finding organs is their very findings of fact. They confirmed that chemical weapons were used many times and in many places in Syria, and that the Syrian government and ISIL were involved. In the author's view, their effectiveness depends on several factors.

First, the availability of feasible or necessary procedures supported by technical expertise is the precondition. In this regard, there has been a "procedures gap" from the outset. All fact-finding organs but the UN Mission were newly established during the ongoing non-international armed conflict in Syria. The OPCW FFM was created by the OPCW Director-General in late April 2014 in a situation where no State Party requested the existing on-site inspections under the CWC, implying that these inspections seemed infeasible during the aforementioned armed conflict. The OPCW-UN JIM and the OPCW IIT were tasked with identifying perpetrators, meaning that the CWC did not include attribution mechanisms. It has been pointed out that "the design of the Chemical Weapons Convention with respect to reactions in the event of non-compliance mainly reflects an inter-state logic."[434] The OPCW-UN JIM was established by the UN Security Council in August 2015, but terminated in November 2017 by Russian veto. The "attribution mechanism gap" was then filled by the creation of the OPCW IIT in 2018,[435] through the implementation of a majority decision of the OPCW Conference of the States Parties.

Second, political support has a significant impact on fact-finding organs. Those organs with broad political support tend to carry out their investigations in a relatively smooth manner, while those organs which encounter opposition are likely to experience difficulty in fulfilling their mandates. The UN Mission received almost universal support from its beginnings, and the OPCW FFM and the OPCW-UN JIM also enjoyed general support at least until mid-2016. While the latter have been criticized by Syria, Russia, and Iran, they did not complain about legitimacy. Such absence of objection was key to the activation of the existing mechanism, i.e., the UN Mission, and the establishment of the new mechanisms, i.e., the OPCW FFM and the OPCW-UN JIM. By contrast, the COI and the OPCW IIT have faced strong opposition from several States including Syria and Russia, causing them difficulties in carrying out their functions. The opposing States argued that these organs are outside

[432] UN Doc. S/24065, 12 June 1992, p. 1, para. 1; UN Doc. S/24344, 24 July 1992, p. 1, para. 3.

[433] UN Doc. S/24065, 12 June 1992, p. 11, para. 36; UN Doc. S/24344, 24 July 1992, p. 8, para. 24.

[434] Sossai, *supra* note 84, p. 227.

[435] While the COI continues to investigate international humanitarian law and identifying perpetrators, its findings have had negligible impact on the most appropriate policy-making organs such as the UN Security Council and the OPCW Executive Council.

the scope of the constitutive documents of the instituting organizations. And while no procedural errors occurred, and a majority decision or resolution might be pragmatic among States with differing views, this runs the risk of weakening the legitimacy of the resulting fact-finding organs. It is thus important to explore consensus decisions to the extent practicable.

Third, independent, objective, impartial and professional investigation upholds the authority of fact-finding organs. It is expected that States will accept the findings of fact-finding organs conducting investigation in these manners. While States agreed on the guiding principles for fact-finding organs activities, they diverge on specific methodological and operational matters, as indicated above. The appointment and composition of investigation teams is critical to their objectivity. If a team member is under the influence of others, including particular States, the fact-finding organ's reliability comes into question. Such matters are left to the relevant "mandating authorities," and as mentioned before, no State raised the issue of the independence of fact-finding organs before early 2017. When Russia and Iran tabled proposals on the matter between April 2017 and April 2018, they encountered strong objections, primarily because they were meant to undermine the very independence of the fact-finding organs. This signifies how the US, the UK, EU Member States and others on the one hand differ from Russia and Syria on the other regarding objectivity and impartiality, as seen in such aspects as the aforementioned on-site visits, chain of custody, open-source materials, standards of proof, and selection of witnesses. Russia and Syria have insisted on strict methodologies and operations and criticized the OPCW FFM, the OPCW-UN JIM, and the OPCW IIT in particular for failing to meet relevant requirements and standard, treating such complaints as a basis for rejecting their findings. By contrast, the US, the UK, EU member States, and others have extended full support to these fact-finding organs, accepting relatively flexible methodologies and operations on their part. This political divide has thus kept the fact-finding organs from functioning effectively. In the author's view, a primary factor in this divide lies in the ongoing armed conflict in Syria itself. Sites of alleged chemical weapons use are at the heart of the battlefield. Safety and security should accordingly be prerequisites for any investigations. It is thus understandable that the OPCW FFM and the OPCW-UN JIM decided in many instances not to visit such sites. Perhaps there should be examinations of general understanding on acceptable methodologies and operations for fact-finding missions during armed conflict without undermining objectivity and impartiality. Turning to professionalism, technical expertise in particular sampling and analysis contributes significantly to fact-finding missions by offering scientific assessments of collected information. The UN Mission and the OPCW FFM have benefitted from the OPCW-designated laboratories network, relying extensively on the result of the latter's off-site analysis of samples.

Fourth, the cooperation of Syria is indispensable for the functioning of the fact-finding organs. Syria and the fact-finding organs have asymmetric relations, in that the latter need the former's cooperation to carry out their missions, especially on-site visits. As mentioned, Syria has cooperated with the OPCW FFM and the OPCW-UN JIM, allowing them into its territory and providing unfettered access to sites and persons subject to security conditions. UN Security Council Resolution 2235 clarified the scope of Syria's obligation to cooperate with the OPCW and the UN under UN Security Council Resolution 2118, which includes the obligation to cooperate with these fact-finding organs. While Syria has complained about the methodologies and operations of these organs, it has continued to accept their investigations on its territory, and the fact-finding organs will be able to fulfill their mandates so long as Syria does so. By contrast, it took more than four months to for Syria and the UN to finalize negotiations on modalities of the UN Mission. Syria has also refused the COI and the OPCW IIT permission to enter its territory, because, according to Syria, their functions were outside the mandates of the UNHRC and the OPCW, respectively. Moreover, Syria's refusal to allow the OPCW IIT in its territory is a clear violation of Syrian obligations under UN Security Council Resolution 2118 and the CWC. The fact that these fact-finding organs were established without Syrian consent is offset, however, by this objection by Syria to their legitimacy. This confrontational attitude is an obstacle to ensuring the effective functioning of the fact-finding organs.

(c) **Implications**

The fact-finding organs have proved to be its effectiveness and will thus continue to contribute to addressing potential non-compliance with the obligation not to use chemical weapons. Irrespective of their mandates to determine whether chemical weapons were used or identify perpetrators, these organs investigate and produce reports on their findings, which serve as the basis for the policy-making organs to make assessments and take action. The fact-finding organs thus play an important role in controlling potential non-compliance issues. In this regard, there are two challenges to be addressed in the contemporary information and communication technology (ICT) era.

The first challenge is the shift from whether chemical weapons are used to who are the perpetrators. In many instances during the non-international armed conflict in Syria, both parties have criticized each other for using chemical weapons, and even disseminated allegations the world over via social media. If both parties do not deny the fact that chemical weapons were used, then it would be quite natural that the fact-finding organ reaches an affirmative conclusion. Perhaps in some cases, the affirmative conclusion is highly plausible. As such, attribution mechanisms become more important, as identifying perpetrators may contribute to discouraging repeated chemical weapons use. The second challenge is the need for more careful examination of facts. The aforementioned dissemination of information via social media is a useful and, in some case, even effective means to attract the attention of and make an impression on the international community. It is not only States or governments but also non-State actors including opposition groups, terrorists, and even individuals that benefit from rapid developments in ICT. In the present context, both parties to the non-international armed conflict in Syria are technically and instantly able to manipulate information. This is one of the main issues between the US, the UK, and the EU on the one hand, and Russia and Syria on the other. The fact-finding organs are thus required to collect more reliable evidence on which to base their conclusions.

At the same time, contemporary fact-finding has some limitations. First, there is room for doubt whether the findings of fact-finding organs will enjoy universal acceptance. While it may be easier for fact-finding organs to commence investigations because contemporary fact-finding in principle does not require the consent of States being investigated, this flexibility may be discounted by possible objections by concerned States to findings of fact. It is also doubtful whether fact-finding organs prevent further use of chemical weapons. These have been used frequently in Syria despite confirmation of their use and identification of perpetrators. While one could argue that the drastic reduction in allegations since mid-2018 is a point in this assertion's favor, it is unclear whether fact-finding organs caused this development. It is highly likely that the Assad regime's military victory over Syrian opposition groups will not require further use of chemical weapons.

Perhaps contemporary fact-finding is, by its nature, presumed to play a limited role in resolving the issue. Its mandates extend only to finding of facts, identification of perpetrators, and reporting to relevant policy-making organs for consideration. Additional measures are required.

3.3.3 *Responding to Non-compliance*

(1) **Background**

As described above, fact-finding organs have ascertained the use of chemical weapons in Syria and even identified perpetrators. The international community is unanimous in the opinion that such use violates international law, and that those involved in such use should be held accountable. The next step is thus how to respond to such non-compliance with the prohibition again chemical weapons use. Any response to non-compliance is necessarily *ex post*.

Generally speaking, non-compliance with the obligation of omission would be addressed under the general international law of State responsibility. A responsible State is obliged to take remedies for an injured State. However, non-international armed conflict requires additional consideration. Since the obligation not to use chemical weapons in non-international armed conflict is non-reciprocal, there are no injured State, in the classical sense, rendering ineffective traditional such reparations as restitution in kind, compensation, or satisfaction. Against this backdrop, the most straightforward way to respond to chemical weapons use would be collective measures by OPCW and UN policy-making organs. Practice shows that they have taken various possible measures. In this regard, consensus should be pursued in arriving at decisions or resolutions, as doing so makes same more conducive to being generally observed. While rulings may also be arrived at by majority vote, difficulties may arise in their implementation. If policy-making organs are unable to decide necessary measures, for whatever reason, then interested States may take unilateral and, in some cases, controversial actions.

(2) Institutional Mechanisms to Respond to Non-compliance

(a) Mandates of International Organizations

Available policy-making organs and their mandates vary depending on the situation. Regarding the use of chemical weapons in Syria before and on 21 August 2013, the UN Security Council fulfilled its primary responsibility for maintaining international peace and security in response to non-compliance with the obligation not to use chemical weapons under customary international law, in close cooperation with the OPCW Executive Council. As the attack in question took place on 21 August 2013, that is, before the CWC entered into force for Syria, or Syria's provisional application thereto, the actions of the OPCW Executive Council cannot be regarded as those in response non-compliance with obligations under the CWC. On the contrary, the OPCW policy-making organs, the Executive Council and the Conference of the States Parties, and the UN Security Council treat further chemical attacks after April 2014 as constituting non-compliance with the aforementioned obligations under the CWC and UN Security Council Resolution 2118. The Executive Council and the Conference of the States Parties have mandates to consider non-compliance in accordance with operative relevant CWC provisions,[436] while the Security Council has its primary responsibility for maintaining international peace and security, as mentioned, and a special mandate to impose measures under Chapter VII "in the event of non-compliance with this resolution, including unauthorized transfer of chemical weapons, or *any use of chemical weapons* by anyone in the Syrian Arab Republic" (emphasis added) in accordance with operative para. 21 of Resolution 2118,[437] though there has been a lack of follow-through despite allegations of further chemical attacks.[438] The UNHRC also assumes mandates regarding

[436] Article VIII, paras 35 and 36 and Article XII.

[437] UN Doc. S/RES/2118 (2013), 27 September 2013, operative para. 21. This reference implied the use of force based on the UN Security Council authorization (Peter van Ham, Sico van der Meer and Malik Ellahi, *Chemical Weapons Challenges Ahead: The Past and Future of the OPCW—With a Case Study on Syria*, Clingendael Report (2017), https://www.clingendael.org/sites/default/files/pdf/Clingendael_Report_Chemical_Weapons_Challenges_Ahead_2017.pdf, accessed 22 April 2023, p. 31. It is extremely rare that the Security Council commits itself to future acts under a specific Chapter of the UN Charter Marie Jacobsson, "Syria and the Issue of Chemical Weapons: A Snapshot of a Legal Time-frame: the United Nations Security Council Resolution 2118 (2013) and the OPCW Executive Council Decision," in Jonas Ebbesson et al (eds.), *International Law and Changing Perceptions of Security: liber amicorum Said Mahmoudi* (Brill Nijhoff, 2014), p. 134, p. 149). This formulation is thus a strong signal by the Security Council to the parties to the conflict in Syria that they are compelled to act in accordance with Resolution 2118. See also UN Doc. S/RES/2209 (2015), 6 March 2015, operative para. 7; UN Doc. S/RES/2235 (2015), 7 August 2015, operative para. 15; UN Doc. S/RES/2314 (2016), 31 October 2016, operative para. 2; UN Doc. S/RES/2319 (2016), 17 November 2016, operative para. 3.

[438] Yasmine Nahlawi, *The Responsibility to Protect in Libya and Syria: Mass Atrocities, Human Protection, and International Law* (Routledge 2020), p. 133, p. 135.

human rights and international humanitarian law, which undoubtedly cover chemical weapons use.

(b) Syrian Obligations

Should the UN Security Council take legally binding action against Syria, Syria will perforce be obliged by same. Otherwise, Syria will face at most demands for specific responses. While the aforementioned traditional forms of reparation, such as restitution in kind, compensation, or satisfaction, may be unfeasible for non-compliance with the non-reciprocal prohibition against chemical weapons use in non-international armed conflict, Syria nonetheless remains obliged by said prohibition.

(c) Implementation: Response to Use

(i) Elimination

Breakthrough

The following skeptical remarks by US Secretary of State John Kerry on 9 September 2013. provided an unexpected breakthrough in avoiding unilateral military action in response to the alleged use of chemical weapons in East Ghouta on 21 August 2013, opening the door instead to international efforts to eliminate the Syrian chemical weapons program: "Sure. He [Assad] could turn over every single bit of his chemical weapons to the international community in the next week. Turn it over, all of it, without delay, and allow a full and total accounting for that. But he isn't about to do it, and it can't be done, obviously."[439]

In an immediate response, Russian Foreign Minister Sergey Lavrov called on Syria "not only to allow their chemical weapons storage places to fall under international control, but also to their further destruction, as well as to accede to the Organisation for the Prohibition of Chemical Weapons in full."[440] This appeal led to Syrian Foreign Minister Walid Al-Muallem's declaration that "the Syrian Arab Republic welcomes Russia's initiative, on the basis that the Syrian leadership cares about the lives of our citizens and the security in our country."[441] He also mentioned the Syrian government's confidence in "the wisdom of the Russian government, which is trying

[439] Remarks, John Kerry, Secretary of State, United Kingdom Foreign and Commonwealth Office, London, United Kingdom, 9 September 2013, https://2009-2017.state.gov/secretary/remarks/2013/09/213956.htm, accessed 22 April 2023.

[440] Press statement by Russian Foreign Minister Sergey Lavrov regarding the Syrian chemical weapons situation, Moscow, 9 September 2013, https://www.mid.ru/en/web/guest/foreign_policy/international_safety/conflicts/-/asset_publisher/xIEMTQ3OvzcA/content/id/97430, accessed 22 April 2023.

[441] CNN, Obama: Russia proposal for Syria 'positive development'—if it's real, 9 September 2013, https://edition.cnn.com/2013/09/09/politics/syria-kerry/index.html, accessed 22 April 2023; Los Angeles Times, John Kerry's me-and-my-big-mouth solution on Syria, https://www.latimes.com/opinion/la-xpm-2013-sep-09-la-ol-kerry-syria-russia-turn-over-chemical-weapons-20130909-story.html, accessed 21 January 2023.

to prevent an American aggression against our people."[442] That moment crystalized the movement to eliminate Syrian chemical weapons, even as the UN Mission continued its investigation.

On 10 September 2013, France, having recognized this development, tabled a draft UN Security Council resolution under Chapter VII on placing the Syrian chemical weapons stockpile under international control.[443] It encompassed actions for Syria to carry out, including eliminating all chemical and biological weapons programs under international supervision (operative para. 6), submitting declarations to the UN Secretary-General (operative para. 7), providing immediate, unconditional and unrestricted access (operative para. 9), and requesting the UN Mission to submit monthly reports (operative para. 11). It appeared that France preferred putting the UN at the center of these efforts, with the OPCW providing support as necessary. However, as this draft included several paragraphs singling out "the Syrian authorities" as the perpetrators and imposing sanctions thereon,[444] Russia and Syria were bound to reject it.

US-Russia Joint National Paper

On 14 September 2013, after three days of negotiations, Russia and the US released a joint national paper, titled "Framework for Elimination of Syrian Chemical Weapons,"[445] which incorporated "their joint determination to ensure the destruction of the Syrian chemical weapons program (CW) in the soonest and safest manner." For this purpose, they expressed their intention to submit a draft OPCW Executive Council decision, which would be backed up by UN Security Council resolution.[446]

---

[442] CNN, Obama: Russia proposal for Syria 'positive development'—if it's real, 9 September 2013, https://edition.cnn.com/2013/09/09/politics/syria-kerry/index.html, accessed 22 April 2023; Los Angeles Times, John Kerry's me-and-my-big-mouth solution on Syria, https://www.latimes.com/opinion/la-xpm-2013-sep-09-la-ol-kerry-syria-russia-turn-over-chemical-weapons-20130909-story.html, accessed 21 January 2023.

[443] Chicago Tribune, French U.N. Security Council draft on Syria chemical weapons, 10 September 2013, https://www.chicagotribune.com/news/ct-xpm-2013-09-10-sns-rt-us-syria-crisis-un-draft-text-20130910-story.html, accessed 22 April 2023; The Telegraph, The full text of the French UN resolution on Syria, 11 September 2013, http://www.telegraph.co.uk/news/worldnews/middleeast/syria/10301732/The-full-text-of-the-French-UN-resolution-on-Syria.html, accessed 21 January 2023.

[444] Relevant paragraphs included the affirmation and condemnation of the use of chemical weapons by the Syrian authorities (preamble para. 4, operative para. 1), the affirmation of the use of chemical weapons by the Syrian authorities (preamble para. 4), the demand for the immediate cessation of the use of chemical weapons by the Syrian authorities (operative para. 3), the prohibition of trade related chemical and biological weapons with Syria (operative para. 12), the travel ban and asset freeze against individuals (operative para. 14), and the referral of the situation in Syria subsequent to March 2011 to the Office of the Prosecutor (OTP) of the International Criminal Court (ICC) (operative para. 15).

[445] OPCW Doc. EC-M-33/NAT.1, 17 September 2013; UN Doc. S/2013/565, 24 September 2013.

[446] It has been argued that "[a] decision of the Executive Council of the OPCW and a resolution of the UN Security Council would be used in the implementation of this agreement" (Mika Hayashi, "Benefits of a Legally Non-Binding Agreement: The Case of the 2013 US-Russian Agreement on the Elimination of Syrian Chemical Weapons," *International Community Law Review*, Vol. 20,

In this regard, Annex A of the document identified principles for a draft OPCW Executive Council decision, covering the following: scope, specific timelines including a deadline of "the first half of 2014" for complete elimination of Syrian chemical weapons, unprecedented use of CWC procedures, verification and monitoring, destruction of Syrian chemical weapons including the possibility of removing said weapons from Syria for destruction, and consequences.[447] Annex B also addressed a "Joint Framework on Destruction of Syrian CW," further highlighting the scope and timelines for said destruction of Syrian chemical weapons.

This paper has a unique status, in that it is a political instrument, rather than a legally binding document.[448] And it has been argued that being non-binding, it enjoyed two benefits that a formal treaty would have lacked. First, it enabled the US and Russia to reach agreement rapidly. The formal procedures and requirements for concluding a treaty "would have served very little purpose"[449] when dealing with such an urgent matter. Second, it established actions to be taken by a third party, in this case, Syria. For instance, Syria was expected to submit comprehensive data within a week of the date the document was issued. Syria must also provide the OPCW, the UN, and other supported personnel with the immediate and unfettered right to inspect any and all sites. A commentator, having mentioned the *pacta tertiis* rule of the law of treaties under which no third party is obliged by a treaty unless it expressly accepts said obligation in writing, stressed that "this agreement does something that a treaty technically could not do."[450] In the author's view, whether a document can establish such a legally binding obligation of a third party is one thing; whether it can include actions to be taken by the third party is another. On the one hand, as it has been established that the US-Russian joint national paper is not a legally binding document, it cannot establish a legally binding obligation of a third party. The *pacta tertiis* rule is thus irrelevant. On the other hand, it can include actions to be taken by said third party, because there is no restriction on what may be included in any document, regardless of legal status, except for treaty clauses against *jus cogens*. The problem, rather, is that such inclusions per se are no guarantee

Issue 2 (2018), p. 252, p. 257). In the author's view, the language "the implementation of this agreement" could be misleading, because the joint national paper envisaged actions being taken by such third parties such as Syria, the OPCW, and the UN, as it was technically impossible to "implement" the actions without the consent of said third parties, irrespective of the paper's legal status. As the Russian Foreign Minister indicated, the US-Russian agreement needed to be actuated in a formal document (US Department of State, Remarks With Russian Foreign Minister Sergey Lavrov After Their Meeting, 14 September 2013, https://2009-2017.state.gov/secretary/remarks/2013/09/214250.htm, accessed 22 April 2023 ("And we proposing—making our proposals, we are intent, with our American colleagues, to work jointly, especially in the framework of the Executive Committee of the OPCW, where we—and with other members of this organ—have to translate this document with any dual—possible interpretations, logical—legal form, legal language")).

[447] US Department of State, Remarks With Russian Foreign Minister Sergey Lavrov After Their Meeting, 14 September 2013, https://2009-2017.state.gov/secretary/remarks/2013/09/214250.htm, accessed 22 April 2023.

[448] Hayashi, *supra* note 446, p. 261.

[449] *Ibid.*, p. 262.

[450] Article 35, VCLT.

that said actions will in fact be taken. Notwithstanding, there was no mistaking the practical message:[451] politically, Syria must act in accord with this agreement. This strongly suggests that these two powers actually controlled the fate of the Middle Eastern State.

Report of the UN Mission

Meanwhile, on 16 September 2013, the UN Mission published its report, in which it concluded that "chemical weapons have been used in the ongoing conflict between the parties in the Syrian Arab Republic, also against civilians, including children, on a relatively large scale."[452] As mentioned elsewhere, this was the first time in more than twenty years that an international independent investigating body had established such chemical weapons use.

Resolution 2118 Regime

On 27 September 2013, the OPCW Executive Council, at its thirty-third meeting in the Hague, having recognized "the extraordinary character of the situation posed by Syrian chemical weapons,"[453] adopted Decision EC-M-33/DEC.1. In New York that same day, the UN Security Council adopted Resolution 2118, endorsing Decision EC-M-33/DEC.1,[454] and incorporating same as its Annex I (the Resolution 2118 Regime). The primary purpose of the Resolution 2118 Regime was to establish a framework to achieve the elimination of Syrian chemical weapons in the most rapid and safe manner in response to Syrian use of chemical weapons, which constituted a violation of international law.

It should be duly noted that both Decision EC-M-33/DEC.1 and Resolution 2118 referred to the aforementioned UN Mission report on the alleged use of chemical weapons in Syria on 21 August 2013,[455] clearly indicating that even though the US and Russia had reached the aforementioned bilateral agreement before the publication of the UN Mission report, the OPCW Executive Council and the UN Security Council kept their efforts to eliminate Syrian chemical weapons on a solid footing by relying on the objective findings of this third international impartial fact-finding mission.[456]

---

[451] Hayashi, *supra* note 446, p. 263.

[452] UN Doc. A/67/997–S/2013/553, 16 September 2013, p. 8, para. 27.

[453] OPCW Doc. EC-M-33/DEC.1, 27 September 2013, preamble para 9. See also *ibid.*, operative para. 3(d).

[454] UN Doc. S/RES/2118 (2013), 27 September 2013, preamble para 11. and operative para. 3.

[455] OPCW Doc. EC-M-33/DEC.1, 27 September 2013, preamble para. 3; UN Doc. S/RES/2118 (2013), 27 September 2013, preamble para. 7.

[456] The UN General Assembly also cited the UN Mission report in its resolutions (UN Doc. A/RES/68/45, 5 December 2013, preamble para. 4; UN Doc. A/RES/68/182, 18 December 2013, preamble para. 9, and operative para. 1. This is understandable because, as previously mentioned, the UN Mission was established based on UN General Assembly Resolution 42/37C. Thus, it was required to submit its report through the UN Secretary-General to the UN General Assembly, as the UN missions in Azerbaijan and Mozambique had also done (UN Doc. A/24065, 12 June 1992; UN Doc. A/24344, 24 July 1992).

The Resolution 2118 Regime created a division of roles between the OPCW Executive Council and the UN Security Council.[457] For its part, the Executive Council made the list of specific requirements for Syria to fulfill including the aforementioned rapid submission of information and initial declaration, elimination of all chemical weapons materials and equipment by a given deadline, destruction of chemical weapons production and mixing/filling equipment by other given deadlines, cooperation with all aspects of the implementation of the decision, and designation of a contact point with authority to ensure the decision's full implementation.[458] On the other hand, the Security Council made the necessary arrangements for said implementation, making the abovementioned requirements binding on Syria with reference to Article 25 of the UN Charter in Resolution 2118.[459] The authorization to transfer Syrian chemical weapons to other States Parties addressed legal obstacles posed by the CWC so that the chemical weapons could be destroyed outside Syria.[460] The Security Council also decided full cooperation with the OPCW and the UN, including the provision of immediate and unfettered access to any sites and those individuals who are believed to be of importance to the OPCW mandate, as well as the same degree of cooperation by "all parties in Syria."[461] The Resolution 2118 Regime included other measures related to the elimination of Syrian chemical weapons, including OPCW and UN monitoring, which will be discussed in detail in Chapter 4.

The launching of international efforts to eliminate Syrian chemical weapons is a unique measure in response to the use of chemical weapons. It can be understood in different ways. At one end of the spectrum, the US, the UK, and France would take the position that imposing on Syria the obligation to eliminate its chemical

---

[457] This indicates that it would have been difficult for Syrian chemical weapons to be eliminated within the regular CWC legal framework (Karim Makdisi and Coralie Pison Hindawi, "The Syrian Chemical Weapons Disarmament Process in Context: Narratives of Coercion, Consent, and Everything in Between," *Third World Quarterly*, Vol. 38, Issue 8 (2017), p. 1691, p. 1702).

[458] OPCW Doc. EC-M-33/DEC.1, 27 September 2013, operative para. 1. The OPCW Executive Council added a reporting requirement at a later stage (OPCW Doc. EC-M-34/DEC.1, 15 November 2013, operative para. 19). The term "elimination" was used so as to allow the Syrian chemical weapons to be destroyed outside Syrian territory irrespective of the CWC provisions requiring such destruction to take place in the territory of the possessor State (Jacobsson, *supra* note 437, pp. 141–142).

[459] UN Doc. S/RES/2118 (2013), 27 September 2013, preamble para. 14. See also UN Doc. S/PV.7038, 27 September 2013, pp. 5 (US), 6 (UK), 6 (Luxembourg), 8 (Azerbaijan), 9 (Republic of Korea), 13 (Argentina), 15 (Australia).

This is a rare instance of the Security Council eschewing the formulation "acting under Chapter VII," and instead referring only to Article 25 of the UN Charter to make the measures binding (Tatsuya Abe, "Effectiveness of the Institutional Approach to An Alleged Violation of International law: The Case of Syrian Chemical Weapons," *Japanese Yearbook of International Law*, Vol. 57 (2014), p. 333, pp. 358–359). Omitting this language ensured that this resolution would not imply a use of force authorization. See UN Doc. S/PV.7038, 27 September 2013, p. 4 (Russia); Jacobsson, *supra* note 437, p. 148; John R. Crook, "United States Threatens Military Strikes Against Syria, Then Joins in Diplomatic Efforts to Control Syrian Chemical Weapon," *American Journal of International Law*, Vol. 107, No. 4 (2013), p. 900, p. 905.

[460] UN Doc. S/RES/2118 (2013), 27 September 2013, operative para. 10.

[461] *Ibid.*, operative para. 7.

weapons is a kind of punishment of or sanction against Syria because they believe that the Assad regime used sarin which was exactly the same chemicals whose precursors Syria declared. At the other end of the spectrum, Russia and Syria would maintain the position that there is no direct link between said use and elimination, because it was not the Assad regime that used chemical weapons, but someone else. Notwithstanding, Syria agreed to the international efforts to eliminate its chemical weapons because it would be preferable to unilateral military action by the US and its allies.

The Resolution 2118 Regime offered no clue as to how to understand the relation between the use and the elimination. In the author's view, the entire Regime should be regarded as sanctions against Syria. It is true that the Regime does not include prototype elements of non-military sanctions such as arms embargos, asset freezes, or travel bans,[462] that Syria was not singled out as the perpetrator of the chemical attacks, and that Syria even accepted Russia's proposal to rapidly place its chemical weapons under international control.[463] However, it is also true that Syria was unable to prevent use of chemical weapons in its territory, whether by the Assad regime or another party to the ongoing non-international armed conflict there. What matters is what the resolution establishes.[464] The Resolution 2118 Regime specified measures in response to use of chemical weapons in Syria, including imposing on Syria the obligation to eliminate and prohibit same. Certainly, Syria agreed to the Russian proposal. Politically, it had no other option.

(ii) **Statements**

The relevant policy-making organs made statements on chemical weapons use, thereby committing themselves to respond to non-compliance under international law. The most important such statements were the legal assessments.

Some statements focused on chemical weapons use in Syria. The Security Council was "[d]eeply outraged by the use of chemical weapons on 21 August 2013 in Rif Damascus, as concluded in the Mission's report," "condemn[ed] the killing of civilians that resulted from it,"[465] "[d]etermin[ed] that the use of chemical weapons in the Syrian Arab Republic constitutes a threat to international peace and security,"[466] and "[c]ondemns in the strongest terms any use of chemical weapons in the Syrian Arab Republic, in particular the attack on 21 August 2013, in violation of international law."[467] The UN General Assembly and UNHRC also "strongly condemn[ed] the use

---

[462] Jacobsson, *supra* note 437, p. 147.

[463] CNN, Obama: Russia proposal for Syria "positive development"—if it's real, 9 September 2013, https://edition.cnn.com/2013/09/09/politics/syria-kerry/index.html, accessed 22 April 2023; Los Angeles Times, John Kerry's me-and-my-big-mouth solution on Syria, https://www.latimes.com/opinion/la-xpm-2013-sep-09-la-ol-kerry-syria-russia-turn-over-chemical-weapons-20130909-story.html, accessed 21 January 2023; UN Doc. A/68/PV.21, 30 September 2013, p. 10 (Syria).

[464] Jacobsson, *supra* note 437, p. 143.

[465] UN Doc. S/RES/2118 (2013), 27 September 2013, preamble para 8.

[466] *Ibid.*, preamble para 13.

[467] *Ibid.*, operative para 2.

of chemical weapons in the Syrian Arab Republic, which is prohibited under international law, amounts to a serious crime and has a devastating impact on civilians."[468] The relevant policy-making organs thus entered the stage where they were required to respond to non-compliance with the obligation under international law. Other texts addressed use of chemical weapons more generally. The OPCW Executive Council condemned "in the strongest possible terms the use of chemical weapons."[469] The UN General Assembly also condemned "in the strongest possible terms the use of chemical weapons"[470] and affirmed that "the use of chemical weapons constitutes a serious violation of international law."[471] The UN Security Council further affirmed that "the use of chemical weapons constitutes a serious violation of international law."[472] In any way, the finding that international law was violated has implications, offering strong evidence for the existence of customary international law on the prohibition of chemical weapons use in non-international armed conflict, as discussed above.[473]

The Security Council also declared that "the use of chemical weapons anywhere constitutes a threat to international peace and security."[474] For the first time, the use of chemical weapons, a category of weapons of mass destruction (WMD), was qualified as a threat to peace within the meaning of Article 39 of the UN Charter. And while this was "no more than an abstract statement that requires a concrete determination in each and every case to be put into effect so that the Council may actually resort to Chapter VII measures,"[475] such a finding itself clearly indicates that the UN Security Council is ready to consider such measures in response to future chemical weapons use.[476] Luxembourg stated that "[this determination] authorizes the Council to be seized automatically of the issue [of the use of chemical weapons] in future."[477] France argued that "[t]he Security Council can therefore act on this issue at any time in the future and will be the guarantor of chemical disarmament."[478] Morocco pointed out that "[this determination] will make it easier for the Security Council to deal with such weapons in the future."[479] Australia said that "[t]he statement should

468 UN Doc. A/HRC/RES/24/22, 27 September 2013, operative para. 6; UN Doc. A/RES/68/182, 18 December 2013, operative para. 1. See also UN Doc. A/RES/68/182, 18 December 2013, preamble para. 9.

469 OPCW Doc. EC-M-33/DEC.1, 27 September 2013, preamble para 4.

470 UN Doc. A/RES/68/45, 5 December 2013, preamble para. 5.

471 UN Doc. A/RES/68/182, 18 December 2013, preamble para. 9.

472 UN Doc. S/RES/2118 (2013), 27 September 2013, preamble para 8.

473 Asada, *supra* note 21, pp. 201–202.

474 UN Doc. S/RES/2118 (2013), 27 September 2013, operative para 1.

475 Asada, *supra* note 21, p. 200.

476 Abe, *supra* note 459, p. 353.

477 UN Doc. S/PV.7038, 27 September 2013, p. 6 (Luxembourg).

478 *Ibid.*, p. 7 (France).

479 *Ibid.*, p. 12 (Morocco).

act as a strong deterrent to anyone who might contemplate using chemical weapons in the future."[480]

(iii) **Accountability**

The relevant policy-making organs also addressed the accountability issue, which is also closely related to the use of chemical weapons, again both in Syria and more generally.

The UN Security Council "[e]xpresses its strong conviction that those individuals responsible for the use of chemical weapons in the Syrian Arab Republic should be held accountable,"[481] though no measures in this regard were incorporated, including referrals to the ICC.[482] As indicated above, there was a difference of opinion between the US, the UK, and France on the one hand, and Syria and Russia on the other, over who the perpetrators were, making it practically impossible for the Security Council to enact further measures in this regard. Such lack of identification of perpetrators may have actually enabled the Resolution 2118 Regime. The General Assembly instead indirectly mentioned the attribution of chemical weapons use to the Syrian government in its resolution, noting Resolution 7667 of the Ministerial Council of the League of Arab States, the text of the final communiqué of its Annual Coordination Meeting of the Ministers of Foreign Affairs of 27 September 2013,[483] and the report of the UN mission "which provides clear evidence that surface-to-surface rockets were fired on 21 August from Government-held territory into opposition areas, using professionally made munitions containing sarin."[484] Logically, there must be attribution before there can be accountability, making attribution mechanisms a critical concern going forward.

Both the UN Security Council and General Assembly also took the general approach to the accountability issue, "stressing that those responsible for any use of chemical weapons must be held accountable."[485] The US expressed the view that "[t]hose responsible for the use of chemical weapons must be held accountable."[486]

---

[480] UN Doc. S/PV.7038, 27 September 2013, p. 15 (Australia).

[481] UN Doc. S/RES/2118 (2013), 27 September 2013, operative para 15.

[482] Argentina and Australia supported referring Syria to the ICC (UN Doc. S/PV.7038, 27 September 2013, pp. 13 (Argentina), 15 (Australia)).

[483] UN Doc. A/RES/68/182, 18 December 2013, preamble para. 10. OIC Doc. OIC/ACM-2013/FC, Final communiqué of the Annual Coordination Meeting of Ministers of Foreign Affairs of the OIC Member States, United Nations Headquarters, New York, 27 September 2013, para. 27, https://www.oic-oci.org/docdown/?docID=512&refID=45, accessed 22 April 2023.

[484] UN Doc. A/RES/68/182, 18 December 2013, operative para. 1. The original draft included the phrase "… which strongly points to use by the Syrian Government" at the end of this paragraph (UN Doc. A/C.3/68/L.42, 31 October 2013). During Third Committee discussions, Pakistan and Argentina expressed negative views on this point (UN Doc. A/C.3/68/SR.48, 19 November 2013, p. 6, para. 28 (Pakistan), pp. 8–9, para. 42 (Argentina), and it was struck from a revised draft (UN Doc. A/C.3/68/L.42/Rev.1, 19 November 2013).

[485] UN Doc. S/RES/2118 (2013), 27 September 2013, preamble para 8; UN Doc. A/RES/68/182, 18 December 2013, preamble para. 9.

[486] The White House, Office of the Press Secretary, Statement by Principal Deputy Press Secretary Josh Earnest on Allegations of Chemical Weapons Use in Syria, August 21,

The NATO Secretary-General also took the position that "[t]hose responsible [for any use of chemical weapons] must be held accountable."[487] As depicted above, the French-sponsored draft UN Security Council resolution of 10 September 2013 included a preamble paragraph stating that "[s]tressing that those responsible for attacks on civilians, and any attacks using chemical weapons, including attacks by forces under their control, must be held accountable."[488] UN policy-making organs incorporated these views.

(iv) **Comprehensive ban**

The UN Security Council also addressed the comprehensive ban on chemical weapons activities in Syria, stating that it "[d]ecides that the Syrian Arab Republic shall not use, develop, produce, otherwise acquire, stockpile or retain chemical weapons, or transfer, directly or indirectly, chemical weapons to other States or non-State actors"[489] and "[u]nderscores that no party in Syria should use, develop, produce, acquire, stockpile, retain, or transfer chemical weapons."[490] The former passage, which recapitulates Article I, para. 1(a) and (b) of CWC, has a declaratory effect, because the CWC applied to Syria provisionally before its entry into force, while the latter passage draws the attention of non-State actors to these prohibited acts.[491] And while the term "should" therein might suggest that non-State actors are not legally prohibited from carrying out such acts by this language, it does not exempt them from such bans either. Article VII, para. 1 of the Convention obliges States Parties to take necessary measures to implement their obligations under the Convention in their domestic legal order. Those who are under jurisdiction or control of States Parties thus have the same obligations under the CWC, including the aforementioned Article I, para. 1(a) and (b). Moreover, non-State actors are obliged not to use chemical weapons in non-international armed conflict under customary international law, as discussed above and as indicated by Resolution 2118 operative para. 1.[492]

(v) **Non-proliferation**

The UN Security Council also tightened its non-proliferation regime, imposing trade sanctions against Syria by obliging UN Member States to prohibit the procurement

2013, https://obamawhitehouse.archives.gov/the-press-office/2013/08/21/statement-principal-deputy-press-secretary-josh-earnest-allegations-chem, accessed 22 April 2023.

487 NATO Secretary General Statement on North Atlantic Council Meeting on Syria, 28 August 2013, https://www.nato.int/cps/en/natolive/news_102605.htm, accessed 22 April 2023.

488 Chicago Tribune, French U.N. Security Council draft on Syria chemical weapons, 10 September 2013, https://www.chicagotribune.com/news/ct-xpm-2013-09-10-sns-rt-us-syria-crisis-un-draft-text-20130910-story.html, accessed 22 April 2023; The Telegraph, The full text of the French UN resolution on Syria, 11 September 2013, http://www.telegraph.co.uk/news/worldnews/middleeast/syria/10301732/The-full-text-of-the-French-UN-resolution-on-Syria.html, accessed 21 January 2023.

489 UN Doc. S/RES/2118 (2013), 27 September 2013, operative para. 4.

490 *Ibid.*, operative para. 5.

491 Asada, *supra* note 21, p. 203.

492 *Ibid.*, p. 204.

of chemical weapons, related equipment, goods and technology or assistance from Syria.[493] More generally, the UN Security Council acted as follows. First, having reaffirmed the proliferation of chemical weapons and their means of delivery as a threat to international peace and security,[494] and recalled the obligation of all States on non-proliferation of weapons of mass destruction including chemical weapons to non-State actors under Resolution 1540,[495] it decided that "Member States shall inform immediately the Security Council of any violation of resolution 1540 (2004), including acquisition by non-State actors of chemical weapons, their means of delivery and related materials in order to take necessary measures therefore."[496] Second, it reaffirmed the obligation of all Member States on non-proliferation of WMD, including chemical weapons, to non-State actors, and called upon all Member States, particularly Member States neighboring the Syrian Arab Republic, to report any violations of this obligation to the Security Council immediately.[497] Third, it similarly demanded that non-State actors not participate in proliferation of WMD, including chemical weapons, and called upon all Member States, particularly Member States neighboring the Syrian Arab Republic, to report any actions inconsistent with this language to the Security Council immediately.[498] It is anticipated that these new reporting requirements will aid effective implementation of relevant obligations.

(d) **Implementation: Response to Further Use**

As discussed above, there have been a number of allegations of the further use of chemical weapons since April 2014. As described above, the OPCW FFM, the OPCW-UN JIM, the OPCW IIT, and the COI have conducted investigations confirming use of chemical weapons and/or identifying perpetrators in accordance with their mandates.

The policy-making organs of the relevant international organizations have responded to further use of chemical weapons through subsequent decisions and resolutions. One OPCW Executive Council decision[499] and three UN Security Council resolutions[500] were adopted by consensus, while others were passed by vote. These include expressions of concern and condemnation, declaring violations of international law, stressing accountability, demanding specific acts or omissions, and

493 UN Doc. S/RES/2118 (2013), 27 September 2013, operative para. 20.

494 *Ibid.*, preamble para. 3.

495 *Ibid.*, preamble para. 9.

496 *Ibid.*, operative para. 14.

497 *Ibid.*, operative para. 18.

498 *Ibid.*, operative para. 19.

499 OPCW Doc. EC-M-50/DEC.1, 23 November 2015.

500 UN Doc. S/RES/2235 (2015), 7 August 2015; UN Doc. S/RES/2314 (2016), 31 October 2016; UN Doc. S/RES/2319 (2016), 17 November 2016.

imposing sanctions. At the same time, they also address the use of chemical weapons in the more general context.

(i) **Statements**

Violation

As with the use of chemical weapons in Syria on 21 August 2013, the most important statements on further use of chemical weapons were the legal evaluations. The policy-making organs of the OPCW and the UN Security Council have declared that use of chemical weapons in Syria is a violation of the CWC and UN Security Council Resolution 2118, thereby contravening international norms and standards.[501] The UN General Assembly, including the UNHRC, has also stated that use of chemical weapons in Syria or use of chemical weapons by the Syrian authorities constitutes a violation of the CWC, UN Security Council Resolution 2118, and international humanitarian law.[502] These statements have led the policy-making organs to further actions in response to non-compliance. Moreover, the policy-making organs have stressed that any use of chemical weapons constitutes a violation of international law and would be contrary to the legal norms and standards of the international community,[503] and that any use of chemical weapons anywhere, at any time, by

501 UN Doc. S/RES/2209 (2015), 6 March 2015, preamble para. 3 and UN Doc. S/RES/2235 (2015), 7 August 2015, preamble para. 2; UN Doc. S/RES/2209 (2015), 6 March 2015, operative para. 2; OPCW Doc. EC-83/DEC.5, 11 November 2016, operative para. 3.

502 Without identifying perpetrators: UN Doc. A/HRC/RES/27/16, 25 September 2014, operative para. 18; UN Doc. A/HRC/RES/28/20, 27 March 2015, operative para. 10; UN Doc. A/HRC/RES/38/16, 6 July 2018, operative para. 28; UN Doc. A/HRC/RES/39/15, 28 September 2018, operative para. 33; UN Doc. A/HRC/RES/40/17, 22 March 2019, operative para. 35; UN Doc. A/HRC/RES/41/23, 12 July 2019, operative para. 37; UN Doc. A/HRC/RES/42/27, 27 September 2019, operative para. 41; UN Doc. A/HRC/RES/43/28, 22 June 2020, operative para. 49. UN Doc. A/RES/69/189, 18 December 2014, operative para. 3; UN Doc. A/RES/70/234, 23 December 2015, operative para. 3; UN Doc. A/RES/71/203, 19 December 2016, operative para. 9; UN Doc. A/RES/72/191, 19 December 2017, operative para. 12; UN Doc. A/RES/73/182, 17 December 2018, operative para. 10; UN Doc. A/RES/74/169, 18 December 2019, operative para. 11; UN Doc. A/RES/75/193, 16 December 2020, operative para. 11; UN Doc. A/RES/76/228, 24 December 2021, operative para. 10; UN Doc. A/RES/77/230, 15 December 2022, operative para. 10. With indirectly identified perpetrators: UN Doc. A/HRC/RES/34/26, 24 March 2017, operative para. 26; UN Doc. A/HRC/RES/35/26, 23 June 2017, operative para. 26; UN Doc. A/HRC/RES/36/20, 29 September 2017, operative para. 26. With identified perpetrators: UN Doc. A/RES/72/191, 19 December 2017, preamble para. 5; UN Doc. A/RES/73/182, 17 December 2018, preamble para. 5, operative para. 4; UN Doc. A/RES/74/169, 18 December 2019, preamble para. 5, operative para. 4; UN Doc. A/RES/75/193, 16 December 2020, preamble para. 5, operative para. 4; UN Doc. A/RES/76/228, 24 December 2021, preamble para. 6, operative para. 4. UN Doc. A/HRC/RES/45/21, 6 October 2020, operative para. 9; UN Doc. A/HRC/RES/46/22, 24 March 2021, operative para. 32; UN Doc. A/RES/77/230, 15 December 2022, preamble para. 6.

503 OPCW Doc. EC-M-48/DEC.1, 4 February 2015, preamble para. 1 and OPCW Doc. EC-M-50/DEC.1, 23 November 2015, preamble para. 1; OPCW Doc. EC-M-48/DEC.1, 4 February 2015, operative para. 3 and OPCW Doc. EC-M-50/DEC.1, 23 November 2015, operative para. 4; OPCW Doc. C-SS-4/DEC.3, 27 June 2018, operative para. 1 and OPCW Doc. C-25/DEC.9, 21 April 2021, operative para. 1; UN Doc. S/RES/2209 (2015), 6 March 2015, preamble para. 8, UN Doc. S/RES/

anyone, under any circumstances is violation of international law.[504] These general statements further contribute to the strengthening international law on non-use of chemical weapons.

Concern

Another statement on chemical weapons use is "concern." The policy-making organs have taken an indirect approach, expressing serious or grave "concern," not about specific uses of chemical weapons per se, but about the findings of fact-finding organs.[505] This means that the policy-making organs have relied strongly on the

2235 (2015), 7 August 2015, preamble para. 4, UN Doc. S/RES/2314 (2016), 31 October 2016, preamble para. 4, and UN Doc. S/RES/2319 (2016), 17 November 2016, preamble para. 4. See also OPCW Doc. C-SS-4/DEC.3, 27 June 2018, operative para. 3.

[504] The UN General Assembly adopted the resolutions by vote, paragraph-by-paragraph on request, which was not made for the concerned paragraphs (UN Doc. A/RES/70/41, 7 December 2015, preamble para. 6; UN Doc. A/RES/71/69, 5 December 2016, operative para. 1; UN Doc. A/RES/72/43, 4 December 2017, operative para. 1; UN Doc. A/RES/73/45, 5 December 2018, operative para. 1; UN Doc. A/RES/74/40, 12 December 2019, operative para. 1; UN Doc. A/RES/75/55, 7 December 2020, operative para. 1; UN Doc. A/RES/76/29, 6 December 2021, operative para. 1; UN Doc. A/RES/77/73, 7 December 2022, operative para. 1). For other resolutions, no paragraph-by-paragraph vote was conducted (UN Doc. A/RES/72/191, 19 December 2017, operative para. 5; UN Doc. A/RES/73/182, 17 December 2018, preamble para. 15; UN Doc. A/RES/74/169, 18 December 2019, preamble para. 16; UN Doc. A/RES/75/193, 16 December 2020, preamble para. 19; UN Doc. A/RES/76/228, 24 December 2021, preamble para. 21). The UNHRC adopted the resolutions by simple vote (UN Doc. A/HRC/RES/37/29, 23 March 2018, preamble para. 14; UN Doc. A/HRC/RES/38/16, 6 July 2018, preamble para. 13; UN Doc. A/HRC/RES/39/15, 28 September 2018, preamble para. 13; UN Doc. A/HRC/RES/40/17, 22 March 2019, preamble para. 14; UN Doc. A/HRC/RES/41/23, 12 July 2019, preamble para. 15; UN Doc. A/HRC/RES/42/27, 27 September 2019, preamble para. 15; UN Doc. A/HRC/RES/43/28, 22 June 2020, preamble para. 18).

[505] Findings of FFM: OPCW Doc. EC-M-48/DEC.1, 4 February 2015, operative para. 1; UN Doc. S/RES/2209 (2015), 6 March 2015, operative para. 2; OPCW Doc. EC-M-50/DEC.1, 23 November 2015, operative para. 1; OPCW Doc. C-SS-4/DEC.3, 27 June 2018, operative para. 9 ("Notes with concern that the Fact-Finding Mission has identified further uses of chemical weapons in the Syrian Arab Republic at Ltamenah on 24, 25 and 30 March 2017 and at Saraqib on 4 February 2018,"). UN Doc. A/HRC/RES/28/20, 27 March 2015, operative para. 10; UN Doc. A/HRC/RES/35/26, 23 June 2017, operative para. 23; UN Doc. A/HRC/RES/36/20, 29 September 2017, operative para. 22; UN Doc. A/HRC/RES/37/29, 23 March 2018, operative para. 27; UN Doc. A/HRC/RES/38/16, 6 July 2018, operative para. 30; UN Doc. A/HRC/RES/39/15, 28 September 2018, operative para. 35; UN Doc. A/HRC/RES/40/17, 22 March 2019, operative para. 37; UN Doc. A/HRC/RES/41/23, 12 July 2019, operative para. 39; UN Doc. A/HRC/RES/42/27, 27 September 2019, operative para. 45; UN Doc. A/HRC/RES/43/28, 22 June 2020, operative para. 53; UN Doc. A/HRC/RES/40/17, 22 March 2019, operative para. 39; UN Doc. A/HRC/RES/41/23, 12 July 2019, operative para. 43; UN Doc. A/HRC/RES/42/27, 27 September 2019, operative para. 47; UN Doc. A/HRC/RES/43/28, 22 June 2020, operative para. 55. UN Doc. A/RES/73/182, 17 December 2018, preamble operative para. 16; UN Doc. A/RES/73/45, 5 December 2018, operative para. 3; UN Doc. A/RES/74/40, 12 December 2019, operative para. 3; UN Doc. A/RES/74/169, 18 December 2019, preamble para. 17; UN Doc. A/RES/75/55, 7 December 2020, operative para. 4; UN Doc. A/RES/75/193, 16 December 2020, preamble para. 20; UN Doc. A/RES/76/29, 6 December 2021, operative para. 4; UN Doc. A/RES/77/73, 7 December 2022, operative para. 4. JIM Findings: OPCW Doc. EC-83/DEC.5, 11 November 2016, operative para. 1. UN Doc. A/HRC/RES/33/23, 30 September 2016, operative para. 21; UN Doc. A/HRC/RES/34/26, 24 March 2017, operative para. 25; UN Doc. A/HRC/RES/35/26, 23 June

results of investigations by the fact-finding bodies, and not established facts on their own assessment.

Condemn

Another such statement is "condemnation." The UN Security Council consistently uses such key language in its resolutions as "condemning/condemns," "in the strongest terms," "any use of any toxic chemical as a weapon," and "in the Syrian Arab Republic."[506] By contrast, the OPCW policy-making organs have taken a dual approach. On the one hand, they directly or indirectly condemn the Syrian government for using chemical weapons, with explicit reference to OPCW-UN JIM and OPCW IIT reports.[507] On the other hand, they express general condemnation in their decisions, including such language as "reaffirms its condemnation" or "condemns," "in the strongest terms," "the use of chemical weapons," and "by anyone under any circumstances."[508] For its part, the UN General Assembly, including the UNHRC, uses the following: condemn the use of chemical weapons in Syria,[509] condemn the

---

2017, operative para. 26; UN Doc. A/HRC/RES/36/20, 29 September 2017, operative para. 26; UN Doc. A/HRC/RES/37/29, 23 March 2018, operative para. 25; UN Doc. A/HRC/RES/38/16, 6 July 2018, operative para. 29; UN Doc. A/HRC/RES/39/15, 28 September 2018, operative para. 34; UN Doc. A/HRC/RES/40/17, 22 March 2019, operative para. 36; UN Doc. A/HRC/RES/41/23, 12 July 2019, operative para. 38; UN Doc. A/HRC/RES/42/27, 27 September 2019, operative para. 44; UN Doc. A/HRC/RES/43/28, 22 June 2020, operative para. 52. UN Doc. A/RES/71/203, 19 December 2016, preamble para. 13; UN Doc. A/RES/72/191, 19 December 2017, preamble para. 11; UN Doc. A/RES/71/203, 19 December 2016, operative para. 6; UN Doc. A/RES/72/191, 19 December 2017, preamble para. 11; UN Doc. A/RES/72/191, 19 December 2017, operative para. 8; UN Doc. A/RES/72/191, 19 December 2017, operative para. 9. IIT Findings: UN Doc. A/RES/75/265, 3 March 2021, operative para. 7. COI Findings: UN Doc. A/HRC/RES/27/16, 25 September 2014, operative para. 18; UN Doc. A/HRC/RES/28/20, 27 March 2015, operative para. 10; UN Doc. A/HRC/RES/36/20, 29 September 2017, operative para. 23; UN Doc. A/HRC/RES/37/29, 23 March 2018, operative para. 26; UN Doc. A/HRC/RES/39/15, 28 September 2018, operative para. 37; UN Doc. A/HRC/RES/40/17, 22 March 2019, operative para. 38; UN Doc. A/HRC/RES/41/23, 12 July 2019, operative para. 40; UN Doc. A/HRC/RES/42/27, 27 September 2019, operative para. 46; UN Doc. A/HRC/RES/43/28, 22 June 2020, operative para. 54; UN Doc. A/HRC/RES/46/22, 24 March 2021, operative para. 32.

[506] UN Doc. S/RES/2209 (2015), 6 March 2015, operative para. 1; UN Doc. S/RES/2235 (2015), 7 August 2015, preamble para. 3, para. 1; UN Doc. S/RES/2314 (2016), 31 October 2016, preamble para. 3; UN Doc. S/RES/2319 (2016), 17 November 2016, preamble para. 3.

[507] OPCW Doc. EC-83/DEC.5, 11 November 2016, operative para. 3; OPCW Doc. C-SS-4/DEC.3, 27 June 2018, operative para. 6; OPCW Doc. EC-94/DEC.2, 9 July 2020, operative para. 1 and OPCW Doc. C-25/DEC.9, 21 April 2021, operative para. 2.

[508] OPCW Doc. EC-M-48/DEC.1, 4 February 2015, operative para. 2; OPCW Doc. EC-M-50/DEC.1, 23 November 2015, operative para. 3; OPCW Doc. C-SS-4/DEC.3, 27 June 2018, operative para. 1; OPCW Doc. C-25/DEC.9, 21 April 2021, operative para. 1. See also OPCW Doc. C-SS-4/DEC.3, 27 June 2018, operative para. 3.

[509] UN Doc. A/HRC/RES/25/23, 28 March 2014, operative para. 14; UN Doc. A/HRC/RES/26/23, 27 June 2014, operative para. 13; UN Doc. A/HRC/RES/27/16, 25 September 2014, operative para. 18; UN Doc. A/HRC/RES/28/20, 27 March 2015, operative para. 9; UN Doc. A/HRC/RES/29/16, 2 July 2015, operative para 6; UN Doc. A/HRC/RES/30/10, 1 October 2015, operative para. 9; UN Doc. A/HRC/RES/31/17, 23 March 2016, operative para. 14; UN Doc. A/HRC/RES/32/25, 1 July 2016, operative para. 17; UN Doc. A/HRC/RES/33/23, 30 September 2016, operative para.

use of chemical weapons by the Syrian regime/Authorities and ISIL,[510] condemn the use of chemical weapons as reported by the OPCW-UN JIM and the OPCW IIT, implying that the Syrian government and ISIL were perpetrators,[511] and condemn the use of chemical weapons in general.[512] The policy-making organs named and criticized the Syrian government for using chemical weapons after August 2016, when the OPCW-UN JIM released its report identifying the Syrian government as the perpetrators. While maintaining a careful attitude on this sensitive issue prior to

---

20; UN Doc. A/HRC/RES/37/29, 23 March 2018, operative para. 24; UN Doc. A/HRC/RES/46/22, 24 March 2021, operative para. 32; UN Doc. A/HRC/RES/47/18, 13 July 2021, operative para. 7; UN Doc. A/HRC/RES/48/15, 8 October 2021, operative para. 17. UN Doc. A/RES/69/189, 18 December 2014, operative para. 19; UN Doc. A/RES/70/234, 23 December 2015, operative para. 29; UN Doc. A/RES/71/203, 19 December 2016, operative para. 4; UN Doc. A/RES/72/191, 19 December 2017, preamble para. 5, operative para. 4; UN Doc. A/RES/73/182, 17 December 2018, preamble para. 5, operative paras. 4 and 5; UN Doc. A/RES/74/169, 18 December 2019, preamble para. 5, operative paras. 4 and 5; UN Doc. A/RES/75/193, 16 December 2020, preamble para. 5, operative paras. 4 and 5; UN Doc. A/RES/76/228, 24 December 2021, preamble para. 6, operative para 4; UN Doc. A/RES/77/230, 15 December 2022, preamble para. 6.

[510] UN Doc. A/HRC/RES/34/26, 24 March 2017, operative para. 16; UN Doc. A/HRC/RES/38/16, 6 July 2018, operative para. 28; UN Doc. A/HRC/RES/39/15, 28 September 2018, operative para. 33; UN Doc. A/HRC/RES/40/17, 22 March 2019, operative para. 35; UN Doc. A/HRC/RES/41/23, 12 July 2019, operative para. 37; UN Doc. A/HRC/RES/42/27, 27 September 2019, operative para. 41; UN Doc. A/HRC/RES/43/28, 22 June 2020, operative para. 49. UN Doc. A/RES/69/189, 18 December 2014, operative para. 3; UN Doc. A/RES/70/234, 23 December 2015, operative para. 3; UN Doc. A/RES/71/203, 19 December 2016, operative para. 9; UN Doc. A/RES/72/191, 19 December 2017, operative paras 7 and 12; UN Doc. A/RES/73/182, 17 December 2018, preamble para. 16; UN Doc. A/RES/73/182, 17 December 2018, operative para. 10; UN Doc. A/RES/74/169, 18 December 2019, preamble para. 17, operative para. 11; UN Doc. A/RES/75/193, 16 December 2020, preamble para. 20, operative para. 11; UN Doc. A/RES/76/228, 24 December 2021, preamble para. 22, operative para. 10; UN Doc. A/RES/77/230, 15 December 2022, preamble para. 25, operative para. 8.

[511] UN Doc. A/HRC/RES/34/26, 24 March 2017, operative para. 26; UN Doc. A/HRC/RES/35/26, 23 June 2017, operative para. 26; UN Doc. A/HRC/RES/36/20, 29 September 2017, operative para. 26. UN Doc. A/RES/71/69, 5 December 2016, operative para. 2; UN Doc. A/RES/72/43, 4 December 2017, operative para. 2; UN Doc. A/RES/73/45, 5 December 2018, operative para. 2; UN Doc. A/RES/74/40, 12 December 2019, operative para. 2; UN Doc. A/RES/75/55, 7 December 2020, operative para. 3; UN Doc. A/RES/76/29, 6 December 2021, operative para. 3; UN Doc. A/RES/77/73, 7 December 2022, operative para. 3.

[512] The UN General Assembly adopted the resolutions by vote, paragraph-by-paragraph on request, which was not made for paragraphs regarding condemnations (UN Doc. A/RES/70/41, 7 December 2015, preamble para. 6; UN Doc. A/RES/71/69, 5 December 2016, operative para. 1; UN Doc. A/RES/72/43, 4 December 2017, operative para. 1; UN Doc. A/RES/73/45, 5 December 2018, operative para. 1; UN Doc. A/RES/74/40, 12 December 2019, operative para. 1; UN Doc. A/RES/75/55, 7 December 2020, operative para. 1; UN Doc. A/RES/76/29, 6 December 2021, operative para. 1; UN Doc. A/RES/77/73, 7 December 2022, operative para. 1). No such paragraph-by-paragraph vote was conducted for other resolutions (UN Doc. A/RES/72/191, 19 December 2017, operative para. 5; UN Doc. A/RES/73/182, 17 December 2018, preamble para. 15; UN Doc. A/RES/74/169, 18 December 2019, preamble para. 16; UN Doc. A/RES/75/193, 16 December 2020, preamble para. 19; UN Doc. A/RES/76/228, 24 December 2021, preamble para. 21).

that time, they took firmer stance, thereafter, making this period a significant turning point.

(ii) **Demands**

In addition to their statements on use of chemical weapons per se, policy-making organs have demanded that concerned parties take action.

Demands for Cessation

The OPCW policy-making organs called on all parties to immediately desist from any further use for the first time in its decision of November 2016,[513] and demanded that the Syrian Arab Republic immediately cease all use of chemical weapons in its subsequent decisions of June 2018, July 2020, and April 2021.[514] The UN General Assembly, including the UNHRC, has also demanded that all parties or the perpetrators desist immediately from any use of chemical weapons,[515] and that the Syrian Republic/authorities/regime immediately cease use of same.[516] The General Assembly also demanded that ISIL desist from any further use of chemical weapons.[517] Such demands accord fully with Article 30 of the Articles on the Responsibility of States for Internationally Wrongful Acts (ARSIWA).

513 OPCW Doc. EC-83/DEC.5, 11 November 2016, operative para. 3.

514 OPCW Doc. C-SS-4/DEC.3, 27 June 2018, operative para. 7; OPCW Doc. EC-94/DEC.2, 9 July 2020, operative para. 2; OPCW Doc. C-25/DEC.9, 21 April 2021, operative para. 4.

515 UN Doc. A/HRC/RES/34/26, 24 March 2017, operative para. 27; UN Doc. A/HRC/RES/35/26, 23 June 2017, operative para. 27; UN Doc. A/HRC/RES/36/20, 29 September 2017, operative para. 24; UN Doc. A/HRC/RES/37/29, 23 March 2018, operative para. 29; UN Doc. A/HRC/RES/38/16, 6 July 2018, operative para. 33; UN Doc. A/HRC/RES/39/15, 28 September 2018, operative para. 39; UN Doc. A/HRC/RES/40/17, 22 March 2019, operative para. 41; UN Doc. A/HRC/RES/41/23, 12 July 2019, operative para. 43; UN Doc. A/HRC/RES/42/27, 27 September 2019, operative para. 42; UN Doc. A/HRC/RES/43/28, 22 June 2020, operative para. 56; UN Doc. A/HRC/RES/45/21, 6 October 2020, operative para. 9; UN Doc. A/HRC/RES/46/22, 24 March 2021, operative para. 32; UN Doc. A/HRC/RES/47/18, 13 July 2021, operative para. 7; UN Doc. A/HRC/RES/48/15, 8 October 2021, operative para. 17.

516 UN Doc. A/HRC/RES/33/23, 30 September 2016, operative para. 22. UN Doc. A/RES/69/189, 18 December 2014, operative para. 2; UN Doc. A/RES/70/234, 23 December 2015, operative para. 2; UN Doc. A/RES/71/203, 19 December 2016, operative para. 3; UN Doc. A/RES/72/191, 19 December 2017, operative para. 4; UN Doc. A/RES/73/182, 17 December 2018, operative para. 5; UN Doc. A/RES/74/169, 18 December 2019, operative para. 5; UN Doc. A/RES/75/193, 16 December 2020, operative para. 5; UN Doc. A/RES/72/191, 19 December 2017, operative para. 7.

517 UN Doc. A/RES/72/191, 19 December 2017, operative para. 4; UN Doc. A/RES/73/182, 17 December 2018, operative para. 5; UN Doc. A/RES/74/169, 18 December 2019, operative para. 5; UN Doc. A/RES/75/193, 16 December 2020, operative para. 5.

Demands for cooperation

Policy-making organs have also demanded cooperation. While all parties were called upon to extend their full cooperation to the OPCW FFM,[518] the OPCW-UN JIM,[519] and the OPCW and the UN in general;[520] the Syrian Arab Republic was singled out by name to cooperation with the OPCW FFM[521] and the OPCW IIT.[522]

(iii) **Accountability**

The policy-making organs have also dealt with the accountability issue, expressing not only their general convictions that those individuals responsible for the use of chemical weapons must and should be held accountable,[523] but also emphasizing the

[518] OPCW Doc. EC-M-48/DEC.1, 4 February 2015, operative para. 6; OPCW Doc. EC-M-50/DEC.1, 23 November 2015, operative para. 7; UN Doc. S/RES/2209 (2015), 6 March 2015, operative para. 6.

[519] UN Doc. S/RES/2335 (2015), 7 August 2015, operative para. 4. The UN Security Council also called upon all other States to cooperate fully with the OPCW-UN JIM, especially by providing information (*ibid.*, operative para. 8).

[520] *Ibid.*, operative para. 7.

[521] UN Doc. A/RES/69/189, 18 December 2014, operative para. 20.

[522] OPCW Doc. EC-94/DEC.2, 9 July 2020, operative para. 3; OPCW Doc. C-25/DEC.9, 21 April 2021, operative para. 6. UN Doc. A/HRC/RES/46/22, 24 March 2021, operative para. 33.

[523] OPCW Doc. EC-M-48/DEC.1, 4 February 2015, operative para. 4 and OPCW Doc. EC-M-50/DEC.1, 23 November 2015, operative para. 5; UN Doc. S/RES/2209 (2015), 6 March 2015, preamble para. 8 and UN Doc. S/RES/2235 (2015), 7 August 2015, preamble para. 4; UN Doc. S/RES/2209 (2015), 6 March 2015, operative para. 6 and UN Doc. S/RES/2235 (2015), 7 August 2015, operative para. 4; UN Doc. S/RES/2314 (2016), 31 October 2016, preamble para. 4 and UN Doc. S/RES/2319 (2016), 17 November 2016, preamble para. 4; OPCW Doc. C-SS-4/DEC.3, 27 June 2018, preamble para. 5, OPCW Doc. EC-94/DEC.2, 9 July 2020, operative para. 9 and OPCW Doc. C-25/DEC.9, 21 April 2021, operative para. 9. The UN General Assembly adopted the resolutions by voting, paragraph-by-paragraph upon request, which was not made for the paragraphs regarding accountability (UN Doc. A/RES/70/41, 7 December 2015, preamble para. 6; UN Doc. A/RES/71/69, 5 December 2016, operative para. 1; UN Doc. A/RES/72/43, 4 December 2017, operative para. 1; UN Doc. A/RES/73/45, 5 December 2018, operative para. 1; UN Doc. A/RES/74/40, 12 December 2019, operative para. 1; UN Doc. A/RES/75/55, 7 December 2020, operative para. 1; UN Doc. A/RES/76/29, 6 December 2021, operative para. 1; UN Doc. A/RES/77/73, 7 December 2022, operative para. 1). For other resolutions, no paragraph-by-paragraph vote was conducted (UN Doc. A/RES/72/191, 19 December 2017, operative para. 5; UN Doc. A/RES/73/182, 17 December 2018, preamble operative para. 15; UN Doc. A/RES/74/169, 18 December 2019, preamble para. 16; UN Doc. A/RES/75/193, 16 December 2020, preamble para. 19; UN Doc. A/RES/76/228, 24 December 2021, preamble para. 21). The UNHRC adopted the resolutions by simple vote (UN Doc. A/HRC/RES/28/20, 27 March 2015, operative para. 10; UN Doc. A/HRC/RES/34/26, 24 March 2017, operative para. 26; UN Doc. A/HRC/RES/35/26, 23 June 2017, operative para. 26; UN Doc. A/HRC/RES/36/20, 29 September 2017, operative para. 26; UN Doc. A/HRC/RES/37/29, 23 March 2018, preamble para. 14, operative para. 24; UN Doc. A/HRC/RES/38/16, 6 July 2018, preamble para. 13, operative para. 33; UN Doc. A/HRC/RES/39/15, 28 September 2018, preamble para. 13, operative para. 39; UN Doc. A/HRC/RES/40/17, 22 March 2019, preamble para. 14, operative para. 41; UN Doc. A/HRC/RES/41/23, 12 July 2019, preamble para. 15, operative para. 43; UN Doc. A/HRC/RES/42/27, 27 September 2019, preamble para. 15, operative para. 42; UN Doc. A/HRC/RES/43/28, 22 June 2020, preamble para. 18, operative para. 56; UN Doc. A/HRC/RES/45/21, 6 October 2020, operative para. 9; UN Doc. A/HRC/RES/46/22, 24 March 2021, operative para.

importance of the accountability of those who were involved in the use of chemical weapons in Syria in their decisions and resolutions.[524] The issue nonetheless remains unresolved.

Attempt to refer to the International Criminal Court (ICC)

Given that a domestic law enforcement approach would be ineffective, it is necessary to explore international approaches, the most realistic existing option thereof being the ICC, whose Statute encompasses crimes related to use of chemical weapons, including murder committed as part of a widespread or systematic attack directed against any civilian population (Article 7, para. 1(a)), violence against life and person (Article 8, para. 2(c)(i)), and intentionally directing attacks against civilian populations (Article 8, para. 2(e)(i)).[525] The 2010 Kampala review conference added "employing asphyxiating, poisonous or other gases, and all analogous liquids, materials or devices," which is the traditional formulation of chemical weapons in the 1925 Geneva Protocol, to the list of war crimes in non-international armed conflict as new Article 8, para. 2(e)(xiv). The Rome Statute offers three options for referring cases to the OTP: referral by a State Party, referral by the UN Security Council acting under Chapter VII, and initiation by the OTP itself (Article 13). Of these, UN Security Council referral was the only viable option, due to Syria being a non-State Party to the Rome Statue and having made no declaration of acceptance of ICC jurisdiction.[526]

In May 2014, France led sixty-five States in proposing a draft Security Council resolution in an attempt to make such a referral of the situation in Syria since March

---

32; UN Doc. A/HRC/RES/47/18, 13 July 2021, operative para. 7; UN Doc. A/HRC/RES/48/15, 8 October 2021, operative para. 17). Moreover, the OPCW States Parties issued the Ieper Declaration on 21 April 2015, in which they "express their strong conviction that those responsible for the use of chemical weapons should be held accountable" (Declaration on the Occasion of the Centennial Commemoration of the First Large-Scale Use of Chemical Weapons at Ieper (Ieper Declaration), OPCW Doc. S/1214/2014/Add.2, 14 April 2015, Annex 1, p. 3; see also OPCW News, OPCW States Parties issue historic Declaration on the centenary of the first large-scale use of chemical weapons in Ieper, 21 April 2015, https://www.opcw.org/media-centre/news/2015/04/opcw-states-parties-issue-historic-declaration-centenary-first-large, accessed 22 April 2023).

[524] OPCW Doc. EC-83/DEC.5, 11 November 2016, operative para. 4; OPCW Doc. EC-94/DEC.2, 9 July 2020, operative para. 9. UN Doc. A/HRC/RES/30/10, 1 October 2015, operative para. 10; UN Doc. A/HRC/RES/31/17, 23 March 2016, operative para. 13; UN Doc. A/HRC/RES/33/23, 30 September 2016, operative para. 19; UN Doc. A/HRC/RES/34/26, 24 March 2017, operative para. 24; UN Doc. A/HRC/RES/35/26, 23 June 2017, operative para. 21; UN Doc. A/HRC/RES/36/20, 29 September 2017, operative para. 21; UN Doc. A/HRC/RES/37/29, 23 March 2018, operative para. 23. UN Doc. A/RES/70/234, 23 December 2015, operative para. 30; UN Doc. A/RES/71/203, 19 December 2016, operative para. 5; UN Doc. A/RES/72/191, 19 December 2017, operative paras. 6 and 7.

[525] Andreas Zimmermann and Meltem Şener, "Chemical Weapons and the International Criminal Court," *American Journal of International Law*, Vol. 108, No. 3 (2014), p. 436, p. 448.

[526] It has been pointed out that the ICC may not exercise jurisdiction through UN Security Council referral over newly introduced war crimes, including Article 8, para. 2(e)(xiv) in relation to non-State Parties to the Rome Statute, owing to varying formulations of applicability of amendments in the relevant resolutions at the 2010 Kampala review conference (*ibid.*, pp. 444–447).

2011, which is described as "the widespread violations of human rights and international humanitarian law by the Syrian authorities and pro-government militias, as well as the human rights abuses and violations of international humanitarian law by non-State armed groups, all committed in the course of the ongoing conflict in the Syrian Arab Republic since March 2011"—implicitly including the use of chemical weapons,[527] which China and Russia vetoed.[528] Russia explained its veto by pointing out that the referral of the situation in Libya by the UN Security Council "did not help resolve the crisis, but added fuel to the flamens of conflict," that the US insisted on an exemption for itself and its citizens, and that the Geneva communiqué of 30 June 2012 leaves the leading role in the accountability and national reconciliationprocess to the Syrians themselves.[529] For its part, China justified its veto by expressing its "principled position" that "any action to seek recourse to the International Criminal Court (ICC) to prosecute the perpetrators of serious violations should be conducted on the basis of respect for State judicial sovereignty and the principle of complementarity" and that "China always has reservations concerning the referral by the Security Council of particular country situations to the ICC."[530] It also attached importance to efforts made by the international community to push for a political settlement and the unity and coordination of the members of the UN Security Council on the question of Syria.[531] Since then, several European States have reiterated their positions that the

---

[527] UN Doc. S/2014/348, 22 May 2014. The sponsors were Albania, Andorra, Australia, Austria, Belgium, Botswana, Bulgaria, Canada, Central African Republic, Chile, Côte d'Ivoire, Croatia, Cyprus, Czech Republic, Democratic Republic of the Congo, Denmark, Estonia, Finland, France, Georgia, Germany, Greece, Hungary, Iceland, Ireland, Italy, Japan, Jordan, Latvia, Libya, Liechtenstein, Lithuania, Luxembourg, Malta, Marshall Islands, Mexico, Monaco, Montenegro, Netherlands, New Zealand, Norway, Panama, Poland, Portugal, Qatar, Republic of Korea, Republic of Moldova, Romania, Samoa, San Marino, Saudi Arabia, Senegal, Serbia, Seychelles, Slovakia, Slovenia, Spain, Sweden, Switzerland, The former Yugoslav Republic of Macedonia, Turkey, Ukraine, United Arab Emirates, UK, and US.

[528] UN Doc. S/PV.7180, 22 May 2014, p. 4.

[529] *Ibid.*, p. 13 (Russia).

[530] *Ibid.*, p. 13 (China). The Security Council adopted Resolutions 1593 (Darfur) and 1970 (Libya), which refer the respective situations to the ICC. China abstained on the former (UN Doc. S/PV.5158, 31 March 2005, p. 2), but voted in favor of the latter (UN Doc. S/PV.6491, 26 February 2011, p. 2). See also UN Doc. S/PV.5158, 31 March 2005, p. 5 (China) and UN Doc. S/PV.6491, 26 February 2011, p. 4 (China).

[531] UN Doc. S/PV.7180, 22 May 2014, pp. 13–14 (China).

Syrian situation should be referred to the ICC.[532] Notwithstanding, there has been no further action in this regard as of this writing.[533]

International, Impartial and Independent Mechanism (IIIM)

In a sign of growing frustration with the Security Council deadlock, thirty-nine States tabled a draft resolution at the General Assembly which explored an alternate path to progress toward Syrian accountability.[534] In December 2016, the General Assembly passed a resolution creating the International, Impartial and Independent Mechanism to Assist in the Investigation and Prosecution of Persons Responsible for the Most Serious Crimes under International Law Committed in the Syrian Arab Republic since March 2011 (IIIM),[535] over several States' objections. Syria opposed the proposed mechanism on the grounds that the resolution "runs counter to Article 2, paragraph 7 of the UN Charter," the General Assembly does not have the power to establish the mechanism, which would require Secretary-General authorization and consent of the affected State, and the mechanism would not be financially independent.[536] Russia stressed that the General Assembly exceeded its mandate through direct interference in the internal affairs of a UN Member State, a violation of that State's sovereignty.[537] Ecuador pointed out "the sovereign jurisdiction of States and, at the same time, [the resolutions] seriously weakens the structure of international justice established by the Rome Statute and its mechanisms by eroding the authority of the International Criminal Court and, in particular, the Office of the Prosecutor."[538] Cuba indicated that "its provisions run entirely counter to that commitment and to

---

[532] UN Doc. S/PV.7401, 6 March 2015, p. 4 (UK); UN Doc. S/PV.7915, 5 April 2017, p. 8 (Italy); UN Doc. S/PV.7919, 7 April 2017, p. 9 (France); Ireland, https://www.opcw.org/sites/default/files/documents/EC/M-54/en/Ireland_ECM54.pdf, accessed 22 April 2023; OPCW Doc. EC-86/NAT.29 (Switzerland),10 October 2017, p. 1; OPCW Doc. EC-M-56/NAT.8 (Switzerland), 9 November 2017, p. 1; UN Doc. S/PV.8174, 5 February 2018, p. 14 (Netherlands); UN Doc. S/PV.8164, 23 January 2018, p. 7 (Netherlands); UN Doc. S/PV.8221, 4 April 2018, p. 5 (Netherlands); UN Doc. S/PV.8225, 9 April 2018, p. 10 (Netherlands); UN Doc. S/PV.8344, 6 September 2018, p. 13 (Netherlands); UN Doc. S/PV.8390, 5 November 2018, p. 13 (Netherlands).

[533] It has been argued that given the lack of any current possibility of either a Security Council referral to the ICC or an agreement to create an *ad hoc* international tribunal, the only viable option would be prosecution before domestic courts based on universal jurisdiction (Sossai, *supra* note 84, p. 227).

[534] Ingrid Elliott, "A Meaningful Step towards Accountability," *Journal of International Criminal Justice*, Vol. 15, No. 2 (2017), p. 239, pp. 240–241.

[535] UN Doc. A/RES/71/248, 21 December 2016, para. 4. This resolution was adopted by a vote of 105 in favor to 15 against (Algeria, Belarus, Bolivia, Burundi, China, Cuba, Democratic People's Republic of Korea, Iran, Kyrgyzstan, Nicaragua, Russia, South Sudan, Syria, Venezuela, Zimbabwe), with 52 abstentions (UN Doc. A/71/PV.66, 21 December 2016, pp. 29–30). The UN Secretary-General included IIIM terms of reference its report (UN Doc. A/71/755, 19 November 2017, Annex), as requested by the UN General Assembly (UN Doc. A/RES/71/248, 21 December 2016, operative para. 5). It is anticipated that this mechanism will operate until UN General Assembly terminates its mandate, because the resolution set no expiration date.

[536] UN Doc. A /71/PV.66, 21 December 2016, pp. 21–22 (Syria).

[537] *Ibid.*, p. 23 (Russia).

[538] *Ibid.*, p. 25 (Ecuador).

the fundamental principles enshrined in the Charter of the United Nations and international law" and that "it is impossible to ensure the independence and impartiality of a mechanism that would enter into force and initially function through voluntary donations."[539] South Africa asserted that "the Assembly cannot deal with an issue that is before the Security Council unless it is authorized to do so by the Council."[540] Iran argued that "the draft resolution in its entirety is in violation of the Charter and its fundamental principle of State sovereignty" because the enforcement of laws and prosecution of criminals fall strictly within the domestic jurisdictions of States and that "establishing such a mechanism without the consent of the State concerned would utterly disregard the sovereignty of the Syrian Arab Republic."[541] For its part, Thailand was concerned about the lack of clarity with regard to the IIIM's terms of reference and its relationship with the COI.[542] These arguments were not widely supported, however, as the General Assembly resolution itself puts the IIIM on sound legal footing.

The IIIM's primary tasks are "to collect, consolidate, preserve and analyse evidence of violations of international humanitarian law and human rights violations and abuses" and "to prepare files in order to facilitate and expedite fair and independent criminal proceedings."[543] As implied in the statement by Thailand, it is closely related to the COI in the sense that both deal with violations of international humanitarian law and international human rights law. They take different approaches, however. The former concentrates on collecting information and preparing files for future criminal investigation and prosecution, while the latter examines incidents in the light of relevant international law and submits reports to Member States with recommendations.[544] With this difference in mind, the UN General Assembly instructed the former to "closely cooperate with" the latter "in all aspects of its

539 *Ibid.*, pp. 25–26 (Cuba).

540 *Ibid.*, p. 26 (South Africa). In response, the President of the General Assembly explained that "Article 12 does not prevent the General Assembly from generally considering, discussing and making recommendations on items that are on the agenda of the Security Council, in particular when the item before the Council and the Assembly are not identical,"and "[t]he accepted practice of the General Assembly to consider, in parallel with the Security Council, the same matter concerning the maintenance of international peace and security has also been noted by the International Court of Justice in its advisory opinion of 2004" (UN Doc. A /71/PV.66, 21 December 2016, pp. 28–29 (President)).

541 UN Doc. A /71/PV.66, 21 December 2016, p. 27 (Iran).

542 *Ibid.*, p. 35 (Thailand). See also *ibid.*, p. 34 (Singapore); p. 34 (Kyrgyzstan).

543 UN Doc. A/RES/71/248, 21 December 2016, operative para. 4.

544 The COI considers human rights violations and submits reports on its findings with its recommendations to Member States, while the IIIM collects information and prepares files for use in future criminal investigation and prosecution (UN Doc. A/71/755, 19 January 2017, p. 6, paras. 30–32, Annex, p. 14, para. 30).

work."[545] A key aspect of such cooperation is providing information,[546] in which sense the latter has transmitted the vast majority of its evidence and information underlying its lists of individual perpetrators to the former.[547]

In the context of the investigation of chemical weapons use, the IIIM has benefited from both the COI's work[548] and the activities of the OPCW fact-finding organs.[549] In June 2018, the OPCW Conference of the States Parties decided that the Technical Secretariat "shall preserve and provide information to" the International, Impartial and Independent Mechanism (IIIM).[550] This paved the way for the latter to obtain access to relevant materials from the former,[551] whereupon the IIIM and the OPCW concluded a memorandum of understanding on 26 September 2018,[552] which was welcomed by the UN General Assembly.[553] Pursuant thereto, the OPCW IIT transferred materials to the IIIM on 2 October and 20 November 2020,[554] while the UN Secretary-General issued a bulletin in April 2019 which made the records and archives of the OPCW-UN Joint Investigative accessible to third parties in accordance

[545] UN Doc. A/RES/71/248, 21 December 2016, operative para. 7. The UN Secretary-General recognizes the "complimentary" relation between two organs (UN Doc. A/71/755, 19 January 2017, Annex, p. 14, para. 30). The UNHRC has also stressed this point (UN Doc. A/HRC/RES/34/26, 24 March 2017, para. 40; UN Doc. A/HRC/RES/35/26, 23 June 2017, para. 39; UN Doc. A/HRC/RES/36/20, 29 September 2017, para. 39; UN Doc. A/HRC/RES/37/29, 23 March 2018, para. 34; UN Doc. A/HRC/RES/38/16, 6 July 2018, para. 37; UN Doc. A/HRC/RES/39/15, 28 September 2018, para. 43; UN Doc. A/HRC/RES/40/17, 22 March 2019, para. 45; UN Doc. A/HRC/RES/41/23, 12 July 2019, para. 47; UN Doc. A/HRC/RES/42/27, 27 September 2019, para. 54; UN Doc. A/HRC/RES/43/28, 22 June 2020, para. 62).

[546] UN Doc. A/71/755, 19 January 2017, p. 6, paras. 30 and 31, Annex, p. 11, para. 5(a), p. 14, and 30. In March 2018, the COI and IIIM concluded a memorandum of understanding which enables the latter to acquire the majority of the material collected by the former, https://iiim.un.org/documents-and-reports/un-entities-w/, accessed 22 April 2023.

[547] UN Doc. A/HRC/46/54, 21 January 2021, para. 83.

[548] UN Doc. A/HRC/RES/40/17, 22 March 2019, preamble para. 15.

[549] UN Doc. A/71/755, 19 January 2017, Annex, p. 11, para. 5(a).

[550] OPCW Doc. C-SS-4/DEC.3, 27 June 2018, operative para. 12.

[551] UN Doc. A/73/295, 3 August 2018, p. 14, para. 59. See also UN Doc. A/75/311 13 August 2020, para. 14; UN Doc. A/75/743, 12 February 2021, para. 11; UN Doc. A/76/690*, 11 February 2022, para. 14.

[552] Memorandum of Understanding Between the Organisation for the Prohibition of Chemical Weapons and the International, Impartial and Independent Mechanism to Assist in the Investigation and Prosecution of Persons Responsible for the Most Serious Crimes Under International Law Committed in the Syrian Arab Republic Since March 2011, Regarding Provision of Access, Storage, and Handling of Information and Evidence, 26 September 2018 (OPCW Doc. C-24/4, 28 November 2019, pp. 18–19, para. 1.62, Annex 8, p. 61). Russia argued that "the Secretariat did not have the mandate to sign an international agreement involving key functions and obligations under the Convention, including the handling of confidential information" (OPCW Doc. EC-91/NAT.44 (Russia), 9 July 2019 p. 2).

[553] UN Doc. A/RES/74/169, 18 December 2019, operative para. 7; UN Doc. A/RES/75/193, 16 December 2020, operative para. 7; UN Doc. A/RES/76/228, 24 December 2021, operative para. 6.

[554] OPCW Doc. EC-96/DG.19, p. 3, para. 25. OPCW Doc. EC-97/NAT.50 (Russia), 6 July 2021, p. 2.

with relevant procedures.[555] The IIIM had sought access to classified materials in these archives and made efforts to meet the requirements thereof under the bulletin, which includes express consent of concerned Member States or third parties, as well as UN Secretary-General approval.[556] Accordingly, the UN General Assembly has called upon the Secretary-General, Member States, and other relevant actors to ensure expeditious processing of relevant materials to be shared with the IIIM without further delay.[557]

The IIIM has adopted "criminal law standards" as its standards of proof,[558] although it is unclear whether this is equivalent to "beyond reasonable doubt." It is argued that the IIIM, "unlike a court," does not make findings beyond a reasonable doubt in light of the fact that even after its creation, chemical weapons use has persisted.[559] Perhaps it can be said that "criminal law standards of proof" are at least higher standards than the "reasonable grounds" or "sufficient evidence" that other fact-finding organs use. The IIIM has "a quasi-prosecutorial function,"[560] which, as mentioned above, encompasses collecting evidence of violations of international humanitarian law and international human rights law and preparing files to assist in future criminal proceedings.[561] Such evidence must meet high standards of proof indeed if relevant persons are to be held accountable for the most serious crimes under international law. Thus, the different standards of proof applied by the various fact-finding missions implies that the information obtained from OPCW and materials available from OPCW-UN JIM archives might serve as a useful reference for IIIM investigations, but not as reliable evidence in legal proceedings.

While the IIIM has made considerable progress toward its objectives, it has also been stymied by the Syrian government who refuses access to its territory, prevents

---

[555] UN Doc. ST/SGB/2019/4, 18 April 2019.

[556] UN Doc. A/76/690, 11 February 2022, pp. 5–6, para. 15. See also UN Doc. A/75/311, 13 August 2020, p. 5, para. 14; UN Doc. A/75/743, 12 February 2021, p. 5, para. 12.

[557] UN Doc. A/RES/74/169, 18 December 2019, operative para. 8; UN Doc. A/RES/75/193, 16 December 2020, operative para. 8; UN Doc. A/RES/76/228, 24 December 2021, operative para. 7.

[558] UN Doc. A/71/755, 19 November 2017, p. 5, para. 23 and Annex (Terms of reference), p. 13, para. 17.

[559] Yasmin Naqvi, "Crossing the red line: The use of chemical weapons in Syria and what should happen now," *International Review of the Red Cross*, Vol. 99, No. 3 (2017), p. 959, p. 993.

[560] UN Doc. A/71/755, 19 November 2017, p. 6, para. 32.

[561] UN Doc. A/RES/71/248, 21 December 2016, operative para. 4.

on-site visits, and ignores requests for relevant material.[562] It has thus relied on "open-source materials" for the purpose of the collection of relevant records.[563]

(iv) **Sanctions**

Finally, having recognized a lack of improvement of situation, the policy-making organs have explored options to take sanctions measures against the Syrian government. As mentioned, August 2016 was a turning point for the Syrian chemical weapons matter, when the OPCW-UN JIM concluded in its third report that the Syrian government had used chemical weapons, which it could not do if it had placed all chemical weapons under international control for destruction. The fact that the Syrian government used chemical weapons meant that it still held undeclared chemical weapons. Therefore, chemical weapons use was logically linked with chemical weapons declarations.[564] The policy-making organs thus treated them as a single instance of non-compliance. Subsequent portions of the decisions concentrated on uses of chemical weapons.

On 11 November 2016, the OPCW Executive Council adopted Decision EC-83/DEC.5.[565] While its primary purpose was to task the Technical Secretariat with the new inspections scheme, it included such statements on the use of chemical weapons as "grave concern" with the findings of the OPCW-UN JIM reports,[566] condemnations[567] of violations of the CWC, UN Security Council Resolution 2118, and decisions of the Executive Council,[568] and a call to all parties to immediately desist from any further such use.[569] It also stressed the importance of accountability,[570] and in connection therewith, called upon States Parties to provide information on "past or future allegations of use of chemical weapons" within the territory of Syria to the Director-General.[571]

---

562 UN Doc. A/72/764, 28 February 2018, p. 17, para. 70; UN Doc. A/73/295, 3 August 2018, p. 10, para. 40; UN Doc. A/73/741, 13 February 2019, p. 5, para. 13; UN Doc. A/74/313, 22 August 2019, p. 5, para. 16; UN Doc. A/74/699, 13 February 2020, p. 10, para. 34; UN Doc. A/75/311, 13 August 2020, p. 5, para. 15; UN Doc. A/75/743, 12 February 2021, p. 5, para. 14; UN Doc. A/76/690*, 11 February 2022, p. 6, para. 18.

563 UN Doc. A/73/741, 13 February 2019, p. 4, para. 10. See also UN Doc. A/73/741, 13 February 2019, p. 7, para. 24; UN Doc. A/74/313, 22 August 2019, p. 5, para. 14; UN Doc. A/74/699, 13 February 2020, p. 4, para. 10; UN Doc. A/75/311, 13 August 2020, p. 6, para. 19; UN Doc. A/76/690*, 11 February 2022, p. 5, para. 13.

564 OPCW Doc. EC-83/NAT.5 (US), 11 October 2016 p. 2; OPCW Doc. EC-83/NAT.14 (UK), 12 October 2016, p. 2. See also OPCW Doc. C-SS-4/DEC.3, 27 June 2018, operative para. 7; OPCW Doc. EC-94/DEC.2, 9 July 2020, operative para. 2; OPCW Doc. C-25/DEC.9, 21 April 2021, operative para 4.

565 OPCW Doc. EC-83/DEC.5, 11 November 2016. The vote was 28 in favor to four against, with nine abstentions (OPCW Doc. EC-83/5, 11 November 2016, para. 6.27).

566 OPCW Doc. EC-83/DEC.5, 11 November 2016, operative para. 1.

567 *Ibid.*, operative para. 3.

568 *Ibid.*, operative para. 3.

569 *Ibid.*, operative para. 3.

570 *Ibid.*, operative para. 4.

571 *Ibid.*, operative para. 8.

Meanwhile, the UK and France explored sanctions,[572] and the UN Security Council debated a draft resolution on the subject on 28 February 2017,[573] with forty-two co-sponsors proposed several sanction measures against Syria under Chapter VII of the UN Charter, particularly Article 41.[574] The draft resolution expressed grave concern about the findings of the OPCW-UN JIM, declared a that Resolution 2118 and international law had both been violated, and condemned the use of chemical weapons in Syria.[575] It called for all parties in Syria to cease any use of toxic chemicals as weapons immediately and permanently.[576] More importantly, it also instigated a prototype sanctions regime, including measures on asset freezes, travel bans, embargos, a sanctions committee, a panel of experts, reporting requirements, and lists of entities and individuals to be targeted.[577] Russia and China vetoed this draft as well.[578] Russia expressed concerns about credibility of facts on which the OPCW-UN JIM based its conclusions, lack of analysis of information about alleged use of toxic substances by opposition groups, and the geographic balance of OPCW-UN JIM experts, and suggested a "national investigation."[579] China and Kazakhstan stressed relevant conclusions based on a need for more convincing evidence.[580] Bolivia, Egypt, and Ethiopia pointed out lack of due process in making the lists of individuals and entities subject to sanctions.[581] France, the UK, Japan, and Italy

[572] A draft resolution was first prepared "at the beginning of December 2016" (UN Doc. S/PV.7893, 28 February 2017, p. 6 (Russia)). See also Security Council Report, What's In Blue, Syria: Draft Resolution Imposing Sanctions Regarding the Use and Production of Chemical Weapons, 25 February 2017, https://www.securitycouncilreport.org/whatsinblue/2017/02/syria-draft-resolution-imposing-sanctions-regarding-the-use-and-production-of-chemical-weapons.php, accessed 22 April 2023.

[573] UN Doc. S/2017/172, 28 February 2017.

[574] *Ibid.*, preamble para. 16. France, the UK, and Japan referred to operative para. 21 of Resolution 2118, which stipulates "in the event of non-compliance with this resolution, including unauthorized transfer of chemical weapons, or any use of chemical weapons by anyone in the Syrian Arab Republic, to impose measures under Chapter VII of the United Nations Charter" (UN Doc. S/PV. 7893, 28 February 2017, pp. 2 (France), 5 (UK), 8 (Japan)).

[575] UN Doc. S/2017/172, 28 February 2017, operative paras. 1–3. It also included a statement on chemical weapons use in general (*ibid.*, preamble para. 3), as well as by non-State actors (*ibid.*, operative paras. 1–3, 8, See also *ibid.*, operative paras. 9–10).

[576] *Ibid.*, operative para. 4.

[577] *Ibid.*, operative para. 13–31. It is reported that some States questioned the appropriateness of designating individuals in the draft resolution rather than leaving this role to the sanctions committee (Security Council Report, What's In Blue, Syria: Draft Resolution Imposing Sanctions Regarding the Use and Production of Chemical Weapons, 25 February 2017, https://www.securitycouncilreport.org/whatsinblue/2017/02/syria-draft-resolution-imposing-sanctions-regarding-the-use-and-production-of-chemical-weapons.php, accessed 22 April 2023).

[578] UN Doc. S/PV.7893, 28 February 2017, p. 4. The vote was nine in favor to three against (Bolivia, China and Russia), with three abstentions (Egypt, Ethiopia and Kazakhstan).

[579] *Ibid.*, p. 7 (Russia). The "national investigation" idea provides Syria with an opportunity to verify the facts laid out in the OPCW-UN JIM report "in accordance with its obligations under article VII of the Chemical Weapons Convention.".

[580] *Ibid.*, pp. 9 (China), 14 (Kazakhstan).

[581] *Ibid.*, pp. 11 (Bolivia), 12 (Egypt), 13 (Ethiopia).

countered by endorsing the impartial, objective, independent, and professional investigation of the OPCW-UN JIM,[582] while the US and the UK expressed doubt about Russia's "national investigation" suggestion.[583]

In light of the ongoing Security Council deadlock, the roles and functions of the OPCW policy making-organs took on greater importance. As illustrated above, in June 2018, the OPCW Conference of the States Parties adopted Decision C-SS-4/DEC.3 at its fourth special session, endorsing the revival of the attribution mechanism within the OPCW,[584] though some States Parties were strongly opposed. On 8 April 2020, the OPCW IIT, a new attribution mechanism established pursuant to this decision, published its first report, concluding that "there are reasonable grounds to believe that the Syrian Arab Republic used chemical weapons."[585] In response, in July 2020, the Executive Council at its ninety-fourth regular session adopted Decision EC-94/DEC.2,[586] which explicitly referred to Article VIII, paras. 35 and 36 of the Convention,[587] meaning that the OPCW Executive Council was dealing with Syrian non-compliance as well. While its key elements were a request that Syria redress outstanding declarations issues and the introduction of another inspections scheme, it also referred to the findings of the OPCW-UN JIM and the OPCW IIT,[588] condemned the use of chemical weapons conducted by the Syria Arab Republic,[589] expressed deep concern about the direct implication by the use of chemical weapons of Syria's failure to declare and destroy all chemical weapons and chemical weapons production facilities,[590] and demanded that Syria immediately cease all use of chemical weapons.[591] It further emphasized the importance of assistance in connection with criminal investigations or proceedings relating to chemical weapons use by the Syrian Arab Republic,[592] and expressed its full support for relevant investigatory entities established under the auspices of the UN.[593] The OPCW Conference of the

---

582 *Ibid.*, pp. 2 (France), 5 (UK), 8 (Japan), 10 (Italy).

583 *Ibid.*, pp. 5 (US), 6 (UK).

584 OPCW Doc. C-SS-4/DEC.3, 27 June 2018.

585 OPCW Doc. S/1867/2020, 8 April 2020, p. 58, para. 14.

586 OPCW Doc. EC-94/DEC.2, 9 July 2020. The vote was 29 in favor (Argentina, Australia, Austria, Belgium, Brazil, Bulgaria, Cameroon, Chile, El Salvador, France, Germany, Ghana, Guatemala, Italy, Japan, Lithuania, Mexico, Morocco, Norway, Peru, the Philippines, Poland, Republic of Korea, Romania, Saudi Arabia, Senegal, Spain, UK, and US) to three against (China, Iran, and Russia), with nine abstentions (Algeria, Bangladesh, India, Kenya, Nigeria, Pakistan, South Africa, Sudan, and United Arab Emirates) (OPCW Doc. EC-94/4, 9 July 2020, para. 6.31). The CWC mandates a two-thirds vote of OPCW Executive Council membership, i.e., 28 out of 41 votes, to adopt decisions in substance (Article VIII, para. 29), showing how narrow the margin of passage was in this instance.

587 OPCW Doc. EC-94/DEC.2, 9 July 2020, preamble paras. 14 and 15, operative paras. 5 and 7.

588 *Ibid.*, preamble paras. 5 and 9.

589 *Ibid.*, operative para. 1.

590 *Ibid.*, operative para. 2.

591 *Ibid.*, operative para. 2.

592 *Ibid.*, operative para. 10.

593 *Ibid.*, operative para. 11.

States Parties additionally adopted Decision C-25/DEC.9 at its twenty-fifth session in April 2021.[594] Having recapitulated all relevant elements of Decision EC-94/DEC.2 in terms of the use of chemical weapons, including the reference to the findings of the OPCW-UN JIM and the OPCW IIT,[595] the condemnation,[596] the deep concern about the direct implication by use of chemical weapons of Syria's failure to declare and destroy all chemical weapons and chemical weapons production facilities,[597] and the demand for immediate cessation,[598] for the first time in OPCW history, the OPCW Conference of the States Parties took substantive sanction measures against a Member state, i.e., Syria, including suspension of the rights and privileges of Syria (a) to vote in the Conference or the Council, (b) to stand for election to the Council, and (c) to hold any office of the Conference, the Council, or any subsidiary organs, in accordance with Article VIII, para. 21(k) and Article XII, para. 2 of the Convention.[599]

(3) Unilateral Measures to Response to Non-compliance

(a) Non-Military Actions

(i) Autonomous Sanction Measures[600]

Several States have individually or collectively taken autonomous sanction measures in response to the use of chemical weapons. This section discusses the practice of Australia, Canada, the EU, Switzerland, and the US by focusing on their approach, relevant legal authorities, measures, designations and legality, as well as additional measures taken by France.

Approach

Practice indicates country-specific and thematic approaches to autonomous sanction measures, respectively. The former targets Syria itself in the wider context of the serious or grave situation of the non-international armed conflict that began in March 2011 and persists as of this writing. Autonomous sanction measures have been taken against Syria since the early stages of this conflict, and those taken in response to the use of chemical weapons should be understood in this same context. The latter addresses chemical weapons or other WMD per se. As mentioned before, there were concerns about Syrian chemical weapons proliferation before the present conflict, with some States having already introduced autonomous sanction measures to prevent

[594] OPCW Doc. C-25/DEC.9, 21 April 2021. The vote was 87 in favor to 15 against, with 34 abstentions (OPCW Doc. C-25/5, 22 April 2021, para. 9.24).

[595] *Ibid.*, preamble paras. 11 and 15.

[596] *Ibid.*, operative para. 2.

[597] *Ibid.*, operative paras. 4 and 6.

[598] *Ibid.*, operative paras. 4 and 6.

[599] *Ibid.*, operative para. 7.

[600] This section is a revision of an article by the present author titled "Syria: The chemical weapons question and autonomous sanctions," in Masahiko Asada (ed.), *Economic Sanctions in International Law and Practice* (Routledge, 2020), pp. 200–222.

such proliferation and possible use, while other States adopted autonomous sanction measures focusing on the illegal production, possession and use of chemical weapons in response to repeated Syrian use of chemical weapons despite the obligations to eliminate same under the Resolution 2118 Regime.

- ***Country-specific approach***

As mentioned above, Australia, Canada, the EU, Switzerland, and the US have adopted a country-specific approach to the autonomous sanction measures. Once enacted, they are amended to update their list of designated targets:

- Australia has imposed its country-specific Syria sanctions regime "to reflect Australis's grave concern at the Syrian regime's deeply disturbing and unacceptable use of violence against its people." Its core legal instruments are the Autonomous Sanctions Act 2011 and the Autonomous Sanctions Regulations 2011, with the former creating a general framework for sanction scheme, while the latter, with amendments, includes the details about tailor-made country-specific measures. Practical and operational aspects are supplemented by such instruments as Specifications, Designations, and Lists. The Autonomous Sanctions (Designated Persons and Entities and Declared Persons—Syria) List 2012 of 7 March 2012, amended 31 May 2013, 26 February 2015, and 12 February 2018,[601] and the Autonomous Sanctions (Designated Persons and Entities and Declared Persons—Syria) List 2017 of 17 August 2017 play key roles in specifying targets of autonomous sanctions against Syria.[602]
- Canada adopted the country-specific Special Economic Measures (Syria) Regulations (SOR/2011–114) on 24 May 2011 in accordance with subsections 3.4(1) to (3) of the Special Economic Measures Act of 4 June 1992.[603] Its purpose was to respond to the situation in Syria, which constitutes "a grave breach of international peace and security that has resulted or is likely to result in a serious international crisis."[604] The Regulations constitute a package of sanctions, including lists of targeted individuals and entities, which have been amended fourteen times to

---

[601] Autonomous Sanctions (Designated Persons and Entities and Declared Persons—Syria) List 2012, https://www.legislation.gov.au/Details/F2012L00482, accessed 22 April 2023; Autonomous Sanctions (Designated Persons and Entities and Declared Persons—Syria) Amendment List 2013, https://www.legislation.gov.au/Details/F2013C00664, accessed 22 April 2023; Autonomous Sanctions (Designated Persons and Entities and Declared Persons—Syria) Amendment List 2015 (No.1), https://www.legislation.gov.au/Details/F2015C00369, accessed 22 April 2023; Autonomous Sanctions (Designated Persons and Entities and Declared Persons—Syria) Continuing Effect Declaration and Revocation Instrument 2018, https://www.legislation.gov.au/Details/F2018C00133, accessed 22 April 2023.

[602] Autonomous Sanctions (Designated Persons and Entities and Declared Persons—Syria) List 2017, https://www.legislation.gov.au/Details/F2017L01080, accessed 22 April 2023.

[603] Government of Canada, Canadian Sanctions Related to Syria, https://www.international.gc.ca/world-monde/international_relations-relations_internationales/sanctions/syria-syrie.aspx?lang=eng, accessed 22 April 2023.

[604] The Special Economic Measures Act of 4 June 1992 specifies "a grave breach of international peace and security that has resulted or is likely to result in a serious international crisis" as one of the circumstances triggering Special Economic Measures (section 3.4(1), subsection (1.1)).

expand their scope, adding individuals and entities to same.[605] The most relevant of these amendments to chemical weapons use in Syria are the Regulations Amending the Special Economic Measures (Syria) Regulations (SOR/2017–69) of 20 April 2017.[606]

- The EU enacted the country-specific "Restrictive Measures in view of the Situation in Syria" in May 2011. Article 215 of the Treaty on the Functioning of the European Union provides the European Council (EC) with mandates to interrupt or reduce the EU's economic and financial relations with one or more third countries, and to identify a list of comprehensive restrictive measures to be implemented by its members.[607] The EC adopted the original Council Decision 2011/273/CFSP regarding "Restrictive Measures in view of the Situation in Syria" on 9 May 2011, which has subsequently been replaced three times, with the latest, Council Decision 2013/255/CFSP, enacted on 31 May 2013 with 46 amendments as of 21 July 2022.[608]
- Switzerland enacted the country-specific "Measures against Syria" (Mesures à l'encontre de la Syrie/ Massnahmen gegenüber Syrien) based on the Federal Act on the Implementation of International Sanctions of 22 March 2002 to respond to the violent repression that the Syrian army and security forces carry out against civilians. The State Secretariat for Economic Affairs (SECO) issued the first order on 18 May 2011 replacing it on 8 June 2012, with 41 amendments as of 27 September 2022. In summary, Switzerland enacts sanctions practically identical to those of the EU.[609]
- The US has enacted the country-specific "Syria sanctions program"[610] to respond to the Syrian government's policies based on such legal authorities as Presidential Executive Orders (E.O.), Congressional statutes, and regulations established by the Office of Foreign Assets Control (OFAC) of the Department of the Treasury (DOT). Instruments relevant to Syrian chemical weapons use include E.O. 13572

---

605 Government of Canada, Justice Laws Website, Special Economic Measures (Syria) Regulations (SOR/2011–114), Full Documents available for previous versions, https://laws-lois.justice.gc.ca/eng/regulations/SOR-2011-114/PITIndex.html, accessed 22 April 2023.

606 Government of Canada, Canada announces new sanctions against Syrian leadership with links to chemical weapons, https://www.canada.ca/en/global-affairs/news/2017/04/canada_announcesnewsanctionsagainstsyrianleadershipwithlinkstoch.html, accessed 22 April 2023.

607 Francesco Giumelli, "From Effective to Useful Sanctions: Lessons Learned from the Experience of the European Union," in Natalino Ronzitti (ed.), *Coercive Diplomacy, Sanctions and International Law* (Brill, Nijhoff, 2016), p. 246, pp. 253–254.

608 Consolidated text: Council Decision 2013/255/CFSP of 31 May 2013 concerning restrictive measures in view of the situation in Syria, https://eur-lex.europa.eu/legal-content/EN/TXT/?uri=CELEX%3A02013D0255-20220721, accessed 22 April 2023.

609 Secrétariat d'Etat à l'économie, Mesures à l'encontre de la Syrie, https://www.seco.admin.ch/seco/fr/home/Aussenwirtschaftspolitik_Wirtschaftliche_Zusammenarbeit/Wirtschaftsbeziehungen/exportkontrollen-und-sanktionen/sanktionen-embargos/sanktionsmassnahmen/massnahmen-gegenueber-syrien.html, accessed 22 April 2023.

610 U.S. Department of the Treasury, "Syria Sanctions," https://home.treasury.gov/policy-issues/financial-sanctions/sanctions-programs-and-country-information/syria-sanctions, accessed 22 April 2023.

of 29 April 2011 (human rights abuse in Syria), E.O. 13573 of 18 May 2011 (targeting the senior officials of the Syrian government), and E.O. 13582 of 18 August 2011 (targeting the Syrian government and transactions with respect to Syria). Target lists are frequently revised.

- ***Thematic approach***

The EU, France, and the US have also taken a thematic approach, combining two approaches to autonomous sanction measures in response to the Syrian chemical weapons matter, again, with lists of targeted individuals and entities renewed and updated as necessary:

- The EU introduced the "Restrictive Measures against the Proliferation and Use of Chemical Weapons" on 15 October 2018, drawing on Council Decision (CFSP) 2018/1544 for legal basis, and keeping "under constant review." As of 11 October 2021, the EC has renewed it annually in accordance with relevant provisions,[611] and amended it five times.[612]
- In addition to the implementation of the EU autonomous sanction measures as a Member State, France has taken its own additional measures in accordance with Articles L.562–3 of the Monetary and Financial Code, which authorizes the Minister of the Economy and Finance to freeze funds and economic resources. Orders of 18 January 2018[613] and 18 May 2018[614] specifically address the use

---

[611] Council Decision (CFSP) 2019/1722, 14 October 2019; Council Decision (CFSP) 2020/1466, 12 October 2020; Council Decision (CFSP) 2021/1799, 11 October 2021; Council Decision (CSFP) 2022/1944, 13 October 2022.

[612] Consolidated text: Council Decision (CFSP) 2018/1544 of 15 October 2018 concerning restrictive measures against the proliferation and use of chemical weapons, https://eur-lex.europa.eu/legal-content/EN/TXT/?uri=CELEX%3A02018D1544-20211013, accessed 22 April 2023.

[613] Arrêté du 18 janvier 2018 portant application des articles L. 562–3 et suivants du code monétaire et financier, NOR: ECOT1801616A; and Arrêté du 18 janvier 2018 portant application des articles L. 562–3 et suivants du code monétaire et financier, NOR: ECOT1801617A (JORF n° 0018 du 23 janvier 2018, https://www.legifrance.gouv.fr/download/pdf?id=YAsnf6hnz13zdM0JqE I861Isrsa00QFujiQScSI_fAU , accessed 22 April 2023).

[614] Arrêté du 17 mai 2018 portant application des articles L. 562–3 et suivants du code monétaire et financier, NOR: ECOT1813351A; Arrêté du 17 mai 2018 portant application des articles L. 562–3 et suivants du code monétaire et financier, NOR: ECOT1813353A; and Arrêté du 17 mai 2018 portant application des articles L. 562–3 et suivants du code monétaire et financier, NOR: ECOT1813357A (JORF n° 0113 du 18 mai 2018, https://www.legifrance.gouv.fr/download/pdf?id=YzfAQ9HliDL0 5e8UDezovk1tUE4pff_NWtPY0T-2KIM =, accessed 22 April 2023).

of chemical weapons in Syria. France has repeated six-month extension of these measures.[615]

- The US issued E.O. 13382 on 28 June 2005 to address the thematic issue of proliferation of WMD and delivery means thereof. This legal authority was used even before the Syrian civil war due to such concerns. The US Congress also provides for visa restrictions against those foreign officials involved in "a gross violation of human rights" in section 7031(c) of the Department of State, Foreign Operations, and Related Programs Appropriations Act 2014,[616] which has been renewed annually as of this writing.[617]

Measures

Sanctions measures are more or less similar across the board, with trade restrictions, asset freeze, and travel bans most frequently imposed:

- Australia's Autonomous Sanctions Regulations 2011 stipulate such sanction measures against Syria as restrictions on export or supply of certain items, including arms, equipment and technology for the oil, gas, and petrochemical industry, equipment and technology for monitoring telecommunications, luxury goods (Part 2, para. 4, Item 4), restrictions on imports of crude oil, petroleum, and petrochemical products (Part 2, para. 4A, Item 2), restrictions on export or

[615] Extensions were granted on 20 July 2018, https://www.legifrance.gouv.fr/download/pdf?id=Z3lP30Pz8A6yvdh9MTR8jGxoCtqh9SJ32VBSCt4dzzI=, accessed 22 April 2023; 18 January 2019, https://www.legifrance.gouv.fr/download/pdf?id=MO3sOiB2V9T8-32qnfVMcGxoCtqh9SJ32VBSCt4dzzI=, accessed 22 April 2023; 18 July 2019, https://www.legifrance.gouv.fr/download/pdf?id=xMSi0N3U_upeHZ81FBHgoGxoCtqh9SJ32VBSCt4dzzI=, accessed 22 April 2023; 17 January 2020, https://www.legifrance.gouv.fr/download/pdf?id=n39uhKySYsCKKR2QQh_3o6BVOO4Ees1U922iCwIn4_8=, accessed 22 April 2023; 16 July 2020, https://www.legifrance.gouv.fr/download/pdf?id=0Pniniz7KL1G3zKMT0eFGt2zup93I6QTVIOrDQLksWk=, accessed 22 April 2023; 15 January 2021, https://www.legifrance.gouv.fr/download/pdf?id=Liw289pOQhZyem6XgFjnQN2zup93I6QTVIOrDQLksWk=, accessed 22 April 2023; 13 July 2021, https://www.legifrance.gouv.fr/download/pdf?id=-Qex6PBdrEX-xi7cWXbhbk1tUE4pff_NWtPY0T-2KIM=, accessed 22 April 2023; 11 January 2022, https://www.legifrance.gouv.fr/download/pdf?id=0_T6sZoNN_IlzohYbHru4RwZjgCJ5g7nDrxqDEoMGrY=, accessed 22 April 2023; and 11 July 2022, https://www.legifrance.gouv.fr/download/pdf?id=YMizwrv-8cJZZCOYEDxtSBwZjgCJ5g7nDrxqDEoMGrY=, accessed 22 April 2023.

[616] Public Law 113–76, 16 December 2014, 128 Stat. 2620 ("Officials of foreign governments and their immediate family members about whom the Secretary of State has credible information have been involved in significant corruption, including corruption related to the extraction of natural resources, or a gross violation of human rights shall be ineligible for entry into the United States."). See also Anton Moiseienko, *Corruption and Targeted Sanctions: Law and Policy of Anti-Corruption Entry Bans* (Brill, 2019), p. 42; Liana W. Rosen and Michael A. Weber, "FY 2020 Foreign Operations Appropriations: Targeting Foreign Corruption and Human Rights Violations," Congressional Research Service, 17 April 2020, https://www.everycrsreport.com/files/2020-04-17_IF10905_b16f232c9119307cbb910cc16ac2ba9af70af6f9.pdf, accessed 22 April 2023.

[617] Public Law 114–11, 18 December 2015, 129 Stat. 2755, Public Law 115–31, 5 May 2017, 131 Stat. 640; Public Law 115–141, 23 March 2018, 132 Stat. 884; Public Law 116–6, 15 February 2019, 133 Stat. 319; Public Law 116–94, 20 December 2019, 133 Stat. 2865; Public Law 116–260, 27 December 2020, 134 Stat. 1743; Public Law 117–103, 15 March 2022, 136 Stat. 615.

provision of such services as military action and manufacture, maintenance or use of Syrian export-sanctioned goods (Part 2, para. 5, Item 4) and commerce by the Syrian oil, petroleum, and petrochemical industry (Part 2, para. 5A, Items 4—7), and travel bans on designated persons (Part 2, para. 6, Item 7).[618] Specifications, Designations and Lists elaborate on practical and operational aspects.

- Canada's Special Economic Measures (Syria) Regulations (SOR/2011–114) have expanded the scope of sanction measures through amendments to include financial prohibitions in relation to designated persons i.e., freezing assets, export bans on goods used for monitoring telecommunications and luxury goods, and import prohibitions on all goods from Syria. It is also prohibited for any person in Canada and any Canadian outside Canada to import, purchase, acquire, carry, or ship chemical weapons and equipment, goods, or dual-use technologies from Syria as well as to transfer, acquire, or purchase technical assistance related to chemical weapons and equipment, goods, or dual-use technologies from Syria.[619]
- EU Council Decision 2013/255/CFSP of 31 May 2013 with amendments covers export restrictions of items including equipment, goods, and technology used for internal repression, equipment for use in monitoring by the Syrian regime, jet fuel, and luxury goods (chapter I), import restrictions of items such as weapons, crude oil and petroleum products, and cultural properties (chapter I), restrictions on financing of specified enterprises (chapter II), restrictions on infrastructure projects (chapter III), restrictions on financial support for trade (chapter IV), financial activities (chapter V), transfer activities (chapter VI), travel bans (chapter VII), and freezing of assets and economic resources (chapter VIII). Council Decision (CFSP) 2018/1544 of 15 October 2018 also provides for travel bans and freezing of assets and economic resources of certain individuals and entities involved in manufacturing or using chemical weapons or engaging in preparations for the use of chemical weapons.
- As mentioned, France has added its own measures to EU sanctions. The funds and economic resources of targeted individuals and entities are subject to asset freezing measures for six months in accordance with Articles L.562–3 of the Monetary and Financial Code.
- Switzerland's domestic order of 8 June 2012 with amendments parallels EU actions, including trade restrictions on items such as armaments, oil and oil products, technologies for exploitation and production of oil and natural gas, jet fuel, electricity generation, equipment, technology, and software for surveillance, precious metals and diamonds, luxury goods, and cultural properties, as well as asset freezes, including restrictions on financial activities, and travel bans.

[618] Autonomous Sanctions Regulations 2011, https://www.legislation.gov.au/Details/F2022C00057.

[619] Government of Canada, Canadian Sanctions Related to Syria, https://www.international.gc.ca/world-monde/international_relations-relations_internationales/sanctions/syria-syrie.aspx?lang=eng, accessed 22 April 2023.

Table 3.1 Designations

	Australia	Canada	EU	Switzerland	US
Individuals	40	21	39	37	293
Entities	20	13	22	22	25

- The US sanctions program blocks the property and interests in property of the government of Syria, including its agencies, instrumentalities, and controlled entities which are in the US or within the possession or control of its citizens, pursuant to E.O. 13582, blocks the property and interests in property of persons listed in an Annex to, or that are determined by the Secretary of the Treasury in consultation with the Secretary of State, to meet the criteria described in, E.O. 13338, E.O. 13572, E.O. 13573, and E.O. 13582, and prohibits transactions or dealings with respect to Syria pursuant to E.O. 13582.[620] E.O. 13382 freezes the assets of proliferators of WMD and their supporters, and isolates them financially. The denial of entry into the US is also covered by section 7031(c) of the Department of State, Foreign Operations, and Related Programs Appropriations Act.

Designations

Participating States and the EU have designated individuals and entities to target with autonomous sanction measures. While such designations can be diverse because each sovereign State or regional organization has full discretion in this regard, they must also be coordinated for best effect.

- ***Status***

Designations are as described in Table 3.1, counting individuals and entities on the website of the France-initiated "Chemical Weapons No Impunity!"[621] campaign.

Out of 322 individuals and 42 entities on the "Chemical Weapons No Impunity!" list, fourteen individuals and ten entities are commonly designated by Australia, Canada, the EU, Switzerland, and the US, meaning that they are key targets involved in chemical weapons use (Tables 3.2 and 3.3).

Particulars of naming and timing of abovementioned targets—identified by the number —and naming thereof by sanctioning authority are also described in Appendix D and E.

- ***Comparative analysis***

Comparative analysis of designations, especially the data on naming and timing of particular targets, yields a number of findings. First, participating States and the EU

[620] Office of Foreign Assets Control, Department of the Treasury, "Syria Sanctions Program," pp. 4–5, https://home.treasury.gov/system/files/126/syria.pdf, accessed 22 April 2023.

[621] Chemical Weapons No Impunity! Sanctions List (322 individuals and 42 entities as of 29 October 2020), https://www.noimpunitychemicalweapons.org/-en-.html, accessed 22 April 2023.

Table 3.2 Fourteen commonly designated individuals

#	Name	Position
1	Ghassan Abbas[a]	Brigadier-General, Syrian Scientific Studies and Research Centre (SSRC/CERS)
2	Suhayl Hasan Al-Hasan[a]	Colonel, Syrian Air Force Intelligence
3	Amr Armanazi[a]	Director-General, Syrian Scientific Studies and Research Centre (SSRC/CERS)
4	Ahmad Ballul[a]	Major-General, Commander, Syrian Arab Air Force and Syrian Arab Air Defense Forces
5	Muhammad Nafi Bilal[a]	Colonel, Syrian Air Force Intelligence Service
6	Bayan Bitar[a]	Managing Director, Organisation for Technological Industries (OTI)
7	Samir Dabul[a]	Brigadier-General, Syrian Scientific Studies and Research Centre (SSRC/CERS)
8	Yasin Ahmad Dahi	Brigadier-General, Syrian Military Intelligence
9	Saji Darwish[a]	Major-General, Syrian Air Force
10	Muhammed Ibrahim[a]	Brigadier-General, Syrian Air Force
11	Muhammad Mahmud Mahalla	Major-General, Director, Syrian Military Intelligence
12	Badi' Mu'Alla	Brigadier-General, Syrian Air Force
13	Jawdat Salbi Mawas	Major-General, Syrian Artillery and Missile Directorate, Syrian Armed Forces
14	Ali Wanus	Brigadier-General, Syrian Scientific Studies and Research Centre (SSRC/CERS)

[a] Individuals also included on the draft UN sanctions list (UN Doc. S/2017/172, 28 February 2017, Annex I)

have dealt with these two categories of targets in the almost same way. There is a sharp contrast between designations of individuals and those of entities for sanctions.

On the one hand, the majority of entities were designated for sanctions before use or alleged use of chemical weapons. By June 2005, the US had designated the Syrian Scientific Studies and Research Center (SSRC) or Centre d'études et de recherches scientifiques (CERS) (#16), the most important target of proliferation concerns,[622] as one of eight entities subject to the aforementioned E.O. 13382,

[622] W. Seth Carus, "Chemical Weapons in the Middle East," *Policy Focus, The Washington Institute for Near East Policy*, No. 9 (December 1988), p. 5, https://www.washingtoninstitute.org/media/3670, accessed 22 April 2023; and Shlomo Gazit (ed.), *The Middle East Military Balance, 1993–1994* (Boulder, CO: Westview Press for the Jaffee Center for Strategic Studies, 1994), p. 229. See also BBC News, "Syria's Chemical Weapons Stockpile," 30 January 2014, www.bbc.com/news/world-middle-east-22307705, accessed 22 April 2023.

Table 3.3 Ten commonly designated entities

#	Name	Description
15	Business Labo[a]	Front company for acquisition of sensitive equipment by SSRC/CERS
16	Syrian Scientific Studies and Research Centre (SSRC) or Centre d'études et de recherches syrien (CERS)[a]	Operating in the chemical weapons proliferation sector…responsible for developing and producing chemical and other non-conventional weapons and delivery systems
17	Expert Partners[a]	SSRC/CERS proxy
18	Handasieh—Organization for Engineering Industries[a]	Front company for acquisition of sensitive equipment by SSRC/CERS
19	Higher Institute for Applied Sciences and Technology (HISAT)[a]	SSRC subsidiary
20	Industrial Solutions[a]	Front company for acquisition of sensitive equipment by SSRC/CERS
21	Mechanical Construction Factory (MCF)[a]	Front company for acquisition of sensitive equipment by SSRC/CERS
22	National Standards & Calibration Laboratory (NCSL)[a]	SSRC subsidiary
23	Organisation for Technological Industries (OTI)[a]	Syrian Ministry of Defence subsidiary
24	Syrinocs—Syrian Arab Co. For Electronic Industries[a]	Front company for acquisition of sensitive equipment by SSRC/CERS

[a] Entities also included on the UN draft sanctions list (UN Doc. S/2017/172, 28 February 2017, Annex I).

which was "aimed at freezing the assets of proliferators of weapons of mass destruction and their supporters and isolating them financially."[623] In January 2007, the US added SSRC subsidiaries Higher Institute for Applied Sciences and Technology (HISAT) (#19) and National Standards & Calibration Laboratory (NCSL) (#22).[624] In December 2011, the EU designated SSRC and five front companies working for acquisition of sensitive equipment by SSRC as subject to sanctions, Business Labo (#15), Handasieh (Organization for Engineering Industries) (#18), Industrial Solutions (#20), Mechanical Construction Factory (MCF) (#21), and Syrinocs (Syrian Arab Co. For Electronic Industries) (#24).[625] Canada, Switzerland, and Australia added the same institutions to their sanctions lists in December 2011 and in February

[623] US Department of State, Executive Order 13,382, https://2009-2017.state.gov/t/isn/c22080.htm, accessed 22 April 2023.

[624] US Department of the Treasury, Three Entities Targeted by Treasury for Supporting Syria's WMD Proliferation, 4 January 2007, https://home.treasury.gov/news/press-releases/hp216, accessed 22 April 2023.

[625] Council Decision 2011/782/CFSP, 1 December 2011.

and March 2012, respectively.[626] The US added the aforementioned front companies to its list in July 2012.[627] As mentioned before, Syria finally acknowledged possessing chemical weapons on 23 July 2012,[628] showing that proliferation concerns were justified in this instance. The abovementioned entities were included on "Chemical Weapons No Impunity!" list primarily because they contributed to producing chemical weapons to be used during the Syrian non-international armed conflict.[629]

On the other hand, all individuals designated by the US and Australia, except Amr Armanazi, Director-General of the SSRC (#3), were included in the sanctions lists of relevant States and the EU after the use of chemical weapons was confirmed. The EU designated Brigadier-General Ghassan Abbas, manager of the SSRC (#1), who was "involved in the proliferation of chemical weapons and the organisation of chemical weapons attacks, including in Ghouta in August 2013," and Bayan Bitar, managing director of the Organization for Technological Industries (OTI) (#6), which assisted in "the production of chemical weapons for the Syrian regime" in March 2015,[630] as well as Major General Jawdat Salbi Mawas (#13), who was "responsible for violent repression against the civilian population, including the use of missiles and chemical weapons by Brigades under his command in highly populated civilian areas in 2013 in Ghouta" in October 2016.[631] It also included Colonel Suhayl Hasan Al-Hasan of Syrian Air Force Intelligence (#2), Amr Armanazi (#3), Colonel Muhammad Nafi Bilal of Syrian Air Force Intelligence Service (#5), and Major General Muhammad Mahmud Mahalla, Director of Syrian Military Intelligence (#11), on the sanctions list between July 2014 and May 2015.[632] The US sanctioned other Syrian military officials in January 2017 "in response to the Organization for the Prohibition of Chemical Weapons (OPCW)—United Nations (UN) Joint Investigative Mechanism (JIM) findings that the Syrian regime used industrial chlorine as a weapon against its own people," including Brigadier-General Yasin Ahmad Dahi of Syrian

[626] Canada, Regulations Amending the Special Economic Measures (Syria) Regulations, P.C. 2011–1727 (December 22, 2011); Switzerland, Ordonnance du 18 mai 2011 instituant des mesures à l'encontre de la Syrie (Etat le 7 février 2012)/ Verordnung über Massnahmen gegenüber Syrien vom 18. Mai 2011 (Stand am 7. Februar 2012); Australia, Autonomous Sanctions (Designated Persons and Entities and Declared Persons—Syria) List 2012, https://www.legislation.gov.au/Details/F2012L00482, accessed 22 April 2023.

[627] US Department of the Treasury, Treasury Increases Sanctions Against Syria, 18 July 2012, https://home.treasury.gov/news/press-releases/tg1642, accessed 22 April 2023.

[628] Reuters, "Syria Says Could Use Chemical Arms Against Foreigners," 23 July 2012, www.reuters.com/article/us-syria-crisis/syria-says-could-use-chemical-arms-against-foreigners-idUSBRE8610SH20120723, accessed 22 April 2023; New York Times, "Syria Threatens Chemical Attack on Foreign Force," 23 July 2012, www.nytimes.com/2012/07/24/world/middleeast/chemical-weapons-wont-be-used-in-rebellion-syria-says.html, accessed 21 January 2023.

[629] This also means that the States and organizations in question were unable to prevent chemical weapons attacks through autonomous sanction measures against concerned entities, raising the question of how to ensure the effectiveness of such sanctions in future.

[630] Council Implementing Decision (CFSP) 2015/383, 6 March 2015.

[631] Council Implementing Decision (CFSP) 2016/1897, 27 October 2016.

[632] Council Decision 2014/488/CFSP, 22 July 2014; Council Decision 2014/730/CFSP, 20 October 2014; Council Decision (CFSP) 2015/837, 28 May 2015.

Military Intelligence (#8) pursuant to E.O. 13572, Major-General Ahmad Ballul, Commander of Syrian Arab Air Force and Syrian Arab Air Defense Forces (#4), Major-General Saji Jamil Darwish of Syrian Arab Air Force (#9), Brigadier-General Badi' Mualla of Syrian Arab Air Force (#12), and Brigadier-General Muhammad Ibrahim of Syrian Air Force (#10), per E.O. 13573, and Brigadier-General Ali Wanus (#14) and Brigadier General Samir Dabul of SSRC (#7), in accordance with E.O. 13382.[633] The EU and the US update their lists to incorporating targets designated by one or the other. Switzerland follows EU action, typically within two months. Australia and Canada have designated all of these individuals based on only one or two actions, respectively.[634]

Second, participating States and the EU adopted a moratorium on sanctions designations, enacting no additional autonomous sanction measures between August 2013 and July 2014, not even when the UN Mission confirmed sarin use in September 2013. As mentioned above, chemical weapons use in Syria led to an unexpected agreement on the elimination of Syrian chemical weapons in exchange for abandoning a plan by which the US, the UK (at the early stage), and France would attack Syria. The Resolution 2118 Regime set a deadline of June 2014 for the project. Perhaps no State wanted to spoil the international efforts during this period. Thanks to worldwide cooperation and assistance, chemical weapons were successfully removed from Syria on 23 June 2014.[635] However, the moratorium was over at least for the EU, followed by Switzerland, after the deadline passed, as indicated below.

Third, decisions by States or organizations tend to affect subsequent decisions by others. It goes without saying that the EU and the US have taken the initiative in designating sanctions targets, most likely because they have actionable intelligence. Their designations have been followed by Australia, Canada, and Switzerland, showing their division of roles. Swiss practice is crystal clear. Switzerland replicates most EU sanctions and maintains an identical sanctions list, though not all. It is pointed out that the Swiss Federal Council must rule case by case whether to align Switzerland with the EU, after a careful consideration of all the interests involved.[636] Australian and Canadian practice suggests the various actions they have taken between before and after the use of chemical weapons. On the one hand,

---

[633] US Department of the Treasury, Treasury Sanctions Syrian Officials in Connection With OPCW-UN Findings of Regime's Use of Chemical Weapons on Civilians, 12 January 2017, https://home.treasury.gov/news/press-releases/jl0701, accessed 22 April 2023.

[634] Australia, Minister for Foreign Affairs, The Hon Julie Bishop MP, Sanctions targeting Syria's chemical weapons program, 24 August 2017, https://www.foreignminister.gov.au/minister/julie-bishop/media-release/sanctions-targeting-syrias-chemical-weapons-program, accessed 22 April 2023. Canada, Regulations Amending the Special Economic Measures (Syria) Regulations, P.C. 2017–405, 13 April 2017 and P.C. 2017–407, 20 April 2017.

[635] OPCW Doc. EC-76/6, 11 July 2014, para. 6.14.

[636] Marco Gestri, "Sanctions Imposed by the European Union: Legal and Institutional Aspects," in Natalino Ronzitti (ed.), *Coercive Diplomacy, Sanctions, and International Law* (Brill, Nijhoff, 2016), p. 70, pp. 76–77. Article 1 of the Federal Act on the Implementation of International Sanctions of 22 March 2002 stipulates that "[t]he Confederation may enact compulsory measures in order to implement sanctions that have been ordered by the United Nations Organisation, by the Organisation for Security and Cooperation in Europe, or by Switzerland's most significant trading partners and

they too shared EU chemical weapons proliferation concerns before their use was confirmed, and designated the exact same entities for sanctions. On the other hand, they did not act before the publication of the OPCW-UN JIM report that identified the Syrian government as the perpetrator or the vote on a UN Security Council draft resolution that included targeted sanctions against individuals and entities involved in use of chemical weapons. It appears that they were motivated to action by the sarin gas attack on Khan Shaykhun on 4 April 2017.

Fourth, the EU and the US have complimented each other in the abovementioned initiative in sanctions designations, a circumstance possibly affected by changes in US administrations. Before fighting broke out in March 2011, the US acted alone. As mentioned, the US designated SSRC by mid-2005 and its subsidiaries in early 2007. While the EU, Canada, Switzerland, and Australia also designated SSRC for sanctions between December 2011 and March 2012, they did not so designate its subsidiaries until later. The EU added them to the list in July 2014, followed by Switzerland in September. Canada and Australia followed suit in April and August 2017, respectively.

In December 2011, the EU designated SSRC and the front companies working for acquisition of sensitive equipment by the SSRC as sanctions targets. Canada, Switzerland, and Australia followed suit between late December 2011 and early February 2012. The US added the entities to its list in July 2012. During the Obama administration, the US let the EU lead. For instance, the EU designated one entity (#17) in October 2012, while the US did so in July 2014. The EU also sanctioned one individual (#2) in July 2014, another (#5) in October 2014, two individuals (#1 and #6) and an entity (#23) in March 2015, and still another individual (#11) in May 2015, while the US added these targets to its list in January 2017. It should also be noted that the EU's designation of these individuals for sanctions was in response to the sarin gas attack of 21 August 2013, which the US did nothing about, despite joining the UK and France in criticizing the Assad regime over this incident.[637]

which serve to secure compliance with international law, and in particular the respect of human rights." Needless to say, the EU is one of "Switzerland's most significant trading partners.".

[637] US, Government Assessment of the Syrian Government's Use of Chemical Weapons on August 21, 2013, https://obamawhitehouse.archives.gov/the-press-office/2013/08/30/government-assessment-syrian-government-s-use-chemical-weapons-august-21, accessed 22 April 2023; UK, Letter from the Chairman of the Joint Intelligence Committee (JIC) about reported chemical weapons use in Syria, 29 August 2013, www.gov.uk/government/uploads/system/uploads/attachment_data/file/235094/Jp_115_JD_PM_Syria_Reported_Chemical_Weapon_Use_with_annex.pdf, accessed 22 April 2023; France, Syrian Chemical Programme—National Executive Summary of Declassified Intelligence, 2 September 2013, www.diplomatie.gouv.fr/en/IMG/pdf/Syrian_Chemical_Programme.pdf, accessed 22 April 2023. The US designated a total of eight entities close to the SSRC for sanctions, taking E.O. 13,382 to be its legal basis (US Department of the Treasury, "Treasury Sanctions Companies for Aiding the Syrian Regime," 9 July 2014, https://home.treasury.gov/news/press-releases/jl2558, accessed 22 April 2023; US Department of the Treasury, "Treasury Targets Syrian Regime Financial and Weapons," 31 March 2015, https://home.treasury.gov/news/press-releases/JL10013, accessed 22 April 2023; US Department of the Treasury, "Treasury Sanctions Networks Providing Support to the Government of Syria," 21 July 2016, https://home.treasury.gov/news/press-releases/jl0526, accessed 22 April 2023.

On one of the last days of the Obama administration in January 2017, the US acted for the first time in the context of the use of chemical weapons, designating seven individuals for sanctions (#4, #7, #8, #9, #10, #12 and #14), referring to the OPCW-UN JIM reports of August and October 2016. The significance of this was that the Obama administration acted based on third-party confirmation that the Assad had regime used chlorine gas as a weapon. These sanctions were followed by a draft UN Security Council resolution on sanctions. Given that Russia and China vetoed said draft resolution, the EU and Switzerland added to their sanction lists the individuals and entities that they had not yet themselves so designated.[638] Canada and Australia followed suit in April and August 2017.[639]

As described above, on 4 April 2017, another instance of chemical weapons use was alleged, with media reports suggesting that victims showed signs sarin poisoning.[640] The OPCW FFM began to investigate almost immediately,[641] confirming that sarin was used at Khan Shaykhun.[642] Following this finding, the OPCW-UN JIM concluded that the Syrian Arab Republic was involved.[643] Contrary to its predecessor, the Trump administration did not wait for these investigations, but took prompt military action against the Assad regime on 6 April to be discussed

[638] EU, Council Implementing Decision (CFSP) 2017/485, 20 March 2017; Switzerland, Ordonnance du 8 juin 2012 instituant des mesures à l'encontre de la Syrie (Etat le 28 mars 2017)/ Verordnung über Massnahmen gegenüber Syrien vom 8. Juni 2012 (Stand am 28. März 2017).

[639] Canada, Regulations Amending the Special Economic Measures (Syria) Regulations, P.C. 2017–407, 20 April 2017; Australia, Autonomous Sanctions (Designated Persons and Entities and Declared Persons—Syria) List 2017, https://www.legislation.gov.au/Details/F2017L01080, accessed 22 April 2023.

[640] Reuters, "Scores Reported Killed in Gas Attack on Syrian Rebel Area," 4 April 2017, www.reuters.com/article/us-mideast-crisis-syria-idlib/scores-reported-killed-in-gas-attack-on-syrian-rebel-area-idUSKBN1760IB, accessed 22 April 2023; The Guardian, "Syria Chemical Weapons Attack Toll Rises to 70 as Russian Narrative Is Dismissed," 5 April 2017, www.theguardian.com/world/2017/apr/04/syria-chemical-attack-idlib-province, accessed 22 April 2023. The US, the UK and France argued that sarin was used by the Assad regime (US, www.opcw.org/fileadmin/OPCW/EC/M-54/en/United_States_ECM54_Statement.pdf, accessed 22 April 2023; White House, The Assad Regime's Use of Chemical Weapons on April 4, 2017; OPCW Doc. EC-M-54/NAT.19 (UK), 13 April 2017; National Evaluation, Chemical Attack of April 4, 2017 (Khan Sheikhoun), Clandestine Syrian Chemical Weapons Program, www.diplomatie.gouv.fr/IMG/pdf/170425_-_evaluation_nationale_-_anglais_-_final_cle0dbf47-1.pdf, accessed 22 April 2023).

[641] OPCW Press Release on Allegations of Chemical Weapons Use in Southern Idlib, Syria, 4 April 2017, www.opcw.org/news/article/opcw-press-release-on-allegations-of-chemical-weapons-use-in-southern-idlib-syria/, accessed 22 April 2023.

[642] OPCW Doc. S/1510/2017, 29 June 2017, paras. 6.4 and 6.25.

[643] UN Doc. S/2017/904, 26 October 2017, p. 10, para. 46.

hereinafter,[644] and extended its sanctions regime pursuant to E.O. 13582 by adding 271 employees of the SSRC to the list on its sole initiative on 24 April.[645]

Legality

These autonomous sanction measures have been taken in accordance with domestic law or EU law. This raises the question of their lawfulness in light of international law. The UN General Assembly Resolution 2625 (XXV) on the Friendly Relations Declaration stipulates that "[n]o State may use or encourage the use of economic political or any other type of measures to coerce another State in order to obtain from it the subordination of the exercise of its sovereign rights and to secure from it advantages of any kind."[646] Given that the Friendly Relations Declaration is generally considered to be an authoritative interpretation of the principles in Article 2 of the UN Charter, this provision could offer a basis for arguing that autonomous sanction measures as such are unlawful. However, even if autonomous sanction measures are incompatible with the non-interference obligation, they might be justified under the law on State responsibility.[647]

The ARSIWA accommodates responses to violations of obligations under international law, with countermeasures being most relevant to autonomous sanction measures. The wrongfulness of such sanction measures may be precluded if strict conditions for countermeasures are met, including violations against other State. Given that the aforementioned autonomous sanction measures have been taken in response to chemical weapons use,[648] one such condition is thus satisfied. There is an obstacle, however. The ARSIWA distinguishes between "an injured State" under Article 42 and "a State other than an injured State" under Article 48, and does not explicitly entitle the latter to resort to countermeasures. In the present instance of chemical weapons use against citizens in the Syrian non-international armed conflict, it might be difficult to recognize those States and members of regional organizations that have taken autonomous sanction measures as "an injured State" due to lack of material damage on their part. This does not necessarily mean that the ARSIWA completely excludes the possibility of "a State other than an injured State" to resort to countermeasures. It endorses the right of "a State other than an injured State" to take "lawful measures" against a State that has violated international law, per Article

---

644 US Department of Defense, "Trump Orders Missile Attack in Retaliation for Syrian Chemical Strikes," 6 April 2017, www.defense.gov/News/Article/Article/1144601/trump-orders-missile-attack-in-retaliation-for-syrian-chemical-strikes/, accessed 22 April 2023.

645 US Department of the Treasury, "Treasury Sanctions 271 Syrian Scientific Studies and Research Center Staff in Response to Sarin Attack on Khan Sheikhoun," 24 April 2017, www.treasury.gov/press-center/press-releases/Pages/sm0056.aspx, accessed 22 April 2023. 258 of 271 individuals are on "Chemical Weapons No Impunity!" list.

646 UN Doc. A/RES/2625 (XXV), 24 October 1970.

647 Matthew Happold, "Economic Sanctions and International Law: An Introduction," in Matthew Happold and Paul Eden (eds.), *Economic Sanctions and International Law* (Hart Publishing, 2016), pp. 2–3.

648 While some autonomous sanctions were originally enacted in reaction to proliferation concerns, they should be understood as being enacted in like context following actual chemical weapons use.

54. Thus, whether "a State other than an injured State" can take countermeasures depends upon the interpretation of "lawful measures." If it means only retorsion as an originally lawful act, it limits the options of the third States.[649] If not, then Article 54 is practically meaningless, because retorsion is lawful. Its identity as a provision in Chapter II, titled "Countermeasures," is also questionable.[650] The ILC leaves this issue to "the further development of international law."[651]

Given the foregoing, it is possible that the abovementioned autonomous sanction measures might be justified by countermeasures. Syria is obliged not to produce or possess chemical weapons under the CWC and UN Security Council Resolution 2118.[652] As stated above, the Syrian government's use of chemical weapons shows that it produced and possessed chemical weapons in violation of these obligations. Autonomous sanction measures could thus be taken in response to such violations. Article 42, para. (b)(ii) of the ARSIWA stipulates that "[a] State is entitled as an injured State to invoke the responsibility of another State if the obligation breached is owed to…a group of States including that State, or the international community as a whole, and the breach of the obligation…is of such a character as radically to change the position of all the other States to which the obligation is owed with respect to the further performance of the obligation." The ILC specifies "a disarmament treaty" as an example of this special category of obligations.[653] The US, the EU, and Australia referred to such obligations concerning both chemical weapons use and the production or proliferation of chemical weapons pursuant to the CWC and UN Security Council Resolution 2118.[654]

[649] Hayashi, *supra* note 446, pp. 92–93.

[650] Masahiko Asada, "Definition and Legal Justification of Sanctions," in Masahiko Asada (ed.), *Economic Sanctions in International Law and Practice* (Routledge, 2020), p. 3, pp. 16–17.

[651] *Yearbook of the International Law Commission 2001*, Vol. II, Part Two, p. 139, para. (6).

[652] Article 1, para. (1)(a), Chemical Weapons Convention; UN Doc. S/RES/2118 (2013), 27 September 2013, operative para. 4.

[653] *Yearbook of the International Law Commission 2001*, Vol. II, Part Two, p. 119, para. (13).

[654] U.S. Department of the Treasury, Press Release, Treasury Sanctions Syrian Officials In Connection With OPCW-UN Findings Of Regime's Use Of Chemical Weapons On Civilians, 12 January 2017, https://home.treasury.gov/news/press-releases/jl0701, accessed 22 April 2023; U.S. Department of the Treasury, Press Release, Treasury Sanctions 271 Syrian Scientific Studies and Research Center Staff in Response to Sarin Attack on Khan Sheikhoun, 24 April 2017, https://home.treasury.gov/news/press-releases/sm0056, accessed 22 April 2023; U.S. Department of the Treasury, Press Release, The United States and France Take Coordinated Action on Global Procurement Network for Syria's Chemical Weapons Program, 25 July 2018, https://home.treasury.gov/news/press-releases/sm443, accessed 22 April 2023; Council Implementing Decision (CFSP) 2017/1341, 17 July 2017; Council Implementing Decision (CFSP) 2018/421, 19 March 2018; Council Implementing Regulation (EU) 2022/2228, 14 November 2022; Minister for Foreign Affairs, The Hon Julie Bishop MP, Media release, Sanctions targeting Syria's chemical weapons program, 24 August 2017, https://www.foreignminister.gov.au/minister/julie-bishop/media-release/sanctions-targeting-syrias-chemical-weapons-program, accessed 22 April 2023.

Features

Autonomous sanction measures may vary among States and regional organizations, owing to discretion on the part of each such party. While relevant States and the EU perforce have their own approaches to autonomous sanction measures against Syria, their legal authorities must be consistent with their respective legislative procedures. The timing of designations may vary among them. Domestic politics may also affect decisions. At the same time, autonomous sanction measures tend to be uniform among designators because collective actions can be more effective than individual ones. Participating States and the EU have designated the same twenty-four key targets irrespective of timing, and regard SSRC (#12) the most critical institution. Overall, de facto cooperative practices appear to exist that would make autonomous sanction measures not autonomous, though as indicated above, final decisions are left to each State or regional organizations. In any event, the point is not the enactment of sanction measures as such but achieving their purpose. It is argued that imposing sanctions does not necessarily have a deterrent effect.[655] In fact, further use of chemical weapons in Syria could be understood as an indication of malfunctioning of sanction measures. The relevant States and regional organizations need to explore ways to overcome this situation.

(ii) **Accountability: International Partnership against Impunity**

On 23 January 2018, France launched an intergovernmental initiative titled the International Partnership against Impunity for the Use of Chemical Weapons, i.e., the aforementioned "Chemical Weapons No Impunity!" campaign, with a view to dealing with the issue of impunity for the perpetrators of chemical weapons, as the title suggests.[656] Participating States have agreed as follows:

- Collect, compile, retain, and preserve relevant information to support efforts to hold accountable those responsible for the proliferation or use of chemical weapons;
- Facilitate the sharing of such information, with participating States, and international, or regional organisation as appropriate, so that those responsible may be brought to justice;
- Use relevant mechanisms to designate individuals, entities, groups and governments involved in the proliferation or use of chemical weapons for sanctions, as appropriate;

[655] Michelle Almary, "The Necessity for a Permanent Disincentive: Examining the Use of Chemical Weapons with a Focus on Syria's Civil War," *Southwestern Journal of International Law*, Vol. 24, Issue 2 (2018), p. 301, p. 317.

[656] France Diplomacy, Launch of the International Partnership against Impunity for the Use of Chemical Weapons, 23 January 2018, https://www.diplomatie.gouv.fr/en/french-foreign-policy/security-disarmament-and-non-proliferation/disarmament-and-non-proliferation/fighting-chemical-weapons/international-partnership-against-impunity-for-the-use-of-chemical-weapons/events/article/chemical-weapons-ending-impunity-23–01-18, accessed 22 April 2023.

- Publicize the names of individuals, entities, groups or governments placed under sanctions for their involvement in the proliferation or use of chemical weapons through a dedicated website;
- Strengthen the capacity of Participating States, through national and supranational measures, to hold accountable those involved in the use of chemical weapons, including by enhancing the legal and operational capabilities of States to identify and sanction or prosecute individuals and entities involved in the proliferation or use of chemical weapons; and
- Support, where appropriate, common positions in existing fora regarding the use of chemical weapons, for example the OPCW Executive Council and the UN Security Council and General Assembly.[657]

As mentioned above, the International Partnership has published and updated a sanctions list on its official website, and it is anticipated that it will facilitate a more effective implementation of autonomous sanction measures. Participants have made statements at the group's own meetings,[658] UN General Assembly regular sessions,[659] and on such other occasions as the adoption of the decision at the fourth special session the OPCW Conference of the States Parties on 28 June 2018[660]

[657] Fighting Impunity: International Partnership against Impunity for the Use of Chemical Weapons, Declaration of Principles, https://www.diplomatie.gouv.fr/IMG/pdf/international_partnership_against_impunity_for_the_use_of_chemical_weapons_declaration_of_principles2_en_cle818838-1.pdf, accessed 22 April 2023.

[658] France Diplomacy, International partnership against impunity for the use of chemical weapons—Joint Ministerial Declaration of State Participants (Paris, 18 May 2018), https://www.diplomatie.gouv.fr/en/french-foreign-policy/security-disarmament-and-non-proliferation/disarmament-and-non-proliferation/fighting-chemical-weapons/international-partnership-against-impunity-for-the-use-of-chemical-weapons/events/article/international-partnership-against-impunity-for-the-use-of-chemical-weapons-235380, accessed 22 April 2023. France released a watchlist of 48 individuals that France deemed to have highly likely been involved in the development and use of chemical weapons, https://www.diplomatie.gouv.fr/IMG/pdf/liste_de_vigilance_cle8c911c.pdf, accessed 22 April 2023.

[659] France Diplomacy, New meeting between the participating States of the International Partnership against Impunity for the Use of Chemical Weapons, https://www.diplomatie.gouv.fr/en/french-foreign-policy/security-disarmament-and-non-proliferation/disarmament-and-non-proliferation/fighting-chemical-weapons/international-partnership-against-impunity-for-the-use-of-chemical-weapons/events/article/new-meeting-between-the-participating-states-of-the-international-partnership, accessed 22 April 2023. See also Joint statement by the Participating States, https://www.diplomatie.gouv.fr/IMG/pdf/impunity_initiative_draft_declaration_october_2018_final_cle4a11f1.pdf, accessed 22 April 2023.

[660] France Diplomacy, OPCW—Fight against impunity for the use of chemical weapons—Statement by Jean-Yves Le Drian (28 June 2018), https://www.diplomatie.gouv.fr/en/french-foreign-policy/security-disarmament-and-non-proliferation/disarmament-and-non-proliferation/fighting-chemical-weapons/international-partnership-against-impunity-for-the-use-of-chemical-weapons/events/article/opcw-fight-against-impunity-for-the-use-of-chemical-weapons-statement-by-jean, accessed 22 April 2023.

and the publication of the OPCW IIT reports.[661] As of late 2022, the International Partnership comprises 40 States and the EU. Its activities appear to overlap to some extent with those of the IIIM concerning chemical weapons use in Syria, possibly boosting IIIM's to fulfil its mandate.[662]

(b) Military Actions

(i) Possible Military Options in August–September 2013

Exploring Unilateral Military Options

As previously mentioned, the press first reported on chemical weapons use in Syria on 21 August 2013[663] during the ongoing UN Mission investigation of other such allegations. The UN Mission was accordingly allowed to shift to this incident. It was only a matter of time before the allegations were confirmed,[664] whereupon France,[665]

---

661 France Diplomacy, Statement of the International Partnership against impunity for the use of chemical weapons (24 Apr. 20), https://www.diplomatie.gouv.fr/en/french-foreign-policy/security-disarmament-and-non-proliferation/news/news-about-disarmament-and-non-proliferation/article/statement-of-the-international-partnership-against-impunity-for-the-use-of, accessed 22 April 2023; Statement of the Partnership—"Supporting the OPCW upon the delivery of the second IIT report" (May 18, 2021), https://www.noimpunitychemicalweapons.org/IMG/pdf/21_05_17_pai_statement_-_supporting_the_opcw_upon_the_delivery_of_the_second_itt_report_-_saraqib_-_vf_en-2.pdf, accessed 22 April 2023; Statement of the Partnership—"Supporting the OPCW upon the delivery of the third IIT report" (February 13, 2023), https://www.noimpunitychemicalweapons.org/IMG/pdf/the_statement_in_english.pdf, accessed 22 April 2023.

662 Naqvi, *supra* note 559, p. 979.

663 The Telegraph, Syrian "poison gas attack" would be worst use of nerve gas in 25 years, 21 August 2013, https://www.theguardian.com/world/2013/sep/16/syrian-chemical-attack-sarin-says-un#:~:text=9%20years%20old-,Syrian%20chemical%20attack%20used%20sarin%20and,in%2025%20years%2C%20says%20UN&text=The%20UN%20has%20confirmed%20that,suburbs%20of%20the%20Syrian%20capital, accessed 22 April 2023.

664 The UN Mission was tasked with determining whether chemical weapons were used. Attribution was beyond the scope of its mandate.

665 Conférence de presse de M. Laurent Fabius, ministre des affaires étrangères, sur les négociations israélo-palestiniennes et sur l'hypothèse de l'utilisation d'armes chimiques en Syrie, à Jérusalem le 25 août 2013, https://www.vie-publique.fr/discours/188841-conference-de-presse-de-m-laurent-fabius-ministre-des-affaires-etrange, accessed 22 April 2023; Syria/Syrian chemical programme—National executive summary of declassified intelligence, https://www.diplomatie.gouv.fr/IMG/pdf/Syrian_Chemical_Programme.pdf, accessed 22 April 2023.

the UK,[666] and the US[667] criticized the Assad regime[668] and explored "a strong response," hinting at military options, while the Syrian government categorically denied responsibility.[669] In fact, by August 2012 the US, the UK, and France had shared their concerns about possible chemical weapons use in Syria. US President Barack Obama warned the Assad regime not to transport or utilize chemical weapons, calling doing so a "red line."[670] Obama and UK Prime Minister David Cameron had a phone call and "both agreed that the use—or threat—of chemical weapons was completely unacceptable and would force them to revisit their approach so far."[671] French President François Hollande said "we remain very vigilant with our allies to

---

666 Foreign Secretary: We cannot allow chemical weapons to be used with impunity, 25 August 2013, https://www.gov.uk/government/news/foreign-secretary-we-cannot-allow-chemical-weapons-to-be-used-with-impunity, accessed 22 April 2023; Syria: reported chemical weapons use—letter from the Chairman of the Joint Intelligence Committee, https://assets.publishing.service.gov.uk/government/uploads/system/uploads/attachment_data/file/235094/Jp_115_JD_PM_Syria_Reported_Chemical_Weapon_Use_with_annex.pdf, accessed 22 April 2023.

667 PBS interview, 28 August 2013, https://www.pbs.org/video/obama-no-decision-on-syria-taking-action-on-voting-rights-1384898134/, accessed 22 April 2023; Government Assessment of the Syrian Government's Use of Chemical Weapons on August 21, 2013, 30 August 2013, https://obamawhitehouse.archives.gov/the-press-office/2013/08/30/government-assessment-syrian-government-s-use-chemical-weapons-august-21, accessed 22 April 2023; Syria: Damascus Areas of Influence and Areas Reportedly Affected by 21 August Chemical Attack, https://obamawhitehouse.archives.gov/sites/default/files/docs/2013-08-30_map_accompanying_usg_assessment_on_syria.pdf, accessed 22 April 2023.

668 Many commentators share this view (Daniela Abratt, "U.S. Intervention in Syria: A Legal Responsibility to Protect," *Denver Law Review*, Vol. 95, Issue 1 (2017), p. 21, p. 25; Jacob Behmer, "The Legality of President Trump's Missile Strike on Al-Shayrat Air Force Base in Syria," *University of St. Thomas Journal of Law and Public Policy (Minnesota)*, Vol. 13, Issue 2 (2019), p. 83, p. 86; Andrew M. Bell, "Using Force against the Weapons of the Weak: Examining a Chemical-Biological Weapons Usage Criterion for Unilateral Humanitarian Intervention under the Responsibility to Protect," *Cardozo Journal of International and Comparative Law*, Vol. 22, Issue 2 (2014), p. 261, p. 264; Philipp C. Bleek and Nicholas J. Kramer, "Eliminating Syria's chemical weapons: implications for addressing nuclear, biological and chemical threats," *The Nonproliferation Review*, Vol. 23, Nos 1-2 (2016), p. 197, p. 205; Jonathan McLaughlin, "A Resilient Threat: SSRC's Role in Syria's Chemical Weapon Program," Wisconsin Project on Nuclear Arms Control (2018), https://www.wisconsinproject.org/a-resilient-threat-ssrcs-role-in-syrias-chemical-weapon-program/, accessed 22 April 2023; Malcolm N. Shaw, *International Law*, ninth edition (Cambridge University Press, 2021), p. 1018). However, no third-party international attribution mechanism has established responsibility on the part of the Assad regime.

669 Syrian President Assad denied the accusations. Bashar al-Assad: «All contracts signed with Russia are implemented», 26 August 2013, https://iz.ru/news/556048, accessed 22 April 2023.

670 The White House, Remarks by the President to the White House Press Corps, 20 August 2012, https://obamawhitehouse.archives.gov/the-press-office/2012/08/20/remarks-president-white-house-press-corps, accessed 22 April 2023.

671 Prime Minister's phone calls with Presidents Hollande and Obama, 23 August 2012, https://www.gov.uk/government/news/prime-ministers-phone-calls-with-presidents-hollande-and-obama, accessed 22 April 2023.

prevent the use of chemical weapons by the [Assad] regime, which would be for the international community a legitimate cause of direct intervention."[672]

These States preferred to obtain UN Security Council authorization, as such would constitute undisputed lawful use of force under the UN Charter. On 28 August 2013, the UK offered a draft resolution[673] with a formulation reportedly almost identical to that of Resolution 1973 of 2011, which authorized the military action against Libya that eventually led to the downfall of Muammar Gaddafi.[674] Russia and China, strong supporters of the Assad regime, had, however, vetoed three previous UN Security Council resolutions since the start of the Syrian uprising,[675] and were likely to do so again. Hence, the draft resolution was not tabled at any formal Security Council meeting, leaving little doubt that early on the US, the UK, and France considered unilateral military measures a viable response to non-compliance with the international obligation on non-use of chemical weapons. On 29 August 2013, UK Prime Minister Cameron put forward a motion on military action against Syria, which the House of Commons voted down.[676] Two days later, US President Obama, while maintaining his determination to "take military action against Syrian regime targets," left the final decision to Congress.[677] This was an extraordinary act on his part, as he had discretion to take military action without Congressional approval. On 9 September 2013, Russia made the aforementioned proposal to place Syrian chemical weapons under international control,[678] avoiding military action against Syria.[679]

---

[672] Déclaration de M. François Hollande, Président de la République, sur les défis et priorités de la politique étrangère de la France, à Paris le 27 août 2012, https://www.vie-publique.fr/discours/185772-declaration-de-m-francois-hollande-president-de-la-republique-sur-les.

[673] Syria: UK to put forward United Nations Security Council resolution, 28 August 2013, https://www.gov.uk/government/news/syria-uk-to-put-forward-united-nations-security-council-resolution, accessed 22 April 2023.

[674] Telegraph, Britain launches last-ditch bid for UN approval for military strikes on Syria with resolution calling for "all necessary measures," 28 August 2013, https://www.proquest.com/docview/1428437503/B76C8E0AA8E64483PQ/37?accountid=8333, accessed 22 April 2023.

[675] China and Russia vetoed draft resolutions on Syria on 4 October 2011, 4 February 2012, 19 July 2012.

[676] The House of Commons rejected the motion on military action in Syria by a vote of 272 for to 285 against (UK Parliament, Syria and the Use of Chemical Weapons, Vol. 566: debated on Thursday 29 August 2013, columns 1552–1555, https://hansard.parliament.uk/commons/2013-08-29/debates/13082980000001/SyriaAndTheUseOfChemicalWeapons, accessed 22 April 2023).

[677] Statement by the President on Syria, 31 August 2013, https://obamawhitehouse.archives.gov/the-press-office/2013/08/31/statement-president-syria, accessed 22 April 2023.

[678] Announcement by the Russian Foreign Minister Sergey Lavrov for the mass media regarding the situation with Syrian chemical weapons, Moscow, 9 September 2013, https://www.mid.ru/en/web/guest/foreign_policy/international_safety/conflicts/-/asset_publisher/xIEMTQ3OvzcA/content/id/97430, accessed 22 April 2023.

[679] On 10 September 2013, US President Barack Obama requested that Congress postpone the vote (Remarks by the President in Address to the Nation on Syria, 10 September 2013, https://obamawhitehouse.archives.gov/the-press-office/2013/09/10/remarks-president-address-nation-syria, accessed 22 April 2023.

Legality

This raised the question of whether these States' attempt to take military action against Syria constitutes a violation of the obligation to refrain from "threat of force" under Article 2, para. 4 of the UN Charter. While no indication about the interpretation of "threat of force" exists neither in the UN Charter or General Assembly resolutions, academic doctrine has attached importance to specific demands for targeted State to carry out particular conduct. According to Brownlie, "a threat of force consists in an express or implied promise by a government of a resort to force conditional on non-acceptance of certain demands of that government."[680] Sadurske defines a threat of force as "a message, explicit or implicit, formulated by a decision maker and directed to the target audience, indicating that force will be used if a rule or demand is not complied with."[681] Stürchler demonstrates that "another state is faced point-blank with a 'last clear chance,' the unequivocal promise that unless it complies with a specific demand, the use of force will result."[682] Tsagourias argues that "a threat of force exists when a demand is made, upon which the eventual use of force is contingent."[683] For Randelzhofer and Dörr, "the threat of force…requires a coercive intent directed towards specific behaviour on the part of another State."[684] Corten points out that "the existence of a threat supposes that things said and done are observed from which demands inherent to the ultimatum can be identified."[685] International judicial and fact-finding organs affirm these views. In its Nuclear Weapons advisory opinion, the ICJ took the position that "it would be illegal for a State to threaten force to secure territory from another State, or to cause it to follow or not follow certain political or economic paths."[686] The Arbitral Tribunal in the Guyana-Suriname case mentioned that "the order…constituted an explicit threat that force might be used if the order was not complied with."[687] The Independent International Fact-Finding Mission on the Conflict in Georgia indicated that "[t]he requirement is that there

---

680 Ian Brownlie, *International Law and the Use of Force by States* (Clarendon Press, 1963), p. 364.

681 Romana Sadurska, "Threats of Force," *American Journal of International Law*, Vol. 82, Issue 2 (1988), p. 239, p. 242.

682 Nikolas Stürchler, *The Threat of Force in International Law* (Cambridge University Press, 2007), p. 259.

683 Nicholas Tsagourias, "The Prohibition of Threats of Force," in Nigel D. White and Christian Henderson (eds.), *Research Handbook on International Conflict and Security Law:* Jus ad Bellum, Jus in Bello and Jus post Bellum (Edward Elgar, 2013), p. 67, p. 76.

684 Albrecht Randelzhofer and Oliver Dörr, "Article 2 (4), in Bruno Simma, Daniel-Erasmus Khan, Gerg Nolte and Andreas Paulus (eds.), *The Charter of the United Nations, A Commentary*, third edition, volume I (Oxford, 2013), p. 200, p. 218.

685 Olivier Corten, *The Law Against War*, second edition (Hart Publishing, 2021), p. 123.

686 *Legality of the Threat or Use of Nuclear Weapons, Advisory Opinion, I.C.J. Reports 1996*, p. 226, p. 246, para. 47.

687 Award in the arbitration regarding the delimitation of the maritime boundary between Guyana and Suriname, Award of 17 September 2007, Reports of International Arbitral Awards, Vol. XXX, p. 1, p. 123, para. 439.

be some specificity in formulating demands and in clarifying what happens if these demands are not met."[688]

Apparently, no demands were addressed to Syria pertaining to the possible military action by the US, the UK, and France. Instead, they responded punitively to try to deter other such incidents.[689] It might be formalistic to conclude that these States' statements do not qualify as threats of force due to an absence of precise demands. As mentioned, one purpose of the possible military action was to prevent further chemical weapons attacks. This was a clear message to Syria, as it was thereby being implicitly urged to comply with the obligation not to use chemical weapons in future.[690] Perhaps specific demands have several formulations, and this reference to deterrence should be regarded as one such.

Credibility is probably more important than specific demands in threats of force.[691] The work of the ILC makes a useful allusion in its commentary on the draft code of crimes against the peace and security of mankind, where it defined the threat of aggression as "declarations, communications, demonstrations of force or any other measures which would give good reason to the Government of a State to believe that aggression is being seriously contemplated against that State."[692] Stürchler points out that "[a]ll that matters is that the use of force is sufficiently alluded to and that it is made clear that it may be put to use."[693] International practice also supports this approach. Once more citing its Nuclear Weapons advisory opinion, the ICJ linked threat of force to "a signalled intention to use force" and "the stated readiness to use."[694] The Independent International Fact-Finding Mission on the Conflict in Georgia held that "[a] threat is credible when it appears rational that it may be implemented, when there is a sufficient commitment to run the risk of armed encounter."[695]

The statements of the US, the UK, and France on military action expressed their intent to intervene by force. They were also formulated in a specific context and under specific circumstances. It is thus obvious that they constituted "good reasons" to believe that these States "seriously" contemplated use of force against Syria, and

---

688 Report of the Independent International Fact-Finding Mission on the Conflict in Georgia, Vol. II, p. 232.

689 Anne Lagerwall, "Threats of and Actual Military Strikes Against Syria—2013 and 2017," in Tom Ruys and Olivier Corten (eds.), *The Use of Force in International Law: A Case-based Approach* (Cambridge University Press, 2018), p. 828, p. 841.

690 *Ibid.*

691 Stürchler, *supra* note 682, p. 259. See also Corten, *supra* note 685, p. 123.

692 *Yearbook of the International Law Commission 1989*, Vol. II, Part Two, p. 68 (Commentary of Article 13 (Threat of aggression), Draft Code of Crimes against the Peace and Security of Mankind).

693 Stürchler, *supra* note 682, p. 259. The same phrase appears in the report of the Independent International Fact-Finding Mission on the Conflict in Georgia (Report of the Independent International Fact-Finding Mission on the Conflict in Georgia, Vol. II, p. 232).

694 *Legality of the Threat or Use of Nuclear Weapons, Advisory Opinion, I.C.J. Reports 1996*, p. 226, p. 246, para. 47.

695 Report of the Independent International Fact-Finding Mission on the Conflict in Georgia, Vol. II, p. 232.

that they can therefore be considered as threats of force within the scope of Article 2, para. 4 of the UN Charter.[696]

(ii) **Military Actions in April 2017 and April 2018**

US Airstrikes in April 2017

The allegations of chemical weapons use in Khan Shaykhoun were reported on 4 April 2017. During the discussion in the Security Council, Russia claimed that airstrikes against a large warehouse belonging to "terrorists" released chemical weapons stockpiled there.[697] The UK and the US argued that this incident "bears all the hallmarks of the Al-Assad regime" in terms of the use of chemical weapons.[698] France also recalled facts that contradicted Russia's argument.[699] Later, the US and France drew on collected intelligence to further rebut Russia.[700] Most Security Council members referred to the OPCW FFM and the OPCW-UN JIM. Some expressed support, while others welcomed their fact-finding, and still others stressed the urgent need to establish the facts.[701] On 7 April 2017 local time, the US launched airstrikes against Syria, firing fifty-nine Tomahawk cruise missiles from the destroyers USS Porter and USS Ross in the eastern Mediterranean Sea against aircraft, hardened aircraft shelters, petroleum and logistical storage, ammunition supply bunkers, air defense systems, and radar.[702]

Tripartite Airstrikes in April 2018

Nearly one year later, another allegation was reported on 7 April 2018, this time in Douma. At an emergency Security Council meeting, Syria expressed doubt about the credibility of the report, arguing that elements of armed terrorist groups fabricated information.[703] Russia denied the attack itself, pointing out that no one with symptoms of sarin or chlorine poisoning had been admitted at the local hospital and that

---

[696] Lagerwall, *supra* note 689, p. 842; Corten, *supra* note 685, p. 135.

[697] UN Doc. S/PV.7915, 5 April 2017, p. 16 (Russia).

[698] *Ibid.*, pp. 5 (UK), 17–18 (US).

[699] *Ibid.*, p. 4 (France).

[700] New York Times, Declassified U.S. Report on Chemical Weapons Attack, 11 April 2017, https://www.nytimes.com/interactive/2017/04/11/world/middleeast/document-Syria-Chemical-Weapons-Report-White-House.html, accessed 21 January 2023; France, Syrie - Attaque chimique - Déclaration de M. Jean-Marc Ayrault, ministre des affaires étrangères et du développement international, à l'issue du Conseil restreint de défense - Paris, 26 avril 2017, https://onu.delegfrance.org/Syrie-chimique-le-rapport-de-la-France-accuse-Damas, accessed 22 April 2023. See also. UN Doc. S/PV.7915, 5 April 2017, p. 4 (France).

[701] UN Doc. S/PV.7915, 5 April 2017, pp. 4 (France), 6 (Bolivia), 7 (China), 8 (Japan), 8 (Italy), 9 (Egypt), 10 (Uruguay), 10 (Kazakhstan), 11 (Sweden), 12 (Ethiopia), 14 (Senegal).

[702] US Department of Defense, DOD News, Trump Orders Missile Attack in Retaliation for Syrian Chemical Strikes, 6 April 2017, https://www.defense.gov/News/News-Stories/Article/Article/1144601/trump-orders-missile-attack-in-retaliation-for-syrian-chemical-strikes/, accessed 22 April 2023.

[703] UN Doc. S/PV.8225, 9 April 2018, p. 25 (Syria). Syria stressed that it "does not use these substances because it does not possess them to begin with" (*ibid.*).

no bodies of people who had died from being poisoned were found.[704] In response, the US and the UK criticized the Assad regime for again using chemical weapons.[705] France also strongly suggested the Syrian armed forces were involved.[706] Irrespective of their positions, Syria announced its readiness to cooperate with the OPCW and receive an OPCW fact-finding mission to Douma.[707] Russia offered logistical and security support to the OPCW experts.[708] Other States also welcomed the dispatchment of the OPCW FFM.[709] There was also a consensus on the need to re-establish an attribution mechanism,[710] though the UN Security Council failed to adopt either

[704] *Ibid.*, p. 7 (Russia). See also Russia, https://www.opcw.org/sites/default/files/documents/EC/M-58/en/Statement_by_the_Head_of_the_Russian_Delegation__Permanent_Representative_of_the_Russian_Federation_to_the_OPCW__Ambassador_A.V._Shulgin_at_the_58th_Meeting_of_the_Executive_Council_16_April.pdf, accessed 22 April 2023.

[705] UN Doc. S/PV.8225, 9 April 2018, pp. 10 (US), 14 (UK). See also OPCW Doc. EC-M-58/NAT.2 (US), 16 April 2018, p. 1; OPCW Doc. EC-M-58/NAT.4 (UK), 16 April 2018, p. 1.

[706] UN Doc. S/PV.8225, 9 April 2018, p. 12 (France). See also OPCW Doc. EC-M-58/NAT.1 (France), 16 April 2018, p. 3; OPCW Doc. EC-M-58/NAT.3 (France), 17 April 2018.

[707] UN Doc. S/PV.8225, 9 April 2018, pp. 25–26 (Syria).

[708] *Ibid.*, p. 7 (Russia). The UK expressed interest, stressing the importance of the OPCW mission's "complete freedom of action and freedom of access" (*ibid.*, p. 14 (UK)).

[709] *Ibid.*, pp. 10 (Netherlands), 14 (China), 15 (Sweden), 16–17 (Ethiopia), 18 (Equatorial Guinea), 19 (Kazakhstan), 21 (Bolivia); UN Doc. S/PV.8228, 10 April 2018, pp. 6 (China), 7 (Bolivia). See also UN Doc. S/PV.8233, 14 April 2018, pp. 10 (China), 13 (Netherlands), 16 (Ethiopia), 17 (Equatorial Guinea), 18 (Côte d'Ivoire), 18 (Peru). OPCW Doc. EC-M-58/NAT.1 (France), 16 April 2018, p. 3; OPCW Doc. EC-M-58/NAT.4 (UK), 16 April 2018, p. 1; OPCW Doc. EC-M-58/NAT.6 (Switzerland), 16 April 2018, p. 1; OPCW Doc. EC-M-58/NAT.11 (Switzerland), 16 April 2018, p. 2; OPCW Doc. EC-M-58/NAT.13 (Italy), 16 April 2018, p. 1; OPCW Doc. EC-M-58/NAT.14 (Croatia), 16 April 2018, p. 1; OPCW Doc. EC-M-58/NAT.15 (Bulgaria on behalf of the EU), 16 April 2018, p. 1; OPCW Doc. EC-M-58/NAT.17 (Sweden), 16 April 2018, p. 1; OPCW Doc. EC-M-58/NAT.18 (Turkey), 16 April 2018, p. 1; OPCW Doc. EC-M-58/NAT.19 (India), 16 April 2018, p. 1; OPCW Doc. EC-M-58/NAT.21 (Canada), 16 April 2018, p. 2; OPCW Doc. EC-M-58/NAT.24 (Albania), 16 April 2018, p. 1; OPCW Doc. EC-M-58/NAT.25 (Portugal), 16 April 2018, p. 1; Russia, https://www.opcw.org/sites/default/files/documents/EC/M-58/en/Statement_by_the_Head_of_the_Russian_Delegation__Permanent_Representative_of_the_Russian_Federation_to_the_OPCW__Ambassador_A.V._Shulgin_at_the_58th_Meeting_of_the_Executive_Council_16_April.pdf, accessed 22 April 2023; Austria, https://www.opcw.org/sites/default/files/documents/EC/M-58/en/Statement_by_Austria_at_the_58th_Meeting_of_the_Executive_Council__16_April_2018.pdf, accessed 22 April 2023; Estonia, https://www.opcw.org/sites/default/files/documents/EC/M-58/en/Statement_by_Estonia_to_the_OPCW_58th_Meeting_of_the_Executive_Council_16_April_2018.pdf, accessed 22 April 2023; Finland, https://www.opcw.org/sites/default/files/documents/EC/M-58/en/Statement_on_behalf_of_the_Republic_of_Finland_ECM-58.pdf, accessed 21 January 2023; Latvia, https://www.opcw.org/sites/default/files/documents/EC/M-58/en/Latvia_statement_EC-M-58.pdf, accessed 22 April 2023; Netherlands, https://www.opcw.org/sites/default/files/documents/EC/M-58/en/EC-M-58_-_Statement_the_Netherlands.pdf, accessed 22 April 2023; Norway, https://www.opcw.org/sites/default/files/documents/EC/M-58/en/EC-M-58_Statement_Norway_-_Amb._Martin_Soerby__2_.pdf, accessed 22 April 2023; Slovenia, https://www.opcw.org/sites/default/files/documents/EC/M-58/en/Statement_EC-M-58_Slovenia.pdf, accessed 22 April 2023.

[710] UN Doc. S/PV.8225, 9 April 2018, pp. 9 (Netherlands), 11 (US), 13 (France), 14 (UK), 14 (China), 16 (Sweden), 16 (Poland), 17 (Ethiopia), 17–18 (Côte d'Ivoire), 18 (Equatorial Guinea), 20–21 (Kuwait), 21 (Bolivia), 22 (Peru).

a draft resolution by Russia or by the US and other States.[711] Even at this stage, several States reminded the Security Council of its general rejection of unilateral use of force.[712] On 14 April 2018, the US, the UK, and France launched airstrikes against Syria, targeting a SSRC facility in the greater Damascus area for research, development, production and testing of chemical and biological warfare technology, a chemical weapons storage facility west of Homs, and a chemical weapons equipment storage facility that was also an important command post.[713]

Legality

The use of force is prohibited under Article 2, para. 4 of the UN Charter and customary international law,[714] while it is also universally recognized that exceptions include right of self-defense and UN Security Council authorization. In this context, self-defense clearly does not apply to these military actions as none of participating States were themselves attacked, while on the other hand, the UN Security Council has taken no action, or more precisely, is deadlocked. Therefore, these military actions require another justification. Two possibilities will be examined: theory of humanitarian intervention, and enforcement of countermeasures.

- ***Use of Force: Theory of Humanitarian Intervention***

As will be discussed, the UK relied on the theory of humanitarian intervention to justify its military actions against Syria, referring to lawful use of force by one State against another for the purpose of terminating the latter's abuse of its own nationals.[715] It dates back to nineteenth-century European claims of right to rescue Christians

---

[711] The UN Security Council deliberated on a draft resolution submitted by Russia (UN Doc. S/2018/175, 10 April 2018), and another submitted by the US and others (UN Doc. S/2018/321, 10 April 2018), but failed to adopt either. Russia's draft was rejected by a vote of six in favor (Bolivia, China, Equatorial Guinea, Ethiopia, Kazakhstan, and Russia) to seven against (France, Netherlands, Peru, Poland, Sweden, UK, and US), with two abstentions (Côte d'Ivoire and Kuwait) (UN Doc. S/PV.8228, 10 April 2018, p. 9). Russia vetoed the other draft (UN Doc. S/PV.8228, 10 April 2018, p. 5).

[712] UN Doc. S/PV.8225, 9 April 2018, pp. 15 (China), 21 (Bolivia), 22 (Peru); UN Doc. S/PV.8228, 10 April 2018, p. 6 (China).

[713] US Department of Defense, Briefing by Secretary Mattis on U.S. Strikes in Syria, 13 April 2018, https://www.defense.gov/News/Transcripts/Transcript/Article/1493658/briefing-by-secretary-mattis-on-us-strikes-in-syria/, accessed 22 April 2023; Government of the UK, News story, RAF jets strike chemical weapon facility in Syria, 14 April 2018, https://www.gov.uk/government/news/raf-jets-strike-chemical-weapon-facility-in-syria, accessed 22 April 2023; UN Doc. S/PV.8233, 14 April 2018, p. 6 (UK).

[714] *Military and Paramilitary Activities in and against Nicaragua (Nicaragua v. United States of America), Jurisdiction and Admissibility, Judgment, I.C.J. Reports 1984*, p. 392, p. 424, para. 73; *Military and Paramilitary Activities in and against Nicaragua (Nicaragua v. United States of America), Merits, Judgment, I.C.J. Reports 1986*, p. 14, pp. 98–102, paras. 187–192.

[715] Tom J. Farer, "An Inquiry into the Legitimacy of Humanitarian Intervention," in Lori Fisler Damrosch and David J. Scheffer (eds.), *Law and Force in the New International Order* (Westview Press, 1991), p. 185, p. 185.

persecuted under the Ottoman Empire.[716] The contemporary issue is whether this theory survives after the UN Charter, which prohibits use of force of one State against another. The preponderant view is that this theory has no place in contemporary international law.[717]

This theory relies on two supportive arguments, depending on sources. One is that it can be derived from a flexible interpretation of Article 2, para. 4 of the UN Charter, especially the last twenty-three words, in which humanitarian intervention is not directed "against the territorial integrity or political independence of any state,"[718] but rather, to put UN purposes into practice.[719] Such interpretation does not take into account the *travaux préparatoires* of this article, however. The language in question was added to emphasize the prohibition of the use of force by giving a typical example of illegal use of force. There was no intention to allow a humanitarian intervention exception.[720] The other is that this theory remains valid under customary international law irrespective of Article 2, para. 4 of the UN Charter. It has been argued that the post-UN practice of humanitarian intervention, seen in the cases of the Congo in 1964 and the Dominican Republic in 1965, affirms the continuing validity of the theory and the conditions under which it will be deemed lawful, and that as long as these conditions are met, use of force for humanitarian purposes will be lawful under the Charter as well as under general international law.[721] However, post-UN practice in other cases, including India's intervention in East Pakistan (Bangladesh) and Viet Nam's in Cambodia, has been understood differently.[722] It has been pointed out that in virtually all such instances, intervening States relied on a basis other than humanitarian intervention, raising doubt about acceptance of the theory, and showing that the international community was highly critical of most cases of intervention

---

716 Thomas M. Franck and Nigel S. Rodley, "After Bangladesh: The Law of Humanitarian Intervention by Military Force," *American Journal of International Law*, Vol. 67, Issue 2 (1973), p. 275, pp. 277–283.

717 Sir Nigel Rodley, "'Humanitarian Intervention'," in Marc Weller (ed.), *The Oxford Handbook of the Use of Force in International Law* (Oxford, 2015), p. 775, pp. 775–776. See also Carsten Stahn, "Syria and the Semantics of Intervention, Aggression and Punishment; On Red Lines and Blurred Lines," *Journal of International Criminal Justice*, Vol. 11, Issue 5 (December 2013), p. 955, p. 965.

718 Richard B. Lillich, "Forcible Self-Help by States to Protect Human Rights," *Iowa Law Review*, Vol. 53, Issue 2 (1967), p. 325, p. 336; Michael Reisman and Myres S. McDougal, "Humanitarian Intervention to Protect the Ibos," in Richard B. Lillich (ed.), *Humanitarian intervention and the United Nations* (University Press of Virginia, 1973), p. 167, p. 177; Anthony Clark Arend and Robert J. Beck, *International Law and the Use of Force: Beyond the UN Charter Paradigm* (Routledge, 1993), p. 134.

719 Arend and Beck, *supra* note 718, p. 134; Fernando R. Tesón, *Humanitarian Intervention: An Inquiry into Law and Morality*, second edition (Transnational, 1997), p. 151.

720 Albrecht Randelzhofer, "Article 2 (4)," in Bruno Simma (ed.), *The Charter of the United Nations: A Commentary* (Oxford University Press, 1994), p. 106, pp. 117–118.

721 Reisman and McDougal, *supra* note 718, p. 187.

722 Sean D. Murphy, *Humanitarian Intervention: The United Nations in an Evolving World Order* (University of Pennsylvania Press, 1996), pp. 92–97. See also Farer, *supra* note 715, p. 193.

and not in favor of the humanitarian intervention exception to the general prohibition on use of force.[723]

NATO's military action in 1999 during the Kosovo crisis revived discussion on the theory of humanitarian intervention. It should be noted that the NATO States did not assert this theory particularly strongly, with only Belgium explicitly relying on the "intervention humanitaire armée" during the oral proceedings of the ICJ.[724] Other NATO States alluded to "humanitarian catastrophe," "humanitarian disaster," "humanitarian suffering," "humanitarian crisis," and "humanitarian considerations" at the meeting of the UN Security Council,[725] obfuscating their positions on the theory. By contrast, several States opposed NATO's military actions, suggesting their denial of the theory. Russia stressed that attempts to justify the NATO strikes with arguments about preventing a humanitarian catastrophe in Kosovo were "in no way based on the Charter or other generally recognized rules of international law."[726] According to China, "[t]his act amounts to a blatant violation of the United Nations Charter and of the accepted norms of international law."[727] Belarus argued that use of military force against Yugoslavia without UN Security Council authorization and dispatching foreign military contingents against the will of the government of Yugoslavia "qualify as an act of aggression."[728] India pointed out that the attacks against Yugoslavia "have not been authorized by the [UN Security] Council, acting under Chapter VII, and are therefore completely illegal."[729] Yugoslavia itself said that there is no evidence of the doctrine of humanitarian intervention in customary international law.[730] The Group of 77 has rejected the "right" of humanitarian intervention, because of a lack of legal basis under either the UN Charter or general principles of international law.[731]

723 Murphy, *supra* note 722, p.143.

724 CR 99/15, 10 May 1999, pp. 16–17 (Ergec).

725 UN Doc. S/PV.3988, 24 March 1999, pp. 4–5 (US), 5–6 (Canada), 8 (Netherlands), 8–9 (France), 11–12 (UK), 16–18 (Germany).

726 *Ibid.*, p. 2 (Russia).

727 *Ibid.*, p. 12 (China).

728 *Ibid.*, p. 15 (Belarus).

729 *Ibid.*, p. 16 (India).

730 CR 99/14, 10 May 1999, p. 36 (Brownlie).

731 Group of 77, Declaration of the South Summit, 14 April 2000, para. 54, https://www.g77.org/summit/Declaration_G77Summit.htm, accessed 22 April 2023. See also UN Doc. A/57/759–S/2003/332, 18 March 2003, Annex I, Final Document, 13th Summit of Heads of State and Government of the Non-Aligned Movement, para. 16; UN Doc. A/61/472–S/2006/780, 29 September 2006, Annex I, Final Document, 14th Summit of Heads of State and Government of the Non-Aligned Movement, para. 249; UN Doc. A/62/929, 11 August 2008, Annex, Final Document, 15th Ministerial Conference and Commemorative Meeting of the Non-Aligned Movement, para. 335; UN Doc. A/65/896–S/2011/407, 7 July 2011, Annex I, Final Document, 16th Ministerial Conference and Commemorative Meeting of the Non-Aligned Movement, para. 520; UN Doc. A/68/966–S/2014/573, 19 August 2014, Annex I, Final Document, 17th Ministerial Conference and Commemorative Meeting of the Non-Aligned Movement, para. 673; UN Doc. A/74/584*, 15 November 2019, Annex, Final Document, 18th Summit of Heads of State and Government of the Non-Aligned Movement (NAM 2019/CoB/Doc.1), para. 1012.

Opinions varied in academia, with a few writers supporting the theory of humanitarian intervention. Greenwood wrote that "modern customary international law recognizes a right of military intervention on humanitarian grounds by States, or by an organization like NATO."[732] Reisman argued that when the UN Security Council cannot take action to enforce human rights by military means, "the legal requirement continues to be to save lives."[733] According to Wedgwood, "[t]he aims of the UN Charter are to guarantee human rights and international security, and while the danger of increasing the scale of a conflict is always to be considered, the use of military action to protect a beleaguered population may advance humane values without significant danger to stability."[734] The majority of commentators opposed it, however. Simma maintained that "[i]n the absence of such authorization [by the UN Security Council], military coercion...constitutes a breach of Article 2 (4) of the Charter."[735] Bilder held that "most scholars have rejected the claim that humanitarian intervention is a legitimate exception to the prohibition of the use of force in the UN Charter."[736] Henkin argued that "by the sum (or product) of law and politics, humanitarian intervention by any state was prohibited; humanitarian intervention was permissible if authorized by the Security Council, but a single permanent member could prevent such authorization."[737] For Charney, "[t]he doctrine of 'humanitarian intervention' is not well defined, and the evidence does not establish a rule of law permitting the use of force against a state in situations like that of Kosovo."[738] Brownlie pointed out that "there is very little evidence to support assertions that a new principle of customary law legitimating humanitarian intervention has crystallised."[739] According to Matheson, "many NATO states-including the United States-had not accepted the doctrine of humanitarian intervention as an independent legal basis for military action that was not justified by self-defense or the authorization of the Security Council."[740] Goodman indicated that "the consensus of opinion among governments and jurists favors requiring Security Council approval

[732] Christopher Greenwood, "Humanitarian Intervention: The Case of Kosovo," *Finnish Yearbook of International Law*, Vol. 10 (1999), p. 141, p. 170.

[733] W. Michael Reisman, "Kosovo's Antinomies," *American Journal of International Law Journal*, Vol. 92, Issue 4 (1999), p. 860, p. 862.

[734] Ruth Wedgwood, "NATO's Campaign in Yugoslavia," *American Journal of International Law Journal*, Vol. 92, Issue 4 (1999), p. 828, p. 833.

[735] Bruno Simma, "NATO, the UN and the Use of Force: Legal Aspects," *European Journal of International Law*, Vol. 10, No. 1 (1999), p. 1, p. 5.

[736] Richard B. Bilder, "Kosovo and the New Interventionism: Promise or Peril," *Journal of Transnational Law and Policy*, Vol. 9, No.1 (1999), p. 153, p. 161.

[737] Louis Henkin, "Kosovo and the Law of 'Humanitarian Intervention,'" *American Journal of International Law*, Vol. 93, Issue 4 (1999), p. 824, p. 825.

[738] Jonathan I. Charney, "Anticipatory Humanitarian Intervention in Kosovo," *Vanderbilt Journal of Transnational Law*, Vol. 32, No. 5 (November 1999), p. 1231, p. 1235.

[739] Ian Brownlie, "International Law and the Use of Force by States Revisited," *Australian Yearbook of International Law*, Vol. 21 (2000), p. 21, pp. 34 –35.

[740] Michael J. Matheson, "Justification for the NATO Air Campaign in Kosovo," *American Society of International Law Proceedings*, Vol. 94 (2000), p. 301, p. 301.

for humanitarian intervention."[741] It follows that as of the end of the twentieth century, the validity of the theory of humanitarian law under international law was in doubt.

The international community strove to find a way forward in response to situations where citizens confront human rights violations within State territories following the Kosovo crisis. The idea of "Responsibility to Protect" accordingly was introduced in the 2001 Report of the Canadian-sponsored International Commission on Intervention and State Sovereignty (ICISS), representing a fundamental conceptual change from the right to protect, i.e., the right of unilateral intervention by another State, to the responsibility to protect, i.e., the primary responsibility of the territorial State and the supplementary responsibility of the international community. Procedures for implementation have mattered more to the state of international law, however. At the October 2005 World Summit, the UN General Assembly endorsed a watered-down version of "Responsibility to Protect" in its Resolution 60/1, clarifying that the international community has the responsibility to help to protect populations from genocide, war crimes, ethnic cleansing and crimes against humanity and that collective action will be taken "through the Security Council, in accordance with the Charter."[742] This means that the concept of "Responsibility to Protect" neither replaces the theory of humanitarian intervention nor allows unilateral military action to protect populations who face genocide, war crimes, ethnic cleansing, or crimes against humanity in the territory of a sovereign State, and thus has almost no effect on international law.[743]

When chemical weapons were used in Syria in August 2013, the US, the UK, and France explored military options, as mentioned above, with the UK explicitly relying on the theory of humanitarian intervention for justification.[744] According to its legal position paper, the UK would be permitted under international law to

---

[741] Ryan Goodman, "Humanitarian Intervention and Pretexts for War," *American Journal of International Law*, Vol. 100, No. 1 (2006), p. 107, p. 108.

[742] UN Doc. A/RES/60/1, 24 October 2005, para. 139.

[743] Dapo Akande, "The Legality of Military Action in Syria: Humanitarian Intervention and Responsibility to Protect," *EJIL Talk*!, 28 August 2013, https://www.ejiltalk.org/humanitarian-intervention-responsibility-to-protect-and-the-legality-of-military-action-in-syria/, accessed 22 April 2023. See also Michael N. Schmitt, "The Syrian Intervention: Assessing the Possible International Law Justifications," *International Law Studies Series*, US Naval War College, Vol. 89 (2013), p. 744, p. 753; Carsten Stahn, "Between Law-Breaking and Law-Making: Syria, Humanitarian Intervention and What the Law Ought to Be," *Journal of Conflict and Security Law*, Vol. 19, Issue 1 (2014), p. 25, p. 30; Bell, *supra* note 668, pp. 287–288; Christian Henderson, "The UK Government's Legal Opinion on Forcible measures in Response to the Use of Chemical Weapons by the Syrian Government," *International and Comparative Law Quarterly*, Vol. 64, No. 1 (2015), p. 179, p. 192.

[744] Policy paper, Chemical weapon use by Syrian regime: UK government legal position, Published 29 August 2013, https://assets.publishing.service.gov.uk/government/uploads/system/uploads/attachment_data/file/235098/Chemical-weapon-use-by-Syrian-regime-UK-government-legal-position.pdf, accessed 22 April 2023; https://www.gov.uk/government/publications/chemical-weapon-use-by-syrian-regime-uk-government-legal-position/chemical-weapon-use-by-syrian-regime-uk-government-legal-position-html-version, accessed 22 April 2023. The UK changed its position of 1986 that "the overwhelming majority of contemporary legal opinion comes down against the existence of a right of humanitarian intervention" (UK Foreign Office Policy Document No. 148 (British Yearbook of International Law, Vol. 57 (1986), p. 614, p. 619).

take exceptional measures without Security Council authorization if the following conditions were met:

- there is convincing evidence, generally accepted by the international community as a whole, of extreme humanitarian distress on a large scale, requiring immediate and urgent relief;
- it must be objectively clear that there is no practicable alternative to use of force if lives are to be saved; and
- the proposed use of force must be necessary and proportionate to the aim of relief of humanitarian need and must be strictly limited in time and scope to this aim (i.e. the minimum necessary to achieve that end and for no other purpose).

The UK government stressed that military action would be carried out to alleviate the overwhelming humanitarian catastrophe in Syria by deterring further chemical weapons use by the Syrian regime.[745]

While Denmark supported the right to use force for humanitarian purposes under customary international law,[746] several States objected. On 28 August 2013, Russia indicated that "[i]f force is used with regard to Syria bypassing the UN Security Council, it would be a most grave violation of international law,"[747] adding thereafter that "armed interference under [the concept of the 'responsibility to protect']...may be possible only when sanctioned by the UNSC (2005 World Summit Outcome, p. 193)," and that "the attempts to revive the notorious concept of 'humanitarian

[745] See also Syria: transcript of PM's interview, 27 August 2013, https://www.gov.uk/government/speeches/syria-transcript-of-pms-interview, accessed 22 April 2023. The US indicated that the purpose of any military action would be to (1) respond to the use of WMDs by the Syrian government, (2) deter Syria's use of chemical weapons in order to protect the national security interests of the US and to protect its allies and partners (3) degrade Syria's capacity to use chemical weapons in future, and (4) prevent the transfer of any weapons of mass destruction to terrorist groups or other State or non-State actors within Syria (S. J. Res. 21, 4 September 2013, 113th Congress, 1st Session, p. 4. See also Statement by the President on Syria, 31 August 2013, https://obamawhitehouse.archives.gov/the-press-office/2013/08/31/statement-president-syria, accessed 22 April 2023; UN Doc. A/68/PV.5, 24 September 2013, p. 12). France also indicated preventing future use of chemical weapons and sanctioning their actual use as primary ends for military action (Interview de M. François Hollande, Président de la République, dans "Le Monde" du 30 août 2013, sur l'utilisation d'armes chimiques en Syrie et sur les réformes engagées depuis le début de son quinquennat, https://www.elysee.fr/francois-hollande/2013/08/30/interview-de-m-francois-hollande-president-de-la-republique-dans-le-monde-du-30-aout-2013-sur-lutilisation-darmes-chimiques-en-syrie-et-sur-les-reformes-engagees-depuis-le-debut-de-son-quinquennat, accessed 22 April 2023; Assemblée nationale, XIVe législature, Deuxième session extraordinaire de 2012–2013, Compte rendu intégral, Première séance du mercredi 04 septembre 2013, https://www.assemblee-nationale.fr/14/cri/2012-2013-extra2/20132001.asp, accessed 22 April 2023; UN Doc. A/68/PV.5, 24 September 2013, p. 32).

[746] Danish Ministry of Foreign Affairs, "General Principled Considerations on the Legal Basis for a Possible Military Operation in Syria," 30 August 2013, https://www.ft.dk/samling/20121/almdel/upn/bilag/298/1276299/index, accessed 22 April 2023.

[747] The Embassy of the Russian Federation to the United Kingdom of Great Britain and Northern Ireland, Press release, Use of force without UN decision will be a grave violation of international law—DFM Gennady Gatilov, 28 August 2013, https://london.mid.ru/en/press-centre/gb_en_fnapr_3113/, accessed 22 April 2023.

intervention'...was not generally accepted."[748] During general debate at the UN General Assembly in September 2013, Brazil stressed that "[u]nder all circumstances and in any case, we repudiate unilateral interventions in violation of international law and without authorization by the Security Council."[749] For South Africa, "any political transition in Syria must come about as a result of the will of the Syrian people and not through the force of arms."[750] Iran warned that "any illegitimate and ineffective threat of use, or the actual use of, force will only lead to the further exacerbation of violence and crisis in the region."[751] According to Argentina, "[m]y country opposed direct intervention—bombing."[752] Niger indicated that "[w]e have always rejected violence and foreign interference."[753] Many other States refrained from touching upon this topic during their statements.

Few international law scholars agreed with the UK government's legal position, apparently putting forward *lex ferenda* arguments. Bethlehem considered that "[d]rawing all of these—as well as other (such as developments in the law on human rights)—threads together, there is a case to be made in favour of the emergence of a tightly constrained principle of humanitarian intervention that is consistent with traditional conceptions of customary international law."[754] Koh demonstrated an idea for lawful use of force in response to the use of chemical weapons under the following conditions: disruptive consequences likely to lead to imminent threat; exhaustion; limited, necessary, proportionate, and humanitarian use of force; collective action; illegal means; and avoidance of illegal ends.[755] By contrast, majority expressed doubt about the existence of the theory of humanitarian intervention itself. Hayashi indicated that "[f]rom the perspective of law, a more fundamental, theoretical issue is that humanitarian intervention has not achieved the status of an established, accepted

[748] Comment by the Information and Press Department of the Russian Ministry of Foreign Affairs regarding a possible forceful action by the United States against Syria, 4 September 2013, https://archive.mid.ru/en/web/guest/foreign_policy/international_safety/conflicts/-/asset_publisher/xIEMTQ3OvzcA/content/id/98022, accessed 22 April 2023. Having noted that Syria is bound by the Geneva Protocol, Russia admitted that "[i]ts violation, if proven, may be qualified as a violation of applicable international law." See also President of Russia, Events, Interview to Channel One and Associated Press news agency, 4 September 2013, http://en.kremlin.ru/events/president/news/19143, accessed 22 April 2023.

[749] UN Doc. A/68/PV.5, 24 September 2013, p. 10 (Brazil).

[750] *Ibid.*, p. 50 (South Africa).

[751] UN Doc. A/68/PV.6, 24 September 2013, p. 15 (Iran).

[752] UN Doc. A/68/PV.7, 24 September 2013, p. 11 (Argentina).

[753] UN Doc. A/68/PV.17, 27 September 2013, p. 3 (Niger).

[754] Daniel Bethlehem, "Stepping Back a Moment-The Legal Basis in Favour of a Principle of Humanitarian Intervention," *EJIL: Talk!*, 12 September 2013, https://www.ejiltalk.org/stepping-back-a-moment-the-legal-basis-in-favour-of-a-principle-of-humanitarian-intervention/, accessed 22 April 2023. Henderson pointed out that the argument of Bethlehem took "little satisfactory consideration" of Article 2, para. 4 of the UN Charter (Henderson, *supra* note 743, p. 191).

[755] Harold Hongju Koh, "Syria and the Law of Humanitarian Intervention (Part II: International Law and the Way Forward)," *EJIL: Talk!*, 4 October 2013, https://www.ejiltalk.org/syria-and-the-law-of-humanitarian-intervention-part-ii-international-law-and-the-way-forward/, accessed 22 April 2023.

legal doctrine."[756] Schmitt pointed out was of the view that "the very existence of such as right [of humanitarian intervention] in international law is highly controversial" and that "the United States has never explicitly accepted the doctrine *de jure*."[757] Ssenyonjo was of the view that "the unilateral use of force without an armed attack on any State threatening to use force in Syria and in the absence of the UN Security Council resolution, would be unlawful under current international law," and that "the use of armed force in Syria undertaken without the mandate or the authorisation of the Security Council and in absence of a claim of self-defence, in reaction to the alleged use of chemical weapons, does not meet the permitted exceptions to the prohibition on the use of force under the UN Charter."[758] Henderson also rejected the theory of humanitarian intervention as *lex lata* based on analysis of interpretations of Article 2 para. 4 and State practice.[759]

US justification for its April 2017 airstrike was unclear. President Donald Trump stressed that "[i]t is in this vital national security interest of the United States to prevent and deter the spread and use of deadly chemical weapons,"[760] while the US Permanent Representative to the OPCW explained that the strike was "a direct response to this horrific atrocity" and "proportional, targeted, and limited in scope."[761] These oral texts clarified the purposes, the reasons and the manner of military actions; however, they did not touch upon legal basis. In response, Syria strongly condemned "this act of aggression by the United States" as "a grave violation of the Charter of the United Nations as well of as all international norms and laws."[762] Other States took a variety of positions. One group supported US military action without reference to legal assessments,[763] while alluding to objectives: "to save lives by ensuring that such acts never happen again" and "intended to

---

[756] Mika Hayashi, "Reacting to the Use of Chemical Weapons: Options for Third States," Journal on Use of Force and International Law, Vol. 1, No.1 (2014), p. 80, p. 116.

[757] Schmitt, *supra* note 743, p. 755.

[758] Manisuli Ssenyonjo, "Unilateral Military Action in the Syrian Arab Republic: A Right to Humanitarian Intervention or a Crime of Aggression," *International Human Rights Law Review*, Vol. 2, Issue 2 (2013), p. 323, pp. 335, 338.

[759] Henderson, *supra* note 743, pp. 183–192.

[760] White House, Statement by President Trump on Syria, 6 April 2017, https://www.whitehouse.gov/the-press-office/2017/04/06/statement-president-trump/syria, accessed 10 April 2017; U.S. Embassy & Consulates in Russia, Statement by President Trump on Syria, 6 April 2017, https://ru.usembassy.gov/statement-president-trump-syria/, accessed 22 April 2023. See also UN Doc. S/PV.7919, 7 April 2017, p. 17 (US).

[761] US, https://www.opcw.org/sites/default/files/documents/EC/M-54/en/United_States_ECM54_Statement.pdf, accessed 22 April 2023.

[762] UN Doc. S/PV.7919, 7 April 2017, p. 18 (Syria). See also UN Doc. S/2017/299, 7 April 2017 (Syria), pp. 1–2.

[763] Chris O'Meara, "United States' Missile Strikes in Syria: Should International Law Permit Unilateral Force to Protect Human Rights?," *EJIL:Talk!*, 18 April 2017, https://www.ejiltalk.org/united-states-missile-strikes-in-syria-should-international-law-permit-unilateral-force-to-protect-human-rights/, accessed 22 April 2023.

deter further attack" (UK),[764] "deterrent to the risk of any further use of chemical weapons in Syria" (Italy),[765] "important reminder that the future use of such weapons will not be tolerated" (France),[766] "to prevent and deter the further use of chemical weapons" (Australia),[767] "to degrade the Assad regime's ability to launch any more chemical weapons attacks" (Canada),[768] and "clear signal that the use of WMDs will no longer be tolerated" (Ukraine).[769] Other statements addressed the reasons for such action: "response to unspeakable acts that gave rise to overwhelming humanitarian distress" and "response to a heinous act by a brutal and uncaring dictator" (UK),[770] "response to a prolonged sense of impunity" (Italy),[771] "response to the chemical attack" (France),[772] and "a direct consequence of the Syrian Arab Republic's continued, and illegal, use of chemical weapons against its own people" (New Zealand).[773] Still others mentioned the manner: "proportionate response" and "appropriate response" (UK),[774] "proportionate in time and manner" (Italy),[775] "a proportionate and calibrated response" (Australia),[776] "limited and focused action" (Canada),[777] and "appropriate and proportionate response" (Ukraine).[778] While Japan supported "the determination of the United States Government to never allow the spread or use of chemical weapons" rather than the airstrike as such,[779] it may be categorized in the first group, because Japan understood the aim as preventing further aggravation of the situation.[780] The second group opposed the US airstrikes against Syria. Russia took the position that the attack constitutes "a flagrant violation of international law and an act of aggression" and "a gross violation of the norms of international law, including the provisions of the United

[764] UN Doc. S/PV.7919, 7 April 2017, p. 5 (UK); OPCW Doc. EC-M-54/NAT.18 (UK), 13 April 2017, pp. 1–2.

[765] UN Doc. S/PV.7919, 7 April 2017, p. 8 (Italy).

[766] *Ibid.*, p. 9 (France).

[767] OPCW Doc. EC-M-54/NAT/8 (Australia), 13 April 2017, p. 1.

[768] Canada, https://www.opcw.org/sites/default/files/documents/EC/M-54/en/Canada_ECM-54.pdf, accessed 22 April 2023.

[769] UN Doc. S/PV.7919, 7 April 2017, p. 16 (Ukraine).

[770] *Ibid.*, pp. 5–6 (UK).

[771] *Ibid.*, p. 8 (Italy).

[772] *Ibid.*, p. 9 (France).

[773] OPCW Doc. EC-M-54/NAT.4 (New Zealand), 13 April 2017, p. 1.

[774] UN Doc. S/PV.7919, 7 April 2017, pp. 5–6 (UK); OPCW Doc. EC-M-54/NAT.18 (UK), 13 April 2017, pp. 1–2.

[775] UN Doc. S/PV.7919, 7 April 2017, p. 8 (Italy).

[776] OPCW Doc. EC-M-54/NAT/8 (Australia), 13 April 2017, p. 1.

[777] Canada, https://www.opcw.org/sites/default/files/documents/EC/M-54/en/Canada_ECM-54.pdf, accessed 22 April 2023.

[778] UN Doc. S/PV.7919, 7 April 2017, p. 16 (Ukraine).

[779] UN Doc. S/PV.7919, 7 April 2017, p. 10 (Japan); OPCW Doc. EC-M-54/NAT/6 (Japan), 13 April 2017, p. 1.

[780] UN Doc. S/PV.7919, 7 April 2017, p. 10 (Japan); OPCW Doc. EC-M-54/NAT/6 (Japan), 13 April 2017, p. 1.

Nations Charter."[781] Bolivia claimed that the unilateral attack is "an extremely serious violation of international law."[782] Iran argued that the US action is "a violation of international laws and the Charter of the United Nations."[783]Cuba also expressed that the airstrike is "a grave violation of the Charter of the United Nations and the International Law."[784] Several States seemed to reject the action though such indirect language as "[a] military solution will not work" (China),[785] "[w]e have always rejected the unilateral use of force" (Uruguay),[786] "resolved peacefully" (Mexico),[787] "the resolution of conflicts exclusively by peaceful means" (Kazakhstan),[788] and "through dialogue and an inclusive political process, not through military actions" (Indonesia).[789] Sweden also raised doubts about "the compatibility with international law."[790] As mentioned, the last group expressed no opinion, while most States participating in UN Security Council and/or OPCW Executive Council meetings continued to emphasize the importance of OPCW FFM investigations,[791] calling on either the Syrian government or all parties to the non-international armed conflict in Syria to cooperate.[792]

---

781 UN Doc. S/PV.7919, 7 April 2017, p. 10 (Russia); OPCW Doc. EC-M-54/NAT.15 (Russia), 13 April 2017, pp. 2 and 6; OPCW Doc. EC-M-54/NAT.13 (Russia), 19 April 2017, p. 1.

782 UN Doc. S/PV.7919, 7 April 2017, p. 3 (Bolivia).

783 OPCW Doc. EC-M-54/NAT/9 (Iran), 13 April 2017, p. 1.

784 Cuba, https://www.opcw.org/sites/default/files/documents/EC/M-54/en/Cuba_ECM54.pdf, accessed 22 April 2023.

785 UN Doc. S/PV.7919, 7 April 2017, p. 10 (China).

786 *Ibid.*, p. 7 (Uruguay).

787 OPCW Doc. EC-M-54/NAT.17 (Mexico), 13 April 2017, p. 1.

788 UN Doc. S/PV.7919, 7 April 2017, p. 13 (Kazakhstan).

789 Indonesia, https://www.opcw.org/sites/default/files/documents/EC/M-54/en/Indonesia_ECM54.pdf, accessed 22 April 2023.

790 UN Doc. S/PV.7919, 7 April 2017, p. 14 (Sweden).

791 UN Doc. S/PV.7919, 7 April 2017, pp. 9 (France), 10 (Japan), 13 (Senegal), 14 (Sweden); OPCW Doc. EC-M-54/NAT.1 (Brazil), 13 April 2017, p. 1; OPCW Doc. EC-M-54/NAT.2 (Norway), 13 April 2017, pp. 1–2; OPCW Doc. EC-M-54/NAT/6 (Japan), 13 April 2017, p. 1; OPCW Doc. EC-M-54/NAT/8 (Australia), 13 April 2017, p. 2; OPCW Doc. EC-M-54/NAT.11 (France), 13 April 2017, pp. 1 and 3; OPCW Doc. EC-M-54/NAT.17 (Mexico), 13 April 2017, p. 1; OPCW Doc. EC-M-54/NAT.19 (Portugal), 13 April 2017, p. 1; Malta behalf of the EU, https://www.opcw.org/sites/default/files/documents/EC/M-54/en/Malta_ECM54.pdf, accessed 22 April 2023; Belgium, https://www.opcw.org/sites/default/files/documents/EC/M-54/en/Belgium_ECM54.pdf, accessed 22 April 2023; Indonesia, https://www.opcw.org/sites/default/files/documents/EC/M-54/en/Indonesia_ECM54.pdf, accessed 21 January 2023; Ireland, https://www.opcw.org/sites/default/files/documents/EC/M-54/en/Ireland_ECM54.pdf, accessed 22 April 2023; Sweden, https://www.opcw.org/sites/default/files/documents/EC/M-54/en/Sweden_ECM-54.pdf, accessed 22 April 2023; US, https://www.opcw.org/sites/default/files/documents/EC/M-54/en/United_States_ECM54_Statement.pdf, accessed 22 April 2023.

792 UN Doc. S/PV.7922, 12 April 2017, pp. 2 (UK), 5 (Egypt), 5 (Italy), 6 (Japan), 8 (Ethiopia), 9 (Sweden); OPCW Doc. EC-M-54/NAT.1 (Brazil), 13 April 2017; OPCW Doc. EC-M-54/NAT.8 (Australia), 13 April 2017, p. 2.

The UK again relied on the theory of humanitarian intervention to justify participating in the April 2018 airstrikes,[793] essentially recapitulating its position of 2013, including the requisite conditions:

- there is convincing evidence, generally accepted by the international community as a whole, of extreme humanitarian distress on a large scale, requiring immediate and urgent relief;
- it must be objectively clear that there is no practicable alternative to the use of force if lives are to be saved; and
- the proposed use of force must be necessary and proportionate to the aim of relief of humanitarian suffering and must be strictly limited in time and in scope to this aim (i.e. the minimum necessary to achieve that end and for no other purpose).

While the UK determined that these conditions had been satisfied in this instance,[794] neither of its partners mentioned any such legal basis.[795] President Trump addressed the nation about the objectives of the action, i.e., the establishment of "a strong deterrent against the production, spread, and use of chemical weapons" and the protection of "a vital national security interest of the United States," and the reason for same, to wit, response to atrocities.[796] The US also claimed that it acted with its partners not in revenge, not in punishment, but that the responses were justified, legitimate, and proportionate.[797] French President Emmanuel Macron stressed that the "redline"[798] had been crossed and that the response is limited to chemical weapons-related facilities for the purpose of preventing "the normalization of the employment of chemical weapons, which is an immediate danger to the Syrian people and to

---

[793] UK, Policy paper, Syria action—UK government legal position, 14 April 2018, https://www.gov.uk/government/publications/syria-action-uk-government-legal-position/syria-action-uk-government-legal-position, accessed 22 April 2023; UN Doc. S/PV.8233, 14 April 2018, pp. 7 and 25 (UK); OPCW Doc. EC-M-58/NAT.4 (UK), 16 April 2018 p. 3.

[794] UK, Policy paper, Syria action—UK government legal position, 14 April 2018.

[795] Corten, *supra* note 685, pp. 534–535. See also Shaw, *supra* note 668, p. 1019.

[796] US President Trump Delivers an Address to the Nation, 13 April 2018, https://www.youtube.com/watch?v=iZ0PA1KnTBE, accessed 22 April 2023. The White House, Office of the Press Secretary, United States Government Assessment of the Assad Regime's Chemical Weapons Use, https://dod.defense.gov/portals/1/features/2018/0418_syria/img/United-States-Assessment-of-the-Assad-Regime%E2%80%99s-Chemical-Weapons-Use.pdf, accessed 22 April 2023.

[797] UN Doc. S/PV.8233, 14 April 2018, p. 5 (US); OPCW Doc. EC-M-58/NAT.2 (US), 16 April 2018, p. 1.

[798] On 29 May 2017, the French President Macron made it clear that use of chemical weapons is a "redline" (Conférence de presse conjointe de MM. Emmanuel Macron, Président de la République, et Vladimir Poutine, Président de la Fédération de Russie, sur les relations franco-russes et sur les conflits en Syrie et en Ukraine, à Versailles le 29 mai 2017, https://www.vie-publique.fr/discours/203301-conference-de-presse-conjointe-de-mm-emmanuel-macron-president-de-la-r, accessed 22 April 2023).

our collective security."[799] France also argued that the action was a justified, proportionate response to an unacceptable situation, i.e., the chemical attacks in Syria, and that its objectives were not only to put an end to the tragedy and prevent a repetition, but also to defend the multilateral system and chemical disarmament architecture.[800] The UK added that there was no alternative means available. For its part, Syria, needless to say, condemned the attack in the strongest terms, describing it as a "flagrant violation of the principles of international law and the United Nations Charter."[801]

Other States' positions could again be classed as supporting, opposing, and no opinion.[802] The first group supported the action, though again without recourse to legal assessment. It comes as little surprise that this group and its statements were practically unchanged from the previous year. Some spoke of objectives: "designed to put an end to the Syrian regime's chemical attacks against its own population" (Belgium),[803] "to degrade the Assad regime's ability to launch chemical weapons attacks against its own people" (Canada),[804] "response to prevent the Syrian government from further violating the Convention" (Germany),[805] "against the use and distribution of chemical weapons" (Israel),[806] "to prevent any further use of chemical weapons against Syrian civilians" (Latvia),[807] "reducing the capabilities

[799] France Diplomatie, Communiqué de presse du Président de la République sur l'intervention des forces armées françaises en réponse à l'emploi d'armes chimiques en Syrie—14.04.2018, https://www.diplomatie.gouv.fr/fr/dossiers-pays/syrie/article/communique-de-presse-du-president-de-la-republique-sur-l-intervention-des, accessed 22 April 2023; France Diplomacy, Press statement by the President of the French Republic on the intervention of the French armed forces in response to the use of chemical weapons in Syria (14 April 2018), https://www.diplomatie.gouv.fr/en/country-files/syria/news/article/statement-by-the-president-of-the-french-republic-on-the-intervention-of-the, accessed 22 April 2023.

[800] UN Doc. S/PV.8233, 14 April 2018, p. 9 (France); OPCW Doc. EC-M-58/NAT.1 (France), 16 April 2018, p. 3.

[801] UN Doc. S/PV.8233, 14 April 2018, pp. 21–22 (Syria).

[802] Corten, *supra* note 685, pp. 536–537. See also Alonso Gurmendi Dunkelberg, Rebecca Ingber, Priya Pillai and Elvina Pothelet, "Mapping States' Reactions to the Syria Strikes of April 2018," Just Security Just Security, https://www.justsecurity.org/55157/mapping-states-reactions-syria-strikes-april-2018/, accessed 22 April 2023.

[803] OPCW Doc. EC-M-58/NAT.22 (Belgium), 16 April 2018, p. 1.

[804] Statement by the Prime Minister on airstrikes in Syria, 13 April 2018, https://pm.gc.ca/en/news/statements/2018/04/14/statement-prime-minister-airstrikes-syria, accessed 22 April 2023.

[805] OPCW Doc. EC-M-58/NAT.11 (Germany), 16 April 2018, p. 1.

[806] Israeli Missions Around the World, PM Netanyahu's statement regarding attack in Syria, 14 April 2018, https://embassies.gov.il/MFA/PressRoom/2018/Pages/PM-Netanyahu-s-statement-regarding-attack-in-Syria-14-April-2018.aspx, accessed 22 April 2023.

[807] Latvia, https://www.opcw.org/sites/default/files/documents/EC/M-58/en/Latvia_statement_EC-M-58.pdf, accessed 22 April 2023.

to execute future chemical attacks" (Netherlands),[808] "intended to deter chemical-weapons attacks against the people of Syria" (Poland),[809] "to degrade the production capacity of a type of weapons" (Portugal),[810] "to protect the Syrian people and deny the regime the use of internationally prohibited weapons" (Qatar),[811] and "intended to prevent Syrian authorities to use chemical weapons" and "aimed at destroying the remaining Syrian Army capacities for the use of chemical weapons" (Slovenia).[812] Others mentioned reasons: "response to the abhorrent use of chemical weapons in the Syrian Arab Republic, especially against civilians and children" (Albania),[813] "response to the repeated use of chemical weapons by the Syrian regime against the Syrian people" (Estonia),[814] "to this atrocity" (Finland),[815] and "response to the chemical weapons attack which caused the deaths of many civilians in Douma on 7 April" (Turkey).[816] Still others referred to means: "proportionate response" (Albania),[817] "calibrated, proportionate and targeted response" (Australia),[818] "proper and proportionate response" (Estonia),[819] "proportionate and necessary response" (Germany),[820] and "targeting a limited number of military

---

[808] UN Doc. S/PV.8233, 14 April 2018, p. 13 (Netherlands); Netherlands, https://www.opcw.org/sites/default/files/documents/EC/M-58/en/EC-M-58_-_Statement_the_Netherlands.pdf, accessed 21 22 April 2023.

[809] UN Doc. S/PV.8233, 14 April 2018, p. 11 (Poland).

[810] OPCW Doc. EC-M-58/NAT.25 (Portugal), 16 April 2018, p. 1.

[811] Qatar, https://www.mofa.gov.qa/en/statements/qatar-supports-operations-against-specific-military-targets-used-by-syrian-regime-in-its-chemical-attacks, accessed 22 April 2023.

[812] Slovenia, https://www.opcw.org/sites/default/files/documents/EC/M-58/en/Statement_EC-M-58_Slovenia.pdf, accessed 22 April 2023.

[813] OPCW Doc. EC-M-58/NAT.24 (Albania), 16 April 2018, p. 1.

[814] Estonia, https://www.opcw.org/sites/default/files/documents/EC/M-58/en/Statement_by_Estonia_to_the_OPCW_58th_Meeting_of_the_Executive_Council_16_April_2018.pdf, accessed 22 April 2023.

[815] Finland, https://www.opcw.org/sites/default/files/documents/EC/M-58/en/Statement_on_behalf_of_the_Republic_of_Finland_ECM-58.pdf, accessed 22 April 2023.

[816] Republic of Turkey, Ministry of Foreign Affairs, No: 105, 14 April 2018, Press Release Regarding the Military Operation Against Certain Points in Syria by the US, the UK and France, https://www.mfa.gov.tr/no_-105_-abd-ingiltere-fransa-n%C4%B1n-suriye-rejimine-ait-noktalar%C4%B1-hedef-alan-operasyonu-hk_en.en.mfa, accessed 22 April 2023; OPCW Doc. EC-M-58/NAT.18 (Turkey), 16 April 2018.

[817] OPCW Doc. EC-M-58/NAT.24 (Albania), 16 April 2018, p. 1.

[818] Australian Government, Department of Foreign Affairs and Trade, Response to targeted strikes in Syria, 14 April 2018, https://www.dfat.gov.au/news/news/Pages/response-to-targeted-strikes-in-syria, accessed 22 April 2023; OPCW Doc. EC-M-58/NAT.12 (Australia), 16 April 2018, p. 2.

[819] Estonia, https://www.opcw.org/sites/default/files/documents/EC/M-58/en/Statement_by_Estonia_to_the_OPCW_58th_Meeting_of_the_Executive_Council_16_April_2018.pdf, accessed 22 April 2023.

[820] OPCW Doc. EC-M-58/NAT.11 (Germany), 16 April 2018, p. 1.

facilities" (Netherlands).[821] Japan recapitulated its unclear position of tacit acceptance, stating its support of "the present determination of the United States, the United Kingdom, and France not to accept the proliferation of the use of chemical weapons".[822] Also as before, the second group opposed the airstrike. Russia again rejected the theory of humanitarian intervention,[823] considering the action "a perfidious act of aggression, a gross violation of the UN Charter and of the fundamental norms of international law."[824] It even submitted a draft resolution to the UN Security Council condemning "the aggression against the Syrian Republic by the US and its allies" and demanding cessation thereof,[825] which was voted down.[826] China also stressed that the actions "violate the basic principle of prohibition of use of force in international law and run contrary to the UN Charter."[827] Bolivia, Equatorial Guinea, and Iran shared this view.[828] Kazakhstan and South Africa pointed out that there was no Security Council authorization.[829] Viet Nam made a vague comment on the importance of dispute resolution "by peaceful means."[830] Sweden implied its objection by referring to its position that actions must be consistent with the UN Charter and international law in general.[831] The third group again maintained its silence.

---

[821] UN Doc. S/PV.8233, 14 April 2018, p. 13 (Netherlands); Netherlands, https://www.opcw.org/sites/default/files/documents/EC/M-58/en/EC-M-58_-_Statement_the_Netherlands.pdf, accessed 22 April 2023.

[822] Extraordinary Press Conference by Foreign Minister Taro Kono, 14 April 2018, Front Entrance Hall, Ministry of Foreign Affairs, https://www.mofa.go.jp/press/kaiken/kaiken4e_000489.html, accessed 22 April 2023.

[823] UN Doc. S/PV.8233, 14 April 2018, p. 25 (Russia).

[824] Russia, https://www.opcw.org/sites/default/files/documents/EC/M-58/en/Statement_by_the_Head_of_the_Russian_Delegation__Permanent_Representative_of_the_Russian_Federation_to_the_OPCW__Ambassador_A.V._Shulgin_at_the_58th_Meeting_of_the_Executive_Council_16_April.pdf, accessed 22 April 2023. See also UN Doc. S/PV.8233, 14 April 2018, p. 3 (Russia); OPCW Doc. EC-M-58/NAT.8 (Russia), 26 April 2018, p. 2.

[825] UN Doc. S/2018/355, 14 April 2018.

[826] UN Doc. S/PV.8233, 14 April 2018, pp. 22–23. The vote was three in favor (Bolivia, China, Russia) to eight against (Côte d'Ivoire, France, Kuwait, Netherlands, Poland, Sweden, UK, and US), with four abstentions (Equatorial Guinea, Ethiopia, Kazakhstan, Peru).

[827] Foreign Ministry Spokesperson Hua Chunying's Regular Press Conference on April 16, 2018, https://www.fmprc.gov.cn/mfa_eng/xwfw_665399/s2510_665401/2511_665403/t1551458.shtml, accessed 22 April 2023. See also UN Doc. S/PV.8233, 14 April 2018, pp. 10, 24 (China).

[828] UN Doc. S/PV.8233, 14 April 2018, pp. 14 (Bolivia), 17 (Equatorial Guinea); OPCW Doc. EC-M-58/NAT.16 (Iran), 16 April 2018, p. 1.

[829] UN Doc. S/PV.8233, 14 April 2018, p. 10 (Kazakhstan); South Africa, Department of International Relations and Cooperation, Media Statement, 13 April 2018, http://www.dirco.gov.za/docs/2018/syri0416.htm, accessed 8 April 2021. See also Foreign Ministry Spokesperson Hua Chunying's Regular Press Conference on April 16, 2018, https://www.fmprc.gov.cn/mfa_eng/xwfw_665399/s2510_665401/2511_665403/t1551458.shtml, accessed 8 April 2021.

[830] Vietnam, https://www.opcw.org/sites/default/files/documents/EC/M-58/en/Statement_of_Vietnam_at_the_Fifty-Eighth_Meeting_of_the_Executive_Council_-_16_April_2018.pdf, accessed 22 April 2023.

[831] UN Doc. S/PV.8233, 14 April 2018, p. 23 (Sweden).

Scholars of international law have also further debated the legality of these airstrikes. Abratt was one of the few commentators who claimed that the actions were legal, although he relied on the concept of "Responsibility to Protect" as laid down by the International Commission on the Intervention and State Sovereignty, rather than the theory of humanitarian intervention.[832] Scharf, who advocated the "Grotian moment concept" which endorses rapid formulation of customary international law,[833] seemed to favor the legality of the theory of humanitarian law, arguing that "a common justification" by the US, the UK, and France, to wit, humanitarian intervention made such formulation of customary international law that much harder.[834] Others objected, with Hayashi maintaining that the theory of humanitarian intervention remains a controversial justification without Security Council authorization in cases of humanitarian distress, and cannot thus be easily upheld as a rule of positive law.[835] Clapham held that "only a few states have in recent decades come close to officially endorsing the idea of this sort of humanitarian intervention."[836] Henriksen argued that "the strike was motivated by a less ambitious (some might say cynical) attempt to merely stop those parts of the human atrocities that are perpetrated by chemical weapons."[837] Corten pointed out that the US and France made no reference to a legally framed right of humanitarian intervention as the British did.[838] Kleczkowska did not regard the cautious comments of other States as unambiguous indicators of legalization of such intervention.[839] Opponents also cite less attention on the part of proponents to non-Western States' opposition.[840]

It follows that there is neither a right to use of force in international law based on the theory of humanitarian intervention, particularly under Article 2, para. 4 of the UN Charter, nor evidence of State practice supporting an establishment of new customary international law allowing for such intervention, because States do not

---

[832] Abratt, *supra* note 668, pp. 57–68.

[833] Michael P. Scharf, Milena Sterio and Paul R. Williams, *The Syrian Conflict's Impact on International Law* (Cambridge University Press, 2020), p. 28.

[834] Michael P. Scharf, "Striking a Grotian Movement: How the Syrian Airstrikes Changed International Law Relating to Humanitarian Intervention," *Chicago Journal of International Law*, Vol. 19, Issue 2 (2019), p. 586, pp. 613–614; Scharf, Sterio and Williams, *supra* note 833, p. 89.

[835] Mika Hayashi, "The U.S. Airstrike After the Use of Chemical Weapons in Syria: National Interest, Humanitarian Intervention, or Enforcement Against War Crimes?," *ASIL Insights*, Vol. 21, Issue 8, 13 July 2017, https://www.asil.org/insights/volume/21/issue/8/us-airstrike-after-use-chemical-weapons-syria-national-interest, accessed 22 April 2023

[836] Andrew Clapham, *War* (Oxford University Press, 2021), p. 168.

[837] Anders Henriksen, "Trump's Missile Strike on Syria and the Legality of Using Force to Deter Chemical Warfare," *Journal of Conflict and Security Law*, Vol. 23, Issue 1 (2018), p. 33, pp. 38–40. See also Corten, *supra* note 685, p. 535; Agata Kleczkowska, "The Illegality of Humanitarian Intervention: The Case of the UK's Legal Position concerning the 2018 Strikes in Syria," Utrecht *Journal of International and European Law*, Vol. 35, Issue 1 (2020), p. 35, pp. 41–42.

[838] Corten, *supra* note 685, p. 535.

[839] Kleczkowska, *supra* note 837, p. 42.

[840] Henriksen, *supra* note 837, p. 38.

appear to use force for humanitarian purposes on the basis of rules clearly obliging them to do so.[841]

- ***Use of Force: Armed Reprisals/Countermeasures***

References to non-compliance with the obligation not to use chemical weapons and emphasis on the objective of preventing further such use invited commentators to discuss whether the actions against Syria could be justified as armed reprisals or countermeasures.[842] While Buchan and Tsagourias claimed that emerging State practice supports the argument that armed reprisals are a "necessary evil" and even a "desirable tool," because they can enhance compliance with international law, and the potential risk of undermining the prohibition on the use of force can be adequately mitigated by the requirements of proportionality,[843] they are almost entirely alone in this opinion. Others stress that armed reprisals are prohibited under international law. Milanovic holds that "[i]nternational law does not permit forcible reprisals that would breach Article 2(4), even if the purpose of the reprisal is to induce the other party to comply with its legal obligations."[844] De Beer argued that "[a]rmed reprisals are widely regarded as unlawful and there is no exception for an armed reprisal for humanitarian purposes."[845] Henriksen, having expressed doubt whether a non-injured State is entitled to engage in countermeasures, added that armed countermeasures are prohibited.[846] The 1970 UN General Assembly Resolution 2265 (XXV) on the Friendly Relations Declaration stipulates that "States have a duty to refrain from the acts of reprisal which involve the use of force."[847] According to Article 50, para. 1(a) of the ARSIWA, countermeasures shall not affect the obligation to refrain from the threat or use of force under the UN Charter, with relevant commentary confirming that this provision "excludes forcible measures from the ambit of permissible countermeasures."[848] It has also been pointed out that the US, the UK, and France never spoke of armed reprisal or relied on the doctrine of countermeasures.[849] Such lack of explicit reference to the legal concepts diminishes the validity of the argument that armed reprisals/countermeasures constitute justification for the military actions. All in all, it is clear that international law has not recognized

---

841 Aniel Caro de Beer and Dire Tladi, "The Use of Force against Syria in Response to Alleged Use of Chemical Weapons by Syria: A Return to Humanitarian Intervention?" *Zeitschrift Für Ausländisches öffentliches Recht Und Vökerrecht*, Vol. 79 (2019), p. 205, pp. 238–239; Henriksen, *supra* note 837, p. 38. See also Shaw, *supra* note 668, p. 1018.

842 Corten, *supra* note 685, p. 535; de Beer and Tladi, *supra* note 841, pp. 224–225.

843 Russell Buchan and Nicholas Tsagourias, *Regulating the Use of Force in International Law* (Edward Elgar Publishing, 2021), p. 106.

844 Marko Milanovic, "The Clearly Illegal US Missile Strike in Syria," *EJIL:Talk!*, 7 April 2017, https://www.ejiltalk.org/the-clearly-illegal-us-missile-strike-in-syria/, accessed 22 April 2023.

845 De Beer and Tladi, *supra* note 841, pp. 224–225.

846 Henriksen, *supra* note 837, p. 45.

847 UN Doc. A/RES/2625 (XXV), 24 October 1970.

848 *Yearbook of the International Law Commission 2001*, Vol. II, Part Two, p. 132.

849 Scharf, *supra* note 834, p. 606; Corten, *supra* note 685, pp. 232–233.

an exception to the prohibition on use of force in response to use of chemical weapons or to deter same. No treaty, state practice, or *opinio juris* supports this notion.[850]

(4) Evaluation

(a) Potential References

Syria was the first State who used chemical weapons since the entry into force of the CWC. To find undisputed use of chemical weapons, we must once against go back to the Iran-Iraq war. Several investigative missions that the UN Secretary-General dispatched upon request by Iran confirmed the use of chemical weapons, and identified Iraq as the perpetrator in some instances. The UN Security Council deliberated over the mission reports and responded with the aforementioned presidential notes and resolutions. In the former, the Security Council indicated with particular concern the mission's conclusion that chemical weapons were used, condemned such use, and called on the States concerned to adhere to their obligations under the Geneva Protocol.[851] In the latter, the Security Council further deplored the violation of international humanitarian law and other laws of armed conflict, especially use of chemical weapons contrary to obligations under the Geneva Protocol,[852] affirmed the urgent necessity of strict observance of the Geneva Protocol,[853] condemned the use of chemical weapons contrary to and in violation of the obligations under the Geneva Protocol,[854] and expected Iran and Iraq to refrain from future use of chemical weapons.[855] While the Security Council could have taken more stringent measures including non-military sanctions, having determined in its Resolution 598 that there was "a breach of the peace,"[856] it instead merely expressed disapproval for political reasons,[857] signifying that politics plays a key role in responses to non-compliance with obligations against using chemical weapons. And no State took unilateral action against Iraqi non-compliance.

(b) Effectiveness

The effectiveness of mechanisms to respond to non-compliance with obligations against chemical weapons use varies. Such non-compliance must first be ascertained. Policy-making organs relied on reports by fact-finding missions to determine whether the party concerned complied with said obligations. The OPCW Executive Council, the UN Security Council, and the UN General Assembly referred in their respective

---

[850] De Beer and Tladi, *supra* note 841, p. 237.

[851] UN Doc. S/16454, 30 March 1984, p. 1; UN Doc. S/17130, 25 April 1985, p. 1; UN Doc. S/17932, 21 March 1986, p. 1; UN Doc. S/18863, 14 May 1987, p. 1.

[852] UN Doc. S/RES/598 (1987), 20 July 1987, preamble para. 4.

[853] UN Doc. S/RES/612 (1988), 9 May 1988, operative para. 1.

[854] UN Doc. S/RES/612 (1988), 9 May 1988, operative para. 2; UN Doc. S/RES/620 (1998), 26 August 1988, operative para. 1.

[855] UN Doc. S/RES/612 (1988), 9 May 1988, operative para. 3.

[856] UN Doc. S/RES/598 (1987), 20 July 1987, preamble para. 9.

[857] Jozef Goldblat, *Arms Control: The New Guide to Negotiations and Agreements*, second edition (SAGE Publications, 2002), p. 338.

resolutions and decisions to the UN Mission report of 16 September 2013 which concluded that chemical weapons were used, and determined that use of chemical weapons in Ghouta and other places constituted a violation of international law. These policy-making organs acted only on receipt of the official UN Mission report, and they were also unlikely to act if the UN Mission had been unable to confirm the use of chemical weapons. Other OPCW FFM, OPCW-UN JIM, OPCW IIT, and COI reports also provided facts to the policy-making organs of the OPCW and the UN, which determined in their respective resolutions and decisions that there had been a violation of obligations under the CWC and UN Security Council Resolution 2118. The OPCW-UN JIM reports which identified the Syrian government as the perpetrator also served as useful contextual information for those States that took non-military autonomous sanction measures against targets involved in the chemical attacks. The exceptions are the possible and actual unilateral military measures in 2013, 2017, and 2018, when the US, the UK, and France took or attempted to take military action on their own judgment, though they released unclassified information as the basis for that judgment. In August 2013, the UN Mission was in the midst of its investigation on the ground in Syria, while the OPCW FFM was being deployed in April 2017 and April 2018. Several States Parties stressed the importance of these investigations, even though the missions had no mandate to identify perpetrators.

The next step is to take *ex post* measures. The UN Security Council and the OPCW Executive Council took several actions in accordance with their respective mandates in reaction to the chemical attack in East Ghouta on 21 August 2013, with the agreement between the US and Russia the decisive factor. In the author's view it was possible because perpetrators went unidentified, allowing both States to maintain their respective views on who was responsible.[858] Procedures for responding to non-compliance under the CWC, the UN Charter and the Resolution 2118 Regime are available in reaction to further use of chemical weapons since April 2014. The OPCW policy-making organs have general mandates to address non-compliance in accordance with relevant provisions of the CWC,[859] while the UN Security Council is responsible for maintaining international peace and security. The Resolution 2118 Regime provides the Security Council with specific mandates under Chapter VII of the UN Charter in the event of non-compliance with Resolution 2118, especially unauthorized transfer, or any use, of chemical weapons by anyone in Syria.[860] The

[858] The relevant measures should be regarded as having been imposed not against a violation of international law by Syria, but in response to use of chemical weapons, which constituted just such violation of international law. While UN Security Council Resolution 2118 described the incident as "in violation of international law," it did not identify the perpetrators.

[859] Article VIII, paras 35 and 36, and Article XII. The Chemical Weapons Convention enable the OPCW policy-making organs to refer such matters to the UN Security Council and UN General Assembly (Article VIII para. 36 and Article XII, para. 4).

[860] UN Doc. S/RES/2118 (2013), 27 September 2013, operative para. 21. This reference implied use of force with UN Security Council authorization (van Ham, van der Meer and Ellahi, *supra* note 437, p. 31. It is rare that the Security Council commits itself to act in future under specific UN Charter Chapter (Jacobsson, *supra* note 437, p. 149). This formulation is thus a strong signal

relevant policy-making organs have thus sufficient mandates. The point is the collective political will. Russian vetoes deadlocked the Security Council, preventing it from adopting legally binding enforcement measures, including collective economic sanctions. By contrast, the OPCW Executive Council and the Conference of the States Parties have adopted decisions to redress the situation of non-compliance, apparently not hesitating to rely on non-unanimous decisions since the OPCW-UN JIM identified the Syrian government as the perpetrators in August 2016. The UN General Assembly, including the UNHRC, has also taken several *ex post* institutional measures.

Despite these *ex post* institutional measures, repeated chemical weapons use in Syria between 2014 and 2018 in particular suggests that they have failed to prevent further such use. Statements on such use, including confirmations of violations of international law, condemnations thereof, calls to hold perpetrators to account, and demands for cessation of such use had no impact on Syria's attitude, even though they reflected the collective policy-making organs' views. Effects of the suspension of Syrian rights and privileges in the OPCW remain to be seen, although strong and consistent political support from Russia, China, and Iran, who consistently vote against relevant decisions and resolutions, may take some pressure off Syria. The effectiveness of *ex post* unilateral measures is likewise unclear. While autonomous sanction measures and targets lists may be frequently updated, only a limited number of States have taken such autonomous sanction measures, and the Assad regime probably does not care in any event. And while military action would be the only means of enforcing obligations under international law, they appear surgical even as a last resort, leaving open the question of whether they have the intended effect either.[861] Unilateral use of force also stands on dubious legal footing. Also, while eliminating Syrian chemical weapons might be understood as one of the few tangible successful responses to chemical weapons use in Syria, the sarin gas attack in Khan Shaykhoun in April 2017 meant that Syria still possessed chemical weapons that should have been declared and eliminated under the Resolution 2118 Regime, revealing the limitations of this project.

The issue of accountability is more serious. One of the most desirable *ex post* actions to redress non-compliance with the obligation not to use chemical weapons is the criminal punishment of perpetrators, necessitating a shift from State–level non-compliance to the personal war crime of chemical weapons use. While the formulation "those who used chemical weapons must be accountable" is commonly held among States, the international community has not managed to match words with deeds.[862] Basically, war crimes in non-international armed conflict needs to be enforced under the domestic legal order. This approach will function under at least two conditions. First, this crime should be committed by the opposition group

of Security Council intent to deter the parties to conflict in Syria from acting in ways inconsistent with Resolution 2118.

[861] Edward M. Spiers, *Agents of War: A History of Chemical and Biological Weapons*, expanded second edition (Reaktion Books, 2021), p. 175.

[862] Stahn pointed out the "inherent contradictions" of the Resolution 2118 Regime, which addresses consequences of breaches of the norm on the universal ban on use of chemical weapons through

rather than the government forces. Second, the legitimate government is willing and able to enforce this crime. If these two conditions are not met. The international community should act. The relevant procedures—the referral to the ICC—already existed, however, the referral has not yet been realized due to a lack of collective political will of the UN Security Council. "The International Partnership against Impunity for the Use of Chemical Weapons!" has not yet achieved its goal. The more impunity continues, the weaker the norm becomes.

Perhaps we should not be surprised at this unsatisfactory outcome. It is another example of the difficulty in enforcing obligations under international law when no enforcement is available absent Security Council authorization. The abovementioned measures were intended to put pressure on the Assad regime in the long run, not to bring about a rapid resolution. Given these circumstances, measures must be maintained and strengthened, not abandoned.

(c) **Implications**

The institutional mechanism to respond to non-compliance has both positive and negative implications.

First, the institutional mechanisms for responding to non-compliance will continue to strengthen the substantive obligation against chemical weapons use. The international community has fully shared universal consensus on the twofold importance of the obligation not to use chemical weapons under international law and of accountability of the perpetrators. OPCW Executive Council and Conference of the States Parties decisions and UN Security Council, General Assembly, and UNHRC resolutions have repeatedly reflected these views, contributing to strengthening substantive obligations under international humanitarian law. Ironically, the obligation of omission and its legal consequence are almost always strengthened and reaffirmed when acts against these obligations occur. Referring again to the Nicaragua case, the ICJ stated that "instances of State conduct inconsistent with a given rule should generally have been treated as breaches of that rule, not as indications of the recognition of a new rule."[863] Condemnation and illegality, whether specific to Syria or more generally, offer evidence of the aforementioned *opinio juris* as one of two components of customary international law.[864]

Second, the "general purpose criteria" under the CWC will continue to be valid. Article II, para. 1(a) introduced this concept under which all toxic chemicals or precursors are regarded as chemical weapons unless they have been developed,

---

disarmament obligations and enforcement measures, rather than through instruments of accountability and criminal justice (Stahn, "Syria and the Semantics of Intervention, Aggression and Punishment; On Red Lines and Blurred Lines," *supra* note 717, pp. 974–976).

[863] *Military and Paramilitary Activities in and against Nicaragua (Nicaragua v. United States of America), Merits, Judgment, I.C.J. Reports 1986*, p. 14, p. 98, para. 186.

[864] Conclusion 10, para. 2, Conclusions on the Identification of Customary International Law (*Yearbook of the International Law Commission 2018*, Vol. II, Part Two, p. 91).

produced, stockpiled, or used for purposes not prohibited under the Convention, irrespective of whether they are listed in the Schedules.[865] The OPCW Executive Council and the UN Security Council affirmed the concept's validity by responses to use of chlorine, a non-scheduled chemical frequently used in Syria, including noting the use of chlorine or any other toxic chemical as a chemical weapon in Syria is a violation of obligation,[866] expressing concern and condemnation thereon,[867] establishing a mechanism to identify parties involved in so using chlorine and other chemicals as weapon,[868] stressing accountability of such perpetrators,[869] and demanding that Syria declare all chemical weapons it currently possesses, including chlorine not intended for purposes not prohibited under the Convention.[870] The abovementioned validity of "general purpose criteria" should contribute to preventing further use of such non-Scheduled chemicals.

Third, as described elsewhere, institutional mechanisms are capable of redressing non-compliance, subject to UN Security Council detemination of threats to the peace. In Resolution 2118, for the first time, the Security Council qualified the use of chemical weapons, a WMD category, as a threat to peace, a clear indication that the Security Council is prepared to consider coercive measures under Chapter VII in response to future such use. Several States alluded to the implications, and it was argued that said determination facilitates an aforementioned Chapter VII-based referral under Article 13(b) of the Rome Statute.[871] A draft Security Council resolution on sanctions against Syria included language "[r]eaffirming its determination that the use of chemical weapons anywhere constitutes a threat to international peace and security."[872] The UN Secretary-General also referred to this determination in his April 2017 monthly report, expressing his hope that the Security Council would take "concrete steps to ensure that those who have used chemical weapons are held accountable, in order to deter and put an end to those inhumane acts."[873]

---

[865] Walter Krutzsch, Eric Myjer and Ralf Trapp (eds.), *The Chemical Weapons Convention: A Commentary* (Oxford University Press, 2014), p. 77.

[866] UN Doc. S/RES/2209 (2015), 6 March 2015, preamble para. 3; UN Doc. S/RES/2235 (2015), 7 August 2015, preamble para. 2.

[867] OPCW Doc. EC-M-48/DEC.1, 4 February 2015, operative para. 1; OPCW Doc. EC-M-50/DEC.1, 23 November 2015, operative para. 1; OPCW Doc. EC-94/DEC.2, 9 July 2020, operative para. 1; OPCW Doc. C-25/DEC.9, 21 April 2021, operative para. 2. UN Doc. S/RES/2209 (2015), 6 March 2015, operative para. 1; UN Doc. S/RES/2235 (2015), 7 August 2015, operative para. 1.

[868] UN Doc. S/RES/2235 (2015), 7 August 2015, operative para. 5.

[869] UN Doc. S/RES/2209 (2015), 6 March 2015, operative para. 6; UN Doc. S/RES/2235 (2015), 7 August 2015, operative para. 4.

[870] OPCW Doc. EC-94/DEC.2, 9 July 2020, operative para. 5.

[871] Zimmermann and Şener, *supra* note 525, p. 448. See also Naqvi, *supra* note 559, p. 974.

[872] UN Doc. S/2017/172, 28 February 2017, preamble para. 15.

[873] UN Doc. S/2017/373, 28 April 2017, p. 1. See also UN Doc. S/PV.7915, 5 April 2017, p. 3 (Under-Secretary-General and High Representative for Disarmament Affairs); UN Doc. S/2017/469, 1 June 2017, p. 2; UN Doc. S/2017/564, 30 June 2017, p. 2; UN Doc. S/2017/658, 31 July 2017, p. 2; UN Doc. S/2017/815, 29 September 2017, pp. 1–2; UN Doc. S/2017/916, 31 October 2017, p. 2.

Fourth, institutional responses to non-compliance with the obligation not to use chemical weapons in non-international armed conflict are always *ex post*, essentially punitive, preventive, and confrontational. Those against the State or government concerned include condemnation, demands, and sanctions, while those against concerned persons are targeted sanctions and criminal punishment. Hence, they may not be effective in either context. Adopting such measures requires that relevant policy-making organs obtain sufficient support from their members. This is particularly true for the UN Security Council. ICC referrals of non-State Parties to the Rome Statute depend on the political will of Security Council members, especially the permanent ones. And even if relevant policy-making organs do adopt decisions or resolutions, doubt remains about the effectiveness of such measures. Concerned States are highly likely to ignore them. States with close relations with said State may refuse to cooperate. Thus, such confrontational measures may not bring about short-term solutions. And while there are various responses to non-compliance, there may be no single decisive step, though that does not necessarily mean that such measures will be indefinitely ineffective. As mentioned above, maintaining and strengthening such measures over the long term is essential.

Fifth, with these deficiencies in mind, some States may resort to unilateral action, the lawfulness of which must be closely examined in light of the current state of international law. While unilateral non-military sanctions may not be an issue if the States concerned have no multilateral obligation to maintain specific legal relations that could interfere with such measures, unilateral military measures, on the other hand, pose the serious problem of *jus ad bellum*. While there is the aforementioned consensus on the prohibition of chemical weapons use and the necessity to hold perpetrators accountable, the majority of States and commentators reject unilateral use of force against States allegedly using chemical weapons against their civilian populations, as this does not fit with the exceptions to the use of force prohibition under the UN Charter, i.e., right of self-defense or Security Council authorization. Enough States oppose enshrining the theory of humanitarian intervention in international law, and the lawful military action argument is weakened because, except for the UK, those States which took military action did not offer legal justification, while those which expressed support refrained from clarifying their own legal positions. The international community should explore a UN Security Council resolution which authorizes Member States to use all necessary means to respond to chemical weapons use.

3.4 Conclusion

The foregoing shows what was originally asserted: the obligation not to use chemical weapons, that is, the obligation of omission, has been handled through *ad hoc* compliance/non-compliance control based on *ex post* measures. In normal circumstances where chemical weapons are not used, this obligation is fully complied with, obviating the need for mechanisms to ensure such compliance. Potential or actual non-compliance becomes an issue only when is there an alleged or actual use of chemical weapons. Although the comprehensive ban on chemical weapons under the CWC makes the use or alleged use of chemical weapons less likely, such incidents could still theoretically happen *ad hoc*, and there were many such attacks in Syria, irrespective of it being a State Party to the CWC. It is thus anticipated that *ad hoc* mechanisms will address potential non-compliance and respond to actual non-compliance with *ex post* measures.

Syria has been obliged not to use chemical weapons. The prohibition on chemical weapons use can be found in customary international law and the CWC. The former binds Syria by definition, while, as mentioned above, the latter was first provisionally applied to Syria prior to formally entering into force on 14 October 2013. In addition, UN Security Council Resolution 2118, adopted in response to the sarin gas attack of 21 August 2013, imposed a like obligation on Syria.

Regarding the compliance/non-compliance control mechanisms, the OPCW policy-making organs and the UN Security Council have conducted the *ad hoc* institutional compliance/non-compliance control over the use or alleged use of chemical weapons by Syria, while several States have taken unilateral action.

The primary function of the mechanism for addressing potential non-compliance is finding facts. In many instances of alleged use of chemical weapons, parties to armed conflict, and their supporters, have different views on the facts rather than law. One could often encounter a situation where one party criticizes the other for using chemical weapons, while the latter categorically denies this allegation and, in some cases, puts forward counterargument that the former used them. In fact, this narrative has been repeated during the armed conflict in Syria.

The UN Mission, OPCW FFM, OPCW-UN JIM, OPCW IIT, and COI have investigated the allegations to determine whether chemical weapons were used and who was responsible for any such use. Their reports have confirmed that the Syrian government and ISIL were involved in these chemical incidents and thus served as useful inputs for the policy-making organs for considering the necessary actions. These are the most important accomplishments. At the same time, the results of investigation as such proved that these fact-finding bodies failed to prevent further use of chemical weapons at least until the middle of 2018.

The effectiveness of this mechanism depends on the availability of feasible procedures and the technical expertise to carry them out. In this regard, a procedural gap arose, because the existing procedures in the CWC were not used and all of the fact-finding organs but the UN Mission were newly established. Thus, the CWC initially lacked the feasible procedures and technical expertise to investigate the allegations during non-international armed conflict in Syria, including identifying perpetrators, necessitating collective action by the UN Security Council and the OPCW policy-making organs and an OPCW Director-General's initiative to instigate same.

Political support is important for the fact-finding organs and their activities. Some enjoy broad political support, and thus function relatively smoothly, while others encounter opposition complicating their functions. So long as no procedural errors arise, majority decisions might be pragmatic when consensus cannot be found. Lack of such consensus risks undermining fact-finding organs' legitimacy, however.

Such legitimacy on the part of fact-finding mission and the authority that derives therefrom are underpinned by the guiding principles of independence, objectivity, impartiality, and professionalism in their investigations. While States generally find common ground on said principles, views diverse on specific methodological and operational issues, including composition of and appointments to investigation teams, on-site visits by such teams, chains of custody, open-source materials, standards of proof, and selection of witnesses. Russia and Syria have insisted on strict methodologies and operations, criticized fact-finding bodies for failing to meet relevant requirements and standards, and used such criticisms as a basis to reject their findings. By contrast, others, led by the US, the UK, and the EU give their full support to these fact-finding bodies and accept relatively flexible methodologies and operations. In the author's view, a primary factor for these differences of opinion lies in the ongoing armed conflict in Syria, which has imposed limitations on fact-finding from the outset. It might behoove parties to seek common ground also on acceptable methodologies and operations for fact-finding during armed conflict so as to avoid undermining such missions' objectivity and impartiality.

For the effective functioning of the fact-finding organs, the cooperation of Syria is indispensable. There is an asymmetric relation between the fact-finding organs and Syria: the former fulfill mandates, while the latter provides cooperation. In fact, Syria has cooperated with some fact-finding missions, allowing them to enter Syria and providing them with unfettered access to sites and persons as security permits. As long as Syria is cooperative, these organs will be able to fulfill their mandates. Others have instead faced resistance. Syria opposed the establishment of the COI and OPCW IIT, and denied them access to its territory, creating serious obstacles to their effective function.

Practice shows that there are institutional and unilateral responses to non-compliance with the obligation against using chemical weapons in the ongoing non-international armed conflict in Syria. Both kinds of responses begin by ascertaining non-compliance. The key here is who determines non-compliance based on what information. Institutional decisions based on objective findings are more convincing, reliable, and legitimate than unilateral subjective assessments. Next is decisions on measures to be taken. One purpose of such action is to prevent further use of chemical weapons. Another is to punish such use, including holding perpetrators to account. While institutional action is, again, preferable, its absence may open the door to unilateral action.

A determination of non-compliance is a clear prerequisite for measures to be taken against same, and institutional and unilateral responses alike have relied on the reports of the aforementioned fact-finding organs to arrive at such determinations. The UN Mission report of 16 September 2013 and the OPCW FFM reports of 29 October 2015 were universally accepted, with relevant policy-making organs explicitly referring to them in their consensus resolutions and decisions that chemical weapons use in Syria constitutes a violation of international law. Other reports provided these same policy-making organs with the basis for majority resolutions and decisions that obligations under the CWC and UN Security Council Resolution 2118 were violated. Some of them also serve as useful background information for States taking non-military autonomous sanction measures against the targets involved in such chemical weapons use. Exceptions are the planned and actual unilateral military actions in 2013, 2017, and 2018, when the US, the UK, and France took or attempted to take military action on their own judgment because of the sense of urgency when the relevant fact-finding bodies were still at work or not yet deployed.

Taking actions is the next step. In response to the chemical attack in East Ghouta of 21 August 2013, the UN Security Council and the OPCW Executive Council took several measures in accordance with their respective mandates. Regarding use of chemical weapons after April 2014, procedures for responding to non-compliance under the CWC, and the Resolution 2118 Regime are available. The latter particularly provides the UN Security Council with mandates to act under Chapter VII of the UN Charter in the event of non-compliance with Resolution 2118, especially unauthorized transfer of chemical weapons, or any use of chemical weapons by anyone in Syria. In this regard, what matters is the political will to implement them. While the UN Security Council particularly failed to adopt legally binding enforcement measures, including collective economic sanctions, the OPCW policy-making organs have taken actions to redress non-compliance, albeit not unanimously.

These positive developments notwithstanding, the institutional measures are too weak to prevent further use of chemical weapons in Syria. Verbal statements have had almost no impact. The effectiveness of unilateral measures is also unclear, as only a limited number of States have enacted and maintained autonomous sanction measures. Military action appears, not to completely eliminate possible future chemical attacks, in addition to being on fundamentally dubious legal footing. Almost all of these measures have punitive aspects as well, as it is assumed that Syria has suffered economic, political, and other damage. It is an open question, however, what kind of action resolves non-compliance, at least regarding obligations applicable to non-international armed conflict under international humanitarian law. The focus is thus on individuals rather than States, giving rise to more serious accountability concerns. ICC referrals have yet to be made due to the aforementioned political deadlock at the UN Security Council. Nor has "The International Partnership against Impunity for the Use of Chemical Weapons!" produced tangible results. Again, the longer impunity continues, the weaker the norms.

Perhaps we should not be surprised at these unsatisfactory situations. The abovementioned measures were intended to put pressure on the Assad regime in the long run, not to bring about short-term solutions. In this circumstance, the point is that these measures must be maintained and strengthened, not abandoned.

Chapter 4
International Disarmament Law: Systematic and Continuous Compliance/Non-compliance Control Based on Combined *Ex Ante* and *Ex Post* Measures

Abstract In response to the sarin gas attack in East Ghouta of 21 August 2013, the UN Security Council, in cooperation with the OPCW Executive Council, established the Resolution 2118 Regime, obliging Syria to submit declarations, remove chemical weapons, and destroy chemical weapons and chemical weapons production facilities, by June 2014. The Resolution 2118 Regime introduced *systematic* and *continuous* compliance/non-compliance control based on combined *ex ante* and *ex post* measures. Initially, it ensured Syrian compliance, but encountered potential non-compliance with the obligations to submit full and complete declaration and to meet deadlines later on. The OPCW-UN JIM conclusion that the Syrian government used chemical weapons led logically to the implication that Syria had failed to submit a full and complete declaration. The OPCW policy-making organs took *ex post* punitive sanction measures against Syria, including the suspension of its rights and privileges as a State Party to the CWC. As Syria has refused to redress the situation, there is no prospect of resolving the resulting stalemate in the near future.

4.1 Introduction

As mentioned above, there were dramatic developments in the Syrian chemical weapons issue in September 2013. Unilateral military action in response to alleged use of chemical weapons in East Ghouta on 21 August 2013 was avoided in exchange for a US-Russian agreement on placing Syrian chemical weapons under international control. The US and Russia submitted their joint national paper, which included a framework for the elimination of the Syrian chemical weapons program "in the soonest and safest manner."[1] Syria accepted, even becoming the 190th State Party to the CWC. The OPCW Executive Council and the UN Security Council adopted

[1] OPCW Doc. EC-M-33/NAT.1, 17 September 2013, Annex, p. 2. See also UN Doc. S/RES/2118 (2013), 27 September 2013, preamble para. 10, operative para. 10. The OPCW Executive Council and the UN Security Council also used the expressions "in the most rapid and safe manner" (OPCW Doc. EC-M-33/DEC.1, 27 September 2013, operative para. 9) and "in the most expedient and safest manner" (UN Doc. S/RES/2118 (2013), 27 September 2013, operative para. 3), respectively.

T. Abe, *Syrian Chemical Weapons and International Law*,
https://doi.org/10.1007/978-981-99-3700-4_4

Decision EC-M-33/DEC.1 and Resolution 2118, respectively, inaugurating the Resolution 2118 Regime. While this Regime addressed the Syrian chemical weapons issue specifically as well as the broader issues of chemical weapons use and non-proliferation, its primary purpose was to establish extraordinary procedures for the safe and expeditious elimination of the Syrian chemical weapons program, including compliance and non-compliance control ("verification" would be the more familiar term in disarmament circles) mechanisms. The situation required the Resolution 2118 Regime to strengthen, augment, and even deviate from CWC provisions in several aspects, as discussed hereinafter. A key element was the removal of chemical weapons from Syria to another State Party for destruction. While the CWC envisages such destruction taking place on the territory of possessor State Parties, UN Security Council authorization addressed this legal obstacle, because, in accordance with Article 103 of the UN Charter, UN Charter prevails over those under other international agreements.

International disarmament law features a combination of substantive objective, or non-reciprocal, obligations relevant to the destruction of specific weapons, i.e., the obligations to act, and compliance/non-compliance control comprising mechanisms for ensuring compliance with these obligations, addressing potential non-compliance, and responding to non-compliance, as required.[2] The Resolution 2118 Regime essentially took the same standard approach to eliminating the Syrian chemical weapons program, obligating Syria to destroy all chemical weapons and chemical weapons production facilities by the deadline. OPCW Executive Council Decision EC-M-34/DEC.1 clarified category-by-category timelines for steps related to such elimination, including removal of chemical weapons and destruction of chemical weapons and chemical weapons production facilities. Furthermore, the Regime introduced a systematic and continuous compliance/non-compliance control mechanism to be implemented and operated by the OPCW and the UN. Such *ex ante* design was crucial, because the mechanism for ensuring compliance with the obligation to eliminate the chemical weapons program, that is, the obligation to act, needed to be placed in advance of the aforementioned destruction. Initially, the focus was on monitoring implementation. The Resolution 2118 Regime functioned as the mechanism for ensuring compliance, so long as Syria complied with its obligations. Non-compliance arose during that selfsame implementation, however.

It has been pointed out that international disarmament law suggests that many non-compliance issues may be addressed by a "pragmatic approach"[3] in a cooperative atmosphere. Perhaps non-compliance would be acceptable when a possessor State is willing but unable to fulfill its obligations. In these cases, the international community

[2] Examples include the 1987 Treaty between the United States of America and the Union of Soviet Socialist Republics on the Elimination of Their Intermediate-Range and Shorter-Range Missiles (INF Treaty), the 1991 Treaty Between the United States of America and the Union of Soviet Socialist Republics on the Reduction and Limitation of Strategic Offensive Arms (START I Treaty), the 1993 Chemical Weapons Convention (CWC); UN Doc. S/RES/687 (1991) C, 3 April 1991 and UN Doc. S/RES/1441 (2002), 8 November 2002.

[3] Jozef Goldblat, *Arms Control: The New Guide to Negotiations and Agreements*, second edition (SAGE Publications, 2002) p. 310.

has provided technical, financial, personnel, logistical, and other assistance to a possessor State to redress its non-compliance.[4] On the contrary, non-compliance would be unacceptable when a possessor State is unwilling to fulfill its obligations. This situation is most likely addressed by confrontation. The Resolution 2118 Regime has taken different approaches to the issues of potential non-compliance or even non-compliance depending on the situation.

This chapter begins with the substantive obligation, then discusses how the international community has grappled with the unprecedented challenges of the elimination of Syrian chemical weapons through the compliance/non-compliance control under the Resolution 2118 Regime, considers how to ensure compliance, how to address potential non-compliance, and how to respond to non-compliance. This chapter ends with conclusion.

4.2 Substantive Obligation: Obligation to Act

(1) Background

The CWC imposes obligations on State Parties possessing chemical weapons to destroy such weapons and their production facilities "in accordance with the provisions of this Convention," (Article I, paras. 2 and 4). Specific procedures are stipulated in Article IV and Verification Annex Part IV(A) and Article V and Verification Annex Part V, respectively. The structure of obligations under the CWC indicates that complete destruction is a "core" substantive obligation, with subsidiary substantive obligations to submit declarations and to meet deadlines for such destruction, and procedural obligations to provide reports and receive inspections. These collectively fall under the heading of obligations to act, in that possessor States Parties must take relevant action for their fulfillment.

(2) Substance

Being a State Party, Syria was required to fulfill these same CWC obligations, though the Resolution 2118 Regime allowed some modifications to account for its extraordinary situation.[5]

[4] Albania was unable to meet the deadline of 29 April 2007 for the destruction of its chemical weapons for technical reasons. At its forty-ninth session, the OPCW Executive Council requested that Albania, under the terms of Article VIII, para. 36 of the Convention, take measures to redress the situation by meeting its obligation to complete said destruction without further delay (OPCW Doc. EC-49/5, 29 June 2007, para. 5.7). It also noted the importance of planned, coordinated, targeted, and effectively utilized international assistance for Albania (*ibid*., para. 5.8). Albania completed said destruction by 11 July 2007 (OPCW News, Albania the First Country to Destroy All Its Chemical Weapons, https://www.opcw.org/media-centre/news/2007/07/albania-first-country-destroy-all-its-chemical-weapons, accessed 22 April 2023).

[5] The UN Security Council typically adopts resolutions "acting under Chapter VII." Resolution 2118, however, relied only on Article 25 of the Charter to make Resolution 2118 Regime measures

(a) Chemical Weapons Program Declarations

(i) CWC

Submission of declarations is an "indispensable starting point"[6] for disarmament under international verification and a prerequisite to destruction of banned weapons, as it clarifies types and quantities of weapons to be destroyed and provides an overall plan for such destruction. This information enables international monitoring organs to develop plans for verification of same. The CWC obliges States Parties to submit initial declarations on chemical weapons and chemical weapons production facilities to the OPCW within 30 days after entry into force (Article III, para. 1). More specifically, a possessor States Parties are required to specify "the precise location, aggregate quantity and detailed inventory of chemical weapons" (Article III, para. 1(a)(ii)) and "any chemical weapons production facility" (Article III, para. 1(c)(ii)), and to provide "its general plan for destruction" of chemical weapons and any chemical weapons production facility (Article III, para. 1(a)(v) and (c)(v)). Relevant provisions of Verification Annex Parts IV(A) and V describe items to be declared.

(ii) US–Russia Joint National Paper

In this instrument, the US and Russia prioritized "the immediate international control over chemical weapons and their components in Syria." In this context, they introduced a new concept of "initial information" which Syria would submit to the OPCW on a tight schedule and in advance of the submission of "the formal CWC declaration," i.e., its initial declaration under the CWC.[7] By this, they expected that Syria would accordingly submit this "initial information" within one week (Table 4.1), and that it should include "a comprehensive listing, including names, types, and quantities of its chemical weapons agents, types of munitions, and location and form of storage, production, and research and development facilities."[8] This was only ever a non-binding recommendation on Syria, however.

---

binding. During negotiations, the US led others in preferring a clear reference to Chapter VII, with Russia opposed. A compromise was reached, combining omitting a reference to Chapter VII in the preamble with mentioning possible future measures under Chapter VII in the operative part (Marie Jacobsson, "Syria and the Issue of Chemical Weapons: A Snapshot of a Legal Timeframe: the United Nations Security Council Resolution 2118 (2013) and the OPCW Executive Council Decision," in Jonas Ebbesson et al (eds.), *International Law and Changing Perceptions of Security: liber amicorum Said Mahmoudi* (Brill Nijhoff, 2014), p. 134, p. 142). Lack of reference to Chapter VII has no legal significance, however, because the UN Charter does not oblige the Security Council to specify the relevant Chapter under which a resolution is adopted (*ibid.*, p. 143). Also, in its Namibia case, the ICJ dismissed the argument that "Article 25 of the Charter applies only to enforcement measures adopted under Chapter VII of the Charter" (*Legal Consequences for States of the Continued Presence of South Africa in Namibia (South West Africa) notwithstanding Security Council Resolution 276 (1970), Advisory Opinion of 21 June 1971, I.C.J. Reports 1971*, p. 16, pp. 52–53, para. 113).

[6] Goldblat, *supra* note 3, p. 311.

[7] OPCW Doc. EC-M-33/NAT.1, 17 September 2013, p. 4, Annex A, para. 5.

[8] *Ibid.*, p. 2, para. 6.

(iii) **Resolution 2118 Regime**

On 27 September 2013, the OPCW Executive Council adopted Decision EC-M-33/DEC.1, requiring Syria to submit two different but overlapping types of declarations to the OPCW (Table 4.1). The first type is "further information, to supplement that provided on 19 September 2013, on the chemical weapons as defined in Article II, para. 1 of the Convention that the Syrian Arab Republic owns or possesses, or has under its jurisdiction or control." The items in detail are "in particular" as follows:

- the chemical name and military designator of each chemical in its chemical weapons stockpile, including precursors and toxins, and quantities thereof;
- the specific type of munitions, sub-munitions and devices in its chemical weapons stockpile, including specific quantities of each type that are filled and unfilled; and
- the location of all of its chemical weapons, chemical weapons storage facilities, chemical weapons production facilities, including mixing and filling facilities, and chemical weapons research and development facilities, providing specific geographic coordinates.[9]

The deadline for the submission of "further information" was given as "not later than seven days after its adoption." Unlike the joint national paper, this decision was legally binding. UN Security Council Resolution 2118, adopted the same day, removed doubt on this point by referring to Article 25 of the UN Charter and including the following language: "*[d]ecides* that the Syrian Arab Republic shall comply with all aspects of the decision of the OPCW Executive Council of 27 September 2013 (Annex I)."[10] Its scope appeared broader than the obligations under the CWC.

The second type is the initial declarations required by Article III of the CWC, for which the OPCW Executive Council established the deadline for submission as "not later than 30 days after the adoption of this decision,"[11] that is, 27 October 2013, which was earlier than the deadline of "not later than 30 days after the entry into force of the Convention" under Article III. As mentioned above, Article 103 of the UN Charter, made this possible, clarifying as it does the primacy of obligations under the UN Charter over other international agreements. It is understood that "obligations under the UN Charter" include those under UN Security Council resolution, as indicated by the ICJ in its Lockerbie rulings.[12]

---

[9] OPCW Doc. EC-M-33/DEC.1, 27 September 2013, operative para. 1(a).

[10] UN Doc. S/RES/2118 (2013), 27 September 2013, preamble para. 14 and operative para. 6. Jacobsson, *supra* note 5, p. 146.

[11] OPCW Doc. EC-M-33/DEC.1, 27 September 2013, operative para. 1(b).

[12] *Questions of Interpretation and Application of the 1971 Montreal Convention arising from the Aerial Incident at Lockerbie (Libyan Arab Jamahiriya* v. *United Kingdom), Provisional Measures, Order of 14 April 1992, I.C.J. Reports 1992*, p. 15, para. 39; *Questions of Interpretation and Application of the 1971 Montreal Convention arising from the Aerial Incident at Lockerbie (Libyan Arab Jamahiriya* v. *United States of America), Provisional Measures, Order of 14 April 1992, I.C.J. Reports 1992*, p. 126, para. 42.

Table 4.1 Information to be submitted by Syria

Type	Deadline
Initial information	Within one week (21 September 2013)
Further information	Not later than 7 days after the adoption of the decision (4 October 2013)
Initial declarations	Not later than 30 days after the adoption of the decision (27 October 2013)

The OCPW Technical Secretariat was tasked with forwarding submitted declarations them to all States Parties within five days of receipt, initiating inspections as soon as possible, though not later than 1 October 2013, and conducting inspections of all declared facilities not later than 30 days after the adoption of the decision, that is, 27 October 2013.[13]

(b) **Removal of Chemical Weapons**

(i) **CWC**

It should be noted again that the CWC bans transfer of chemical weapons (Article 1, para. 1 (a)), and has no explicit exception for transfer of same for destruction, unlike the Anti-Personnel Landmine Convention or the Cluster Munitions Convention.[14]

Notwithstanding, the OPCW had established the practice of allowing transportation of old chemical weapons for the destruction thereof from one State Party to another. The first such case involved transporting three such old chemical weapons from Austria to Germany. At its forty-eighth session in March 2007, the OPCW Executive Council approved a proposal by Austria and Germany to transport them to Germany for destruction, noting information submitted by these States Parties about the discovery and declarations of such old chemical weapons, as well as a technical assessment by the Technical Secretariat that they posed an imminent danger to the environment.[15] The second instance was the transportation of one old chemical weapon from the Netherlands to Belgium, which was addressed by "using an OPCW procedure that Austria employed in 2007,"[16] although the OPCW Executive Council

[13] OPCW Doc. EC-M-33/DEC.1, 27 September 2013, operative para. 2(a)–(c).

[14] Article 3, para. 2 of the Anti-Personnel Landmine Convention; Article 3, para. 7 of the Cluster Munitions Convention.

[15] OPCW Doc. EC-50/3, C-12/3, 26 September 2007, para. 2.32. The Executive Council approved the proposal on the understanding that "(a) nothing can alter the general obligation of each State Party … never under any circumstances to transfer chemical weapons, directly or indirectly, to anyone, or the obligation of each State Party that declares OCWs to destroy them under the terms of the Convention; (b) the OCWs discovered by Austria shall remain under the ownership and control of Austria during the process of destruction; (c) these OCWs shall be destroyed as soon as possible, but no later than the Forty-Ninth Session of the Council; (d) the Secretarial would continuously monitor the whole process and report to the Council at its Forty-Ninth Session on the destruction of these OPCWs; and (e) this case shall not establish a precedent for any future cases.".

[16] Dominique Anelli, "Old Chemical Weapons: Moving the OPCW to an Active Role," *Arms Control Today*, June 2020, https://www.armscontrol.org/act/2020-06/features/old-chemical-weapons-moving-opcw-active-role, accessed 22 April 2023

took no formal action at its seventy-third session in July 2013 to approve and impose conditions, instead merely noting the information provided by the Technical Secretariat and the Netherlands.[17] Both Austria and the Netherlands relied on neighboring States Parties with extensive experience of and active facilities for the destruction of such old chemical weapons. Such practice suggests that collective decisions may facilitate deviations from the text of the CWC, when necessary, on a case-by-case basis. Syria's ongoing armed conflict requires exceptional measures to overcome this legal obstacle.

(ii) **US–Russia Joint National Paper**

The US and Russia set "ambitious goals" in their joint national paper for the destruction of the Syrian chemical weapons program by mid-2014 and tabled the idea of destruction of chemical weapons outside of the territory of Syria, to fulfill the abovementioned objective of doing so. They "determined that the most effective control of these weapons may be achieved by removal of the largest amounts of weapons feasible, under OPCW supervision, and their destruction outside of Syria, if possible."[18] The phrase "if possible" implied that they were not entirely certain how feasible the idea was.

(iii) **Resolution 2118 Regime**

OPCW Executive Council Decision EC-M-33/DEC.1

On 27 September 2013, the OPCW Executive Council in the Hague adopted Decision EC-M-33/DEC.1, in which it did not mention the destruction of chemical weapons outside of Syria, but instead elaborated on a requirement that such destruction be completed not later than 15 November 2013.[19] In New York, later the same day, the UN Security Council explored the idea of destroying Syrian chemical weapons outside of Syria, adopting a resolution in which it "*decides* to authorize Member States to acquire, control, transport, transfer and destroy chemical weapons identified by the Director-General of the OPCW, consistent with the objective of the CWC, to ensure the elimination of the Syrian Arab Republic's chemical weapons program in the soonest and safest manner."[20] In light of the status of such Security Council decisions, which, as mentioned above, are legally binding (Article 25 of the UN Charter) and prevails over obligations under other international agreements (Article 103 of the UN Charter), this decision removed legal obstacles to Syrian chemical

[17] OPCW Doc. EC-73/6, 19 July 2013, para. 6.12. Robert A. Friedman, "Legal Aspects of Weapons of Mass Destruction Elimination Contingencies," *The Nonproliferation Review*, Vol. 23, Nos. 1–2 (2016), p. 61, p. 68.

[18] OPCW Doc. EC-M-33/NAT.1, 17 September 2013, p. 2, para. 7.

[19] OPCW Doc. EC-M-33/DEC.1, 27 September 2013, operative para. 1(c).

[20] UN Doc. S/RES/2118 (2013), 27 September 2013, operative para. 10. Resolution 2118 was officially transmitted by the OPCW Director-General to the OPCW Executive Council (OPCW Doc. EC-M-34/DEC.1, 15 November 2013, preamble para. 5).

Table 4.2 Chemical weapons to be removed from Syria

Types	Deadlines
Priority 1: mustard agent and the key binary chemical weapon components DF, A, B, and BB, including BB salt declared by Syria	31 December 2013
Priority 2: all other chemicals declared by Syria	5 February 2014

weapons being destroyed outside of Syria, irrespective of the prohibition of transfer under the CWC. Syria, in its initial declaration to the OPCW on 23 October 2013, also acknowledged the need to have its chemical weapons destroyed outside its territory, under strict OPCW verification, with a view to meeting the requirements established by the aforementioned OPCW Executive Council Decision EC-M-33/DEC.1.[21]

On 5 November 2013, at the thirty-fourth meeting of the OPCW Executive Council, the OPCW Director-General expressed his view that the destruction of Syrian chemical weapons outside its territory constitutes "the most viable option" available to fulfil the requirements established under OPCW Executive Council Decisions and UN Security Council Resolution 2118 for the safe and expeditious elimination of chemical weapons in Syria,[22] lending impetus to consultations among States Parties on drafting a resolution.

OPCW Executive Council Decision EC-M-34/DEC.1

The thirty-fourth meeting of the OPCW Executive Council adopted a decision on detailed requirements for destroying Syrian chemical weapons.[23] Having noted that the OPCW Director-General identified chemical weapons that could be transported for destruction outside the territory of the Syrian Arab Republic, pursuant to operative para. 10 of Resolution 2118,[24] the OPCW Executive Council formally decided on the removal of some chemical weapons from Syria to be destroyed outside Syria and the destruction of other chemical weapons within Syrian territory,[25] specifying deadlines for such removal as follows (Table 4.2).

This endorsement of the removal of chemical weapons outside Syria marked a significant deviation from the CWC, leading to the separation of obligations at the transportation and destruction stages.[26] The OPCW Executive Council affirmed that Syria "maintains ownership of its chemical weapons until they are destroyed, wherever the destruction might take place,"[27] while recognizing that "upon removal

[21] OPCW Doc. EC-M-34/DEC.1, 15 November 2013, preamble para. 4.

[22] Director-General's Statement at the 34th Meeting of the Executive Council, 5 November 2013, https://www.opcw.org/sites/default/files/documents/ODG/uzumcu/DG_Statement_-_EC-M-34.pdf, accessed 22 April 2023.

[23] OPCW Doc. EC-M-34/DEC.1, 15 November 2013.

[24] *Ibid.*, preamble para. 6.

[25] *Ibid.*, operative para. 2(a).

[26] OPCW Doc. EC-M-36/DG.5, 17 December 2013, p. 2.

[27] OPCW Doc. EC-M-34/DEC.1, 15 November 2013, operative para. 4.

of declared chemical weapons from its territory, the Syrian Arab Republic no longer has possession, nor jurisdiction, nor control over these chemical weapons."[28] This decision implied that Syria had the obligation to remove such weapons and would responsible for safe packaging and transportation thereof until they were loaded onto vessels, but that Syria would have no obligation to destroy such chemicals after they were removed from its territory, as mentioned by Syria itself.[29]

(c) **Destruction of Chemical Weapons**

(i) **CWC**

International disarmament treaties typically establish deadlines for destroying banned weapons,[30] a subsidiary obligation that facilitates implementing the core obligation of the complete destruction of same. The CWC likewise stipulates that chemical weapons are to be destroyed within ten years of CWC entry into force (Article IV, para. 6), with an extension of up to five years (Verification Annex Part IV(A), paras. 24–26).[31] The Convention also includes a stringent order of chemical weapons destruction in specific intermediate phases (Verification Annex Part IV(A), para. 17). For those States Parties who join the CWC after the ten-year period for destruction, chemical weapons shall be destroyed "as soon as possible," with order and procedures to be determined by the OPCW Executive Council (Article IV, para. 8), allowing same to devise a destruction order and procedures suited to Syria's situation.[32]

(ii) **US–Russia Joint National Paper**

In their joint national paper of 14 September 2013, the US and Russia set ambitious goals for the destruction of all chemical weapons categories by the end of "the first half of 2014," under stringent special verification measures to be provided by OPCW Executive Council decision.[33] Calling for destruction to be carried out in such a short

---

[28] *Ibid.*

[29] OPCW Doc. EC-M-34/NAT.4 (Syria), 15 November 2013, p. 2.

[30] Article 2, Biological Weapons Convention; Articles 4 and 5, Intermediate-Range Nuclear Forces Treaty.

[31] Requests for conversion are approved by the Conference of the States Parties on Executive Council recommendation (Article V, para. 13).

[32] Iraq became a State Party to the CWC after the ten-year chemical weapons destruction period and declared its possession of chemical weapons remnants stored in two storage bunkers at the Al Muthana site. The OPCW Executive Council adopted a decision entitled "General Plan for Destruction and Establishment of the Deadlines for the destruction of Chemical Weapon Remnants Stored at the Al Muthana Site" in March 2017 (OPCW Doc. EC-84/2, 9 March 2017, para. 6.26). The Director-General submitted a note on Iraq 's completing the destruction of remnants, which the Executive Council noted (OPCW Doc. EC-87/2, 15 March 2018, para. 7.12; See also OPCW News, OPCW Director-General Congratulates Iraq on Complete Destruction of Chemical Weapons Remnants, 13 March 2018, https://www.opcw.org/media-centre/news/2018/03/opcw-director-general-congratulates-iraq-complete-destruction-chemical, accessed 22 April 2023).

[33] OPCW Doc. EC-M-33/NAT.1, 17 September 2013.

time, achievable or not, clearly indicates their determination to urgently address the elimination of the Syrian chemical weapons. It was anticipated that stringent special verification measures would be extraordinary in nature, because the joint national paper suggested "the largest amounts of [chemical] weapons feasible" should be destroyed outside of Syria, which the OPCW had never before conducted, although there were no legal obstacles in terms of destruction timelines or procedures, given the OPCW Executive Council mandate to rule on same (Article IV, para. 8), which pertains to States joining the Convention ten years after its entry into force.

(iii) **Resolution 2118 Regime**

OPCW Executive Council Decision EC-M-33/DEC.1

On 27 September 2013, the OPCW Executive Council adopted its decision on the elimination of Syrian chemical weapons. This decision addressed the issue by first, endorsing the abovementioned ambitious goals of the joint national paper by specifying "the first half of 2014" as the deadline that Syria would be required to meet for the complete elimination of all chemical weapons material and equipment,[34] and second, deferring the elaboration on detailed requirements for said destruction to 15 November 2013 at the latest.[35] The OPCW Executive Council decided to consider "the funding mechanisms" urgently, intending to defray "the activities carried out by the [Technical] Secretariat with respect to the Syrian Arab Republic."[36] Also as previously discussed, the UN Security Council adopted Resolution 2118 that same day, making the OPCW Executive Council decision obligatory and 30 June 2014 a legally binding deadline for Syria.

OPCW Executive Council Decision EC-M-34/DEC.1

The OPCW Executive Council adopted a decision on detailed requirements for the destruction at its thirty-fourth meeting on 15 November 2013.[37] It formally decided that some chemical weapons would be removed and destroyed outside Syria, others in Syria. Established timelines for such destruction by category are as Table 4.3.[38]

The OPCW Executive Council relied on relevant CWC procedures for destroying chemical weapons in Syria, requesting that Syria submit its plan to the OPCW Executive Council for destroying isopropanol and residual mustard agent in containers previously containing mustard agent not later than 1 and 15 January 2014, respectively.[39]

There were several issues concerning destroying chemical weapons outside of Syria, beginning with the status of Syria and that of those States Parties involved in the transportation and destruction of Syrian chemical weapons to be removed from

[34] OPCW Doc. EC-M-33/DEC.1, 27 September 2013, operative para. 1(c).

[35] *Ibid.*, operative para. 1(c).

[36] *Ibid.*, operative para. 3(a).

[37] OPCW Doc. EC-M-34/DEC.1, 15 November 2013.

[38] *Ibid.*, operative paras. 2(a) and 3(a).

[39] *Ibid.*, operative para. 9.

Table 4.3 Chemical weapons to be destroyed either within or outside Syria

Type	Site	Deadline
Unfilled munitions	In Syria	31 January 2014
Isopropanol	In Syria	1 March 2014
Containers previously containing mustard agent	In Syria	1 March 2014
Mustard agent and the key binary chemical weapon components DF, A, B, and BB, including BB salt (Priority 1 chemicals)	Outside of Syria	31 March 2014
Resulting reaction mass	Outside of Syria	To be decided
Other chemicals (Priority 2 chemicals)	Outside of Syria	30 June 2014

Syria. The Chemical Weapons Convention obliges a State Party to destroy "chemical weapons it owns or possesses, or that are located in any place under its jurisdiction or control" (Article I, para. 2). Once removed from Syrian territory, Syrian chemical weapons would be destroyed by States or actors other than Syria. As mentioned above, Syria would maintain ownership of its chemical weapons stockpiles until they were destroyed, but no longer have possession, nor jurisdiction, nor control over its chemical weapons after their removal from Syrian territory,[40] as opposed to Austria, who had ownership of and control over its newly discovered old chemical weapons,[41] perhaps because Austria was able to take control, while Syria was not expected to do so. The OPCW Executive Council also clarified the status of the aforementioned State Parties involved in transporting and destroying Syrian chemical weapons, indicating that they shall not be regarded as possessor States Parties nor incur obligations of same,[42] making ambiguous who is thus obligated to destroy Syrian chemical weapons outside of Syrian territory.[43]

The OPCW Executive Council directed the Director-General to submit a plan for destroying Syrian chemical weapons outside Syria for Executive Council consideration no later than 17 December 2013[44] as well as the Technical Secretariat to submit a detailed plan for verification and draft facility agreement to the OPCW Executive Council for review and approval before said facility commences operations.[45] The OPCW Executive Council also requested that the Technical Secretariat confirm the completion of each stage of destruction,[46] ensuring regular OPCW Executive Council monitoring based on verification conducted by the Technical Secretariat.

[40] *Ibid.*, operative paras. 4 and 5.

[41] OPCW Doc. EC-50/3, C-12/3, 26 September 2007, para. 2.32.

[42] OPCW Doc. EC-M-34/DEC.1, 15 November 2013, operative para. 12(a).

[43] OPCW Doc. EC-M-34/NAT.4 (Syria), 15 November 2013, p. 2 ("my country welcomes the decision's confirmation that … it shall not be burdened with any financial obligations for destruction activities outside its territory.").

[44] OPCW Doc. EC-M-34/DEC.1, 15 November 2013, operative para. 8.

[45] *Ibid.*, operative para. 15.

[46] *Ibid.*, operative para. 21.

Once chemical weapons were removed from Syria, their destruction would be left to other States Parties in a position to do so. The OPCW Executive Council at its thirty-fourth meeting welcomed offers from States Parties to assist in the destruction of Syrian chemical weapons.[47] It requested that these States Parties make further arrangements, including providing access and granting privileges and immunities to the Technical Secretariat for verification purposes, holding consultations with and providing information to the OPCW Director-General, facilitating observation of transportation and destruction of Syrian chemical weapons by Syrian representatives, taking measures to implement the decision, and meeting human and environmental safety requirements under Article IV, para. 10.[48] In the meantime, the OPCW Executive Council explored options regarding using commercial facilities to disposal of effluent resulting from destroying Priority 1 and 2 chemicals, again requesting that the OPCW Director-General submit a plan for destruction of same including his findings on this topic for OPCW Executive Council consideration.[49] Additionally, Syria had already indicated that it could neither afford to destroy its chemical weapons nor meet to the costs of the verification and inspection owing to its current economic difficulties, the economic sanctions imposed on it, and the priority of fulfilling its citizens' basic needs.[50] In acknowledgment, the OPCW Executive Council requested that the Director-General establish a special trust fund, limited to destruction of Syrian chemical weapons outside the territory of Syria,[51] and invited all States Parties in a position to do so to make voluntary contributions. Syria thus remained responsible for financing the destruction of its chemical weapons in its territory.

Offers for Destruction

As mentioned above, multiple States Parties offered assistance in destroying Syrian chemical weapons, including the US, which informed the OPCW Director-General in November 2013 of its plan to supply the technology and full operational support for neutralizing mustard agent and key binary chemical weapon components DF and A with a hydrolysis system aboard the US vessel M/V Cape Ray in the Mediterranean Sea.[52] In addition, the UK sponsored Veolia in destroying the Priority 1 binary

[47] *Ibid.*, preamble para. 10.

[48] *Ibid.*, operative para. 12(b)–(f).

[49] OPCW Doc. EC-M-34/DEC.1, 15 November 2013, operative para. 24.

[50] OPCW Doc. EC-M-34/NAT.4 (Syria), 15 November 2013, p. 2.

[51] OPCW Doc. EC-M-34/DEC.1, 15 November 2013, preamble para. 6.

[52] OPCW Doc. EC-M-37/DG.1, 23 December 2013, para. 11; OPCW Doc. EC-76/DG.16, 4 July 2014, para. 22. The US could not assist in funding construction of destruction facilities in Syria, because it designated Syria as a State sponsor of terrorism (Albert J. Mauroni, "Eliminating Syria's Chemical Weapons," *The Counterproliferation Papers Future Warfare Series*, No. 58 (June 2017), p. 20). While Italy, Jordan, France, Belgium, Norway, Russia, and Germany considered hosting the destruction, they ultimately declined. Albania was approached as a possible candidate but also declined following protests (*ibid.*, p. 22; Philipp C. Bleek and Nicholas J. Kramer, "Eliminating Syria's chemical weapons: implications for addressing nuclear, biological and chemical threats," *The Nonproliferation Review*, Vol. 23, Nos. 1-2 (2016), p. 197, p. 213).

chemical weapon components B and BB at a commercial facility,[53] while Germany sponsored GEKA in disposing of approximately 370 metric tons of effluent created on board the M/V Cape Ray during the aforementioned mustard agent neutralization thereon.[54]

The OPCW Technical Secretariat issuing a call for expressions of interest on 21 November 2013, in response to an Executive Council request to explore other options to disposal by commercial facilities of effluent resulting from destroying Priority 1 and 2 chemicals.[55] Upon reviewing responses, it submitted the Director-General's note on a call for proposals for the treatment and disposal of chemicals, effluent, and packaging materials with respect to the destruction of Syrian chemical weapons, which was noted by OPCW Executive Council Decision.[56] On 20 December, the Technical Secretariat initiated the tendering process, receiving proposals from fourteen companies.[57] Following technical and commercial evaluations, it was announced on 14 February 2014 that contracts had been awarded to Ekokem Oy Ab of Finland, and US-based Veolia Environmental Services Technical Solutions, LLC.[58]

States Parties made other offers for transportation and destruction of Syrian chemical weapons, including Denmark and Norway respectively providing the cargo ships Ark Futura and Taiko to transport chemicals from Syria to ports of States Parties where the chemicals would be destroyed,[59] Russia, China, and the UK providing naval escort for these ships,[60] Italy offering the port of Gioia Tauro for transloading chemicals from the Ark Futura and Taiko to the M/V Cape Ray,[61] the UK also offering the equipment for neutralizing chemical warfare agents aboard the M/V Cape Ray,[62] and Finnish chemical weapons emergency services,[63] while still other State Parties made the aforementioned voluntary financial contributions.[64]

Syria, the OPCW, and the United Nations agreed to a trilateral arrangement regarding the shipping by Denmark and Norway,[65] wherein personnel and assets of the multinational maritime transport operation would be considered only on government non-commercial service and enjoying State immunity, and Syria, Denmark,

---

[53] OPCW Doc. EC-M-37/DG.1, 23 December 2013, paras. 11 and 18; OPCW Doc. EC-76/DG.16, 4 July 2014, para. 24.

[54] OPCW Doc. EC-M-38/DG.1, 23 January 2014, para. 14(d); OPCW Doc. EC-76/DG.16, 4 July 2014, para. 24.

[55] OPCW Doc. S/1142/2013, 22 November 2013.

[56] OPCW Doc. EC-M-37/DG.1, 23 December 2013, para. 16.

[57] OPCW Doc. EC-M-38/DG.1, 23 January 2014, para. 11.

[58] OPCW Doc. EC-75/DG.6, 25 February 2014, para. 11.

[59] OPCW Doc. EC-M-37/DG.1, 23 December 2013, para. 19.

[60] OPCW Doc. EC-M-38/DG.1, 23 January 2014, para. 14(a)(b)(e).

[61] *Ibid.*, para. 14(f).

[62] *Ibid.*, para. 14(e).

[63] OPCW Doc. EC-M-37/DG.1, 23 December 2013, para. 19.

[64] OPCW Doc. EC-76/DG.16, 4 July 2014, para. 14. See also https://opcw.unmissions.org/sites/default/files/donor_factsheet_310714_final.pdf, accessed 22 April 2023.

[65] UN Doc. S/2013/774, 27 December 2013, pp. 3–4.

and Norway would accordingly enjoy the rights and obligations related to warships or government ships operated for non-commercial purposes provided for in UN Convention on the Law of the Sea (UNCLOS) Articles 30, 31, 32, 96, and 236, notwithstanding that Syria is not a State Party thereto.[66]

Overview of the Destruction Plan

The destruction plan itself divided chemicals into two categories, as described in Tables 4.2 and 4.3, establishing different schemes for each.[67] Priority 1 chemicals, i.e., a small amount of mustard agent and precursors of sarin, would be transported by the Ark Futura from Latakia, Syria to Gioia Tauro, Italy, where some 600 metric tons of would be transloaded to the US M/V Cape Ray for neutralization on the Mediterranean Sea, with OPCW inspectors present to verify same. Upon completing said neutralization, the M/V Cape Ray would transport the resulting effluent to Hamina Kotka, Finland and Bremen, Germany. The effluent created by the neutralization of mustard agent, i.e., the HD and DF effluent, will be destroyed at the Finnish hazardous waste management company Ekokem AB and the German facility GEKA. The remaining 150 metric tons of chemicals would be transported by the Ark Futura to Ellesmere Port, UK, for destruction by the commercial waste processing company Veolia (UK). Priority 2 chemicals would be transported by the Taiko from Latakia, Syria to Finland and the US, offloading 360 metric tons at Hamina Kotka, Finland for destruction by Ekokem AB, with the remaining 145 metric tons unloaded Port Arthur, Texas, for destruction by Veolia (US).

(d) Destruction of Chemical Weapons Production Facilities

(i) CWC

The CWC also establishes ten-year deadlines for the destruction of chemical weapons production facilities (Article V, para. 8) and stringent order of destruction for specific intermediate phases or periods (Verification Annex Part V, para. 30). It allows converting such facilities to purposes not prohibited by the Convention, in exceptional cases of compelling need (Article V, para. 13).[68] For States Parties who joins the Convention after the ten-year period for destruction, as with chemical weapons, the CWC obliges these States Parties to destroy such facilities "as soon as possible," with order and procedures to be determined by the OPCW Executive Council (Article V, para. 10).

[66] Exchange of letters constituting an agreement between the Organisation for the Prohibition of Chemical Weapons, the United Nations and the Government of the Syrian Arab Republic concerning the multinational maritime transport operation for the removal and transport of Syrian chemical agents. The Hague, 5 January 2014, New York, 5 January 2014, and Damascus, 6 January 2014, *UN Treaty Series*, No. 51679.

[67] OPCW, Removal and Destruction of Syrian Chemical Weapons, https://www.opcw.org/sites/default/files/documents/files/Syra_Infographic.pdf, accessed 22 April 2023.

[68] Requests for conversion will be approved by the Conference of the States Parties based on the Executive Council recommendation (Article V, para. 13).

(ii) **US–Russia Joint National Paper**

In the joint national paper, the US and Russia stressed that "the elimination process must include the facilities for the development and production of these weapons."[69] They also identified ten principles for incorporation in OPCW Executive Council decision, including language from Article V, para. 10 of the CWC of "a schedule for the rapid destruction of Syrian chemical weapons capabilities," and intermediate and shortest possible final deadlines.[70]

(iii) **Resolution 2118 Regime**

OPCW Executive Council Decision EC-M-33/DEC.1

To reiterate, the OPCW Executive Council adopted its decision on the elimination of Syrian chemical weapons on 27 September 2013. It also decided that Syria "shall complete as soon as possible and in any case not later than 1 November 2013, the destruction of chemical weapons production and mixing/filling equipment."[71] This was obviously essential to preventing more chemical munitions being produced for potential use in the ongoing Syrian conflict. The UN Security Council made it clear that this decision binds on Syria under its Resolution 2118, adopted the same day,[72] while details for said destruction would be determined by the OPCW Executive Council no later than 15 November 2013.[73]

OPCW Executive Council Decision EC-M-34/DEC.1

The OPCW Executive Council duly adopted the requisite decision on that date,[74] which first established timelines according to risk-based criteria as Table 4.4.[75]

Next, it called on the Technical Secretariat to prepare a plan to verify the destruction of Syrian chemical weapons production facilities based on plans submitted by Syria, and to submit the combined plans for destruction and verification for OPCW Executive Council consideration no later than 9 December 2013, thereby demonstrating the OPCW Executive Council's intent to monitor said destruction in accordance with CWC provisions that other State Parties had followed.[76] Meanwhile, the OPCW Executive Council decided not to insist on facility agreements between Syria and the OPCW, given that all chemical weapons production facilities declared by the Syrian Arab Republic had already been inspected and would soon be destroyed.[77]

---

[69] OPCW Doc. EC-M-33/NAT.1, 17 September 2013, p. 3.

[70] *Ibid.*, p. 4.

[71] OPCW Doc. EC-M-33/DEC.1, 27 September 2013, operative para. 1(d).

[72] UN Doc. S/RES/2118 (2013), 27 September 2013, operative para. 6.

[73] OPCW Doc. EC-M-33/DEC.1, 27 September 2013, operative para. 1(c).

[74] OPCW Doc. EC-M-34/DEC.1, 15 November 2013.

[75] *Ibid.*, operative para. 2(b); OPCW News, OPCW adopts plan for destruction of Syria's chemical weapons programme in the first half of 2014, 15 November 2013, https://www.opcw.org/media-centre/news/2013/11/opcw-adopts-plan-destruction-syrias-chemical-weapons-programme-first-half, accessed 22 April 2023.

[76] OPCW Doc. EC-M-34/DEC.1, 15 November 2013, operative para. 16.

[77] *Ibid.*, operative para. 17.

Table 4.4 Chemical weapons production facilities to be destroyed by Syria

Type	Deadline
Facilities with mobile units/systems designed for mixing and filling, and mixing and filling facilities where specialized equipment is not yet dismantled, collocated with storage sites for binary components and/or empty munitions	15 December 2013
Facilities with disconnected or intact (not yet dismantled) equipment train/lines for production of chemical agents or binary components	15 January 2014
Facilities with dismantled equipment for production and dismantled equipment for mixing and filling	15 February 2014
Facilities for production of other chemicals (thiodiglycol, acetic acid, etc.)	15 March 2014
Facilities that do not hold either specialized or standard equipment	15 March 2014

4.3 Compliance/Non-compliance Control

As described elsewhere, the Resolution 2118 Regime introduced systematic and continuous compliance/non-compliance control based on combined *ex ante* and *ex post* measures. While it continues to control Syrian compliance/non-compliance with its obligations, said Regime's function has transformed over time from ensuring compliance to addressing potential non-compliance and responding to actual non-compliance, tasking the OPCW and the UN with monitoring Syria to this end, and with both organizations accordingly expected and required to closely cooperate and collaborate with each other during the parallel implementation process.

Fortunately, these organizations had experience in just such cooperation. In 1999, the OPCW Technical Secretariat had the opportunity to assist the United Nations Special Commission in closing its chemical laboratory in the Baghdad Monitoring and Verification Centre, including the destruction of seven VX reference standards, a two-week mission involving the deployment of four specialists.[78] Their relations were subsequently formalized and governed by the Agreement concerning the Relationship between the United Nations and the Organisation for the Prohibition of Chemical Weapons of 17 October 2000.[79] There have been such additional exercises as the OPCW Director-General's annual briefings at the plenary session or the First

[78] OPCW News, OPCW Experts Mission to Iraq: An Update, 20 July 1999, https://www.opcw.org/media-centre/news/1999/07/opcw-experts-mission-iraq-update, accessed 17 August 2021; OPCW News, OPCW Mission in Baghdad Successfully Completed, 29 July 1999, https://www.opcw.org/media-centre/news/1999/07/opcw-mission-baghdad-successfully-completed, accessed 22 April 2023. For VX issues, see also UN Doc. S/1998/176, 27 February 1998; UN Doc. S/1998/995, 26 October 1998; UN Doc. S/1998/1008, 28 October 1998; UN Doc. S/1999/831, 28 July 1999; UN Doc. S/1999/897, 20 August 1999.

[79] *United Nations Treaty Series*, Vol. 2160, II-1240, p. 209. See also OPCW Doc. C-VI/DEC.5, 17 May 2001; UN Doc. A/RES/55/283, 24 September 2001. The Agreement, which entered into force on 26 September 2001, covers general matters, cooperation, coordination, reporting, reciprocal representation, agenda items, the ICJ, UN resolutions, UN laisses-passer, personnel arrangements, budgetary and financial matters, expenses, protection of confidentiality, implementation, amendments, and entry into force.

Committee of the UN General Assembly,[80] statements by the UN Secretary-General or high-level representative at the annual session of the Conference of the States Parties,[81] and the adoption of resolutions on the CWC and the OPCW at the UN General Assembly.[82] In addition, needless to say, the OPCW Technical Secretariat was providing personnel and technical resources to the UN Mission to investigate an alleged use of chemical weapons in Syria when OPCW Executive Council Decision EC-M-33/DEC.1 and UN Security Council Resolution 2118 were adopted. All of these served to facilitate continuous cooperation between these organizations in the wider context of the Syrian chemical weapons issue.

This section will discuss the unique quadruple compliance/non-compliance control—in which the OPCW Technical Secretariat, the UN Secretariat, the OPCW Executive Council, and the UN Security Council are involved—to implement the Resolution 2118 Regime.

4.3.1 Ensuring Compliance

(1) **Background**

As previously mentioned, the obligation to eliminate chemical weapons programs is a non-reciprocal act within the territories of concerned States, and its implementation

[80] UN Doc. A/C.1/52/PV.6, 16 October 1997, pp. 23–28; UN Doc. A/C.1/53/PV.9, 19 October 1998, pp. 20–25; UN Doc. A/55/PV.38, 20 October 2000, pp. 27–32; UN Doc. A/56/PV.77, 6 December 2001, pp. 4–10; UN Doc. A/C.1/57/PV.19, 23 October 2002, pp. 1–5; UN Doc. A/57/PV.53, 20 November 2002, pp. 5–8; UN Doc. A/C.1/58/PV.3, 7 October 2003, pp. 23–26; UN Doc. A/C.1/59/PV.4, 7 October 2004, pp. 23–25; UN Doc. A/59/PV.38, 21 October 2004, pp. 4–7; UN Doc. A/C.1/60/PV.8, 10 October 2005, pp. 16–21; UN Doc. A/C.1/61/PV.8, 9 October 2006, pp. 6–11; UN Doc. A/61/PV.38, 20 October 2006, pp. 5–9; UN Doc. A/C.1/62/PV.9, 17 October 2007, pp. 7–12; UN Doc. A/C.1/62/PV.12, 19 October 2007, pp. 3–7; UN Doc. A/C.1/63/PV.9, 15 October 2008, pp. 6–9; UN Doc. A/63/PV.36, 3 November 2008, pp. 19–23; UN Doc. A/C.1/64/PV.12, 16 October 2009, pp. 1–6; UN Doc. A/C.1/65/PV.9, 13 October 2010, pp. 4–6; UN Doc. A/C.1/66/PV.10, 12 October 2011, pp. 5–7; UN Doc. A/C.1/67/PV.7, 15 October 2012, pp. 3–6; UN Doc. A/67/PV.40, 19 November 2012, pp. 4–7. See also UN Doc. A/C.1/68/PV.10, 17 October 2013; UN Doc. A/C.1/69/PV.9, 16 October 2014.

[81] C-V/2, 15 May 2000 (Message from the Secretary-General of the United Nations for the Opening Ceremony of the Fifth Session of the Conference of the States Parties to the Chemical Weapons Convention); C-VI/3, 14 May 2001 (Message From the Secretary-General of the United Nations to the Sixth Session of the Conference of the States Parties to the Chemical Weapons Convention Delivered by Mr. Vladimir Petrovsky, Director-General, United Nations Office at Geneva); C-8/6, 20 October 2003 (Message from the Secretary-General of the United Nations to the Eighth Session of the Conference of the States Parties to the Chemical Weapons Convention); Secretary-General's message to Seventeenth Session of the Conference of State Parties to the Chemical Weapons Convention, 26 November 2012, https://www.un.org/sg/en/content/sg/statement/2012-11-26/secretary-generals-message-seventeenth-session-conference-state; https://www.opcw.org/sites/default/files/documents/CSP/C-17/en/UN-26nov2012_CSP_17.pdf, accessed 22 April 2023.

[82] See Appendix G for a list of UN General Assembly Resolutions.

is accordingly normally invisible to the international community. It is thus necessary to adopt procedures for ensuring compliance by having said concerned States submit information on said implementation to international monitoring bodies. Multilateral treaties on international human rights and environmental protection require States Parties to submit national reports to treaty-based organs, i.e., a committee or a Conference of States Parties (COP), for consideration. Such procedures for ensuring compliance are further strengthened in the field of arms control because implementation of said obligations by possessor States may have a direct impact on the security of other States. International monitoring bodies accordingly verify implementation thereof by comparing the information submitted by the possessor State with the information collected through inspections in the possessor State's territory. The CWC has adopted this methodology, as did the UN Special Commission (UNSCOM) and the UN Monitoring, Verification and Inspection Commission (UNMOVIC), which monitored Iraqi compliance with disarmament obligations per UN Security Council Resolutions.[83] In light of the nature of the obligation to eliminate chemical weapons programs, that is, the aforementioned obligation to act, compliance/non-compliance control can be designed *ex ante* to elimination-related activities, especially ensuring compliance.

(2) **Ensuring Compliance**

The Resolution 2118 Regime has established mechanisms for ensuring Syrian compliance with the obligations to eliminate its chemical weapons program, as shown hereinafter.

(a) **Mandates of International Organizations**

Two organizations have been tasked with implementing these mechanisms, with different mandates for their respective secretariats and policy-making organs.

(i) **Secretariats**

OPCW Technical Secretariat

The OPCW Technical Secretariat was required to fulfill both general verification mandates, including receiving declarations and conducting inspections in accordance with the CWC, as well as the special verification mandates developed by the Resolution 2118 Regime,[84] which are more stringent than those under the CWC in the next three areas.[85]

---

[83] UN Doc. S/RES/687 (1991), 3 April 1991, operative paras. 7–14; UN Doc. S/RES/1284 (1999), 17 December 1999, operative paras. 1–12.

[84] See OPCW Doc. EC-M-33/NAT.20 (Russia), 3 October 2013, p. 1; OPCW Doc. EC-M-33/NAT.18 (Switzerland), 3 October 2013, p. 1. The CWC provides for the Technical Secretariat conducting other verification tasks not covered by the Convention when the OPCW policy-making organs, i.e., the Executive Council and the Conference of the States Parties, decide (Article VIII, para. 37).

[85] Such verification measures are fully consistent with CWC provisions, even though they may be more stringent. Article IV, para. 8 and Article V, para. 10 mandate that the OPCW Executive Council

First, the OPCW Technical Secretariat shall make any information or declaration referred to therein available to all States Parties "within five days of its receipt,"[86] which is extremely expeditious compared with the Confidentiality Annex, para. 2(b) which allows States Parties' data to be "routinely" provided to other States Parties for the assurance of the compliance of said State Parties with the CWC.

Second, the OPCW Technical Secretariat shall conduct special initial inspections "as soon as possible and in any case not later than 1 October 2013," as well as inspections of all facilities to be declared by Syria "not later than 30 days after the adoption of this decision."[87] The CWC is ambiguous with regard to the timeline of initial inspections for chemical weapons and chemical weapons production facilities such as "immediately" and "promptly" (Article IV, para. 4; Article V, para. 6; Verification Annex Part III, para. 1; Verification Annex Part IV(A), para. 38). While such wording may enable inspected States Parties and the OPCW Technical Secretariat to make practical arrangements for smooth conduct of initial inspections, OPCW Executive Council Decision EC-M-33/DEC.1 did specify the special initial inspection timeframe, reflecting an aspect of the US-Russia joint national paper and also showing the OPCW Executive Council's determination to complete the elimination of the Syrian chemical weapons program expeditiously.

Third, the OPCW Technical Secretariat shall submit a monthly report on the implementation of this decision to the Executive Council, which will include Syria's progress in fulfilling the requirements of this decision and the CWC, the activities of the Technical Secretariat, and the needs for technical, personnel and other supplementary resources.[88] OPCW Executive Council Decision EC-M-34/DEC.1 expanded the required reporting to encompass the implementation of the decision itself.[89] The OPCW Director-General was also requested to make monthly reports to the UN Security Council via the UN Secretary-General.[90] Such regular reports are an indispensable tool for the OPCW Executive Council and the UN Security Council to monitor the elimination of the Syrian chemical weapons program and respond to any issues arising therefrom.

In addition, the OPCW Director-General was expected to coordinate support provided by State Parties to enable the OPCW to implement the elimination of the Syrian chemical weapons program.[91]

---

establish stringent verification procedures for States that become parties to the Convention after the ten-year period for destruction (OPCW Doc. EC-M-33/DEC.1, 27 September 2013, preamble para. 16). These provisions apply to Syria, which acceded to the Convention on 14 October 2013, nearly six and a half year after the ten-year period for destruction expired on 29 April 2007.

[86] OPCW Doc. EC-M-33/DEC.1, 27 September 2013, operative para. 2(a).

[87] *Ibid.*, operative para. 2(b) and (c).

[88] *Ibid.*, operative para. 2(f).

[89] OPCW Doc. EC-M-34/DEC.1, 15 November 2013, operative para. 22.

[90] UN Doc. S/RES/2118 (2013), 27 September 2013, operative para. 12.

[91] *Ibid.*, operative para. 10.

Personnel, legal, and financial arrangements were required for the OPCW Technical Secretariat to fulfill these mandates. Accordingly, the Executive Council authorized the Technical Secretariat "to hire, on a short-term basis, qualified inspectors and other technical experts and to rehire, on a short-term basis, inspectors, other technical experts, and such other personnel as may be required whose term of service has recently expired."[92] The context of this authorization is that as of September 2013, the Technical Secretariat lacked sufficient staff to fulfill the above new mandates, and there were ever fewer inspectors with chemical weapons expertise due to other possessor States Parties destroying their stockpiles. The OPCW has a tenure policy, wherein professional staff may work for the Organization for a maximum of seven years, making it legally impossible to rehire any inspectors who had served that long.[93] The OPCW has adhered strictly to this policy[94] since the Conference of the States Parties adopted the relevant decision in April 2003.[95] Thirteen experts were hired or rehired on a short-term basis under the authority thus afforded to the Technical Secretariat.[96]

Another issue was OPCW personnel privileges and immunities.[97] The provisional application of the CWC to Syria might have addressed this issue, because its Verification Annex Part II (B) stipulates the privileges and immunities of the OPCW inspectors, including but not necessarily limited to inviolability of inspectors' persons, living quarters, official premises, papers, correspondence, samples and approved equipment, immunity from criminal jurisdiction, and exemptions from dues and taxes. The UN Security Council resolved this issue in a straightforward way, however, deciding that "OPCW-designated personnel undertaking activities provided for in this resolution or the decision of the OPCW Executive Council of 27 September 2013 shall enjoy the privileges and immunities contained in the Verification Annex, Part II (B) of the Chemical Weapons Convention."[98] As with other relevant decisions, Syria was thus legally bound in accordance with Article 25 of the UN Charter. The phrase "OPCW-designated personnel" implied that the OPCW would dispatch personnel to Syria in addition to inspectors, and that this measure encompassed their privileges and immunities as well.

---

[92] OPCW Doc. EC-M-33/DEC.1, 27 September 2013, operative para. 2(e).

[93] Regulation 4.4, OPCW Staff Regulations (OPCW Doc. C-IV/DEC.25, 2 July 1999).

[94] OPCW Doc. C-11/2 EC-47/3, 8 November 2006, para. 2.67; OPCW Doc. C-12/3 EC-50/3, 26 September 2007, para. 2.64; OPCW Doc. C-13/2 EC-54/4, 15 October 2008, para. 2.72; OPCW Doc. C-16/2 EC-66/3, 5 October 2011, para. 2.70; OPCW Doc. C-17/2 EC-70/4, 28 September 2012, paras. 2.71–2.73; OPCW Doc. C-18/2 EC-74/4, 9 October 2013, para. 2.79.

[95] OPCW Doc. C-SS-2/DEC.1, 30 April 2003.

[96] OPCW Doc. EC-76/DG.16, 4 July 2014, para. 32.

[97] Syria is a party to the Convention on the Privileges and Immunities of the United Nations (See UN Doc. S/RES/2118 (2013), 27 September 2013, operative para. 9). Hence privileges and immunities of UN personnel were not at issue.

[98] *Ibid.*, operative para. 9.

The OPCW Technical Secretariat also desperately needed additional funds to fulfill its new mandates. The Executive Council opted to consider funding mechanisms on an emergency basis, calling upon all States Parties to provide voluntary contributions if they could,[99] creating the OPCW trust fund for the destruction of Syrian chemical weapons to "provide funding to facilitate the technical activities of the OPCW in support of the verification of the destruction of Syrian chemical weapons"[100] and the Syria Trust Fund for the Destruction of Chemical Weapons to support the Technical Secretariat's work in relation to the destruction of Syrian chemical weapons outside Syrian territory.[101] States Parties accordingly made contributions to both funds.[102]

UN Secretariat

For its part, the UN Secretariat was assigned few mandates for the aforementioned verification of the implementation of Syria's obligations. An advance team of UN personnel was authorized "to provide early assistance to OPCW activities in Syria,"[103] thus helping the OPCW, which, up to that time, had no experience in carrying out its own functions in Syria, which was still not a CWC State Party. As mentioned above, the UN Secretary-General was required to submit the OPCW Director-General's monthly reports to the UN Security Council, attaching "relevant information on United Nations activities related to the implementation of this resolution."[104] The UN Secretary-General was also expected to coordinate assistance offered by Member States that would enable the UN to implement the elimination of the Syrian chemical weapons program.[105] Although funding mechanisms were not mentioned in Security Council Resolution 2118, the UN launched its own fund to "support efforts to destroy Syrian chemical weapons in accordance with the United Nations Security Council resolution 2118 (2013) and subsequent resolutions,"[106] to which several Member States contributed.[107]

---

[99] OPCW Doc. EC-M-33/DEC.1, 27 September 2013, operative para. 3(a).

[100] OPCW Doc. S/1132/2013, 16 October 2013, p. 8. Expenses associated with the inspection and verification of the destruction of Syrian chemical weapons include personnel and travel costs, purchasing equipment and protective gear, hiring staff, providing technical assistance, inspections to assess Syria's initial declaration, rendering chemical weapons production facilities inoperable, verifying destruction of Syrian chemical weapons, and any other OPCW activity in line with the obligations of the CWC and Executive Council decision EC-M-33/DEC.1.

[101] OPCW Doc. S/1141/2013, 19 November 2013.

[102] Andorra, Canada, Denmark, the European Union, Estonia, Finland, Germany, Ireland, Latvia, Netherlands, Republic of Korea, Switzerland, UK, the US contributed EUR 6,451,052 as of 31 July 2014 (OPCW-UN Joint Mission in Syria, Status of contributions to the OPCW-UN Joint Mission in Syria, as of July 2014, https://opcw.unmissions.org/sites/default/files/donor_factsheet_310714_final.pdf, accessed 22 April 2023).

[103] UN Doc. S/RES/2118 (2013), 27 September 2013, operative para. 8.

[104] *Ibid.*, operative para. 12.

[105] *Ibid.*, operative para. 10.

[106] See OPCW Doc. S/1132/2013, 16 October 2013, p. 8.

[107] Denmark, Japan, Luxembourg, the Netherlands, Russia, and the US contributed USD 8,014,509 as of 31 July 2014 (OPCW-UN Joint Mission in Syria, Status of contributions to the OPCW-UN

Relation Between Secretariats: OPCW-UN Joint Mission

While the OPCW Technical Secretariat and the UN Secretariat were assigned different mandates, cooperation was essential. The UN Security Council requested that the OPCW Director-General and the UN Secretary-General cooperate closely in implementing Decision EC-M-33/DEC.1 and Resolution 2118 including through their on the ground operations,[108] and further requested that the UN Secretary-General, in consultation with the OPCW Director-General, submit recommendations on the UN's role in the elimination of the Syrian chemical weapons program.[109]

On 8 October 2013, a proposal of "a Joint Mission of the OPCW and the United Nations" was presented.[110] While Resolution 2118 limited the scope of the original request to recommendations the UN's role,[111] the respective organizational chef officers explored a more collaborative approach,[112] establishing the OPCW-UN Joint Mission in Syria on 16 October 2013[113] with UN Security Council authorization,[114] and the OPCW and the UN concluded a supplementary arrangement to provide the legal framework for same.[115]

Joint Mission in Syria, as of July 2014, https://opcw.unmissions.org/sites/default/files/donor_factsheet_310714_final.pdf, accessed 22 April 2023).

[108] UN Doc. S/RES/2118 (2013), 27 September 2013, operative para. 8.

[109] UN Doc. S/RES/2118 (2013), 27 September 2013, operative para. 8.

[110] UN Doc. S/2013/591*, 8 October 2013.

[111] Karim Makdisi and Coralie Pison Hindawi, "Exploring the UN and OPCW Partnership in Syrian Chemical Weapons Disarmament: Interorganizational Cooperation and Autonomy," *Global Governance*, Vol. 25, Issue 4 (2019), p. 535, p. 546.

[112] For organizational preparatory work toward the Joint Mission, see *ibid.*, pp. 546–549.

[113] Joint Statement from the Organisation for the Prohibition of Chemical Weapons (OPCW) and the United Nations (UN), 16 October 2013, https://www.opcw.org/media-centre/news/2013/10/joint-statement-organisation-prohibition-chemical-weapons-opcw-and-united; https://www.un.org/sg/en/content/sg/note-correspondents/2013-10-16/joint-statement-organisation-prohibition-chemical-weapons, accessed 22 April 2023; OPCW Doc. EC-M-34/DG.1, 25 October 2013, para. 17; UN Doc. S/2013/629, 28 October 2013, p. 1. The UN Secretary-General appointed Sigrid Kaag Special Coordinator.

[114] UN Doc. S/2013/603, 11 October 2013.

[115] Supplementary Arrangement concerning Cooperation between the United Nations and the Organisation for the Prohibition of Chemical Weapons for the Implementation of the OPCW Executive Council decision EC-M-33/DEC.1 and United Nations Security Council resolution 2118 (2013) relating to the Elimination of Syrian Chemical Weapons, *United Nations Treaty Series*, Vol. 2966, B-1240, p. 312. This instrument was signed and entered into force on 16 October 2013. See also Agreement between the Organisation for the Prohibition of Chemical Weapons (OPCW), the United Nations and the Government of the Syrian Arab Republic concerning the status of the Joint OPCW-United Nations Mission for the Elimination of Syrian Chemical Weapons, Damascus, 5 February 2014, *United Nations Treaty Series*, I-51957. While the CWC stipulates that the OPCW Executive Council shall "[c]onclude agreements or arrangements with States and international organizations on behalf of the Organization, subject to prior approval by the Conference" and "[a]pprove agreements or arrangements relating to the implementation of verification activities, negotiated by the Technical Secretariat with States Parties" (Article VIII, para. 34(a) and (c)), the Supplementary Arrangement was concluded without Executive Council involvement. Lists of "International Agreements and Instruments registered by the Technical Secretariat" in OPCW annual reports reveal that

There would be a substantial division of roles between the Secretariats within the OPCW-UN Joint Mission, with the OPCW Technical Secretariat concentrating on technical aspects, especially verification, including inspections of chemical weapons, chemical weapons production facilities, and related sites, and the UN Secretariat managing the strategic and operational aspects, including coordination and liaison with relevant parties in Syria, logistical and administrative arrangements, and engaging with regional and international actors and stakeholders.[116] It was estimated that the Joint Mission would expand from the thirty-five member joint advance team to approximately 100 personnel drawn from the respective organizations, subject to operational requirements, and would be led by a civilian Special Coordinator.[117]

The OPCW-UN Joint Mission would begin to fulfill its mandate by establishing an initial presence in Damascus and developing preliminary infrastructure. Then it would conduct initial inspections at declared sites, prepare plans for forthcoming verification, expand its medical and other facilities, enhance its security posture, and commence specialized training. With this infrastructure in place, it would support, monitor, and verify the destruction of the Syrian chemical weapons program between 1 November 2013 and 30 June 2014.[118]

(ii) **Policy-Making Organs**

The primary task of policy-making organs is to monitor the status of implementation. Unlike the Secretariats, the Resolution 2118 Regime did not envisage joint OPCW Executive Council and UN Security Council action to ensure Syria's compliance with the obligation to eliminate its chemical weapons program. The UN Security Council would review the implementation of Resolution 2118,[119] which annexes Executive

the OPCW has concluded international agreements or instruments without policy-making organ approval (OPCW Doc. C-III/3, 20 November 1998, Annex 14; OPCW Doc. C-V/5, 17 May 2000, Annex 12; (OPCW Doc. C-12/6, 6 November 2007, Annex 12; OPCW Doc. C-13/4, 3 December 2008, Annex 12) OPCW Doc. C-14/4, 2 December 2009, Annex 13. See also bilateral instruments regarding sample preparation or evaluation of results for official OPCW Proficiency Tests between OPCW and designated laboratories (OPCW Doc. C-13/4, 3 December 2008, Annex 12; OPCW Doc. C-14/4, 2 December 2009, Annex 13).

116 UN Doc. S/2013/591*, 8 October 2013, pp. 3–4. It has been suggested that this asymmetry in size and resources between the OPCW and the UN was key to their successful cooperation (Makdisi and Hindawi, *supra* note 111, p. 557).

117 The UN Secretary-General proposed resource requirements of USD11,822,900 and 123 posts (UN Doc. A/68/327/Add.8, 6 December 2013). The Advisory Committee on Administrative and Budgetary Questions assessed the proposal and recommended General Assembly approval with minor modifications (UN Doc. A/68/7/Add.18, 13 December 2013).

118 UN Doc. S/2013/591*, 8 October 2013, pp. 5–6.

119 UN Doc. S/RES/2118 (2013), 27 September 2013, operative para. 12.

Council Decision EC-M-33/DEC.1, with the Executive Council overseeing the decision's implementation.[120] Regular reports by the Secretariats would provide the basis for said monitoring by both policy-making organs.[121]

(b) Syrian Obligations

(i) Reporting

OPCW Executive Council Decision EC-M-34/DEC.1 obliges Syria to "provide a monthly report to the [Executive] Council regarding activities on its territory related to the destruction of chemical weapons and chemical weapons production facilities."[122] By contrast, UN Security Council Resolution 2118 was silent about reporting requirements for Syria, suggesting that the Executive Council was assigned the primary task of monitoring the Syrian operations regarding eliminating its chemical weapons. As indicated, regular reports by Syria also provide a key basis for monitoring progress in implementation.

(ii) Cooperation

The CWC stipulates the default obligation of the States Parties to cooperate with the OPCW (Article VII, para. 7), which is manifest in the exercise of all OPCW functions, including the mandate establishing the policy-making organs. Its broad language suffices to encompass any emerging needs for cooperation as OPCW practice evolves over time.[123] The Resolution 2118 Regime reinforced Syria's obligation to cooperate with the OPCW under the CWC. It decided that Syria shall comply with all aspects of OPCW Executive Council Decision EC-M-33/DEC.1,[124] which include Syria's full cooperation "with all aspects of the implementation of this decision, including by providing the OPCW personnel with the immediate and unfettered right to inspect any and all sites in the Syrian Arab Republic."[125] It also decided that Syria shall cooperate fully with the OPCW and the UN, including by complying with their relevant recommendations, by accepting personnel designated by the OPCW or the UN, by providing for and ensuring the security of activities undertaken by these

---

[120] The CWC established the Conference of the States Parties and the Executive Council, with the latter, being "the executive organ of the Organization" (Article VIII, para. 30), taking the lead in reviewing CWC implementation due to meeting more frequently. Article VIII, para. 28 stipulates that "[t]he Executive Council shall meet for regular sessions. Between regular sessions it shall meet as often as may be required for the fulfilment of its powers and functions." The OPCW Executive Council has held four regular sessions annually between 1999 and 2013 and three sessions annually since 2014, with unscheduled meetings as required.

[121] UN Doc. S/RES/2118 (2013), 27 September 2013, operative para. 8; OPCW Doc. EC-M-33/DEC.1, 27 September 2013, operative para. 2(f). It has been pointed out that operative para. 8 of UN Security Council Resolution 2118 linked the OPCW to the UN to implement the elimination of Syrian chemical weapons (Friedman, *supra* note 17, p. 77).

[122] OPCW Doc. EC-M-34/DEC.1, 15 November 2013, operative para. 19.

[123] Walter Krutzsch, Eric Myjer and Ralf Trapp (eds.), *The Chemical Weapons Convention: A Commentary* (Oxford University Press, 2014), p. 211.

[124] UN Doc. S/RES/2118 (2013), 27 September 2013, operative para. 6.

[125] OPCW Doc. EC-M-33/DEC.1, 27 September 2013, operative para. 1(e).

personnel, by providing these personnel with immediate and unfettered access to and the right to inspect, in discharging their functions, any and all sites, and by allowing immediate and unfettered access to individuals that the OPCW has grounds to believe to be of importance for the purpose of its mandate.[126]

(c) **Implementation**

Syria has taken various actions to comply with the obligation to eliminate its chemical weapons program by the deadline designated by OPCW Executive Council Decision EC-M-33/DEC.1. Between September 2013 and June 2014, the OPCW Executive Council held combining two regular sessions and nine irregular meetings[127] at which it evaluated implementation by reviewing the Director-General's monthly reports.[128] The UN Security Council also held informal monthly closed-door consultations to discuss the UN Secretary-General's reports which annexed the OPCW Director-General's reports, and listen to briefings by the Special Coordinator on the implementation of Security Council Resolution 2118.[129] Notwithstanding, it neither held official meetings nor took action before the 30 June 2014 deadline. Apparently, the Security Council carefully observed the considerations and actions of the OPCW Executive Council, while refraining from taking initiative.

(i) **Declaration of Chemical Weapons Program**

Syria submitted information and declarations by the required dates (Table 4.5). It submitted initial information on 19 September 2013, two days before the expected

[126] UN Doc. S/RES/2118 (2013), 27 September 2013, operative para. 7.

[127] The seventy-fourth regular session on 8–11 October 2013; thirty-fourth irregular meeting on 5 and 15 November 2013; thirty-fifth irregular meeting on 26 November 2013; thirty-sixth irregular meeting on 17 December 2013; thirty-seventh irregular meeting on 8 January 2014; thirty-eighth irregular meeting on 30 January 2014; thirty-ninth irregular meeting on 21 February 2014; seventy-fifth regular session on 4–7 March 2014; fortieth irregular meeting on 28 March, and 11 and 29 April 2014; forty-first irregular meeting on 22 May 2014; and forty-second irregular meeting on 17 June 2014 (see http://www.opcw.org/documents-reports/executive-council/, accessed 22 April 2023). In addition, upon request of the OPCW Executive Council (OPCW Doc. EC-75/2, 7 March 2014, para. 7.12), between March and June 2014, either the OPCW Director-General or the Technical Secretariat briefed State Parties weekly on the implementation of the plan for the removal of Syrian chemical weapons (OPCW Doc. EC-M-40/DG.1/Rev.1, 27 March 2014, para. 6; OPCW Doc. EC-M-40/DG.4, 25 April 2014, para. 6; OPCW Doc. EC-M-42/DG.1, 23 May 2014, para. 7; OPCW Doc. EC-76/DG.14, 26 June 2014, para. 7).

[128] OPCW Doc. EC-M-34/DG.1, 25 October 2013; OPCW Doc. EC-M-35/DG.1, 25 November 2013; OPCW Doc. EC-M-37/DG.1, 23 December 2013; OPCW Doc. EC-M-38/DG.1, 23 January 2014; OPCW Doc. EC-75/DG.6, 25 February 2014; OPCW Doc. EC-M-40/DG.1/Rev.1, 27 March 2014; OPCW Doc. EC-M-40/DG.4, 25 April 2014; OPCW Doc. EC-M-42/DG.1. 23 May 2014; OPCW Doc. EC-76/DG.14, 25 June 2014. The OPCW Director-General continued to submit monthly reports after June 2014, submitting 114 reports to the OPCW Executive Council and the UN Security Council as of 24 March 2023. A list is provided in Appendix A.

[129] There were eight such briefings, on 5 November and 4 December in 2013 and 7 January, 6 February, 5 March, 3 April, 5 May, and 4 June in 2014 (https://opcw.unmissions.org/chronology-events, accessed 22 April 2023).

Table 4.5 Information submitted by Syria

Type	Date
Initial information	Submitted on 19 September 2013, two days in advance of the expected date "within a week" after the publication of the US–Russia joint national paper
Further information	Submitted on 4 October 2013, the deadline "not later than 7 days after the adoption of the decision"
Initial declarations	Submitted on 23 October 2013, four days before the deadline "not later than 30 days after the adoption of the decision"

date of "within a week" of the publication of the US-Russia joint national paper.[130] It also provided further information on 4 October 2013, covering approximately 1000 metric tons of Category 1 chemical weapons, 290 metric tons of Category 2 chemical weapons, and 1230 unfilled chemical munitions, as well as 41 chemical weapons-related facilities at 23 sites, including 18 chemical weapons production facilities, eight mobile filling units, 12 chemical weapons storage facilities, and three chemical weapons-related facilities.[131] The Technical Secretariat made the information available to all States Parties within five days of its receipt.[132] Finally, Syria submitted its initial declarations on 23 October 2013, declaring possession of chemical weapons, chemical weapons manufacturing facilities, abandoned chemical weapons, riot control agents, other chemical weapons-related facilities, and information about civilian chemical plants,[133] as well as providing general plans for the destruction of chemical weapons and chemical weapons production facilities.[134] Syria amended its initial declarations five times as of 30 June 2014, leading to technical discussions between the Technical Secretariat and Syria to addressing outstanding issues.[135]

The Technical Secretariat promptly conducted inspections in accordance with the relevant provisions of the Executive Council decision, deploying a team to Syria on 1 October 2013[136] and carrying out on-site inspections at 21 declared sites by the

[130] OPCW Doc. EC-M-33/DEC.1, 27 September 2013, preamble para. 12. While the CWC might provisionally apply to Syria as of 19 September 2013, it was uncertain whether the OPCW had a mandate to receive information that Syria had submitted voluntarily.

[131] OPCW Doc. EC-M-34/DG.1, 25 October 2013, para. 4(a).

[132] OPCW Doc. EC-76/DG.16, 4 July 2014, para. 4.

[133] OPCW Doc. EC-M-35/DG.1, 25 November 2013, para. 5(a).

[134] *Ibid.*, para. 5(b).

[135] OPCW Doc. EC-76/DG.16, 4 July 2014, para. 5. See also OPCW Doc. EC-M-35/DG.1, 25 November 2013, para. 5(a); OPCW Doc. EC-M-38/DG.1, 23 January 2014, para. 4(d); OPCW Doc. EC-75/DG.6, 25 February 2014, para. 4(c); OPCW Doc. EC-M-40/DG.4, 25 April 2014, para. 4(e).

[136] OPCW Doc. EC-M-34/DG.1, 25 October 2013, para. 5.

target date of 27 October 2013.[137] The remaining two sites were inaccessible due to safety and security problems.[138]

(ii) **Removal of Chemical Weapons**

The provisions of Decision EC-M-34/DEC.1 were implemented upon its adoption. On 15 December 2013, the OPCW Director-General submitted a plan for the destruction of chemical weapons outside Syria to the Executive Council, which adopted a decision thereon at its thirty-sixth meeting on 17 December 2013,[139] calling for Syria to package and transport chemical weapons from its storage facilities to the port of embarkation in Latakia, where they would be transported outside Syria for destruction. The OPCW-UN Joint Mission would verify all activities at the chemical weapons storage facilities related to possible reloading and packing by on-site inspection including possible random sampling, and/or remote monitoring, depending upon the security situation. At Latakia, the OPCW-UN Joint Mission would carry out further verification, including inventories of chemicals, storage and shipping containers, inspection of seals, and analysis of representative samples.[140] In the aforementioned decision, the Executive Council welcomed assistance offered for the removal aspects of the plan,[141] including thirteen field kitchens from Belarus,[142] surveillance cameras and ten ambulances from China,[143] fifty Kamaz trucks and twenty-five Ural armored trucks airlifted by Russia,[144] and some 3000 container drums of various capacities, GPS trackers, and loading, transportation, and decontamination equipment from the US.[145]

(iii) **Destruction of Chemical Weapons**

Destruction in Syria

In November 2013, Syria informed the OPCW Secretariat that it had destroyed all declared Category 3 chemical weapons, before the 31 January 2014 deadline.[146]

[137] OPCW Doc. EC-M-34/DG.1, 25 October 2013, para. 8; OPCW Doc. EC-76/DG.16, 4 July 2014, para. 10. The Technical Secretariat was unable to inspect all declared facilities within 30 days for safety and security reasons (OPCW Doc. EC-M-35/DG.1, 25 November 2013, para.7).

[138] OPCW Doc. EC-76/DG.16, 4 July 2014, para. 10. One of the sites was verified by 22 November 2013 with sealed GPS cameras used by Syrian personnel with the inspection team's guidance (OPCW Doc. EC-M-35/DG.1, 25 November 2013, para. 7). The remaining site and a ricin production facility that had been declared on 14 July 2014 were inspected in November 2017 (OPCW Doc. EC-87/DG.4, 24 November 2017, para. 6(a)).

[139] OPCW Doc. EC-M-37/DG.1, 23 December 2013, para. 9.

[140] *Ibid.*, para. 10.

[141] OPCW Doc. EC-76/DG.16, 4 July 2014, para. 14.

[142] OPCW Doc. EC-M-38/DG.1, 23 January 2014, para. 14(a).

[143] OPCW Doc. EC-M-37/DG.1, 23 December 2013, para. 18.

[144] OPCW Doc. EC-M-38/DG.1, 23 January 2014, para. 14(a).

[145] OPCW Doc. EC-M-37/DG.1, 23 December 2013, para. 18.

[146] OPCW Doc. EC-M-35/DG.1, 25 November 2013, para. 5(b).

On 16 December 2013, Syria submitted to the Secretariat a plan for the destruction of isopropanol and residual mustard agent before the 1 January 2014 deadline,[147] submitting a modified version on 16 January 2014.[148] At its thirty-eighth meeting on 30 January the OPCW Executive Council adopted a decision on verifying isopropanol destruction.[149] By 22 February 2014, the OPCW-UN Joint Mission verified the destruction of 93% of the declared amount of isopropanol and 87% of containers that had held mustard agent.[150] The remaining quantity of isopropanol and the remaining containers were located in areas inaccessible at that time for security reasons.[151]

Destruction Outside Syria

The Executive Council approved an agreed detailed plan and a facility agreement for verification of the destruction of chemical weapons at the chemical weapons destruction facility aboard the M/V Cape Ray at its thirty-seventh meeting on 8 January 2014.[152] It also approved a model agreement governing on-site inspections at commercial facilities at its thirty-eighth meeting on 30 January 2014,[153] followed by further approval of facility agreements with Finland, the UK, Germany, and the US.[154] Notwithstanding, delayed removal of chemical weapons from Syria forestalled destruction thereof outside Syria by the 30 June 2014 deadline.

(iv) Destruction of Chemical Weapons Production Facilities

Destruction of Chemical Weapons Production and Mixing/Filling Equipment

Syria destroyed the chemical weapons production and mixing/filling equipment by 22 October 2013 ahead of the target date of 1 November 2013.[155] At the thirty-fourth meeting of the OPCW Executive Council, the Director-General affirmed that Syria completed "functional destruction of critical specialised equipment at all of the declared chemical weapons production facilities and filling and mixing plants both stationary and mobile in Syria" by the aforementioned target date.[156]

---

[147] OPCW Doc. EC-M-37/DG.1, 23 December 2013, para. 5(b).

[148] OPCW Doc. EC-M-38/DG.1, 23 January 2014, para. 4(c).

[149] OPCW Doc. EC-75/DG.6, 25 February 2014, para. 4(d).

[150] *Ibid.*, para. 9.

[151] *Ibid.*, para. 9.

[152] OPCW Doc. EC-76/DG.16, 4 July 2014, para. 22.

[153] OPCW Doc. EC-M-40/DG.1/Rev.1, 27 March 2014, para. 10.

[154] OPCW Doc. EC-75/2, 7 March 2014, paras. 7.25 and 7.26; OPCW Doc. EC-75/DG.6, 25 February 2014, para. 13; OPCW Doc. EC-M-40/DEC.1, 29 April 2014; OPCW Doc. EC-M-42/3, 30 June 2014, para. 5; OPCW Doc. EC-76/DG.14, 25 June 2014, para. 14.

[155] OPCW Doc. EC-M-34/DG.1, 25 October 2013, para. 4(d); OPCW Doc. EC-M-35/DG.1, 25 November 2013, para. 5(c).

[156] Director-General's Statement at the 34th Meeting of the Executive Council, 5 November 2013, https://www.opcw.org/sites/default/files/documents/ODG/uzumcu/DG_Statement_-_EC-M-34.pdf, accessed 22 April 2023. Trapp has pointed out that Syria relied on a binary system, using

Destruction of 26 Chemical Weapons Production Facilities

The first step in destroying Syria's chemical weapons production facilities was the Executive Council's endorsement of the combined verification and destruction plans, which it agreed to at its thirty-sixth meeting on 17 December 2013. These plans addressed fourteen of Syria's declared chemical weapons production facilities, comprising six buildings—Tudmur, Al-Dhamir 1, Al-Dhamir 3, Al-Nasiriyah 2, Tel Kurdi, and 500 (Aleppo)—and eight mobile units.[157] By 22 February 2013, the mobile units had been destroyed and verified, while all declared specialised buildings and equipment had been destroyed and verified at one facility, all declared specialised/standard buildings and equipment had been destroyed with verification pending at four facilities, and one facility remained to be destroyed and verified due to security concerns.[158] By contrast, the Executive Council was still assessing the destruction and verification plans on the remaining twelve chemical weapons production facilities, comprising five underground structures and seven reinforced aircraft hangars known as Shayrat, Tha'lah, Al-Sin, Al-Nasiriyah 3, Baly, Khalkhalah, Dhabaa, Hafir 1, Hafir 2, Al-Sayed, Al-Dhamir 2, and Al-Nasiriyah 1,[159] resulting in none of these being destroyed.[160] The problem was that Syria had proposed to decommission these facilities by, for instance, welding doors shut and constructing interior obstacles,[161] which attracted criticism from States Parties who insisted on physical destruction of all such facilities in accordance with relevant CWC provisions by the 15 March 2014 deadline.[162]

chemical weapons production and mixing/filling equipment to form sarin by mixing two precursors (methylphosphonyl difluoride (DF) and isopropanol) with an acid scavenger (hexamethylene tetramine) shortly before deployment, and that once the chemical weapons production and mixing/filling equipment had been rendered inoperable, Syria had no effective sarin delivery system (Ralf Trapp, "The Use of Chemical Weapons in Syria: implications and Consequences," in Bretislav Friedrich, Dieter Hoffmann, Jürgen Renn, Florian Schmaltz and Martin Wolf (eds.), *One Hundred Years of Chemical Warfare: Research, Deployment, Consequences* (Springer Open, 2017), p. 363, p. 368).

[157] OPCW Doc. EC-M-36/3, 8 January 2014, para. 4; OPCW Doc. EC-M-37/DG.1, 23 December 2013, para. 15.

[158] OPCW Doc. EC-75/DG.6, 25 February 2014, para. 4(c).

[159] OPCW Doc. EC-M-37/DG.1, 23 December 2013, para. 15.

[160] OPCW Doc. EC-75/DG.6, 25 February 2014, para. 4(c).

[161] See OPCW Doc. EC-M-38/NAT.4 (US), 30 January 2014, p. 1.

[162] OPCW Doc. EC-M-38/NAT.2 (France), 30 January 2014, p. 1; OPCW Doc. EC-M-38/NAT.3 (Spain), 30 January 2014, p. 1; OPCW Doc. EC-M-38/NAT.4 (US), 30 January 2014, pp. 2–3; OPCW Doc. EC-M-38/NAT.5 (UK), 30 January 2014, p. 2 OPCW Doc. EC-75/NAT.12 (Netherlands), 4 March 2014, p. 2. See also OPCW Doc. EC-M-39/NAT.4 (Switzerland), 21 February 2014, p. 1; OPCW Doc. EC-M-39/NAT.10 (Japan), 21 February 2014, pp. 1–2; OPCW Doc. EC-M-39/NAT.16 (Germany), 21 February 2014, p. 1; OPCW Doc. EC-75/NAT.9 (Turkey), 4 March 2014, p. 1; OPCW Doc. EC-75/NAT.17 (Japan), 4 March 2014, p. 1; OPCW Doc. EC-75/NAT.23 (Greece on behalf of the EU), 4 March 2014, p. 1; OPCW Doc. EC-75/NAT.27 (Spain), 4 March 2014, p. 1.

Request for Conversion

Syria requested conversion of its twelve chemical weapons production facilities for purposes not prohibited by the CWC, asserting that their destruction would be an added burden on Syria economy and have a harmful impact on natural resources and local infrastructure, while conversion would avoid economic losses resulting from constructing facilities for purposes not prohibited by the CWC and create job opportunities.[163] At its thirty-fourth meeting on 15 November 2013, the Executive Council took no immediate action, leaving the matter pending.[164] At its thirty-fifth meeting on 29 November 2013, however, it decided that the requests were no longer pending, which was understood as rejection of same.[165]

(v) **Reporting and Cooperation**

Syria submitted seven monthly reports to the Executive Council by June 2014.[166] The Director-General's monthly reports indicated that the Syrian authorities continued to extend the necessary cooperation to the OPCW-UN Joint Mission in the conduct of its activities.[167]

(3) **Evaluation**

The Resolution 2118 Regime instigated mechanisms for ensuring compliance with Syria's obligation to eliminate its chemical weapons program. It functioned as intended because it was able to monitor progress in relevant tasks.

(a) **Possible References**

Mechanisms to ensure compliance with Syria's obligation to eliminate its chemical weapons program might benefit from OPCW experience in verifying destruction of chemical weapons and chemical weapons production facilities. Since the

---

[163] OPCW Doc. EC-M-34/NAT.1 (Syria), 15 November 2013.

[164] OPCW Doc. EC-M-34/DEC.1, 15 November 2013, operative para. 26.

[165] OPCW Doc. EC-M-38/NAT.3 (Spain), 30 January 2014, p. 1; OPCW Doc. EC-M-38/NAT.4 (US), 30 January 2014, p. 2; OPCW Doc. EC-M-38/NAT.5 (UK), 30 January 2014), p. 2; OPCW Doc. EC-75/NAT.5 (UK), 4 March 2014, p. 2. This was the first instance of a request for conversion being rejected, which the OPCW policy-making organs had granted for twenty-three chemical weapons production facilities in the UK, Russia, a State Party, Libya, and Iraq, in accordance with relevant CWC provisions.

[166] See OPCW Doc. EC-M-37/DG.1, 23 December 2013, para. 5(c); OPCW Doc. EC-M-38/DG.1, 23 January 2014, para. 4(d); OPCW Doc. EC-75/DG.6, 25 February 2014, para. 4(e); OPCW Doc. EC-M-40/DG.1/Rev.1, 27 March 2014, para. 4(d); OPCW Doc. EC-M-40/DG.4, 25 April 2014, para. 4(d); OPCW Doc. EC-M-42/DG.1, 23 May 2014, para. 4(c); OPCW Doc. EC-76/DG.14, 26 June 2014, para. 4(c). Note that these documents are classified. Syria continued to submit monthly reports to the OPCW Executive Council after June 2014, totaling 112 as of March 2023.

[167] OPCW Doc. EC-M-34/DG.1, 25 October 2013, para. 4(e); OPCW Doc. EC-M-35/DG.1, 25 November 2013, para. 5(d); OPCW Doc. EC-M-37/DG.1, 23 December 2013, para. 5(d); OPCW Doc. EC-M-38/DG.1, 23 January 2014, para. 4(e); OPCW Doc. EC-75/DG.6, 25 February 2014, para. 5; OPCW Doc. EC-M-40/DG.1/Rev.1, 27 March 2014, para. 4(f); OPCW Doc. EC-M-40/DG.4, 25 April 2014, para. 4(f); OPCW Doc. EC-M-42/DG.1. 23 May 2014, para. 4(d); OPCW Doc. EC-76/DG.14, 25 June 2014, para. 4(d).

CWC's entry into force, Albania, India, Iraq, Libya, Russia, the US, and a State Party have declared their chemical weapons, while Bosnia and Herzegovina, China, France, India, Iran, Iraq, Japan, Libya, Russia, the UK, the US, Federal Republic of Yugoslavia, and a State Party have declared their chemical weapons production facilities. The OPCW commenced verification in all these instances on receipt of declarations. The Executive Council made decisions including approving "agreed detailed plans for verification" (Verification Annex Part IV(A), para. 56), "combined plan for destruction and verification" (Verification Annex Part V, para. 38) and facility agreements (Verification Annex part III, para. 3; Article VIII, para. 34(c)), and monitored said destruction pursuant to "detailed annual plans for destruction" (Verification Annex part IV(A), para. 29; Verification Annex part V, para. 8) and "annual reports on destruction" (Verification Annex part IV(A), para. 36; Verification Annex part V, para. 9) provided by the possessor States Parties, together with information gathered by Technical Secretariat inspections. The OPCW was accordingly able to verify the destruction of chemical weapons by the aforementioned a State Party and India by their extended deadlines, the destruction of chemical weapons production facilities by Bosnia and Herzegovina, China, France, Iran, Japan, the UK, the US, and Federal Republic of Yugoslavia by their original deadlines, and the conversion of chemical weapons production facilities by a State Party and the UK by their original deadlines.

(b) **Effectiveness**

As stated above, the mechanisms for ensuring Syrian compliance with its obligation to eliminate its chemical weapons program under the Resolution 2118 Regime functioned as intended overall. The OPCW Technical Secretariat and/or the OPCW-UN Joint Mission verified Syria's initial required steps under the Resolution 2118 Regime despite the ongoing Syrian armed conflict, for the following reasons. First, the Resolution 2118 Regime succeeded in its *ex ante* planning, addressing the overall scheme, required components, and potential and real obstacles, prior to commencing on-site work. The OPCW Executive Council endorsed the necessary arrangements, including the aforementioned approval of the agreed detailed plan for the destruction of chemical weapons, the combined verification and destruction plans for chemical weapons production facilities, and the relevant facility agreements. The UN Security Council resolved legal obstacles including acceptance of OPCW personnel, provision of access, and privileges and immunities of OPCW personnel per relevant text of Resolution 2118. Rather than devising comprehensive mechanisms for ensuring compliance, OPCW Executive Council Decision EC-M-33/DEC.1 and UN Security Council Resolution 2118 established the goal of eliminating the Syrian chemical weapons program by the first half of 2014, and initial obligations and arrangements to that end. The Executive Council addressed the remaining aspects within two months. The innovative idea of the OPCW-UN Joint Mission was instrumental in allocating and implementing both organizations' mandates and facilitating smooth verification the OPCW, which had no official relations with Syria. In short, the Resolution 2118 Regime took incremental approach, with a view to striking a balance between the urgent need to legitimize its purpose, eliminating the Syrian chemical weapons program, and the feasibility of means and method to achieve that objective. *Ex ante* planning accounted for perhaps 90% of the compliance control's success.

Second, Syria was committed to eliminating its chemical weapons program, though the plan derived from the US, not Syria itself, and even the initial US proposal was not entirely serious. Russia, however, seized the opportunity to approach Syria, which almost immediately accepted the plan, going so far as to accede to the CWC and request its provisional application, as previously described. Syria was outside the formal decision-making process of the Resolution 2118 Regime. The key document of the US–Russia joint national paper was unique in that the signatories themselves established the framework for the project to eliminate chemical weapons of other State. The Syrian government was not a party to this instrument. Executive Council Decision EC-M-33/DEC.1 was also a rare action, in that it required a non-State Party in a formal sense to take action, made obligatory by UN Security Council Resolution 2118. Notwithstanding their unusual status, Syria accepted these instruments, as it was clear that the only alternative for Syria (and Russia) was possible US military action. Syria expressed its commitment to the Resolution 2118 Regime by deed, fulfilling obligations including providing further information, submitting its initial declaration, destroying Category 3 chemical weapons, submitting a plan for destroying isopropanol and residual mustard agent, destroying its chemical weapons production and mixing/filling equipment, and destroying some chemical weapons production facilities. It also met the requirement to submit monthly implementation reports to the Executive Council. The Director-General's monthly reports confirmed Syria's cooperation with the OPCW-UN Joint Mission. As long as Syria continues to comply with its obligations, the mechanism for ensuring compliance will accordingly shows that it indeed remains in compliance.

Third, all stakeholders shared the same goal and cooperated with each other, the OPCW, and the UN. It was clear from the outset that Syria was not able to destroy its chemical weapons and chemical weapons production facilities on its own due to security concerns in the ongoing non-international armed conflict and a lack of necessary technical, financial, logistical, and personnel resources. Syria thus requested assistance. No matter what positions States Parties took on the Assad regime, their assistance was indispensable to achieving the ultimate goal of eliminating the Syrian chemical weapons program. To this end, the idea of destroying Syrian chemical weapons outside Syria as such was a good indication of readiness of and necessity for said assistance. As mentioned above, in response to the OPCW Executive Council and UN Security Council's requests, many States Parties made voluntary contributions to the newly established OPCW and UN trust funds amounting to more than EUR fifty million by the end of June 2014, and offered a variety of items, exemplifying a model of concerted international effort and cooperation. In this sense, the Resolution 2118 Regime also functioned to arrange and coordinate assistance by States Parties and the private sector alike.

Despite such effectiveness, however, compliance was by no means complete. The mechanism confronted potential and real non-compliance through verification, transforming to address said non-compliance concerns as discussed hereinafter.

(c) Implications

Perhaps the most significant implication is that the mechanism for ensuring compliance proved that cooperative, rather than coercive, disarmament was possible even in ongoing armed conflict. While it took time to destroy all declared chemical weapons and chemical weapons production facilities under international verification, the mission was completed without any serious problem. This was a rare example of international cooperation and collaboration overcoming differences among concerned States, suggesting that such cooperative disarmament is feasible if (i) the most important interested States, i.e., the US and Russia, permanent UN Security Council members, agree on the goals and frameworks,[168] (ii) the State concerned, Syria in this instance, accepts the obligations, and (iii) the relevant States, organizations, and other stakeholders cooperate in sharing the burden.

Another key to success in this instance was the extraordinary arrangements that were devised. Due to the ongoing Syrian non-international armed conflict the idea of removing chemical weapons from the possessor State and destroying them abroad was explored pragmatically from the outset. The international community feared further use of chemical weapons in the fighting, and the risk of proliferation of same to terrorist groups was also relatively high. The UN Security Council relaxed the prohibition on transfer of chemical weapons under the CWC, avoiding potential legal obstacles. While the operation faced many challenges, including safe domestic and international transportation, determination of sites for destruction, legal and practical arrangements, and collection of funds, most were addressed through cooperation by all concerned. The international community would act similarly three years later, in response to the emerging risk of Libyan chemical weapons proliferation, despite the OPCW ruling that the Syrian arrangement for transferring chemical weapons from the possessor State Party to another State arty for destruction "does not create any precedent for the future."[169]

Libya acceded to the CWC on 5 February 2004 and submitted its initial declarations in accordance with Article III on 5 March 2004,[170] revealing that it possessed 24.7 metric tons of mustard gas (category 1 chemical weapons), 1,390 metric tons of precursor chemicals (category 2 chemical weapons) and 3,563 aerial bombs containing chemical weapons (category 3 chemical weapons).[171] By the end of 2015,

---

[168] In the author's opinion, there was little leeway in agreeing on eliminating Syrian chemical weapons. As stressed previously, the decisive factor was the agreement between the US and Russia, which should be recognized as responding to the chemical attack of 21 August 2013. In light of the divergent views between the US and Russia on who was responsible, it is likely that the agreement was possible only because, while the UN Mission confirmed the attack, it lacked a mandate to identify perpetrators, leaving the attribution issue unresolved.

[169] OPCW Doc. EC-M-34/DEC.1, 15 November 2013, operative para. 27.

[170] OPCW News, Libya Submits Initial Chemical Weapons Declaration, 5 March 2004, https://www.opcw.org/media-centre/news/2004/03/libya-submits-initial-chemical-weapons-declaration, accessed 22 April 2023.

[171] GlobalSecurity.org, Libyan Chemical Weapons, https://www.globalsecurity.org/wmd/world/libya/cw.htm, accessed 22 April 2023.

all category 1 and 3 chemicals weapons had been destroyed, including those discovered and declared in 2011, while 720 metric tons of category 2 chemical weapons remained to be destroyed.[172] Beginning in early 2016, however, Libya faced an emerging risk of losing its chemical weapons to terrorist organizations in an unstable domestic situation where order and security were rapidly deteriorating. Accordingly, on 12 February 2016, Libya requested that OPCW Director-General consider the option of transporting its remaining category 2 chemical weapons to a waste disposal facility outside Libya.[173] The Executive Council responded cautiously, beginning with a request at its fifty-first meeting on 24 February 2016 that the Director-General continue consulting with Libya to determine the most appropriate solution. At this juncture, options for both in-country and out-of-country destruction were on the table.[174]

At its fifty-second meeting on 20 July 2016, in response to a renewed request by Libya for support in ensuring the destruction of its remaining chemical weapons on an expedited basis at a waste treatment facility outside Libya, the Executive Council requested that the Director-General assist Libya in developing a modified plan of destruction for consideration, "along with recommendations from the Director-General for additional measures needed to ensure the expeditious transport, storage, and destruction of Libya's Category 2 chemical weapons."[175] On 22 July 2016, the UN Security Council unanimously adopted Resolution 2298, determining that "the potential for acquisition by non-State actors of chemical weapons in Libya represents a threat to international peace and security,"[176] and, acting under Chapter VII of the UN Charter, "*[d]ecides* to authorize Member States to acquire, control, transport, transfer and destroy chemical weapons identified by the Director-General of the OPCW...to ensure the elimination of Libya's chemical weapons stockpile in the soonest and safest manner."[177] As with Syria, Security Council authorization avoided the legal obstacle under the CWC to removing chemical weapons for destruction outside the territory of a possessor State Party.

When its fifty-second meeting reconvened on 27 July 2016, the OPCW Executive Council elaborated on such requirements as the deadline of 8 September 2016 for the removal of remaining category 2 chemical weapons from Libya and that of 15 months after arrival in the host State Party for destroying same,[178] the status of Libya and of States Parties providing assistance in terms of its chemical weapons,[179] and the establishment of a special trust fund to defray expenses.[180] It also requested that either the Director-General or the Technical Secretariat submit documents including

[172] OPCW Doc. S/1423/2016, 26 September 2016, para. 3.11.

[173] OPCW Doc. EC-M-51/DEC.1, 24 February 2016, operative para. 1.

[174] *Ibid.*, operative para. 2.

[175] OPCW Doc. EC-M-52/DEC.1, 20 July 2016, operative para. 2.

[176] UN Doc. S/RES/2298 (2016), 22 July 2016, preamble para. 8.

[177] *Ibid.*, operative para. 3.

[178] OPCW Doc. EC-M-52/DEC.2, 27 July 2016, operative paras. 2 and 3.

[179] *Ibid.*, operative paras. 5, 6, and 11.

[180] *Ibid.*, operative para. 7.

a plan with options for destroying remaining chemical weapons in chemical disposal facilities, an agreed detailed plan for verification, and a draft facility agreement.[181] The Director-General was also called on to report on the implementation to the Executive Council.[182] These requirements benefited from the experience of, and used an essentially identical formulation to, the removal of the Syrian chemical weapons outside Syria for destruction.

At its reconvened fifty-third meeting on 26 August 2016, the Executive Council adopted a decision noting the destruction plan,[183] in which Libya's remaining chemical weapons would be transported from their storage sites to the port of embarkation, loaded on a Danish ship, transported to Germany, and destroyed at the GEKA facility in Munster.[184] All relevant category 2 chemical weapons were accordingly removed from Libya on 27 August 2016 and transported to Germany for destruction on 9 September 2016,[185] where they were completely destroyed by 23 November 2017.[186]

Removing chemical weapons outside possessor States Parties for destruction may be realistic if the situation demands it, and the international community is united to address the situation, despite it the CWC prohibiting same. As mentioned above, when the Executive Council adopted its decision on the removal of Syrian chemical weapons, it declared that "this decision...does not create any precedent for future."[187] In reality, however, "[t]he destruction of Syrian chemical weapons outside of Syria set a precedent for transporting the precursors out of Libya for destruction."[188] The suitability of this approach obviously varies according to circumstance. While the OPCW Executive Council acknowledged that decisions to remove chemical weapons from Syria and Libya were made "due to the extraordinary character of the situation" posed by their chemical weapons, the situations differed, as mentioned above. The UN Security Council declared that what constituted threats to international peace and security were "the use of chemical weapons" in the Syrian Arab Republic"[189] on the one hand, and "the potential for acquisition by non-State actors of chemical

181 *Ibid.*, operative paras. 9, 13 and 16.

182 *Ibid.*, operative para. 17.

183 OPCW Doc. EC-M-53/DEC.1, 26 August 2016.

184 OPCW Doc. EC-M-53/DG.1, 19 August 2016, paras. 5–10. The OPCW Executive Council decided to remove from Libya all four types of chemicals, 2-chloroethanol, tributylamine, phosphorous trichloride, and thionyl chloride. The US joined the consensus on this decision, although it asserted that extraordinary measures were not necessary for tributylamine due to its lower risk for proliferation, and the associated reduced threat to security (US, https://www.opcw.org/sites/default/files/documents/EC/M-51/en/EC-M_51_USA_Statement.pdf, accessed 22 April 2023).

185 UN Doc. S/2016/943, 8 November 2016, Annex I, Enclosure, paras. 6–7.

186 OPCW Doc. EC-87/DG.6, 22 December 2016, para. 3.

187 OPCW Doc. EC-M-33/DEC.1, 27 September 2013, operative para. 3(d).

188 Kelsey Davenport, "Last CW Materials Removed from Libya," *Arms Control Today* (October 2016), https://www.armscontrol.org/act/2016-09/news/last-cw-materials-removed-libya, accessed 22 April 2023).

189 UN Doc. S/RES/2118 (2013), 27 September 2013, preamble para. 13.

weapons in Libya"[190] on the other, indicating that the international community treats chemical weapons proliferation as being as serious as their actual use. Should similar risks arise in future, similar responses may again be called for.

4.3.2 Addressing Potential Non-compliance

(1) **Background**

Theoretically, there is a clear distinction between compliance and non-compliance. A given State should simply be considered in non-compliance if it does not comply with its obligations. This is much too legalistic, however, failing to take into account that potential non-compliance may occur during dynamic implementation processes.

The first scenario concerns full and complete declaration. All weapons programs that a concerned State retains must be destroyed before said programs may be considered eliminated. All will be well if the State concerned declares all weapons programs it owns, for it will destroy all declared weapons programs, complying fully with its obligation to do so. Should it not make the requisite full and complete declaration, however, then it may conceal some portion of its weapons program while destroying all declared weapons programs, constituting non-compliance. The UN Security Council encountered an issue with Iraq's full implementation of its disarmament obligations under Resolution 687.[191] The problem is that such situations remain unresolved until monitoring organs verify whether concerned States have indeed declared their entire weapons programs, which may put such States in potential non-compliance.

The second scenario pertains to the failure to meet deadlines per the CWC, which is easily and unambiguously identified, unlike the aforementioned declaration issues, and constitutes clear non-compliance in a legalistic sense. The OPCW has heretofore responded pragmatically when confronted with such missing deadlines. One approach is *ex ante* decisions to adopt post-deadline measures, including extensions and expanded reporting scope and frequency. At its sixteenth session in December 2011, the OPCW Conference of the States Parties adopted such a decision regarding the destruction of US, Russian, and Libyan chemical weapons, requiring these possessor States Parties to take specific steps after the 29 April 2012 final extended deadline.[192] The objectivity of deadlines enables international monitoring organs to prepare for impending non-compliance ahead of time. Another approach is *ex post* actions for redress, in response to non-compliance, to be analyzed hereinafter. Such actions emphasize fulfilling substantive obligations to act, including the

[190] UN Doc. S/RES/2298 (2016), 22 July 2016, preamble para. 8. See also statements by the UK, Egypt, Russia, the US, China, and France (UN Doc. S/PV.7743, 22 July 2016, pp. 2–4).

[191] Cf. UN Doc. S/RES/1284 (1999), 17 December 1999; UN Doc. S/RES/1441 (2002), 8 November 2002.

[192] OPCW Doc. C-16/DEC. 11, 1 December 2011.

submission of initial declarations, the conversion of the chemical weapons production facilities, and the completion of destruction of chemical weapons.

(2) Mechanisms to Address Potential Non-compliance

(a) Mandates of International Organizations

Implementing mechanisms for ensuring compliance often suffices to identify potential non-compliance, as such mechanisms operate systematically and continuously. Upon so identifying potential non-compliance, they become mechanisms to address potential non-compliance.

The CWC grants the OPCW policy-making organs general mandates to address "concerns regarding compliance," "doubts or concerns regarding compliance," and "problems with regard to [State Party] compliance" (Article VIII, paras. 35 and 36 and Article XII). It also encompasses specific procedures for consultation, cooperation, and fact-finding, including challenge inspections (Article IX). States Parties are required to cooperate with the OPCW (Article VII, para. 7). These provisions apply without exception to potential Syrian non-compliance.

In addition to these existing procedures, the Resolution 2118 Regime, particularly OPCW Executive Council Decision EC-M-33/DEC.1, established a special type of inspection, more stringent than the challenge inspections under the Convention, to be carried out by the Technical Secretariat. The CWC stipulates that challenge inspections will be carried out, upon request of a State Party, at any facility or location in the territory or in any other place under the jurisdiction or control of any other State Party for the sole purpose of clarifying and resolving any questions concerning possible non-compliance with the Convention (Article IX, para. 8). By contrast, OPCW Executive Council Decision EC-M-33/DEC.1 tasks the Technical Secretariat with conducting this newly established inspection, known as a "section 2(d)" inspection, for "any other site identified by a State Party as having been involved in the Syrian chemical weapons program, unless deemed unwarranted by the Director-General, or the matter resolved through the process of consultations and cooperation."[193] The Director-General may thus instigate the "section 2(d)" inspection bypassing political filter mechanism under which a request for challenge inspection may be rejected by a three-fourths majority of the Executive Council (Article IX, para. 17).[194] Syria would be obligated to accept such inspections because the OPCW Executive Council decided that Syria shall "cooperate fully with all aspects of the implementation of this decision, including by providing the OPCW personnel with the immediate and unfettered right to inspect any and all sites" in its territory,[195] and UN Security Council Resolution 2118 made all aspects of Executive Council Decision EC-M-33/DEC.1 binding, as mentioned above.[196] Despite, or perhaps because

[193] OPCW Doc. EC-M-33/DEC.1, 27 September 2013, operative para. 2(d).

[194] Ralf Trapp, "Elimination of the Chemical Weapons Stockpile of Syria," *Journal of Conflict and Security Law*, Vol. 19, Issue 1 (2014), p. 7, p. 17.

[195] OPCW Doc. EC-M-33/DEC.1, 27 September 2013, operative para. 1(e).

[196] UN Doc. S/RES/2118 (2013), 27 September 2013, operative para. 6.

of, the special nature of "section 2(d)" inspection, available documents indicate that it has yet to be invoked.

(b) Syrian Obligations

Syria remains obliged to submit regular reports to the Executive Council in which it includes actions in response to Executive Council measures and explains potential non-compliance and options to address same. Syria also continues to be bound to cooperate with the OPCW and the UN.[197]

(c) Implementation

In the second half of 2014, the OPCW Executive Council returned to its traditional monitoring modality of holding three regular sessions with irregular meetings as necessary.[198] The Director-General continued to submit monthly reports on implementation to the Executive Council.[199] Either the Director-General or the Technical Secretariat continued to brief States Parties on their activities.[200] The Executive Council has identified several instances of potential non-compliance by assessing implementation and taken action as required. As will be seen hereinafter, Syria maintained its essentially cooperative attitude during this period, although some issues remain unresolved.

(i) Declaration of Chemical Weapons Program

Dispatchment of the Declaration Assessment Team

The OPCW Director-General drew the Executive Council's attention to the Syrian declarations issue for the first time in his sixth monthly report, dated 27 March

---

[197] Article VII, para. 7 of the Chemical Weapons Convention; UN Doc. S/RES/2118 (2013), 27 September 2013, operative para. 7.

[198] At the forty-fourth irregular meeting of the Executive Council on 28 August 2014, Brazil suggested reducing the number of briefings and reports (https://www.opcw.org/index.php?eID=dam_frontend_push&docID=17579, accessed 22 April 2023).

[199] See Appendix A.

[200] OPCW Doc. EC-M-44/DG.1, 25 July 2014, para. 8; OPCW Doc. EC-M-44/DG.2, 25 August 2014, para. 8; OPCW Doc. EC-77/DG.22, 24 September 2014, para. 8; OPCW Doc. EC-M-46/DG.1, 23 October 2014, para. 8; OPCW Doc. EC-78/DG.3, 24 November 2014, para. 8; UN Doc. S/2014/948, 26 December 2014, para. 8; UN Doc. S/2015/56, 26 January 2015, Annex, para. 9; OPCW Doc. EC-78/DG.9, 23 February 2015, para. 9; OPCW Doc. EC-79/DG.1, 23 March 2015, para. 9; OPCW Doc. EC-M-49/DG.1, 23 April 2015, para. 9; OPCW Doc. EC-79/DG.8, 22 May 2015, para. 9; OPCW Doc. EC-79/DG.15, 23 June 2015, para. 9; OPCW Doc. EC-80/DG.2, 23 July 2015, para. 8; OPCW Doc. EC-80/DG.4, 24 August 2015, para. 8; OPCW Doc. EC-80/DG.20, 23 September 2015, para. 9; OPCW Doc. EC-81/DG.1, 22 October 2015, para. 8; OPCW Doc. EC-81/DG.2, 24 November 2015, para. 8; OPCW Doc. EC-81/DG.3, 22 December 2015, para. 8; OPCW Doc. EC-81/DG.5, 25 January 2016, para. 9; OPCW Doc. EC-81/DG.11, 24 February 2016, para. 8; OPCW Doc. EC-82/DG.1, 24 March 2016, para. 8; OPCW Doc. EC-82/DG.5, 22 April 2016, para. 7; OPCW Doc. EC-82/DG.9, 25 May 2016, para. 12; UN Doc. S/2016/577, 28 June 2016, Annex, para. 10; OPCW Doc. EC-83/DG.2, 22 July 2016, para. 11; OPCW Doc. EC-83/DG.6, 22 August 2016, para. 10.

2014, by mentioning that "the [Technical] Secretariat is currently in the process of seeking clarifications" on the 7 March 2014 amendment to Syria's initial declaration of 23 October 2013.[201] This was the third such amendment, following the previous amendments of 21 November 2013 and 6 February 2014.[202] The US, the UK, and the EU responded promptly. stressing the necessity for verifying the accuracy and completeness of the submissions and taking appropriate steps to that end.[203]

On 22 April 2014, the Director-General announced the dispatch of technical experts, later designated the "Declaration Assessment Team (DAT)," to Syria "to meet with Syrian authorities as part of continuing efforts to streamline and complete the data regarding the initial declaration submitted by the Syrian Arab Republic in October 2013, and subsequent amendments, as well as the verification work."[204] This statement suggested that Syria accepted, rather than opposed, the team's visit. The UK, Greece on behalf of the EU, the US, Turkey, New Zealand, the Netherlands, Chile, Peru, Guatemala, Switzerland, Japan, and the Republic of Korea welcomed the decision of the Director-General and called on Syria to provide information and documents to address the issues regarding its initial declaration.[205] They also mentioned the following key aspects of the DAT's work. First, they attached importance to the accuracy and completeness of Syria's declarations.[206] While the CWC

---

201 OPCW Doc. EC-M-40/DG.1/Rev.1, 27 March 2014, para. 4(e). The OPCW Director-General did not raise the issue of the declaration's accuracy prior to this time. The Technical Secretariat, enjoying widespread political support and goodwill, appeared willing to seize the unprecedented opportunity to undertake a disarmament project during an armed conflict (Edward M. Spiers, *Agents of War: A History of Chemical and Biological Weapons*, expanded second edition (Reaktion Books, 2021), p. 166).

202 OPCW Doc. EC-M-35/DG.1, 25 November 2013, para. 5(a); OPCW Doc. EC-75/DG.6, 25 February 2014, para. 4(d).

203 OPCW Doc. EC-M-40/NAT.2 (US), 28 March 2014, p. 2; OPCW Doc. EC-M-40/NAT.4 (US), 11 April 2014, p. 2; OPCW Doc. EC-M-40/NAT.7 (UK), 11 April 2014, p. 2; OPCW Doc. EC-M-40/NAT.8 (Greece on behalf of the EU), 11 April 2014, p. 2.

204 OPCW Doc. EC-M-40/DG.4, 25 April 2014, para. 10.

205 OPCW Doc. EC-M-40/NAT.13 (UK), 29 April 2014, p. 2; OPCW Doc. EC-M-40/NAT.21 (Greece on behalf of the EU), 8 May 2014, p. 2; OPCW Doc. EC-M-40/NAT.23 (US), 8 May 2014, p. 1; OPCW Doc. EC-M-42/NAT.1 (Greece on behalf of the EU), 17 June 2014, p. 2; OPCW Doc. EC-M-42/NAT.2 (Turkey), 17 June 2014, p. 1; OPCW Doc. EC-M-42/NAT.3 (New Zealand, 17 June 2014), p. 1; OPCW Doc. EC-M-42/NAT.4 (UK), 17 June 2014, pp. 1–2; OPCW Doc. EC-M-42/NAT.11 (Netherlands), 17 June 2014, p. 2; OPCW Doc. EC-M-42/NAT.12 (US), 17 June 2014, p. 2; OPCW Doc. EC-76/NAT.8 (Netherlands), 9 July 2014, p. 2; OPCW Doc. EC-76/NAT.9 (Chile), 8 July 2014, p. 1; OPCW Doc. EC-76/NAT.17 (Peru), 8 July 2014, pp. 1–2; OPCW Doc. EC-76/NAT.18 (Guatemala), 8 July 2014, p. 2; OPCW Doc. EC-76/NAT.23 (Switzerland), 9 July 2014, p. 1; OPCW Doc. EC-76/NAT.28 (Japan), 9 July 2014, p. 2; OPCW Doc. EC-76/NAT.32 (UK), 8 July 2014, pp. 1–2; OPCW Doc. EC-76/NAT.39 (US), 8 July 2014, pp. 3–4; Republic of Korea, https://www.opcw.org/sites/default/files/documents/EC/76/en/Republic_of_Korea-09july.pdf, accessed 22 April 2023.

206 OPCW Doc. EC-M-40/NAT.13 (UK), 29 April 2014, p. 2; OPCW Doc. EC-M-40/NAT.21 (Greece on behalf of the EU), 8 May 2014, p. 2; OPCW Doc. EC-M-40/NAT.23 (US), 8 May 2014, p. 1; OPCW Doc. EC-M-41/NAT.4 (Netherlands), 22 May 2013, p. 2; OPCW Doc. EC-M-41/NAT.5 (Germany), 22 May 2013, p. 2; OPCW Doc. EC-M-41/NAT.7 (Greece on behalf of the EU), 22 May 2013, p. 2; OPCW Doc. EC-M-41/NAT.8 (US), 22 May 2013, p. 2; OPCW Doc.

might not explicitly require the OPCW to verify the completeness of declarations,[207] the Executive Council endorsed the concept in the context of the Syrian chemical weapons program at its seventy-six session in July 2014, urging the Technical Secretariat and Syria "to continue to cooperate…on outstanding issues regarding Syria's declaration, with a view to the soonest resolution of questions raised by the [Technical] Secretariat to further the declaration's accuracy and completeness."[208] This measure indirectly expanded the qualitative scope of Syria's obligation on its declarations. Russia implicitly complained about the Technical Secretariat accordingly being more stringent in its verification of same by expressing its hope that future OPCW mission work would "be done exclusively within the framework of Convention requirements and fully in line with the standards and practices of the Organisation with respect to other States Parties."[209] The US immediately rebutted this argument, however, stressing the "special framework" for verifying Syria's declarations, which was essential to eliminating its chemical weapons program.[210] The UN General Assembly also referred to the OPCW Executive Council decision that required Syria "to declare its programme in full,"[211] stressing the importance of fully verifying that its declarations are "accurate and complete."[212]

Second, contrary to this selfsame expansive scope of Syrian obligation, the States Parties appeared reluctant to treat the declarations issue as non-compliance, at least before November 2016. Prior to that time, they referred to it in terms of "gaps, inconsistencies, and discrepancies,"[213] instead of "doubts, ambiguities or uncertainties,"

EC-M-42/NAT.4 (UK), 17 July 2014, p. 2; OPCW Doc. EC-M-42/NAT.12 (US), 17 July 2014, p. 2; OPCW Doc. EC-M-42/NAT.1 (Greece on behalf of the EU), 17 July 2014, p. 2; OPCW Doc. EC-M-42/NAT.2 (Turkey), 17 July 2014, p. 1; OPCW Doc. EC-M-42/NAT.3 (New Zealand), 17 July 2014, p. 1; OPCW Doc. EC-76/NAT.17 (Peru), 8 July 2014, p. 2; OPCW Doc. EC-76/NAT.32 (UK), 8 July 2014, p. 1; OPCW Doc. EC-76/NAT.39 (US), 8 July 2014, pp. 3–4; OPCW Doc. EC-76/NAT.22 (Russia), 8 July 2014, pp. 3–4; OPCW Doc. EC-76/NAT.28 (Japan), 9 July 2014, p. 2.

[207] Report of the Scientific Advisory Board's Temporary Working Group: Verification (June 2015), https://www.opcw.org/sites/default/files/documents/SAB/en/Final_Report_of_SAB_TWG_on_Verification_-_as_presented_to_SAB.pdf, accessed 22 April 2023, p. 22, para. 14 ("A major limitation is that the verification regime of the Convention has no provisions for assessing the completeness of declarations; it is only possible to assess the correctness of declarations, in other words whether what has been declared has been correctly declared, and not whether all that should have been declared has indeed been declared.").

[208] OPCW Doc. EC-76/6, 11 July 2014, para. 6.17. The OPCW Executive Council reiterated the Declaration Assessment Team's mandate in subsequent decisions (OPCW Doc. EC-81/DEC.4, 23 March 2016, preamble para. 6; OPCW Doc. EC-81/DEC.4, 23 March 2016, operative para. 3; OPCW Doc. EC-81/DEC.4, 23 March 2016, operative para. 6; OPCW Doc. EC-83/DEC.5, 11 November 2016, preamble para. 7.

[209] OPCW Doc. EC-M-48/NAT.1 (Russia), 21 January 2015, p. 2.

[210] OPCW Doc. EC-M-48/NAT.4 (US), 21 January 2015, p. 2.

[211] UN Doc. A/RES/69/189, 18 December 2014, operative para. 20; UN Doc. A/RES/70/234, 23 December 2015, operative para. 31.

[212] UN Doc. A/RES/70/41, 7 December 2015, operative para. 10.

[213] OPCW Doc. EC-M-41/NAT.3 (UK), 22 May 2013, p. 2; OPCW Doc. EC-M-42/NAT.1 (Greece on behalf of the EU), 17 July 2014, p. 2; OPCW Doc. EC-M-42/NAT. 3 (New Zealand), 17 July

within the meaning of Article VIII, para. 40 of the CWC.[214] At the Executive Council eightieth session in October 2015, the US argued that "[g]iven the critical importance of this issue, the Director-General should, by the end of January [2016], inform the Council in a report, pursuant to Article VIII, paragraph 40, of all doubts, ambiguities, or uncertainties with Syria's declaration and related submissions that the Secretariat has been unable to resolve or clarify through its consultations with Syria."[215] This statement suggested that the Executive Council was not yet in a position to deal with issues per the aforementioned Article VIII, para. 40. The Executive Council took a collective but less confrontational step in line with this attitude, requesting that the Technical Secretariat and Syria step up their efforts to resolve these "gaps, inconsistencies, and discrepancies."[216] This implies that the Executive Council understood the DAT's work to be "consultations with the State Party concerned" (Article VIII, para. 40), which would precede the Technical Secretariat notifying the Executive Council of such "doubts, ambiguities or uncertainties."[217]

2014, p. 1; OPCW Doc. EC-M-42/NAT.4 (UK), 17 July 2014, p. 1; OPCW Doc. EC-M-42/NAT.12 (US), 17 July 2014, p. 2; OPCW Doc. EC-76/NAT, 16 (Brazil), 8 July 2014, p. 2; OPCW Doc. EC-76/NAT.32 (UK), 8 July 2014, p. 1; OPCW Doc. EC-76/NAT.39 (US),, 8 July 2014 p. 3; OPCW Doc. EC-76/NAT.31 (New Zealand), 9 July 2014, p. 1; OPCW Doc. EC-M-44/NAT.6 (US), 28 August 2014, p. 2; OPCW Doc. EC-M-45/NAT.13 (UK), 26 September 2014, p. 2; OPCW Doc. EC-77/NAT.5 (Italy on behalf of fifty-two States Parties (Albania, Andorra, Australia, Austria, Belgium, Bulgaria, Canada, Croatia, Cyprus, Czech Republic, Denmark, Estonia, France, Finland, Germany, Georgia, Greece, Hungary, Iceland, Ireland, Italy, Japan, Jordan, Republic of Korea, Kuwait, Latvia, Lithuania, Luxemburg, Former Yugoslav Republic of Macedonia, Malta, Moldova, Montenegro, Morocco, Netherlands, New Zealand, Norway, Poland, Portugal, Qatar, Romania, Saudi Arabia, Slovakia, Oman, Slovenia, Spain, Sweden, Switzerland, Turkey, United Arab Emirates, Ukraine, UK, and US)), 10 October 2014, p. 2; OPCW Doc. EC-77/NAT.18 (Turkey), 7 October 2014, p. 1; OPCW Doc. EC-M-46/NAT.5 (Turkey), 19 November 2014, p. 1; OPCW Doc. EC-M-46/NAT.13 (Chile), 19 November 2014, p. 1; OPCW Doc. EC-M-48/NAT.6 (Chile), 21 January 2015, p. 2; OPCW Doc. EC-M-48/NAT.10 (Turkey), 21 January 2015, p. 2; OPCW Doc. EC-78/NAT.17 (Turkey), 17 March 2015, p. 1; EC-M-49/NAT.3 (US), 7 May 2015, p. 1; OPCW Doc. EC-79/NAT.6 (Luxembourg on behalf of the EU), 7 July 2015, p. 1; OPCW Doc. EC-79/NAT.9 (Finland), 7 July 2015, p. 1; OPCW Doc. EC-79/NAT.36 (US), 7 July 2015, p. 2; OPCW Doc. EC-80/NAT.5 (Turkey), 6 October 2015, pp. 1–2; OPCW Doc. EC-80/NAT.6 (New Zealand), 6 October 2015, p. 1; OPCW Doc. EC-80/NAT.7 (Germany), 6 October 2015, p. 1; OPCW Doc. EC-80/NAT.11 (Australia), 6 October 2015, p. 2; OPCW Doc. EC-80/NAT.15 (Republic of Korea), 6 October 2015, p. 2; OPCW Doc. EC-80/NAT.28 (Luxembourg on behalf of the EU), 6 October 2015, p. 2; OPCW Doc. EC-80/NAT.31 (Netherlands), 6 October 2015, p. 1.

[214] Article VIII, para. 40 stipulates that "The Technical Secretariat shall inform the Executive Council of any problem that has arisen with regard to the discharge of its functions, including doubts, ambiguities or uncertainties about compliance with this Convention that have come to its notice in the performance of its verification activities and that it has been unable to resolve or clarify through its consultations with the State Party concerned."

[215] OPCW Doc. EC-80/NAT.33 (US), 6 October 2015, p. 3.

[216] OPCW Doc. EC-80/4*, 8 October 2015, para. 7.19.

[217] While the CWC allowed the OPCW Technical Secretariat to assist the States Parties in preparing their declarations, there were no formal arrangements for doing so, leading to the DAT devising its work *ad hoc* (Peter van Ham, Sico van der Meer and Malik Ellahi, *Chemical Weapons Challenges Ahead: The Past and Future of the OPCW - With a Case Study on Syria* , Clingendael

Table 4.6 Meetings between the DAT and Syria

Round	Date	Place
First[218]	22–28 April 2014	Syria
Second[219]	21–28 May 2014	Syria
Third[220]	30 June–5 July 2014	Syria

Verification Activities Until October 2016

Between April 2014 and October 2016, the Technical Secretariat implemented its mandate to verify Syrian initial declarations through the DAT, under Executive Council guidance.[221] The DAT accordingly held three rounds of meetings with the Syrian authorities between April and July 2014, as Table 4.6.

While Syria submitted amendments to its declarations on 16 April and 14 July 2014,[222] the issues yet remained unresolved. Thus, the DAT and the Syrian authorities held another eight rounds of meetings in a show of continued cooperation between August 2014 and September 2015, again, as Table 4.7.[223]

Report (2017), https://www.clingendael.org/sites/default/files/pdf/Clingendael_Report_Chemical_Weapons_Challenges_Ahead_2017.pdf, accessed 22 April 2023, p. 48).

218 OPCW Doc. EC-M-40/DG.4, 25 April 2014, para. 10; OPCW Doc. EC-M-42/DG.1, 23 May 2014, para. 9.

219 OPCW Doc. EC-76/DG.14, 25 June 2014, para. 10.

220 OPCW Doc. EC-M-44-/DG.1, 25 July 2014, para. 10.

221 The OPCW Executive Council reiterated the DAT's mandate in its decisions (OPCW Doc. EC-81/DEC.4, 23 March 2016, preamble para. 6; OPCW Doc. EC-81/DEC.4, 23 March 2016, operative para. 3; OPCW Doc. EC-81/DEC.4, 23 March 2016, operative para. 6; OPCW Doc. EC-83/DEC.5, 11 November 2016, preamble para. 7.

222 OPCW Doc. EC-M-40/DG.4, 25 April 2014, para. 4(e); OPCW Doc. EC-M-44/DG.1, 25 June 2014, para. 4(b). OPCW Doc. EC-M-45/NAT.10 (Saudi Arabia), 26 September 2014, p. 1 ("[t]he existence of these facilities would not have been revealed had it not been for the excellent verification and follow-up by the OPCW").

223 OPCW Doc. EC-79/DG.8, 22 May 2015, para. 10; OPCW Doc. EC-79/DG.15, 23 June 2015, para. 10; OPCW Doc. EC-80/DG.2, 23 July 2015, para. 9; OPCW Doc. EC-80/DG.4, 24 August 2015, para. 9; OPCW Doc. EC-80/DG.20, 23 September 2015, para. 10.

Table 4.7 Meetings between the DAT and Syria

Round	Date	Place
Fourth[224]	17–19 September 2014	Beirut
Fifth[225]	2–10 November 2014	Syria
Sixth[226]	10–15 December 2014	Syria
Seventh[227]	25 January–5 February 2015	Syria
Eighth[228]	22 March–3 April 2015	Syria
Ninth[229]	17–29 May 2015	Syria
Tenth[230]	19–31 July 2015	Syria
Eleventh[231]	28 August–12 September 2015	Syria

The Technical Secretariat kept the Executive Council informed through status reports and follow-up briefings.[232] A number of States Parties expressed continued concern about lack of progress on the initial declarations, stressed the importance of resolving gaps, inconsistencies, and discrepancies and ensuring accuracy and completeness therein, supported the DAT's work, and called on Syria to cooperate with the Technical Secretariat.[233] There were already indications, even at this stage,

[224] OPCW Doc. EC-77/DG.22, 24 September 2014, para. 10.

[225] OPCW Doc. EC-78/DG.3, 24 November 2014, para. 9.

[226] UN Doc. S/2014/948, 26 December 2014, Annex, para. 9.

[227] OPCW Doc. EC-78/DG.9, 23 February 2015, para. 10.

[228] OPCW Doc. EC-M-49/DG.1, 23 April 2015, para. 10.

[229] OPCW Doc. EC-79/DG.15, 23 June 2015, para. 10.

[230] OPCW Doc. EC-80/DG.4, 24 August 2015, para. 9.

[231] OPCW Doc. EC-80/DG.20, 23 September 2015, para. 10.

[232] OPCW Doc. EC-77/4, 10 October 2014, paras. 6.17 and 6.18; OPCW Doc. EC-M-48/3, 4 February 2015, paras. 4.4 and 4.5; OPCW Doc. EC-78/2, 19 March 2015, paras. 6.17 and 6.18; OPCW Doc. EC-M-49/3, 7 May 2015, paras. 4.3 and 4.4; OPCW Doc. EC-79/6, 9 July 2015, paras. 6.17 and 6.18; OPCW Doc. EC-80/4*, 8 October 2015, paras. 7.16 and 7.17.

[233] OPCW Doc. EC-M-41/NAT.3 (UK), 22 May 2014, p. 2; OPCW Doc. EC-M-42/NAT.1 (Greece on behalf of the EU), 17 July 2014, p. 2; OPCW Doc. EC-M-42/NAT. 3 (New Zealand), 17 July 2014, p. 1; OPCW Doc. EC-M-42/NAT.4 (UK), 17 July 2014, p. 1; OPCW Doc. EC-M-42/NAT.12 (US), 17 July 2014, p. 2; OPCW Doc. EC-76/NAT.16 (Brazil), 8 July 2014, p. 2; OPCW Doc. EC-76/NAT.32 (UK), 8 July 2014, p. 1; OPCW Doc. EC-76/NAT.39 (US), 8 July 2014, p. 3; OPCW Doc. EC-76/NAT.31 (New Zealand), 9 July 2014, p. 1; OPCW Doc. EC-M-44/NAT.6 (US), 28 August 2014, p. 2; OPCW Doc. EC-M-44/NAT.4 (Peru), 28 August 2014, p. 1; OPCW Doc. EC-M-45/NAT.10 (Saudi Arabia), 26 September 2014, p. 1; OPCW Doc. EC-M-45/NAT.13 (UK), 26 September 2014, p. 2; OPCW Doc. EC-77/NAT.5 (Italy on behalf of fifty-two States Parties (Albania, Andorra, Australia, Austria, Belgium, Bulgaria, Canada, Croatia, Cyprus, Czech Republic, Denmark, Estonia, France, Finland, Germany, Georgia, Greece, Hungary, Iceland, Ireland, Italy, Japan, Jordan, Republic of Korea, Kuwait, Latvia, Lithuania, Luxemburg, Former Yugoslav Republic of Macedonia, Malta, Moldova, Montenegro, Morocco, Netherlands, New Zealand, Norway, Poland, Portugal, Qatar, Romania, Saudi Arabia, Slovakia, Oman, Slovenia, Spain, Sweden, Switzerland, Turkey, United Arab Emirates, Ukraine, UK, and US)), 10 October 2014, p. 2; OPCW Doc. EC-77/NAT.9 (Japan), 7 October 2014, p. 1; OPCW Doc. EC-77/NAT.18

of a possible link between the uncertainties in the initial declarations and chemical weapons use.[234]

(Turkey), 7 October 2014, p. 1; OPCW Doc. EC-77/NAT.22 (Netherlands), 7 October 2014, p. 1; OPCW Doc. EC-M-46/NAT.5 (Turkey), 19 November 2014, p. 1; OPCW Doc. EC-M-46/NAT.7 (Japan), 19 November 2014, p. 1; OPCW Doc. EC-M-46/NAT.10 (Spain), 19 November 2014, p. 1; OPCW Doc. EC-M-46/NAT.13 (Chile), 19 November 2014, p. 1; US, https://www.opcw.org/sites/default/files/documents/EC/M-46/USA.pdf, accessed 22 April 2023; OPCW Doc. EC-M-48/NAT.4 (US), 21 January 2015, p. 1; OPCW Doc. EC-M-48/NAT.6 (Chile), 21 January 2015, p. 2; OPCW Doc. EC-M-48/NAT.7 (Peru), 21 January 2015, pp. 1–2; OPCW Doc. EC-M-48/NAT.8 (Uruguay), 21 January 2015, p. 1; OPCW Doc. EC-M-48/NAT.10 (Turkey), 21 January 2015, p. 2; OPCW Doc. EC-M-48/NAT.11 (Netherlands), 21 January 2015, p. 1; Latvia on behalf of the EU, https://www.opcw.org/sites/default/files/documents/EC/M-48/Statement_on_behalf_of_the_European_Union.pdf, accessed 22 April 2023; OPCW Doc. EC-78/NAT.6 (Croatia), 17 March 2015; OPCW Doc. EC-78/NAT.7 (UK), 17 March 2015, p. 1; OPCW Doc. EC-78/NAT.10 (US), 17 March 2015, p. 2; OPCW Doc. EC-78/NAT.11 (Uruguay), 17 March 2015, p. 2; OPCW Doc. EC-78/NAT.15 (Japan), 17 March 2015, p. 2; OPCW Doc. EC-78/NAT.16 (Germany), 17 March 2015, p. 2; OPCW Doc. EC-78/NAT.17 (Turkey), 17 March 2015, p. 1; OPCW Doc. EC-78/NAT.25 (New Zealand), 17 March 2015; OPCW Doc. EC-78/NAT.28 (Switzerland), 17 March 2015, p. 1; OPCW Doc. EC-78/NAT.29 (Australia), 17 March 2015, p. 1; OPCW Doc. EC-78/NAT.31 (Netherlands), 17 March 2015, p. 1; OPCW Doc. EC-78/NAT.33 (Chile), 17 March 2015, p. 2; OPCW Doc. EC-78/NAT.34 (France), 17 March 2015, p. 3; Latvia on behalf of the EU, https://www.opcw.org/sites/default/files/documents/EC/78/en/Latvia.pdf, accessed 22 April 2023; Republic of Korea, https://www.opcw.org/sites/default/files/documents/EC/78/en/Korea.pdf, accessed 22 April 2023; EC-M-49/NAT.3 (US), 7 May 2015, p. 1; EC-M-49/NAT.4 (Peru), 7 May 2015, p. 1; EC-M-49/NAT.5 (Chile), 7 May 2015, p. 1; EC-M-49/NAT.9 (Switzerland), 7 May 2015, p. 1; EC-M-49/NAT.11 (Germany), 7 May 2015, pp. 1–2; UK, https://www.opcw.org/sites/default/files/documents/EC/M-49/FINAL_UK_Statement_for_May_ECM_Syria_v2.pdf, accessed 22 April 2023; OPCW Doc. EC-79/NAT.6 (Luxembourg on behalf of the EU), 7 July 2015, p. 1; OPCW Doc. EC-79/NAT.9 (Finland), 7 July 2015, p. 1; OPCW Doc. EC-79/NAT.10 (Republic of Korea), 7 July 2015, p. 1; OPCW Doc. EC-79/NAT.11 (New Zealand), 7 July 2015, p. 1; OPCW Doc. EC-79/NAT.12 (Turkey), 7 July 2015, p. 2; OPCW Doc. EC-79/NAT.14 (Argentina), 7 July 2015, p. 1; OPCW Doc. EC-79/NAT.16 (Peru), 7 July 2015, p. 1; OPCW Doc. EC-79/NAT.17 (Japan), 7 July 2015, p. 2; OPCW Doc. EC-79/NAT.23 (Switzerland), 7 July 2015, p. 1; OPCW Doc. EC-79/NAT.24 (Peru), 7 July 2015, p. 2; OPCW Doc. EC-79/NAT.25 (France), 7 July 2015, pp. 2–3; OPCW Doc. EC-79/NAT.35 (Netherlands), 7 July 2015, p. 2; OPCW Doc. EC-79/NAT.36 (US), 7 July 2015, p. 2; India, https://www.opcw.org/sites/default/files/documents/EC/79/en/India.pdf, accessed 22 April 2023; UK, https://www.opcw.org/sites/default/files/documents/EC/79/en/EC79_UK_statement.pdf, accessed 22 April 2023; OPCW Doc. EC-80/NAT.5 (Turkey), 6 October 2015, pp. 1–2; OPCW Doc. EC-80/NAT.6 (New Zealand), 6 October 2015, p. 1; OPCW Doc. EC-80/NAT.7 (Germany), 6 October 2015, p. 1; OPCW Doc. EC-80/NAT.8 (Peru), 6 October 2015, p. 1; OPCW Doc. EC-80/NAT.9 (Switzerland), 6 October 2015, p. 1; OPCW Doc. EC-80/NAT.11 (Australia), 6 October 2015, p. 2; OPCW Doc. EC-80/NAT.15 (Republic of Korea), 6 October 2015, p. 2; OPCW Doc. EC-80/NAT.18 (Japan), 6 October 2015, pp. 1–2; OPCW Doc. EC-80/NAT.19 (China), 6 October 2015, p. 2; OPCW Doc. EC-80/NAT.23 (UK), 6 October 2015, p. 1; OPCW Doc. EC-80/NAT.26 (Chile), 6 October 2015, p. 3; OPCW Doc. EC-80/NAT.28 (Luxembourg on behalf of the EU), 6 October 2015, p. 2; OPCW Doc. EC-80/NAT.31 (Netherlands), 6 October 2015, p. 1; OPCW Doc. EC-80/NAT.32 (France), 6 October 2015, p. 2; OPCW Doc. EC-80/NAT.33 (US), 6 October 2015, pp. 2–3; OPCW Doc. EC-80/NAT.3 (Argentina), 7 October 2015, p. 1.

[234] OPCW Doc. EC-M-45/NAT.10 (Saudi Arabia), 26 September 2014, p. 1.

Table 4.8 Meetings between the DAT and Syria

Round	Date	Place
Twelfth[238]	2–12 November 2015	Syria
Thirteenth[239]	13–22 December 2015	Syria
Fourteenth[240]	18–26 January 2016	Syria
Fifteenth[241]	20–25 February 2016	Syria

At its eightieth session in October 2015, the Executive Council took further steps. Having "underscored the substantial unresolved issues, including the gaps, inconsistencies, and discrepancies identified by the Secretariat in its report…and stressed the importance of fully verifying that the declaration and related submissions of the Syrian Arab Republic are accurate and complete," it again requested that the Technical Secretariat and Syria make greater efforts to resolve these gaps, inconsistencies, and discrepancies, and asked the Director-General to submit a report at its next session.[235] Accordingly, the Director-General submitted a classified report to the eighty-first session of the Executive Council on 22 February 2016,[236] detailing all unresolved issues, especially those for which no further progress could be made despite the DAT's fifteen visits to Syria over the past two years, including four visits between November 2015 and February 2016, as Table 4.8.[237]

[235] OPCW Doc. EC-80/4*, 8 October 2015, para. 7.19.

[236] OPCW Doc. EC-81/DG.11, 24 February 2016, para. 10. This report (OPCW Doc. EC-81/HP/DG.1, 22 February 2016) was cited in subsequent UN General Assembly resolutions (UN Doc. A/RES/71/203, 19 December 2016, operative para. 7; UN Doc. A/RES/72/191, 19 December 2017, operative para. 10; UN Doc. A/RES/73/182, 17 December 2018, operative para. 8; UN Doc. A/RES/74/169, 18 December 2019, operative para. 9).

[237] OPCW Doc. EC-82/DG.1, 24 March 2016, para. 9. The Technical Secretariat and the Syrian authorities continued to cooperate (OPCW Doc. EC-81/DG.1, 22 October 2015, para. 9; OPCW Doc. EC-81/DG.2, 24 November 2015, para. 9; OPCW Doc. EC-81/DG.3, 22 December 2015, para. 9; OPCW Doc. EC-81/DG.5, 25 January 2016, para. 10; OPCW Doc. EC-81/DG.11, 24 February 2016, para. 9; OPCW Doc. EC-82/DG.1, 24 March 2016, para. 9).

[238] OPCW Doc. EC-81/DG.2, 24 November 2015, para. 9.

[239] OPCW Doc. EC-81/DG.5, 25 January 2016, para. 10.

[240] OPCW Doc. EC-81/DG.11, 24 February 2016, para. 10.

[241] OPCW Doc. EC-81/DG.11, 24 February 2016, para. 10.

Table 4.9 Meetings between the DAT and Syria

Round	Date	Place
Sixteenth[247]	27–30 April 2016	The Hague
Seventeenth[248]	29 May–4 June 2016	Syria

At its eighty-first session in March 2016, the Executive Council deliberated on the Director-General's report and unanimously adopted a decision to give Syria another chance.[242] Having expressed concern about the report, which concluded that the Technical Secretariat was unable at that time to verify fully the accuracy and completeness of the declaration and related submissions of Syria and that no further progress was possible for nine of seventeen unresolved issues,[243] it requested that the Technical Secretariat continue its efforts to verify the accuracy and completeness of the declaration and related disclosures of Syria and to address the gaps, inconsistencies, and discrepancies.[244] It also requested that the Director-General meet with Syrian officials with the aim of addressing unresolved issues and submit a report at its next session.[245] It further called upon Syria to "cooperate fully with the Director-General's engagement as well as in the continuing activities of the Secretariat's Declaration Assessment Team,"[246] demonstrating the Executive Council's continuing non-confrontational approach. Two additional rounds of consultations between the Declaration Assessment Team and the Syrian authorities took place, as Table 4.9.

The Director-General issued classified and unclassified reports on the outcome of the consultations with Syrian officials to the eighty-second session of the Executive Council on 30 June and 6 July 2016, respectively.[249] While he acknowledged

242 OPCW Doc. EC-81/DEC.4, 23 March 2016. Many States Parties expressed concern and emphasized necessity of additional action (OPCW Doc. EC-81/NAT.6 (Germany), 15 March 2016, p. 1; OPCW Doc. EC-81/NAT.7 (Brazil), 15 March 2016, p. 1; OPCW Doc. EC-81/NAT.9 (Pakistan), 15 March 2016, p. 1; OPCW Doc. EC-81/NAT.14 (New Zealand), 15 March 2016, p. 1; OPCW Doc. EC-81/NAT.15 (Poland), 15 March 2016, p. 1; OPCW Doc. EC-81/NAT.17 (US), 15 March 2016, pp. 1–2; OPCW Doc. EC-81/NAT.19 (Malaysia), 15 March 2016, p. 1; OPCW Doc. EC-81/NAT.25 (Chile), 15 March 2016, pp. 1–2; OPCW Doc. EC-81/NAT.27 (China), 15 March 2016, p. 2; OPCW Doc. EC-81/NAT.31 (France), 15 March 2016, pp. 1–2; OPCW Doc. EC-81/NAT.33 (Australia), 15 March 2016, pp. 2–3; OPCW Doc. EC-81/NAT.35 (Republic of Korea), 15 March 2016, p. 1; OPCW Doc. EC-81/NAT.8 (Finland), 16 March 2016, p. 1; OPCW Doc. EC-81/NAT.13 (Japan), 16 March 2016, p. 1; India, https://www.opcw.org/sites/default/files/documents/EC/81/en/India_EC81.pdf, accessed 22 April 2023; Netherlands on behalf of the EU, https://www.opcw.org/sites/default/files/documents/EC/81/en/NL_Statement_at_the_81th_session_of_the_Executive_Council.pdf, accessed 22 April 2023).

243 OPCW Doc. EC-81/DEC.4, 23 March 2016, operative paras 1–2.

244 *Ibid.*, operative para. 3.

245 *Ibid.*, operative para. 4(a)(b).

246 *Ibid.*, operative para. 6.

247 OPCW Doc. EC-82/DG.9, 25 May 2016, para. 9.

248 UN Doc. S/2016/577, 28 June 2016, Annex, para. 8.

249 EC-83/DG.2, 22 July 2016, paras. 7–8. There were consultations between the Deputy Foreign Minister of Syria and a delegation of experts and the Technical Secretariat at the OPCW Headquarters

Syria's provision of new information on some outstanding issues,[250] his conclusion was unchanged: the Technical Secretariat was "not able to resolve all identified gaps, inconsistencies and discrepancies in Syria's declaration, and therefore cannot fully verify that Syria has submitted a declaration that can be considered accurate and complete in accordance with the Chemical Weapons Convention or [Executive] Council decision EC-M-33/DEC.1, dated 27 September 2013."[251] The OPCW Executive Council deliberated and the US circulated a draft decision, but no consensus was reached.[252] Several States Parties including the EU supported the US draft,[253] while Russia and the NAM CWC States Parties and China called on Syria and the OPCW Technical Secretariat to continue their cooperation.[254] Following this session, the Syrian authorities and the Technical Secretariat exchanged a number of communications in an effort to make progress in clarifying the outstanding issues,[255] resulting in the submission of a declaration on select aspect of the SSRC in a letter dated 13 October 2016.[256] The Technical Secretariat considered this declaration incomplete, however, and urged Syria to declare all relevant parts of the SSRC in accordance with the CWC.[257]

It follows that the Executive Council addressed the declaration issues carefully, spending much time collecting information from Syria via the Technical Secretariat to redress the situation. The issues yet remained unresolved, however, while the international community discovered a connection between the declaration issues

---

from 27 to 30 April 2016 (OPCW Doc. EC-82/DG.9, 25 May 2016, para. 9), at the expert level in Damascus from 29 May to 4 June 2016, and at the senior level at the OPCW Headquarters from 20 to 22 June 2016 (UN Doc. S/2016/577, 28 June 2016, Annex, para. 8).

[250] OPCW Doc. EC-82/DG.18, 6 July 2016, para. 1.

[251] *Ibid.*, para. 8. One key justification was sampling and analysis results that indicated "potentially declarable activities involving five additional chemical agents" (*ibid.*, para. 6).

[252] OPCW Doc. EC-83/DG.2, 22 July 2016, para. 10.

[253] OPCW Doc. EC-82/NAT.10 (Germany), 12 July 2016, p. 1; OPCW Doc. EC-82/NAT.12 (New Zealand), 12 July 2016, p. 1; OPCW Doc. EC-82/NAT.14 (Sweden), 12 July 2016, p. 2; OPCW Doc. EC-82/NAT.15 (Australia), 12 July 2016, pp. 1–2; OPCW Doc. EC-82/NAT.18 (Poland), 12 July 2016, p. 1; OPCW Doc. EC-82/NAT.22 (Slovakia on behalf of the EU), 12 July 2016, pp. 1–2; OPCW Doc. EC-82/NAT.25 (Netherlands), 12 July 2016, pp. 1–2; OPCW Doc. EC-82/NAT.26 (France), 12 July 2016, pp. 1–2.

[254] OPCW Doc. EC-82/NAT.20 (Russia), 12 July 2016, p. 2; OPCW Doc. EC-82/NAT.24 (Iran on behalf of the NAM CWC States Parties and China), 12 July 2016, pp. 2–3.

[255] OPCW Doc. EC-83/DG.6, 22 August 2016, para. 9 (a letter from the OPCW Director-General to the Syrian Deputy Foreign Minister dated 27 July 2016); OPCW Doc. EC-83/DG.18, 26 September 2016, para. 8 (a letter with some information from the Head of the National Authority of Syria to the OPCW Director-General dated 30 August 2016); OPCW Doc. EC-84/DG.1, 25 October 2016, para. 8 (a letter from the OPCW Director-General to the Head of the National Authority of Syria dated 29 September 2016); OPCW Doc. EC-84/DG.1, 25 October 2016, para. 9 (a letter from Syria to the OPCW Technical Secretariat dated 10 October 2016); OPCW Doc. EC-84/DG.4, 23 November 2016, para. 9 (a letter from the OPCW Technical Secretariat to Syria dated 1 November 2016); OPCW Doc. EC-84/DG.6, 22 December 2016, para. 10 (a letter from Syria to the OPCW Technical Secretariat dated 10 November 2016).

[256] OPCW Doc. EC-84/DG.1, 25 October 2016, para. 9.

[257] OPCW Doc. EC-84/DG.4, 23 November 2016, para. 9.

and chemical weapons use in Syria, as mentioned above and elaborated hereinafter, which signified Syrian non-compliance with its obligation to submit full and complete declarations.

(ii) **Removal of Chemical Weapons**

Deadline of 31 December 2013

The Executive Council had its thirty-sixth meeting on 17 December 2013, two weeks before the deadline for removing priority 1 chemicals. The Director-General indicated possible delays in so doing, taking into account schedules being disrupted by "a combination of security concerns, clearance procedures in international transit and even inclement weather conditions," and that there was "continuing heavy fighting in the Qalamoun and surrounding areas and the closure of a major arterial road between Damascus and Homs."[258] The Executive Council noted that "technical factors have caused delays regarding some aspects of removal operations for high-priority chemicals and may also affect future implementation activities,"[259] suggesting that the Executive Council took a wait-and-see attitude. On 28 December 2013, the OPCW-UN Joint Mission issued a statement acknowledging that "at this stage, transportation of the most critical chemical material before 31 December is unlikely."[260]

Deadline of 5 February 2014

On 30 January 2014, less than a week before the deadline for removing priority 2 chemicals, the Executive Council held its thirty-eighth meeting. The Director-General mentioned that "[i]n less than a week, the date set for the removal of all other chemicals will also elapse."[261] The US, the UK, Greece on behalf of the EU, and Ireland also alluded to the 5 February 2014 completion date and the possible failure of Syria to meet it.[262] The Executive Council appeared not to reach consensus on any collective response, while the Director-General requested that Syria revise the deadlines, as discussed hereinafter.

(iii) **Destruction of Chemical Weapons**

[258] OPCW Doc. EC-M-36/DG.5, 17 December 2013, p. 3.

[259] OPCW Doc. EC-M-37/DG.1, 23 December 2013, para. 22.

[260] UN News, 28 December 2013, https://news.un.org/en/story/2013/12/458842-deadline-removing-syrias-chemical-weapons-will-not-be-met-says-opcw-un-mission, accessed 22 April 2023.

[261] OPCW Doc. EC-M-38/DG.2, 30 January 2014, p. 1.

[262] OPCW Doc. EC-M-38/NAT.4 (US), 30 January 2014, p. 1; OPCW Doc. EC-M-38/NAT.5 (UK), 30 January 2014, p. 1; OPCW Doc. EC-M-38/NAT.6 (Greece on behalf of the EU), 30 January 2014, p. 1; OPCW Doc. EC-M-38/NAT.7 (Ireland), 30 January 2014, p. 1.

Deadline of 1 March 2014 for Destruction in Syria

By 22 February 2014, destruction had been verified of 93% of the declared quantity of isopropanol and 87% of containers previously containing mustard agent.[263] While it was likely that the 1 March 2014 deadline for their complete destruction would also be missed, apparently there was no consideration of possible non-compliance beforehand.

Deadline of 31 March 2014 for Destruction Outside Syria

The delay in removing chemicals from Syria made it impossible even to commence their destruction. The Director-General's monthly report dated 27 March 2014 indicated that "the target date of 31 March 2014 for the effective destruction of Priority 1 chemicals…will not be met."[264] As with the 1 March 2014 deadline, however, apparently no discussion on possible non-compliance took place beforehand. It may have appeared premature to deliberate thereon at this time, given the paramount importance of said complete removal.

Deadline of 30 June 2014 for Destruction Outside Syria

The deadline of 30 June 2014 for eliminating the Syrian chemical weapons program was of greater significance. Several States Parties referred in February 2014 to the possibility of missing this deadline in light of the slow progress in removing the chemicals from Syria. Switzerland mentioned then that "the target date of 30 June 2014 might be missed."[265] Turkey indicated that "[d]espite the optimism expressed by the United Nations, in view of the unwillingness of the regime, the 30 June deadline for the complete destruction could hardly be met."[266] The UK, the EU, Denmark, Norway, and the Netherlands expressed like sentiments.[267] At its forty-first meeting on 22 May 2013, the Executive Council called on Syria "to undertake all possible efforts to complete the speedy removal of the remaining chemicals."[268] At the Executive Council forty-second meeting on 17 June 2013, the US stressed that it expected the Executive Council at the next regular session in early July to review objectively the implementation and fulfillment by Syria of its obligations based on what had been accomplished and what had not and to decide how to deal with the factual situation.[269] The Executive Council adopted a decision on "Destruction of

[263] OPCW Doc. EC-75/DG.6, 25 February 2014, para. 9.

[264] OPCW Doc. EC-M-40/DG.1/Rev.1, 27 March 2014, para. 4(b).

[265] OPCW Doc. EC-M-39/NAT.4 (Switzerland), 21 February 2014, p. 1.

[266] OPCW Doc. EC-M-39/NAT.6 (Turkey), 21 February 2014, p. 1.

[267] OPCW Doc. EC-M-40/NAT.7 (UK), 11 April 2014, p. 1; OPCW Doc. EC-M-40/NAT.13 (UK), 29 April 2014, p. 1; OPCW Doc. EC-M-40/NAT.21 (Greece on behalf of the EU), 8 May 2014, p. 1; OPCW Doc. EC-M-41/NAT.7 (Greece on behalf of the EU), 22 May 2014, p. 1; OPCW Doc. EC-M-41/NAT.6 (Denmark and Norway), 22 May 2014, p. 1; OPCW Doc. EC-M-41/NAT.3 (UK), 22 May 2014, p. 2; OPCW Doc. EC-M-42/NAT.1 (Greece on behalf of the EU), 17 June 2014, p. 1; OPCW Doc. EC-M-42/NAT.11 (Netherlands), 17 June 2014, p. 1.

[268] OPCW Doc. EC-M-41/2, 22 May 2013, para. 3.1.

[269] OPCW Doc. EC-M-42/NAT.12 (US), 17 June 2014, p. 1.

Chemical Weapons" by consensus, in which the Director-General was requested (a) to provide an overall report on the elimination of the Syrian chemical weapons program, including whether the elimination of all chemical weapons material and equipment was completed in the first half of 2014; (b) to specify requirements that remain to be implemented by Syria; and (c) to provide recommendations for consideration.[270] This is another indication of the OPCW policy-making organs' reliance on the information that the Secretariat would provide in addressing State Party non-compliance.

(iv) **Destruction of Chemical Weapons Production Facilities**

With the 15 March 2014 deadline for complete destruction of Syrian chemical weapons production facilities approaching, the US made two proposals on 21 February 2014, at the thirty-ninth Executive Council meeting. The first proposal required Syria to collapse the roofs of the aforementioned seven hardened aircraft shelters by the 15 March 2014 deadline, which the US believed would meet the CWC's requirements for such physical destruction. The second proposal allowed extending the deadline for destroying the five aforementioned underground structures, enabling Syria to explore measures to overcome the technical challenges these facilities posed.[271] The Executive Council appeared to have reached no consensus, however. At its seventy-fifth session on 7 March 2014, the Executive Council requested that Syria submit a revised detailed plan for destroying these chemical weapons production facilities to the Technical Secretariat, which would develop and submit combined plans for destruction and verification to the Executive Council.[272]

(v) **Reporting and Cooperation**

Syria continued to submit its monthly reports to the OPCW Executive Council in accordance with Decision EC-M-34/DEC.1.[273] At its seventy-sixth session in July

[270] OPCW Doc. EC-M-42/DEC.1, 17 June 2014, operative para. Apparently the Executive Council did not insist on its measure in Decision EC-M-34/DEC.1 in which it decided that, "with respect to the destruction of chemical weapons removed from the territory of the Syrian Arab Republic, if the Director-General, in close consultation with a State Party hosting a destruction facility and relevant States Parties providing assistance with transport or destruction, determines that it will not be possible to ensure the destruction of chemicals according to a date..., he should immediately notify the Council, specifying the circumstances, and propose an alternative date for its consideration and approval, with a view to completing destruction as soon as possible" (OPCW Doc. EC-M-34/DEC.1, 15 November 2013, operative para. 11). The Director-General did not take specific actions in this regard.

[271] Statement to the Thirty-Ninth Meeting of the Executive Council, Robert P. Mikulak, U.S. Permanent Representative to the Organization for the Prohibition of Chemical Weapons, The Hague, Netherlands, 21 February 2014, https://2009-2017.state.gov/t/avc/rls/2014/221891.htm, accessed 22 April 2023. See also OPCW Doc. EC-75/NAT.6 (US), 4 March 2014, pp. 2–3.

[272] OPCW Doc. EC-75/2, 7 March 2013, para. 7.13.

[273] See OPCW Doc. EC-M-44/DG.1, 25 July 2014, para. 4(d); OPCW Doc. EC-M-44/DG.2, 25 August 2014, para. 4(c); OPCW Doc. EC-77/DG.22, 24 September 2014, para. 4(d); OPCW Doc. EC-M-46/DG.1, 23 October 2014, para. 4(d); OPCW Doc. EC-78/DG.3, 24 November 2014, para. 4(c); UN Doc. S/2014/948, 26 December 2014, Annex, para. 4(b); UN Doc. S/2015/56, 26 January

2014, the Executive Council urged Syria and the Technical Secretariat "to continue to cooperate…on outstanding issues regarding Syria's declaration, with a view to the soonest resolution of questions raised by the [Technical] Secretariat to further the declaration's accuracy and completeness."[274] It also called upon Syria "to cooperate fully with the Director-General's engagement as well as in the continuing activities of the Secretariat's Declaration Assessment Team" at its eighty-first session in March 2016.[275] According to the Director-General's monthly reports, the Secretariat and the Syrian authorities were cooperating between September 2014 and April 2016 on outstanding issues regarding the Syrian initial declaration,[276] The same reports also acknowledged the Syrian authorities' cooperation through August 2016.[277]

2015, Annex, para. 4(b); OPCW Doc. EC-78/DG.9, 23 February 2015, para. 5(b); OPCW Doc. EC-79/DG.1, 23 March 2015, para. 5(b); OPCW Doc. EC-M-49/DG.1, 23 April 2015, para. 5(b); OPCW Doc. EC-79/DG.8, 22 May 2015, para. 5(b); OPCW Doc. EC-79/DG.15, 23 June 2015, para. 5(b); OPCW Doc. EC-80/DG.2, 23 July 2015, para. 5(b); OPCW Doc. EC-80/DG.4, 24 August 2015, para. 5(b); OPCW Doc. EC-80/DG.20, 23 September 2015, para. 5(b); OPCW Doc. EC-81/DG.1, 22 October 2015, para. 5(b); OPCW Doc. EC-81/DG.2, 24 November 2015, para. 5(b); OPCW Doc. EC-81/DG.3, 22 December 2015, para. 5(b); OPCW Doc. EC-81/DG.5, 25 January 2016, para. 5(b); OPCW Doc. EC-81/DG.11, 24 February 2016, para. 5(b); OPCW Doc. EC-82/DG.1, 24 March 2016, para. 5(b); OPCW Doc. EC-82/DG.5, 22 April 2016, para. 5(b); OPCW Doc. EC-82/DG.9, 25 May 2016, para. 5(b); UN Doc. S/2016/577, 26 June 2016, Annex, para. 5(b); OPCW Doc. EC-83/DG.2, 22 April 2016, para. 5(b); OPCW Doc. EC-83/DG.6, 22 August 2016, para. 5(b). They were classified.

[274] OPCW Doc. EC-76/6, 11 July 2014, para. 6.17.

[275] OPCW Doc. EC-81/DEC.4, 23 March 2016, operative para. 6.

[276] OPCW Doc. EC-77/DG.22, 24 September 2014, para. 10; OPCW Doc. EC-M-46/DG.1, 23 October 2014, para. 10; OPCW Doc. EC-78/DG.3, 24 November 2014, para. 9; UN Doc. S/2014/948, 26 December 2014, Annex, para. 9; UN Doc. S/2015/56, 26 January 2015, Annex, para. 10; OPCW Doc. EC-78/DG.9, 23 February 2015, para. 10; OPCW Doc. EC-79/DG.1, 23 March 2015, para. 10; OPCW Doc. EC-M-49/DG.1, 23 April 2015, para. 10; OPCW Doc. EC-79/DG.8, 22 May 2015, para. 10; OPCW Doc. EC-79/DG.15, 23 June 2015, para. 10; OPCW Doc. EC-80/DG.2, 23 July 2015, para. 9; OPCW Doc. EC-80/DG.4, 24 August 2015, para. 9; OPCW Doc. EC-80/DG.20, 23 September 201, para. 10; OPCW Doc. EC-81/DG.1, 22 October 2015, para. 9; OPCW Doc. EC-81/DG.2, 24 November 2015, para. 9; OPCW Doc. EC-81/DG.3, 22 December 2015, para. 9; OPCW Doc. EC-81/DG.5, 25 January 2016, para. 9; OPCW Doc. EC-81/DG.11, 24 February 2016, para. 9; OPCW Doc. EC-82/DG.1, 24 March 2016, para. 9; OPCW Doc. EC-82/DG.5, 22 April 2016, para. 8. Some States Parties welcomed or acknowledged the continued cooperation between Syria and the OPCW (OPCW Doc. EC-82/NAT.24 (Iran on behalf of the NAM States Parties to the CWC and China), 12 July 2016, p. 2). Other States Parties called upon Syria to continue or intensify cooperation with the OPCW (OPCW Doc. EC-79/NAT.23 (Switzerland), 7 July 2015, p. 1; OPCW Doc. EC-79/NAT.13 (China), 7 July 2015, p. 2; OPCW Doc. EC-80/NAT.9 (Switzerland), 6 October 2015, p. 1; OPCW Doc. EC-81/NAT.7 (Brazil), 15 March 2016, p. 1; OPCW Doc. EC-81/NAT.15 (Poland), 15 March 2016, p. 1; OPCW Doc. EC-81/NAT.25 (Chile), 15 March 2016, p. 1; OPCW Doc. EC-82/NAT.9 (Pakistan), 12 July 2016, p. 1; OPCW Doc. EC-82/NAT.24 (Iran on behalf of the NAM States Parties to the CWC and China), 12 July 2016, pp. 2–3). Other States Parties pointed out Syrian non-cooperation (OPCW Doc. EC-80/NAT.32 (France), 6 October 2015, p. 2; OPCW Doc. EC-81/NAT.13 (Japan), 16 March 2016, p. 2; OPCW Doc. EC-82/NAT.22 (Slovakia on behalf of the EU), 12 July 2016, p. 2).

[277] OPCW Doc. EC-M-37/DG.1, 23 December 2013, para. 5(d); OPCW Doc. EC-M-38/DG.1, 23 January 2014, para. 4(e); OPCW Doc. EC-75/DG.6, 25 February 2014, para. 5; OPCW Doc. EC-M-40/DG.1/Rev.1, 27 March 2014, para. 4(f); OPCW Doc. EC-M-40/DG.4, 25 April 2014, para. 4(f);

(3) Evaluation

(a) Possible References

As described above, the OPCW policy-making organs have encountered potential Syrian non-compliance twice. The first was with its obligation to submit full and complete declarations, while the other was with its obligation to meet deadlines for actions including removing chemical weapons from its territory and destroying chemical weapons and chemical weapons production facilities within its borders. The OPCW policy-making organs had no experience in putting the first instance on its agenda, although the US criticized Iran at the CWC First Review Conference in April 2003 for stockpiling blister, blood, and chocking agents, and making nerve agents.[278] By contrast, the OPCW policy-making organs confronted three prior situations where possessor States Parties missed chemical disarmament deadlines. The first was the 29 April 2003 deadline for converting chemical weapons production facilities, where ten of sixteen Russian facilities were not converted in time.[279] As discussed hereinafter, the OPCW policy-making organs did not act until after the deadline had passed. The second was the 29 April 2007 deadline for destroying of chemical weapons production facilities, where one in India, two in Libya, and one in Russia were not destroyed in time.[280] In this instance, the OPCW policy-making organs took no action at all. The third was the 29 April 2012 extended final deadline for the destruction of chemical weapons, which Libya, Russia, and the US missed. In response, the OPCW Conference of the States Parties adopted several *ex ante* measures at its sixteenth

---

OPCW Doc. EC-M-42/DG.1. 23 May 2014, para. 4(d); OPCW Doc. EC-76/DG.14, 25 June 2014, para. 4(d); OPCW Doc. EC-M-44/DG.1, 25 July 2014, para. 4(e); OPCW Doc. EC-M-44/DG.2, 25 August 2014, para. 4(d); OPCW Doc. EC-77/DG.22, 24 September 2014, para. 4(e); OPCW Doc. EC-M-46/DG.1, 23 October 2014, para. 4(e); OPCW Doc. EC-78/DG.3, 24 November 2014, para. 4(d); UN Doc. S/2014/948, 26 December 2014, Annex, para. 4(c); UN Doc. S/2015/56, 26 January 2015, Annex, para. 4(c); OPCW Doc. EC-78/DG.9, 23 February 2015, para. 5(c); OPCW Doc. EC-79/DG.1, 23 March 2015, para. 5(c); OPCW Doc. EC-M-49/DG.1, 23 April 2015, para. 5(c); OPCW Doc. EC-79/DG.8, 22 May 2015, para. 5(c); OPCW Doc. EC-79/DG.15, 23 June 2015, para. 5(c); OPCW Doc. EC-80/DG.2, 23 July 2015, para. 5(c); OPCW Doc. EC-80/DG.4, 24 August 2015, para. 5(c); OPCW Doc. EC-80/DG.20, 23 September 2015, para. 5(c); OPCW Doc. EC-81/DG.1, 22 October 2015, para. 5(c); OPCW Doc. EC-81/DG.2, 24 November 2015, para. 5(c); OPCW Doc. EC-81/DG.3, 22 December 2015, para. 5(c); OPCW Doc. EC-81/DG.5, 25 January 2016, para. 5(c); OPCW Doc. EC-81/DG.11, 24 February 2016, para. 5(c); OPCW Doc. EC-82/DG.1, 24 March 2016, para. 5(c); OPCW Doc. EC-82/DG.5, 22 April 2016, para. 5(c); OPCW Doc. EC-82/DG.9, 25 May 2016, para. 5(c); UN Doc. S/2016/577, 26 June 2016, Annex, para. 5(c); OPCW Doc. EC-83/DG.2, 22 April 2016, para. 5(c); OPCW Doc. EC-83/DG.6, 22 August 2016, para. 5(c).

[278] Stephen G. Rademaker, Assistant Secretary of State for Arms Control, Head of U.S. delegation, Statement to the Conference, The Hague, The Netherlands, 28 April 2003, https://2001-2009.state.gov/t/isn/rls/rm/20099.htm, accessed 22 April 2023. The US Department of State publishes a Compliance Report, in which it designates non-compliant States Parties who are in non-compliance, https://www.state.gov/adherence-to-and-compliance-with-arms-control-nonproliferation-and-disarmament-agreements-and-commitments/, accessed 22 April 2023.

[279] OPCW Doc. C-9/5, 30 November 2004, p. 6, para. 1.21.

[280] OPCW Doc. S/784/2009, 7 August 2009, p. 9, para. 4.2.

session in December 2011, including requiring further reporting by possessor States Parties after the deadline.[281] All of which demonstrates that the OPCW may exercise discretion in its responses to given deadlines being missed.

(b) **Effectiveness**

The OPCW policy-making organs have approached two situations of potential non-compliance in different manners in light of different types of obligation.

As described above, the OPCW Executive Council had an *ex ante* option to avoid non-compliance before deadlines were missed. Implementation made it clear that it was only a matter of time until Syria missed its deadlines. While there might be insufficient time to decide, it would still be possible to preemptively extend these deadlines and thereby avoid non-compliance. The Executive Council instead let time elapse, however, resulting in non-compliance. Possible reasons include the following. First, there might be no incentive to extend the deadlines. With the armed conflict ongoing and security concerns unresolved, it would be unclear whether Syria was able to meet revised deadlines any more than the initial ones. Second, while missing deadlines is legally unacceptable, it might be politically acceptable. Syria's core obligation to eliminate its chemical weapons program is the obligation of result or more precisely, of completion. Non-compliance with the obligation to meet deadlines would be redressed only when the relevant tasks are completed, which would only be a matter of time, practically speaking. If the Executive Council did not consider missing deadlines a threat to the CWC and the Resolution 2118 Regime, then inaction would be pragmatic. What matters is complete resolution irrespective of scheduling, rather than temporary measures for avoiding non-compliance. The Executive Council would still be able to extend the deadline after it had passed in any event. Third, the "first half of 2014" deadline for Syria's complete destruction of its chemical weapons became practically meaningless when the Executive Council decided to remove priority 1 and 2 chemicals from Syrian territory for destruction abroad. While the Executive Council originally intended to consider and approve "an alternative date" to be proposed by the Director-General, apparently it did not insist on this approach when the deadline was approaching. No State Party raised the missed deadline for the destruction of chemical weapons which had been removed from Syria. Thus, it never made it on to the policy-making organs' agenda.

By contrast, the OPCW made efforts to address Syria's potential non-compliance with the full and complete declaration obligation. The problem is that Syria and the Technical Secretariat have different views on declaration. While Syria insisted that its declaration was full and complete, the Technical Secretariat expressed doubt. The situation is unclear and thus in the middle of compliance and non-compliance. In order to clarify the status of implementation of this obligation, the CWC is equipped with the challenge inspection (Article IX and Verification Annex Part X), and the Resolution 2118 Regime introduces the more powerful "section 2(d)" inspection procedure. Syria is obliged to allow OPCW inspection teams access anywhere in its territory

[281] OPCW Doc. C-16/DEC.11, 1 December 2006.

on short notice. Instead of invoking these procedures, however, the OPCW Director-General dispatched the DAT to Syria, per its agreement to address the unresolved Syrian declaration issues. The DAT worked intensively in Syria on the latter's unresolved declaration issues, including meeting with Syrian authorities, visiting chemical weapons related facilities, and collecting samples and other data. It compiled its work and evaluations in reports that it submitted to the Executive Council, which took *ex ante* measures against Syria based on same. The measures the Executive Council took at this stage of potential non-compliance were non-confrontational, in the sense that it called on Syria to submit full and complete declarations. In other words, the OPCW attempted to avoid non-compliance, which would likely require *ex post* confrontational measures, instead giving Syria time to act. It thus relied on Syria's cooperation, and Syria had cooperated with the Technical Secretariat in accepting the DAT's visits. Contrary to the potential non-compliance with the obligation to meet the deadlines, there must be incentive to take *ex ante* measures. The "core" obligation to eliminate the Syrian chemical weapons program is premised on the full and complete declaration. If a portion of chemical weapons remain undeclared, it will become a serious non-compliance with the "core" obligation and poses a significant threat to the CWC and the Resolution 2118 Regime. It is thus important for the Executive Council to induce Syria to submit full and complete declaration. This does not mean that Syria had unlimited time, however. In the event, Syria's consultations with the DAT were unable to bridge the gaps between them, and the Executive Council thus moved to address Syrian non-compliance.

Neither potential non-compliance concerns were resolved, irrespective of how the OPCW responded. Missing deadlines constituted non-compliance. The declaration issue also constituted non-compliance when the OPCW-UN JIM identified the Syrian government as having used chemical weapons, specifically sarin, meaning the Syrian government was concealing chemical weapons, thus failing to submit full and complete declarations. This does not necessarily mean, however, that the Executive Council's *ex ante* measures for addressing potential non-compliance were completely ineffective or meaningless. They drew the policy-making organs' attention to potential Syrian non-compliance with the deadline obligation for their response in the near future, thus giving them the opportunity to prepare. They also helped clarify the full and complete declaration issue, providing the Executive Council with the necessary and sufficient information for treating Syria as being in non-compliance. Between compliance and non-compliance, these *ex ante* measures for addressing potential non-compliance have an intermediate but essential role in managing compliance/non-compliance.

(c) **Implications**

Measures to address potential non-compliance may vary according to types of obligation and the circumstances. There are two options for potential non-compliance with the obligation to meet deadlines: to take actions including the extension of deadlines and to take no action and let the deadline pass. Legally, extending deadlines can avoid a situation of non-compliance with that obligation for a time but future status is unclear, while taking no action will lead to non-compliance. The

State concerned continues to be bound by the obligation for complete destruction of its chemical weapons program in any event. Practically, there is thus almost no difference between two options. The deadline obligation should serve as an accelerator, ensuring compliance with the goal of complete elimination of the said program.

The following implications emerge in terms of potential non-compliance with the obligation to submit full, complete and accurate declarations. Firstly, effective ways to collect relevant information should be explored. As mentioned, the CWC provides the challenge inspection system, which is a useful tool to detect undeclared activities, and the Resolution 2118 Regime introduced the "section 2(d)" inspection, which is more powerful than the challenge inspection as it is not subject to a political filter of the Executive Council. This procedure has the added advantage of obliging Syria to accept an inspection anytime, anywhere. Nonetheless, as mentioned above, it has not been invoked. Possible reasons may be as follows. In the former case, a number of issues arising from ambiguous provisions of the challenge inspection procedure remain unresolved. Some States may be concerned about retaliatory challenge inspection requests. Requesting States Parties run the risk of disclosing their intelligence sources and capabilities. There is also no guarantee that undeclared operations will be detected.[282] Other practical factors are relevant to the Syria situation. Ongoing armed conflict complicates the OPCW inspection team's efforts to follow the rigid timeline specified by the CWC. It also affects Syria's obligation to ensure the inspection team's safety and security during its work. The latter may be affected by a lack of detailed procedures for identification by a State Party and the Director-General consideration. It could also be understood that the Technical Secretariat and Syria are in "the process of consultations and cooperation" (operative para. 2(b) of Executive Council Decision EC-M-33/DEC.1) to clarify and resolve doubts and ambiguities with regard to Syria's initial declaration. This may in fact be a primary reason, considering that the DAT visited Syria several times.[283] In any event, the DAT, rather than these challenge procedures, has played the critical role in collecting information relevant to the declaration matters. It is neither an existing procedure under the CWC nor newly established under the Resolution 2118 Regime. It was introduced on an *ad hoc* basis through the implementation of the mechanisms for addressing potential non-compliance. Its modalities have thus been established through practice. Unlike the challenge procedures, the DAT is a non-confrontational cooperative procedure with some flexibility built in. The Technical Secretariat takes time preparing for DAT visits, negotiating with the Syrian authorities, and dispatches its experts as soon as they reach agreement. Such non-confrontational cooperative procedures may be more acceptable to concerned States than the confrontational challenge procedures.

Secondly, the policy-making organs will be required to move on to the next stage of responding to non-compliance if potential non-compliance remain unresolved. While the mechanisms for addressing potential non-compliance have the advantage

---

[282] Tatsuya Abe, "Challenge inspections under the Chemical Weapons Convention: between ideal and reality," *The Nonproliferation Review*, Vol. 24, Nos. 1–2 (2017), p. 167, pp. 172–176.

[283] *Ibid.*, p. 178.

of avoiding intentional non-compliance, such issues should not remain therewithin long-term. The challenge confronting policy-making organs is finding the right time to do so. Factors to consider include the following. First is the outcome of institutional efforts to address potential non-compliance with the obligation to submit full and complete declaration. If there are tangible improvements, it would be better to await further positive developments. By contrast, if many issues remain unresolved and the list of outstanding issues grows, then waiting may serve no purpose. Second is the concerned State's cooperation, as addressing potential non-compliance requires the State concerned to redress the situation by providing additional explanations, and when necessary, declaring previously undeclared matters. In addition to such substantive cooperation, the concerned State should also cooperate administratively and logistically. Sustained refusals to meet, communicate, or provide facilities could also trigger the decision to treat the concerned State as being in intentional non-compliance.

4.3.3 Responding to Non-compliance

(1) **Background**

The obligation to eliminate chemical weapons program requires a possessor State to act non-reciprocally within its territory. For this type of obligation, a situation of non-compliance will be redressed through its full implementation rather than by traditional remedial measures under the law of State responsibility.

When it comes to a situation of intentional non-compliance with the obligation to submit full and complete declaration, an approach to the State concerned will be hard. For instance, In 2002, the UN Security Council tightened the inspection regime against Iraq partly because Iraq failed to comply with its obligation to submit relevant declarations under Resolution 687.[284] In 2006, the IAEA Board of Governors demanded that Iran take steps because of "Iran's many failures and breaches of its obligations to comply with its NPT Safeguards Agreement," which made it impossible for the IAEA to conclude that there were no undeclared nuclear materials or activities in Iran.[285] While history suggests that it is uncertain whether pressure on concerned States will bring about desired changes in attitude, redressing intentional non-compliance with the obligation to submit full and complete declarations necessitates concerned States' full compliance with same.

By contrast, a cooperative approach would suit non-compliance with the deadline obligation. Deadlines motivate concerned States to fulfill their core obligation and offer international monitoring organs a means to review implementation of same. While deadlines may be missed in the real world, they are often beyond the control of concerned States. Remedies under the law of State responsibility are practically

---

[284] UN Doc. S/RES/1441 (2003), 8 November 2002.

[285] IAEA Doc. GOV/2006/14, 4 February 2006, preamble paras. (f) and (g) and operative paras. 1, 3, 5, and 6. See also UN Doc. S/RES/1696, 31 July 2006, operative paras. 1 and 2.

useless in such instances because the ultimate goal will be achieved only through fulfilling the core obligation to eliminate chemical weapons. The situation will thus be redressed through the provision of technical, financial, personnel, logistical, and other assistance. As long as the State concerned never abandons the aforementioned core obligation, it should be given additional time to complete the work, and such non-compliance would be considered acceptable, as described previously.

(2) **Mechanisms to Respond to Non-Compliance**

(a) **Mandates of International Organizations**

The Resolution 2118 Regime has also functioned as a mechanism for responding to non-compliance with obligations related to eliminating the Syrian chemical weapons program, which differs somewhat from the mechanisms for responding to non-compliance with the obligation against using chemical weapons. While the OPCW Executive Council appears to have the primary role in addressing the former, the OPCW policy-making organs and the UN Security Council respond in tandem, albeit independently, to the latter. The relevant paragraphs endorse this understanding. For instance, the Executive Council will "meet within 24 hours if the Director-General reports delay by the Syrian Arab Republic in meeting the requirements of this decision or the Convention."[286] While UN Security Council Resolution 2118 requested that the OPCW Director-General report non-compliance with Executive Council Decision EC-M-33/DEC.1 to the UN Security Council,[287] it did not single out non-compliance with the obligations related the elimination as a specific case in which the Security Council would impose measures under Chapter VII of the UN Charter.[288] Both Executive Council Decision EC-M-33/DEC.1 and Security Council Resolution 2118 refer to Article VIII, para. 36 of the CWC, on which bases the Executive Council brings particularly urgent non-compliance issues to the UN Security Council.[289]

The distinction derives from the different formulations of substantive obligation. The prohibition against chemical weapons use is stipulated in the CWC and included in UN Security Council Resolution 2118. On the other hand, the obligation to eliminate the Syrian chemical weapons program is established only in Executive

286 OPCW Doc. EC-M-33/DEC.1, 27 September 2013, operative para. 3(b).

287 UN Doc. S/RES/2118 (2013), 27 September 2013, operative para. 12.

288 *Ibid.*, operative para. 21 ("Decides, in the event of non-compliance with this resolution, including unauthorized transfer of chemical weapons, or any use of chemical weapons by anyone in the Syrian Arab Republic, to impose measures under Chapter VII of the United Nations Charter;"). Given that OPCW Executive Council Decision EC-M-33/DEC.1 is annexed in UN Security Council Resolution 2118, the language "non-compliance with this resolution" may be construed as encompassing non-compliance with same. This interpretation does not affect the understanding that the OPCW Executive Council has the primary role in addressing non-compliance with Syria's obligation to eliminate its chemical weapons program.

289 OPCW Doc. EC-M-33/DEC.1, 27 September 2013, preamble para. 13 and operative para. 3(b); UN Doc. S/RES/2118 (2013), 27 September 2013, operative para. 13.

Council Decision EC-M-33/DEC.1. In any event, as there are no additional procedures in Executive Council Decision EC-M-33/DEC.1, except for convening emergency meetings, the OPCW Executive Council thus fulfills its functions in accordance with the relevant provisions of the CWC, including Article VIII, para. 36 thereof.

(b) **Syrian Obligations**

Again, the non-reciprocal nature of the obligations to submit declarations and destroy chemical weapons by specified deadlines makes traditional reparations, such as restitution in kind, compensation, or satisfaction practically useless. Even in a situation of non-compliance, Syria remains obliged to submit full and accurate declarations and destroy its chemical weapons. Full implementation is the only way to redress the situation of non-compliance. Syria is also obliged to submit regular reports to the Executive Council, including steps the Executive Council requires as well as to cooperate with the OPCW and the UN.[290]

(c) **Implementation**

The OPCW policy-making organs have considered non-compliance issues at their regular sessions and, when necessary, in special sessions and other irregular meetings. As also mentioned previously, the Director-General has submitted monthly reports to the Executive Council on the implementation,[291] and either the Director-General or the Technical Secretariat have continued to brief States Parties through at least August 2017.[292] For its part, Syria refuses to implement several measures that the OPCW policy-making organs have called for, as indicated hereinafter.

(i) **Declaration of Chemical Weapons Program**

Logical Implication of Non-Compliance

As discussed, the Executive Council carefully handled the declaration issues, urging Syria to address them in cooperation with the Technical Secretariat. In November 2016, the issue entered a new phase, following the OPCW-UN JIM reports of 24 August and 21 October 2016 in which it identified the Syrian government as the perpetrator of chemical attacks,[293] clearly confirming Syria's non-compliance with the

---

[290] Article VII, para. 7 of the Chemical Weapons Convention; UN Doc. S/RES/2118 (2013), 27 September 2013, operative para. 7.

[291] See Appendix A.

[292] Cf. footnote 200. OPCW Doc. EC-83/DG.18, 26 September 2016, para. 9; OPCW Doc. EC-84/DG.1, 25 October 2016, para. 11; OPCW Doc. EC-84/DG.4, 23 November 2016, para. 12; OPCW Doc. EC-84/DG.6, 22 December 2016, para. 11; OPCW Doc. EC-84/DG.11, 24 January 2017, para. 12; OPCW Doc. EC-84/DG.22, 23 February 2017, para. 12; OPCW Doc. EC-85/DG.2, 23 March 2017, para. 15; OPCW Doc. EC-85/DG.5, 24 April 2017, para. 11; OPCW Doc. EC-85/DG.11, 24 May 2017, para. 11; OPCW Doc. EC-85/DG.21, 23 June 2017, para. 11; OPCW Doc. EC-86/DG.2, 24 July 2017, para. 10; OPCW Doc. EC-86/DG.7, 23 August 2017, para. 11.

[293] UN Doc. S/2016/738/Rev.1, 24 August 2016, paras. 54 and 56; UN Doc. S/2016/888, 21 October 2016, para. 19. The OPCW-UN JIM also identified ISIL as perpetrating the chemical attack on Marea of 21 August 2015 (UN Doc. S/2016/738/Rev.1, 24 August 2016, para. 41).

obligation against chemical weapons use and logically indicating its additional non-compliance with the obligation to submit complete and accurate chemical weapons declarations. Having found a link between these issues,[294] which had thus far been treated separately, the international community was compelled to explore responses to both in tandem.

OPCW Executive Council Decision EC-83/DEC.5

In October 2016, the Executive Council held its eighty-third session. The US, Russia, and Spain tabled draft decisions on Syria's non-compliance, in response to the aforementioned findings of the OPCW-UN JIM. Of these, the US draft decision condemned Syria's use of chemical weapons and expressed grave concern at its failure to declare and destroy its chemical weapons program. It also introduced additional verifications for the declaration and destruction of all chlorine stocks, any other stocks of toxic chemicals, associated munitions, and the equipment and facilities used to produce these weapons.[295] This draft decision received support from several States Parties and the EU,[296] however, Russia rejected it and maintained its own opposing draft.[297] During negotiations, the US and Russia revised their original drafts, only to withdraw them both in the end,[298] leaving only the Spanish draft for deliberation.

On 11 November 2016, at its reconvened eighty-third session, the Executive Council adopted the Spanish draft, resulting in Decision EC-83/DEC.5, by a vote of

[294] OPCW Doc. EC-83/NAT.5 (US), 11 October 2016, p. 2; OPCW Doc. EC-83/NAT.14 (UK), 12 October 2016, p. 2. See also OPCW Doc. C-SS-4/DEC.3, 27 June 2018, operative para. 7; OPCW Doc. EC-94/DEC.2, 9 July 2020, operative para. 2; OPCW Doc. C-25/DEC.9, 21 April 2021, operative para. 4.

[295] OPCW Doc. EC-83/NAT.5 (US), 11 October 2016, p. 3.

[296] OPCW Doc. EC-83/NAT.6 (Australia), 11 October 2016, p. 2; OPCW Doc. EC-83/NAT.8 (Germany), 11 October 2016, p. 2; OPCW Doc. EC-83/NAT.9 (Slovakia on behalf of the EU), 11 October 2016, p. 1; OPCW Doc. EC-83/NAT.11 (Japan), 11 October 2016, p. 1; OPCW Doc. EC-83/NAT.12 (New Zealand), 11 October 2016, p. 1; OPCW Doc. EC-83/NAT.13 (Canada), 11 October 2016, p. 2; OPCW Doc. EC-83/NAT.14 (UK), 12 October 2016, p. 3; OPCW Doc. EC-83/NAT.30 (France), 11 October 2016, p. 2.

[297] OPCW Doc. EC-83/NAT.19 (Russia), 11 November 2016, p. 1. The Russian draft decision included the controversial element of "internal national investigation." Canada objected, pointing out that the Russian draft "ignores the fact that the JIM has already found Syrian government forces responsible for two chemical weapons attacks" (OPCW Doc. EC-83/NAT.13 (Canada), 11 October 2016, p. 2).

[298] OPCW Doc. EC-83/5, 11 November 2016, paras. 6.22, 6.23, 6.25, and 6.26. The NAM CWC States Parties and China maintained their position from the previous session, encouraging both Syria and the OPCW to "continue cooperation" (OPCW Doc. EC-83/NAT.31 (Venezuela on behalf of the Member States of the Non-Aligned Movement that are Parties to the Chemical Weapons Convention and China), 11 October 2016, p. 3).

28 in favor to four against, with nine abstentions.[299] It included several measures in response to Syria's non-compliance with its obligation on declarations:

- It expressed grave concern that, as reported by the Director-General,[300] the Technical Secretariat is not able to resolve outstanding issues and thus cannot verify the accuracy and completeness of Syrian declarations and demanded that Syria comply fully with its obligations under the Chemical Weapons Convention, Decision EC-M-33/DEC.1, and Resolution 2118, including the expeditious resolution of all outstanding issues regarding its initial declaration and related disclosures.[301]
- It also decided that the Technical Secretariat shall conduct two types of inspections. The first type will be conducted at those sites identified by the OPCW-UN JIM in its third and fourth reports as soon as security conditions permit.[302] The second type will be carried out at the SSRC facilities in Barzah and Jamrayah twice a year until the Council decides to cease them.[303] In this context, the OPCW Executive Council decided that the Syrian Arab Republic shall "facilitate promptly, and fully cooperate with, these inspections."[304]
- In addition, the Executive Council tasked the Director-General with informing it and the UN Security Council through the UN Secretary-General about the implementation of this decision as well as reporting to it "any unresolved doubts, ambiguities or uncertainties" regarding the compliance of Syria with the Chemical Weapons Convention in accordance with Article VIII, para. 40.[305]

---

[299] OPCW Doc. EC-83/DEC.5, 11 November 2016. The vote was 28 in favor (Argentina, Australia, Belgium, Brazil, Cameroon, Chile, France, Germany, Guatemala, Italy, Japan, Latvia, Libya, Mexico, Morocco, Panama, Peru, Poland, Republic of Korea, Saudi Arabia, Senegal, Slovakia, Spain, Sweden, Switzerland, UK, US, and Viet Nam) to four against (China, Iran, Russia, and Sudan), with nine abstentions (Algeria, Armenia, Bangladesh, Ghana, India, Iraq, Kenya, Pakistan, and South Africa) (OPCW Doc. EC-83/5, 11 November 2016, para. 6.27).

[300] OPCW Doc. EC-82/DG.18, 6 July 2016.

[301] OPCW Doc. EC-83/DEC.5, 11 November 2016, operative para. 6. The outstanding issues were enumerated as (a) the role of the SSRC in the Syrian Chemical Weapons Programme, (b) the results of the analyses of samples collected at multiple locations in Syria, (c) other chemical weapons-related activities that were undertaken prior to Syria's accession to the CWC (OPCW Doc. EC-84/DG.4, 23 November 2016, para. 10).

[302] *Ibid.*, operative para. 10.

[303] *Ibid.*, operative para. 11.

[304] *Ibid.*, operative para. 11.

[305] *Ibid.*, operative para. 12. At the OPCW Executive Council's eighty-fifth session, the UK mentioned that "[w]e were grateful to receive report EC-85/DG.25 provided for this session under Article 8 paragraph 40 of the Convention, on the work of the Declaration Assessment Team (DAT)" (OPCW Doc. EC-85/NAT.23 (UK), 12 July 2017, p. 1). The OPCW Technical Secretariat submitted the following Director-General's Note to the Executive Council at its ninety-first session: Outcome of Consultations with the Syrian Arab Republic regarding its Chemical Weapons Declaration, which opened by cited the preceding operative para. 12 (OPCW Doc. EC-91/DG.23, 5 July 2019, para. 1). The policy-making organs' decisions also recalled Article VIII, para. 40 in their preambles (OPCW Doc. C-SS-4/DEC.3, 27 June 2018, preamble para. 8; OPCW Doc. EC-94/DEC.2, 9 July 2020, preamble para. 12; OPCW Doc. C-25/DEC.9, 21 April 2021, preamble para. 17).

- It also called upon States Parties to provide information on "any discrepancies in the declaration or related submissions of the Syrian Arab republic" to the Director-General.[306]

This was the first OPCW Executive Council decision to name Syria and implicitly criticize it for its non-compliance with the obligation on declarations, as indicated by the explicit reference to Article VIII, para. 40, and to task the Technical Secretariat to conduct particular inspections. And as the new inspections scheme obliged Syria to cooperate with the Technical Secretariat, this decision should be understood as sanctions against Syria over said non-compliance. Russia argued that demands to conduct inspections contradicted CWC provisions stipulating challenge inspections for such situations, and that the Syrian armed conflict represented "an unprecedented threat to the lives and health of Technical Secretariat staff."[307] While any State Party could indeed request a challenge inspection of the abovementioned Syria's facilities, the new inspections scheme would not undermine the challenge inspection provision for the following reasons. First, the former is more flexible in terms of procedures than the latter, including an innovative multiple inspections concept. As with the OPCW FFM, it is important that the Technical Secretariat have a degree of flexibility in conducting on-site investigations in Syria, given the aforementioned conflict. Second, Decision EC-83/DEC.5 was adopted with a greater than two-thirds vote in favor, sufficient to enable any requested challenge inspection. Third, as mentioned elsewhere, the Resolution 2118 Regime obliges Syria to provide OPCW and UN personnel unfettered access,[308] thereby obliging Syria to receive this new inspection scheme by extension.

Draft UN Security Council Resolution

The UN Security Council likewise dealt with the incomplete declarations in a wider context of the logical linkage between the use of chemical weapons and the submission of declarations. In February 2017, forty-two co-sponsoring States accordingly tabled a draft resolution,[309] in which the Security Council, recalling the abovementioned OPCW Director-General's report and OPCW Executive Council Decision EC-83/DEC.5,[310] and acting under Chapter VII, especially Article 41,[311] expressed

[306] OPCW Doc. EC-83/DEC.5, 11 November 2016, operative para. 8.

[307] OPCW Doc. EC-83/NAT.19 (Russia), 11 November 2016, p. 2; OPCW Doc. EC-83/NAT.24 (Russia), 11 November 2016, p. 1.

[308] OPCW Doc. EC-M-33/DEC.1, 27 September 2013, operative para. 1(e); UN Security Council Resolution 2118 (2013), 27 September 2013, operative para. 7.

[309] UN Doc. S/2017/172, 28 February 2017. The co-sponsors were Albania, Australia, Austria, Belgium, Bulgaria, Canada, Croatia, Cyprus, Czech Republic, Denmark, Estonia, Finland, France, Germany, Greece, Iceland, Ireland, Israel, Italy, Japan, Latvia, Liechtenstein, Lithuania, Luxembourg, Malta, Montenegro, Netherlands, New Zealand, Norway, Poland, Portugal, Qatar, Romania, Saudi Arabia, Slovakia, Spain, Sweden, Turkey, Ukraine, United Arab Emirates, UK, and US.

[310] *Ibid.*, preamble para. 6. This language indicates that the resolution was based on the OPCW Director-General's findings and a collective decision by the OPCW policy making organ.

[311] *Ibid.*, preamble para. 16. The draft resolution also included the language "[r]eaffirming its determination that the use of chemical weapons anywhere constitutes a threat to international peace

grave concern that, the Technical Secretariat is unable to resolve all issues related to Syria's declaration, and therefore cannot fully verify that Syria has submitted an accurate and complete declaration, called upon Syria to comply fully with all obligations including the expeditious resolution of all outstanding issues regarding its declaration, and decided that Syria declare and place under OPCW supervision and control all chemical weapons within thirty days.[312] It was defeated by Russian and Chinese veto.[313]

---

and security" in preamble para. 15. See also UN Doc. S/RES/2118 (2013), 27 September 2013, operative para. 1.

[312] *Ibid.*, operative paras. 5 and 6. The draft resolution obliged Syria to declare and place the following under OPCW supervision and control:

(a) The chemical name and military designator of any chemical which is not specifically held for purposes not prohibited in accordance with Paragraph 9 of Article II of the CWC, that are located, as of the day of adoption of this resolution, on the facilities of the Syrian Arab Armed Forces;
(b) The specific type of any munitions and devices it holds which are capable of deploying chemical weapons, including those which have been adapted or are intended to be adapted for delivery of chlorine, and including specific quantities or each type that are filled and unfilled; and.
(c) The location of any remaining chemical weapons, chemical weapons storage facilities, chemical weapons production facilities and chemical weapons research and development facilities, including sites where chlorine and associated munitions and devices are stored.

[313] UN Doc. S/PV.7893, 28 February 2017, p. 4. The vote was nine in favor to three against (Bolivia, China and Russia), with three abstentions (Egypt, Ethiopia and Kazakhstan).

Table 4.10 Meetings between the DAT and Syria

Round	Date	Place
Eighteenth[316]	16–18 September 2017	The Hague
Nineteenth[317]	4–8 February 2019	Beirut
Twentieth[318]	8–21 March 2019	The Hague
Twenty-first[319]	10–17 April 2019	Syria
Twenty-second[320]	14–23 October 2019	Syria

Additional Efforts and Implementation of the Decision EC-83/DEC.5

The OPCW Technical Secretariat and Syria made further efforts to address the outstanding issues, exchanging more communications[314] and holding more consultations.[315] The DAT also had five further rounds of meetings with the Syrian authorities, including meeting twice in Syria for the first time in almost three years (Table 4.10).

[314] OPCW Doc. EC-84/DG.6, 22 December 2016, para. 10 (letter from the OPCW Technical Secretariat to Syria dated 6 December 2016); OPCW Doc. EC-85/DG.11, 24 May 2017, para. 8 ("additional documents and information" from Syria to the OPCW Technical Secretariat dated 18 May 2017); OPCW Doc. EC-85/DG.21, 23 June 2017, para. 8 (note verbale from the OPCW Technical Secretariat to Syria dated 1 June 2017); OPCW Doc. EC-87/DG.2, 23 October 2017, para. 9 ("submissions" from Syria to the OPCW Technical Secretariat dated 30 September and 2 October 2017); OPCW Doc. EC-87/DG.4, 24 November 2017, para. 10 ("documents" from Syria to the OPCW Technical Secretariat dated 10 November 2017); OPCW Doc. EC-87/DG.16, 23 February 2018, paras. 9–10 (letter from the OPCW Director-General to the Syrian Deputy Foreign Minister dated 29 January 2018); OPCW Doc. Doc. EC-87/DG.16, 23 February 2018, para. 10 (note verbale from Syria to the OPCW Technical Secretariat dated 19 February 2018); OPCW Doc. EC-88/DG.3, 24 April 2018, paras. 10–11 (letter from the OPCW Director-General to the Syrian Deputy Foreign Minister dated 10 April 2018); OPCW Doc. EC-89/DG.1, 24 July 2018, para. 9 (note verbale from Syria to the OPCW Technical Secretariat dated on 10 July 2018); OPCW Doc. EC-90/DG.1, 23 October 2018, para. 10 (letter from the OPCW Director-General to the Syrian Deputy Foreign Minister dated 28 September 2018); OPCW Doc. EC-94/DG.3, 24 April 2020, paras. 13 and 16 (letter from the OPCW Director-General to the Syrian Deputy Foreign Minister dated 21 April 2020); OPCW Doc. EC-94/DG.12*, 24 June 2020, para 12 (letter from the Syrian Deputy Foreign Minister to the OPCW Director-General dated 16 June 2020); OPCW Doc. EC-95/DG.1, 24 July 2020, para. 12 (letter from the OPCW Director-General to the Syrian Deputy Foreign Minister dated 26 June 2020). See also OPCW Doc. EC-84/DG.11, 24 January 2017, para. 10 (letter from the OPCW Technical Secretariat to Syria dated 17 January 2017); OPCW Doc. EC-93/DG.7, 24 January 2020, para. 10 (note verbale from the OPCW Technical Secretariat to Syria dated 6 January 2020); OPCW Doc. EC-93/DG.7, 24 January 2020, para. 10 (note verbale from Syria received by the OPCW Technical Secretariat on 17 January 2020).

[315] OPCW Doc. EC-87/DG.2, 23 October 2017, para. 8 (consultations at high-level at the OPCW Headquarters from 16 to 18 September 2017); OPCW Doc. EC-90/DG.11, 25 February 2019, para. 9 (consultations between the Technical Secretariat and Syria in Beirut from 4 to 8 February 2019).

[316] OPCW Doc. EC-87/DG.2, 23 October 2017, para. 8.

[317] OPCW Doc. EC-90/DG.11, 25 February 2019, para. 9.

[318] OPCW Doc. EC-91/DG.1, 25 March 2019, para. 10.

[319] OPCW Doc. EC-91/DG.2, 4 May 2019, para. 9.

[320] OPCW Doc. EC-93/DG.1, 23 October 2019, para. 10.

Table 4.11 SSRC Facilities Inspections

Round	Date
First[323]	26 February–5 March 2017
Second[324]	14–21 November 2017
Third[325]	6–11 November 2018
Fourth[326]	6–14 December 2018
Fifth[327]	5–13 July 2019
Sixth[328]	6–11 November 2019

While Syria provided additional information several times,[321] little changed as a consequence. In its reports and notes to the Executive Council, the Director-General concluded that the Technical Secretariat was still unable to fully verify that the Syrian Arab Republic had submitted a declaration that could be considered accurate and complete in accordance with the CWC and Executive Council decision EC-M-33/DEC.1.[322]

The Technical Secretariat conducted six rounds of inspections at two SSRC facilities per the specific inspections mandate under operative para. 11 of Decision EC-83/DEC.5 (Table 4.11), but it refrained the conduct of inspections under operative para 10 of said Decision because it continued to "monitor the security situation" or "assess conditions."[329]

[321] OPCW Doc. EC-85/DG.11, 24 May 2017, para. 8; OPCW Doc. EC-87/DG.2, 23 October 2017, para. 9; OPCW Doc. EC-87/DG.4, 24 November 2017, para. 10.

[322] OPCW Doc. EC-88/DG.1, 23 March 2018, para. 9; OPCW Doc. EC-89/DG.1, 24 July 2018, para. 10; OPCW Doc. EC-90/DG.1, 23 October 2018, para. 11; OPCW Doc. EC-90/DG.2, 23 November 2018, para. 9; OPCW Doc. EC-90/DG.4, 21 December 2018, para. 9; OPCW Doc. EC-90/DG.7, 24 January 2019, para. 9; OPCW Doc. EC-90/DG.11, 25 February 2019, para. 10; OPCW Doc. EC-91/DG.1, 25 March 2019, para. 11; OPCW Doc. EC-93/DG.1, 23 October 2019, para. 9.

[323] OPCW Doc. EC-85/DG.2, 23 March 2017, para. 12.

[324] OPCW Doc. EC-87/DG.4, 24 November 2017, para. 1.

[325] OPCW Doc. EC-90/DG.2, 23 November 2018, para. 10.

[326] OPCW Doc. EC-90/DG.4, 21 December 2018, para. 10.

[327] OPCW Doc. EC-92/DG.1, 24 July 2019, para. 14.

[328] OPCW Doc. EC-93/DG.3, 25 November 2019, para. 10.

[329] OPCW Doc. EC-85/DG.2, 23 March 2017, para. 13; OPCW Doc. EC-88/DG.16, 22 June 2018, para. 9; OPCW Doc. EC-89/DG.1, 24 July 2018, para. 11; OPCW Doc. EC-89/DG.10, 24 August 2018, para. 10; OPCW Doc. EC-89/DG.24, 24 September 2018, para. 10; OPCW Doc. EC-90/DG.1, 23 October 2018, para. 12; OPCW Doc. EC-90/DG.2, 23 November 2018, para. 10; OPCW Doc. EC-90/DG.4, 21 December 2018, para. 10; OPCW Doc. EC-90/DG.7, 24 January 2019, para. 10; OPCW Doc. EC-90/DG.11, 25 February 2019, para. 11; OPCW Doc. EC-91/DG.1, 25 March 2019, para. 12; OPCW Doc. EC-91/DG.2, 4 May 2019, para. 11; OPCW Doc. EC-91/DG.7, 24 May 2019, para. 11; OPCW Doc. EC-91/DG.14, 24 June 2019, para. 12; OPCW Doc. EC-92/DG.1, 24 July 2019, para. 11; OPCW Doc. EC-92/DG.6, 23 August 2019, para. 11; OPCW Doc. EC-92/DG.22, 24 September 2019, para. 12; OPCW Doc. EC-93/DG.1, 23 October 2019, para. 11; OPCW Doc. EC-93/DG.3, 25 November 2019, para. 10; OPCW Doc. EC-93/DG.5, 24 December 2019, para. 10; OPCW Doc. EC-93/DG.7, 24 January 2020, para. 11; OPCW Doc. EC-93/DG.12, 24 February 2020, para. 11; OPCW Doc. EC-94/DG.1, 24 March 2020, para. 13; OPCW Doc. EC-94/DG.3, 24 April 2020, para. 14; OPCW Doc. EC-94/DG.5, 25 May 2020, para. 13.

The inspection team did not find any substances or activities inconsistent with the Syria's obligations under the CWC[330] except at the third round when a Scheduled chemical, 2B04 ethyl ethylphosphonate, was detected in samples taken at the Barzah SSRC facilities.[331] The issue remained unresolved despite the communications between the Syrian authorities and the Technical Secretariat.[332]

One faction of State Parties, led by the US and the EU, continued criticizing the incomplete declaration issue,[333] pointing out Syria's lack of cooperation on the

---

[330] OPCW Doc. EC-85/DG.16, 2 June 2017, para. 10; OPCW Doc. EC-88/DG.1, 23 March 2018, para. 11; OPCW Doc. EC-91/DG.14, 24 June 2019, para. 13; OPCW Doc. EC-93/DG.5, 23 December 2019, para. 10; OPCW Doc. EC-94/DG.12*, 24 June 2020, para. 13.

[331] OPCW Doc. EC-91/DG.14, 24 June 2019, para. 13.

[332] OPCW Doc. EC-92/DG.1, 24 July 2019, para. 13; OPCW Doc. EC-93/DG.3, 25 November 2019, para. 11 (note verbale from Syria to the OPCW Technical Secretariat dated 7 November 2019); OPCW Doc. EC-94/DG.1, 24 March 2020, para. 14 (note verbale from the OPCW Technical Secretariat to Syria dated 20 February 2020); OPCW Doc. EC-94/DG.1, 24 March 2020, para. 14 (note verbale from Syria to the OPCW Technical Secretariat dated 12 March 2020); OPCW Doc. EC-94/DG.5, 25 May 2020, para 14 (note verbale from Syria to the OPCW Technical Secretariat dated 20 May 2020); OPCW Doc. EC-94/DG.12*, 24 June 2020, para 14 (note verbale from the OPCW Technical Secretariat to Syria dated 19 June 2020).

[333] OPCW Doc. EC-84/NAT.9 (UK), 7 March 2017, pp. 1–2; OPCW Doc. EC-84/NAT.10 (Malta on behalf of the EU), 7 March 2017, pp. 2–3; OPCW Doc. EC-84/NAT.11 (New Zealand), 7 March 2017, p. 1; OPCW Doc. EC-84/NAT.12 (Germany), 7 March 2017, p. 2; OPCW Doc. EC-84/NAT.17 (Japan), 7 March 2017, p. 2; OPCW Doc. EC-84/NAT.24 (Turkey), 7 March 2017, p. 2; OPCW Doc. EC-84/NAT.29 (Switzerland), 7 March 2017, p. 1; OPCW Doc. EC-84/NAT.33 (Chile), 7 March 2017, p. 2; OPCW Doc. EC-M-54/NAT.2 (Norway), 13 April 2017, p. 1; OPCW Doc. EC-M-54/NAT.11 (France), 13 April 2017, p. 2; OPCW Doc. EC-M-54/NAT.18 (UK), 13 April 2017, p. 2; OPCW Doc. EC-M-54/NAT.19 (Portugal), 13 April 2017, p. 1; OPCW Doc. EC-M-55/NAT.2 (US), 5 July 2017, p. 2; OPCW Doc. EC-M-55/NAT.3 (Turkey), 5 July 2017, p. 2; OPCW Doc. EC-M-55/NAT.4 (UK), 5 July 2017, p. 2; OPCW Doc. EC-M-55/NAT.8 (Netherlands), 5 July 2017, p. 1; OPCW Doc. EC-M-55/NAT.11 (Belgium), 5 July 2017, p. 2; OPCW Doc. EC-M-55/NAT.17 (Portugal), 5 July 2017, p. 1; OPCW Doc. EC-85/NAT.7 (Estonia on behalf of the EU), 11 July 2017, p. 2; OPCW Doc. EC-85/NAT.9 (Sweden), 11 July 2017, p. 1; OPCW Doc. EC-85/NAT.14 (UK), 11 July 2017, pp. 1–2; OPCW Doc. EC-85/NAT.15 (Canada), 11 July 2017, pp. 1–2; OPCW Doc. EC-85/NAT.18 (Australia), 11 July 2017, p. 2; OPCW Doc. EC-85/NAT.19 (Italy), 11 July 2017, p. 2; OPCW Doc. EC-85/NAT.29 (Japan), 11 July 2017, p. 2; OPCW Doc. EC-85/NAT.30 (Switzerland), 11 July 2017, p. 1; OPCW Doc. EC-85/NAT.31 (Netherlands), 11 July 2017, pp. 1–2; OPCW Doc. EC-85/NAT.23 (UK), 12 July 2017, pp. 1–2; OPCW Doc. EC-86/NAT.5 (Estonia on behalf of the EU), 10 October 2017, p. 2; OPCW Doc. EC-86/NAT.13 (New Zealand), 10 October 2017, p. 2; OPCW Doc. EC-86/NAT.19 (Australia), 10 October 2017, p. 2; OPCW Doc. EC-86/NAT.22 (Germany), 10 October 2017 p. 2; OPCW Doc. EC-86/NAT.29 (Switzerland), 10 October 2017, p. 1; OPCW Doc. EC-86/NAT.30 (Belgium), 10 October 2017, p. 1; OPCW Doc. EC-86/NAT.10 (UK), 11 October 2017, p. 2; OPCW Doc. EC-86/NAT.21 (Chile), 10 October 2017, p. 2; OPCW Doc. EC-M-56/NAT.4 (Germany), 9 November 2017, p. 1; OPCW Doc. EC-M-56/NAT.4 (Slovakia), 9 November 2017, p. 1; OPCW Doc. EC-M-56/NAT.8 (Switzerland), 9 November 2017, p. 1; OPCW Doc. EC-M-56/NAT.13 (Chile), 9 November 2017, p. 2; OPCW Doc. EC-87/NAT.37 (Belgium), 14 March 2018, pp. 1–2; OPCW Doc. EC-87/NAT.28 (Morocco), 13 March 2018, p. 3; OPCW Doc. EC-87/NAT.31 (Colombia), 14 March 2018, p. 1; OPCW Doc. EC-87/NAT.17 (Switzerland), 13 March 2018, p. 1; OPCW Doc. EC-87/NAT.38 (Australia), 14 March 2018, p. 2; OPCW Doc. EC-87/NAT.13 (France), 13 March 2018, p. 2; OPCW Doc. EC-87/NAT.36 (Japan), 13 March 2018, p. 2; OPCW Doc. EC-87/NAT.10 (Turley), 13 March 2018, p. 1; OPCW Doc. EC-87/NAT.35

matter,[334] and accordingly urging Syria to cooperate with the Technical Secretariat to resolve the problem.[335] Russia and Iran defended Syria, trying to highlight such

(Italy), 13 March 2018, p. 2; OPCW Doc. EC-87/NAT.11 (Germany), 13 March 2018, p. 2; OPCW Doc. EC-87/NAT.32 (New Zealand), 13 March 2018, p. 2; OPCW Doc. EC-M-58/NAT.2 (US), 16 April 2018, p. 2; OPCW Doc. EC-M-58/NAT.12 (Australia), 16 April 2018, p. 1; OPCW Doc. EC-M-58/NAT.15 (Bulgaria on behalf of the EU), 16 April 2018, pp. 1–2; OPCW Doc. EC-M-58/NAT.21 (Canada), 16 April 2018, p. 2; OPCW Doc. C-SS-4/NAT.5 (Bulgaria on behalf of the EU), 26 June 2018, p. 2; OPCW Doc. EC-88/NAT.7 (Sweden), 10 July 2018, p. 2; OPCW Doc. EC-89/NAT.8 (UK), 9 October 2018, p. 2; OPCW Doc. EC-89/NAT.9 (Netherlands), 9 October 2018, p. 2; OPCW Doc. EC-89/NAT.24 (Chile), 9 October 2018, p. 1; OPCW Doc. EC-89/NAT.30 (Denmark), 9 October 2018, p. 1; OPCW Doc. EC-89/NAT.33 (Italy), 9 October 2018, p. 2; OPCW Doc. EC-89/NAT.37 (New Zealand), 9 October 2018, p. 2; OPCW Doc. EC-90/NAT.7 (US), 12 March 2019, p. 2; OPCW Doc. EC-90/NAT.8 (Romania on behalf of the EU), 12 March 2019, p. 2; OPCW Doc. EC-90/NAT.17 (UK), 12 March 2019, p. 1; OPCW Doc. EC-90/NAT.18 (Republic of Korea), 12 March 2019, p. 2; OPCW Doc. EC-90/NAT.21 (Denmark), 12 March 2019, p. 1; OPCW Doc. EC-90/NAT.22 (Italy), 13 March 2019, p. 2; OPCW Doc. EC-90/NAT.29 (Germany), 12 March 2019, p. 2; OPCW Doc. EC-90/NAT.30 (Peru), 12 March 2019, p. 1; OPCW Doc. EC-90/NAT.33 (Chile), 12 March 2019, p. 2; OPCW Doc. EC-91/NAT.9 (Finland), 9 July 2019, p. 2; OPCW Doc. EC-91/NAT.13 (Germany), 9 July 2019, p. 1; OPCW Doc. EC-91/NAT.16 (UK), 9 July 2019, p. 1; OPCW Doc. EC-91/NAT.17 (Australia), 9 July 2019, p. 2; OPCW Doc. EC-91/NAT.29 (Netherlands), 9 July 2019, p. 1; OPCW Doc. EC-91/NAT.30 (New Zealand), 9 July 2019, p. 1; OPCW Doc. EC-91/NAT.20 (Czech Republic), 10 July 2019, p. 1; OPCW Doc. EC-91/NAT.40 (Canada), 9 July 2019, p. 1; OPCW Doc. EC-92/NAT.7 (Finland on behalf of the EU), 8 October 2019, pp. 3–4; OPCW Doc. EC-92/NAT.11 (Republic of Korea), 8 October 2019, p. 1; OPCW Doc. EC-92/NAT.12 (Switzerland), 8 October 2019, p. 2; OPCW Doc. EC-92/NAT.16 (New Zealand), 9 October 2019, p. 2; OPCW Doc. EC-92/NAT.18 (UK), 8 October 2019, p. 1; OPCW Doc. EC-92/NAT.19 (Czech Republic), 8 October 2019, p. 1; OPCW Doc. EC-93/NAT.13 (Germany), 10 March 2020, p. 1; OPCW Doc. EC-93/NAT.15 (Croatia on behalf of the EU), 10 March 2020, p. 2; OPCW Doc. EC-93/NAT.19 (New Zealand), 10 March 2020, p. 1; OPCW Doc. EC-93/NAT.23 (Finland), 10 March 2020, p. 1; OPCW Doc. EC-93/NAT.24 (UK), 10 March 2020, p. 1; OPCW Doc. EC-93/NAT.38 (Canada), 10 March 2020, p. 1.

[334] OPCW Doc. EC-85/NAT.30 (Switzerland), 11 July 2017, p. 1; OPCW Doc. EC-86/NAT.5 (Estonia on behalf of the EU), 10 October 2017, p. 2.

[335] OPCW Doc. EC-84/NAT.10 (Malta on behalf of the EU), 7 March 2017, p. 2; OPCW Doc. EC-84/NAT.14 (Sweden), 7 March 2017, p. 1; OPCW Doc. EC-84/NAT.17 (Japan), 7 March 2017, p. 2; OPCW Doc. EC-M-55/NAT.11 (Belgium), 5 July 2017, p. 2; OPCW Doc. EC-85/NAT.23 (UK), 12 July 2017, p. 2; OPCW Doc. EC-86/NAT.13 (New Zealand), 10 October 2017, p. 2; OPCW Doc. EC-87/NAT.11 (Germany), 13 March 2018, p. 2; OPCW Doc. EC-87/NAT.32 (New Zealand), 13 March 2018, p. 2; OPCW Doc. EC-87/NAT.35 (Italy), 13 March 2018, p. 2; OPCW Doc. EC-87/NAT.37 (Belgium), 14 March 2018, p. 2; OPCW Doc. EC-88/NAT.10 (Sweden), 10 July 2018, p. 2; OPCW Doc. EC-88/NAT.27 (Denmark), 11 July 2018, p. 1; OPCW Doc. EC-89/NAT.19 (Sweden), 9 October 2018, p. 1; OPCW Doc. EC-90/NAT.18 (Republic of Korea), 12 March 2019, p. 2; OPCW Doc. EC-90/NAT.21 (Denmark), 12 March 2019, p. 1; OPCW Doc. EC-91/NAT.13 (Germany), 9 July 2019, p. 2; OPCW Doc. EC-91/NAT.30 (New Zealand), 9 July 2019, p. 2; OPCW Doc. EC-92/NAT.7 (Finland on behalf of the EU), 8 October 2019, p. 3; OPCW Doc. EC-92/NAT.10 (Germany), 8 October 2019, p. 1; OPCW Doc. EC-92/NAT.11 (Republic of Korea), 8 October 2019, p. 2; OPCW Doc. EC-92/NAT.12 (Switzerland), 8 October 2019, p. 2; OPCW Doc. EC-93/NAT.12 (Sweden) March 2020, p. 1; OPCW Doc. EC-93/NAT.13 (Germany), 10 March 2020, p. 1; OPCW Doc. EC-93/NAT.15 (Republic of Korea), 10 March 2020, p. 2.

positive aspects as "openness that Syria has demonstrated,"[336] "meticulous work,"[337] "substantive results,"[338] and "the few remaining issues."[339] Argentina, Malaysia, China, Morocco, India, Nigeria, and Guatemala adopted a more moderate tone.[340] Other States Parties expressed no opinion.

The OPCW Conference of the States Parties held its fourth special session in June 2018, where it adopted Decision C-SS-4/DEC.3 which, while intended to revive an attribution mechanism, also addressed the declarations issue, noting with concern that Syria's use of chemical weapons established by direct implication that Syria had failed to declare and destroy all chemical weapons and chemical weapons production facilities, and demanding that Syria comply with the relevant obligations.[341] The UN General Assembly, including the UNHRC, also referenced the declarations issue in their resolutions, expressing grave concern with the OPCW Technical Secretariat's conclusions[342] and demanding that the Syrian regime adhere to its international obligations, including those concerning its declarations, with special emphasis on the necessity for Syria to resolve the issues identified by the OPCW Director-General's report.[343] Syria was also called upon to provide further clarification in cooperation with the OPCW.[344]

---

336 OPCW Doc. EC-84/NAT.28 (Russia), 7 March 2017, p. 1.

337 OPCW Doc. EC-86/NAT.24 (Russia), 10 October 2017, p. 2.

338 OPCW Doc. EC-86/NAT.26 (Russia), 11 October 2017, p. 1.

339 OPCW Doc. EC-92/NAT.9 (Iran), 9 October 2019, p. 2.

340 OPCW Doc. EC-86/NAT.11 (Argentina), 10 October 2017, p. 2; OPCW Doc. EC-86/NAT.12 (Malaysia), 10 October 2017, p. 1; OPCW Doc. EC-86/NAT.18 (China), 10 October 2017, p. 2; OPCW Doc. EC-86/NAT.28 (Morocco), 10 October 2017, p. 3; OPCW Doc. EC-86/NAT.34 (India), 10 October 2017, p. 2; OPCW Doc. EC-86/NAT.35 (Morocco on behalf of the African group), 10 October 2017, p. 2; OPCW Doc. EC-87/NAT.19 (China), 13 March 2018, p. 2; OPCW Doc. EC-89/NAT.32 (India), 10 October 2018, p. 2; OPCW Doc. EC-91/NAT.11 (Nigeria), 10 July 2019, p. 2; OPCW Doc. EC-91/NAT.45 (Guatemala), 10 July 2019, p. 1; OPCW Doc. EC-92/NAT.6 (Nigeria), 8 October 2019, pp. 1–2.

341 OPCW Doc. C-SS-4/DEC.3, 27 June 2018, operative para. 7.

342 UN Doc. A/RES/72/43, 4 December 2017, operative para. 15 (138–10–26 by separate vote); UN Doc. A/RES/73/45, 5 December 2018, operative para. 16 (110–15–38 by separate vote); UN Doc. A/RES/74/40, 12 December 2019, operative para. 16 (112–12–36 by separate vote). See also UN Doc. A/RES/71/69, 5 December 2016, operative para. 13. UN Doc. A/HRC/RES/35/26, 23 June 2017, operative para. 24; UN Doc. A/HRC/RES/36/20, 29 September 2017, operative para. 24; UN Doc. A/HRC/RES/37/29, 23 March 2018, operative para. 29; UN Doc. A/HRC/RES/38/16, 6 July 2018, operative para. 32; UN Doc. A/HRC/RES/39/15, 28 September 2018, operative para. 38; UN Doc. A/HRC/RES/40/17, 22 March 2019, operative para. 40; UN Doc. A/HRC/RES/41/23, 12 July 2019, operative para. 42; UN Doc. A/HRC/RES/42/27, 27 September 2019, operative para. 42; UN Doc. A/HRC/RES/43/28, 22 June 2020, operative para. 50.

343 UN Doc. A/RES/71/203, 19 December 2016, operative para. 7; UN Doc. A/RES/72/191, 19 December 2017, operative para. 10; UN Doc. A/RES/73/182, 17 December 2018, operative para. 8; UN Doc. A/RES/74/169, 18 December 2019, operative para. 9.

344 UN Doc. A/HRC/RES/35/26, 23 June 2017, operative para. 24; UN Doc. A/HRC/RES/36/20, 29 September 2017, operative para. 24; UN Doc. A/HRC/RES/37/29, 23 March 2018, operative para. 29; UN Doc. A/HRC/RES/38/16, 6 July 2018, operative para. 32; UN Doc. A/HRC/RES/39/15, 28 September 2018, operative para. 38; UN Doc. A/HRC/RES/40/17, 22 March 2019, operative para. 40; UN Doc. A/HRC/RES/41/23, 12 July 2019, operative para. 42; UN Doc. A/HRC/RES/42/27,

OPCW Executive Council Decision EC-94/DEC.2

The OPCW IIT, a re-established attribution mechanism, published its first report in April 2020, in which it identified the Syrian government as the perpetrator.[345] States Parties remained divided on the declarations question, with the US and EU once more leading a bloc criticizing Syria's failure to provide complete declarations[346] and urging Syria to submit full declarations[347] and to cooperate with the OPCW.[348] India, China, Nigeria, Mexico, and Morocco welcomed Syria's continued cooperation and engagement with the Technical Secretariat.[349] and Iran referred to Syria's cooperative attitude.[350] Other States Parties again expressed no opinion. The Executive Council adopted another decision at its ninety-fourth session in July 2020,[351] in which, having expressed deep concern about the abovementioned implication by Syria's use of chemical weapons of its failure to declare same,[352] it requested that within 90 days, Syria declare facilities relevant to the development, production, stockpiling, and storage of chemical weapons used in the attacks as well as all chemical weapons, chemical weapons production facilities and other related facilities, and resolve all outstanding issues regarding its initial declaration of its chemical weapons stockpile and program.[353] The Executive Council also tasked the Director-General with reporting on implementation thereof within 100 days, especially whether Syria has not completed measures above.[354] The decision referred to Article VIII, para. 36 in deciding to recommend that the Conference of the States Parties adopt a decision if Syria failed to redress the situation by taking said steps.[355] Furthermore, the

---

27 September 2019, operative para. 42; UN Doc. A/HRC/RES/43/28, 22 June 2020, operative para. 50.

345 OPCW Doc. S/1867/2020, 8 April 2020, p. 58, para. 14.

346 OPCW Doc. EC-94/NAT.2 (Sweden), 17 April 2020, p. 1; OPCW Doc. EC-94/NAT.4 (Germany), 15 April 2020, p. 1; OPCW Doc. EC-94/NAT.6 (UK), 14 April 2020, p. 2; OPCW Doc. EC-94/NAT.8 (New Zealand), 21 April 2020, p. 1; OPCW Doc. EC-94/NAT.10 (Czech Republic), 16 April 2020, p. 1; OPCW Doc. EC-94/NAT.15 (Italy), 18 June 2020, p. 1; OPCW Doc. EC-94/NAT.25 (Ireland), 7 July 2020, p. 2; OPCW Doc. EC-94/NAT.34 (Finland), 7 July 2020, p. 1; OPCW Doc. EC-94/NAT.37 (US), 7 July 2020, p. 3; OPCW Doc. EC-94/NAT.42 (Sweden), 7 July 2020, p. 2; OPCW Doc. EC-94/NAT.60 (Peru), 7 July 2020, p. 1; OPCW Doc. EC-94/NAT.65 (Guatemala), 7 July 2020, p. 2.

347 OPCW Doc. EC-94/NAT.8 (New Zealand), 21 April 2020, p. 1.

348 OPCW Doc. EC-94/NAT.24 (Republic of Korea), 7 July 2020, p. 2; OPCW Doc. EC-94/NAT.60 (Peru), 7 July 2020, p. 1.

349 OPCW Doc. EC-94/NAT.31 (Nigeria), 7 July 2020, pp. 1–2; OPCW Doc. EC-94/NAT.39 (India), 7 July 2020, p. 1; OPCW Doc. EC-94/NAT.41 (China), 7 July 2020, p. 1; OPCW Doc. EC-94/NAT.54 (Mexico), 7 July 2020, p. 2; OPCW Doc. EC-94/NAT.58 (India), 7 July 2020, p. 1; OPCW Doc. EC-94/NAT.77 (Morocco), 7 July 2020, p. 2.

350 OPCW Doc. EC-94/NAT.29 (Iran), 7 July 2020, p. 2.

351 OPCW Doc. EC-94/DEC.2, 9 July 2020.

352 *Ibid.* operative para. 2.

353 *Ibid.*, operative para. 5 (a), (b) and (c).

354 *Ibid.*, operative para. 6.

355 *Ibid.*, preamble para. 15 and operative para. 7.

Executive Council instituted another inspections scheme under which the Technical Secretariat would inspect Shayrat and Hama airbases, which the OPCW IIT report identified as directly involved in launching chemical weapons attacks, for as long as the Executive Council deems appropriate.[356]

Further Efforts and the Implementation of the Decision EC-94/DEC.2

While the Syrian authorities and the Technical Secretariat continued to work together, with Syria providing information including two amendments[357] and holding its twenty-third round of consultations with the DAT, these efforts were inadequate, and the Director-General accordingly reported to the Executive Council that the Syrian Arab Republic had neither submitted declarations on all items nor resolved all outstanding issues regarding declarations within the 90-day period under Decision EC-94/DEC.2.[358] Nor did such additional efforts as the twenty-fourth round of consultations between the DAT and the Syrian authorities or the seventh round of inspections at two SSRC facilities finding no activities inconsistent with the CWC[359] help with these outstanding issues, including the aforementioned finding of the Schedule 2B04 chemical during the third round of inspections at the Barzah facilities[360] and the declaration of all chemical warfare agents produced and/or weaponized at a former chemical weapons production facility (Tables 4.12 and 4.13).[361]

Table 4.12 DAT meetings with Syria

Rounds	Dates	Places
Twenty-third[362]	22 September–3 October 2020	Syria
Twenty-fourth[363]	7–25 February 2021	Syria

Table 4.13 SSRC Facilities Inspections

Round	Date
Seventh[364]	8–13 November 2020

356 *Ibid.*, operative para. 8.

357 OPCW Doc. EC-95/DG.19, 24 September 2020, para. 10.

358 OPCW Doc. EC-96/DG.1, 14 October 2020, paras. 5–6. See also OPCW Doc. EC-96/DG.2, 26 October 2020, para. 26.

359 OPCW Doc. EC-97/DG.7, 25 May 2021 para. 17.

360 OPCW Doc. EC-97/DG.2, 24 March 2021, para. 17. Two inspections schemes under Decisions EC-83/DEC.5 and EC-94/DEC.2 were postponed due to "conditions," the "security situation," and the COVID-19 pandemic (OPCW Doc. EC-97/DG.2, 24 March 2021, paras. 15 and 26).

361 OPCW Doc. EC-97/DG.2, 24 March 2021, para. 13 (note verbale from Syria to the OPCW Technical Secretariat dated 9 March 2021). See also OPCW Doc. EC-97/DG.2, 24 March 2021, para. 13 (note verbale from Syria to the OPCW Technical Secretariat dated 21 October 2020).

362 OPCW Doc. EC-96/DG.2, 26 October 2020, para. 11.

363 OPCW Doc. EC-97/DG.2, 24 March 2021 para. 11.

364 OPCW Doc. EC-96/DG.3, 24 November 2020 para. 14.

The Director-General thus reiterated the conclusion that "the declaration submitted by the Syrian Arab Republic still cannot be considered accurate and complete in accordance with the Chemical Weapons Convention, Council decision EC-M-33/DEC.1, and United Nations Security Council resolution 2118 (2013)."[365]

OPCW Conference of the States Parties Decision C-25/DEC.9

As indicated above, in April 2021, the OPCW Conference of the States Parties adopted a decision during the second part of its twenty-fifth session titled "Addressing the Possession and Use of Chemical Weapons by the Syrian Arab Republic."[366] The Conference of the States Parties, recalling operative paras. 5–7 of Decision EC-94/DEC.2, again expressed deep concern that the use of such chemical weapons by the Syrian Arab Republic, by direct implication, established that the Syrian

---

[365] OPCW Doc. EC-94/DG.1, 24 March 2020, para. 11; OPCW Doc. EC-95/DG.1, 24 July 2020, para. 11; OPCW Doc. EC-96/DG.2, 26 October 2020, para. 12; OPCW Doc. EC-96/DG.3, 24 November 2020, para. 12; OPCW Doc. EC-96/DG.4, 24 December 2020, para. 12; OPCW Doc. EC-96/DG.6, 25 January 2021, para. 12; OPCW Doc. EC-96/DG.13, 24 February 2021, para. 13; OPCW Doc. EC-97/DG.2, 24 March 2021, para. 14. The UN General Assembly continued to express grave concern that the OPCW Technical Secretariat could not fully verify the accuracy and completeness of Syria's declaration (UN Doc. A/RES/75/55, 7 December 2020, operative para. 17), and demanded that Syria adhere fully to its international obligations, including the requirement that it declare in full its chemical weapons program (UN Doc. A/RES/75/193, 16 December 2020, operative para. 9).

[366] OPCW Doc. C-25/DEC.9, 21 April 2021. The vote was 87 for (Albania, Andorra, Argentina, Australia, Austria, Bahrain, Belgium, Bosnia and Herzegovina, Botswana, Brazil, Brunei Darussalam, Bulgaria, Canada, Chile, Colombia, Costa Rica, Côte d'Ivoire, Croatia, Cyprus, Czech Republic, Democratic Republic of the Congo, Denmark, Ecuador, El Salvador, Estonia, Fiji, Finland, France, Gambia, Georgia, Germany, Ghana, Greece, Guatemala, Honduras, Hungary, Iceland, Ireland, Italy, Japan, Kuwait, Latvia, Liberia, Liechtenstein, Lithuania, Luxembourg, Maldives, Malta, Marshall Islands, Monaco, Montenegro, Morocco, Netherlands, New Zealand, North Macedonia, Norway, Palau, Panama, Papua New Guinea, Paraguay, Peru, Philippines, Poland, Portugal, Qatar, Republic of Korea, Republic of Moldova, Romania, Saint Lucia, San Marino, Saudi Arabia, Senegal, Seychelles, Singapore, Slovakia, Slovenia, Spain, Sweden, Switzerland, Togo, Turkey, Ukraine, UK, US, Uruguay, Vanuatu, and Zambia) to 15 against (Armenia, Belarus, Bolivia, China, Iran, Kazakhstan, Kyrgyzstan, Myanmar, Nicaragua, Pakistan, the Russian Federation, the State of Palestine, the Syrian Arab Republic, Tajikistan, and Zimbabwe), with 34 abstentions (Afghanistan, Algeria, Bangladesh, Burkina Faso, Burundi, Cameroon, Eswatini, Ethiopia, Holy See, India, Indonesia, Iraq, Jordan, Kenya, Laos, Lebanon, Madagascar, Malawi, Malaysia, Mali, Mexico, Mongolia, Nepal, Nigeria, Oman, Rwanda, South Africa, Sudan, Thailand, Tunisia, Uganda, United Arab Emirates, Uzbekistan, and Viet Nam) (OPCW Doc. C-25/5, 22 April 2021, para. 9.24). States voting against did so primarily on grounds that the decision was based on reporting by an "illegitimate body" established in a manner inconsistent with the CWC and tasked with mandates beyond the scope thereof (OPCW Doc. C-25/NAT.124 (Russia on behalf of the Collective Security Treaty Organization), 20 April 2021, p. 1; OPCW Doc. C-25/NAT.106 (Palestine), 21 April 2021, p. 1; OPCW Doc. C-25/NAT.108 (Iran), 20 April 2021, pp. 1–2; Russia, https://www.opcw.org/sites/default/files/documents/2021/04/Russian%20Federation%20CSP%2025%20Statement%20under%20Agenda%20Item%209d.pdf, 22 April 2023).

Arab Republic failed to declare and destroy all of its chemical weapons and chemical weapons production facilities,[367] expressed grave concern that the Director-General had reported Syria's failure to carry out the steps called for in Decision EC-94/DEC.2,[368] and decided pursuant to Article VIII, para. 21(k) and Article XII, para. 2 to suspend the following rights and privileges of Syria under the Convention: (a) to vote in the Conference and the Council; (b) to stand for election to the Council; and (c) to hold any office of the Conference, the Council, or any subsidiary organs.[369] The Conference of the States Parties also decided that said suspended rights and privileges would be reinstated if the Director-General reported to the Executive Council that Syria has completed the relevant measures.[370]

Aftermath

As anticipated, the adoption of Decision C-25/DEC.9 did not improve matters either. While Syria received the eighth and ninth rounds of inspections at the two SSRC facilities,[371] it neither submitted the required information on the undeclared production and/or weaponization of chemical warfare agents at the former chemical weapons production facility,[372]nor provided sufficient technical information or explanations about the detection of the Schedule 2B04 chemical during the third round of inspections at the Barzah facilities.[373] The Director-General thus reiterated the conclusion that "the declaration submitted by the Syrian Arab Republic still cannot be considered accurate and complete in accordance with the Chemical Weapons Convention, Council decision EC-M-33/DEC.1, and United Nations Security Council resolution 2118 (2013)."[374]

---

[367] OPCW Doc. C-25/DEC.9, 21 April 2021, operative para. 4.

[368] *Ibid.*, operative para. 5.

[369] *Ibid.*, operative para. 6.

[370] *Ibid.*, operative para. 8.

[371] OPCW Doc. EC-99/DG.3, 23 December 2021, para. 21 (eighth round, 10–17 December 2021) and OPCW Doc. EC-101/DG.22, 23 September 2022, para. 17 (ninth round, 11–18 September 2022). Two inspections schemes under the Decisions EC-83/DEC.5 and EC-94/DEC.2 were postponed due to "conditions" and "security concerns," respectively (OPCW Doc. EC-101/DG.2, 22 July 2022, paras. 17 and 35; OPCW Doc. EC-101/DG.4, 24 August 2022, paras. 17 and 33; OPCW Doc. EC-101/DG.22, 23 September 2022, paras 16 and 31; OPCW Doc. EC-102/DG.1, 25 October 2022, paras. 16 and 31; OPCW Doc. EC-102/DG.2, 24 November 2022, paras 20 and 35; OPCW Doc. EC-102/DG.3, 23 December 2022, paras. 19 and 35).

[372] OPCW Doc. EC-101/DG.2, 22 July 2022, para. 14; OPCW Doc. EC-101/DG.4, 24 August 2022, para. 14.

[373] OPCW Doc. EC-101/DG.2, 22 July 2022, para. 20; OPCW Doc. EC-101/DG.4, 24 August 2022, para. 19; OPCW Doc. EC-101/DG.22, 23 September 2022, para 18; OPCW Doc. EC-102/DG.1, 25 October 2022, para. 18; OPCW Doc. EC-102/DG.2, 24 November 2022, para 22; OPCW Doc. EC-102/DG.3, 23 December 2022, para. 21.

[374] OPCW Doc. EC-97/DG.3, 23 April 2021, para. 13; OPCW Doc. EC-97/DG.7, 25 May 2021, para. 15; OPCW Doc. EC-97/DG.13, 22 June 2021, para. 14; OPCW Doc. EC-98/DG.1, 23 July 2021, para. 14; OPCW Doc. EC-98/DG.6, 24 August 2021, para. 14; OPCW Doc. EC-98/DG.24, 24 September 2021, para. 19; OPCW Doc. EC-99/DG.1, 26 October 2021, para. 17; OPCW Doc. EC-99/DG.2, 24 November 2021, para. 18; OPCW Doc. EC-99/DG.3, 23 December 2021, para. 19; OPCW Doc. EC-99/DG.5, 24 January 2022, para. 15; OPCW Doc. EC-99/DG.13, 24 February

The twenty-fifth round of consultations between the DAT and the Syrian authorities, which were originally scheduled to be held in May 2021 and subsequently postponed until October 2021,[375] remained pending primarily because Syria refused an entry visa for one DAT member,[376] and even disallowed this member's participation in "the limited round of consultations" in Lebanon,[377] which several States Parties

2022, para. 15; OPCW Doc. EC-100/DG.2, 24 March 2022, para. 19; OPCW Doc. EC-100/DG.4, 25 April 2022, para. 16; OPCW Doc. EC-100/DG.6, 24 May 2022, para. 17; OPCW Doc. EC-100/DG.14, 23 June 2022, para. 17; OPCW Doc. EC-101/DG.2, 22 July 2022, para. 16; OPCW Doc. EC-101/DG.4, 24 August 2022, para. 16; OPCW Doc. EC-101/DG.22, 23 September 2022, para. 15; OPCW Doc. EC-102/DG.1, 25 October 2022, para. 15; OPCW Doc. EC-102/DG.2, 24 November 2022, para. 19; OPCW Doc. EC-102/DG.3, 23 December 2022, para. 18. The UN General Assembly continued to express grave concern that the OPCW Technical Secretariat could not fully verify the accuracy and completeness of the declaration (UN Doc. A/RES/76/29, 6 December 2021, operative para. 17; UN Doc. A/RES/77/73, 7 December 2022, operative para. 18), and demanded that Syria adhere fully to its international obligations, including the requirement that it declare in full its chemical weapons program (UN Doc. A/RES/76/228, 24 December 2021, operative para. 8; UN Doc. A/RES/77/230, 15 December 2022, operative para. 6).

375 OPCW Doc. EC-97/DG.7, 25 May 2021, para. 14 (note verbale from the OPCW Technical Secretariat to Syria dated 30 April and 14 May 2021); OPCW Doc. EC-97/DG.13, 22 June 2021, para. 13 (note verbale from the OPCW Technical Secretariat to Syria dated 26 May 2021); OPCW Doc. EC-98/DG.6, 24 August 2021, para. 13 (a note verbale from Syria to the OPCW Technical Secretariat dated 16 August 2021); OPCW Doc. EC-98/DG.6, 24 August 2021, para. 14 (note verbale from Syria to the OPCW Technical Secretariat dated 16 August 2021); OPCW Doc. EC-98/DG.24, 24 September, para. 15 (note verbale from the OPCW Technical Secretariat to Syria dated 25 August 2021).

376 OPCW Doc. EC-98/DG.24,24 September 2021, paras.16 note verbale from Syria to the OPCW Technical Secretariat dated 3 September 2021; note verbale from the OPCW Technical Secretariat to Syria dated 20 September 2021) and 17 (reconfirmation of Syria; response of the OPCW Technical Secretariat); OPCW Doc. EC-100/DG.2, 24 March 2022, paras. 14 (note verbale from the OPCW Technical Secretariat to Syria dated 28 February 2022; response from Syria to the OPCW Technical Secretariat dated 3 March 2022), 15 (note verbale from the OPCW Technical Secretariat to Syria dated 7 March 2022) and 16 (note verbale from Syria to the OPCW Technical Secretariat dated 11 March 2022).

377 OPCW Doc. EC-100/DG.4, 25 April 2022, paras. 14 (note verbale from the OPCW Technical Secretariat to Syria dated 11 April 2022) and 15 (note verbale from Syria to the OPCW Technical Secretariat dated 18 April 2022); OPCW Doc. EC-100/DG.6, 24 May 2022, paras. 13 (letter from the Syrian Deputy Foreign Minister to the OPCW Director-General dated 7 May 2022) and 14 (note verbale from the OPCW Technical Secretariat to Syria dated 20 May 2022); OPCW Doc. EC-100/DG.14, 23 June 2022, para. 14 (letter from the Syrian Deputy Foreign Minister to the OPCW Director-General dated 31 May 2022). See also OPCW Doc. EC-99/DG.5, 24 January 2022, para. 20, (letter from the Syrian Deputy Foreign Minister to the OPCW Director-General dated 13 December 2021); OPCW Doc. EC-99/DG.5, 24 January 2022, para. 20, OPCW Doc. EC-100/DG.6, 24 May 2022, para. 14 (letter from the OPCW Director-General to the Syrian Deputy Foreign Minister dated 19 January 2022).

criticized.[378] Syria justified its actions on the basis of "national and sovereign procedures and instructions,"[379] asserting that it had the right to request the replacement of this one DAT expert.[380] In making this assertion, Syria appears to have relied on Verification Annex Part II, para. 2 allowing each State Party to declare non-acceptance of an inspector for "verification activities" on its territory or in any other place under its jurisdiction or control. By contrast, the OPCW Technical Secretariat has adopted a narrow interpretation of "verification activities," limiting same to inspections, chiefly because some OPCW Technical Secretariat personnel involved in data monitoring and evaluating declaration and inspection report data are not designated as inspectors.[381] It has also taken the position that Syria is obliged "to accept and provide immediate and unfettered access to the personnel designated by the Secretariat of the OPCW," in accordance with the aforementioned operative para. 7 of the UN Security Council Resolution 2118,[382] which "shall prevail" over obligations under any other international agreement, in accordance with Article 103 of the UN Charter with no exceptions, even the aforementioned CWC denial procedures. Several States Parties endorse the position of the Technical Secretariat.[383] Hence, Syria's argument

[378] UN Doc. S/PV.8872, 4 October 2021, pp. 6 (US), 8 (Niger), 8–9 (Estonia), 9 (Saint Vincent and the Grenadines), 9–10 (France), 11 (Ireland), 13 (UK), 13 (Mexico), 16 (Turkey); OPCW Doc. EC-98/NAT.14 (Austria), 5 October 2021, p. 1; OPCW Doc. EC-98/NAT.22 (Canada), 5 October 2021, p. 2; OPCW Doc. EC-98/NAT.27 (Slovenia on behalf of the EU), 5 October 2021, p. 2; OPCW Doc. EC-98/NAT.36 (France), 5 October 2021, p. 1; UN Doc. S/PV.8921, 8 December 2021, pp. 6 (US), 9 (Estonia), 16 (Norway); OPCW Doc. EC-99/NAT.9 (Latvia), 8 March 2022, p. 2; Doc. EC-99/NAT.12 (US), 8 March 2022. p. 2; OPCW Doc. EC-99/NAT.13 (Germany), 8 March 2022, p. 2; OPCW Doc. EC-99/NAT.26 (Czech Republic), 8 March 2022, p. 2; OPCW Doc. EC-99/NAT.32 (Australia), 8 March 2022, p. 2; OPCW Doc. EC-99/NAT.41 (France on behalf of the EU), 8 March 2022, p. 3; OPCW Doc. EC-99/NAT.44 (France), 8 March 2022, p. 2; OPCW Doc. EC-99/NAT.55 (Mexico), 8 March 2022, p. 2; OPCW Doc. EC-99/NAT.59 (Spain), 8 March 2022, p. 1; OPCW Doc. EC-99/NAT.74 (Canada), 8 March 2022, p. 2; OPCW Doc. EC-99/NAT.82 (Chile), 8 March 2022, p. 2; UN Doc. S/PV.8990, 10 March 2022, p. 8 (Norway); OPCW Doc. EC-100/NAT.16 (Albania), 5 July 2022, p. 2; OPCW Doc. EC-100/NAT.17 (Norway), 5 July 2022, p. 2; OPCW Doc. EC-100/NAT.19 (Lithuania), 5 July 2022, p. 1; OPCW Doc. EC-100/NAT.24 (Germany), 5 July 2022, p. 2; OPCW Doc. EC-100/NAT.37 (France on behalf of the EU), 5 July 2022, p. 1; OPCW Doc. EC-100/NAT.39 (France on behalf of the EU), 5 July 2022, p. 2; OPCW Doc. EC-100/NAT.44 (Chile), 5 July 2022, p. 2; OPCW Doc. EC-100/NAT.48 (France), 5 July 2022, p. 1; UN Doc. S/PV. 9097, 20 July 2022, pp. 6 (US), 9 (Mexico), 10 (Ghana), 12 (Norway), 15 (Turkey); UN Doc. S/PV.9141, 29 September 2022, pp. 5 (US), 6 (Albania), 12 (Turkey).

[379] UN Doc. S/PV.8872, 4 October 2021, p. 14 (Syria).

[380] OPCW Doc. EC-100/NAT.70 (Syria), 5 July 2022, p. 1.

[381] Krutzsch, Myjer and Trapp, *supra* note 123, pp. 462–463, footnote 14.

[382] OPCW Doc. EC-98/DG.30*, 5 October 2021, para. 13; OPCW Doc. EC-99/DG.2, 24 November 2021, para. 17; OPCW Doc. EC-99/DG.3, 23 December 2021, para. 18; OPCW Doc. EC-99/DG.5, 24 January 2022, para. 13; OPCW Doc. EC-99/DG.13, 24 February 2022, para. 13; OPCW Doc. EC-100/DG.2, 24 March 2022, para. 13; OPCW Doc. EC-100/DG.4, 25 April 2022, para. 13; OPCW Doc. EC-100/DG.6, 24 May 2022, para. 13. See also OPCW Doc. EC-100/DG.14, 23 June 2022, para. 15; OPCW Doc. EC-101/DG.2, 22 July 2022, para. 11; OPCW Doc. EC-101/DG.4, 24 August 2022, para. 11.

[383] UN Doc. S/PV.8872, 4 October 2021, pp. 6 (US), 11 (Ireland), 13 (UK); UN Doc. S/PV.8921, 8 December 2021, p. 16 (Norway); UN Doc. S/PV.8990, 10 March 2022, p. 8 (Norway); OPCW

is unconvincing on its face. Syria has been called on to grant all visas as part of its required cooperation with the OPCW.[384] All of which means Syria had not fulfilled the conditions for reinstating its suspended rights and privileges under para. 5 of the Decision EC-94/DEC.5.[385] It remains unclear when and how the declaration issue will be resolved.[386]

(ii) **Removal of Chemical Weapons**

Missing Deadline of 31 December 2013

It should come as little surprise that Syria did not meet the 31 December 2013 deadline for removal of all priority 1 chemicals.[387] The first lot of chemicals were transported

---

Doc. EC-99/NAT.41 (France on behalf of the EU), 8 March 2022, p. 3; OPCW Doc. EC-99/NAT.44 (France), 8 March 2022, p. 2; OPCW Doc. EC-100/NAT.16 (Albania), 5 July 2022, p. 2; OPCW Doc. EC-100/NAT.17 (Norway), 5 July 2022 p. 2; OPCW Doc. EC-100/NAT.24 (Germany), 5 July 2022, p. 2; OPCW Doc. EC-100/NAT.37 (France on behalf of the EU), 5 July 2022, p. 1; OPCW Doc. EC-100/NAT.39 (France on behalf of the EU), 5 July 2022, p. 2.

[384] OPCW Doc. EC-99/DG.2, 24 November 2021, para. 17; UN Doc. S/PV.8872, 4 October 2021, pp. 6 (US), 11 (Ireland); OPCW Doc. EC-98/NAT.27, 5 October 2021 (Slovenia on behalf of the EU, p. 2; UN Doc. S/PV.8921, 8 December 2021, p. 6 (US); OPCW Doc. EC-99/NAT.26 (Czech Republic), 8 March 2022, p. 2; OPCW Doc. EC-99/NAT.9 (Latvia), 8 March 2022, p. 2; OPCW Doc. EC-99/NAT.41 (France on behalf of the EU), 8 March 2022, p. 3; OPCW Doc. EC-99/NAT.74 (Canada), 8 March 2022, p. 2; OPCW Doc. EC-99/NAT.82 (Chile), 8 March 2022, p. 2; OPCW Doc. EC-100/NAT.16 (Albania), 5 July 2022, p. 2; OPCW Doc. EC-100/NAT.19 (Lithuania), 5 July 2022, p. 1; OPCW Doc. EC-100/NAT.37 (France on behalf of the EU), 5 July 2022, p. 1; OPCW Doc. EC-100/NAT.39 (France on behalf of the EU), 5 July 2022, p. 2. Iran, while taking the position that Syria is "exercising its sovereign rights," encouraged Syria and the OPCW Technical Secretariat to resolve the "minor" issue in good faith (OPCW Doc. EC-99/NAT.25 (Iran), 8 March 2022, p. 1; OPCW Doc. EC-100/NAT.31 (Iran), 5 July 2022, p. 1).

[385] OPCW Doc. EC-101/DG.2, 22 July 2022, para. 37; OPCW Doc. EC-101/DG.4, 24 August 2022, para. 35; OPCW Doc. EC-101/DG.22, 23 September 2022, para. 33; OPCW Doc. EC-102/DG.1, 25 October 2022, para. 33, OPCW Doc. EC-102/DG.2, 24 November 2022, para. 37; OPCW Doc. EC-102/DG.3, 23 December 2022, para. 37.

[386] The UN General Assembly continued to express its grave concern, to underscore the importance of such full verification, and to demand Syria's fulfillment of its obligations including full declaration (UN Doc. A/RES/72/43, 4 December 2017, operative para. 15 (138 in favor, 10 against, and 26 abstentions by separate vote); UN Doc. A/RES/73/45, 5 December 2018, operative para. 16 (110-15-38 by separate vote); UN Doc. A/RES/74/40, 12 December 2019, operative para. 16 (112-12-36 by separate vote); UN Doc. A/RES/75/55, 7 December 2020, operative para. 17 (119-10-35 by separate vote); UN Doc. A/RES/76/29, 6 December 2021, operative para. 17 (109-11-42 by separate vote); UN Doc. A/RES/76/228, 24 December 2021, operative para. 8; UN Doc. A/RES/77/73, 7 December 2022, operative para. 18; UN Doc. A/RES/77/230, 15 December 2022, operative para. 6).

[387] OPCW Doc. EC-M-38/DG.1, 23 January 2014, para. 4(a). Although the Technical Secretariat developed a draft facility agreement for chemical weapons storage facilities and submitted it to Syria for consideration, no agreement was concluded (OPCW EC-M-35/DG.1, 25 November 2013, para. 12; OPCW EC-M-37/DG.1, 23 December 2013, para.13; OPCW Doc. EC-M-38/DG.1, 23 January 2014, para. 13. See also OPCW Doc. EC-75/DG.6, 25 February 2014, para. 14; OPCW Doc. EC-M-40/DG.1/Rev.1, 27 March 2014, para.11; OPCW Doc. EC-M-40/DG.4, 25 April 2014, para. 11; OPCW Doc. EC-M-42/DG.1, 23 May 2014, para. 10; OPCW Doc. EC-76/DG.14, 25 June 2014, para. 12).

to Latakia and loaded onboard ship on 7 January 2014.[388] The Executive Council held its thirty-seventh meeting on 8 January 2014, in light of this development. The Director-General highlighted the beginning of the removal, albeit with "some delay," which he explained was due to circumstances including the security situation, the challenges associated with the procurement and delivery of large quantities of packaging and transportation materials and equipment, and adverse weather conditions. He hoped the transportation and removal would pick up pace and mentioned that high-level Syrian officials agreed on the need to maintain the momentum.[389] The US also acknowledged the start of the removal process as "the extraordinary accomplishments" and urged that "every effort be made to achieve the prompt and complete removal without further delay," without singling out Syria.[390] The Executive Council "noted that, notwithstanding the technical difficulties resulting in delays, the transportation of priority chemicals began on 7 January 2014, and encouraged all States Parties in a position to do so to maintain the momentum."[391]

Despite this action, removal did not speed up, with the second shipment completed on 27 January 2014.[392] At the thirty-eighth meeting of the Executive Council on 30 January 2014, France, Spain, US, UK, Greece on behalf of the EU, Ireland, the Netherlands, Uruguay, and Pakistan expressed concern about further delay, urging Syria to fulfill its obligations as soon as possible.[393] In fact, meeting the deadlines

[388] OPCW Doc. EC-M-38/DG.1, 23 January 2014, para. 4(a).

[389] OPCW Doc. EC-M-37/DG.3, 8 January 2014. Syria requested equipment including armored jackets for shipping containers, electronic countermeasures, and detectors for improvised explosive devices. The OPCW-UN Joint Mission assessed, however, that Syria "has sufficient material and equipment to carry out multiple ground movements to ensure the expeditious removal of chemical weapons material" (UN Doc. S/2014/52, 27 January 2014, p. 3).

[390] OPCW Doc. EC-M-37/NAT.1 (US), 8 January 2014, p. 1.

[391] OPCW Doc. EC-M-37/2, 8 January 2014, para. 5.

[392] OPCW Doc. EC-M-38/DG.2, 30 January 2014.

[393] OPCW Doc. EC-M-38/NAT.2 (France), 30 January 2014, p. 1; OPCW Doc. EC-M-38/NAT.3 (Spain), 30 January 2014, p. 1; OPCW Doc. EC-M-38/NAT.4 (US), 30 January 2014, pp. 1–2; OPCW Doc. EC-M-38/NAT.5 (UK), 30 January 2014, pp. 1–2; OPCW Doc. EC-M-38/NAT.6 (Greece on behalf of the EU), 30 January 2014, p. 1; OPCW Doc. EC-M-38/NAT.7 (Ireland), 30 January 2014, pp. 1–2; OPCW Doc. EC-M-38/NAT.8 (Netherlands), 30 January 2014, p. 1; OPCW Doc. EC-M-38/NAT.13 (Uruguay), 30 January 2014, p. 1. Pakistan noted the concerns of Syria about the security situation but strongly urged it to make all efforts to ensure removal in an expeditious manner (OPCW Doc. EC-M-38/NAT.14 (Pakistan), 30 January 2014, p. 1). Russia called on the OPCW Executive Council to "show patience" (OPCW Doc. EC-M-38/NAT.11 (Russia), 30 January 2014, p. 2). See also like concerns at subsequent meetings and session: OPCW Doc. EC-M-39/NAT.2 (Norway), 21 February 2014, p. 1; OPCW Doc. EC-M-39/NAT.4 (Switzerland), 21 February 2014, p. 1; OPCW Doc. EC-M-39/NAT.5 (Chile), 21 February 2014, p. 1; OPCW Doc. EC-M-39/NAT.6 (Turkey), 21 February 2014, pp. 1–2; OPCW Doc. EC-M-39/NAT.7 (Austria), 21 February 2014, p. 1; OPCW Doc. EC-M-39/NAT.12 (Mexico), 21 February 2014, p. 1; OPCW Doc. EC-M-39/NAT.13 (Greece on behalf of the EU), 21 February 2014, pp. 1–2; OPCW Doc. EC-M-39/NAT.14 (Ireland), 21 February 2014, p. 1; OPCW Doc. EC-M-39/NAT.16, (Germany) 21 February 2014, pp. 1–2; OPCW Doc. EC-75/NAT.5 (UK), 4 March 2014, p. 1; OPCW Doc. EC-75/NAT.6 (US), 4 March 2014, p. 2; OPCW Doc. EC-75/NAT.9 (Turkey), 4 March 2014, p. 1; OPCW Doc. EC-75/NAT.17 (Japan), 4 March 2014, pp. 1–2; OPCW Doc. EC-75/NAT.20 (Qatar), 4 March 2014, p. 2; OPCW Doc. EC-75/NAT.23 (Greece on behalf of the EU), 4 March 2014, p. 2;

was essential, both because it was a legally binding obligation on Syria and because eliminating Syrian chemical weapons was complex and demanded the collective efforts of the OPCW, contributing States Parties, and the private sector, in providing financing, personnel, and time.[394]

Missing Deadline of 5 February 2014

Six days after the thirty-eighth meeting of the Executive Council, it became clear that Syria had not met the 5 February 2014 deadline for removal of priority 2 chemicals either.[395] The UN Security Council held consultations on 6 February 2014, at which, while noting the removal of "limited quantities" of chemical weapons materials from Syria on 7 and 27 January, it expressed "growing concern at the slow pace" of said removal, calling upon Syria to "expedite actions to meet its obligations to transport in a systematic and sufficiently accelerated manner all the relevant materials to Latakia" and "intensify its efforts to expedite in-country movement."[396]

Extension of Deadlines

The OPCW Director-General and the Syrian authorities exchanged communications in which they explored deadline extensions. The Director-General took the initiative in sending a letter on 14 January 2014, requesting that Syrian authorities provide a time frame for removal.[397] In response, on 14 February 2014, Syria provided a new timeline for removing chemicals outside its territory, in which it anticipated completion by the end of May 2014, inducing the Operational Planning Group to make an alternative plan for 31 March 2014.[398] Germany also expressed concern about this proposal, as it would "make it practically impossible to complete the destruction of the Syrian chemical weapons by 30 June 2014."[399] The Director-General requested that Syria give serious consideration to this plan,[400] and on 23 February 2014, Syria

---

OPCW Doc. EC-75/NAT.25 (Saudi Arabia), 4 March 2014, pp. 2–3; OPCW Doc. EC-75/NAT.27 (Spain), 4 March 2014, p. 1.

394 OPCW Doc. EC-M-38/DG.2, 30 January 2014; OPCW Doc. EC-M-38/NAT.4 (US), 30 January 2014, p. 3; OPCW Doc. EC-M-38/NAT.5 (UK), 30 January 2014, pp. 1–2.

395 OPCW Doc. EC-75/DG.6, 25 February 2014, para. 4(a).

396 UN News, 6 February 2014, https://news.un.org/en/story/2014/02/461362-syria-un-calls-speeding-pace-lagging-chemical-weapons-elimination#.UvU7OfldV8G, accessed 22 April 2023.

397 OPCW Doc. EC-M-38/DG.2, 30 January 2014. Pakistan urged Syria to "provide a clear time frame…at the earliest" (OPCW Doc. EC-M-38/NAT.14 (Pakistan), 30 January 2014, p. 1). Russia also held that "these intermediate timelines should be based on reality, and objective reality comes down, in the first place, to security issues," and that "the security situation on the ground is evaluated, above all, by the Syrian Government which is responsible for this operation" (OPCW Doc. EC-M-38/NAT.11 (Russia), 30 January 2014, p. 1).

398 OPCW Doc. EC-75/DG.6, 25 February 2014, para. 4(b).

399 OPCW Doc. EC-M-39/NAT.16 (Germany), 21 February 2014, pp. 1–2.

400 OPCW Doc. EC-75/DG.6, 25 February 2014, para. 4(b). See also OPCW Doc. EC-M-39/NAT.2 (Norway), 21 February 2014, p. 1.

Table 4.14 Extended deadlines for chemical weapons removal

Type	Extended deadline
Priority 1: mustard agent and the key binary chemical weapon components DF, A, B, and BB, including BB salt declared by the Syrian Arab Republic	Original: 31 December 2013 New: 13 April 2014 and 27 April 2014*
Priority 2: all other chemicals declared by the Syrian Arab Republic	Original: 5 February 2014 New: 13 April 2014 and 27 April 2014*

* Stored in inaccessible facilities

revised the schedule, aiming instead to complete removing chemicals from its territory by 13 April 2014, except for chemicals stored in inaccessible facilities, which would be removed by 27 April 2014.[401]

The Executive Council held its seventy-fifth session 4–7 March 2014. India welcomed the revised proposal.[402] The Netherlands regarded the revised plan as "a commitment the Syrian Arab Republic has taken upon itself" and called on Syria to implement it without further delay.[403] As a result of discussion, the Executive Council noted the revised plan for removal (Table 4.14) and requested Syria "to continue systematic, predictable and substantial movements and to accelerate, where possible and in cooperation with the Joint Mission, its efforts in order to complete removal in the shortest possible time."[404] In this context, the Executive Council requested that the Director-General brief delegations each week on progress in implementation for close monitoring purposes.[405]

Developments After the Extension of Completion Dates

Progress still lagged, irrespective of the aforementioned deadline extension, which Syria again missed, chiefly owing to lack of full security control near one storage facility.[406] States Parties continued to raise concerns, urging Syria both before and after the deadline to complete the removal without further delay.[407] At its forty-first

[401] OPCW Doc. EC-75/DG.6, 25 February 2014, para. 4(b).

[402] OPCW Doc. EC-75/NAT.8 (India), 4 March 2014, p. 1.

[403] OPCW Doc. EC-75/NAT.12 (Netherlands), 4 March 2014, pp. 1–2.

[404] OPCW Doc. EC-75/2, 7 March 2014, para. 7.12.

[405] *Ibid.*, para. 7.12.

[406] UN Doc. S/2014/368, 23 May 2014, p. 1.

[407] OPCW Doc. EC-M-40/NAT.1 (Norway), 28 March 2014, p. 1; OPCW Doc. EC-M-40/NAT.2 (US), 28 March 2014, p. 1; OPCW Doc. EC-M-40/NAT.11 (Chile), 28 March 2014, p. 1; OPCW Doc. EC-M-40/NAT.4 (US), 11 April 2014, p. 1; OPCW Doc. EC-M-40/NAT.6 (Turkey), 11 April 2014, p. 1; OPCW Doc. EC-M-40/NAT.8 (Greece on behalf of the EU), 11 April 2014, pp. 1–2; OPCW Doc. EC-M-40/NAT.11 (Chile), 11 April 2014, p. 1; OPCW Doc. EC-M-40/NAT.13 (UK), 29 April 2014, p. 1; OPCW Doc. EC-M-40/NAT.14 (Ireland), 29 April 2014, p. 1; OPCW Doc. EC-M-40/NAT.15 (Turkey), 29 April 2014, p. 1; OPCW Doc. EC-M-40/NAT.24 (Mexico), 29 April 2014, p. 1; OPCW Doc. EC-M-40/NAT.20 (UK), 8 May 2014, pp. 1–2; OPCW Doc. EC-M-40/NAT.21 (Greece on behalf of the EU), 8 May 2014, p. 1; OPCW Doc. EC-M-40/NAT.23 (US), 8 May 2014, p. 2; OPCW Doc. EC-M-41/NAT.1 (Turkey), 22 May 2014, p. 1; OPCW Doc. EC-M-41/NAT.3 (UK), 22 May 2014, pp. 1–2; OPCW Doc. EC-M-41/NAT.4 (Netherlands), 22

meeting, the OPCW Executive Council on 22 May 2014 called on Syria "to undertake all possible efforts to complete the speedy removal of the remaining chemicals."[408] On 20 June 2014, the UN Secretary-General and the OPCW Director-General sent a joint letter urging Syria to remove the chemical weapons as soon as possible.[409]

Completion of Removal

The final shipments took place and all chemicals identified for removal were removed from Syria on 23 June 2014 (Table 4.15).[410] The Technical Secretariat so notified the OPCW Executive Council at its forty-second meeting of the OPCW held on 30 June 2014 and included in its report.[411] In accordance with the relevant paragraph of the Executive Council decision, the Director-General confirmed that 100% of the declared Priority 1 and 2 chemicals had been removed from Syria.[412] In July 2014, at the seventy-sixth session of the Executive Council, Brazil, Peru, NAM CWC States Parties and China, Russia, Cuba, the UK, the Netherlands, New Zealand, Switzerland, Malaysia, Nigeria, India, and the Republic of Korea referred to the complete removal of designated chemicals from Syria in their respective statements.[413] The Executive Council itself "welcomed the significant progress achieved in the elimination of the Syrian chemical weapons programme and noted, in particular, the completed elimination by 23 June 2014, i.e. in the first half of 2014…of all declared chemical

May 2014, p. 1; OPCW Doc. EC-M-41/NAT.5 (Germany), 22 May 2014, pp. 1–2; OPCW Doc. EC-M-41/NAT.6 (Denmark and Norway), 22 May 2014, p. 1; OPCW Doc. EC-M-41/NAT.7 (Greece on behalf of the EU), 22 May 2014, pp. 1–2; OPCW Doc. EC-M-41/NAT.8 (US), 22 May 2014, pp. 1–2; OPCW Doc. EC-M-42/NAT.1 (Greece on behalf of the EU), 17 June 2014, pp. 1–2; OPCW Doc. EC-M-42/NAT.2 (Turkey), 17 June 2014, p. 1; OPCW Doc. EC-M-42/NAT.3 (New Zealand), 17 June 2014, p. 1; OPCW Doc. EC-M-42/NAT.4 (UK), 17 June 2014, p. 1; OPCW Doc. EC-M-42/NAT.7 (Croatia), 17 June 2014, p. 1; OPCW Doc. EC-M-42/NAT.11 (Netherlands), 17 June 2014, p. 1; OPCW Doc. EC-M-42/NAT.12 (US), 17 June 2014, pp. 1–2; OPCW Doc. EC-M-42/NAT.13 (Uruguay), 17 June 2014, p. 1.

408 OPCW Doc. EC-M-41/2, 22 May 2014, para. 3.1.

409 UN Doc. S/2014/444, 26 June 2014, p. 2.

410 OPCW Doc. EC-76/DG.14, 25 June 2014, para. 4(a); OPCW Doc. EC-76/DG.16, 4 July 2014, para. 15.

411 OPCW Doc. EC-M-42/3, 30 June 2014, para. 7.6.

412 OPCW Doc. EC-76/DG.14, 25 June 2014, para. 4(a).

413 OPCW Doc. EC-76/NAT.16 (Brazil), 8 July 2014, p. 1; OPCW Doc. EC-76/NAT.17 (Peru), 8 July 2014, p. 1; OPCW Doc. EC-76/NAT.20 (Iran on behalf of the NAM CWC States Parties and China), 8 July 2014, p. 2; OPCW Doc. EC-76/NAT.22 (Russia), 8 July 2014, p. 2; OPCW Doc. EC-76/NAT.24 (Cuba), 8 July 2014, p. 1; OPCW Doc. EC-76/NAT.32 (UK), 8 July 2014, p. 1; OPCW Doc. EC-76/NAT.8 (Netherlands), 9 July 2014, p. 1; OPCW Doc. EC-76/NAT.31 (New Zealand), 9 July 2014, p. 1; OPCW Doc. EC-76/NAT.23 (Switzerland), 9 July 2014, p. 1; Malaysia, https://www.opcw.org/sites/default/files/documents/EC/76/en/Malaysia-08july.pdf, accesses 20 August 2021; Nigeria, https://www.opcw.org/sites/default/files/documents/EC/76/en/Nigeria-08july.pdf, accessed 22 April 2023; India, https://www.opcw.org/sites/default/files/documents/EC/76/en/India-09july.pdf, accessed 22 April 2023; Republic of Korea, https://www.opcw.org/sites/default/files/documents/EC/76/en/Republic_of_Korea-09july.pdf, accessed 22 April 2023.

Table 4.15 Progress of chemical weapons removal

Deadline	Priority 1	Priority 2
22 January 2014[415]	Limited quantities	N/A
22 February 2014[416]	4.5%	N/A
22 March 2014[417]	Approx. 35%	More than 80%
24 April 2014[418]	96.45%	81.09%
22 May 2014[419]	96.45%	81.09%
23 June 2014	100%	100%

weapons material and equipment from the territory of the Syrian Arab Republic, despite uniquely challenging conditions."[414]

(iii) **Destruction of Chemical Weapons**

Deadline of 1 March 2014 for Destruction in Syria

Syria failed to meet the 1 March 2014 deadline for destroying isopropanol and containers previously containing mustard agent in its territory.[420] The OPCW Executive Council observed without taking action. The Technical Secretariat verified the destruction of the containers and isopropanol as of 24 April and 22 May 2014, respectively.[421] Denmark, Norway, and the Netherlands referred to same in their Executive Council statements.[422]

Deadlines of 31 March 2014 and 30 June 2014 for Destruction Outside Syria

As feared, the delay in removal made it impossible to meet either deadline for destroying chemical weapons outside Syria: 31 March 2013 for mustard agent and key binary chemical weapon components, and 30 June 2014 for other chemicals.[423]

414 OPCW Doc. EC-76/6, 11 July 2014, para. 6.14.

415 OPCW Doc. EC-M-38/DG.1, 23 January 2014, para. 4(a).

416 OPCW Doc. EC-75/DG.6, 25 February 2014, para. 4(a).

417 OPCW Doc. EC-M-40/DG.1/Rev.1, 27 March 2014, para. 4(b).

418 OPCW Doc. EC-M-40/DG.4, 25 April 2014, para. 4(a).

419 OPCW Doc. EC-M-42/DG.1, 23 May 2014, para. 4(a).

420 OPCW Doc. EC-M-40/DG.1/Rev.1, 27 March 2014, para. 4(c).

421 OPCW Doc. EC-M-40/DG.4, 25 April 2014, para. 8; OPCW Doc. EC-M-42/DG.1, 23 May 2014, para. 4(a).

422 OPCW Doc. EC-M-41/NAT.6 (Denmark and Norway), 22 May 2014, p. 1 ("While it is commendable that the remaining isopropanol has been destroyed and that steps have been taken to prepare for the final removal, those steps were already overdue."); OPCW Doc. EC-M-41/NAT.4 (Netherlands), 22 May 2014, p. 1 ("The Netherlands welcomes the news that the remaining isopropanol in Site 2 now has been destroyed. The same, unfortunately, cannot yet be said of the twelve remaining chemical weapon production facilities.").

423 OPCW Doc. EC-M-40/DG.4, 25 April 2014, para. 4(a); OPCW Doc. EC-76/DG.16, 4 July 2014, para. 20.

Nor did the destruction of Priority 1 and Priority 2 chemicals commence according to the original schedule.[424] The seventy-sixth session of the Executive Council in July 2014 presented an opportunity to address Syria's non-compliance with its obligation to complete destruction of all chemical weapons, although Syria had nothing to do after chemical weapons were removed from its territory. During the discussion, the US argued that the Executive Council would need to acknowledge that Syria missed the deadline.[425] Instead of criticizing Syria, the Executive Council noted that destruction of Category 3 chemical weapons, isopropanol, and residual mustard agent was completed, and chemical weapons material removed from the territory of the Syrian Arab Republic, outside its territory had yet to be destroyed.[426]

Further Developments Towards the Completion of Destruction

Priority 1 chemicals were destroyed aboard the M/V Cape Ray between 9 July and 18 August 2014.[427] All liquid waste produced by the HD and DF hydrolysis was transported to the GEKA facility in Münster, Germany and the Ekokem facility in Riihimäki, Finland,[428] which destroyed same as of 21 May and 22 June 2015, respectively.[429] The Ekokem facility in Riihimäki, Finland and the Veolia ES Technical Solutions, L.L.C., in Port Arthur, Texas, US destroyed all Priority 2 chemicals as of 22 September 2014 and the end of 2015, respectively.[430] Veolia Environmental Services (UK) and Mexichem UK Limited also participated in destroying hydrogen fluoride (HF) and hydrochloric acid (HCl) which could not be transported to the US due to the delay in removal of same from Syria,[431] completing their work as of 7 August 2014 and 21 May 2015, respectively.[432] On 4 January 2016, the OPCW announced the complete destruction of declared Syrian chemical weapons (Fig. 4.1; Table 4.16).[433] At the eighty-first Executive Council session in March

[424] OPCW Doc. EC-76/DG.16, 4 July 2014, para. 21.

[425] OPCW Doc. EC-76/NAT.39 (US), 8 July 2014, p. 4.

[426] OPCW Doc. EC-76/6, 11 July 2014, paras. 6.15 and 6.16.

[427] OPCW Doc. EC-M-44/DG.1, 25 July 2014, para. 5(a); The White House, Statement by the President on the Completion by the M/V Cape Ray of the Destruction of Syria's Declared Chemical Weapons, 18 August 2014, https://obamawhitehouse.archives.gov/the-press-office/2014/08/18/statement-president-completion-mv-cape-ray-destruction-syria-s-declared-, accessed 22 April 2023; OPCW News, U.S. Completes Destruction of Sarin Precursors from Syria on the Cape Ray, 13 August 2014, https://www.opcw.org/media-centre/news/2014/08/us-completes-destruction-sarin-precursors-syria-cape-ray, accessed 22 April 2023.

[428] OPCW Doc. EC-M-44/DG.2, 25 August 2014, para. 5(a).

[429] OPCW Doc. EC-79/DG.8, 22 May 2015, para. 6(b); OPCW Doc. EC-79/DG.15, 23 June 2015, para. 6(b).

[430] OPCW Doc. EC-77/DG.22, 24 September 2014, para. 5(b); OPCW Doc. EC-81/DG.5, 25 January 2016, para. 6.

[431] OPCW Doc. EC-76/S/8, 9 July 2014, paras. 2–3; OPCW Doc. EC-M-44/DG.1, 25 July 2014, para. 5(d).

[432] OPCW Doc. EC-M-44/DG.2, 25 August 2014, para. 5(d); OPCW Doc. EC-79/DG.8, 22 May 2015, para. 6(a).

[433] OPCW News, Destruction of declared Syrian chemical weapons completed, 4 January 2016, https://www.opcw.org/media-centre/news/2016/01/destruction-declared-syrian-chemical-weapons-completed, accessed 22 April 2023. See also OPCW Doc. EC-81/DG.5, 25 January 2016, para. 6.

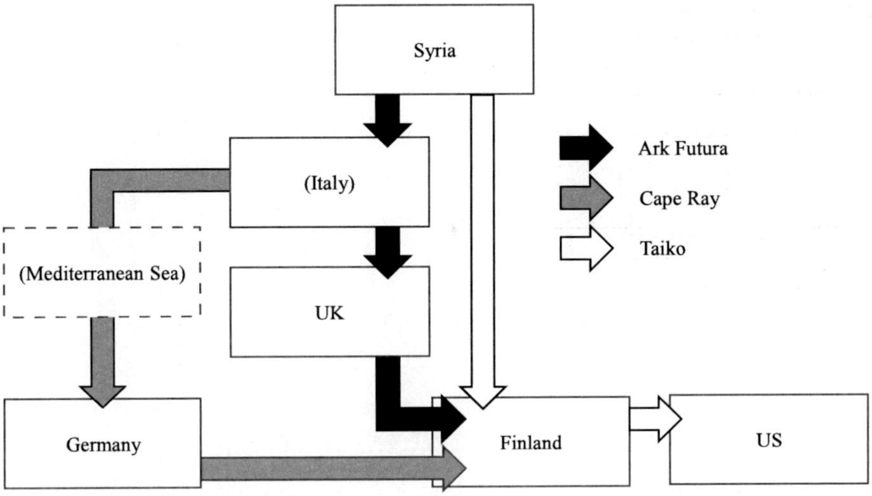

Fig. 4.1 Flow of chemicals[440]

2016, China stated "the set goal of the elimination of the Syrian chemical weapons is close to its attainment."[434] Malaysia, India, and Pakistan welcomed this accomplishment,[435] as did New Zealand, while stressing in its statement that "the Syrian file is far from closed."[436] Japan appreciated the efforts made by the parties.[437] The Republic of Korea reiterated its appreciation of the OPCW team for their devotion and hard work.[438] The Executive Council itself merely noted the relevant monthly reports by the Director-General and Syria.[439]

[434] OPCW Doc. EC-81/NAT.27 (China), 15 March 2016, p. 2.

[435] OPCW Doc. EC-81/NAT.19 (Malaysia), 15 March 2016, p. 1; India, https://www.opcw.org/sites/default/files/documents/EC/81/en/India_EC81.pdf, accessed 22 April 2023; OPCW Doc. EC-81/NAT.9 (Pakistan), 15 March 2016, p. 1.

[436] OPCW Doc. EC-81/NAT.14 (New Zealand), 15 March 2016, p. 1.

[437] OPCW Doc. EC-81/NAT.12 (Japan), 16 March 2016, p. 1.

[438] OPCW Doc. EC-81/NAT.35 (Republic of Korea), 15 March 2016, p. 1.

[439] OPCW Doc. EC-81/2, 23 March 2016, paras. 6.12 and 6.13. Since its ninety-second session in October 2019, the OPCW Executive Council included the following language in its reports: "As stated in the report of the Secretariat (EC-81/DG.5, 25 January 2016), all of the chemicals declared by the Syrian Arab Republic that had been removed from its territory in 2014 had now been destroyed" (OPCW Doc. EC-92/5, 11 October 2019, para. 7.17; OPCW Doc. EC-93/2, 12 March 2020, para. 6.13; OPCW Doc. EC-94/4, 9 July 2020, para. 6.13; OPCW Doc. EC-95/4, 9 October 2020, para. 6.16; OPCW Doc. EC-96/2, 12 March 2021, para. 6.15; OPCW Doc. EC-97/3, 8 July 2021, para. 6.14; OPCW Doc. EC-98/5, 7 October 2021, para. 6.16; OPCW Doc. EC-99/2, 10 March 2022, para. 7.15).

[440] See Dominique Anelli and Mehran Rouzbahani, "Chemical Demilitarisation in Syria: An Overview," *Verification & Implementation 2015* (2015), pp. 121–128, https://www.vertic.org/media/assets/VI%202015/VI%20Chapter%207.pdf, accessed 22 April 2023; OPCW Doc. EC-76/DG.16, 4 July 2014, para. 16.

Table 4.16 Progress of chemical weapons destruction

Date	Isopropanolin Syria (%)	Containers in Syria (%)	Priority 1outside of Syria	Priority 2outside of Syria
24 April 2014	93.1[441]	100[442]		
22 May 2014	100[443]			
7 August 2014			Completed in UK[444]	
18 August 2014			Completed on M/V Cape Ray[445]	
September 2014				Completed in Finland[446]
May 2015			Completed in the UK[447] (HD effluent) Completed in Germany[448]	

(continued)

441 OPCW Doc. EC-M-40/DG.4, 25 April 2014, para. 4(a).

442 *Ibid.*, para. 8.

443 OPCW Doc. EC-M-42/DG.1, 23 May 2014, para. 4(a).

444 OPCW Doc. EC-M-44/DG.2, 25 August 2014, para. 5(d).

445 The White House, Statement by the President on the Completion by the M/V Cape Ray of the Destruction of Syria's Declared Chemical Weapons, 18 August 2014, https://obamawhitehouse.archives.gov/the-press-office/2014/08/18/statement-president-completion-mv-cape-ray-destruction-syria-s-declared-, accessed 22 April 2023; OPCW News, U.S. Completes Destruction of Sarin Precursors from Syria on the Cape Ray, 13 August 2014, https://www.opcw.org/media-centre/news/2014/08/us-completes-destruction-sarin-precursors-syria-cape-ray, accessed 22 April 2023.

446 OPCW Doc. EC-77/DG.22, 24 September 2014, para. 5(b).

447 OPCW Doc. EC-79/DG.8, 22 May 2015, para. 6(a).

448 *Ibid.*, para. 6(b).

Table 4.16 (continued)

Date	Isopropanolin Syria (%)	Containers in Syria (%)	Priority 1outside of Syria	Priority 2outside of Syria
June 2015			(DF effluent) Completed in Finland[449]	
End of 2015				Completed in US[450]

[449] OPCW Doc. EC-79/DG.15, 23 June 2015, para. 6(b).

[450] OPCW Doc. EC-81/DG.5, 25 January 2016, para. 6.

(iv) Destruction of Chemical Weapons Production Facilities

Status of Destruction

Syria failed to destroy all of its chemical weapons production facilities by the 15 March 2014 deadline.[451] The status of twenty-six chemical weapons production facilities was unchanged as of 22 March 2014. One building and the aforementioned five underground structures and seven reinforced aircraft hangars remained to be destroyed and verified.[452] On 14 July 2014, following consultations with the DAT, Syria declared the "Al-Maliha" ricin plant its 27th chemical weapons production facility, although it was located in an area not under government control.[453]

Combined Plans for the Destruction and Verification

On 18 March 2014, Syria presented a revised destruction plan on the aforementioned twelve chemical weapons production facilities to the Technical Secretariat, which thereupon submitted a revised combined destruction and verification plan to the Executive Council on 27 March 2014. At its forty-second meeting on 17 June 2014, however, the Executive Council was unable to reach consensus,[454] owing chiefly to many States Parties continued insistence on the necessity of physical destruction.[455] Accordingly, the Executive Council adopted a decision in which all parties concerned were encouraged to continue their consultations with a view to arriving at an agreement.[456] At a meeting of Syria, the US, Russia, and the OPCW-UN Joint Mission on 27–28 June 2014, the Technical Secretariat presented a proposed compromise which

---

451 OPCW Doc. EC-M-40/DG.1/Rev.1, 27 March 2014, para. 4(c).

452 *Ibid.*, para. 4(c).

453 OPCW Doc. EC-M-44/DG.1, 25 July 2014, para. 4(b).

454 OPCW Doc. EC-M-42/3, 30 June 2014, para. 4.1.

455 OPCW Doc. EC-M-40/NAT.2 (US), 28 March 2014, p. 2 ("The extended completion date, set by the Council by consensus, was two weeks ago."); OPCW Doc. EC-M-40/NAT.2 (US), 28 March 2014, p. 1; OPCW Doc. EC-M-40/NAT.6 (Turkey), 11 April 2014, p. 1; OPCW Doc. EC-M-40/NAT.8 (Greece on behalf of the EU), 11 April 2014, p. 2; OPCW Doc. EC-M-41/NAT.1 (Turkey), 22 May 2014; OPCW Doc. EC-M-41/NAT.3 (UK), 22 May 2014, p. 2; OPCW Doc. EC-M-41/NAT.4 (Netherlands), 22 May 2014, p. 1; OPCW Doc. EC-M-41/NAT.5 (Germany), 22 May 2014, p. 2; OPCW Doc. EC-M-41/NAT.6 (Denmark and Norway), 22 May 2014, p. 1; OPCW Doc. EC-M-41/NAT.7 (Greece on behalf of the EU), 22 May 2014, p. 2; OPCW Doc. EC-M-41/NAT.8 (US), 22 May 2014, p. 2; OPCW Doc. EC-M-42/NAT.1 (Greece on behalf of the EU), 17 June 2014, p. 2; OPCW Doc. EC-M-42/NAT.2 (Turkey), 17 June 2014, p. 1; OPCW Doc. EC-M-42/NAT.3 (New Zealand), 17 June 2014, p. 1; OPCW Doc. EC-M-42/NAT.4 (UK), 17 June 2014, p. 1; OPCW Doc. EC-M-42/NAT.12 (US), 17 June 2014, p. 2. Iran asserted that "it is the right of each State Party to determine the method of destruction for these facilities" (OPCW Doc. EC-M-40/NAT.16 (Iran), 29 April 2014, p. 1.

456 OPCW Doc. EC-M-42/DEC.3, 17 June 2014. This decision also tasked the OPCW Director-General with approaching commercial firms and the UN to assist Syria in destruction activities. On 25 September 2014, the OPCW accordingly concluded a Contribution Agreement with the United Nations Office for Project Services (UNOPS) to provide equipment and services (OPCW Doc. EC-M-46/DG.1, 23 October 2014, para. 11).

would bring the interested States Parties closer together.[457] Consequently, other States Parties called for a quick solution, abandoning their insistence on physical destruction.[458]

On 24 July 2014, at its forty-third meeting, the Executive Council adopted the decision on the combined plans for the destruction and verification of twelve chemical weapons production facilities.[459] It was agreed that the seven hangars would be razed to the ground, the five underground structures would be sealed permanently to make them inaccessible,[460] that special monitoring system equipment would be installed at these underground structures for remote monitoring,[461] and that inspections would be conducted for four of the latter annually until 2020.[462] At its forty-sixth meeting, the Executive Council also adopted a decision on the combined plans for the destruction and verification of the "Al-Maliha" ricin production facility.[463]

Destruction of Twelve Chemical Weapons Production Facilities

Preparations for the destruction of the twelve chemical weapons production facilities were made in the second half of 2014. The Technical Secretariat, the United Nations Office for Project Services (UNOPS), Syria, and Syrian commercial firms held planning meetings to address the arrangements, including procuring necessary services, equipment, explosives, and materials, assigning responsibilities, tasks, and modalities, and estimating costs and schedules.[464] The work began on 24 December 2014,[465] with the underground structures destroyed and verified as of 22 July 2015[466] and the

---

[457] OPCW Doc. EC-M-44/DG.1, 25 July 2014, para. 4(a); OPCW Doc. EC-76/NAT.39 (US), 8 July 2014, p. 3.

[458] OPCW Doc. EC-76/NAT.9 (Chile), 8 July 2014, p. 2; OPCW Doc. EC-76/NAT.16 (Brazil), 8 July 2014, pp. 1–2; OPCW Doc. EC-76/NAT.18 (Guatemala), 8 July 2014, pp. 1–2; OPCW Doc. EC-76/NAT.17 (Peru), 8 July 2014, p. 1; OPCW Doc. EC-76/NAT.32 (UK), 8 July 2014, p. 2; OPCW Doc. EC-76/NAT.8 (Netherlands), 9 July 2014, p. 1; OPCW Doc. EC-76/NAT.21 (Croatia), 9 July 2014, p. 1; OPCW Doc. EC-76/NAT.28 (Japan), 9 July 2014, p. 1; OPCW Doc. EC-76/NAT.31 (New Zealand), 9 July 2014, p. 2. See also OPCW Doc. EC-76/NAT.22 (Russia) 8 July 2014, p. 3.

[459] OPCW Doc. EC-M-43/2, 24 July 2014, para. 4; OPCW Doc. EC-M-44/DG.1, 25 July 2014, para. 4(a).

[460] OPCW News, OPCW Maritime Operation Completes Deliveries of Syrian Chemicals to Commercial Destruction Facilities, 24 July, 2014 https://www.opcw.org/media-centre/news/2014/07/opcw-maritime-operation-completes-deliveries-syrian-chemicals-commercial, accessed 22 April 2023.

[461] See OPCW Doc. EC-M-44/DG.2, 25 August 2014, para. 13.

[462] See OPCW Doc. EC-93/DG.12, 24 February 2020, para. 16.

[463] OPCW Doc. EC-M-46/DEC.1, 19 November 2014.

[464] OPCW Doc. EC-M-44/DG.2, 25 August 2014, para. 4(a); OPCW Doc. EC-77/DG.22, 24 September 2014, para. 4(a); OPCW Doc. EC-M-46/DG.1, 23 October 2014, para. 4(a); OPCW Doc. EC-78/DG.3, 24 November 2014, para. 4(a); UN Doc. S/2014/948, 26 December 2014, Annex, para. 4(a).

[465] UN Doc. S/2015/56, 26 January 2015, Annex, para. 4(a).

[466] OPCW Doc. EC-80/DG.2, 23 July 2015, para. 5(a).

hangars as of 6 June 2017.[467] The Technical Secretariat carried out the mandated annual inspections for the former thereafter.[468]

Destruction of Two Other Chemical Weapons Production Facilities

In July 2017, the security situation surrounding the two remaining chemical weapons production facilities was improved,[469] and Syria requested assistance in their destruction.[470] The Secretariat conducted an initial inspection of these facilities in November 2017.[471] Arrangements to assist Syria in destroying these were completed by June 2018, thanks to the voluntary contributions by States Parties to the Syria Trust Fund for the Destruction of Chemical Weapons, including those made in response to this request.[472]

Completion of Destruction

On 12 July 2018, the Technical Secretariat inspected two remaining facilities and verified that all declared buildings had been razed to ground level and all debris had been removed,[473] meaning the completion of destruction (Table 4.17). States Parties welcomed the completed destruction under OPCW verification.[474] At its eighty-ninth session, the Executive Council noted the monthly reports by the Director-General and Syria.[475] At subsequent sessions, the Executive Council included the following language in its reports: "[t]he Secretariat has also verified the destruction of all twenty-seven chemical weapons production facilities (CWPFs) declared by the Syrian Arab Republic (EC-89/DG.1, dated 24 July 2018)." [476]

---

[467] OPCW Doc. EC-85/DG.21, 23 June 2017, para. 6(a).

[468] OPCW Doc. C-22/4, 29 November 2017, para. 1.33; OPCW Doc. C-23/4, 19 November 2018, para. 1.23.

[469] OPCW Doc. EC-86/DG.2, 24 July 2017, para. 6(b).

[470] OPCW Doc. S/1541/2017, 9 October 2017.

[471] OPCW Doc. EC-87/DG.4, 24 November 2017, para. 6(a).

[472] OPCW Doc. EC-87/DG.10, 22 January 2018, para. 6(a); OPCW Doc. EC-88/DG.16, 22 June 2018, para. 6(a). OPCW Doc. EC-87/NAT.11 (Germany), 13 March 2018 ("In November 2017, Germany contributed more than EUR 700,000 towards the destruction of the last two declared chemical weapons production facilities in the Syrian Arab Republic. Linked to our contribution is the expectation that the Syrian Arab Republic will fully honour its obligations as a State Party to the Chemical Weapons Convention and will finally become a country free of chemical weapons.").

[473] OPCW Doc. EC-89/DG.1, 24 July 2018, para. 6(a).

[474] OPCW Doc. EC-89/NAT.23 (Mexico), 10 October 2018, p. 2; OPCW Doc. EC-89/NAT.32 (India), 10 October 2018, p. 2; OPCW Doc. EC-89/NAT.34 (Morocco), 10 October 2018, p. 2.

[475] OPCW Doc. EC-89/3, 22 October 2018, paras. 6.12 and 6.13.

[476] OPCW Doc. EC-92/5, 11 October 2019, para. 7.17; OPCW Doc. EC-93/2, 12 March 2020, para. 6.13; OPCW Doc. EC-94/4, 9 July 2020, para. 6.13; OPCW Doc. EC-95/4, 9 October 2020, para. 6.16; OPCW Doc. EC-96/2, 12 March 2021, para. 6.15; OPCW Doc. EC-97/3, 8 July 2021, para. 6.14; OPCW Doc. EC-98/5, 7 October 2021, para. 6.16; OPCW Doc. EC-99/2, 10 March 2022, para. 7.15.

Table 4.17 Progress of chemical weapons production facilities destruction

		Declaration	Combined plan	Destruction
1	Mobile unit 1	23 October 2013[477]	17 December 2013[478]	By the end of December 2013[479]
2	Mobile unit 2	23 October 2013	17 December 2013	By the end of December 2013
3	Mobile unit 3	23 October 2013	17 December 2013	By the end of December 2013
4	Mobile unit 4	23 October 2013	17 December 2013	By the end of December 2013
5	Mobile unit 5	23 October 2013	17 December 2013	By the end of December 2013
6	Mobile unit 6	23 October 2013	17 December 2013	By the end of December 2013
7	Mobile unit 7	23 October 2013	17 December 2013	By the end of December 2013
8	Mobile unit 8	23 October 2013	17 December 2013	By the end of December 2013
9	"Tudmur"	23 October 2013	17 December 2013	By 30 June 2014[480]
10	"Al-Dhamir 1"	23 October 2013	17 December 2013	By 30 June 2014
11	"Al-Dhamir 3"	23 October 2013	17 December 2013	By 30 June 2014
12	"Al-Nasiriyah 2"	23 October 2013	17 December 2013	By 30 June 2014
13	"500 (Aleppo)"	23 October 2013	17 December 2013	By 30 June 2014

(continued)

[477] OPCW Doc. EC-M-34/DG.1, 25 October 2013, para. 4(a).

[478] OPCW Doc. EC-M-37/DG.1, 23 December 2013, para. 15.

[479] OPCW Doc. EC-M-37/DG.1, 23 December 2013, para. 5(a); OPCW Doc. EC-M-40/DG.4, 25 April 2014, para. 4(c).

[480] OPCW Doc. EC-76/6, 11 July 2014, para. 6.15(g).

Table 4.17 (continued)

		Declaration	Combined plan	Destruction
14	"Tel Kurdi"	23 October 2013	17 December 2013	Destroyed by 30 June 2014[481] Verified on 12 June 2018[482]
15	Underground structure 1	23 October 2013	24 July 2014[483]	31 January 2015[484]
16	Underground structure 2	23 October 2013	24 July 2014	22 February 2015[485]
17	Underground structure 3	23 October 2013	24 July 2014	By 22 March 2015[486]
18	Underground structure 4	23 October 2013	24 July 2014	By 22 April 2015[487]
19	Underground structure 5	23 October 2013	24 July 2014	8 September 2015[488]
20	Aircraft hangar 1	23 October 2013	24 July 2014	By 22 August 2015[489]
21	Aircraft hangar 2	23 October 2013	24 July 2014	By 22 August 2015
22	Aircraft hangar 3	23 October 2013	24 July 2014	By 22 August 2015
23	Aircraft hangar 4	23 October 2013	24 July 2014	By 22 August 2015
24	Aircraft hangar 5	23 October 2013	24 July 2014	8 September 2015[490]
25	Aircraft hangar 6	23 October 2013	24 July 2014	By 21 October 2015[491]
26	Aircraft hangar 7	23 October 2013	24 July 2014	6 June 2017[492]
27	"Al-Maliha"	14 July 2014[493]	19 November 2014[494]	23 June 2018[495]

[481] *Ibid.*

[482] OPCW Doc. EC-89/DG.1, 24 July 2018, para. 6(a). See also Scott Lucas, Assad Regime Still Hasn't Declared All Its Chemical Weapons, 27 July 2018, https://eaworldview.com/2018/07/assad-regime-still-hasnt-declared-all-its-chemical-weapons/, accessed 22 April 2023.

[483] OPCW Doc. EC-M-44/DG.1, 25 July 2014, para. 4(a).

[484] OPCW Doc. EC-78/DG.9, 23 February 2015, para. 5(a).

[485] *Ibid.*

[486] OPCW Doc. EC-79/DG.1, 23 March 2015, para. 5(a).

[487] OPCW Doc. EC-M-49/DG.1, 23 April 2015, para. 5(a).

[488] OPCW Doc. EC-80/DG.20, 23 September 2015, para. 5(a).

[489] OPCW Doc. EC-80/DG.4, 24 August 2015, para. 5(a).

[490] OPCW Doc. EC-80/DG.20, 23 September 2015, para. 5(a).

[491] OPCW Doc. EC-81/DG.1, 22 October 2015, para. 5(a).

[492] OPCW Doc. EC-85/DG.21, 23 June 2017, para. 6(a).

[493] OPCW Doc. EC-M-44/DG.1, 25 July 2014, para. 4(b).

[494] OPCW Doc. EC-M-46/DEC.1, 19 November 2014.

Annual Inspections of the Underground Structures

The Technical Secretariat continued to fulfill its mandate to conduct annual inspections of the underground structures verified as destroyed.[496] While originally scheduled to expire as of 31 March 2020,[497] the Director-General postponed the final inspections until further notice due to the COVID-19 outbreak.[498] The Technical Secretariat made its final visits to the underground structures in November 2020, where it observed the removal of the monitoring equipment, and informed Syria that the underground structures should remain sealed as part of the destruction plan agreed to by the Executive Council.[499]

(v) **Reporting and Cooperation**

Syria continued to submit its monthly reports to the Executive Council in accordance with Decision EC-M-34/DEC.1.[500] However, the status of its compliance with its

495 Lucas, *supra* note 482.

496 OPCW Doc. C-24/4, 28 November 2019, para. 1.18; OPCW Doc. C-25/4, 20 April 2021, para. 1.14; OPCW Doc. EC-93/DG.3, 25 November 2019, para. 13.

497 OPCW Doc. EC-93/DG.12, 24 February 2020, para. 16.

498 OPCW Doc. EC-94/DG.1, 24 March 2020, para. 18.

499 OPCW Doc. EC-96/DG.3, 24 November 2020, para. 17.

500 See OPCW Doc. EC-83/DG.18, 26 September 2016, para. 5(b); OPCW Doc. EC-84/DG.1, 25 October 2016, para. 5(b); OPCW Doc. EC-84/DG.4, 23 November 2016, para. 6(b); OPCW Doc. EC-84/DG.6, 22 December 2016, para. 6(b); OPCW Doc. EC-84/DG.11, 24 January 2017, para. 6(b); OPCW Doc. EC-84/DG.22, 23 February 2017, para. 6(b); OPCW Doc. EC-85/DG.2, 23 March 2017, para. 6(b); OPCW Doc. EC-85/DG.5, 24 April 2017, para. 6(b); OPCW Doc. EC-85/DG.11, 24 May 2017, para. 6(b); OPCW Doc. EC-85/DG.21, 23 June 2017, para. 6(b); OPCW Doc. EC-86/DG.2, 24 July 2017, para. 6(b); OPCW Doc. EC-86/DG.7, 23 August 2017, para. 6(b); OPCW Doc. EC-86/DG.23, 25 September 2017, para. 6(b); OPCW Doc. EC-87/DG.2, 23 October 2017, para. 6(c); OPCW Doc. EC-87/DG.4, 24 November 2017, para. 6(b); OPCW Doc. EC-87/DG.7, 22 December 2017, para. 6(b); OPCW Doc. EC-87/DG.10, 22 January 2018, para. 6(b); OPCW Doc. EC-87/DG.16, 23 February 2018, para. 6(b); OPCW Doc. EC-88/DG.1, 23 March 2018, para. 6(c); OPCW Doc. EC-88/DG.3, 24 April 2018, para. 6(b); OPCW Doc. EC-88/DG.8, 24 May 2018, para. 6(b); OPCW Doc. EC-88/DG.16, 22 June 2018, para. 6(b); OPCW Doc. EC-89/DG.1, 24 July 2018, para. 6(b); OPCW Doc. EC-89/DG.10, 24 August 2018, para. 6(b); OPCW Doc. EC-89/DG.24, 24 September 2018, para. 6(b); OPCW Doc. EC-90/DG.1, 23 October 2018, para. 6(b); OPCW Doc. EC-90/DG.2, 23 November 2018, para. 6(b); OPCW Doc. EC-90/DG.4, 21 December 2018, para. 6(b); OPCW Doc. EC-90/DG.7, 24 January 2019, para. 6(b); OPCW Doc. EC-90/DG.11, 25 February 2019, para. 6(b); OPCW Doc. EC-91/DG.1, 25 March 2019, para. 6(b); OPCW Doc. EC-91/DG.2, 4 May 2019, para. 6(b); OPCW Doc. EC-91/DG.7, 24 May 2019, para. 6(b); OPCW Doc. EC-91/DG.14, 24 June 2019, para. 6(b); OPCW Doc. EC-92/DG.1, 24 July 2019, para. 6(b); OPCW Doc. EC-92/DG.6, 23 August 2019, para. 6(b); OPCW Doc. EC-92/DG.22, 24 September 2019, para. 6(b); OPCW Doc. EC-93/DG.1, 23 October 2019, para. 6(b); OPCW Doc. EC-93/DG.3, 25 November 2019, para. 6(b); OPCW Doc. EC-93/DG.5, 24 December 2019, para. 6(b); OPCW Doc. EC-93/DG.7, 24 January 2020, para. 6(b); OPCW Doc. EC-93/DG.12, 24 February 2020, para. 6(b); OPCW Doc. EC-94/DG.1, 24 March 2020, para. 8(b); OPCW Doc. EC-94/DG.3, 24 April 2020, para. 8(b); OPCW Doc. EC-94/DG.5, 25 May 2020, para. 8(b); OPCW Doc. EC-94/DG.12*, 24 June 2020, para. 8(b); OPCW Doc. EC-95/DG.1, 24 July 2020, para. 8(b); OPCW Doc. EC-95/DG.4, 24 August 2020, para. 8(b); OPCW Doc. EC-95/DG.19, 24 September 2020, para. 7(b); OPCW Doc. EC-96/DG.2, 26 October 2020, para. 7(b); OPCW Doc. EC-96/DG.3, 24

obligation to cooperate was in doubt. The OPCW Director-General's monthly reports refrained from referring to Syrian cooperation in the specific context of outstanding issues regarding the Syrian initial declaration and more generally since May and September 2016, respectively. States Parties have also pointed out lack of cooperation of Syria,,[501] exemplified by Syria's aforementioned refusing a visa for a DAT member. The notification of the loss of two cylinders "caused by the attack of Israel"[502] also raised doubts about Syria's credibility in preserving evidence.[503]

November 2020, para. 7(b); OPCW Doc. EC-96/DG.4, 24 December 2020, para. 8(b); OPCW Doc. EC-96/DG.6, 25 January 2021, para. 8(b); OPCW Doc. EC-96/DG.13, 24 February 2021, para. 8(b); OPCW Doc. EC-97/DG.2, 24 March 2021, para. 8(b); OPCW Doc. EC-97/DG.3, 23 April 2021, para. 8(b); OPCW Doc. EC-97/DG.7, 25 May 2021, para. 9(b); OPCW Doc. EC-97/DG.13, 22 June 2021, para. 9(b); OPCW Doc. EC-98/DG.1, 23 July 2021, para. 9(b); OPCW Doc. EC-98/DG.6, 24 August 2021, para. 9(b); OPCW Doc. EC-98/DG.24, 24 September 2021, para. 9(b); OPCW Doc. EC-99/DG.1, 26 October 2021, para. 9(b); OPCW Doc. EC-99/DG.2, 24 November 2021, para. 9(b); OPCW Doc. EC-99/DG.3, 23 December 2021, para. 9(b); OPCW Doc. EC-99/DG.5, 24 January 2022, para. 9(b); OPCW Doc. EC-99/DG.13, 24 February 2022, para. 9(b); OPCW Doc. EC-100/DG.2, 24 March 2022, para. 9(b); OPCW Doc. EC-100/DG.4, 25 April 2022, para. 9(b); OPCW Doc. EC-100/DG.6, 24 May 2022, para. 8(b); OPCW Doc. EC-100/DG.14, 23 June 2022, para. 8(b); OPCW Doc. EC-101/DG.2, 22 July 2022, para. 8(b); OPCW Doc. EC-101/DG.4, 24 August 2022, para. 8(b); OPCW Doc. EC-101/DG.22, 23 September 2022, para. 8(b); OPCW Doc. EC-102/DG.1, 25 October 2022, para. 8(b); OPCW Doc. EC-102/DG.2, 24 November 2022, para. 8(b); OPCW Doc. EC-102/DG.3, 23 December 2022, para. 8(b). These documents were classified.

501 OPCW Doc. EC-84/NAT.10 (Malta on behalf of the EU), 7 March 2017, p. 2; OPCW Doc. EC-M-55/NAT.11 (Belgium), 5 July 2017, p. 1; OPCW Doc. EC-90/NAT.17 (UK), 12 March 2019, p. 1; OPCW Doc. EC-91/NAT.30 (New Zealand), 9 July 2019, p. 2. See also OPCW Doc. EC-94/NAT.4 (Germany), 15 April 2020, p. 2; UN Doc. S/2020/1088, 9 November 2020, Annex II (Belgium), p. 4; UN Doc. S/2020/1088, 9 November 2020, Annex V (Estonia), p. 10; UN Doc. S/2020/1088, 9 November 2020, Annex VI (France), p. 11; UN Doc. S/2020/1202, 16 December 2020, Annex VI (Estonia), p. 15; UN Doc. S/2021/226, 8 March 2021, Annex III (Estonia), p. 5; UN Doc. S/2021/446, 10 May 2021, Annex XIX (Turkey), p. 31; OPCW Doc. EC-96/NAT.42 (France), 9 March 2021, p. 2; OPCW Doc. C-25/NAT.103 (France), 20 April 2021, p. 2; OPCW Doc. C-25/NAT.123 (Estonia), 20 April 2021, p. 1; OPCW Doc. EC-97/NAT.34 (Czech Republic), 6 July 2021, p. 1; OPCW Doc. EC-97/NAT.55 (Spain), 6 July 2021, p. 2; UN Doc. S/PV.8872, 4 October 2021, p. 13 (UK); OPCW Doc. EC-98/NAT.14 (Austria), 5 October 2021, p. 1; OPCW Doc. EC-98/NAT.16 (Lithuania), 5 October 2021, p. 2; UN Doc. S/PV.8921, 8 December 2021, pp. 6 (US), 8 (Norway), 9 (Estonia); UN Doc. S/PV.8982, 28 February 2022, p. 9 (Albania); OPCW Doc. EC-99/NAT.13 (Germany), 8 March 2022, p. 2; OPCW Doc. EC-99/NAT.18 (Sweden), 8 March 2022, p. 1; OPCW Doc. EC-99/NAT.26 (Czech), 8 March 2022, p. 2; UN Doc. S/PV.8990, 10 March 2022, p. 7 (Albania); OPCW Doc. EC-100/NAT.17 (Norway), 5 July 2022, p. 2; OPCW Doc. EC-100/NAT.24 (Germany), 5 July 2022, p. 2; UN Doc. S/PV.9141, 29 September 2022, p. 6 (Albania); UN Doc. S/PV.9164, 25 October 2022, p. 7 (Albania).

502 OPCW Doc. EC-98/NAT.1 (Syria), 9 July 2021, Annex. According to Syria, "[t]he 'Al-Nasiriyah 1' site (one of the 5 underground facilities—tunnels—that were sealed with the knowledge of the Technical Secretariat of the OPCW) was flagrantly attacked by the Israel enemy using missiles" resulted in loss of several items including "2 chlorine cylinders related to the alleged Douma incident of (2018)."

503 The Technical Secretariat, having pointed out that "the cylinders were stored and inspected at another declared site approximately 60 km from the location at which they were reportedly destroyed on 8 June 2021," requested that Syria provide all relevant information regarding the movement of the two cylinders (OPCW Doc. EC-98/DG.1, 23 July 2021, paras. 21 and 23). Syria did not comply

Table 4.18 Destruction of chemical weapons

State party	Deadline for complete destruction of chemical weapons	Status
Albania	29 April 2007	Incomplete

Table 4.19 Destruction of chemical weapons production facilities

State party	Deadline for complete destruction of chemical weapons production facilities	Status
India (three CWPFs)	29 April 2007	Incomplete (one CWPF)
Libya (two CWPFs)	29 April 2007	Incomplete (two CWPFs)
Russia (eight CWPFs)	29 April 2007	Incomplete (one CWPF)

(3) Evaluation

(a) Possible References

(i) Deadlines

The OPCW has experienced several cases of missed deadlines for completing disarmament (Table 4.18).[504] Albania failed to meet the deadline for complete destruction of its chemical weapons. At its forty-ninth session in June 2007, the Executive Council reiterated its concern at the delays, requesting under the terms of Article VIII, para. 36 of the Convention that Albania take measures to redress the situation by meeting its obligation to completely destroy its chemical weapons without any further delay,[505] which Albania did on 11 July 2007. At its fiftieth session in September 2007, the Executive Council noted the Director-General's report and the information provided by Albania on this accomplishment.[506]

India, Libya, and Russia missed the deadline for destroying chemical weapons production facilities (Table 4.19).[507] The OPCW Executive Council continued to monitor progress periodically.

(OPCW Doc. EC-98/DG.24, 24 September 2021, para. 24; OPCW Doc. EC-99/DG.1, 26 October 2021, para. 22; OPCW Doc. EC-99/DG.2, 24 November 2021, para. 23; OPCW Doc. EC-99/DG.3, 23 December 2021, para. 24; OPCW Doc. EC-99/DG.5, 24 January 2022, para. 21; OPCW Doc. EC-99/DG.13, 24 February 2022, para. 21; OPCW Doc. EC-100/DG.2, 24 March 2022, para. 24; OPCW Doc. EC-100/DG.4, 25 April 2022, para. 23; OPCW Doc. EC-100/DG.6, 24 May 2022, para. 22; OPCW Doc. EC-100/DG.14, 23 June 2022, para. 22; OPCW Doc. EC-101/DG.2, 22 July 2022, para. 23; OPCW Doc. EC-101/DG.4, 24 August 2022, para. 21; OPCW Doc. EC-101/DG.22, 23 September 2022, para. 20; OPCW Doc. EC-102/DG.1, 25 October 2022, para. 20; OPCW Doc. EC-102/DG.2, 24 November 2022, para. 24; OPCW Doc. EC-102/DG.3, 23 December 2022, para. 23).

504 Missed intermediate deadlines for chemical weapons destruction are not counted herein.

505 OPCW Doc. C-12/3 EC-50/3, 26 September 2007, para. 2.16.

506 OPCW Doc. C-13/2 EC-54/4, 15 October 2008, para. 2.15.

507 OPCW Doc. S/784/2009, 7 August 2009, p. 9, para. 4.2.

Table 4.20 Conversion of chemical weapons production facilities

State party	Deadline for complete conversion of chemical weapons production facilities	Status
Russia (sixteen CWPFs)	29 April 2003	Incomplete (ten CWPFs)

Russia also missed the deadline for converting ten chemical weapons production facilities (Table 4.20).[508] At its thirty-third session in June 2003, the Executive Council established reporting requirements for the concerned State Party and the Director-General, in which the former informs the Executive Council of the conversion status annually at the last regular session, while the latter reports progress of conversion at its first regular session following its regular annual inspection.[509]

(ii) **Declaration**

Albania and Libya informed the newly discovered chemical weapons long period after the submission of its initial declarations. In November 2002, Albania notified the OPCW that it had discovered undeclared chemical weapons agents,[510] which it declared thereafter. The Director-General informed the Executive Council on receipt of said declaration at the thirty-second session in March 2003.[511] In September 2011, after the fall of the Gaddafi regime, Libyan rebels found chemical weapons that the previous government had not declared.[512] On 31 October 2011, the UN Security Council adopted Resolution 2017, calling upon the Libyan authorities "to meet Libya's arms control, disarmament and non-proliferation obligations under international law, through the full implementation of their plans in this regard."[513] Libya submitted a declaration on 28 November 2011.[514] In both cases, the Executive Council took no punitive action, neither expressing concern about nor condemning the previous government's failure to submit complete declarations.

(b) **Effectiveness**

As is the case with potential non-compliance, the OPCW policy-making organs have also approached two situations of non-compliance in different manners in light of different types of obligation and taken *ex post* measures against them.

The OPCW Executive Council has responded to non-compliance with deadlines in different ways, depending on circumstance. First, the Executive Council

508 OPCW Doc. C-9/5, 30 November 2004, p. 6, para. 1.21.

509 OPCW Doc. C-8/3 EC-34/3, 23 September 2003, para. 2.48.

510 OPCW Doc. C-8/5, 22 October 2003, p. 1, para. 3 and p. 6, para. 2.2.

511 CBW Conventions Bulletin, Issue No. 59 (March 2003), p. 2.

512 The Guardian, Libyan rebels discover Gaddafi's chemical weapons, 22 September 2011, https://www.theguardian.com/world/2011/sep/22/libyan-rebels-gaddafis-chemical-weapons , accessed 22 April 2023; The Telegraph, Libyan rebels "capture Gaddafi chemical weapons site," 22 September 2011, http://www.telegraph.co.uk/news/worldnews/africaandindianocean/libya/8780601/Libyan-rebels-capture-Gaddafi-chemical-weapons-site.html, accessed 31 December 2022.

513 UN Doc. S/RES/2017 (2011), 31 October 2011, operative para. 1.

514 OPCW Doc. C-16/DG.18, 28 November 2011, p. 9, para. 40.

established *ex post* new deadlines to remove remaining chemical weapons from its territory, legitimizing the delay and giving Syria additional time to comply. In a formalistic sense, this measure failed, because Syria missed the revised deadlines as well, although its feasibility was always in doubt. The new deadlines were a compromise between Syria's original proposal and an alternative plan offered by the OPCW Operational Planning Group that was intended to put political pressure on Syria to accelerate the removal work. In this sense, the new deadlines brought about the ultimate complete removal of chemical weapons from the Syrian territory. Second, the Executive Council continued monitoring the progress of the destruction of chemical weapons and chemical weapons production facilities in Syria after those deadlines passed. Subsequent developments suggest why. It appears that the Executive Council anticipated that Syria would complete the destruction of chemical weapons in its territory before long, and more importantly, meet the 30 June 2014 deadline for destroying all such chemical weapons. As Syria also showed its commitment to said destruction, the Executive Council may have deemed it unnecessary to respond to this particular non-compliance. The situation with the remaining chemical weapons production facilities was completely different. Syria struggled to destroy these due to technical issues for twelve facilities and security concerns for two. The Executive Council also acknowledged these problems, which were likely to preclude setting new deadlines. Despite the expired deadline, the risk of the remaining chemical weapons production facilities being used declined, partly because the chemical agents necessary for producing chemical weapons were almost destroyed or removed, and partly because, as with its chemical weapons, Syria remained fully committed to the destruction of the remaining chemical weapons production facilities as well. Third, the Executive Council practically ignored the deadline for destroying chemical weapons outside Syria. Given that Syria's participation in this phase ended when its chemical weapons were removed from its territory, Syria was technically no longer obligated to meet this deadline. Instead, the Executive Council continued to monitor this phase without further reference to deadlines. All of these approaches were non-confrontational, rather than punitive, and achieved positive results in that non-compliance was redressed due to designated tasks being completed. It follows that the mechanisms for responding to non-compliance with the obligation to meet deadlines proved effective.

By contrast, the Executive Council has taken *ex post* confrontational measures in response to non-compliance with the obligation to submit full and complete declarations, which appear ineffective to-date. The incomplete declaration has been a continuous issue since the stage of potential non-compliance. The linkage between chemical weapons use and incomplete declaration triggered the move of the policy-making organs of the OPCW and the UN to the next stage of non-compliance. They no longer took *ex ante* non-confrontational approach to Syria but decided *ex post* confrontational punitive measures. As mentioned above, the UN Security Council drafted a legally binding resolution under Chapter VII that would oblige Syria to declare all undeclared chemical weapons and place them under OPCW supervision and control, which Russia and China vetoed. This malfunctioning of the UN Security Council led the OPCW policy-making organs, for the first time in OPCW history, into imposing the abovementioned *ex post* punitive sanctions which suspended the rights and privileges of Syria as a Member State of the OPCW. The UN General Assembly including the UNHRC also called on Syria to take necessary action. Syria has criticized these measures and further refused to redress the matter. As mentioned, strong and consistent political support from Russia, China, and Iran may take some pressure off Syria. There is no prospect of the stalemate being resolved in the near future.

(c) **Implications**

The discussion on the mechanism to respond to non-compliance has some general implications.

First, the policy-making organs attach importance to objective information as a basis for decision-making, as is the case with the issue of non-compliance with the obligation not to use chemical weapons. The OPCW Executive Council cited the Director-General's reports and notes that included the DAT's evaluations, in addressing incomplete declarations. It also referred to the Director-General's affirmation to whether specific deadlines were met. In both cases, the OPCW Executive Council never made subjective assessment but relied on the objective information collected or confirmed by the Director-General. There are degrees of objectivity between these obligations. None will dispute the objectiveness of information about non-compliance with deadlines. Confirmation is easy, given viable verification. By contrast, the State concerned may raise questions about the validity of monitoring organs' evaluations concerning the obligation to submit complete declarations. The State concerned may insist that specific items and facilities are not subject to declaration, while the monitoring organs may disagree. Policy-making organs must bear this in mind when relying on "objective" information.

Second, an approach to redressing non-compliance depends on the situation. It may stand to reason that non-compliance should preferably be redressed as soon as possible, to avoid both undermining obligations and risking further non-compliance. Hence, measures to redress non-compliance tend to be punitive, confrontational, or at least demanding. The record shows that the OPCW policy-making organs have taken, and the UN Security Council attempted to take, just such stringent measures. In response to non-compliance with the obligation to submit complete declarations, they imposed sanctions on Syria for the first time in OPCW history. However, at the same time, the OPCW policy-making organs have demonstrated flexibility, establishing new deadlines, exploring actions conducive to compliance, and even pragmatic inaction, as seen in their response to Syria's non-compliance with its obligation on the deadlines. This suggests that there is more than one approach to redressing non-compliance, and that there are acceptable and non-acceptable kinds of non-compliance, at least in the limited context of the elimination of (chemical) weapons. Policy-making organs are thus compelled to choose appropriate measures in any given instance of non-compliance.

Third, no effective *ex post* measures for resolving incomplete declarations have yet been developed. As indicated, monitoring organs treat this as non-compliance, compelling concerned States to make redress by clarifying ambiguities and, when necessary, to submit additional information. If concerned States disagree, however, they will see no need to take action. Although policy-making organs may take *ex post* punitive and confrontational action, concerned States will not respond. Nor will they respond to tightening of such measures, creating a vicious circle. In practically all cases of weapons subject to international verification, including chemical weapons, the only effective remedy appears to be sanctions enacted by UN Security Council resolution. Given the current structure of co-existing of sovereign States and the dependence on their good faith, it is very difficult to discover clandestine weapons programs. History shows that whenever undeclared weapons or related weapons program were discovered, again, including chemical weapons, they were revealed by persons either directly or indirectly involved with same. Albania and Libya announced the discovery of chemical weapons stockpiles concealed by old regimes in 2002 and 2011,[515] proving that even including the challenge inspection provisions in the CWC did not prevent incomplete declarations. As with measures against non-compliance with the obligation against use chemical weapons, policy-making organs must continue to put pressure on concerned States to change their behavior.

4.4 Conclusion

The foregoing indicates that the obligation to eliminate chemical weapons, that is, the obligation to act, requires systematic and continuous compliance/non-compliance control based on combined *ex ante* and *ex post* measures. As concerned States will themselves eliminate their chemical weapons, international law thus imposes such relevant substantive obligations on said States as the obligations to submit declarations and to meet deadlines. Institutional mechanisms for ensuring compliance are required as these obligations are non-reciprocal in nature. Verification is the mechanism usually applied in international disarmament law, and it must be designed *ex ante*, so that it may be fully implemented from the outset. Should doubts arise about

[515] The CBW Conventions Bulletin, Issue No. 59 (March 2003), pp. 2 and 6. The Guardian, Libyan rebels discover Gaddafi's chemical weapons, 22 September 2011, https://www.theguardian.com/world/2011/sep/22/libyan-rebels-gaddafis-chemical-weapons, accessed 21 January 2023; The Telegraph, Libyan rebels "capture Gaddafi chemical weapons site," 22 September 2011, https://www.telegraph.co.uk/news/worldnews/africaandindianocean/libya/8780601/Libyan-rebels-capture-Gaddafi-chemical-weapons-site.html, accessed 21 January 2023; OPCW News, Captured Chemical Weapons in Libya Were Declared to the OPCW by Former Government, 28 September 2011, https://www.opcw.org/media-centre/news/2011/09/captured-chemical-weapons-libya-were-declared-opcw-former-government, accessed 22 April 2023; UN Doc. S/RES/2017 (2011), 31 October 2011, para. 1; OPCW Doc. S/1042/2012/Rev.2, 19 December 2012, para. 3.9(c). See also OPCW Doc. C-16/DG.18, 28 November 2011, p. 9, para. 40; OPCW Doc. C-16/NAT.24 (Libya), 29 November 2011. cf. Samuel Nurding, "Libya destroys 'Category 1' chemical weapons," *Trust and Verify*, Issue Number 144 (January-March 2014), Verification Research, Training and Information Center (VERTIC), p. 4.

compliance, the institutional verification mechanism may address the potential non-compliance either by taking *ex ante* measures, or continuing to monitor the situation. The primary purpose of such *ex ante* measures is to induce the State concerned to comply with their obligations. Should this non-confrontational approach fail, the institutional mechanism must respond to actual non-compliance, taking *ex post* measures and continuing to monitor the situation until the completion of the obliged acts by the State concerned.

We have seen that Syria has been subject to obligations under both the CWC and the Resolution 2118 Regime, said frameworks conferring soundness, flexibility and stringency toward eliminating the Syrian chemical weapons program "in the most expedient and safest manner."

Regarding the obligations under the Chemical Weapons Convention, they are nothing new. They have existed since the Convention's entry into force and applied to all States Parties, including Syria. As previously described, they encompass the core substantive obligation to destroy chemical weapons and chemical weapons production facilities, and such subsidiary obligations as submitting declarations and cooperating with inspections. These are the basic components of disarmament obligations which contribute to ensuring soundness of the whole process of elimination of Syrian chemical weapons program. When it comes to the obligation to meet deadlines for elimination of chemical weapons program, the deadlines as such appeared very stringent and ambitious, though the OPCW Executive Council established them by fulfilling its mandate to decide the order of destruction and procedures for latecomer States Parties (Article IV, para. 8 and Article V, para. 10). One exceptional measure was taken under the Resolution 2118 Regime. Syria was exempted from its obligation to destroy its chemical weapons on its own soil. While the OPCW had experience in transferring old chemical weapons from one State Party to another for destruction based on *ad hoc* OPCW Executive Council measures, despite no explicit provisions for doing so, there were both qualitative and quantitative differences between a handful of non-usable remnants and large quantities of chemicals that could easily be weaponized. The only legal avenue was for the UN Security Council to authorize the transfer of Syrian chemical weapons. The Security Council accordingly did so, drawing on the flexibility that the UN Charter offered.

Regarding the obligations under the Resolution 2118 Regime, they are newly introduced to strengthen compliance/non-compliance control and supplement the existing CWC obligations, thereby making the Resolution 2118 Regime itself and its implementation sound. The Regime begins by obligating Syria to comply with all aspects of OPCW Executive Council Decision EC-M-33/DEC.1 in accordance with Article 25 of the UN Charter, precluding any interpretation other than that OPCW Executive Council Decision EC-M-33/DEC.1 is binding on Syria. It also obliges Syria to cooperate with the OPCW and the UN. In this regard, the UN Security Council ensures the privileges and immunities of the OPCW personnel who carry out the mandates under the Resolution 2118 Regime, addressing a legal gap in the period between the adoption of the Resolution 2118 Regime and the entry into force of the CWC for Syria. The Regime further obligates Syria to submit regular reports to the OPCW Executive Council. Turning once more to completeness of declaration, while this concept is apparently not included in the CWC, it nonetheless emerged as a key requirement for Syria through discourse among States Parties at the policy-making organs during implementation, indicating the Resolution 2118 Regime's stringency.

As previously described, the Resolution 2118 Regime introduced systematic and continuous compliance/non-compliance control based on combined *ex ante* and *ex post* measures. While it continued to control compliance/non-compliance of Syria with the relevant obligations, as the situations progress, its function transformed from a mechanism to ensure compliance to that to address potential non-compliance to that to respond to non-compliance.

Initially, the Resolution 2118 Regime functioned to ensure compliance with Syrian chemical weapons elimination obligations. Its approach was essentially standard. The OPCW Technical Secretariat's role in the OPCW-UN Joint Mission was verifying Syrian compliance with the aforementioned obligations, especially submitting declarations, meeting destruction deadlines, and accepting inspections. The OPCW Executive Council was responsible for monitoring the entire process of eliminating Syrian chemical weapons. To this end, it met as frequently as Syria's extraordinary situation demanded, monthly at least. Overall, the mechanisms for ensuring Syrian compliance with its obligation to eliminate its chemical weapons program worked as intended, for the following reasons. First, the Resolution 2118 Regime succeeded in its *ex ante* design, taking an incremental approach so as to strike a balance between the urgent need to legitimize its objectives and the feasibility of means and methods for achieving same. At the outset, the OPCW Executive Council made arrangements as the CWC required, while the UN Security Council resolved legal obstacles to the verification work. The OPCW-UN Joint Mission was established to facilitate smooth verification activities. Second, Syria was committed to eliminating its chemical weapons program. It almost immediately agreed, even acceding to the CWC and accepting the Resolution 2118 Regime. It also fulfilled obligations, including submitting monthly implementation reports to the OPCW Executive Council. The OPCW Director-General's monthly reports also confirmed Syria's cooperation with the OPCW-UN Joint Mission. All would be well so long as Syria fully complied with said obligations. Third, all stakeholders cooperated toward the same goal. It was clear from the beginning that Syria was unable to destroy its chemical weapons and chemical weapons production facilities alone due to security concerns and a lack of various resources. Regardless of their positions on the Assad regime, State Parties offered assistance in a variety of forms, exemplifying international cooperation.

Compliance/non-compliance control may identify doubts about compliance. Early on, the Resolution 2118 Regime functioned to address such potential non-compliance, while the OPCW Executive Council has taken different approaches to address potential non-compliance with different obligations. Non-compliance with the deadline obligation is highly predictable. While a concerned State technically remains always in compliance before a deadline passes, if the tasks in question are likely to remain undone, then non-compliance is only a matter of time. An *ex ante* option thus exists to extend the deadline. The OPCW Executive Council instead let the deadline elapse, resulting in Syrian non-compliance. As described above, there might be a number of reasons for doing so. Setting new deadlines might not be realistic; missing deadlines would also be regarded as politically acceptable non-compliance; the deadline of "first half of 2014" for complete destruction of chemical weapons became almost meaningless. By contrast, the OPCW strove to address potential Syrian non-compliance with the obligation to submit full and complete declarations. Despite the availability of challenge inspections under the CWC and the more powerful "section 2(d)" inspection under the Resolution 2118 Regime, the OPCW Director-General dispatched the DAT to Syria, per its prior agreement to address unresolved issues related to the Syrian declaration. Based on the DAT reports, the Executive Council took *ex ante* measures against Syria, which were essentially non-confrontational in that it called on Syria to fulfill this prerequisite obligation to submit full and complete declarations. As a matter of fact, the OPCW failed to resolve either instance of potential non-compliance, irrespective of approach, which does not necessarily mean that the *ex ante* measures for address potential non-compliance itself were meaningless. They enabled the policy-making organs to identify the nature of said non-compliance as well as the timing of next steps.

In the later stages, the Resolution 2118 Regime functioned to respond to non-compliance. The policy-making organs have taken several *ex post* measures in this regard. The OPCW Executive Council has responded to Syrian non-compliance with the deadline obligation as follows. First, it set a new *ex post* deadline for chemical weapons removal, Syria nonetheless failed to meet the new deadline, however, suggesting that it was intended as political pressure on Syria to accelerate the removal. Second, the Executive Council continued monitoring the destruction of chemical weapons and chemical weapons production facilities on Syrian soil after the deadlines expired, appearing to opt for inaction in light of the likelihood that said destruction would be completed sooner or later. Third, the Executive Council practically ignored the deadline for the destruction of chemical weapons outside Syria, as the removal of same from Syria precluded Syrian participation therein, though it continued to monitor the destruction of same. All of these approaches were non-confrontational, rather than punitive, and led to positive results in that non-compliance was ultimately redressed through said completion of tasks. Hence, the mechanisms for responding to non-compliance were flexible enough to resolve the non-compliance with the deadline obligation. By contrast, the policy-making organs have taken or attempted to take confrontational *ex post* measures in response to Syrian non-compliance with its obligation to submit full and complete declaration. While the UN Security Council attempted to adopt legally binding sanctions under Chapter VII, obliging Syria to declare all undeclared chemical weapons and place them under OPCW supervision and control, which Russia and China vetoed, thus leaving the OPCW policy-making organs with sole responsibility. Having encountered the refusal of Syria to redress the situation, the OPCW Conference of the States Parties, for the first time, suspended Syria's rights and privileges as an OPCW Member State. So far, these punitive sanctions make no impact on the attitude of Syria. Further efforts are required to solve this stalemate.

Chapter 5
Conclusion

Abstract The discussion in main Chapters leads to the following conclusions. On the one hand, there are several differences between these compliance/non-compliance controls deriving from the assumed different natures of the substantive obligations. The mechanism for ensuring compliance is required only for compliance/non-compliance control concerning the obligation to eliminate chemical weapons programs because it is an obligation to act. The natures of obligations also characterize the concept of compliance/non-compliance control and purposes of *ex post* measures. On the other hand, there are similarities between these compliance/non-compliance controls, which the author holds indicate the objective and non-reciprocal nature of both obligations. Both compliance/non-compliance controls rely on objective information, need cooperation of Syria, find unique value of the second mechanism for addressing potential non-compliance, and require political support. The Syrian chemical weapons problem poses challenges and opportunities for the CWC and beyond. It is clear that the CWC is neither perfect nor comprehensive enough to address all chemical weapons issues. A holistic approach should be taken. Other relevant institutional frameworks should collaborate with the OPCW. In this context, the most important such organ remains the UN Security Council, because it has the power to impose and enforce obligations on concerned States, as well as the authority to modify applications of treaty provisions.

5.1 Introduction

This monograph has discussed Syrian chemical weapons issues from an international law perspective, with attention chiefly paid to Syrian compliance with its obligations under international humanitarian law and international disarmament law. Chapter 2 provided an overview of relevant international law, spanning the 1925 Geneva Protocol, the 1993 Chemical Weapons Convention (CWC), the 1998 Rome Statute of the International Criminal Court (ICC), customary international law, and UN Security Council Resolution 1540. It then explained the contexts of legally binding instruments, development of customary rules, implementation thereof, and how these relate to Syria. Chapters 3 and 4 examined Syrian compliance/non-compliance

T. Abe, *Syrian Chemical Weapons and International Law*,
https://doi.org/10.1007/978-981-99-3700-4_5

with its obligations through the analytical framework of compliance/non-compliance control, which may comprise any of mechanisms for ensuring compliance, addressing potential non-compliance, and responding to actual non-compliance, as appropriate. Chapter 3 focused on compliance/non-compliance control with obligations under international humanitarian law, i.e., the prohibition against using chemical weapons, while Chapter 4 was devoted to obligations under international disarmament law, i.e., destroying Syria's chemical weapons program. Underpinning this approach of treating these topics in their own respective chapters was an assumption of their differences in terms of approaches, methodologies, and measures, deriving logically from their respective substantive natures. This approach revealed similarities as well as the suggested differences. This concluding chapter will summarize the entire discussion by highlighting compliance/non-compliance control characteristics in the Syrian chemical weapons context, as well as implications for the CWC and beyond.

5.2 Characteristics

(1) Differences

The preceding denotes several differences between these compliance/non-compliance controls deriving from the assumed different natures of the substantive obligations.

- ***With or without the first mechanism***

The most significant difference is whether the first mechanism for ensuring compliance is required. This is true only of compliance/non-compliance control concerning the obligation to eliminate chemical weapons programs, and not compliance/non-compliance control concerning the obligation against chemical weapons use in non-international armed conflict. While both obligations must be fulfilled within the concerned State's territory and the implementation thereof should be made visible to the international community, issues therewith arise independently. On the one hand, the entire implementation is at issue where the obligation to eliminate chemical weapons programs, an obligation to act, is concerned. Syria is obliged to submit full, accurate and complete declarations, to remove chemical weapons outside its territory, and to destroy both other chemical weapons and chemical weapons production facilities on its soil. It is also obligated to meet deadlines for completing relevant tasks, beginning with submitting its declarations. Compliance/non-compliance control begins here and must be sustained through such tasks of elimination as removal and destruction even when deadlines are missed. Full compliance with the obligation to eliminate the chemical weapons program is to be verified. On the other hand, issues arise with the obligation against using chemical weapons only after their alleged or actual use, as this is an obligation of omission. This means that under normal circumstances, where the obligation is upheld, compliance is ensured, obviating the need for mechanisms for ensuring compliance with same. Mechanisms for addressing potential non-compliance and responding to actual non-compliance are sufficient.

- ***Systematic and continuous or* ad hoc**

The natures of obligations characterize their concepts of compliance/non-compliance control. Where the obligation to eliminate chemical weapons programs is concerned, compliance/non-compliance control is systematic and continuous. As mentioned, it should function from the outset, making its *ex ante* design essential. The substantive components include regular reports on implementation by Syria, as well as by the OPCW Director-General and the UN Secretary-General based on information collected through verification, and OPCW Executive Council and UN Security Council assessments based on said reports. The emphasis here is on collecting facts because such facts themselves prove whether Syria complies with its obligations. For the relevant organs to fulfill their mandates, personnel, logistical, financial, and legal issues need to have been addressed *ex ante*. When deadlines are missed or concerns about declarations arise, this mechanism may shift either to addressing potential non-compliance or responding to actual non-compliance. When there is real or potential non-compliance, such controls rely on *ex post* measures, although *ex ante* actions may also be possible depending on particulars. In any event the goal of such compliance/non-compliance control is to verify the elimination of Syrian chemical weapons. By contrast, compliance/non-compliance control where the obligation against using chemical weapons is concerned will always be *ad hoc*. That is, when chemical weapons use is alleged, *ex post* measures are taken to determine the facts of such allegations. When allegations are confirmed and perpetrators identified, *ex post* measures are taken to redress such non-compliance. The policy-making organs may thus address potential or actual non-compliance by fulfilling their mandates.

- ***Purposes of* ex post *measures***

The different natures of obligation require the different purposes of *ex post* measures against Syria. For the obligation to eliminate chemical weapons, *ex post* measures are aimed to induce full compliance the elimination of Syria's chemical weapons program as soon as possible. As described herein, the record shows that Syria was in potential and actual non-compliance with both the declaration and deadline obligations. Syria has been called upon to submit full, accurate, and complete declarations, which is the only means of redressing same. Regarding the latter, the OPCW Executive Council let deadlines expire, monitoring developments, except for its *ex post* extension deadlines for removal of chemicals for destruction outside Syria. It appears that the Executive Council regarded impending and actual non-compliance with the deadline obligation less seriously, given the expectation of complete destruction of weapons and facilities in the near future.

Ex post measures have interlinked preventive and punitive purposes where the obligation against chemical weapons use is concerned. While many such measures have been taken, institutional and unilateral, military and non-military alike, they have all proven ineffective in preventing further such use. This suggests the difficulty in ensuring compliance with the obligation of omission where the only enforcement mechanism is UN Security Council resolutions. Syria may have suffered some economic or political damage due to the *ex post* punitive measures taken against it, especially sanctions. It remains an open question whether such punitive measures redress non-compliance, at least, with obligations under international humanitarian law applicable to non-international armed conflict.

(2) **Similarities**

As alluded to above, there are similarities between these compliance/non-compliance controls, which the author holds indicate the objective and non-reciprocal nature of both obligations.

- ***Facts (Objective information)***

The preceding also shows that both controls rely on objective information, i.e., facts, which are indispensable because if they conform with what is required by international obligation, the State concerned will be assessed as being compliant. As mentioned above, assessing facts matters to the obligation against chemical weapons use, and the UN Mission and the OPCW FFM investigated allegations of same, while the OPCW-UN JIM and the OPCW IIT examined the question of attribution thereof. On the other hand, the declaration obligation hinges on completeness and accuracy, i.e., the absence of undeclared chemical weapons and chemical weapons production facilities. The OPCW Director-General also established the DAT, which has worked with the Syrian authorities to resolve outstanding issues with this obligation. All in all, monitoring organs, including ad hoc fact-finding teams, play the key role of independent and impartial third parties, collecting objective facts in Syrian territory. They fulfill their own mandates pursuant to the CWC or provided by policy-making organs, with the consent of Syria, thus guaranteeing the objectivity of their reporting. The policy-making organs take action only after these organs submit their reports, showing that they refrain from making decisions while uncertain about facts. Several States have also relied on these reports when enacting autonomous sanction measures.

- ***Cooperation of Syria***

As acts within Syrian territory are the subjects of compliance/non-compliance control, the monitoring organs are tasked with collecting and/or verifying information, necessitating Syrian cooperation. It is therefore significant that operative para. 7 of UN Security Council Resolution 2118 imposes on Syria the obligation to cooperate with the UN and the OPCW. While the scope of this obligation initially appeared to be verification concerning eliminating Syrian chemical weapons, the Security Council expanded it to investigating allegations of chemical weapons use as well, by stressing that this obligation included the cooperation with the OPCW Director-General, the OPCW FFM, and the OPCW-UN JIM. The OPCW policy-making organs have taken the position that the OPCW IIT's work is also covered by UN Security Council Resolution 2118 operative para. 7, and that CWC Article VII, para. 7 stipulates State Party obligations to cooperate with the OPCW, which covers such teams as the FFM, the DAT, and the IIT. Additionally, while OPCW Director-General reports prior to August 2016 indicate that Syria has continued to extend the necessary cooperation in accordance with the implementation of para. 1(e) of EC-M-33/DEC.1 and operative para. 7 of UN Security Council Resolution 2118, this language was omitted thereafter.

Given the reciprocal and bilateral nature of this obligation, it should be comparatively straightforward to assess non-compliance with same, which is admittedly a task for policy-making organs rather than secretariats. In this regard, the OPCW policy-making organs have expressed deep concern that the Syrian Arab Republic did not cooperate with, and provide access to, the IIT as required by UN Security Council Resolution 2118. Non-compliance with the obligation on cooperation also provides justification for said policy-making organs to enact collective sanctions.

- ***Unique value of the second mechanism for addressing potential non-compliance***

The elements of objective information and cooperation of Syria are closely related to the unique value of the mechanism for addressing potential non-compliance, which represents an ambiguous situation between compliance and non-compliance. Ideally, the ambiguity is clarified or redressed, resulting in compliance being confirmed, which applies to some allegations of chemical weapons use. Fact-finding bodies investigated and concluded that the allegations were not proved. Syria also resolved some doubts, ambiguities, and inconsistencies in declaration by submitting amendments. These were exceptions, however. All other such situations, other allegations of chemical weapons use, missed deadlines and other declaration problems, resulted in actual non-compliance.

Notwithstanding, mechanisms for addressing potential non-compliance still have value, because they assess information to clarify non-compliance and/or induce Syria to comply with its obligations before it can be found intentionally non-compliant. The policy-making organs wait on the fact-finding bodies' assessments of allegations of chemical weapons use to rule whether Syria is in non-compliance. The policy-making organs are also constrained when one party to the armed conflict criticizes another for using chemical weapons, and the latter categorically denies same or counters that the former used chemical weapons instead. Potential Syrian non-compliance has tended to last longer because the division of roles between the OPCW FFM and such attribution mechanisms as the OPCW-UN JIM and the OPCW IIT require additional time to find facts, including identifying perpetrators. The policy-making organs also delayed finding Syria in non-compliance on declarations, taking advantage of the ensuing ambiguity to try to induce Syria to comply with its obligations. As described elsewhere, the OPCW Director-General dispatched the DAT to Syria fifteen times between April 2014 and June 2016 to resolve such outstanding issues, and the Executive Council called on Syria to continue cooperating with the Director-General and the DAT. The Executive Council also adopted a decision to redress the situation in

November 2016, even after the OPCW-UN JIM reports of August and October 2016 that identified the Syrian government as having used chemical weapons.

- ***Political support***

The effectiveness of measures depends significantly on the conditions under which they are adopted. Prior to August 2016, the UN Security Council and the OPCW Executive Council showed a collective will by adopting resolutions and decisions concerning the Syrian chemical weapons program essentially unanimously. Syria also cooperated with the UN and the OPCW, as indicated above. After the OPCW-UN JIM submitted its report of August 2016, however, which identified the Syrian government as responsible for using chemical weapons, Syria and Russia objected. Russian, and sometimes Chinese, vetoes have since deadlocked the Security Council, while the OPCW policy-making organs have been visibly divided. The Executive Council adopted two decisions by narrow margins, while the Conference of the States Parties adopted as many with some votes against, as well as abstentions. Russia, Iran, and China opposed all of these, and Syria has refused to accept the OPCW IIT, which was established by Conference of the States Parties Decision C-SS-4/DEC.3, as well as to implement Executive Council Decision EC-94/DEC.2. The Conference of the States Parties consequently imposed sanctions on Syria under Decision C-25/DEC.9. Balancing how a given measure is adopted with its effectiveness remains a challenge (Table 5.1).

Table 5.1 Votes on OPCW decisions

Date	Decision	Result
27 September 2013	OPCW Doc. EC-M-33/DEC.1 (elimination)	Consensus
4 February 2015	OPCW Doc. EC-M-48/DEC.1 (use)	40 in favor, 1 against
23 November 2015	OPCW Doc. EC-M-50/DEC.1 (use)	Consensus
23 March 2016	OPCW Doc. EC-81/DEC.4 (declaration)	Consensus
11 November 2016	OPCW Doc. EC-83/DEC.5 (use and declaration)	28 in favor, 4 against and 9 abstentions
27 June 2018	OPCW Doc. C-SS-4/DEC.3 (use)	82 in favor, 24 against and 0 abstention (46 States Parties did not participate in the vote.)
9 July 2020	OPCW Doc. EC-94/DEC.2 (possession and use)	29 in favor, 3 against and 9 abstentions
21 April 2021	OPCW Doc. C-25/DEC.9 (possession and use)	103 in favor, 14 against and 13 abstentions (9 States Parties did not participate in the vote.)

(3) **Logical Linkage**

Initially, the OPCW policy-making organs addressed the abovementioned non-compliance issues, real and potential alike, of incomplete declarations and chemical weapons use independently. The reason was that the different chemicals fell into different categories, with the precursors of sarin and mustard subject to destruction under the Resolution 2118 Regime, while chlorine, which was not declared as weapons, was used frequently, against the CWC and UN Security Council Resolution 2118. Then came the OPCW-UN JIM report of October 2017, which confirmed the Syrian government's use of sarin in Khan Shaykhun in April 2017, showing that Syria still possessed sarin, which, as mentioned above, should have been destroyed under the Resolution 2118 Regime. Both non-compliance matters thus became intertwined. The sarin attack was evidence of Syrian non-compliance with the obligation to submit full and complete declaration, and raised further concerns about other possible undeclared chemical weapons.

While this instance may be unique, either circumstance could occur again if conditions are met, summarized as follows: (i) use of certain weapons is prohibited; (ii) an obligation to destroy specific chemicals configuring said weapons is imposed; and, (iii) other chemicals configuring such weapons that are not subject to destruction are diverted for military purposes, then the respective non-compliance matters would be handled independently. Two different dual-use chemicals could give rise to such conditions. On the other hand, the respective non-compliance matters would be intertwined if, in addition to (i) and (ii) above, (iii) the said obligation to destroy is fulfilled, and (iv) notwithstanding, said specific chemicals are used. While destruction may succeed in the former instance, it clearly fails in the latter, making it the more serious circumstance.

5.3 Challenges and Opportunities

This monograph ends with a description of challenges and opportunities that the Syrian chemical weapons problem poses for the CWC and beyond. First, the CWC is not a perfect instrument for eliminating chemical weapons under international verification. Its fundamental obligations, the prohibition and destruction of chemical weapons, are strict, as they should be. Other aspects are too strict, however, and while such strictness may avoid disputes in interpretation and application, they may also pose obstacles to achieving the Convention's objectives when extraordinary circumstances arise. One example is challenge inspections. The CWC describes detailed procedures that allow only State Parties to request this powerful short-notice verification tool. Yet no such request has been made against Syria, despite the need to clarify or resolve such "questions concerning possible non-compliance" as chemical weapons use and incomplete declarations, possibly owing to limited scope for *ratione personae*. Other States Parties would consider requesting a challenge inspection during the Syrian armed conflict infeasible due to inability to guarantee safety and security of Technical Secretariat personnel.[1] Instead, the OPCW explored alternatives, in which the OPCW Director-General took the initiative, establishing the OPCW FFM to investigate allegations of chemical weapons attacks, as well as dispatching the DAT to Syria to resolve the declaration problems with the Syrian authorities. Syria accepted these teams and the OPCW Executive Council endorsed them. Another example was transferring Syrian chemical weapons to other States Parties for destruction, which the CWC prohibits "under any circumstances." While the OPCW admittedly has experience addressing the transfer of old chemical weapons to other State Party for destruction by *ad hoc* Executive Council endorsement, the transfer of usable chemical weapons abroad for destruction would have a qualitatively different meaning for the CWC. External flexibility was thus required to bridge this legal gap, in the form of explicit reference to Article 25 of the UN Charter in UN Security Council Resolution 2118. This arrangement suggests that expediency took precedence over strict prohibition in this instance.

Second, the CWC is also insufficiently comprehensive. Its chief emphasis is on States,[2] and thus it does not encompass acts by individuals. While it obliges States Parties to take national implementation measures, including penal legislation, each State Party is left to its own devices. Nor are there any prosecution or extradition provisions. To address these problems, the UN Security Council instituted the OPCW–UN JIM to identify those responsible for using chemical weapons in Syria. This might suggest that the UN Security Council was the most appropriate venue for establishing attribution mechanisms, and that the OPCW might have no mandate in this regard. The vetoing of the renewal of the OPCW–UN JIM's mandate led to further developments. The OPCW Conference of the States Parties voted to adopt a decision paving the way for creating the OPCW IIT, with the same mandate as the OPCW–UN JIM. Those States Parties that opposed this decision stressed the lack of OPCW mandate regarding attribution, refusing to cooperate with the OPCW IIT or accept the findings of its reports. In any event, even if the OPCW had such a mandate, criminal proceedings against individuals are beyond the CWC's scope, falling instead to either State Parties' domestic legal systems or the ICC.

Given that the CWC is thus not comprehensive, a holistic approach should be taken to resolving chemical weapons issues. Other relevant institutional frameworks should collaborate with the OPCW, as denoted above. In this context, the most important such organ remains the UN Security Council, because it has the power to impose and enforce obligations on concerned States, as well as the authority to

[1] Tatsuya Abe, "Challenge inspections under the Chemical Weapons Convention: between ideal and reality," The Nonproliferation Review, Vol. 24, Nos. 1-2 (2017), p. 167, 182.

[2] Mirko Sossai, "Identifying the Perpetrators of Chemical Attacks in Syria: The Organisation for the Prohibition of Chemical Weapons as Part of the Fight against Impunity," Journal of International Criminal Justice, Vol. 17, Issue 2 (May 2019), p. 211, 227.

modify applications of treaty provisions. It also has the mandate to make referrals to the ICC. And as indicated above, the UN Security Council has indeed bridged some gaps concerning the Syrian chemical weapons program. Even if the UN Security Council is deadlocked, other actors should continue to explore ways to ensure that the Security Council fulfills its primary responsibility to maintain international peace, however difficult this may prove.

Appendix A
OPCW Director-General/UN Secretary-General Monthly Reports

	OPCW Director-General monthly reports	OPCW Executive Council	UN Secretary-General monthly reports	UN Security Council
1	EC-M-34/DG.1, 25 October 2013	Noted (EC-M-34/3, 15 November 2013, para. 3.3)	S/2013/629, 28 October 2013	Informal briefing, 5 November 2013
2	EC-M-35/DG.1, 25 November 2013	Noted (EC-77/3 C-19/2, 9 October 2014, para. 2.30)	S/2013/700, 27 November 2013	Informal briefing, 4 December 2013
3	EC-M-37/DG.1, 23 December 2013	Noted (EC-M-37/2, 8 January 2014, para. 3.1)	S/2013/774, 27 December 2013	Informal briefing, 7 January 2014
4	EC-M-38/DG.1, 23 January 2014	Received (EC-77/3 C-19/2, 9 October 2014, para. 2.30)	S/2014/52, 27 January 2014	Informal briefing, 6 February 2014
5	EC-75/DG.6, 25 February 2014	Noted (EC-75/2, 7 March 2014, para. 7.10)	S/2014/133, 27 February 2014	Informal briefing, 5 March 2014
6	EC-M-40/DG.1/Rev.1, 27 March 2014	Received (EC-77/3 C-19/2, 9 October 2014, para. 2.30)	S/2014/220, 26 March 2014	Informal briefing, 3 April 2014
7	EC-M-40/DG.4, 25 April 2014	Received (EC-77/3 C-19/2, 9 October 2014, para. 2.30)	S/2014/300, 25 April 2014	Informal briefing, 5 May 2014
8	EC-M-42/DG.1, 23 May 2014	Noted (EC-M-42/3, 30 June 2014, para. 3.2)	S/2014/368, 23 May 2014	Informal briefing, 4 June 2014

(continued)

T. Abe, *Syrian Chemical Weapons and International Law*,
https://doi.org/10.1007/978-981-99-3700-4

(continued)

	OPCW Director-General monthly reports	OPCW Executive Council	UN Secretary-General monthly reports	UN Security Council
9	EC-76/DG.14, 25 June 2014	Noted (EC-76/6, 11 July 2014, para. 6.10)	S/2014/444, 26 June 2014	
10	EC-M-44/DG.1, 25 July 2014	Noted (EC-M-44/2, 28 August 2014, para. 3.4)	S/2014/533, 25 July 2014	
11	EC-M-44/DG.2, 25 August 2014	Noted (EC-M-44/2, 28 August 2014, para. 3.4)	S/2014/622, 25 August 2014	
12	EC-77/DG.22, 24 September 2014	Noted (EC-77/4, 10 October 2014, para. 6.10)	S/2014/706, 26 September 2014	
13	EC-M-46/DG.1, 23 October 2014	Noted (EC-M-46/3, 19 November 2014, para. 3.2)	S/2014/767, 27 October 2014	
14	EC-78/DG.3, 24 November 2014	Noted (EC-M-48/3, 4 February 2015, para. 4.2)	S/2014/853, 28 November 2014	
15	EC-M-48/DG.1, 23 December 2014 (not publicly available)	Noted (EC-M-48/3, 4 February 2015, para. 4.2)	S/2014/948, 26 December 2014	
16	EC-78/DG.5, 23 January 2015 (not publicly available)	Noted (EC-78/2, 19 March 2015, para. 6.10)	S/2015/56, 26 January 2015	
17	EC-78/DG.9, 23 February 2015	Noted (EC-78/2, 19 March 2015, para. 6.10)	S/2015/138, 25 February 2015	
18	EC-79/DG.1, 23 March 2015	Noted (EC-M-49/3, 7 May 2015, para. 4.1)	S/2015/211, 25 March 2015	
19	EC-M-49/DG.1, 23 April 2015	Noted (EC-M-49/3, 7 May 2015, para. 4.1)	S/2015/295, 28 April 2015	
20	EC-79/DG.8, 22 May 2015	Noted (EC-79/6, 9 July 2015, para. 6.11)	S/2015/391, 28 May 2015	
21	EC-79/DG.15, 23 June 2015	Noted (EC-79/6, 9 July 2015, para. 6.11)	S/2015/485, 26 June 2015	
22	EC-80/DG.2, 23 July 2015	Noted (EC-80/4*, 8 October 2015, para. 7.10)	S/2015/572, 29 July 2015	
23	EC-80/DG.4, 24 August 2015	Noted (EC-80/4*, 8 October 2015, para. 7.10)	S/2015/668, 27 August 2015	

(continued)

(continued)

	OPCW Director-General monthly reports	OPCW Executive Council	UN Secretary-General monthly reports	UN Security Council
24	EC-80/DG.20, 23 September 2015	Noted (EC-80/4*, 8 October 2015, para. 7.10)	S/2015/737, 24 September 2015	
25	EC-81/DG.1, 22 October 2015	Noted (EC-81/2, 23 March 2016, para. 6.13)	S/2015/820, 26 October 2015	
26	EC-81/DG.2, 24 November 2015	Noted (EC-81/2, 23 March 2016, para. 6.13)	S/2015/908, 24 November 2015	
27	EC-81/DG.3, 22 December 2015	Noted (EC-81/2, 23 March 2016, para. 6.13)	S/2015/1049, 29 December 2015	
28	EC-81/DG.5, 25 January 2016	Noted (EC-81/2, 23 March 2016, para. 6.13)	S/2016/85, 28 January 2016	
29	EC-81/DG.11, 24 February 2016	Noted (EC-81/2, 23 March 2016, para. 6.13)	S/2016/196, 26 February 2016	
30	EC-82/DG.1, 24 March 2016	Noted (EC-83/4 C-21/2, 11 November 2017, para. 2.23)	S/2016/285, 29 March 2016	
31	EC-82/DG.5, 22 April 2016	Noted (EC-83/4 C-21/2, 11 November 2017, para. 2.23)	S/2016/391, 27 April 2016	
32	EC-82/DG.9, 25 May 2016	Noted (EC-83/4 C-21/2, 11 November 2017, para. 2.23)	S/2016/494, 27 May 2016	
33	EC-82/DG.17, 24 June 2016 (not publicly available)	Noted (EC-83/4 C-21/2, 11 November 2017, para. 2.23)	S/2016/577, 28 June 2016	
34	EC-83/DG.2, 22 July 2016	Noted (EC-83/5, 11 November 2016, para. 6.13)	S/2016/678, 3 August 2016	
35	EC-83/DG.6, 22 August 2016	Noted (EC-83/5, 11 November 2016, para. 6.13)	S/2016/748, 29 August 2016	
36	EC-83/DG.18, 26 September 2016	Noted (EC-83/5, 11 November 2016, para. 6.13)	S/2016/825, 30 September 2016	

(continued)

(continued)

	OPCW Director-General monthly reports	OPCW Executive Council	UN Secretary-General monthly reports	UN Security Council
37	EC-84/DG.1, 25 October 2016	Noted (EC-84/2, 9 March 2017, para. 6.18)	S/2016/928, 2 November 2016	
38	EC-84/DG.4, 23 November 2016	Noted (EC-84/2, 9 March 2017, para. 6.18)	S/2016/998, 29 November 2016	
39	EC-84/DG.6, 22 December 2016	Noted (EC-84/2, 9 March 2017, para. 6.18)	S/2016/1131, 29 December 2016	
40	EC-84/DG.11, 24 January 2017	Noted (EC-84/2, 9 March 2017, para. 6.18)	S/2017/86, 30 January 2017	
41	EC-84/DG.22, 23 February 2017	Noted (EC-84/2, 9 March 2017, para. 6.18)	S/2017/175, 27 February 2017	
42	EC-85/DG.2, 23 March 2017	Noted (EC-86/9 C-22/2, 12 October 2017, para. 2.35)	S/2017/260, 28 March 2017	
43	EC-85/DG.5, 24 April 2017	Noted (EC-86/9 C-22/2, 12 October 2017, para. 2.35)	S/2017/373, 28 April 2017	
44	EC-85/DG.11, 24 May 2017	Noted (EC-86/9 C-22/2, 12 October 2017, para. 2.35)	S/2017/469, 1 June 2017	
45	EC-85/DG.21, 23 June 2017	Noted (EC-86/9 C-22/2, 12 October 2017, para. 2.35)	S/2017/564, 30 June 2017	
46	EC-86/DG.2, 24 July 2017	Noted (EC-86/11, 13 October 2017, para. 6.18)	S/2017/658, 31 July 2017	
47	EC-86/DG.7, 23 August 2017	Noted (EC-86/11, 13 October 2017, para. 6.18)	S/2017/756, 5 September 2017	
48	EC-86/DG.23, 25 September 2017	Noted (EC-86/11, 13 October 2017, para. 6.18)	S/2017/815, 29 September 2017	
49	EC-87/DG.2, 23 October 2017	Noted (EC-87/2, 15 March 2018, para. 7.17)	S/2017/916, 31 October 2017	

(continued)

(continued)

	OPCW Director-General monthly reports	OPCW Executive Council	UN Secretary-General monthly reports	UN Security Council
50	EC-87/DG.4, 24 November 2017	Noted (EC-87/2, 15 March 2018, para. 7.17)	S/2017/1005, 1 December 2017	
51	EC-87/DG.7, 22 December 2017	Noted (EC-87/2, 15 March 2018, para. 7.17)	S/2017/1119, 27 December 2017	
52	EC-87/DG.10, 22 January 2018	Noted (EC-87/2, 15 March 2018, para. 7.17)	S/2018/84, 1 February 2018	
53	EC-87/DG.16, 23 February 2018	Noted (EC-87/2, 15 March 2018, para. 7.17)	S/2018/182, 5 March 2018	
54	EC-88/DG.1, 23 March 2018	Noted (EC-88/4, 12 July 2018, para. 6.12)	S/2018/283, 2 April 2018	
55	EC-88/DG.3, 24 April 2018	Noted (EC-88/4, 12 July 2018, para. 6.12)	S/2018/408, 1 May 2018	
56	EC-88/DG.8, 24 May 2018	Noted (EC-88/4, 12 July 2018, para. 6.12)	S/2018/523, 1 June 2018	
57	EC-88/DG.16, 22 June 2018	Noted (EC-88/4, 12 July 2018, para. 6.12)	S/2018/644, 28 June 2018	
58	EC-89/DG.1, 24 July 2018	Noted (EC-89/3, 22 October 2018, para. 6.12)	S/2018/745, 30 July 2018	
59	EC-89/DG.10, 24 August 2018	Noted (EC-89/3, 22 October 2018, para. 6.12)	S/2018/804, 31 August 2018	
60	EC-89/DG.24, 24 September 2018	Noted (EC-89/3, 22 October 2018, para. 6.12)	S/2018/875, 28 September 2018	
61	EC-90/DG.1, 23 October 2018	Noted (EC-92/4 C-24/2, 10 October 2019, para. 2.21)	S/2018/971, 31 October 2018	
62	EC-90/DG.2, 23 November 2018	Noted (EC-92/4 C-24/2, 10 October 2019, para. 2.21)	S/2018/1071, 30 November 2018	
63	EC-90/DG.4, 21 December 2018	Noted (EC-92/4 C-24/2, 10 October 2019, para. 2.21)	S/2018/1166, 28 December 2018	

(continued)

(continued)

	OPCW Director-General monthly reports	OPCW Executive Council	UN Secretary-General monthly reports	UN Security Council
64	EC-90/DG.7, 24 January 2019	Noted (EC-92/4 C-24/2, 10 October 2019, para. 2.21)	S/2019/91, 29 January 2019	
65	EC-90/DG.11, 25 February 2019	Noted (EC-92/4 C-24/2, 10 October 2019, para. 2.21)	S/2019/201, 1 March 2019	
66	EC-91/DG.1, 25 March 2019	Noted (EC-92/4 C-24/2, 10 October 2019, para. 2.21)	S/2019/279, 29 March 2019	
67	EC-91/DG.2, 4 May 2019	Noted (EC-92/4 C-24/2, 10 October 2019, para. 2.21)	S/2019/355, 30 April 2019	
68	EC-91/DG.7, 24 May 2019	Noted (EC-92/4 C-24/2, 10 October 2019, para. 2.21)	S/2019/447, 30 May 2019	
69	EC-91/DG.14, 24 June 2019	Noted (EC-92/4 C-24/2, 10 October 2019, para. 2.21)	S/2019/541, 28 June 2019	
70	EC-92/DG.1, 24 July 2019	Noted (EC-92/5, 11 October 2019, para. 7.18)	S/2019/601, 26 July 2019	
71	EC-92/DG.6, 23 August 2019	Noted (EC-92/5, 11 October 2019, para. 7.18)	S/2019/697, 30 August 2019	
72	EC-92/DG.22, 24 September 2019	Noted (EC-92/5, 11 October 2019, para. 7.18)	S/2019/784, 2 October 2019	
73	EC-93/DG.1, 23 October 2019	Noted (EC-93/2, 12 March 2020, para. 6.14)	S/2019/854, 1 November 2019	
74	EC-93/DG.3, 25 November 2019	Noted (EC-93/2, 12 March 2020, para. 6.14)	S/2019/915, 29 November 2019	
75	EC-93/DG.5, 24 December 2019	Noted (EC-93/2, 12 March 2020, para. 6.14)	S/2019/1016, 31 December 2019	
76	EC-93/DG.7, 24 January 2020	Noted (EC-93/2, 12 March 2020, para. 6.14)	S/2020/82, 30 January 2020	

(continued)

(continued)

	OPCW Director-General monthly reports	OPCW Executive Council	UN Secretary-General monthly reports	UN Security Council
77	EC-93/DG.12, 24 February 2020; EC-93/DG.12/Corr.1, 27 February 2020	Noted (EC-93/2, 12 March 2020, para. 6.14)	S/2020/164, 2 March 2020	
78	EC-94/DG.1, 24 March 2020	Noted (EC-94/4, 9 July 2020, para. 6.14)	S/2020/262, 1 April 2020	
79	EC-94/DG.3, 24 April 2020	Noted (EC-94/4, 9 July 2020, para. 6.14)	S/2020/348, 30 April 2020	
80	EC-94/DG.5, 25 May 2020	Noted (EC-94/4, 9 July 2020, para. 6.14)	S/2020/456, 29 May 2020	
81	EC-94/DG.12*, 24 June 2020	Noted (EC-94/4, 9 July 2020, para. 6.14)	S/2020/620, 30 June 2020	
82	EC-95/DG.1, 24 July 2020	Noted (EC-95/4, 9 October 2020, para. 6.17)	S/2020/769, 3 August 2020	
83	EC-95/DG.4, 24 August 2020	Noted (EC-95/4, 9 October 2020, para. 6.17)	S/2020/871, 1 September 2020	Video-teleconference, 10 September 2020 (S/2020/902, 15 September 2020)
84	EC-95/DG.19, 24 September 2020	Noted (EC-95/4, 9 October 2020, para. 6.17)	S/2020/961, 1 October 2020	
85	EC-96/DG.2, 26 October 2020	Noted (EC-96/2, 12 March 2021, para. 6.16)	S/2020/1056, 29 October 2020	Video-teleconference, 5 November 2020 (S/2020/1088, 9 November 2020)
86	EC-96/DG.3, 24 November 2020	Noted (EC-96/2, 12 March 2021, para. 6.16)	S/2020/1152, 30 November 2020	Video-teleconference, 11 December 2020 (S/2020/1202, 16 December 2020)
87	EC-96/DG.4, 24 December 2020	Noted (EC-96/2, 12 March 2021, para. 6.16)	S/2020/1300, 29 December 2020	Video-teleconference, 5 January 2021 (S/2021/22, 7 January 2021)
88	EC-96/DG.6, 25 January 2021	Noted (EC-96/2, 12 March 2021, para. 6.16)	S/2021/84, 27 January 2021	Video-teleconference, 3 February 2021 (S/2021/109, 11 February 2021)
89	EC-96/DG.13, 24 February 2021	Noted (EC-96/2, 12 March 2021, para. 6.16)	S/2021/200, 1 March 2021	Video-teleconference, 4 March 2021 (S/2021/226, 9 March 2021)
90	EC-97/DG.2, 24 March 2021	Noted (EC-97/3, 8 July 2021, para. 6.16)	S/2021/305, 30 March 2021	Video-teleconference, 6 April 2021 (S/2021/337, 9 April 2021)
91	EC-97/DG.3, 23 April 2021	Noted (EC-97/3, 8 July 2021, para. 6.16)	S/2021/422, 3 May 2021	Video-teleconference, 6 May 2021 (S/2021/446, 10 May 2021)

(continued)

(continued)

	OPCW Director-General monthly reports	OPCW Executive Council	UN Secretary-General monthly reports	UN Security Council
92	EC-97/DG.7, 25 May 2021	Noted (EC-97/3, 8 July 2021, para. 6.16)	S/2021/514, 28 May 2021	Briefing, 3 June 2021 (S/PV.8785, 3 June 2021)
93	EC-97/DG.15, 24 June 2021 (not publicly available)	Noted (EC-97/3, 8 July 2021, para. 6.16)	S/2021/615, 30 June 2021	
94	EC-98/DG.1, 23 July 2021	Noted (EC-98/5, 7 October 2021, para. 6.18)	S/2021/692, 30 July 2021	Briefing, 4 August 2021 (S/PV.8830, 4 August 2021)
95	Doc. EC-98/DG.6, 24 August 2021	Noted (EC-98/5, 7 October 2021, para. 6.18)	S/2021/764, 31 August 2021	Briefing, 2 September 2021 (S/PV.8849, 2 September 2021)
96	EC-98/DG.24, 24 September 2021	Noted (EC-98/5, 7 October 2021, para. 6.18)	S/2021/842, 1 October 2021	Briefing, 4 October 2021 (S/PV.8872, 4 October 2021)
97	EC-99/DG.1, 26 October 2021	Noted (EC-99/2, 10 March 2022, para. 7.17)	S/2021/911, 1 November 2021	
98	EC-99/DG.2, 24 November 2021	Noted (EC-99/2, 10 March 2022, para. 7.17)	S/2021/989, 1 December 2021	Briefing, 3 December 2021 (S/PV.8921, 3 December 2021)
99	EC-99/DG.3, 23 December 2021	Noted (EC-99/2, 10 March 2022, para. 7.17)	S/2021/1103, 29 December 2021	Briefing, 5 January 2022 (S/PV.8943, 5 January 2022)
100	EC-99/DG.5, 24 January 2022	Noted (EC-99/2, 10 March 2022, para. 7.17)	S/2022/76, 1 February 2022	Briefing, 28 February 2022 (S/PV.8982, 28 February 2022)
101	EC-99/DG.13, 24 February 2022	Noted (EC-99/2, 10 March 2022, para. 7.17)	S/2022/181, 7 March 2022	Briefing, 10 March 2022 (S/PV.8990, 10 March 2022)
102	EC-100/DG.2, 24 March 2022	Noted (EC-101/3, 4 October 2022, para. 2.17)	S/2022/281, 31 March 2022	Briefing, 29 April 2022 (S/PV.9026, 29 April 2022)
103	EC-100/DG.4, 25 April 2022	Noted (EC-101/3, 4 October 2022, para. 2.17)	S/2022/365, 3 May 2022	
104	EC-100/DG.6, 24 May 2022	Noted (EC-101/3, 4 October 2022, para. 2.17)	S/2022/441, 31 May 2022	
105	EC-100/DG.14, 23 June 2022	Noted (EC-101/3, 4 October 2022, para. 2.17)	S/2022/530, 1 July 2022	Briefing, 20 July 2022 (S/PV.9097, 20 July 2022)
106	EC-101/DG.2, 22 July 2022	Noted (EC-101/5, 7 October 2022, para. 6.19)	S/2022/585, 29 July 2022	

(continued)

(continued)

	OPCW Director-General monthly reports	OPCW Executive Council	UN Secretary-General monthly reports	UN Security Council
107	EC-101/DG.4, 24 August 2022	Noted (EC-101/5, 7 October 2022, para. 6.19)	S/2022/658, 31 August 2022	Briefing, 29 September 2022 (S/PV.9141, 29 September 2022)
108	EC-101/DG.22, 23 September 2022	Noted (EC-101/5, 7 October 2022, para. 6.19)	S/2022/727, 30 September 2022	Briefing, 25 October 2022 (S/PV.9164, 25 October 2022)
109	EC-102/DG.1, 25 October 2022	Noted (EC-102/2, 17 March 2023, para. 6.15)	S/2022/828, 3 November 2022	
110	EC-102/DG.2, 24 November 2022	Noted (EC-102/2, 17 March 2023, para. 6.15)	S/2022/897, 30 November 2022	Briefing, 5 December 2022 (S/PV.9207, 5 December 2022)
111	EC-102/DG.3, 23 December 2022	Noted (EC-102/2, 17 March 2023, para. 6.15)	S/2022/1016, 30 December 2022	Briefing, 5 January 2023 (S/PV.9235, 5 January 2023)
112	EC-102/DG.4, 24 January 2023	Noted (EC-102/2, 17 March 2023, para. 6.15)	S/2023/69, 30 January 2023	Briefing, 7 February 2023 (S/PV.9255, 7 February 2023)
113	EC-102/DG.14, 24 February 2023	Noted (EC-102/2, 17 March 2023, para. 6.15)	S/2023/158, 1 March 2023	Briefing, 6 March 2023 (S/PV.9275, 6 March 2023)
114	EC-103/DG.2, 24 March 2023		S/2023/231, 30 March 2023	

Appendix B
Findings by Fact-Finding Organs

Locations and dates	Chemical agents (FFM reports)	Perpetrators (JIM/IIT reports)
Kafr-Zita, 11 April 2014	Chlorine (OPCW Doc. S/1212/2014, 10 September 2014, p. 8, para. 29; OPCW Doc. S/1230/2014, 18 December 2014, pp. 3–4, paras. 1.6–1.10)	N/A (UN Doc. S/2016/738/Rev.1, 24 August 2016, p. 17, para. 74)
Al-Tamanah, 12 April 2014	Chlorine (OPCW Doc. S/1212/2014, 10 September 2014, p. 8, para. 29; OPCW Doc. S/1230/2014, 18 December 2014, pp. 3–4, paras. 1.6–1.10)	
Kafr-Zita, 18 April 2014	Chlorine (OPCW Doc. S/1212/2014, 10 September 2014, p. 8, para. 29; OPCW Doc. S/1230/2014, 18 December 2014, pp. 3–4, paras. 1.6–1.10)	N/A (UN Doc. S/2016/738/Rev.1, 24 August 2016, p. 15, para. 61) N/A (UN Doc. S/2016/888, 21 October 2016, p. 5, para. 15)
Al-Tamanah, 18 April 2014	Chlorine (OPCW Doc. S/1212/2014, 10 September 2014, p. 8, para. 29; OPCW Doc. S/1230/2014, 18 December 2014, pp. 3–4, paras. 1.6–1.10)	
Talmenes, 21 April 2014	Chlorine (OPCW Doc. S/1212/2014, 10 September 2014, p. 8, para. 29; OPCW Doc. S/1230/2014, 18 December 2014, pp. 3–4, paras. 1.6–1.10)	Syrian Arab Armed Forces (UN Doc. S/2016/738/Rev.1, 24 August 2016, p. 13, para. 54)
Al-Tamanah, 29 and 30 April 2014	Chlorine (OPCW Doc. S/1212/2014, 10 September 2014, p. 8, para. 29; OPCW Doc. S/1230/2014, 18 December 2014, pp. 3–4, paras. 1.6–1.10)	N/A (UN Doc. S/2016/738/Rev.1, 24 August 2016, p. 18, para. 76)
Al-Tamanah, 25 and 26 May 2014	Chlorine (OPCW Doc. S/1212/2014, 10 September 2014, p. 8, para. 29; OPCW Doc. S/1230/2014, 18 December 2014, pp. 3–4, paras. 1.6–1.10)	N/A (UN Doc. S/2016/738/Rev.1, 24 August 2016, p. 18, para. 78)

(continued)

T. Abe, *Syrian Chemical Weapons and International Law*,
https://doi.org/10.1007/978-981-99-3700-4

(continued)

Locations and dates	Chemical agents (FFM reports)	Perpetrators (JIM/IIT reports)
Sarmin, 16 March 2015	Chlorine (OPCW Doc. S/1319/2015, 29 October 2015, pp. 94 and 96, paras 5.8 and 5.19)	Syrian Arab Armed Forces (UN Doc. S/2016/738/Rev.1, 24 August 2016, p. 13, para. 56)
Qmenas, 16 March 2015	Chlorine (OPCW Doc. S/1319/2015, 29 October 2015, pp. 94 and 96, paras 5.8 and 5.19)	N/A (UN Doc. S/2016/738/Rev.1, 24 August 2016, p. 15, para. 65) Syrian Arab Armed Forces (UN Doc. S/2016/888, 21 October 2016, p. 6, para. 19)
Binnish, 24 March 2015	Chlorine (OPCW Doc. S/1319/2015, 29 October 2015, pp. 94 and 96, paras 5.8 and 5.19)	N/A (UN Doc. S/2016/738/Rev.1, 24 August 2016, p. 16, para. 69) N/A (UN Doc. S/2016/888, 21 October 2016, p. 7, para. 24)
Marea, 21 August 2015	Sulfur mustard (OPCW Doc. S/1320/2015, 29 October 2015, p. 23, para. 4.6)	ISIL (UN Doc. S/2016/738/Rev.1, 24 August 2016, p. 14, para. 58)
Marea, 1 September 2015	Sulfur mustard (OPCW Doc. S/2017/2022*, 24 January 2022, p. 26, para. 8.10)	
Um-Housh, 15 and 16 September 2016	Sulfur mustard (OPCW Doc. S/1491/2017, 12 May 2017, p. 22, para. 6.3)	ISIL (UN Doc. S/2017/904, 26 October 2017, p. 9, para. 36)
Ltamenah, 24 March 2017	Sarin (OPCW Doc. S/1636/2018*, 13 June 2018, p. 29, para. 6.8)	Syrian Arab Air Force (OPCW Doc. S/1867/2020, 8 April 2020, p. 53, para. 11.1)
Ltamenah, 25 March 2017	Chlorine (OPCW Doc. S/1636/2018*, 13 June 2018, p. 30, para. 6.9)	Syrian Arab Air Force (OPCW Doc. S/1867/2020, 8 April 2020, p. 56, para. 12.1)
Ltamenah, 30 March 2017	Sarin (OPCW Doc. S/1548/2017, 2 November 2017, p. 26, para. 6.9)	Syrian Arab Air Force (OPCW Doc. S/1867/2020, 8 April 2020, p. 53, para. 11.1)
Khan Shaykhun, 4 April 2017	Sarin (OPCW Doc. S/1510/2017, 29 June 2017, p. 53, para. 6.25; cf. OPCW Doc. S/1497/2017, 12 May 2017, p. 3, paras. 3.2–3.4)	Syrian Arab Republic (UN Doc. S/2017/904, 26 October 2017, p. 10, para. 46)
Saraqib, 4 February 2018	Chlorine (OPCW Doc. S/1626/2018, 15 May 2018, p. 26, para. 7.4)	Syrian Arab Air Force (OPCW Doc. S/1943/2021, 12 April 2021, p. 45, para. 10.1)
Douma, 7 April 2018	Chlorine (OPCW Doc. S/1731/2019, 19 March 2019, pp. 31–32, para. 9.12; cf. OPCW Doc. S/1645/2018, 6 July 2018)	Syrian Arab Air Force (OPCW Doc. S/2125/2023, 27 January 2023, p. 119, para. 10.1)

Appendix C
Reports of Fact-Finding Organs and Actions of Policy-Making Organs

Locations and dates	UN mission reports		COI reports	OPCW policy-making organs	UN policy-making organs
Khan Al-Assal, 19 March 2013			COI report of 12 February 2014[1]		
Saraqib, 29 April 2013			COI report of 12 February 2014[2]		
East Ghouta, 21 August 2013			COI report of 12 February 2014[3]		
East Ghouta, 21 August 2013	UN mission reports of 16 September and 13 December 2013[4]			OPCW EC[5]	UNSC[6]; UNGA[7]

[1] UN Doc. A/HRC/25/65, 12 February 2014.

[2] *Ibid.*

[3] *Ibid.*

[4] UN Doc. A/67/997–S/2013/553, 16 September 2013; UN Doc. A/68/663–S/2013/735, 13 December 2013.

[5] OPCW Doc. EC-M-33/DEC.1, 27 September 2013 (consensus), preamble para. 3.

[6] UN Doc. S/RES/2118 (2013), 27 September 2013 (unanimous), preamble paras. 7 and 8.

[7] UN Doc. A/RES/68/45, 5 December 2013 (consensus), preamble para. 4; UN Doc. A/RES/68/182, 18 December 2013, preamble para. 9, operative para. 1.

T. Abe, *Syrian Chemical Weapons and International Law*,
https://doi.org/10.1007/978-981-99-3700-4

Locations and dates	FFM reports	JIM/IIT reports (perpetrators)	COI reports	OPCW policy-making organs	UN policy-making organs
Kafr Zeita, 11, 12, 16, and 18 April 2014			COI report of 13 August 2014[8]		UNGA[9]; UNHRC[10]
Kafr-Zita, between 10 April and 30 August 2014	FFM report of 16 June 2014[11]			OPCW EC[12]	UNSC[13]
Kafr-Zita, between 10 April and 30 August 2014	FFM reports of 10 September and 18 December 2014[14]			OPCW EC[15]	UNSC[16]; UNHRC[17]
Al-Tamana'a, 12, 18, and 29 April 2014			COI report of 13 August 2014[18]		UNGA[19]; UNHRC[20]
Al-Tamanah, 12, 18 and 30 April 2014 and 22 and 25 May 2014	FFM report of 16 June 2014[21]			OPCW EC[22]	UNSC[23]
Al-Tamanah, 12, 18 and 30 April 2014 and 22 and 25 May 2014	FFM reports of 10 September and 18 December 2014[24]			OPCW EC[25]	UNSC[26]; UNHRC[27]

(continued)

[8] UN Doc. A/HRC/27/60, 13 August 2014.

[9] UN Doc. A/RES/69/189, 18 December 2014 (127–13–48), operative para. 19.

[10] UN Doc. A/HRC/RES/27/16, 25 September 2014 (32–5–10), operative para. 18; UN Doc. A/HRC/RES/28/20, 27 March 2015 (29–6–12), operative para. 10.

[11] OPCW Doc. S/1191/2014, 16 June 2014.

[12] OPCW Doc. EC-M-48/DEC.1, 4 February 2015 (40–1–0) preamble para. 3, operative para. 1.

[13] UN Doc. S/RES/2209 (2015), 6 March 2015 (14–0–1), preamble paras. 5, 6, operative para. 2.

[14] OPCW Doc. S/1212/2014, 10 September 2014; OPCW Doc. S/1230/2014, 18 December 2014.

[15] OPCW Doc. EC-M-48/DEC.1, 4 February 2015 (40–1–0) preamble para. 3, operative para. 1.

[16] UN Doc. S/RES/2209 (2015), 6 March 2015 (14–0–1), preamble paras. 5, 6, operative para. 2.

[17] UN Doc. A/HRC/RES/28/20, 27 March 2015 (29–6–12), operative para. 10.

[18] UN Doc. A/HRC/27/60, 13 August 2014.

[19] UN Doc. A/RES/69/189, 18 December 2014 (127–13–48), operative para. 19.

[20] UN Doc. A/HRC/RES/27/16, 25 September 2014 (32–5–10), operative para. 18; UN Doc. A/HRC/RES/28/20, 27 March 2015 (29–6–12), operative para. 10.

[21] OPCW Doc. S/1191/2014, 16 June 2014.

[22] OPCW Doc. EC-M-48/DEC.1, 4 February 2015 (40–1–0) preamble para. 3, operative para. 1.

[23] UN Doc. S/RES/2209 (2015), 6 March 2015 (14–0–1), preamble paras. 5, 6, operative para. 2.

[24] OPCW Doc. S/1212/2014, 10 September 2014; OPCW Doc. S/1230/2014, 18 December 2014.

[25] OPCW Doc. EC-M-48/DEC.1, 4 February 2015 (40–1–0) preamble para. 3, operative para. 1.

[26] UN Doc. S/RES/2209 (2015), 6 March 2015 (14–0–1), preamble paras. 5, 6, operative para. 2.

[27] UN Doc. A/HRC/RES/28/20, 27 March 2015 (29–6–12), operative para. 10.

(continued)

Locations and dates	FFM reports	JIM/IIT reports (perpetrators)	COI reports	OPCW policy-making organs	UN policy-making organs
Tal Minnis, 21 April 2014			COI report of 13 August 2014[28]		UNGA[29]; UNHRC[30]
Talmenes, 21 and 24 April 2014	FFM report of 16 June 2014[31]			OPCW EC[32]	UNSC[33]
Talmenes, 21 and 24 April 2014	FFM reports of 10 September and 18 December 2014[34]			OPCW EC[35]	UNSC[36]; UNHRC[37]
Talmenes, 21 April 2014		JIM report of 24 August 2016[38] (Syrian government)		OPCW EC[39]; OPCW CSP[40]	UNGA[41]; UNHRC[42]

(continued)

[28] UN Doc. A/HRC/27/60, 13 August 2014.

[29] UN Doc. A/RES/69/189, 18 December 2014 (127–13–48), operative para. 19.

[30] UN Doc. A/HRC/RES/27/16, 25 September 2014 (32–5–10), operative para. 18; UN Doc. A/HRC/RES/28/20, 27 March 2015 (29–6–12), operative para. 10.

[31] OPCW Doc. S/1191/2014, 16 June 2014.

[32] OPCW Doc. EC-M-48/DEC.1, 4 February 2015 (40–1–0) preamble para. 3, operative para. 1.

[33] UN Doc. S/RES/2209 (2015), 6 March 2015 (14–0–1), preamble paras. 5, 6, operative para. 2.

[34] OPCW Doc. S/1212/2014, 10 September 2014; OPCW Doc. S/1230/2014, 18 December 2014.

[35] OPCW Doc. EC-M-48/DEC.1, 4 February 2015 (40–1–0) preamble para. 3, operative para. 1.

[36] UN Doc. S/RES/2209 (2015), 6 March 2015 (14–0–1), preamble paras. 5, 6, operative para. 2.

[37] UN Doc. A/HRC/RES/28/20, 27 March 2015 (29–6–12), operative para. 10.

[38] UN Doc. S/2016/738/Rev.1, 24 August 2016.

[39] OPCW Doc. EC-83/DEC.5, 11 November 2016 (28–4–9), preamble paras. 10, 12 and operative paras. 1, 2, 3.

[40] OPCW Doc. C-SS-4/DEC.3, 27 June 2018 (82–24–0), operative para. 6.

[41] UN Doc. A/RES/71/69, 5 December 2016, operative para. 2 (139–12–20 by separate vote); UN Doc. A/RES/71/203, 19 December 2016 (116–16–52), preamble para. 13, operative para. 6; UN Doc. A/RES/72/43, 4 December 2017, operative para. 2 (133–12–25 by separate vote); UN Doc. A/RES/72/191, 19 December 2017 (109–17–58), operative para. 9; UN Doc. A/RES/73/45, 5 December 2018, operative para. 2 (122–13–26 by separate vote); UN Doc. A/RES/73/182, 17 December 2018 (111–15–55), preamble para. 16; UN Doc. A/RES/74/40, 12 December 2019, operative para. 2 (119–11–30 by separate vote); UN Doc. A/RES/74/169, 18 December 2019 (106–15–57), preamble para. 17; UN Doc. A/RES/75/55, 7 December 2020, operative para. 3 (123–11–31 by separate vote); UN Doc. A/RES/75/193, 16 December 2020 (101–13–62), preamble para. 20; UN Doc. A/RES/76/29, 6 December 2021, operative para. 3 (118–13–34 by separate vote); UN Doc. A/RES/76/228, 24 December 2021 (93–16–52), preamble para. 22; UN Doc. A/RES/77/73, 7 December 2022 (155–6–19), operative para. 3; UN Doc. A/RES/77/230, 15 December 2022 (92–14–71), preamble para. 25.

[42] UN Doc. A/HRC/RES/33/23, 30 September 2016 (24–7–14), operative para. 21; UN Doc. A/HRC/RES/34/26, 24 March 2017 (27–7–13), operative paras. 25, 26; UN Doc. A/HRC/RES/35/26, 23 June 2017 (27–8–12), operative paras. 25, 26; UN Doc. A/HRC/RES/36/20, 29 September

(continued)

Locations and dates	FFM reports	JIM/IIT reports (perpetrators)	COI reports	OPCW policy-making organs	UN policy-making organs
Idlib Governorate (Qmenas, Sarmin, Binnish, Idlib City, Al-Nerab, and Saraqib), between 16 March and 20 May 2015	FFM report of 29 October 2015[43]			OPCW EC[44]	
Qmenas, 16 March 2015		JIM report of 21 October 2016[45] (Syrian government)		OPCW EC[46]; OPCW CSP[47]	UNGA[48]; UNHRC[49]

(continued)

2017 (27–7–13), operative paras. 25, 26; UN Doc. A/HRC/RES/37/29, 23 March 2018 (27–4–16), operative para. 25; UN Doc. A/HRC/RES/38/16, 6 July 2018 (26–5–15), operative para. 29; UN Doc. A/HRC/RES/39/15, 28 September 2018 (27–4–16), operative para. 34; Doc. A/HRC/RES/40/17, 22 March 2019 (28–5–14), operative para. 36; UN Doc. A/HRC/RES/41/23, 12 July 2019 (26–7–14), operative para. 38; UN Doc. A/HRC/RES/42/27, 27 September 2019 (27–6–13), operative para. 44; UN Doc. A/HRC/RES/43/28, 22 June 2020 (27–2–18), operative para. 52.

[43] OPCW Doc. S/1319/2015, 29 October 2015.

[44] OPCW Doc. EC-M-50/DEC.1, 23 November 2015 (consensus), preamble para. 4. cf. *ibid.*, operative para.1.

[45] UN Doc. S/2016/888, 21 October 2016.

[46] OPCW Doc. EC-83/DEC.5, 11 November 2016 (28–4–9), preamble paras. 11, 12 and operative paras. 1, 3.

[47] OPCW Doc. C-SS-4/DEC.3, 27 June 2018 (82–24–0), operative para. 6.

[48] UN Doc. A/RES/71/69, 5 December 2016, operative para. 2 (139–12–20 by separate vote); UN Doc. A/RES/71/203, 19 December 2016 (116–16–52), preamble para. 13, operative para. 6; UN Doc. A/RES/72/43, 4 December 2017, operative para. 2 (133–12–25 by separate vote); UN Doc. A/RES/72/191, 19 December 2017 (109–17–58), operative paras. 7 and 9; UN Doc. A/RES/73/45, 5 December 2018, operative para. 2 (122–13–26 by separate vote); UN Doc. A/RES/73/182, 17 December 2018 (111–15–55), preamble para. 16; UN Doc. A/RES/74/40, 12 December 2019, operative para. 2 (119–11–30 by separate vote); UN Doc. A/RES/74/169, 18 December 2019 (106–15–57), preamble para. 17; UN Doc. A/RES/75/55, 7 December 2020, operative para. 3 (123–11–31 by separate vote); UN Doc. A/RES/75/193, 16 December 2020 (101–13–62), preamble para. 20; UN Doc. A/RES/76/29, 6 December 2021, operative para. 3 (118–13–34 by separate vote); UN Doc. A/RES/76/228, 24 December 2021 (93–16–52), preamble para. 22; UN Doc. A/RES/77/73, 7 December 2022 (155–6–19), operative para. 3; UN Doc. A/RES/77/230, 15 December 2022 (92–14–71), preamble para. 25.

[49] UN Doc. A/HRC/RES/34/26, 24 March 2017 (27–7–13), operative paras. 25, 26; UN Doc. A/HRC/RES/35/26, 23 June 2017 (27–8–12), operative paras. 25, 26; UN Doc. A/HRC/RES/36/20 29 September 2017 (27–7–13), operative paras. 25, 26; UN Doc. A/HRC/RES/37/29, 23 March 2018 (27–4–16), operative para. 25; UN Doc. A/HRC/RES/38/16, 6 July 2018 (26–5–15), operative para. 29; UN Doc. A/HRC/RES/39/15, 28 September 2018 (27–4–16), operative para. 34; Doc. A/HRC/RES/40/17, 22 March 2019 (28–5–14), operative para. 36; UN Doc. A/HRC/RES/41/23, 12 July 2019 (26–7–14), operative para. 38; UN Doc. A/HRC/RES/42/27, 27 September 2019 (27–6–13), operative para. 44; UN Doc. A/HRC/RES/43/28, 22 June 2020 (27–2–18), operative para. 52.

(continued)

Locations and dates	FFM reports	JIM/IIT reports (perpetrators)	COI reports	OPCW policy-making organs	UN policy-making organs
Sarmin, 16 March 2015		JIM report of 24 August 2016[50] (Syrian government)		OPCW EC[51]; OPCW CSP[52]	UNGA[53]; UNHRC[54]
Marea, 21 August 2015	FFM report of 29 October 2015[55]			OPCW EC[56]	
Marea, 21 August 2015		JIM report of 24 August 2016[57] (ISIL)		OPCW CSP[58]	UNGA[59]

(continued)

[50] UN Doc. S/2016/738/Rev.1, 24 August 2016.

[51] OPCW Doc. EC-83/DEC.5, 11 November 2016 (28–4–9), preamble paras. 10, 12 and operative paras. 1, 2, 3.

[52] OPCW Doc. C-SS-4/DEC.3, 27 June 2018 (82–24–0), operative para. 6.

[53] UN Doc. A/RES/71/69, 5 December 2016, operative para. 2 (139–12–20 by separate vote); UN Doc. A/RES/71/203, 19 December 2016 (116–16–52), preamble para. 13, operative para. 6; UN Doc. A/RES/72/43, 4 December 2017, operative para. 2 (133–12–25 by separate vote); UN Doc. A/RES/72/191, 19 December 2017 (109–17–58), operative para. 9; UN Doc. A/RES/73/45, 5 December 2018, operative para. 2 (122–13–26 by separate vote); UN Doc. A/RES/73/182, 17 December 2018 (111–15–55), preamble para. 16; UN Doc. A/RES/74/40, 12 December 2019, operative para. 2 (119–11–30 by separate vote); UN Doc. A/RES/74/169, 18 December 2019 (106–15–57), preamble para. 17; UN Doc. A/RES/75/55, 7 December 2020, operative para. 3 (123–11–31 by separate vote); UN Doc. A/RES/75/193, 16 December 2020 (101–13–62), preamble para. 20; UN Doc. A/RES/76/29, 6 December 2021, operative para. 3 (118–13–34 by separate vote); UN Doc. A/RES/76/228, 24 December 2021 (93–16–52), preamble para. 22; UN Doc. A/RES/77/73, 7 December 2022 (155–6–19), operative para. 3; UN Doc. A/RES/77/230, 15 December 2022 (92–14–71), preamble para. 25.

[54] UN Doc. A/HRC/RES/33/23, 30 September 2016 (24–7–14), operative para. 21; UN Doc. A/HRC/RES/34/26, 24 March 2017 (27–7–13), operative paras. 25, 26; UN Doc. A/HRC/RES/35/26, 23 June 2017 (27–8–12), operative paras. 25, 26; UN Doc. A/HRC/RES/36/20, 29 September 2017 (27–7–13), operative paras. 25, 26; UN Doc. A/HRC/RES/37/29, 23 March 2018 (27–4–16), operative para. 25; UN Doc. A/HRC/RES/38/16, 6 July 2018 (26–5–15), operative para. 29; UN Doc. A/HRC/RES/39/15, 28 September 2018 (27–4–16), operative para. 34; Doc. A/HRC/RES/40/17, 22 March 2019 (28–5–14), operative para. 36; UN Doc. A/HRC/RES/41/23, 12 July 2019 (26–7–14), operative para. 38; UN Doc. A/HRC/RES/42/27, 27 September 2019 (27–6–13), operative para. 44; UN Doc. A/HRC/RES/43/28, 22 June 2020 (27–2–18), operative para. 52.

[55] OPCW Doc. S/1319/2015, 29 October 2015.

[56] OPCW Doc. EC-M-50/DEC.1, 23 November 2015 (consensus), preamble para. 4. cf. *ibid.*, operative para. 1.

[57] UN Doc. S/2016/738/Rev.1, 24 August 2016.

[58] OPCW Doc. C-SS-4/DEC.3, 27 June 2018 (82–24–0), operative para. 15.

[59] UN Doc. A/RES/71/69, 5 December 2016, operative para. 2 (139–12–20 by separate vote); UN Doc. A/RES/71/203, 19 December 2016 (116–16–52), preamble para. 13, operative para. 6; UN Doc. A/RES/72/43, 4 December 2017, operative para. 2 (133–12–25 by separate vote); UN Doc. A/RES/72/191, 19 December 2017 (109–17–58), operative para. 9; UN Doc. A/RES/73/45,

(continued)

Locations and dates	FFM reports	JIM/IIT reports (perpetrators)	COI reports	OPCW policy-making organs	UN policy-making organs
Marea, 1 and 3 September 2015	FFM report of 24 January 2022[60]				UNGA[61]; UNHRC[62]
al-Sukkari, 6 September 2016			COI report of 2 February 2017[63]		UNHRC[64]
Um-Housh, 15 and 16 September 2016	FFM report of 12 May 2017[65]				UNHRC[66]
Um-Housh, 15 and 16 September 2016		JIM report of 26 October 2017[67] (ISIL)		OPCW CSP[68]	UNGA[69]; UNHRC[70]

(continued)

5 December 2018, operative para. 2 (122–13–26 by separate vote); UN Doc. A/RES/73/182, 17 December 2018 (111–15–55), preamble para. 16; UN Doc. A/RES/74/40, 12 December 2019, operative para. 2 (119–11–30 by separate vote); UN Doc. A/RES/74/169, 18 December 2019 (106–15–57), preamble para. 17; UN Doc. A/RES/75/55, 7 December 2020, operative para. 3 (123–11–31 by separate vote); UN Doc. A/RES/75/193, 16 December 2020 (101–13–62), preamble para. 20; UN Doc. A/RES/76/29, 6 December 2021, operative para. 3 (118–13–34 by separate vote); UN Doc. A/RES/76/228, 24 December 2021 (93–16–52), preamble para. 22; UN Doc. A/RES/77/73, 7 December 2022 (155–6–19), operative para. 3; UN Doc. A/RES/77/230, 15 December 2022 (92–14–71), preamble para. 25.

60 OPCW Doc. S/2017/2022*, 24 January 2022.

61 UN Doc. A/RES/77/73, 7 December 2022 (155–6–19), operative para. 4.

62 UN Doc. A/HRC/RES/49/27, 1 April 2022 (23–7–16), operative para. 20.

63 UN Doc. A/HRC/34/64, 2 February 2017.

64 UN Doc. A/HRC/RES/34/26, 24 March 2017 (27–7–13), operative para. 16.

65 OPCW Doc. S/1491/2017, 12 May 2017.

66 UN Doc. A/HRC/RES/35/26, 23 June 2017 (27–8–12), operative para. 22; UN Doc. A/HRC/RES/36/20, 29 September 2017 (27–7–13), operative para. 22.

67 UN Doc. S/2017/904, 26 October 2017.

68 OPCW Doc. C-SS-4/DEC.3, 27 June 2018 (82–24–0), operative para. 15.

69 UN Doc. A/RES/72/43, 4 December 2017, operative para. 2 (133–12–25 by separate vote); UN Doc. A/RES/72/191, 19 December 2017 (109–17–58), preamble para. 11, operative para. 9; UN Doc. A/RES/73/45, 5 December 2018, operative para. 2 (122–13–26 by separate vote); UN Doc. A/RES/73/182, 17 December 2018 (111–15–55), preamble para. 16; UN Doc. A/RES/74/40, 12 December 2019, operative para. 2 (119–11–30 by separate vote); UN Doc. A/RES/74/169, 18 December 2019 (106–15–57), preamble para. 17; UN Doc. A/RES/75/55, 7 December 2020, operative para. 3 (123–11–31 by separate vote); UN Doc. A/RES/75/193, 16 December 2020 (101–13–62), preamble para. 20; UN Doc. A/RES/76/29, 6 December 2021, operative para. 3 (118–13–34 by separate vote); UN Doc. A/RES/76/228, 24 December 2021 (93–16–52), preamble para. 22; UN Doc. A/RES/77/73, 7 December 2022 (155–6–19), operative para. 3; UN Doc. A/RES/77/230, 15 December 2022 (92–14–71), preamble para. 25.

70 UN Doc. A/HRC/RES/37/29, 23 March 2018 (27–4–16), operative para. 25; UN Doc. A/HRC/RES/38/16, 6 July 2018 (26–5–15), operative para. 29; UN Doc. A/HRC/RES/39/15, 28 September 2018 (27–4–16), operative para. 34; UN Doc. A/HRC/RES/40/17, 22 March 2019 (28–5–14), operative para. 36; UN Doc. A/HRC/RES/41/23, 12 July 2019 (26–7–14), operative para. 38; UN

(continued)

Locations and dates	FFM reports	JIM/IIT reports (perpetrators)	COI reports	OPCW policy-making organs	UN policy-making organs
Kafr Zeita, 1 October 2016	FFM report of 31 January 2022[71]				UNGA[72]; UNHRC[73]
Eastern Aleppo, 1 October 2016			COI report of 2 February 2017[74]		UNHRC[75]
al-Kalasa, 8 December 2016			COI report of 2 February 2017[76]		UNHRC[77]
Ltamenah, 24 and 25 March 2017	FFM report of 13 June 2018[78]			OPCW CSP[79]; OPCW EC[80]	UNHRC;[81] UNGA[82]

(continued)

Doc. A/HRC/RES/42/27, 27 September 2019 (27–6–13), operative para. 44; UN Doc. A/HRC/RES/43/28, 22 June 2020 (27–2–18), operative para. 52.

[71] OPCW Doc. S/2020/2022, 31 January 2022.

[72] UN Doc. A/RES/77/73, 7 December 2022 (155–6–19), operative para. 4.

[73] UN Doc. A/HRC/RES/49/27, 1 April 2022 (23–7–16), operative para. 20.

[74] UN Doc. A/HRC/34/64, 2 February 2017, 2 February 2017.

[75] UN Doc. A/HRC/RES/34/26, 24 March 2017 (27–7–13), operative para. 16.

[76] UN Doc. A/HRC/34/64, 2 February 2017, 2 February 2017.

[77] UN Doc. A/HRC/RES/34/26, 24 March 2017 (27–7–13), operative para. 16.

[78] OPCW Doc. S/1636/2018*, 13 June 2018.

[79] OPCW Doc. C-SS-4/DEC.3, 27 June 2018 (82–24–0), operative para. 9; OPCW Doc. C-25/DEC.9, 21 April 2021 (103–14–13), preamble para. 15.

[80] OPCW Doc. EC-94/DEC.2, 9 July 2020 (29–3–9), preamble para. 9.

[81] UN Doc. A/HRC/RES/38/16, 6 July 2018 (26–5–15), operative para. 30; UN Doc. A/HRC/RES/39/15, 28 September 2018 (27–4–16), operative para. 35; UN Doc. A/HRC/RES/40/17, 22 March 2019 (28–5–14), operative para. 37; UN Doc. A/HRC/RES/41/23, 12 July 2019 (26–7–14), operative para. 39; UN Doc. A/HRC/RES/42/27, 27 September 2019 (27–6–13), operative para. 45; UN Doc. A/HRC/RES/43/28, 22 June 2020 (27–2–18), operative para. 53.

[82] UN Doc. A/RES/73/45, 5 December 2018, operative para. 3 (122–13–30 by separate vote); UN Doc. A/RES/74/40, 12 December 2019, operative para. 3 (120–11–26 by separate vote); UN Doc. A/RES/75/55, 7 December 2020, operative para. 4 (124–10–30 by separate vote); UN Doc. A/RES/76/29, 6 December 2021, operative para. 4 (111–10–40 by separate vote): UN Doc. A/RES/77/73, 7 December 2022 (155–6–19), operative para. 4.

(continued)

Locations and dates	FFM reports	JIM/IIT reports (perpetrators)	COI reports	OPCW policy-making organs	UN policy-making organs
Ltamenah, 24 and 25 March 2017		IIT report of 8 April 2020[83] (Syrian government)		OPCW CSP[84]; OPCW EC[85]	UNGA[86]; UNHRC[87]
Al-Latamneh, 30 March 2017			COI report of 8 August 2017[88]		UNHRC[89]; UNGA[90]
Ltamenah, 30 March 2017	FFM report of 2 November 2017[91]			OPCW CSP[92]; OPCW EC[93]	UNGA[94]; UNHRC[95]

(continued)

[83] OPCW Doc. S/1867/2020, 8 April 2020.

[84] OPCW Doc. C-25/DEC.9, 21 April 2021 (103–14–13), preamble para. 15 and operative para. 2.

[85] OPCW Doc. EC-94/DEC.2, 9 July 2020 (29–3–9), preamble para. 10 and operative para. 1.

[86] UN Doc. A/RES/75/55, 7 December 2020, operative para. 3 (123–11–31 by separate vote); UN Doc. A/RES/75/193 (101–13–62), 16 December 2020, preamble para. 20; UN Doc. A/RES/75/265, 3 March 2021, operative para. 7 (77–10–25 by separate vote); UN Doc. A/RES/76/29, 6 December 2021, operative para. 3 (118–13–34 by separate vote); UN Doc. A/RES/76/228, 24 December 2021(93–16–52), preamble para. 22; UN Doc. A/RES/77/73, 7 December 2022 (155–6–19), operative para. 3; UN Doc. A/RES/77/230, 15 December 2022 (92–14–71), preamble paras. 7 and 25.

[87] UN Doc. A/HRC/RES/46/22, 24 March 2021 (27–6–14), operative para. 33; UN Doc. A/HRC/RES/49/27, 1 April 2022 (23–7–16), operative para. 20; UN Doc. A/HRC/RES/51/26, 7 October (25–6–16), preamble para. 13.

[88] UN Doc. A/HRC/36/55, 8 August 2017.

[89] UN Doc. A/HRC/RES/36/20, 29 September 2017, (27–7–13), operative para. 23; UN Doc. A/HRC/RES/37/29, 23 March 2018 (27–4–16), operative para. 26.

[90] UN Doc. A/RES/72/191, 19 December 2017 (109–17–58), operative para. 7.

[91] OPCW Doc. S/1548/2017, 2 November 2017.

[92] OPCW Doc. C-SS-4/DEC.3, 27 June 2018 (82–24–0), operative para. 9; OPCW Doc. C-25/DEC.9, 21 April 2021 (103–14–13), preamble para. 15.

[93] OPCW Doc. EC-94/DEC.2, 9 July 2020 (29–3–9), preamble para. 9.

[94] UN Doc. A/RES/73/45, 5 December 2018, operative para. 3 (122–13–30 by separate vote); UN Doc. A/RES/73/182, 17 December 2018 (115–15–55), preamble para. 16; UN Doc. A/RES/74/40, 12 December 2019, operative para. 3 (120–11–26 by separate vote); UN Doc. A/RES/74/169, 18 December 2019 (106–15–57), preamble para. 17; UN Doc. A/RES/75/55, 7 December 2020, operative para. 4 (124–10–30 by separate vote); UN Doc. A/RES/76/29, 6 December 2021, operative para. 4 (111–10–40 by separate vote); UN Doc. A/RES/77/73, 7 December 2022 (155–6–19), operative para. 4.

[95] UN Doc. A/HRC/RES/37/29, 23 March 2018 (27–4–16), operative para. 27.

(continued)

Locations and dates	FFM reports	JIM/IIT reports (perpetrators)	COI reports	OPCW policy-making organs	UN policy-making organs
Ltamenah, 30 March 2017		IIT report of 8 April 2020[96] (Syrian government)		OPCW CSP[97]; OPCW EC[98]	UNGA[99]; UNHRC[100]
Khan Shaykhun, 4 April 2017	FFM reports of 12 May and 29 June 2017[101]				UNHRC[102]
Khan Shaykhun, 4 April 2017			COI report of 8 August 2017[103] (Syrian government)		UNGA[104]; UNHRC[105]

(continued)

[96] OPCW Doc. S/1867/2020, 8 April 2020.

[97] OPCW Doc. C-25/DEC.9, 21 April 2021 (103–14–13), preamble para. 15 and operative para. 2.

[98] OPCW Doc. EC-94/DEC.2, 9 July 2020 (29–3–9), preamble para. 10 and operative para. 1.

[99] UN Doc. A/RES/75/55, 7 December 2020, operative para. 3 (123–11–31 by separate vote); UN Doc. A/RES/75/193 (101–13–62), 16 December 2020, preamble para. 20; UN Doc. A/RES/75/265, 3 March 2021, operative para. 7 (77–10–25 by separate vote); UN Doc. A/RES/76/29, 6 December 2021, operative para. 3 (118–13–34 by separate vote); UN Doc. A/RES/76/228, 24 December 2021(93–16–52), preamble para. 22; UN Doc. A/RES/77/73, 7 December 2022 (155–6–19), operative para. 3; UN Doc. A/RES/77/230, 15 December 2022 (92–14–71), preamble paras. 7 and 25.

[100] UN Doc. A/HRC/RES/46/22, 24 March 2021 (27–6–14), operative para. 33; UN Doc. A/HRC/RES/49/27, 1 April 2022 (23–7–16), operative para. 20; UN Doc. A/HRC/RES/51/26, 7 October (25–6–16), preamble para. 13.

[101] OPCW Doc. S/1497/2017, 12 May 2017; OPCW Doc. S/1510/2017, 29 June 2017.

[102] UN Doc. A/HRC/RES/35/26, 23 June 2017 (27–8–12), operative para. 23; UN Doc. A/HRC/RES/36/20, 29 September 2017 (27–7–13), operative para. 22.

[103] UN Doc. A/HRC/36/55, 8 August 2017.

[104] UN Doc. A/RES/72/191, 19 December 2017 (109–17–58), operative para. 7.

[105] UN Doc. A/HRC/RES/36/20, 29 September 2017 (27–7–13), operative para. 23; UN Doc. A/RES/72/191, 19 December 2017 (109–17–58), operative para. 7; UN Doc. A/HRC/RES/37/29, 23 March 2018 (27–4–16), operative para. 26.

(continued)

Locations and dates	FFM reports	JIM/IIT reports (perpetrators)	COI reports	OPCW policy-making organs	UN policy-making organs
Khan Shaykhun, 4 April 2017		JIM report of 26 October 2017[106] (Syrian government)		OPCW CSP[107]; OPCW EC[108]	UNGA[109]; UNHRC[110]
Ayn Tarma, 1 July 2017			COI report of 8 August 2017[111]		UNHRC[112]
Zamalka, 2 July 2017			COI report of 8 August 2017[113]		UNHRC[114]
Jowbar, 6 July 2017;			COI report of 8 August 2017[115]		UNHRC[116]
Saraqueb, 4 February 2018			COI report of 8 August 2017[117]		UNHRC[118]

(continued)

[106] UN Doc. S/2017/904, 26 October 2017.

[107] OPCW Doc. C-SS-4/DEC.3, 27 June 2018 (82–24–0), operative para. 6; OPCW Doc. C-25/DEC.9, 21 April 2021 (103–14–13), preamble para. 11.

[108] OPCW Doc. EC-94/DEC.2, 9 July 2020 (29–3–9), preamble para. 5.

[109] UN Doc. A/RES/72/43, 4 December 2017, operative para. 2 (133–12–25 by separate vote); UN Doc. A/RES/72/191, 19 December 2017 (109–17–58), preamble para. 11, operative para. 9; UN Doc. A/RES/73/45, 5 December 2018, operative para. 2 (122–13–26 by separate vote); UN Doc. A/RES/73/182, 17 December 2018 (111–15–55), preamble para. 16; UN Doc. A/RES/74/40, 12 December 2019, operative para. 2 (119–11–30 by separate vote); UN Doc. A/RES/74/169, 18 December 2019 (106–15–57), preamble para. 17; UN Doc. A/RES/75/55, 7 December 2020, operative para. 3 (123–11–31 by separate vote); UN Doc. A/RES/75/193, 16 December 2020 (101–13–62), preamble para. 20; UN Doc. A/RES/76/29, 6 December 2021, operative para. 3 (118–13–34 by separate vote); UN Doc. A/RES/76/228, 24 December 2021 (93–16–52), preamble para. 22; UN Doc. A/RES/77/73, 7 December 2022 (155–6–19), operative para. 3; UN Doc. A/RES/77/230, 15 December 2022 (92–14–71), preamble para. 25.

[110] UN Doc. A/HRC/RES/37/29, 23 March 2018 (27–4–16), operative para. 25.

[111] UN Doc. A/HRC/36/55, 8 August 2017.

[112] UN Doc. A/HRC/RES/36/20, 29 September 2017 (27–7–13), operative para. 23; UN Doc. A/RES/72/191, 19 December 2017 (109–17–58), operative para. 7; UN Doc. A/HRC/RES/37/29, 23 March 2018 (27–4–16), operative para. 26.

[113] UN Doc. A/HRC/36/55, 8 August 2017.

[114] UN Doc. A/HRC/RES/36/20, 29 September 2017, (27–7–13), operative para. 23; UN Doc. A/RES/72/191, 19 December 2017 (109–17–58), operative para. 7; UN Doc. A/HRC/RES/37/29, 23 March 2018 (27–4–16), operative para. 26.

[115] UN Doc. A/HRC/36/55, 8 August 2017.

[116] UN Doc. A/HRC/RES/36/20, 29 September 2017, (27–7–13), operative para. 23; UN Doc. A/RES/72/191, 19 December 2017 (109–17–58), operative para. 7; UN Doc. A/HRC/RES/37/29, 23 March 2018 (27–4–16), operative para. 26.

[117] UN Doc. A/HRC/36/55, 8 August 2017.

[118] UN Doc. A/HRC/RES/36/20, 29 September 2017, (27–7–13), operative para. 23; UN Doc. A/RES/72/191, 19 December 2017 (109–17–58), operative para. 7; UN Doc. A/HRC/RES/37/29, 23 March 2018 (27–4–16), operative para. 26.

(continued)

Locations and dates	FFM reports	JIM/IIT reports (perpetrators)	COI reports	OPCW policy-making organs	UN policy-making organs
Saraqib, 4 February 2018	FFM report of 15 May 2018[119]			OPCW CSP[120]	UNHRC[121]; UNGA[122]
Saraqib, 4 February 2018		IIT report of 12 April 2021[123] (Syrian government)			UNGA[124]; UNHRC[125]
Douma, 7 April 2018			COI report of 9 August 2018[126]		UNGA[127]; UNHRC[128]

(continued)

[119] OPCW Doc. S/1626/2018, 15 May 2018.

[120] OPCW Doc. C-SS-4/DEC.3, 27 June 2018 (82–24–0), operative para. 9.

[121] UN Doc. A/HRC/RES/38/16, 6 July 2018 (26–5–15), operative para. 30; UN Doc. A/HRC/RES/39/15, 28 September 2018 (27–4–16), operative para. 35; UN Doc. A/HRC/RES/40/17, 22 March 2019 (28–5–14), operative para. 37; UN Doc. A/HRC/RES/41/23, 12 July 2019 (26–7–14), operative para. 39; UN Doc. A/HRC/RES/42/27, 27 September 2019 (27–6–13), operative para. 45; UN Doc. A/HRC/RES/43/28, 22 June 2020 (27–2–18), operative para. 53.

[122] UN Doc. A/RES/73/45, 5 December 2018, operative para. 3 (122–13–30 by separate vote); UN Doc. A/RES/73/182, 17 December 2018 (115–15–55), preamble para. 16; UN Doc. A/RES/74/40, 12 December 2019, operative para. 3 (120–11–26 by separate vote); UN Doc. A/RES/74/169, 18 December 2019 (106–15–57), preamble para. 17; UN Doc. A/RES/75/55, 7 December 2020, operative para. 4 (124–10–30 by separate vote); UN Doc. A/RES/75/193, 16 December 2020 (101–13–62), preamble para. 20; UN Doc. A/RES/76/29, 6 December 2021, operative para. 4 (111–10–40 by separate vote); UN Doc. A/RES/77/73, 7 December 2022 (155–6–19), operative para. 4.

[123] OPCW Doc. S/1943/2021, 12 April 2021.

[124] UN Doc. A/RES/76/29, 6 December 2021, operative para. 3 (118–13–34 by separate vote); UN Doc. A/RES/76/228, 24 December 2021 (93–16–52), preamble para. 22; UN Doc. A/RES/77/73, 7 December 2022 (155–6–19), operative para. 3; UN Doc. A/RES/77/230, 15 December 2022 (92–14–71), preamble paras. 7 and 25.

[125] UN Doc. A/HRC/RES/49/27, 1 April 2022 (23–7–16), operative para. 20; UN Doc. A/HRC/RES/51/26, 7 October (25–6–16), preamble para. 13.

[126] UN Doc. A/HRC/39/65, 9 August 2018.

[127] UN Doc. A/RES/73/182, 17 December 2018 (111–15–55), operative para. 6; UN Doc. A/RES/74/169, 18 December 2019 (106–15–57), operative para. 6; UN Doc. A/RES/75/193, 16 December 2020 (101–13–62), operative para. 6.

[128] UN Doc. A/HRC/RES/39/15, 28 September 2018 (27–4–16), preamble para. 15 and operative para. 37; UN Doc. A/HRC/RES/40/17, 22 March 2019 (28–5–14), preamble para. 17 and operative para. 38; UN Doc. A/HRC/RES/41/23, 12 July 2019 (26–7–14), operative para. 40; UN Doc. A/HRC/RES/42/27, 27 September 2019 (27–6–13), operative para. 46; UN Doc. A/HRC/RES/43/28, 22 June 2020 (27–2–18), operative para. 54.

(continued)

Locations and dates	FFM reports	JIM/IIT reports (perpetrators)	COI reports	OPCW policy-making organs	UN policy-making organs
Douma, 7 April 2018	FFM report of 6 July 2018 and 1 March 2019[129]				UNGA[130]; UNHRC[131]
Douma, 7 April 2018		IIT report of 27 January 2023[132] (Syrian government)			

129 OPCW Doc. S/1645/2018, 6 July 2018; OPCW Doc. S/1731/2019, 1 March 2019.

130 UN Doc. A/RES/73/45, 5 December 2018, operative para. 3 (122–13–30 by separate vote); UN Doc. A/RES/73/182, 17 December 2018 (111–15–55), preamble para. 16, operative para. 5; UN Doc. A/RES/74/40, 12 December 2019, operative para. 3 (120–11–26 by separate vote); UN Doc. A/RES/74/169, 18 December 2019 (106–15–57), preamble para. 17, operative para. 6; UN Doc. A/RES/75/55, 7 December 2020, operative para. 4 (124–10–30 by separate vote); UN Doc. A/RES/75/193, 16 December 2020 (101–13–62), preamble para. 20, operative para. 6; UN Doc. A/RES/76/29, 6 December 2021, operative para. 4 (111–10–40 by separate vote); UN Doc. A/RES/77/73, 7 December 2022 (155–6–19), operative para. 4).

131 UN Doc. A/HRC/RES/40/17, 22 March 2019 (28–5–14), operative para. 39; UN Doc. A/HRC/RES/41/23, 12 July 2019 (26–7–14), operative para. 41; UN Doc. A/HRC/RES/42/27, 27 September 2019 (27–6–13), operative para. 47; UN Doc. A/HRC/RES/43/28, 22 June 2020 (27–2–18), operative para. 55.

132 OPCW Doc. S/2125/2023, 27 January 2023.

Appendix D
Overall Autonomous Sanction Measures Against Entities

D.1 Designations June 2005–December 2012

Australia	Canada	EU	Switzerland	US
				28 Jun. 2005 1 entity [**16**]
				4 Jan. 2007 2 entity [**19**,**22**]
		1 Dec. 2011 6 entities [**15**,16,**18**,**20**,**21**,**24**]		
	23 Dec. 2011 6 entities [15,16,18,20,21,24]			
			7 Feb. 2012 6 entities [15,16,18,20,21,24]	
7 Mar. 2012 6 entities [15,16,18,20,21,24]				
				18 Jul. 2012 5 entities [15,18,20,21,24]
Confirmation of possession of chemical weapons by Syria on 23 July 2012				
				19 Sept. 2012
		15 Oct. 2012 2 entities [**17**]		
			27 Oct. 2012 2 entities [17]	
	26 Nov. 2012 2 entities [17]			

Numbers in brackets indicate the entities on the list in Table 3.3

T. Abe, *Syrian Chemical Weapons and International Law*,
https://doi.org/10.1007/978-981-99-3700-4

D.2 Designations January 2013–December 2015

Australia	Canada	EU	Switzerland	US
Use of sarin in East Ghouta on 21 August 2013				
Removal and elimination of chemical weapons				
				9 Jul. 2014
				2 entities [17]
		22 Jul. 2014		
		2 entities [19,22]		
			9 Sept. 2014	
			2 entities [19,22]	
		20 Oct. 2014		
			16 Dec. 2014	
				17 Dec. 2014
		6 Mar. 2015		
		1 entity [23]		
			17 Mar. 2015	
			1 entity [23]	
				31 Mar. 2015
				3 entities
		28 May 2015		
			16 June 2015	

Numbers in brackets indicate the entities on the list in Table 3.3

D.3 Designations January 2016–March 2017

Australia	Canada	EU	Switzerland	US
				21 Jul. 2016
				4 entities
Third report of the OPCW-UN Joint Investigative Mechanism on 24 August 2016				
		27 Oct. 2016		
			7 Nov. 2016	
				23 Dec. 2016
				2 entities
				12 Jan. 2017
				1 entity [23]
Failure of the UN Security Council to adopt collective sanction measures on 28 February 2017				
		20 Mar. 2017		
			27 Mar. 2017	

Numbers in brackets indicate the entities on the list in Table 3.3

D.4 Designations April 2017–March 2018

Australia	Canada	EU	Switzerland	US
Use of sarin in Khan Shaykhun on 4 April 2017				
	13 Apr. 2017			
	20 Apr. 2017 5 entities [19,22,23]			
				24 Apr. 2017
				16 May 2017
		17 Jul. 2017		
			2 Aug. 2017	
17 Aug. 2017 14 entities [17,19,22,23]				
		19 Mar. 2018		
			26 Mar. 2018	

Numbers in brackets indicate the entities on the list in Table 3.3

D.5 Designations April 2018–December 2022

Australia	Canada	EU	Switzerland	US
Use of chlorine in Douma on 7 April 2018				
				25 Jul. 2018
				5 entities
		21 Jan. 2019		
				7 Dec. 2021
				24 Oct. 2022
		14 Nov. 2022		
		1 entity		

Appendix E
Overall Autonomous Sanction Measures Against Individuals

E.1 Designations June 2005—December 2012

Australia	Canada	EU	Switzerland	US
				28 Jun. 2005
				4 Jan. 2007
		1 Dec. 2011		
	23 Dec. 2011			
			7 Feb. 2012	
7 Mar. 2012				
				18 Jul. 2012
Confirmation of possession of chemical weapons by Syria on 23 July 2012				
				19 Sept. 2012 1 individual [3]
		15 Oct. 2012		
			27 Oct. 2012	
	26 Nov. 2012 1 individual [3]			

Numbers in brackets indicate the individuals on the list in Table 3.2

T. Abe, *Syrian Chemical Weapons and International Law*,
https://doi.org/10.1007/978-981-99-3700-4

E.2 Designations January 2013–December 2015

Australia	Canada	EU	Switzerland	US
Use of sarin in East Ghouta on 21 August 2013				
Removal and elimination of chemical weapons				
				9 Jul. 2014
		22 Jul. 2014 5 individuals [**2**,3]		
			9 Sept. 2014 3 individuals [2,3]	
		20 Oct. 2014 1 individual [**5**]		
			16 Dec. 2014 1 individual [5]	
				17 Dec. 2014 1 individual
		6 Mar. 2015 3 individuals [**1**,**6**]		
			17 Mar. 2015 3 individuals [1,6]	
				31 Mar. 2015
		28 May 2015 1 individual [**11**]		
			16 June 2015 1 individual [11]	

Numbers in brackets indicate the individuals on the list in Table 3.2

E.3 Designations January 2016–March 2017

Australia	Canada	EU	Switzerland	US
				21 Jul. 2016 2 individuals
Third report of the OPCW-UN Joint Investigative Mechanism on 24 August 2016				
		27 Oct. 2016 3 individuals **[13]**		
			7 Nov. 2016 3 individuals [13]	
				23 Dec. 2016 1 individual
				12 Jan. 2017 17 individuals [1,2,**4**,5,6,**7**,**8**,**9**,**10**,11,**12**,**14**]
Failure of the UN Security Council to adopt collective sanction measures on 28 February 2017				
		20 Mar. 2017 4 individuals [4,9,10,12]		
			27 Mar. 2017 4 individuals [4,9,10,12]	

Numbers in brackets indicate the individuals on the list in Table 3.2

E.4 Designations April 2017–March 2018

Australia	Canada	EU	Switzerland	US
Use of sarin in Khan Shaykhun on 4 April 2017				
	13 Apr. 2017 3 individuals [13]			
	20 Apr. 2017 17 individuals [1,2,4,5,6,7,8,9,10,11,12,14]			
				24 Apr. 2017 258 individuals
				16 May 2017 1 individual
		17 Jul. 2017 16 individuals [7,8,14]		
			2 Aug. 2017 16 individuals [7,8,14]	
17 Aug. 2017 40 individuals [1,2,3,4,5,6,7,8,9,10,11,12,13,14]				
		19 Mar. 2018 4 individuals		
			26 Mar. 2018 4 individuals	

Numbers in brackets indicate the individuals on the list in Table 3.2

E.5 *Designations April 2018–December 2022*

Australia	Canada	EU	Switzerland	US
Use of chlorine in Douma on 7 April 2018				
				25 Jul. 2018 8 individuals
		21 Jan. 2019 2 individuals		
				7 Dec. 2021 2 individuals
				24 Oct. 2022 3 individuals [13]
		14 Nov. 2022 2 individuals		

Numbers in brackets indicate the individuals on the list in Table 3.2

Appendix F
State/Regional Organization-Specific Autonomous Sanction Measures

F.1 Australia: 20 Entities and 40 Individuals

7 March 2012[133]	6 entities
17 August 2017[134]	14 entities and 40 individuals

[133] Autonomous Sanctions (Designated Persons and Entities and Declared Persons—Syria) List 2012, https://www.legislation.gov.au/Details/F2012L00482, accessed 22 April 2023.

[134] Autonomous Sanctions (Designated Persons and Entities and Declared Persons–Syria) List 2017, https://www.legislation.gov.au/Details/F2017L01080, accessed 22 April 2023; Minister for Foreign Affairs, The Hon Julie Bishop MP, Media release, Sanctions targeting Syria's chemical weapons program, 24 August 2017 ("Today I have sanctioned 40 individuals and 14 entities linked to the Syrian regime's chemical weapons program. These individuals and entities are now subject to targeted financial sanctions, with individuals also subject to travel bans. The Organisation for the Prohibition of Chemical Weapons and the UN have confirmed that the Syrian military has used chemical weapons on several occasions. We urge the Syrian regime to fully comply with its 2013 commitment to dismantle and destroy its chemical weapons program."), https://www.foreignminister.gov.au/minister/julie-bishop/media-release/sanctions-targeting-syrias-chemical-weapons-program, accessed 22 April 2023.

T. Abe, *Syrian Chemical Weapons and International Law*,
https://doi.org/10.1007/978-981-99-3700-4

F.2 Canada: 13 Entities and 21 Individuals

23 December 2011[135]	6 entities
26 November 2012[136]	2 entities and 1 individual
13 April 2017[137]	3 individuals
20 April 2017[138]	5 entities and 17 individuals

F.3 EU: 22 Entities and 39 Individuals

	Council decision 2013/255/CFSP of 31 May 2013	Council decision (CFSP) 2018/1544
1 December 2011[139]	6 entities	
15 October 2012[140]	2 entities	
22 July 2014[141]	2 entities and 5 individuals	
20 October 2014[142]	1 individual	

(continued)

[135] Regulations Amending the Special Economic Measures (Syria) Regulations, P.C. 2011-1727, 22 December 2011, https://gazette.gc.ca/rp-pr/p2/2012/2012-01-04/html/sor-dors330-eng.html, accessed 22 April 2023; SOR/2011-330, 23 December 2011; Special Economic Measures (Syria) Regulations, SOR/2011-114, Version of document from 2011-12-23 to 2012-01-24, https://laws-lois.justice.gc.ca/eng/regulations/sor-2011-114/20111223/P1TT3xt3.html, accessed 22 April 2023.

[136] Regulations Amending the Special Economic Measures (Syria) Regulations, P.C. 2012-1577, 26 November 2012, https://gazette.gc.ca/rp-pr/p2/2012/2012-12-19/html/sor-dors249-eng.html, accessed 22 April 2023; SOR/2012-249, 26 November 2012; Special Economic Measures (Syria) Regulations, SOR/2011-114, Version of document from 2012-11-26 to 2014-01-28, https://laws-lois.justice.gc.ca/eng/regulations/sor-2011-114/20121126/P1TT3xt3.html, accessed 22 April 2023.

[137] Regulations Amending the Special Economic Measures (Syria) Regulations, P.C. 2017-405, 13 April 2017, https://gazette.gc.ca/rp-pr/p2/2017/2017-05-03/html/sor-dors62-eng.html, accessed 22 April 2023; SOR/2017-62, 13 April 2017; Special Economic Measures (Syria) Regulations, SOR/2011-114, Version of document from 2017-04-13 to 2017-04-19, https://laws-lois.justice.gc.ca/eng/regulations/sor-2011-114/20170413/P1TT3xt3.html, accessed 22 April 2023.

[138] Regulations Amending the Special Economic Measures (Syria) Regulations, P.C. 2017-407, 20 April 2017, https://gazette.gc.ca/rp-pr/p2/2017/2017-05-03/html/sor-dors69-eng.html, accessed 22 April 2023.

[139] Council Decision 2011/782/CFSP, 1 December 2011.

[140] Council Decision 2012/634/CFSP, 15 October 2012.

[141] Council Decision 2014/488/CFSP, 22 July 2014.

[142] Council Decision 2014/730/CFSP, 20 October 2014.

(continued)

	Council decision 2013/255/CFSP of 31 May 2013	Council decision (CFSP) 2018/1544
6 March 2015[143]	1 entity and 3 individuals	
28 May 2015[144]	1 individual	
27 October 2016[145]	3 individuals	
20 March 2017[146]	4 individuals	
17 July 2017,[147]	16 individuals	
19 March 2018,[148]	4 individuals	
21 January 2019,[149]		2 individuals
14 November 2022,[150]		1 entity and 2 individuals

[143] Council Implementing Decision (CFSP) 2015/383, 6 March 2015.

[144] Council Decision (CFSP) 2015/837, 28 May 2015.

[145] Council Implementing Decision (CFSP) 2016/1897, 27 October 2016.

[146] Council Implementing Decision (CFSP) 2017/485, 20 March 2017.

[147] Council Implementing Decision (CFSP) 2017/1341, 17 July 2017; Council of the EU, Press release, Use of chemical weapons in Syria: EU imposes sanctions against 16 additional persons, 17 July 2017, https://www.consilium.europa.eu/en/press/press-releases/2017/07/17/sanctions-syria/, accessed 22 April 2023.

[148] Council Implementing Decision (CFSP) 2018/421, 19 March 2018; Council of the EU, Press release, Use of chemical weapons in Syria: EU adds 4 persons to sanctions list, 19 March 2018, https://www.consilium.europa.eu/en/press/press-releases/2018/03/19/use-of-chemical-weapons-in-syria-eu-adds-4-persons-to-sanctions-list/, accessed 22 April 2023.

[149] Council Implementing Regulation (EU) 2019/84, 21 January 2019; Council of the EU, Press release, Chemical weapons: the EU places nine persons and one entity under new sanctions regime, 21 January 2019, https://www.consilium.europa.eu/en/press/press-releases/2019/01/21/chemical-weapons-the-eu-places-nine-persons-and-one-entity-under-new-sanctions-regime/, accessed 22 April 2023.

[150] Council Implementing Regulation (EU) 2022/2228, 14 November 2022; Council of the EU, Press release, Chemical weapons: EU imposes further restrictive measures on ten individuals and one entity, 14 November 2022, https://www.consilium.europa.eu/en/press/press-releases/2022/11/14/chemical-weapons-eu-imposes-further-restrictive-measures-on-ten-individuals-and-one-entity/, accessed 22 April 2023.

F.4 France: 24 Entities and 14 Individuals

18 January 2018[151]	14 entities and 11 individuals
18 May 2018[152]	10 entities and 3 individuals

F.5 Switzerland: 22 Entities and 37 Individuals

7 February 2012[153]	6 entities
27 October 2012[154]	2 entities
10 September 2014[155]	2 entities and 3 individuals
18 March 2015[156]	1 entity and 3 individuals
16 June 2015[157]	1 individual

(continued)

[151] Arrêté du 18 janvier 2018 portant application des articles L. 562-3 et suivants du code monétaire et financier, NOR: ECOT1801616A; and Arrêté du 18 janvier 2018 portant application des articles L. 562-3 et suivants du code monétaire et financier, NOR: ECOT1801617A (JORF n° 0018 du 23 janvier 2018, https://www.legifrance.gouv.fr/download/pdf?id=YAsnf6hnz13zdM0JqEI861Isrsa00QFujiQScSI_fAU, accessed 22 April 2023.

[152] Arrêté du 17 mai 2018 portant application des articles L. 562-3 et suivants du code monétaire et financier, NOR: ECOT1813351A; Arrêté du 17 mai 2018 portant application des articles L. 562-3 et suivants du code monétaire et financier, NOR: ECOT1813353A; and Arrêté du 17 mai 2018 portant application des articles L. 562-3 et suivants du code monétaire et financier, NOR: ECOT1813357A (JORF n° 0113 du 18 mai 2018, https://www.legifrance.gouv.fr/download/pdf?id=YzfAQ9HliDL05e8UDezovk1tUE4pff_NWtPY0T-2KIM, accessed 22 April 2023).

[153] Ordonnance instituant des mesures à l'encontre de la Syrie du 18 mai 2011 (Etat le 7 février 2012).

[154] Ordonnance instituant des mesures à l'encontre de la Syrie du 8 juin 2012 (Etat le 27 octobre 2012).

[155] Modification du 09.09.2014, avec entrée en vigueur le 10.09.2014 à 18 heures, https://www.seco.admin.ch/dam/seco/de/dokumente/Aussenwirtschaft/Wirtschaftsbeziehungen/Exportkontrollen/Sanktionen/Verordnungen/Syrien/Syrien_Delta_2014-09-10.pdf.download.pdf/Syrien_Delta_2014-09-10.pdf, accessed 22 April 2023.

[156] Modification du 10.03.2015, avec entrée en vigueur le 11.03.2015 à 18 heures, https://www.seco.admin.ch/dam/seco/fr/dokumente/Aussenwirtschaft/Wirtschaftsbeziehungen/Exportkontrollen/Sanktionen/Verordnungen/Syrien/Syrien_Delta_2015-03-17.pdf.download.pdf/Syrie_Delta_2015-03-17.pdf, accessed 22 April 2023.

[157] Modification du 16.06.2015, avec entrée en vigueur le 17.06.2015 à 18 heures, https://www.seco.admin.ch/dam/seco/fr/dokumente/Aussenwirtschaft/Wirtschaftsbeziehungen/Exportkontrollen/Sanktionen/Verordnungen/Syrien/Syrien_Delta_2015-06-16.pdf.download.pdf/Syrie_Delta_2015-06-16.pdf, accessed 22 April 2023.

(continued)

7 November 2016[158]	3 individuals
27 March 2017[159]	4 individuals
2 August 2017[160]	16 individuals
26 March 2018[161]	4 individuals

F.6 US: 25 Entities and 291 Individuals

	E.O. 13382 of 28 June 2005	E.O. 13572 of 29 April 2011	E.O. 13573 of 18 May 2011	E.O. 13582 of 17 August 2011	Section 7031(c)
28 June 2005[162]	1 entity				
4 January 2007[163]	2 entities				
18 July 2012[164]	5 entities				

(continued)

[158] Modification du 07.11.2016, avec entrée en vigueur le 08.11.2016 à 18 heures, https://www.seco.admin.ch/dam/seco/de/dokumente/Aussenwirtschaft/Wirtschaftsbeziehungen/Exportkontrollen/Sanktionen/Verordnungen/Syrien/Syrien%20Delta%202016-11-07.pdf.download.pdf/Syrien%20Delta%202016-11-07.pdf, accessed 22 April 2023.

[159] Modification du 27.03.2017, avec entrée en vigueur le 28.03.2017 à 18 heures, https://www.seco.admin.ch/dam/seco/de/dokumente/Aussenwirtschaft/Wirtschaftsbeziehungen/Exportkontrollen/Sanktionen/Verordnungen/Syrien/Syrien_Delta_2017-03-27.pdf.download.pdf/Syrien_Delta_2017-03-27.pdf, accessed 22 April 2023.

[160] Modification du 02.08.2017, avec entrée en vigueur le 03.08.2017 à 18 heures, https://www.seco.admin.ch/dam/seco/de/dokumente/Aussenwirtschaft/Wirtschaftsbeziehungen/Exportkontrollen/Sanktionen/Verordnungen/Syrien/Syrien%20Delta%202017-08-02.pdf.download.pdf/Syrien%20Delta%202017-08-02.pdf, accessed 22 April 2023.

[161] Modification du 26.03.2018, avec entrée en vigueur le 27.03.2018 à 18 heures, https://www.seco.admin.ch/dam/seco/fr/dokumente/Aussenwirtschaft/Wirtschaftsbeziehungen/Exportkontrollen/Sanktionen/Verordnungen/Syrien/Syrien_Delta_2018-03-26.pdf.download.pdf/Syrien_Delta_2018-03-26.pdf, accessed 22 April 2023.

[162] U.S. Department of the Treasury, Press Release, Statement of Secretary Snow on WMD Proliferation Financing Executive Order, 29 May 2005, https://home.treasury.gov/news/press-releases/js2613, accessed 22 April 2023; U.S. Department of the Treasury, Recent Actions, Non-Proliferation Designations; Issuance of new Executive Order on Non-Proliferation, 29 May 2005, https://home.treasury.gov/policy-issues/financial-sanctions/recent-actions/20050629, accessed 22 April 2023.

[163] U.S. Department of the Treasury, Press Release, Three Entities Targeted by Treasury for Supporting Syria's WMD Proliferation, 4 January 2007, https://home.treasury.gov/news/press-releases/hp216, accessed 22 April 2023.

[164] U.S. Department of the Treasury, Press Release, Treasury Increases Sanctions Against Syria, 18 July 2012, https://home.treasury.gov/news/press-releases/tg1642, accessed 22 April 2023.

(continued)

	E.O. 13382 of 28 June 2005	E.O. 13572 of 29 April 2011	E.O. 13573 of 18 May 2011	E.O. 13582 of 17 August 2011	Section 7031(c)
19 September 2012[165]	1 individual				
17 December 2012 [166]				1 individual	
9 July 2014[167]	2 entities				
31 March 2015[168]	3 entities				
21 July 2016[169]	3 entities and 1 individual			1 entity and 1 individual	
23 December 2016[170]	1 entity and 1 individual			1 entity	
12 January 2017[171]	1 entity and 7 individuals	5 individuals	4 individuals[172]	1 individual[173]	

(continued)

165 U.S. Department of the Treasury, Press Release, Treasury Designates Syrian Entity, Others Involved in Arms and Communications Procurement Networks and Identifies Blocked Iranian Aircraft, 19 September 2012, https://home.treasury.gov/news/press-releases/tg1714, accessed 22 April 2023.

166 U.S. Department of the Treasury, Press Release, Treasury Designates Lebanese Agent Working On Behalf Of The Asad Regime, 17 December 2012, https://home.treasury.gov/news/press-releases/tg1807, accessed 22 April 2023.

167 U.S. Department of the Treasury, Press Release, Treasury Sanctions Companies for Aiding the Syrian Regime, 9 July 2014, https://home.treasury.gov/news/press-releases/jl2558, accessed 22 April 2023.

168 U.S. Department of the Treasury, Press Release, Treasury Targets Syrian Regime Financial and Weapons Networks, 31 March 2015, https://home.treasury.gov/news/press-releases/JL10013, accessed 22 April 2023.

169 U.S. Department of the Treasury, Press Release, Treasury Sanctions Networks Providing Support to the Government of Syria, 21 July 2016, https://home.treasury.gov/news/press-releases/jl0526, accessed 22 April 2023.

170 U.S. Department of the Treasury, Press Release, Treasury Sanctions Additional Individuals and Entities in Response to Continuing Violence in Syria, 23 December 2016, https://home.treasury.gov/news/press-releases/jl0690, accessed 22 April 2023.

171 U.S. Department of the Treasury, Press Release, Treasury Sanctions Syrian Officials In Connection With OPCW-UN Findings of Regime's Use of Chemical Weapons on Civilians, 12 January 2017, https://home.treasury.gov/news/press-releases/jl0701, accessed 22 April 2023.

172 While Major-General Talal Shafiq Makhluf, commander of the Syrian Arab Republican Guard, was also designated, he is not on the "Chemical Weapons No Impunity!" sanctions list.

173 While the Syrian Arab Air Force, Syrian Arab Air Defense Forces, Syrian Arab Army, Syrian Arab Navy, and Syrian Arab Republican Guard were also designated, they are not on the "Chemical Weapons No Impunity!" sanctions list.

(continued)

	E.O. 13382 of 28 June 2005	E.O. 13572 of 29 April 2011	E.O. 13573 of 18 May 2011	E.O. 13582 of 17 August 2011	Section 7031(c)
24 April 2017[174]				258 individuals[175]	
16 May 2017[176]	1 individual				
25 July 2018[177]	5 entities and 8 individuals				
7 December 2021[178]		2 individuals			
24 October 2022[179]					2 individuals

[174] U.S. Department of the Treasury, Press Release, Treasury Sanctions 271 Syrian Scientific Studies and Research Center Staff in Response to Sarin Attack on Khan Sheikhoun, 24 April 2017, https://home.treasury.gov/news/press-releases/sm0056, accessed 22 April 2023. Thirteen out of 271 staff members of the SSRC are not on the "Chemical Weapons No Impunity!" sanctions list.

[175] The names of 13 individuals are missing in the list of "Chemical Weapons No Impunity!" (https://www.noimpunitychemicalweapons.org/-en-.html, accessed 22 April 2023).

[176] U.S. Department of the Treasury, Press Release, Treasury Sanctions Additional Individuals and Entities In Response to Continuing Violent Attacks on Syrian Citizens by the Syrian Government, 16 May 2017, https://home.treasury.gov/news/press-releases/sm0087, accessed 22 April 2023.

[177] U.S. Department of the Treasury, Press Release, The United States and France Take Coordinated Action on Global Procurement Network for Syria's Chemical Weapons Program, 25 July 2018, https://home.treasury.gov/news/press-releases/sm443, accessed 22 April 2023.

[178] U.S. Department of the Treasury, Press Release, Treasury Targets Repression and the Undermining of Democracy, 7 December 2021, https://home.treasury.gov/news/press-releases/jy0517, accessed 22 April 2023.

[179] U.S. Department of the State, Press Statement, Designation of Three Syrian Military Officials Due to Involvement in Gross Violations of Human Rights, 24 October 2022, https://www.state.gov/designation-of-three-syrian-military-officials-due-to-involvement-in-gross-violations-of-human-rights/, accessed 22 April 2023. One out of three designated Syrian military officials is not on the sanctions of "Chemical Weapons No Impunity!".

Appendix G
UN General Assembly Resolutions

	Implementation of the convention on the prohibition of the development, production, stockpiling and use of chemical weapons and on their destruction		Cooperation between the United Nations and the organization for the prohibition of chemical weapons	
1997	A/RES/52/38T, 9 December 1997	Without vote		
1998	A/RES/53/77R, 4 December 1998	Without vote		
1999	A/RES/54/54E, 1 December 1999	Without vote		
2000	A/RES/55/33H, 20 November 2000	Without vote		
2001	A/RES/56/24K, 29 November 2001	Without vote	A/RES/55/283, 7 September 2001; A/RES/56/42, 7 December 2001	Without vote; without vote
2002	A/RES/57/82, 22 November 2002	Without vote	A/RES/57/45, 21 November 2002	Without vote
2003	A/RES/58/52, 8 December 2003	Without vote		
2004	A/RES/59/72, 3 December 2004	Without vote	A/RES/59/7, 22 October 2004	Without vote
2005	A/RES/60/67, 8 December 2005	Without vote		
2006	A/RES/61/68, 6 December 2006	Without vote	A/RES/61/224, 20 December 2006	Without vote
2007	A/RES/62/23, 5 December 2007	Without vote		

(continued)

T. Abe, *Syrian Chemical Weapons and International Law*,
https://doi.org/10.1007/978-981-99-3700-4

(continued)

	Implementation of the convention on the prohibition of the development, production, stockpiling and use of chemical weapons and on their destruction		Cooperation between the United Nations and the organization for the prohibition of chemical weapons	
2008	A/RES/63/48, 2 December 2008	Without vote	A/RES/63/115, 5 December 2008	Without vote
2009	A/RES/64/46, 2 December 2009	Without vote		
2010	A/RES/65/57, 8 December 2010	Without vote	A/RES/65/236, 22 December 2010	Without vote
2011	A/RES/66/35, 2 December 2011	Without vote		
2012	A/RES/67/54, 3 December 2012	Without vote	A/RES/67/8, 19 November 2012	Without vote
2013	A/RES/68/45, 5 December 2013	Without vote		
2014	A/RES/69/67, 2 December 2014	181–0–1[180]	A/RES/69/14, 11 November 2014	108–0–1[181]
2015	A/RES/70/41, 7 December 2015	174–0–4[182]		
2016	A/RES/71/69, 5 December 2016	160–6–15[183]	A/RES/71/250, 22 December 2016	145–0–0[184]
2017	A/RES/72/43, 4 December 2017	159–7–14[185]		

(continued)

[180] 181 votes to none, with one abstention (Saudi Arabia) (UN Doc. A/69/PV.62, 2 December 2014, pp. 30–31), though subsequently, the delegation of Saudi Arabia informed the Secretariat that it had intended to vote in favor (UN Doc. A/69/PV.62, 2 December 2014, p. 31).

[181] 108 votes to none, with one abstention (Guyana) (UN Doc. A/69/PV.48, 11 November 2014, p. 28), although the delegations of Cambodia, Guyana, Laos, and Philippines subsequently informed the Secretariat that they had intended to vote in favor (UN Doc. A/69/PV.48, 11 November 2014, p. 28).

[182] 174 votes to none, with four abstentions (China, Iran, Russia, and Syria) (UN Doc. A/70/PV.67, 7 December 2015, p. 18).

[183] 160 votes to six (Burundi, China, Iran, Kyrgyzstan, Russia, and Syria), with 15 abstentions (Armenia, Belarus, Bolivia, Cuba, Kenya, Lebanon, Nicaragua, Samoa, South Africa, South Sudan, Sudan, Uganda, Tanzania, Venezuela, and Zimbabwe) (UN Doc. A/71/PV.51, 5 December 2016, p. 36).

[184] 145 votes to none, with no abstentions (UN Doc. A/71/PV.67, 22 December 2016, pp. 6–7).

[185] 159 votes to seven (Burundi, China, DPRK, Iran, Russia, Syria, and Zimbabwe), with 14 abstentions (Angola, Armenia, Belarus, Bolivia, Cuba, Kenya, Kyrgyzstan, Lebanon, Mali, Nicaragua, Rwanda, Uganda, Tanzania, and Venezuela) (UN Doc. A/72/PV.62, 4 December 2017, p. 21).

(continued)

	Implementation of the convention on the prohibition of the development, production, stockpiling and use of chemical weapons and on their destruction		Cooperation between the United Nations and the organization for the prohibition of chemical weapons	
2018	A/RES/73/45, 5 December 2018	152–7–22[186]	A/RES/73/258, 20 December 2018	142–0–12[187]
2019	A/RES/74/40, 12 December 2019	151–8–21[188]		
2020	A/RES/75/55, 7 December 2020	152–8–23[189]	A/RES/75/265, 3 March 2021	109–3–11[190]
2021	A/RES/76/29, 6 December 2021	154–8–21[191]		
2022	A/RES/77/73, 7 December 2022	155–6–19	A/RES/77/272, 20 February 2023	112–7–18

[186] 152 votes to seven (Cambodia, China, Iran, Nicaragua, Russia, Syria, and Zimbabwe), with 22 abstentions (Algeria, Armenia, Belarus, Bolivia, Burundi, Comoros, Cuba, Egypt, Kazakhstan, Kenya, Kyrgyzstan, Lebanon, Madagascar, Mali, Myanmar, Niger, Rwanda, Suriname, Uganda, Tanzania, Uzbekistan, and Venezuela) (UN Doc. A/73/PV.45, 5 December 2018, pp. 19–20).

[187] 142 votes to none, with 12 abstentions (Belarus, Cambodia, China, Cuba, DPRK, Iran, Mali, Myanmar, Nicaragua, Russia, Syria, and Zimbabwe) (UN Doc. A/73/PV.63, 20 December 2018, p. 7).

[188] 151 votes to eight (Cambodia, China, Congo, Iran, Nicaragua, Russia, Syria, and Zimbabwe), with 21 abstentions (Algeria, Armenia, Belarus, Bolivia, Burundi, Cuba, Egypt, Kazakhstan, Kenya, Kyrgyzstan, Lebanon, Mali, Mongolia, Myanmar, Rwanda, Suriname, Tajikistan, Tunisia, Uganda, Uzbekistan, and Venezuela) (UN Doc. A/74/PV.46, 12 December 2019, pp. 18–19).

[189] 152 votes to eight (Cambodia, China, Iran, Nicaragua, Russia, Syria, Venezuela, and Zimbabwe), with 23 abstentions (Algeria, Armenia, Belarus, Bolivia, Comoros, Cuba, Djibouti, Egypt, Eritrea, Kazakhstan, Kyrgyzstan, Lebanon, Madagascar, Mali, Mauritania, Mongolia, Myanmar, Sudan, Suriname, Tajikistan, Tunisia, Uganda, and Uzbekistan) (UN Doc. A/75/PV.37, 7 December 2020, pp. 29–30).

[190] 109 votes to three (China, Russia, and Syria), with 11 abstentions (Algeria, Angola, Belarus, Bolivia, Cambodia, Côte d'Ivoire, Cuba, Madagascar, Nicaragua, Venezuela, and Zimbabwe) (UN Doc. A/75/PV.56, 3 March 2021, p. 18).

[191] 154 votes to eight (Cambodia, China, Iran, Nicaragua, Russia, Syria, Venezuela, and Zimbabwe), with 21 abstentions (Algeria, Armenia, Belarus, Bolivia, Burundi, Cuba, Djibouti, Egypt, Eritrea, Kazakhstan, Kenya, Kyrgyzstan, Lebanon, Mali, Mongolia, Rwanda, Sudan, Tajikistan, Tunisia, Uganda, and Uzbekistan) (UN Doc. A/76/PV.45, 6 December 2021, p. 16).

References

Treaties

Protocol for the Prohibition of the Use of Asphyxiating, Poisonous or Other Gases, and of Bacteriological Methods of Warfare. Geneva, 17 June 1925, *League of Nations Treaty Series*, Vol. XCIV, No. 2138, p. 65.

Convention on the Prohibition of the Development, Production, Stockpiling, and Use of Chemical Weapons and on Their Destruction, *United Nations Treaty Series*, Vol. 1974, No. 33757, p. 45.

Amendment to Article 8 of the Rome Statute of the International Criminal Court, 10 June 2010, *United Nations Treaty Series*, Vol. 2868, No. 38544, p. 197.

Publications

Tatsuya Abe, "Effectiveness of the Institutional Approach to An Alleged Violation of International law: The Case of Syrian Chemical Weapons," *Japanese Yearbook of International Law*, Vol. 57 (2014), pp. 333–370.

Tatsuya Abe, "Syria: The chemical weapons question and autonomous sanctions," in Masahiko Asada (ed.), *Economic Sanctions in International Law and Practice* (Routledge, 2020), pp. 200–222.

Tatsuya Abe, "Challenge inspections under the Chemical Weapons Convention: between ideal and reality," *The Nonproliferation Review*, Vol. 24, Nos. 1–2 (2017), pp. 167–184.

Daniela Abratt, "U.S. Intervention in Syria: A Legal Responsibility to Protect," *Denver Law Review*, Vol. 95, Issue 1 (2017), pp. 21–72.

Nadia Ahmad, "Legalizing Humanitarian Intervention in Response to Chemical Weapon Usage: Syrian Conflict's Impact on International Law," *Willamette Journal of International Law and Dispute Resolution*, Vol. 29, Issue 2 (2022), pp. 155–186.

Dapo Akande, "The Legality of Military Action in Syria: Humanitarian Intervention and Responsibility to Protect," *EJIL Talk!*, 28 August 2013, https://www.ejiltalk.org/humanitarian-intervention-responsibility-to-protect-and-the-legality-of-military-action-in-syria/.

Michelle Almary, "The Necessity for a Permanent Disincentive: Examining the Use of Chemical Weapons with a Focus on Syria's Civil War," *Southwestern Journal of International Law*, Vol. 24, Issue 2 (2018), pp. 301–336.

Philip Alston, "Commissions of Inquiry as Human Rights Fact-Finding Tools," *American Society of International Law Proceedings*, Vol. 105 (2011), pp. 81–85.

T. Abe, *Syrian Chemical Weapons and International Law*,
https://doi.org/10.1007/978-981-99-3700-4

Dominique Anelli and Mehran Rouzbahani, "Chemical Demilitarisation in Syria: An Overview," *Verification & Implementation 2015* (2015), pp. 121–128, https://www.vertic.org/media/assets/VI%202015/VI%20Chapter%207.pdf.

Dominique Anelli, "Old Chemical Weapons: Moving the OPCW to an Active Role," *Arms Control Today*, June 2020, https://www.armscontrol.org/act/2020-06/features/old-chemical-weapons-moving-opcw-active-role.

Anthony Clark Arend and Robert J. Beck, *International Law and the Use of Force: Beyond the UN Charter Paradigm* (Routledge, 1993).

Masahiko Asada, "A Path to a Comprehensive Prohibition of the Use of Chemical Weapons under International Law: From the Hague to Damascus," *Journal of Conflict and Security Law*, Vol. 21, No. 2 (2016), pp. 153–208.

Masahiko Asada, "Definition and Legal Justification of Sanctions," in Masahiko Asada (ed.), *Economic Sanctions in International Law and Practice* (Routledge, 2020), pp. 3–23.

Masahiko Asada, "International Law of Nuclear Non-Proliferation and Disarmament," *Recueil des cours*, Vol. 424 (2022), pp. 9–726.

Rebecca Barber, "Uniting for Peace Not Aggression: Responding to Chemical Weapons in Syria Without Breaking the Law," *Journal of Conflict and Security Law*, Vol. 24, No. 1 (2019), pp. 71–110.

R.R. Baxter and Thomas Buergenthal, "Legal Aspects of the Geneva Protocol of 1925," *American Journal of International Law*, Vol. 64, No. 5 (1970), pp. 853–879.

Michael A. Becker and Sarah M.H. Nouwen, "International Commissions of Inquiry: What Difference Do They Make? Taking an Empirical Approach," *The European Journal of International Law*, Vol. 30, No. 3 (2019), pp. 819–841.

Jacob Behmer, "The Legality of President Trump's Missile Strike on Al-Shayrat Air Force Base in Syria," *University of St. Thomas Journal of Law and Public Policy (Minnesota)*, Vol. 13, Issue 2 (2019), pp. 83–102.

Andrew M. Bell, "Using Force against the Weapons of the Weak: Examining a Chemical-Biological Weapons Usage Criterion for Unilateral Humanitarian Intervention under the Responsibility to Protect," *Cardozo Journal of International and Comparative Law*, Vol. 22, Issue 2 (2014), pp. 261–320.

Michelle Bentley, *Syria and the Chemical Weapons Taboo* (Manchester University Press, 2016).

Daniel Bethlehem, "Stepping Back a Moment-The Legal Basis in Favour of a Principle of Humanitarian Intervention," *EJIL: Talk!*, 12 September 2013, https://www.ejiltalk.org/stepping-back-a-moment-the-legal-basis-in-favour-of-a-principle-of-humanitarian-intervention/.

Richard B. Bilder, "Kosovo and the New Interventionism: Promise or Peril," *Journal of Transnational Law and Policy*, Vol. 9, No.1 (1999), pp. 153–182.

Alison Bisset, "Community of Inquiry and Procedural Fairness," in Christian Henderson (ed.), *Commissions of Inquiry: Problems and Prospects* (Hart Publishing, 2017), pp. 309–335.

Philipp C. Bleek and Nicholas J. Kramer, "Eliminating Syria's chemical weapons: implications for addressing nuclear, biological and chemical threats," *The Nonproliferation Review*, Vol. 23, Nos 1–2 (2016), pp. 197–230.

William H. Boothby, *Weapons and the Law of Armed Conflict* (Oxford University Press, 2009).

Michael Bothe, "Fact-finding as a means of ensuring respect for international humanitarian law," in W Heintschel von Heinegg and V Epping (eds), *International Humanitarian Law Facing New Challenges* (Springer, 2007), pp. 249–267.

Théo Boutruche, "Credible Fact-Finding and Allegations of International Humanitarian Law Violations: Challenges in Theory and Practice," *Journal of Conflict and Security Law*, Vol. 16, No. 1 (2011), pp. 105–140.

Théo Boutruche, "Selectivity and Choices in Human Rights Fact-finding: Reconciling Subjectivity with Objectivity?" in Christian Henderson (ed.), *Commissions of Inquiry: Problems and Prospects* (Hart Publishing, 2017), pp. 287–308.

Ian Brownlie, *International Law and the Use of Force by States* (Clarendon Press, 1963).

Ian Brownlie, "International Law and the Use of Force by States Revisited," *Australian Yearbook of International Law*, Vol. 21 (2000), pp. 21–38.
Robert J. Bunker Dr., *Contemporary Chemical Weapons Use in Syria and Iraq by the Assad Regime and the Islamic State* (US Army War College Press, 2019), https://press.armywarcollege.edu/monographs/383.
George Bunn, "Banning Poison Gas and Germ Warfare: Should the United States Agree?," *Wisconsin Law Review*, Vol. 1969, No. 2 (1969), pp. 375–420.
Patrick Butchard and Christian Henderson, "A Functional Typology of Commissions of Inquiry," in Christian Henderson (ed.), *Commissions of Inquiry: Problems and Prospects* (Hart Publishing, 2017), pp. 11–34.
Russell Buchan and Nicholas Tsagourias, *Regulating the Use of Force in International Law* (Edward Elgar Publishing, 2021).
Sean Butler, "To Unite Our Strength to Maintain International Peace and Security: The International Response to the Syrian Civil War & the Global Discourse on State Sovereignty," *Irish Yearbook of International Law*, Vol. 9 (2014), pp. 7–24.
W. E. Butler (ed.), *Control over Compliance with International Law* (Martinus Nijhoff Publishers, 1991).
W. E. Butler, "Ensuring Compliance with Arms Control Agreements: Legal Responses," in W. E. Butler (ed.), *Control over Compliance with International Law* (Martinus Nijhoff Publishers, 1991), pp. 31–39.
W. Seth Carus, "Chemical Weapons in the Middle East," *Policy Focus, The Washington Institute for Near East Policy*, No. 9 (1988).
Antonio Cassese, *International Law, second edition* (Oxford University Press, 2005).
Antonio Cassese, "Fostering Increased Conformity with International Standards: Monitoring and Institutional Fact-finding," in Antonio Cassese (ed.), *Realizing Utopia: The Future of International Law* (Oxford University Press, 2012), pp. 295–303.
Jonathan I. Charney, "Anticipatory Humanitarian Intervention in Kosovo," *Vanderbilt Journal of Transnational Law*, Vol. 32, No. 5 (1999), pp. 1231-1248.
Abram Chayes and Antonia Handler Chayes, *The New Sovereignty: Compliance with International Regulatory Agreements* (Harvard University Press, 1995).
Simon Chesterman, "Responsibility to Protect and Humanitarian Intervention From Apology to Utopia and Back Again", in Robin Geiß and Nils Melzer (eds.), *The Oxford Handbook of the International Law of Global Security* (Oxford University Press, 2021), pp. 808–820.
Andrew Clapham, *Brierly's Law of Nations*, seventh edition (Oxford University Press, 2012).
Andrew Clapham, *War* (Oxford University Press, 2021).
Olivier Corten, *The Law Against War*, second edition (Hart Publishing, 2021).
John R. Crook, "United States Threatens Military Strikes Against Syria, Then Joins in Diplomatic Efforts to Control Syrian Chemical Weapon," *American Journal of International Law*, Vol. 107, No. 4 (2013), pp. 900–907.
Kelsey Davenport, "Last CW Materials Removed from Libya," *Arms Control Today* (October 2016), https://www.armscontrol.org/act/2016-09/news/last-cw-materials-removed-libya.
Aniel Caro de Beer and Dire Tladi, "The Use of Force against Syria in Response to Alleged Use of Chemical Weapons by Syria: A Return to Humanitarian Intervention?" *Zeitschrift Für Ausländisches öffentliches Recht Und Vökerrecht*, Vol. 79 (2019), pp. 205–239.
Yoram Dinstein, *Non-International Armed Conflicts in International Law* (Cambridge University Press, 2014).
Yoram Dinstein, *The Conduct of Hostilities under the Law of International Armed Conflict*, third edition (Cambridge University Press, 2016).
Alonso Gurmendi Dunkelberg, Rebecca Ingber, Priya Pillai and Elvina Pothelet, "Mapping States' Reactions to the Syria Strikes of April 2018," Just Security, https://www.justsecurity.org/55157/mapping-states-reactions-syria-strikes-april-2018/.
Treasa Dunworth and Anna Hood (eds.), *Disarmament Law* (Routledge, 2021).
Pierre-Marie Dupuy and Yann Kerbrat, *Droit international public, 16e édition* (Dalloz, 2022).

Ingrid Elliott, "A Meaningful Step towards Accountability," *Journal of International Criminal Justice*, Vol. 15, No. 2 (2017), pp. 239–256.

Tom J. Farer, "An Inquiry into the Legitimacy of Humanitarian Intervention," in Lori Fisler Damrosch and David J. Scheffer (eds.), *Law and Force in the New International Order* (Westview Press, 1991), pp. 185–201.

Michelle Farrell and Ben Murphy, "Hegemony and Counter-Hegemony: The Politics of Establishing United Nations Commissions of Inquiry," in Christian Henderson (ed.), *Commissions of Inquiry: Problems and Prospects* (Hart Publishing, 2017), pp. 35–64.

Ana Maria Carvalho Ferreira da Silva Correia, "International Humanitarian Law and Weapons of Mass Destruction: The Case of Syria," *Portuguese Journal of Military Sciences*, May, IX (1), pp. 187–207.

Dieter Fleck, "6. Means of Combat, III. Weapons of Mass Destruction," in Dieter Fleck (ed.), *The Handbook of International Humanitarian Law*, fourth edition (Oxford University Press, 2021), pp. 156–169.

Thomas M. Franck and Nigel S. Rodley, "After Bangladesh: The Law of Humanitarian Intervention by Military Force, "*American Journal of International Law*," Vol. 67, Issue 2 (1973), pp. 275–305.

Thomas M. Franck, "Fairness in the International Legal and Institutional System: General Course on Public International Law," *Recueil des Cours*, Vol. 240 (1993-III) 240, pp. 9–498.

Robert A. Friedman, "Legal Aspects of Weapons of Mass Destruction Elimination Contingencies," *The Nonproliferation Review*, Vol. 23, Nos. 1–2 (2016), pp. 61–82.

Micaela Frulli, "Fact-Finding or Paving the Road to Criminal Justice: Some Reflections on United Nations Commissions of Inquiry," *Journal of International Criminal Justice*, Vol. 10, No. 5 (2012), pp. 1323–1338.

Shlomo Gazit (ed.), *The Middle East Military Balance, 1993–1994* (Boulder, CO: Westview Press for the Jaffee Center for Strategic Studies, 1994).

Marco Gestri, "Sanctions Imposed by the European Union: Legal and Institutional Aspects," in Natalino Ronzitti (ed.), *Coercive Diplomacy, Sanctions, and International Law* (Brill, Nijhoff, 2016), pp. 70–102.

Francesco Giumelli, "From Effective to Useful Sanctions: Lessons Learned from the Experience of the European Union," in Natalino Ronzitti (ed.), *Coercive Diplomacy, Sanctions and International Law* (Brill, Nijhoff, 2016), pp. 246–269.

Jozef Goldblat, *Arms Control: The New Guide to Negotiations and Agreements, fully revised and updated second edition* (SAGE Publications, 2002).

Juan Manuel Gómez-Robledo, "The Provisional Application of Treaties," *University of Vienna Law Review*, Vol. 2:2 (2018), pp. 182–197.

Ryan Goodman, "Humanitarian Intervention and Pretexts for War," *American Journal of International Law*, Vol. 100, No. 1 (2006), pp. 107–141.

Rob Grace, "From Design to Implementation: The Interpretation of Fact-Finding Mandates," *Journal of Conflict and Security Law*, Vol. 20, No. 1 (2015), pp. 27–60.

Christine Gray, "The Use of Force for Humanitarian Purposes," in Nigel D. White and Christian Henderson (eds.), *Research Handbook on International Conflict and Security Law:* Jus ad Bellum, Jus in Bello and Jus post Bellum (Edward Elgar, 2013), pp. 229–255.

Morris Greenspan, *The Modern Law of Land Warfare* (University of California Press, 1959).

Christopher Greenwood, "Humanitarian Intervention: The Case of Kosovo," *Finnish Yearbook of International Law*, Vol. 10 (1999), pp. 141–176.

John Hart, "8. Reducing security threats from chemical and biological materials," SIPRI Yearbook 2014, Armaments, Disarmament and International Security (Oxford University Press, 2014), pp. 387–416.

John Hart, "13. Chemical and biological security threats," SIPRI Yearbook 2015, Armaments, Disarmament and International Security (Oxford University Press, 2015), pp. 557–585.

John Hart, "18. Chemical and biological security threats," SIPRI Yearbook 2016, Armaments, Disarmament and International Security (Oxford University Press, 2016), pp. 709–739.

John Hart, "13. Chemical and biological security threats," SIPRI Yearbook 2017, Armaments, Disarmament and International Security (Oxford University Press, 2017), pp. 511–541.
John Hart, "8. Chemical and biological security threats," SIPRI Yearbook 2018, Armaments, Disarmament and International Security (Oxford University Press, 2018), pp. 347–378.
Monica Hakimi, "The Attack on Syria and the Contemporary Jus ad Bellum," *EJIL Talk!*, 15 April 2018, https://www.ejiltalk.org/the-attack-on-syria-and-the-contemporary-jus-ad-bellum/.
Mika Hayashi, "Benefits of a Legally Non-Binding Agreement: The Case of the 2013 US-Russian Agreement on the Elimination of Syrian Chemical Weapons," *International Community Law Review*, Vol. 20, Issue 2 (2018), pp. 252–277.
Mika Hayashi, "Reacting to the Use of Chemical Weapons: Options for Third States," *Journal on Use of Force and International Law*, Vol. 1, No.1 (2014), pp. 80–121.
Mika Hayashi, "The U.S. Airstrike After the Use of Chemical Weapons in Syria: National Interest, Humanitarian Intervention, or Enforcement Against War Crimes?," *ASIL Insights*, Vol. 21, Issue 8, 13 July 2017, https://www.asil.org/insights/volume/21/issue/8/us-airstrike-after-use-chemical-weapons-syria-national-interest.
Jean-Marie Henckaerts and Louise Doswald-Beck, *Customary International Humanitarian Law*, Volume I Rules (Cambridge University Press, 2005).
Christian Henderson, "The UK Government's Legal Opinion on Forcible measures in Response to the Use of Chemical Weapons by the Syrian Government," *International and Comparative Law Quarterly*, Vol. 64, No. 1 (2015), pp. 179–196.
Christian Henderson (ed.), *Commissions of Inquiry: Problems and Prospects* (Hart Publishing, 2017).
Anders Henriksen and M Schack, "The Crisis in Syria and Humanitarian Intervention," *Journal on the Use of Force and International Law* (2014), Vol. 1, No. 1, pp. 122–147.
Anders Henriksen, "Trump's Missile Strike on Syria and the Legality of Using Force to Deter Chemical Warfare," *Journal of Conflict and Security Law*, Vol. 23, Issue 1 (2018), pp. 33–48.
Corinne Heaven, "A Visible College: The Community of Fact-Finding Practice," in Christian Henderson (ed.), *Commissions of Inquiry: Problems and Prospects* (Hart Publishing, 2017), pp. 337–359.
Louis Henkin, "Kosovo and the Law of 'Humanitarian Intervention,'" *American Journal of International Law*, Vol. 93, Issue 4 (1999), pp. 824–828.
Harold Hongju Koh, "Syria and the Law of Humanitarian Intervention (Part II: International Law and the Way Forward)," *EJIL: Talk!*, 4 October 2013, https://www.ejiltalk.org/syria-and-the-law-of-humanitarian-intervention-part-ii-international-law-and-the-way-forward/.
Una Jakob, "12. Chemical, biological and health security threats," *SIPRI Yearbook 2022, Armaments, Disarmament and International Security* (Oxford University Press, 2022), pp. 496–503.
Agnieszka Jachec Neale, "Human Rights Fact-Finding into Armed Conflict and Breaches of the Laws of War," *American Society of International Law Proceedings*, Vol. 105 (2011), pp. 85–89.
Agnieszka Jachec-Neale, "Fact-Finding," in Rüdiger Wolfrum (ed.), *The Max Planck Encyclopedia of Public International Law*, Vol. 4 (Oxford University Press, 2012), pp. 1077–1084.
Marie Jacobsson, "Syria and the Issue of Chemical Weapons: A Snapshot of a Legal Time-frame: the United Nations Security Council Resolution 2118 (2013) and the OPCW Executive Council Decision," in Jonas Ebbesson et al (eds.), *International Law and Changing Perceptions of Security: liber amicorum Said Mahmoudi* (Brill Nijhoff, 2014), pp. 134–151.
John Janzekovic, "OPCW," in Daniel Silander and Don Wallace (eds.), *International Organizations and the Implementation of the Responsibility to Protect: the Humanitarian Crisis in Syria* (Routledge, 2015).
Michael Kirby and Rebecca LaForgia, "Fact-Finding and Report Writing by UN Human Rights Mandate Holders," *Adelaide Law Review*, Vol. 38, No. 2 (2017), pp. 463–482.
Agata Kleczkowska, "The Illegality of Humanitarian Intervention: The Case of the UK's Legal Position concerning the 2018 Strikes in Syria," *Utrecht Journal of International and European Law*, Vol. 35, Issue 1 (2020), pp. 35–49.

Robert Kolb, "Note on Humanitarian Intervention," *International Review of Red Cross*, Vol. 85, No. 849 (2003), pp. 119–134.

Walter Krutzsch, Eric Myjer and Ralf Trapp (eds.), *The Chemical Weapons Convention: A Commentary* (Oxford University Press, 2014).

Anne Lagerwall, "Threats of and Actual Military Strikes Against Syria—2013 and 2017," in Tom Ruys and Olivier Corten (eds.), *The Use of Force in International Law: A Case-based Approach* (Cambridge University Press, 2018), pp. 828–854.

H. E. Nicolas Lang, "The Path to Better Compliance with International Humanitarian Law," *Military Law and Law of War Review*, Vol. 52, No. 1 (2013), pp. 131–144.

Hersch Lauterpacht (ed), *Oppenheim's International Law: a treatise*, 7th edition (Longmans, Green and Co., 1955).

Richard B. Lillich, "Forcible Self-Help by States to Protect Human Rights," *Iowa Law Review*, Vol. 53, Issue 2 (1967), pp. 325–351.

Richard B. Lillich (ed.), *Humanitarian intervention and the United Nations* (University Press of Virginia, 1973).

M. I. Lazarev, "On a Theoretical Concept of Control over the Fulfilment of International Obligations of State," in W. E. Butler (ed.), *Control over Compliance with International Law* (Martinus Nijhoff Publishers, 1991), pp. 17–22.

Anne Lorenzat, "The Current State of Customary International Law with regard to the Use of Chemical Weapons in Non-International Armed Conflicts," *Military Law and Law of War Review*, Vol. 56, Issue 2 (2017–2018), pp. 349–404.

Vaughan Lowe, *International Law* (Oxford University Press, 2007).

I. I. Lukashuk, "Control in Contemporary International Law," in W. E. Butler (ed.), *Control over Compliance with International Law* (Martinus Nijhoff Publishers, 1991), pp. 5–16.

Karim Makdisi and Coralie Pison Hindawi, "The Syrian Chemical Weapons Disarmament Process in Context: Narratives of Coercion, Consent, and Everything in Between," *Third World Quarterly*, Vol. 38, Issue 8 (2017), pp. 1691–1709.

Karim Makdisi and Coralie Pison Hindawi, "Exploring the UN and OPCW Partnership in Syrian Chemical Weapons Disarmament: Interorganizational Cooperation and Autonomy," *Global Governance*, Vol. 25, Issue 4 (2019), pp. 535–562.

Howard Mann, "Arms Control Verification and the United Nations: The Chemical Weapons Experience of the 1980s," *Canadian Yearbook of International Law*, Vol. 26 (1988), pp.185–214.

Herbert F. Manisty, "The Use of Poison Gas in War," *Transactions of the Grotius Society*, Vol. 9, Problems of Peace and War, Papers Read before the Society in the Year 1923 (1923), pp. 17–28.

Thilo Marauhn, "Sailing Close to the Wind: Human Rights Council Fact-Finding in Situations of Armed Conflict—The Case of Syria," *California Western International Law Journal*, Vol. 43, No. 2 (2013), pp. 401–460.

Thilo Marauhn, "The Prohibition to Use Chemical Weapons," *Yearbook of International Humanitarian Law*, Vol. 17 (2014), pp. 25–44.

Triestino Mariniello, "The Impact of International Commissions of Inquiry on the Proceedings before the International Criminal Court," in Christian Henderson (ed.), *Commissions of Inquiry: Problems and Prospects* (Hart Publishing, 2017), pp. 171–196.

Michael J. Matheson, "Justification for the NATO Air Campaign in Kosovo," *American Society of International Law Proceedings*, Vol. 94 (2000), p. 301.

Albert J. Mauroni, "Eliminating Syria's Chemical Weapons," *The Counterproliferation Papers Future Warfare Series*, No. 58 (2017), https://media.defense.gov/2019/Apr/11/2002115522/-1/-1/0/58ELIMINATINGSYRIACW.PDF.

Kenneth R. Mayer, "Executive Power in the Obama Administration and the Decision to Seek Congressional Authorization for a Military Attack against Syria: Implications for Theories of Unilateral Action," *Utah Law Review*, Vol. 2014, Issue 4 (2014), pp. 821–842.

Myres S. McDougal and Florentino P. Feliciano, *Law and Minimum World Public Order* (Yale University Press, 1961).

Jonathan McLaughlin, "A Resilient Threat: SSRC's Role in Syria's Chemical Weapon Program," Wisconsin Project on Nuclear Arms Control (2018), https://www.wisconsinproject.org/a-resilient-threat-ssrcs-role-in-syrias-chemical-weapon-program/.

Caitriona McLeish, "8. Chemical and biological security threats," *SIPRI Yearbook 2019, Armaments, Disarmament and International Security* (Oxford University Press, 2019), pp. 397–445.

Caitriona McLeish, "12. Chemical and biological security threats," *SIPRI Yearbook 2020, Armaments, Disarmament and International Security* (Oxford University Press, 2020), pp. 437–481.

Caitriona McLeish, "12. Chemical and biological security threats," *SIPRI Yearbook 2021, Armaments, Disarmament and International Security* (Oxford University Press, 2021), pp. 445–502.

Marko Milanovic, "The Clearly Illegal US Missile Strike in Syria," *EJIL:Talk!*, 7 April 2017, https://www.ejiltalk.org/the-clearly-illegal-us-missile-strike-in-syria/.

Marko Milanovic, "The Syria Strikes: Still Clearly Illegal," *EJIL:Talk!*, 15 April 2018, https://www.ejiltalk.org/the-syria-strikes-still-clearly-illegal/.

Marjorie Millace Whiteman, *Digest of International Law*, Vol. 10 (U.S. Department of State, 1968).

Anton Moiseienko, *Corruption and Targeted Sanctions: Law and Policy of Anti-Corruption Entry Bans* (Brill, 2019).

Hilly Moodrick-Even Khen, Nir T. Boms, and Sareta Ashraph (eds.), *The Syrian War: Between Justice and Political Reality* (Cambridge University Press, 2020).

John Norton Moore, "Ratification of the Geneva Protocol on Gas and Bacteriological Warfare: A Legal and Political Analysis," *Virginia Law Review*, Vol. 58, No. 3 (1972), pp. 419–509.

Sean D. Murphy, *Humanitarian Intervention: The United Nations in an Evolving World Order* (University of Pennsylvania Press, 1996).

Sean D. Murphy, "Current Developments," *American Journal of International Law*, Vol. 115, Issue 4 (2021), pp. 671–687.

Yasmine Nahlawi, "The Responsibility to Protect and Obama's Red Line on Syria," *Global Responsibility to Protect*, Vol. 8, Issue 1 (2016), pp. 76–101.

Yasmine Nahlawi, *The Responsibility to Protect in Libya and Syria: Mass Atrocities, Human Protection, and International Law* (Routledge 2020).

Yasmin Naqvi, "Crossing the red line: The use of chemical weapons in Syria and what should happen now," *International Review of the Red Cross*, Vol. 99, No. 3 (2017), pp. 959–993.

Yasmin Naqvi and Olfemi Elias, "Chemical Weapons and Non-State Actors," in Ezequiel Heffes, Marcos D. Kotlik and Manuel J. Ventura (eds.), *International Humanitarian Law and Non-State Actors* (Springer, 2020), pp. 115–148.

Vincent Nordin, "A Humanitarian Exception: The International Legal Justification for U.S. Military Action Against the Syrian Regime," *Santa Clara Law Review*, Vol. 61, Issue 3 (2021), pp. 811–838.

Samuel Nurding, "Libya destroys 'Category 1' chemical weapons," *Trust and Verify*, Issue Number 144 (January-March 2014), Verification Research, Training and Information Center (VERTIC), p. 4.

Marco Odello, "The Interplay between International Human Rights Law and International Humanitarian Law in the Practice of Commissions of Inquiry," in Christian Henderson (ed.), *Commissions of Inquiry: Problems and Prospects* (Hart Publishing, 2017), pp. 199–229.

Stefan Oeter, "Methods and Means of Combat," in Dieter Fleck (ed.), *The Handbook of International Humanitarian Law* (Oxford University Press, 1999), pp. 105–207.

Stefan Oeter, "Methods and Means of Combat," in Dieter Fleck (ed.), *The Handbook of International Humanitarian Law*, second edition (Oxford University Press, 2008), pp. 119–235.

Stefan Oeter, "Methods and Means of Combat," in Dieter Fleck (ed.), *The Handbook of International Humanitarian Law*, third edition (Oxford University Press, 2013), pp. 115–230.

Chelsea O'Donnell, "The Development of the Responsibility to Protect: An Examination of the Debate over the Legality of Humanitarian Intervention," *Duke Journal of Comparative and International Law*, Vol. 24, Issue 3 (Spring 2014), pp. 557–588.

Chris O'Meara, "United States' Missile Strikes in Syria: Should International Law Permit Unilateral Force to Protect Human Rights?," *EJIL:Talk!*, 18 April 2017, https://www.ejiltalk.org/united-states-missile-strikes-in-syria-should-international-law-permit-unilateral-force-to-protect-human-rights/.

Alexander Orakhelashvili, "Sanctions and Fundamental Rights of States: The case of EU Sanctions Against Iran and Syria," in Matthew Happold and Paul Eden (eds.), *Economic Sanctions and International Law* (Hart Publishing, 2016), pp. 13–36.

Alexander Orakhelashvili, "Commissions of Inquiry and Traditional Mechanisms of Dispute Settlement," in Christian Henderson (ed.), *Commissions of Inquiry: Problems and Prospects* (Hart Publishing, 2017), pp. 119–143.

Alexander Orakhelashvili, "The Attribution Decision Adopted by the OPCW's Conference of States Parties and Its Legality," *International Organizations Law Review*, Vol. 17, Issue 3 (2020), pp. 664–681.

Bertrand G. Ramcharan (ed.), *International Law and Fact-Finding in the Field of Human Rights*, revised and edited reprint version (Brill Nijhoff, 2014).

Albrecht Randelzhofer, "Article 2 (4)," in Bruno Simma (ed.), *The Charter of the United Nations: A Commentary* (Oxford University Press, 1994), pp. 106–128.

Albrecht Randelzhofer and Oliver Dörr, "Article 2 (4), in Bruno Simma, Daniel-Erasmus Khan, Gerg Nolte and Andreas Paulus (eds.), *The Charter of the United Nations, A Commentary*, third edition, volume I (Oxford, 2013), pp. 200–234.

W. Michael Reisman, "Humanitarian Intervention and Fledging Democracies," *Fordham International Law Journal*, Vol. 18, Issue 3 (1994), pp. 794–805.

Michael Reisman and Myres S. McDougal, "Humanitarian Intervention to Protect the Ibos," in Richard B. Lillich (ed.), *Humanitarian intervention and the United Nations* (University Press of Virginia, 1973), pp. 167–195.

W. Michael Reisman, "Kosovo's Antinomies," *American Journal of International Law Journal*, Vol. 92, Issue 4 (1999), pp. 860–862.

Julian Perry Robinson, "Chemical-Weapons Proliferation in the Middle East," in Efraim Karsh, Martin S. Navias and Philip Sabin (eds.), *Non-Conventional-Weapons Proliferation in the Middle East: Tackling the Spread of Nuclear, Chemical, and Biological Capabilities* (Clarendon Press, 1993), pp. 69–98.

Sir Nigel Rodley, "'Humanitarian Intervention'," in Marc Weller (ed.), *The Oxford Handbook of the Use of Force in International Law* (Oxford, 2015), pp. 775–796.

Liana W. Rosen and Michael A. Weber, "FY 2020 Foreign Operations Appropriations: Targeting Foreign Corruption and Human Rights Violations," Congressional Research Service, 17 April 2020, https://www.everycrsreport.com/files/2020-04-17_IF10905_b16f232c9119307cbb910cc16ac2ba9af70af6f9.pdf.

Tom Ruys, "Digest of State Practice 1 July 2013–December 2013," *Journal on the Use of Force and International Law*, Vol. 1, Issue 1 (2014), pp. 149–189.

Tom Ruys, Luca Ferro and Carl Vander Maelen, "Digest of State Practice 1 January 2013–30 June 2017," *Journal on the Use of Force and International Law*, Vol. 4, Issue 2 (2017), pp. 371–418.

Tom Ruys, Carl Vander Maelen and Sebastiaan Van Severen, "Digest of State Practice: 1 July 2017– 31 December 2017," *Journal on the Use of Force and International Law*, Vol. 5, Issue 1 (2017), pp. 145–187.

Tom Ruys, Carl Vander Maelen and Sebastiaan Van Severen, "Digest of State Practice: 1 January–30 June 2018," *Journal on the Use of Force and International Law*, Vol. 5, Issue 2 (2018), pp. 324–394.

Leila Sadat, "The Seventh Annual Chautauqua Declaration," *International Legal Materials*, Vol. 53, Issue 4 (2014), pp. 739–743.

Romana Sadurska, "Threats of Force," *American Journal of International Law*, Vol. 82, Issue 2 (1988), pp. 239–268.

Michael P. Scharf, "Striking a Grotian Movement: How the Syrian Airstrikes Changed International Law Relating to Humanitarian Intervention," *Chicago Journal of International Law*, Vol. 19, Issue 2 (2019), pp. 586–614.

Michael P. Scharf, "Responding to Chemical Weapons Use in Syria," *Case Western Reserve Journal of International Law*, Vol. 51 (2019), pp. 189–200.

Michael P. Scharf, Milena Sterio and Paul R. Williams, *The Syrian Conflict's Impact on International Law* (Cambridge University Press, 2020).
Michael N. Schmitt, "The Syrian Intervention: Assessing the Possible International Law Justifications," *International Law Studies Series*. US Naval War College, Vol. 89 (2013), pp. 744–756.
Henry G. Schermers and Niels M. Blokker, *International Institutional Law: Unity within Diversity*, fifth revised edition (Martinus Nijhoff Publishers, 2011).
Malcolm N. Shaw, *International Law*, ninth edition (Cambridge University Press, 2021).
Bruno Simma, "NATO, the UN and the Use of Force: Legal Aspects," *European Journal of International Law*, Vol. 10, No. 1 (1999), pp. 1–22.
Sandesh Sivakumaran, *The Law of Non-International Armed Conflict* (Oxford University Press, 2012).
Gary D. Solis, *The Law of Armed Conflict: International Humanitarian law in War*, third edition (Cambridge University Press, 2022).
Mirko Sossai, "Identifying the Perpetrators of Chemical Attacks in Syria: The Organisation for the Prohibition of Chemical Weapons as Part of the Fight against Impunity," *Journal of International Criminal Justice*, Vol. 17, Issue 2 (May 2019), pp. 211–227.
Edward M. Spiers, *Agents of War: A History of Chemical and Biological Weapons*, expanded second edition (Reaktion Books, 2021).
Manisuli Ssenyonjo, "Unilateral Military Action in the Syrian Arab Republic: A Right to Humanitarian Intervention or a Crime of Aggression," *International Human Rights Law Review*, Vol. 2, Issue 2 (2013), pp. 323–343.
Carsten Stahn, "Syria and the Semantics of Intervention, Aggression and Punishment; On Red Lines and Blurred Lines," *Journal of International Criminal Justice*, Vol. 11, Issue 5 (December 2013), pp. 955–977.
Carsten Stahn, "Between Law-Breaking and Law-Making: Syria, Humanitarian Intervention and What the Law Ought to Be," *Journal of Conflict and Security Law*, Vol. 19, Issue 1 (2014), pp. 25–48.
Ash Stanley-Ryan, "Achieving Chemical Weapons Convention Compliance in the Aftermath of Khan Shaykhun," *New Zealand Journal of Public and International Law*, Vol. 16, No. 1 (November 2018), pp. 39–66.
Milena Sterio, "Humanitarian Intervention Post-Syria: Legitimate and Legal," *Brooklyn Journal of International Law*, Vol. 40, Issue 1 (2014), pp. 109–170.
Nikolas Stürchler, *The Threat of Force in International Law* (Cambridge University Press, 2007).
Lisa Tabassi and Olufemi Elias, "18—Disarmament," in Michael J. Bowman (ed.), *Conceptual and Contextual Perspectives on the Modern Law of Treaties* (Cambridge University Press, 2018), pp. 578–620.
Fernando R. Tesón, *Humanitarian Intervention: An Inquiry into Law and Morality*, second edition (Transnational, 1997).
Hugh Thirlway, *The Sources of International Law, second edition* (Oxford University Press, 2019).
Ann Van Wynen Thomas and Aaron Joshua Thomas, *Legal Limits on the Use of Chemical and Biological Weapons* (Southern Methodist University Press, 1970).
Ralf Trapp, "Elimination of the Chemical Weapons Stockpile of Syria," *Journal of Conflict and Security Law*, Vol. 19, Issue 1 (2014), pp. 7–24.
Ralf Trapp, "The Use of Chemical Weapons in Syria: implications and Consequences," in Bretislav Friedrich, Dieter Hoffmann, Jürgen Renn, Florian Schmaltz and Martin Wolf (eds.), *One Hundred Years of Chemical Warfare: Research, Deployment, Consequences* (Springer Open, 2017), pp. 363–375.
Ralf Trapp, "Compliance Management under the Chemical Weapons Convention," *UNIDIR, WMD Compliance and Enforcement Series, Paper Three* (2019), https://unidir.org/sites/default/files/2019-12/UNID%20WMD%20CE%20-%20Paper%203%20v3.pdf.
Nicholas Tsagourias, "The Prohibition of Threats of Force," in Nigel D. White and Christian Henderson (eds.), *Research Handbook on International Conflict and Security Law:* Jus ad Bellum, Jus in Bello and Jus post Bellum (Edward Elgar, 2013), pp. 67–88.

Robert W. Tucker, *The Law of War and Neutrality at Sea* (United States Government Printing Office, 1957).

Larissa J. Van Den Herik, "An Inquiry into the Role of Commissions of Inquiry in International Law: Navigating the Tensions between Fact-Finding and Application of International Law," *Chinese Journal of International Law*, Vol. 13, No. 3 (2014), pp. 507–538.

Johan D van der Vyver, "Military Intervention in Syria: The American, British and French Alternatives and the Russian Option," *De Jure*, Vol. 48, No. 1 (2015), pp. 36–54.

Pieter van Dijk, "Normative Force and Effectiveness of International Norms," *Germany Yearbook of International Law*, Vol. XXX (1987), pp. 9–35.

Peter van Ham, Sico van der Meer and Malik Ellahi, *Chemical Weapons Challenges Ahead: The Past and Future of the OPCW—With a Case Study on Syria* , Clingendael Report (2017), https://www.clingendael.org/sites/default/files/pdf/Clingendael_Report_Chemical_Weapons_Challenges_Ahead_2017.pdf.

Beth Van Schaack, *Imagining Justice for Syria: Water Always Finds its Way* (Oxford University Press, 2020).

Mindia Vashakmadze, "Legality of Foreign Military Intervention in International Law: Four Case Studies," *Max Planck Yearbook of United Nations Law*, Vol. 18 (2014), pp. 462–506.

WD Verwey, "Chemical Warfare in Vietnam: Legal or Illegal?," *Netherlands International Law Review*, Vol. 18, Issue 2 (1971), pp. 217–244.

Wil D. Verwey, *Riot Control Agents and Herbicides in War: Their humanitarian, toxicological, ecological, military, polemological, and legal aspects* (A. W. Sijthoff, 1977)

Paul Walker, "Syrian Chemical Weapons Destruction: Taking Stocks and Looking Ahead," *Arms Control Today* (December 2014), https://www.armscontrol.org/act/2014-12/features/syrian-chemical-weapons-destruction-taking-stock-looking-ahead.

Kenneth Watkin, "Chemical Agents and Expanding Bullets: Limited Law Enforcement Exceptions or Unwarranted Handcuffs," Israel Yearbook on Human Rights, Vol. 36 (2006), pp. 43–69.

Kenneth Watkin, "Humanitarian Intervention and the Responsibility to Protect: Where It Stands in 2020: Fighting in the Law's Gaps," *Southwestern Journal of International Law*, Vol. 26, Issue 2 (2020), pp. 213–240.

Stephen Wilkinson, "Finding the Facts' Standards of Proof and Information Handling in Monitoring, Reporting and Fact-Finding Missions," Working Paper, Monitoring, Reporting, and Fact-Finding (MRP) project, Program on Humanitarian Policy and Conflict Research (HPCR) at Harvard University (2014). https://ssrn.com/abstract=2400927.

Stephen Wilkinson, "Standards of Proof in International Humanitarian and Human Rights Fact-Finding and Inquiry Missions," Geneva academy of international humanitarian law and human rights (2012), https://www.geneva-academy.ch/joomlatools-files/docman-files/Standards%20of%20Proof%20in%20Fact-Finding.pdf.

Ruth Wedgwood, "NATO's Campaign in Yugoslavia," *American Journal of International Law Journal*, Vol. 92, Issue 4 (1999), pp. 828–834.

Richard Weitz, "Syria and Beyond: The Future of the Chemical Weapons Threat," *Proliferation Papers*, No. 51 (December 2014), https://www.ifri.org/sites/default/files/atoms/files/pp51weitz.pdf.

Andreas Zimmermann and Meltem Şener, "Chemical Weapons and the International Criminal Court," *American Journal of International Law*, Vol. 108, No. 3 (2014), pp. 436–448.

Marten Zwanenburg and Guido den Dekker, "Prosecutor v. Frans van Anraat—Case No. 07/10742.2009 Nederlandse Jurisprudentie 481," *American Journal of International Law*, Vol. 104, No. 1 (2010), pp. 86–94.

Jurisprudence

International Court of Justice

North Sea Continental Shelf, Judgment, I.C.J. Reports 1969, p. 3.

Continental Shelf (Libyan Arab Jamahiriya/Malta), Judgment, I.C.J. Reports 1985, p. 13.

Military and Paramilitary Activities in and against Nicaragua (Nicaragua v. United States of America), Merits, Judgment, I.C.J. Reports 1986, p. 14.

Territorial Dispute (Libyan Arab Jamahiriya/Chad), Judgment, I.C.J. Reports 1994, p. 6.

Legality of the Use by a State of Nuclear Weapons in Armed Conflict, Advisory Opinion, I.C.J. Reports 1996(I), p. 66.

Legality of the Threat or Use of Nuclear Weapons, Advisory Opinion, I.C.J. Reports 1996, p. 226.

Kasikili/Sedudu Island (Botswana/Namibia), Judgment, I.C.J. Reports 1999(II), p. 1045.

Sovereignty over Pulau Ligitan and Pulau Sipadan (Indonesia/Malaysia), Judgment, I.C.J. Reports 2002, p. 625.

Jurisdictional Immunities of the State (Germany v. Italy: Greece intervening), Judgment, I.C.J. Reports 2012, p. 99.

Legal Consequences of the Separation of the Chagos Archipelago from Mauritius in 1965, Advisory Opinion, I.C.J. Reports 2019, p. 95.

Arbitration

Award in the arbitration regarding the delimitation of the maritime boundary between Guyana and Suriname, Award of 17 September 2007, Reports of International Arbitral Awards, Vol. XXX, p. 1.

International Criminal Tribunal for Former Yugoslavia

Prosecutor v. Dusko Tadić a/k/a "Dule", Decision on the Defence Motion for Interlocutory Appeal on Jurisdiction, IT-94–01, 2 October 1995.

Domestic Courts of the Netherlands

Judgment LJN: AX6406, Rechtbank 's-Gravenhage (Regional Court of The Hague), 09/751003-04, 23 December 2005.

Judgment LJN: BA6734, Gerechtshof 's-Gravenhage (Court of Appeal of The Hague), 2200050906-2, 9 May 2007.

Judgment LJN: BG4822, Hoge Raad der Nederlanden (Supreme Court of the Netherlands), 07/10742, 30 June 2009.

Index

T. Abe, *Syrian Chemical Weapons and International Law*,
https://doi.org/10.1007/978-981-99-3700-4

D

J

K

L

M

Q

R

S

T

U

V

W

Y